Communicating across Cultures at Work

Third Edition

MAUREEN GUIRDHAM

palgrave
macmillan

First published 1999 as *Communicating Across Cultures*
Second edition 2005
Third edition 2011
PALGRAVE MACMILLAN

Palgrave Macmillan in the UK is an imprint of Macmillan Publishers Limited, registered in England, company number 785998, of Houndmills, Basingstoke, Hampshire RG21 6XS.

Palgrave Macmillan in the US is a division of St Martin's Press LLC, 175 Fifth Avenue, New York, NY 10010.

Palgrave Macmillan is the global academic imprint of the above companies and has companies and representatives throughout the world.

Palgrave® and Macmillan® are registered trademarks in the United States, the United Kingdom, Europe and other countries.

ISBN: 978–0–230–28369–5

This book is printed on paper suitable for recycling and made from fully managed and sustained forest sources. Logging, pulping and manufacturing processes are expected to conform to the environmental regulations of the country of origin.

A catalogue record for this book is available from the British Library.

A catalog record for this book is available from the Library of Congress.

10 9 8 7 6 5 4 3 2 1
20 19 18 17 16 15 14 13 12 11

Printed in China

For Damon and Oliver

Contents

List of Figures and Tables

Figures

Tables

Preface

The overall effect of the changes made in this third edition of *Communicating across Cultures at Work* includes a further increase in the focus on work and business. The second edition expanded this coverage by including a chapter on work activities such as negotiating and management; this edition includes a new chapter, Chapter 9, on international intercultural work communication, covering working in virtual teams, offshoring, working in international alliances, working in multinational enterprises and international business-to-business relations. The chapter begins with conceptual topics that are common to these contexts – technology-mediated communication, knowledge transfer and co-ordination. A further change is an increase in the focus on Asia to complement the focus of earlier editions on Europe. Europe is 'a complex environment affected by diverse and intense pressure of national cultures'.[1] The continent therefore supplies a valuable canvas on which to depict the impact of culture, cultural difference and intercultural communication on work. The same is true of Asia, which also supplies some comparisons and contrasts with Europe that are less clear-cut within that continent. In a world in which the Asian countries are increasingly important economically, these introductions also have their own intrinsic value.

The intention in this new edition of *Communicating across Cultures at Work* is to retain and improve the features of the earlier editions that were most valued by its users, while adding the new dimensions just described that were not previously covered. The practical focus of the chapters on how to communicate interculturally and how to function internationally has been retained; so has the breadth of diversity covered, so that ethnicity, gender, age, social class and religious subcultures are covered, and not just national cultures. The book also continues to rely heavily on published research for its main conclusions, while many illustrations are drawn from the author's own published and unpublished research and from current news reports.

---

[1] Muzychenko, O. (2006) 'Cross-cultural entrepreneurial competence in identifying international business opportunities', *European Journal of Management*, **26**(6): 366–77.

A NOTE ON TERMINOLOGY

References in the text to cultures and subcultures as distinct concepts use the terms without brackets. To cover the combined concepts the terms (sub)culture and (sub)cultural are generally used; however, when referring to communication and interactions between members of different groups, I prefer the term 'intercultural', to avoid the clumsiness of 'inter(sub)cultural'. Similarly, I use 'cross-cultural' rather than 'cross(sub) cultural' for comparisons. To refer to members of groups other than a communicator's own, I generally use the terminology, which is gradually becoming current, of 'different others', and, to capture the quality of their difference, 'otherness'. However, certain intercultural communication theories use the term 'strangers' instead of 'different others', and where that is so the author's original terminology is retained. Again, I generally use the term 'interpersonal' to mean 'between people'. Interpersonal communication now comprehends both face-to-face and mediated communication. However, in some writings on intercultural communication 'interpersonal' is used in contrast to 'inter-group' and 'intercultural', in the sense that an encounter, even between only two people, may occur on an inter-group, intercultural or interpersonal level. Again, in these cases I follow the terminology of the writer but try to make the difference clear. Labels for societal groups are always problematic – the subject is discussed in the section on inclusive language in Chapter 6. The term 'minority' is often used not literally, but defined as a group in a subordinate position irrespective of relative size; for example, it can be applied to women in Britain or Black people in South Africa, both of whom are numeric majorities. This usage can be sensitive because of its indirect reference to subordinate status, but, in the absence of any other accepted general term and because it is adopted by the UK Commission for Racial Equality, it is the usage of this book.

USING THIS BOOK

As far as possible, this book is based on research material. Because the field, though rapidly developing, is still a young one, this necessarily limits its coverage. Nevertheless, it has proved possible to cover adequately most topics needed for an understanding of cultural and intercultural communication and to provide guidance on applying these understandings at work. The underpinnings of cultural theory, psychology, social psychology, communication studies and interactive behaviour are touched on, but readings such as those given in Further Reading are needed for full comprehension.

Each of the nine chapters contains a conclusion, questions and exercises as well as the core sections. The questions and exercises offer a range of learning opportunities, including case analyses, group discussions, role plays and self-completion question-naires. The Appendix shows how to score and interpret these questionnaires.

The boxes in the text provide illustrative material. Many are based on the author's own interviews. Some are referred to in the text; others are not, allowing readers to interpret them for themselves.

Acknowledgements

The author wishes to thank the following for permission to use a diagram:

Figure 9.1 Reprinted with permission from Srikanth, K. and Puranam, P. (2010) 'Integrating distributed work: comparing task design, communication, and tacit co-ordination mechanisms', *SSRN Working Paper Series*, URL: http://ssrn.com/abstract= 1125924.

Culture and Communication at Work

chapter one

Introduction

In modern societies, interpersonal communication is central to most forms of work, and that communication often takes place between people who come from different backgrounds. At work interpersonal communication – two-way interaction between individuals or within groups – impacts on everything, from just getting basic tasks done at all to the overall organizational performance. For instance, many professional roles depend critically on communication – those of doctors and lawyers cannot be performed at all without frequent communication with patients and clients, while near-continuous communication is intrinsic to the role of a teacher. In business, communication is central to the activities of buying and selling. For managers of people, the activities generally understood as central to the role – motivating, facilitating, even directing and controlling – are primarily communication activities. All organizations depend on communication for the purposes of co-ordination and so for the processes

Box 1.1

Even in software development, which is often regarded as an area where interpersonal communication is not a central issue, two studies have found that performance depends on task-related internal communication. 'High communication facilitates project performance, especially in early stages of the project life-cycle and when standardization of methods and tools is low.'[a]

'Software development, particularly in the early stages, requires much communication. In fact, software projects have two complementary communication needs. First, the more formal, official communications need a clear, well-understood interface. [Second,] informal "corridor talk" helps people stay aware of what is going on around them, what other people are working on, what states various parts of the project are in, who has expertise in what area, and many other essential pieces of background information that enable developers to work together efficiently.'[b]

Sources: (a) Brodbeck, F.C. (2001) 'Communication and performance in software development projects', _European Journal of Work and Organizational Psychology,_ **10**(1): 73–94

(b) Herbsleb, J.D. and Moitra, D. (2001) 'Global software development', _IEEE Software,_ March/April: 16–20

of organization itself. In our twenty-first-century 'age of information', organizations also depend on communication to transfer knowledge; communication failures can leave pockets of information isolated and often useless. Furthermore, for individuals, job satisfaction and career success depend on good relations with superiors, colleagues and subordinates, and these only flow from skilled and sincere communication.

A feature of modern societies and organizations is that they are composed of people who differ widely in terms of nationality, ethnicity, gender, sexual orientation, age, education, social class or level of (dis)ability – in other words, in terms of their demographic profile or social background. The countries of world regions (such as Europe and Asia[1]) are becoming integrated, their markets and workforces diverse and their organizations international. At work, therefore, more people than ever before now interact with 'different others' – people whose demographic profile or social background is different from their own. Individuals are now likely to interact with a highly diverse range of people as colleagues, subordinates, managers, clients, patients, customers, students, professional advisers and other service providers, sales representatives and other interface workers.

There is a naïve view that interpersonal communication at work is unproblematic – that it just happens without people needing to attend to it or be skilled at it. This view is mistaken, as research has conclusively shown. All communication is error-prone: it is liable to lead to misunderstanding or even conflict because of poor encoding of messages by senders, or because of transmission failures or distortion by receivers who are inattentive or emotionally aroused. These problems can arise even between two people from identical backgrounds and who have a large measure of shared experience. They are, however, undoubtedly exacerbated when interactors are from different backgrounds. People from different cultures (nationalities, ethnicities or religions) and subcultures (genders, age groups, sexual orientations or levels of [dis]ability) may communicate differently and may have differences of attitudes or beliefs. These differences can add to their difficulties in communicating with one another.

This book is about the different ways in which people at work communicate, about how those differences can lead to misunderstanding, conflict and low performance. More positively, it is also about how understanding between people who communicate differently can be increased, conflict avoided and performance enhanced. In particular, it is about differences in how people communicate that originate in their background – their culture or their subculture. It also deals with communication problems and breakdowns that occur, not because of differences in ways of communicating or lack of communication skill, but because of differences in attitudes and beliefs that originate in their background.

About this book

Part I of the book analyses diversity at work in terms of cultures and subcultures. It also analyses cultural and subcultural similarities and differences in how we communicate at work and how the factors such as motives and the processes such as perception that influence communication are affected by (sub)culture. This chapter (Chapter 1) has three main purposes: to begin describing what intercultural communication is by clarifying 'work communication' and 'culture' and to begin to substantiate the claim that intercultural communication at work is of great and growing importance and the further claim that it is not unproblematic and so requires and justifies study and skill development. Some of the material in this chapter serves all three purposes. For instance, facts about the size and employment position of different societal groups demonstrate the amount and range of intercultural encounters that must be happening. These facts are also relevant to the beliefs, attitudes and so to the communication behaviours of the participants. Admittedly, there is a problem with this last point: it is people's perceptions that influence their beliefs and attitudes, rather than any 'objective' facts, and in individual cases the two may diverge quite widely. Nevertheless, the facts are useful as an overall foundation for understanding how people view the intercultural social world of work.

Nearly half a century of cross-cultural research has firmly established that there are differences in the ways that members of different societal groups behave, both in private life and at work. Chapter 2 analyses cultural differences, using a range of models. Many of these models are taxonomies based on underlying factors, such as values; others are based on communication itself, such as Hall's (1976) 'high-context/low-context communication' distinction. The three final sections of Chapter 2 consider the impact of culture and cultural difference on work behaviour, on work organization and management and on aspects of organizational environments. Chapters 3 and 4 cover communication at work and the effects of (sub)cultural differences. The subject of human communication is a huge one, and radical selection has been necessary for this book: it has been done by selecting those elements of general communication which differ between cultures, such as the concept of 'politeness', and those which feed in directly to intercultural communication, such as 'elaborated and restricted codes'. Chapter 3 deals with analyses of overt communication behaviour at an individual level; Chapter 4 expands the analysis into the intrapersonal level and covers the psychological factors and processes affecting behaviour, including, of course, communication behaviour.

Part II of the book is about intercultural communication at work. Chapter 5 presents the argument that intercultural communication is problematic in particular ways. It describes the wide range of barriers that apply. It both deals with 'universal' factors, such as stereotyping, prejudice and discrimination, and builds on the analyses of Chapters 2, 3 and 4, by showing how (sub)cultural differences also impede intercultural communication. Chapter 6 is concerned with how intercultural communication can be made more effective. Its coverage ranges from inclusive language to the practical application of a number of intercultural communication theories. Attention is paid to behaviours and traits such as tolerance for ambiguity, mindfulness and self-monitoring. There is discussion of the underlying motivations, goals, emotions and cognitions as well as the processes of intercultural encounters.

Part III consists of applications and extensions of the understanding of (sub)cultural difference and intercultural communication developed in Parts I and II of the book. Chapter 7 deals with the different situation that arises when the work context is that of a culture other than the individual's own. Sojourners and people on international assignments need additional skills and new attitudes to work effectively in a foreign culture. Chapter 8 discusses cultural differences in, and effective intercultural communication for, selection interviewing, service encounters, mentoring, conflict resolution (mediating), negotiating, working in groups or teams, and leadership and management. Chapter 9 draws out the effect of five important contexts for working and communicating interculturally: working in virtual teams, offshoring, international joint ventures and other intercultural alliances, multinational enterprises and business-to-business relations. In addition to the impact of these contexts on intercultural communication and of cultural differences on these contexts, there are issues around computer-mediated communication, knowledge transfer and co-ordination,

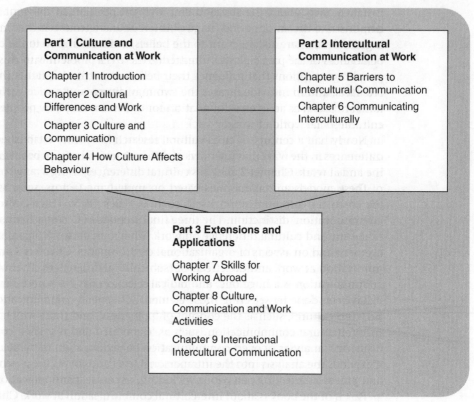

Part 1 Culture and Communication at Work

Chapter 1 Introduction

Chapter 2 Cultural Differences and Work

Chapter 3 Culture and Communication

Chapter 4 How Culture Affects Behaviour

Part 2 Intercultural Communication at Work

Chapter 5 Barriers to Intercultural Communication

Chapter 6 Communicating Interculturally

Part 3 Extensions and Applications

Chapter 7 Skills for Working Abroad

Chapter 8 Culture, Communication and Work Activities

Chapter 9 International Intercultural Communication

Figure 1.1   *The structure of this book*

which are discussed at the start of this chapter. Figure 1.1 shows the structure of this book in a diagram.

> This book is about culture, subculture and the impact of these on how people at work communicate with one another. It is also about how to overcome the obstacles to communication that (sub)cultural differences may create. This knowledge leads to understanding how to communicate effectively at work with people from different backgrounds.[2]

1.1   THE IMPORTANCE OF WORK COMMUNICATION

Communication can be defined as the 'collective and interactive process of generating and interpreting messages'.[3] Work communication is essential for co-ordinating activities; co-ordination is fundamental to organization. Work communication also leads to both understanding or misunderstanding and good or poor work relationships. All communication is complex; work communication is less complex in some ways, more complex in others. Focus on tasks may reduce work communication complexity but it is made more complex by continuous interaction, often with 'different others', by the high stakes often involved for both individuals and organizations, by the conflicting motivations of participants and by the need to work in groups.

The significance of any activity at work can be judged by the amount of time employees spend at it, and by its impact on how effectively and efficiently the work is carried out, on job satisfaction and career success for individuals, and on profits or other measures of results for organizations. By all these measures, it is likely that communication is the most important work activity, especially in modern, service-oriented, team-based organizations. Communication has been described as a revolutionary discovery,[4] energized by technological development, increasing global literacy and 'the philosophies of progressivism and pragmatism, which stimulated a desire to improve society through widespread social change'.[5] In the world of work and organization, many scholars now acknowledge the central role of communication, and there is a large literature devoted to it.[6]

The new recognition that, in order to compete, modern organizations need to tap the creativity, expertise and know-how of all their employees places a premium on interpersonal communication. There is considerable evidence that both individual achievement in organizations and organizational effectiveness are closely related to the communication abilities of staff. Research in a large insurance company and two other organizations showed that persuasive ability was a relatively strong predictor of performance appraisal ratings, job level and upward mobility.[7] Another study investigated the link between communication abilities and organizational achievement among 394 employees of three south-east US organizations. This research established that communication abilities and achievement were closely linked for both men and women. The researchers concluded: 'The results lend additional support to the claim that these abilities help people attain desired social outcomes.'[8] It has also been shown that small business owners who give directions and control to their employees in a 'person-centred' way – that is, skilfully adjust their instructions and feedback to the characteristics of the individual employee – are perceived more positively as leaders by their employees. Research has linked person-centred communication by doctors to health outcomes, including the degree to which patients comply with 'doctors' orders'.[9] There is a developing body of work showing that teacher communication methods influence student empowerment.[10]

New technologies have increased communication opportunities but also their complexity. For instance, call centre staff in Asia, responding to callers from the UK, must adjust to time-of-day differences and may need to respond to comments on local UK concerns such as soccer results. Again, staff who need to send frequent emails to colleagues or customers in another continent can experience difficulty if they have never visited it and have no first-hand knowledge of local conditions. Chapter 9 describes some effects of technological mediation on interpersonal communication.

> Communication can claim to be the most important single work activity, and interpersonal communication has increased in importance with organizations' new emphasis on individuals and teams. Technology has expanded the scope of work communication while often adding to its complexity.

1.2 THE GROWTH IN CONTACT WITH 'DIFFERENT OTHERS' AT WORK

Several trends of the late twentieth and early twenty-first centuries increased the number and types of 'different others' that many people meet through work. These trends included the phenomenal growth of both international communications and business and the increasing diversity of domestic workforces.

Prior to the 1980s, telecommunication monopolies were generally under the direct control of state ministries of postal services and telecommunications, and these monopolistic national networks co-ordinated international traffic flows using standard rate-sharing formulae. This changed rapidly in the 1980s and 1990s as a transnational commercial communication system was set up; this resulted from major improvements in communication technology and from barriers to the commercialization of media and communication systems being relaxed. 'The recent expansion of global access to voice telephony has been almost violent. During the 1990s, wire-line phone access shot upward; while, increasing from a tiny base as recently as 1990, 1 billion mobile phones were in use by 2002.' In addition to the growth of international dial-up circuits, activated international private line circuits (the in-house corporate and organizational telecommunication networks that employ leased circuits and other proprietary facilities on a full-time basis) grew exponentially, increasing tenfold in the years 1997 to 2000 alone. As a result, business users assimilated networks into a vast and growing range of business processes: payroll accounting, employment relations, inventory, sales, marketing, research and development, and so on. 'By revolutionizing network systems and services, large corporations acquired new freedom of manoeuvre in their attempts to reintegrate their operations...on a broadened, supranational basis.' Transnationally, organized networks employed a lengthening list of media, including wireless, telephone lines, cable television systems, fibre optics and satellites, plus the software-defined means for network access, operation and management. This development expanded the geographical organization of business: by 1997 to 1999 fully half of global telecommunication investment was being absorbed by developing and transitional countries.[11] This global expansion of telecommunications connectivity not only enabled a huge growth of work-related interpersonal contact within and between organizations, but also supported other trends that reinforced the amount of that communication through developments such as offshoring, virtual teams, the application of social networking to work and the growth of world trade, especially in services.

Although world trade is affected by recessions, between 2000 and 2008 world exports grew by an average 5 per cent year on year; most regions of the world shared in this growth. Over the same period of 2000 to 2008, Asian exports rose by 10 per cent a year; while those of the 27 countries of the European Union (EU) increased by only 3.5 per cent annually, this still meant that they nearly doubled from 683 to 1306 thousand million euros between 1999 and 2008.[12] Service business tends to involve more interpersonal contact than other sectors. The service component of many developed economies grew dramatically in the late twentieth and early twenty-first centuries, both in absolute terms and as a share of their total gross national product, pointing to a very large increase in the number of enterprises engaged in the service economy. Global trade in services grew even faster than that in merchandise, at 12 per cent per annum for the years 2000 to 2008.

During the late twentieth and early twenty-first centuries, workforces in many parts of the world became increasingly diverse – that is, they came to be composed of people from many different national and ethnic backgrounds, of women to nearly the same degree as men, and to include more people with disabilities. Workforces came to reflect legal recognition that people are entitled to differing sexual orientations, religious affiliations and family structures. The extension of working age limits and the cumulative effects of the open labour market also expanded the diversity of people at work in regions such as Europe. Additionally, in some countries, such as Japan, India and those of the EU, substantially increased legal rights increased the visibility and voice of women and minority groups, who were increasingly found in positions of power and influence. Furthermore, for most people the diversity of the people they met through work – as patients, students, pupils and their parents, clients, customers, suppliers, advisers, accountants, bankers and lawyers – was already wider than that among their colleagues alone and was growing. For business executives and managers, for instance, the diversity of the backgrounds of their contacts increased even faster than the rate at which it increased among colleagues, due to globalization. For the caring professions, because people were living longer and, as they aged, needed more medical and support services, mainly young or middle-aged nurses, doctors and care workers were dealing with more and more elderly or very elderly people; women live longer than men and so were disproportionately served by doctors who were still predominantly male (though decreasingly so); members of ethnic minorities had a higher birth rate and so used more maternity services; and so on.

Although organizations often fail to notice the benefits of diversity, a growing number do, and encourage it in their workforces, thereby increasing it. The benefits are of two kinds. The first kind has been defined as affecting divergent activities. These are those activities where creativity is required, which range from generating strategies to writing advertising copy, from developing new products to improving systems. When people of different ethnic, national, gender, religious, sexual orientation, social class and specialist backgrounds share perspectives and approaches, it helps ferment ideas, while the tests applied by such a cross-section help filter out the good ideas from the bad. Diversity also helps guard against the dangers of over-conformity and groupthink, which are real perils in organizations. The second benefit of diversity in organizations is that it gives them an increased capacity for dealing with the inescapable diversity that exists in the environment, for domestic and international organizations alike, in markets, user groups and publics, and, for international organizations, in governments. A study of the success of nine organizations confirmed that companies benefit from valuing 'diverse cultural modes of being and interacting', where 'all cultural voices … participate fully in setting goals and making decisions'. Managers in these companies assessed cultural biases and devised new ways for people to work together. These included extensive cultural awareness training at all levels, from entry employees to senior staff; analysis of interpersonal communication and interactive styles; active support groups to share issues and mentor all employees; increased assistance to parents in the form of daycare and flexible leave; and bias-free hiring, evaluating, and promoting.[13]

Different societal groups

The rest of this section shows the context of communication at work in terms of societal diversity. It discusses the position of different societal groups.

Nationality and ethnicity

Nationality, as the term is used here, is decided by a person's national status, which is a legal relationship involving allegiance on the part of an individual and (usually) protection on the part of the state. This usage distinguishes nationality from ethnicity, since a nation may be composed of many ethnic groups but only one nationality, no matter how many foreign nationals or people with dual citizenship live within its borders. However, the importance of nationality itself to how people behave, and so to its impact on work communication, is far from clear. In multi-ethnic countries, many peoples contribute to the creation of the national culture.

An ethnic unit is 'a population whose members believe that in some sense they share common descent and a common cultural heritage or tradition, and who are so regarded by others'.[14] Another definition of ethnic identity reflects a similar idea: it is 'identification with and perceived acceptance into a group with shared heritage and culture'.[15] Thus ethnicity is socially constructed.[16] Minority ethnic groups share a sense of heritage, history and origin from an area outside or preceding the creation of their present nation state; they often also share a language or dialect. Ethnic identity is situational; it is possible to be simultaneously English, British and European, stressing these identities more or less strongly in different aspects of everyday life. Similarly, a person might self-identify as Gujarati, Indian, East African, Asian or British depending on the situation, his or her immediate objectives and the responses and behaviour of others.

The significance of national and ethnic differences for communication at work is affected by the size of the stock of foreign population living in a country or region, by the stock of ethnic minorities in a population and by the labour market participation and employment rates of foreign nationals and ethnic minorities. Although affected by recession, indications are that the long-term trend in these factors was a rising one in many parts of the world during the late twentieth and early twenty-first centuries.

Gender

Gender differences have growing significance for communication at work. Gender has been defined as 'patterned, socially produced distinctions between female and male.…Gender is not something that people are…rather for the individual and the collective, it is daily accomplished'.[17] The term gender, therefore, refers to a society's beliefs about the differences between the sexes and its rules for appropriate behaviour for males and females.

In the world as a whole, men outnumber women in the ratio 100 to 98.6, and in Asia (where the ratio is distorted by the cultural preference for male children) by 105 to 100, but in Europe women outnumber men by 105 to 100. The proportion of women in the European labour market continued to increase more important between 2000 and 2006, as it had over the previous 15 years; in Asia it declined slightly and varied from China's 66 per cent down to Pakistan's 20 per cent (in 2008). In the EU, labour market participation and employment rates are correlated with level of educational qualification: the higher the educational attainment, the higher the employment rate. This finding applies to both sexes but is more significant for women than for men. As the educational qualification level of women continues to increase, female employment rates are also expected to rise. Unemployment rates in Asia and Europe slightly favoured women by the year 2009, when the unemployment rate for women in the EU27 was for the first time lower than that for men.

Despite their growing participation in labour markets and their unemployment advantage, women face 'harsh realities'. They are more likely to be in part-time work (which is generally less secure, less protected, less well paid and more lacking in benefits than full-time work). As a result of these and other factors, women are disproportionately represented among the low-paid. Again, while women managers 'appear to have achieved parity in salaries', when differences in productivity, behavioural

Box 1.2

'Within the next few months women will cross the 50 per cent threshold and become the majority of the American workforce. Women already make up the majority of university graduates in the OECD [Organisation for Economic Co-operation and Development] countries and the majority of professional workers in several rich countries, including the United States. Women run many of the world's great companies, from PepsiCo in America to Areva in France.

Women's economic empowerment is arguably the biggest social change of our times. Just a generation ago, women were largely confined to repetitive, menial jobs. They were routinely subjected to casual sexism and were expected to abandon their careers when they married and had children. Today they are running some of the organizations that once treated them as second-class citizens. Millions of women have been given more control over their own lives. And millions of brains have been put to more productive use. Societies that try to resist this trend – most notably the Arab countries, but also Japan and some southern European countries – will pay a heavy price in the form of wasted talent and frustrated citizens.'

The Economist, 30 December 2009

factors and age are controlled for, it is clear that 'gender plays a significant role in salary determination'.[18] The supply of women qualified for jobs in management, or in executive, administrative and managerial occupations, continued to increase as more women accumulated work experience and completed management and professional education programmes. However, although women made progress in obtaining managerial jobs, their median weekly earnings continued to be well below those of male managers.

Younger and older people

Age distributions of working age populations (15 to 65) show wide variations by region. In Asia, excluding the Near East, in 2009, 26.1 per cent of the population was aged between 15 and 29, while 18.8 per cent was in the age range of 45 to 65; in Western Europe the equivalent figures were 17.8 per cent and 26.6 per cent respectively and for Eastern Europe they were 21.6 per cent and 26.4 per cent.[19] Projected age distributions for the developed world show an ageing population, while the developing world outside China is expected to continue to benefit from continued growth in its young working age population. The unemployment facts both in Europe and some parts of Asia point to a serious disadvantage for young people; however, the predominant cause is less likely to be discrimination than labour market rigidities: the difficulty for younger people is to gain entry. Most job opportunities arise only as the total number of jobs expands or as natural wastage creates vacancies. People in the age group 25 to 49 tend to have a degree of tenure in the jobs they occupy. Worldwide, the unemployment rate for the 15–24 age group is twice as high as for the workforce as a whole, and it has been increasing over the last 18 years.[20] In Europe and some parts of Asia (Japan and China, but not India) an existing situation of disadvantage for both younger and older workers may be about to change, however, as Box 1.3 suggests.

Box 1.3

'Companies in the rich world are confronted with a rapidly ageing workforce. Nearly one in three American workers will be over 50 by 2012, and America is a young country compared with Japan and Germany. China is also ageing rapidly, thanks to its one-child policy. This means that companies will have to learn how to manage older workers better. ... How do you encourage older people to adapt to new practices and technologies? How do they get senior people to take orders from young whippersnappers? Happily a few companies have started to think seriously about these problems and generate insights that their more stick-in-the-mud peers can imitate. The leaders in this area are retail companies. Asda, a subsidiary of the equally gerontophile Wal-Mart, is Britain's biggest employer of over-50s. Netto, a Danish supermarket group, has experimented with shops that employ only people aged 45 and over. ... When BMW decided to staff one of its production lines with workers of an age likely to be typical at the firm in 2017, at first "the pensioners' line" was less productive. But the firm brought it up to the level of the rest of the factory by introducing 70 relatively small changes, such as new chairs, comfier shoes, magnifying lenses and adjustable tables.'

Source: The Economist, 4 February 2010

People with disabilities

Persons defined as having disabilities are those with physical, sensory or mental impairments that can make performing an everyday task more difficult. Most disabilities are not 'handicaps' in the sense of making people unable to work and take part in community life on an equal footing with others. This includes severe disabilities such as being confined to a wheelchair. Often it is only the fact that an environment is not adapted – there are no wheelchair ramps or lifts – that makes full participation difficult for people with such impairments. A qualified person with a disability is someone who, with or without reasonable adjustment by the employer, can perform the essential function of the employment position that s/he holds or desires. Disability increases with age in a rising curve.

People with disabilities are a significant part of the European workforce (no figures are available for Asia). For instance in Great Britain in 2009 nearly one in five people of working age (7 million, or 18.6 per cent) had a disability. There were 1.3 million disabled people in the UK who were available for, and wanted to, work. Although only half of disabled people of working age were in work (50 per cent compared with 80 per cent of non-disabled people), that still meant that around 650,000 people with disabilities were at work in the UK. Employment rates varied greatly according to the type of impairment a person had; only 20 per cent of people with mental health problems were in employment.[21] Data from the European Community Household Panel for the period 1995–2001 for 13 European countries showed that people with disabilities were more likely to be self-employed than people without disabilities. Self-employment provides flexibility and a better adjustment between disability status and working life. (Moreover, the levels of satisfaction with job, type of job and working conditions of self-employed disabled people are higher than those reported by disabled people who are wage and salary earners.[22]) Whether self-employed or employed, people with disabilities are an important part of workforces and are significantly involved in work-related communication of all kinds.

Homosexuals

Estimates for the numbers of male homosexuals and lesbians are, for obvious reasons, unreliable: the figures quoted for the EU range from 2 per cent to 10 per cent; none are available for Asia, where discrimination remains strong and most homosexuals stay 'in the closet'. Anecdotal evidence suggests that homosexuals often attain seniority at work more rapidly than the majority population; this is sometimes attributed to their greater commitment, owing to the demands of family life being lower for them than for heterosexuals. Although homosexuals may be affected by prejudice (discussed in Chapter 5), they constitute an important sector of the working community and are extensively involved in all kinds of communication at work.

Religious groups

Across the world, Christians were estimated at 32.88 per cent in 1999, Muslims 19.54 per cent, Hindus 13.34 per cent, and Buddhists at 5.92 per cent, with the rest of the world population spread across various religions and atheism.[23] No figures are available for labour market participation or employment by religious group, but it is likely that cultural values reduce participation by some groups (Muslim women, for instance). Lack of accommodation to religious needs, such as Muslims' need to worship five times a day or the need of Orthodox Jews to be home by sunset on Fridays, distorts the employment pattern towards self-employment or part-time working. Clearly, though, the adherents of the various religions compose the majority of workforces worldwide, and participate, therefore, in work communication to an important extent.

Social class, education and other differences

Social class is one dimension on which Western European societies became less diverse during the last quarter of the twentieth century, with the growth of a large category of 'intermediate' and other non-manual workers and a decrease in the percentage of all manual workers, especially the unskilled. These changes were largely a result of the decline of manufacturing and heavy industry. These trends are set to continue, reinforced by government policies that see an increase in the educational and technical skill levels of the population as essential to international competitiveness. In Asia, increasing industrialization led to a major shift away from rural employment to urban, and to substantial growth in the size of the middle class.

Final educational level is undeniably a major source of difference between individuals in the workplace. There is in the EU, for instance, a considerable amount of initial job segregation of graduates, 18-year-old school leavers with higher-level school qualifications (such as A-Level), 16-year-old school leavers with qualifications and those who leave school at the earliest legal date without qualifications. In this respect, the UK, for instance, is still elitist, despite recent changes, compared with some international competitors, such as the USA or South Korea, where about 70 per cent of the population receive university-level qualifications.

Other educational/professional differences also create significant differences between groups of people at work. Examples include subject specialization (especially science versus arts), independent versus state-maintained schooling (because of its perceived implications for social class) and professional training (consider the problems created by legal jargon, 'academese' and civil-servant-speak.) These non-cultural differences are not, however, a main focus of this book.

Box 1.4

'In Britain, class and money overlap, but only partially, like circles in a Venn diagram. Not all posh people are rich (some are shabby genteel, scrimping and saving for the school fees), and vice versa. Class is a magical amalgam of education, occupation, accent, vocabulary ("lounge" or "sitting room"), outlook and habit.

There is no denying that class is alive and potent. The structure of the British economy has changed, with the proletariat shrinking and the middle class bulging; celebrities have ousted aristocrats in the gossip columns. But most Britons still instinctively filter themselves and others into social classes, with attendant suspicions and snobberies.'[a]

'Sixty years after India's constitution banned caste discrimination, Hinduism's millennia-old hierarchy retains a tight grip. Lonely-hearts ads in the newspapers are classified by caste and sub-caste. Brahmins, at the top, dominate many professions. There are still hundreds of "honour killings" by which families avenge inter-caste marriages and liaisons. Caste discrimination is still drearily evident in the wretched lives of *dalits*, formerly "untouchables", who remain India's poorest and least educated people.'[b]

Sources: (a) *The Economist*, 10 December 2009
(b) *The Economist*, 10 June 2010

By the beginning of the third millennium, several forces were bringing about a great expansion in the amount and range of contacts with 'different others' experienced by people round the globe through their work. This section has shown that, numerically, both the population at large and the workforces in Europe and Asia are diverse and are continuing to become more so. This implies a significant increase in the amount, and therefore the importance, of intergroup (intercultural) interpersonal communication at work. This section has also shown that, despite an improvement in their societal position, minorities' earnings, employment rates and career prospects are still below those of the majority group. Furthermore, there is an increasingly important interface between workers in developing countries such as India and workers or customers in the developed countries. The inevitable discrepancies in economic security and disposable income are part of the context of intercultural communication at work.

1.3 THE GROWING IMPORTANCE OF (SUB)CULTURAL DIVERSITY AT WORK

The diversity described in the previous section was demographic. There is some agreement that demographic factors are important particularly for their effects on psychological factors, such as values, beliefs and attitudes, and thus on behaviour, especially communication behaviour. Arguing that researchers should examine other facets of diversity in addition to demographic background traits, Dansby and Knouse (1999) pointed out that, in a group dynamics study, as the time that group members worked together increased, the effects of surface-level diversity (demographic and physical differences) decreased, whereas those of deep-level diversity (attitudes, beliefs and values) increased.[24] As later chapters will show, differences in attitudes, beliefs and values are related to culture. This section makes the case for linking diversity with (sub)cultural differences in the context of work. There are many different understandings of culture. These will be discussed in Sections 1.4 and 1.5, but for now we will use the term to mean a society or social system from the point of view of its members' shared beliefs and preferred ways of doing things. Subcultures are groupings that exist within or cut across cultures – 'French women' or 'women' respectively, for example. The meaning of subculture will also be discussed in Section 1.5.

In the late twentieth and early twenty-first centuries, the trends described in Section 1.2 substantially increased the need to adapt to cultural difference at work: it started to become a major concern of general management, marketing and human resource management. Among the reasons were the exponential growth in the amount of contact among 'different others' at work, noted above. Another was the demonstration by researchers that from the point of view of work the significant differences among 'different others' included cultural differences as well as those of language, education and experience. Researchers also showed for the first time that cultural differences between modern societies are profound, significantly affect how people behave, may be less amenable to training or retraining than other sources of difference and are not disappearing, so that the 'investment' to adjust for them was seen as worthwhile. In the words of one author: 'Culture pervades and radiates meanings into every aspect of the enterprise.'[25] The following are some 'aspects of the enterprise' affected by culture and the reasons for their increasing importance:

- Cultural differences are known to affect people's purchasing behaviour, and therefore the most effective ways of marketing to them. Content analyses of Chinese and US food advertisements showed that community, popular, ornamental, status, health and nutrition appeals were more frequently used in China than in the USA, where independence appeals were more common. These differences were linked to cultural differences between the two countries: China is collectivist, high in power distance and has a strong long-term orientation; the USA is more individualistic. Overall, the findings suggested that advertising appeals in global markets reflected the dominant cultural values in each country.[26] Another 11-country study found that cultural variables influenced the focus of consumers' product information search activities.[27] With spreading globalization, more organizations must take these kinds of difference into account. Factors that influence perceived service quality, such as reliability, responsiveness, assurance, tangibles and empathy, are influenced by culture.[28]

Box 1.5

'As consumers, Koreans look for a complex product and service. This explains the failure of Walmart in Korea. Korean superstores, such as those of Emart, which is the dominant chain, unlike Walmart are attractively laid out and provide helpful assistants. Westerners are more practical in their shopping; Koreans are more emotional, and seek a pleasant shopping experience. Again, South Korean IT is unique – it shows high creativity and innovativeness. The country has 7 or 8 web search engines and they are very different in style from Google or Yahoo. Each page is much more densely filled with a variety of content. This may reflect a culturally-influenced, more holistic, less "linear" way of using information and thinking. Again, for Koreans, their mobile is a navigation tool – it has been developed to have that functionality. Korea developed a social networking web service before Facebook, called "I Love School".

Source: interview with a South Korean executive, author's research

- A study of adoptions by medium-sized companies in ten European countries found that national cultural differences helped explain the variance in firms' decisions to adopt innovations such as Enterprise Resource Planning (ERP) software. This finding indicates that globalizing business-to-business marketing as well as consumer marketing requires allowing for cultural difference.[29]

- In service businesses, success depends on effective interactions and communications between people. 'Delivering service products requires employees with well-developed interpersonal skills; cultural similarity between the service provider and the customer may improve the effectiveness of service delivery and the perceived quality of service.'[30] The clear implication here is that culture influences the interactions between services providers and their customers. Several studies have found that ethnicity and gender affect interactions between employees and customers in service businesses. Organizations may better understand and meet customers' needs in ethnic and international markets if they not only have a diverse workforce but also 'listen' to its diverse contributions.

- The importance of culture for international business and the problems managers have in dealing with it have been summarized as follows: 'As markets globalize, the need for standardization in organizational design, systems and procedures increases. Yet managers are also under pressure to adapt their organization to the local characteristics of the market, the legislation, the fiscal regime, the socio-political system and the cultural system.'[31]

- Diversity in domestic organizations became a growing concern, 'as more and more minorities are brought into domestic work forces.'[32] From about 1960, fairness concerns and pressure from minority groups led many countries to pass equal opportunities legislation. It became unlawful to discriminate in employment against people on the grounds of their 'race' (ethnicity) or gender. Over subsequent years, the coverage and demands of this kind of legislation gradually expanded. However, traditional equal opportunities approaches came to be criticized for denying differences. 'Equal rights necessarily came to mean we are all the same.'[33] A later trend was towards valuing diversity, which means 'viewing people as having equal rights while being different'. Valuing diversity in the workplace 'is about recognising, valuing, and managing people's differences and about sharing power and communicating'. Workplace diversity focuses on 'empowering people of all kinds to develop and contribute their own unique talents to solving our business problems', rather than having employees 'give up their own ethnic, gender, or individual identities to be successful'. Heightened concern with diversity stems not only from the growing presence of women and minorities in the work force, but also from modern organizational strategies that require more interaction among employees of different functional backgrounds. The effects on performance were, and still are, unclear. Studies have found both positive and negative effects of workforce diversity on performance. Some have shown that group diversity both enhances and diminishes task performance. The negative effects may result from poor management of diversity. Even though working with diversity is intrinsically more demanding, good management of diversity can enhance overall performance.[34]

Tung (1993) argued that there are important similarities, as well as differences, in managing diversity in international and national contexts. There was a need, however, for more emphasis on the domestic issue rather than the international one.[35] In a later presentation, Tung (1996) explained why: '[First] due to the localization policies of most host countries and the rising costs of expatriation, there will be a decrease in the number of expatriates. In comparison, the problem of managing intra-national diversity is definitely increasing in size and magnitude...;

[second]…expatriates involved in managing cross-national diversity do so on a short-term basis (2 to 3 years). In contrast, in light of the changing demographics of the…workforce, those involved in managing intra-national diversity are expected to have a long-term (permanent) commitment to such policies and practices.'[36]

In addition to these trends that increased the importance of cultural difference at work, there was also concern with 'capturing individual capabilities and motivating the entire organization to respond to the demands of the environment'. Earlier, companies were mainly concerned with strategy; organizational structures were designed to support strategy. Companies believed that by changing their structure they automatically changed the 'shared norms, values and beliefs that shape the way individual managers think and act'.[37]

Box 1.6

The 500 employees of a British-owned start-up in India are all Indians but they speak nine different languages as their mother tongue. The working language is English, but away from the office they speak to one another in Hindi, unless they are from South India. Hindi is the common language of North Indians but is little known and less used in the south. In spoken Hindi there is a strong admixture of English words, and not only for technical or modern terms or where there is no Hindi equivalent. For instance, the Hindi for 'table' is 'mez', but 'table' is used.

Source: author's research

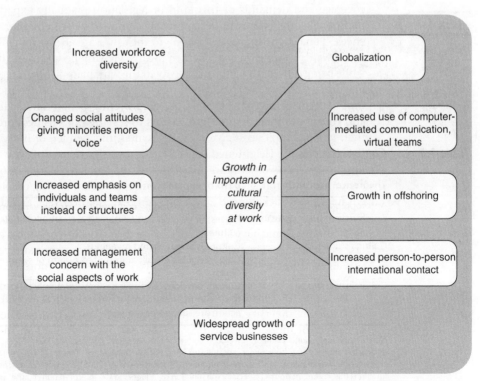

Figure 1.2   *Factors increasing the importance of cultural diversity at work*

Because these assumptions of managerial responsiveness were false, many organizations were incapable of carrying out the sophisticated strategies they developed.

Recognizing the constraints placed on strategy implementation by individuals' limitations brought a shift in organizational priorities; there was a new emphasis on individual capabilities and motivations as key factors for implementing strategy. Growth, development and prosperity were seen to depend on developing a creative, consultative culture in which individuals could contribute fully. Human capital came to be regarded as the strategic resource of the future;[38] the role of managers began to change from directing to facilitating, coaching and mentoring.[39] Organizations started to try 'to build into their very structure' the capacity for individual learning and development.[40] Finally, the increasing use of teams as a way of organizing work added to the pressure for attending to the social aspects of work.[41]

Figure 1.2 summarizes these influences on the growing importance of cultural diversity at work.

1.4 WHAT IS CULTURE?

Individuals are rarely conscious of their culture, yet culture affects practically all aspects of the way the people of a society or societal group interact with each other or with outsiders. There is a whole range of ways of defining culture, many of which provide complementary views of what it is.[42] Table 1.1 briefly describes those understandings of culture that are drawn on in this book as underpinning for the study of cultural differences in communication.

Box 1.7

A dataset of 41 large European firms in the banking and insurance industry found that entry into new foreign markets and new cultural zones was associated with higher levels of international capacity at top management team level.

Source: Greve, P., Nielsen, S. and Ruigrok, W. (2003) 'Transcending borders with international top management teams: a study of European financial multinational corporations', *European Management Journal*, **27**(3): 213–24

Table 1.1   *Cultural theories*

Theoretical approach	Basis of explanation
Anthropological	Core values shared by communities explain variations in behaviours.
Communication perspective	Process, interaction and meaning are central; people co-create their culture.
Cultural studies	Culture is about shared meanings.
Social identity	Culture is a historically transmitted system of symbols, meanings and norms.
Cultural psychology	Culture provides 'symbolic systems' and only by participating in these can the intentional states by which human experience and action are shaped be realized.

Note: Other definitional elements have been added by other scholars. For instance, Hall (1997) saw culture as drawing arbitrary lines between acceptable and unacceptable behaviour;[43] Triandis (1994) emphasized a characteristic way of perceiving a social environment;[44] Spencer-Oatey (2005) brought in a description of the functions that culture performs, especially the function of influencing the interpretation of other people's behaviour.[45]

Cultural diversity assumed greater importance as organizations came to recognize that increased demographic diversity meant increased cultural diversity and that culture affects many aspects of business and management.

Values as the basis of culture

Values have been defined as follows: 'Concepts or beliefs that pertain to desirable end states or behaviors, transcend specific situations, guide selection or evaluation of behavior and events and are ordered by relative importance'.[46] Values are also broad tendencies to prefer certain states of affairs to others. Terms like good or evil and dirty or clean usually express values. Many values have to do with someone's position on, and the importance they attach to, various moral, religious, political or ecological issues. They have been described as 'the most important indicator in the analyses and prediction of human action and behavior' and 'a means to understanding the underlying motivation (the "why") behind individual behavior'.[47] A literature review found that values are related to such practical work concerns as decision style, strategic action, innovation, creativity, commitment, managerial satisfaction and organizational competitiveness.

A major part of cross-cultural research has sought to identify values or motivational goals that differentiate cultures. This emphasis on values was advocated by Rokeach (1993), who wrote: 'The value concept, more than any other, should occupy a central position....able to unify the apparently diverse interests of all the sciences concerned with human behavior.'[48] Within this approach, values are viewed as the criteria people use to select and justify actions and to evaluate people (including the self) and events. Societal institutions such as the family, education, economic, political and religious systems function according to, and their goals and their modes of operation express, cultural value priorities. For example, in societies where individual ambition and success are highly valued, the organization of the economic and legal systems is likely to be competitive. In contrast, a cultural emphasis on group well-being is likely to be expressed in more co-operative economic and legal systems. Because cultural value priorities are shared, role incumbents in social institutions can draw on them to select socially appropriate behaviour and to justify to others their behavioural choices, such as to go to war or to fire employees.[49] Section 2.3 describes values approaches in more depth.

Communication as the basis of culture

Over a number of years, approaches that place communication at the centre of culture have gained increasing acceptance. For instance Aldridge (2002) defined culture as follows:

> [Culture is] the shared system of symbolic knowledge and patterns of behavior, derived from speech communication, that human individuals carry to provide predictable internal and external psychological stability so as to prevent chaos among human individuals. We learn cultural codes for social life, role expectations, common definitions of situations, and social norms in order to provide predictability and survival of the human species. Human language (spoken and written) is the symbolic glue for human culture.[50]

A communication perspective emphasizes process, interaction and meaning. Most communication theorists argue that people are not passive representatives of culture but regulators of a complex system, which they co-create during interaction.

For Kincaid *et al.* (1983), communication was the work required to sustain a human group; it consists of the transfer of information among individuals, groups or cultures. Groups cluster together according to common beliefs, values and behaviour. Cultures are nothing more than common ways of thinking and acting, which develop because of relatively isolated within-group communication. Cultures differ from one another because there is less contact between cultures than within them. If everybody communicated with people outside their culture as much as they do with people within it, cultures would soon disappear.[51] Haslett (1989) held that culture and communication are acquired simultaneously: neither exists without the other. Culture by definition was a 'shared, consensual way of life and sharing and consensus is made possible only by communication'; in turn, humans communicate in a cultural environment that constrains the form and nature of communication. Through communication, members of a culture share a perspective or world view, although members may not share that perspective equally or in every aspect of experience.[52] According to Burke *et al.* (2002), too, culture and communication are closely linked.

Culture as communication is the process of creating and using shared meanings within a specific community and its history. This cultural approach to communication emphasizes that people exist in a world of shared meanings, which they (usually) take for granted. Additionally, members of a culture continually participate in the production, maintenance and reproduction of a shared sense of what is real.[53,54] (Thus this cultural model of communication is based within the theories associated with the social construction of reality.) Human beings live in a world whose meaning they have produced through their own culture. This notion is reinforced by most theories of socialization, which suggest that within modern societies certain activities and institutions, such as religions, families and schools, function to tell citizens or group members who they are and how they are to behave.

Shared meanings as the basis of culture

For scholars in the cultural studies tradition, such as Stuart Hall (1997), culture is about 'shared meanings'. Meanings are produced and exchanged through language, which is

---

Box 1.8

'There are some commonly held attitudes in our [Italian] culture which are different from those in other European countries and which must be taken into consideration if we want to study in more depth the anomalous situation of the Italian family in a European context. We have found some aspects which are…strongly anchored in tradition: the lack of development of a "single" way of life, "over-coddling", the protection offered by the family, the desire for certain guarantees in order to leave home without running any risks and the emphasis placed on the parental role. These are all aspects which show the importance and the role of the family in Italy and which provide an answer – a family one – to the structural difficulties encountered by young people which have led them to "emancipate themselves within the family rather than to emancipate themselves from the family". Two elements have emerged that indicate a change in family characteristics, i.e. a change in the parent/child relationship and an attenuation in gender differences due to the female entrance in the labour force.'

Source: Menniti, A., Misiti, M. and Savioli, M. 'Italian stay-at-home children: attitudes and constraints', URL: www.demogr.mpg.de/Papers/workshops/000906_paper01.pdf (internal references omitted), last accessed on 14 December 2010

the medium through which we 'make sense' of things. Meanings can only be shared through language. Thus, 'to say that two people belong to the same culture is to say that they interpret the world in roughly the same ways and can express themselves, their thoughts and feelings about the world, in ways which will be understood by each other.' To communicate, people must speak the 'same language' – broadly, be able to use the same 'cultural codes'; they must interpret visual images, sounds, body language and facial expressions in broadly similar ways. They must also know how to translate their feelings and ideas into these various codes.[55]

'This is not to deny that, within a culture, there may be different meanings, even for the same word or symbol, or that people within a culture may feel that they belong to different groups, have different identities or think different thoughts.'[56] Furthermore, culture is not only 'in the head'; it organizes and regulates social lives. It is a process or set of practices which means that individuals function within a context of cultural assumptions as well as a network of social, political and economic factors. Cultural studies treats discourses as ways of referring to or constructing knowledge about a particular topic or practice: they reflect the ideas and assumptions implicit in the communication of a group or society. For example, medical discourse refers to the ideas and assumptions associated with the medical world. While any one society includes multiple discourses, some discourses may be dominant in their influence and ability to shape what is defined as reality. This means that discourses have power relations embedded in them. For instance, the phrase 'doctor's orders' expresses the power exerted over patients by doctors – power based on their expertise and assumed beneficence.[57] Following this logic, culture can be defined as the way of life of a group or society including meanings, the transmission, communication and alteration of those meanings and the power relations that decide which meanings are accepted and which have more significance than others.

As an example of the practical application of the 'shared meaning' view of culture, it has been argued that 'brand personalities' are symbols and carriers of culture. Research found that Spanish brand personalities had some dimensions in common with North American (sincerity, excitement and sophistication) and others that differed – passion (Spanish) and competence and ruggedness (American). Japanese brand personalities shared sincerity, excitement, competence and sophistication with American, but also had the dimension of peacefulness.[58]

Figure 1.3 shows the key ideas of the 'culture as communication' theorists described in this chapter.

Social or cultural identities as the basis of culture

Communication and culture are seen as inextricably intertwined within another approach – cultural identity theory. A cultural identity is part of an individual's self-construal, or sense of selfhood. (Self-construals are explained further in Chapter 4.) Cultural identity is the part of the self-construal that derives from a person's knowledge of his or her membership in a cultural group (or groups), together with the value and emotional significance attached to that membership. A cultural identity is an aspect of social identity. That part of the self-construal not accounted for by social identity is personal identity. Within cultural identity theory, culture is defined as a historically transmitted system of symbols, meanings and norms. Symbols and meanings are what groups of people say, do, think and feel. To be a member of a group is to communicate with other members. This interpretation of culture is radically different from those approaches in which cultural status is determined mainly by birth rather than by subscribing to a system of symbols and meanings.

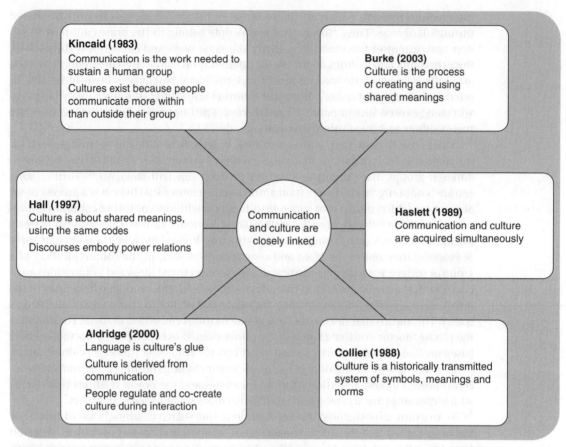

Figure 1.3   *Key ideas of culture theorists for whom communication is central to culture*

Box 1.9

'Switzerland's EU ties are governed by a web of some 120 agreements and treaties, and this bilateral approach is still the preferred choice of government, business and most voters.
Swiss people fear their identity might "dissolve" in the EU, says Ms. Calmy-Rey [the Swiss foreign minister]. It is an identity that revolves around neutrality and an awkward tradition of citizens' referendums.'

_____

Source: *The Economist*, 3 December 2009

The close link between communication and identity is reflected in findings that inter-group identity issues appeared to account better than either power differentials or language competence for conversation style differences observed when discourse analysis was applied to intercultural decision-making meetings, specifically those involving US-born native English speakers and participants from East Asian countries.[59]

Core symbols are particularly important. For example, a core symbol for collectivist cultures, such as Mexico's, may be bondedness, whereas a core symbol for a more individualist culture, such as mainstream culture in the US, may be individual accomplishment.[60] Meanings include metaphors, stories and myths. Norms are patterns of appropriate ways of communicating; attached to norms are prescriptions, proscriptions and social sanctions, while stories that are told often relate to norm violations and how they are punished. For example, the Biblical story of Sodom and Gomorrah refers to Hebrew norms against certain sexual practices; the folk tale of the fisherman who was granted three wishes but lost everything through asking for too much refers to a widespread norm against greed.

There are different types of culture corresponding to different types of groups which, according to cultural identity theorists, meet the requirements for being a culture. Cultural groups include corporations, support groups, national groups or civil rights groups; cultural groups are any such groups that are bounded (have restricted membership), have histories and are significant to individuals. This is why each individual has a range of cultures to which s/he belongs. Symbols and norms change over the lifetime of culture systems, but there is enough consistency in what is handed down to make it possible to define the boundaries between systems and distinguish members of one cultural system from those of another.

Thus, for cultural identity theorists, national cultures are only one type among many. (This, of course, exposes the theory to the criticism that you end up with a 'culture of one'.) In fact, because many people contribute to the creation of a national culture's symbols, meanings and norms, national culture is diffuse. Ethnicity, gender, profession, geographical area and organization are other bases for cultural difference. The meanings and associations attributed to any category of people 'are a product of the enduring images and characteristics people have ascribed and assigned to men [sic] in groups over time'.[61] For instance, masculinity can be defined as a social and symbolic construct. Based upon a survey of contemporary published research regarding masculinity, Chesebro and Fuse (2001) concluded that masculinity is now a construct that attributes ten traits to people viewed as masculine. These traits, it is suggested, overlap with, but are not identical with, those that would have been part of the construct of masculinity at other times. Cultural identities are enduring yet dynamic; for instance, the idea of what it means to be a woman changed considerably during the twentieth century, but the underlying idea of difference from men persisted.[62] A further point was made by Delmestri (2006), who argued that individuals are able to participate in multiple cultural traditions and to maintain distinctive and inconsistent action frames. Quantitative information on 418 Italian middle managers, working for local and international firms in Italy, and qualitative information on 113 of them, revealed that, whereas the majority in Italian firms enacted a traditional Italian identity, the majority in international firms enacted Anglo-Saxon identities, and more so in US and British firms.[63]

An identity to which people normally pay little attention becomes more important to them when, for instance, they meet for the first time with people whom they perceive to have a different cultural identity – for example, when they travel abroad. This point will be seen to have considerable importance in Chapter 6 when intercultural communication is considered.

> The cultural theories relevant to this book variously emphasize values, communication, shared meanings and identity. Culture and communication are strongly related in the last three of these approaches.

1.5 OTHER CONCEPTUAL ISSUES

A number of important conceptual issues remain to be discussed – the questions of whether the very concept of 'culture' is an error, of how explanatory and how general-izable concepts of culture are, of whether intracultural behaviours can be generalized to intercultural situations and of whether cultures are converging.

Is to use the term 'culture' to fall into an essentialist error?

The assertion that the term 'culture' is a reification has gained ground since about the year 2000. For example, Gjerde (2004) wrote: 'Cultural psychology, as conceived by many [cultural psychologists] is typically based on the supposition of unified groups that can be studied in their organic totality. The result is essentialism: the assumption that a group contains features emblematic of all its members. This assumption is peril-ous because it easily can lead people to be viewed as exchangeable carbon copies and promote disregard for heterogeneity, agency, and individuality.'[64] Clearly, if that was the assumption of cultural psychologists, it would be an error. However, the assertion seems disputable. For example, Markus and Kitayama (1991), in one of the articles cited by Gjerde (2004) as falling into the essentialist error, includes in its conclusion the words 'Is it the case, as we suggest here, that these norms can sometimes be inter-nalised to the extent that they determine the nature of one's experience?'[65] The use of the unanswered question and the word 'sometimes' surely exonerate Markus and Kitayama (1991) from a charge of supposing that unified groups can be studied in their organic totality. Equally, Hofstede (1981) made it clear that not all members of a culture would hold the culture's values to the same degree,[66] as Section 2.1 of this book explains. Certainly the position taken here is that culture can be and is often, but not always, an influence; but it is never a determinant.

How much does culture explain?

Given that any one individual is potentially a member of multiple cultural and subcul-tural groups, how can behaviours be identified with any one type of group? Secondly, with so many factors influencing behaviour, including genetic, epigenetic, familial, local, social (such as the environment of a particular school or a particular set of friends) and individual experience, how can we know what behaviours to attribute to culture? As Hickson and Pugh (1995) pointed out, it may be hard to determine whether a 'highly personal, verbal practice of communication [in an organization] is due to a culture that values person-to-person contact or to illiteracy among employees who could not read written instructions'.[67]

When transcripts of intercultural negotiations between Taiwanese and US Americans were analysed to compare the two cultures in their use of self-positive, other-positive, self-negative and other-negative facework, it was found that culture and other aspects of an interaction combined to influence communication choices, rather than culture playing the dominant role. This contradicts a perspective that culture has a global influence.[68] As Hickson and Pugh (1995) suggested, 'Perhaps it helps most to see the world as multi-causal, with many factors acting and interacting simultaneously.... Whatever one's view, a sensitivity to the part likely to be played by societal cultures does aid understanding. Difficult though it may be to say exactly what that part is, the notion of culture is persistently useful and its manifestations are persistently recognizable.'

How broadly can concepts of culture be applied?

National boundaries are a convenient synonym for a culture. This framing of the concept is somewhat imprecise, however, since no nation is so pure that all of its members share a worldview. Nevertheless, members of a nation face a set of common experiences, themes and institutions that help shape their values and ways of viewing the world. These shared experiences include geography, climate, economy, political system, racial mix, religious mix, media, language, educational system and so on. They result in a unique national character that is often more apparent to foreigners than to the nationals themselves.[69] Some scholars have argued that particular types of national culture, such as a country's political culture, are most relevant for certain analyses. For instance, 'At first sight, Switzerland is a country with multiple internal cultures and borders; [however] a closer analysis shows that the Swiss people share a common political culture based upon attachment to local communities and institutions, to government through consensus and to conflict solving by resorting to arbitration and pragmatism.' In the Swiss case, it is argued, management practices are embedded in national political cultures.[70]

There seems to be agreement that the term 'culture' can be applied to a much wider range of groupings than the national or ethnic. For example, Kim (1988) wrote: 'Culture is not viewed as limited to the life patterns of conventionally recognizable culture groups such as national, ethnic or racial. Instead it is viewed as potentially open to all levels of groups whose life patterns.... influence individuals' behaviour.'[71] Hofstede (1981) wrote: 'The word culture is used here in the sense of the "collective programming of the mind" which distinguishes the members of one category of people from another. The "category of people" can be a nation, regional or ethnic group (national etc. culture), women versus men (gender culture), old versus young (generation culture), a social class, a profession or occupation (occupational culture), a type of business, a work organization or part of it (organizational culture) or even a family.'[72] However, Hofstede also considered that gender, generation and class cultures can only partly be classified by the dimensions found for national cultures. This was because they are not *groups* but *categories* of people. Countries (and ethnic groups too) are integrated social systems. The dimensions (individualism–collectivism, power distance, uncertainty avoidance and masculinity/femininity – see Chapter 2, Section 1) apply to the basic problems of such systems. Categories such as gender, generation or class are only parts of social systems and therefore not all dimensions apply to them. Gender, generation and class cultures should be described in their own terms, Hofstede (1981) argued, based on special studies of such cultures.

Surface culture differences are to be found in all types of grouping – age groups (e.g., the different ways pensioners and teenagers dress), religions (the Muslim shalwar kameez versus Western Christian teenagers' mini-skirts), genders (skirts versus trousers), occupations (the relative formality of most bankers' work clothes with the shirt-sleeve approach in the creative departments of advertising agencies). With deep culture, however, the case appears less clear. As Chapters 3 and 4 will show, research has found significant differences among genders, age groups, religious groups and so on in some communication behaviours and in some underlying values, attitudes, orientations and motivations. In Switzerland, empirically measurable differences in attitudes, openness to technical communication forms and ethnocentricity clearly correlated with the linguistically distinct cultures of the German-speaking and Latin areas.[73] Other studies have shown that subgroups that vary in acculturation may have similar cultural values. A scale of cultural identity developed for Latino adolescents included cultural values such as *respeto* (respect for authority) and *feminismo* (attitudes towards traditional sex roles). However, those cultural values did not differentiate among sub-groups of Latinos identified as Latino, American or bicultural.[74] In most cases it has not been demonstrated whether or not specific subcultural differences extend beyond broader cultural or civilizational boundaries. For example, the declining communica-tive abilities of people over the age of 65, widely observed in the West, may or may not extend to those collectivist countries where the elderly are revered. We simply do not know as yet.

In this book nationality, ethnicity and religion are regarded as full cultural div-isions. Of these, the term 'culture' is widely applied only to 'nationality'; 'ethnicity', where it does not correspond to nationality, has not been well researched, so that the interaction of the two variables is not understood, while there is disagreement over whether religion is a fundamental influence on culture. (Hofstede (1981) saw language and religion as rather insignificant in cultural terms, but Huntington (1997) saw them as 'the central elements of any culture or civilization'[75]). However, nearly all the generalizations about cultural influences in this book apply to these three categories of groups. A statement such as 'Culture implies a shared world view and set of values which are largely held unconsciously because they were inculcated in childhood' would apply to most members (not all) of the same national, ethnic or religious groups. The members of some other social categories, such as gender, social class or occupational groups, typically conform to many of the norms and values of their dominant culture, but also have beliefs, attitudes, habits and forms of behaviour that deviate from those of others in their society. This reasoning leads them to be treated here as subcultures. The statement 'Culture implies a shared world view, etc.' would not apply easily to gender groups. Women with different religious beliefs do not share a world view; generally, men from Japan are positioned well apart from men from the USA on some cultural dimensions, whereas Americans of both genders and all social classes are closer together. On the other hand, a statement such as 'Cultural differences lead to differences in communication styles' does apply to gender, social class and occupational groups: women communicate differently from men, working-class people differently from upper-class people, engineers from publishers (especially at work) across national, ethnic and religious boundaries. Overall, however, gender, social class, sexual orientation, age and educational, technical, professional and experiential background, though having a profound effect on the way people think and behave, do not meet the full criteria for cultures. For these societal subdivisions, some, but not all, generalizations about cultural influences will apply. Disability and sexual orientation are to some degree unknown. Some people with disabilities were born with them, and may have acquired particular world views and values as they grew up. Others will not have.

All these distinctions have fuzzy boundaries. There is substantial intra-group vari-ation as well as inter-group difference. Not every Japanese person has a highly col-lectivist outlook; not every Muslim practises polygamy. The important point is to be aware of cultural and subcultural influences and how they may be affecting one's own and others' behaviour, while still remembering that individual variations due to differ-ences in heredity, family, schooling and experience sometimes modify and outweigh those influences.

There is a view that groupings below the level of nation, such as those based on age, class, sex, education, ethnicity, religion, abilities or sexual orientation, and other unifying elements, should be termed co-cultures. 'The term co-culture is embraced over other terminology to signify the notion that no one culture … is inherently

Box 1.10

Although less well known in the West than the Chinese Feng Shui system of architectural design, India has its own, called Vaastu, which is widely adhered to. New homes are advertised as 'Vaastu compliant' and newspaper columns are devoted to solving the problems caused by a lack of Vaastu compliance in the home. The term Vaastu, a Sanskrit term meaning a dwelling place, was initially used to refer to the homes of gods. However, with time, it came to be associated with the right location as well as design of almost any structure. Some examples of Vaastu principles are that the kitchen should be in the South-East, the dining room in the West, the living room and the master bedroom in the South-West, the guest bedroom in the North-West, the bath room in the East or the North, the prayer room in the North-East and so also the well and water supply. Such general principles are, however, inadequate to make a building fully Vaastu compliant, and detailed charts are used to ensure compliance.

Source: author's research and URL: http://www.homedesignfind.com/how-to-tips-advice/principles-of-vaastu-shastra/, last accessed on 14 December 2010

superior (though it may be dominant) over other co-existing cultures. The intention is to avoid the negative or inferior connotations of past descriptions (i.e., *sub*culture) while acknowledging the great diversity of influential cultures that simultaneously exist.'[76] In this book, the term subculture will be retained, but it is not intended to connote inferiority, only that we are talking about a level of analysis below that of broad cultures.

Can intracultural behaviours be generalized to intercultural situations?

This question is clearly important. Although cultural differences in behaviour are intrinsically interesting, a major part of the concern with them has been with a view to facilitating intercultural communication. Unfortunately, we do not really have an answer to the question. There has been a tendency to assume that intracultural interactive behaviours will generalize to intercultural situations, but a serious argument has been made in the context of negotiating that this may be a false assumption, particularly among people from cultures where ingroups are treated very differently from outgroups:

'Intracultural dyads with collectivist cultural values were found to be more likely to emphasize certain cooperatively oriented tactics than intracultural dyads with individualist cultural values.'[77] 'In a negotiation with an out-group member, however, a negotiator with collectivist values may strongly discriminate against the out-group, since mistrust and suspicion of out-group members is high.'[78]

As this researcher concluded, 'One should not assume that intracultural processes and behaviors of a cultural group will generalize to the intercultural context.' The position taken here is that, except in the one or two instances where research has demonstrated a disjunction between intracultural and intercultural behaviour, it is as well to keep in mind the possibility of cultural influence on the behaviour of different others, though without a mind closed to alternative interpretations. As far as the intercultural communication behaviours advocated in Chapter 6 are concerned, moreover, most of them would be worth practising in any communication context.

Are cultures converging?

Some readers may wonder whether cultural differences are disappearing so fast that it is unnecessary to allow for them. People increasingly buy the same products, use the same labour-saving, transportation and communication devices, are entertained in the same way by television and music systems. Many now dress in Western-style clothes, live in Western-style houses, work at Western-style jobs and conduct many of their conversations in English. Does this mean that cultures are converging? Are people worldwide coming to share the same values, world view, kinship system and social organization? This is a question that a number of scholars and researchers have addressed. The answers vary. For instance, Pinker (1994) noted that the difference between two cultures generally correlates with how long ago they separated; this suggests that cultures evolve.[79] On the level of individuals, research undertaken to extend the understanding of how culture functions investigated the cultural orientations of people originating from one nation, but working in two different national settings. The cultural dimensions of 429 Indian natives living and working in India were compared with those of 151 Indian migrants living and working in the USA. The study found significant cultural value differences between the two groups, both in terms of their total populations and in terms of breakdowns by occupation, gender, age, and level of education. The results suggested that the cultural values of individuals are more malleable than previously thought when they are exposed to another culture. (This may be particularly true when that culture is an aspirational one for many people.[80])

Li and Karakowsky (2002) argued that national culture and cultural influences on businesses are not necessarily stable, enduring characteristics. They can be altered, for instance, by consistent government policies. For example, in recent years, because of the effects of such policies, respect for authority, a traditional element in ethnic Chinese culture, has become less salient in both Hong Kong and Taiwan.[81] On the other hand, Hofstede's (1981) study provided little evidence of global convergence, but this was based on a comparison between points of time only four years apart – 1968 and 1972. However, Hofstede concluded, on more general grounds, 'There is very little evidence of international convergence over time, except an increase of individualism for countries that have become richer. Value differences between nations described by authors centuries ago are still present today, in spite of close contacts. For the next few hundred years, countries will remain culturally very diverse.'[82] As Aldridge (2002) pointed out, 'Each culture provides predictability, thus changing culture can be quite difficult unless the cultural value being changed has been demonstrated to be of less value or no longer useful to a particular group.'[83]

Empirically, the conclusion drawn from an analysis of the longitudinal World Values Surveys is that, if anything, values are diverging, and that change is being brought about, not by poorer countries adopting rich country values as a result of exposure to mass media, but by rich country values changing rapidly while poor country values are changing more slowly. Furthermore, it is a myth that there is a single 'Western' culture for other cultures to converge towards:

> The results of the analysis...suggest some important points that the convergence thesis overlooks or underestimates. The evidence indicates that culture in post-industrial nations is far from static or uniform. Convergence implicitly assumes that unchanging cultural values exist in richer nations, and exaggerates the degree of consensus between the core values of Americans and Europeans. The convergence thesis then goes on to assume that developing societies assimilate this monolithic American/Western culture.

But post-industrial societies themselves are experiencing profound long-term processes of value change – and they also differ significantly amongst themselves. There is a wealth of research demonstrating that the younger generation in rich nations differs significantly from their parents and grand-parents on self-expression values, such as tolerance of homosexuality, support for gender equality, concern about environmental protection, and willingness to...take part in direct political action. Far from being a static and homogeneous 'Western culture', the process of value change creates a moving target that affects all countries in the world....Moreover important cultural differences exist between Protestant and Catholic Europe, and between Western and Orthodox Europe, as well as between Europe and the United States. The persistent imprint of deep-rooted cultural traditions, left by given societies' religious heritage, as well as by distinctive historical experiences, ethnic cleavages, and social structures, means that the values found in contemporary post-industrial societies differ in important ways.[84]

Concerning subcultures, there are indications that ethnic, gender, sexual orientation and religious consciousness are increasing among some groups, and that the claims for rights made by these groups are evidence of an increased cultural and subcultural awareness and sense of difference. In the USA, and to a lesser extent in Western Europe, the ideal of a pluralistic, multicultural society has largely replaced the old ideal of the melting pot. Minorities that sought to preserve and enhance their sense of a separate identity have now come to be seen to have a strong moral case. In earlier times they were often seen by the majority as eccentric. There are backlashes, including among members of ethnic minorities themselves, but these may be regarded as signs of a general acceptance of the multicultural ideal. On gender rights, some developing countries are witnessing divergent trends. On the one hand, technological advance has facilitated the old cultural preference for boy children, leading to a situation described as '10 million missing girls'; on the other hand, affirmative action in education, public sector jobs and government has increased the influence of women. In the *panchayats* or village councils of India, for instance, reservations for women have led to an increased emphasis on health care, education for girls, road building and connectivity.[85] India decriminalized homosexuality in the 1990s, and by 2010 was contemplating introducing same-sex marriages; elsewhere, however, the trend was in the other direction: Uganda's mix of vigorous heterosexuality and religiosity led in 2009 to a proposed new law against homosexuals, whose supporters claimed it was needed to shore up family values.[86]

In a work context, Chiang and Birtch (2007) found empirical evidence to suggest both (national) cultural similarities and differences in employee reward preferences, but concluded that their study suggested that, although culture may impinge on reward preferences, its influence might be diminishing or giving way to a range of other contextual forces.[87] A study of how leaders from eight Central Eurasian countries perceived the work-related values of effective organizational leaders suggested that there is a cultural convergence of Central Eurasian values, norms, and practices toward those of Western cultures regarding how effective leadership in organizations ought to be executed.[88] However, data on the adoption of contingent employment practices in Europe suggested that convergence is limited by the institutional embeddedness of organizations. The data were drawn from organizations operating in Germany, Spain, Sweden, the Netherlands and the UK in 1991.[89]

In business, cultural difference has been expressed as 'cultural distance', which can be measured and compared. Characteristics such as dominant religion, business language, form of government, economic development and levels of emigration indicate two countries' cultural distance from one another. Cultural distance between countries may be reduced by increased communication, geographical proximity (leading to more contact) and cultural attractiveness. For individuals, foreign experience and acculturation may also decrease cultural distance. For organizations, the presence of 'bicultural' individuals may have a bridging effect. A 1997 report on a study of international joint ventures found no decrease in the effect of cultural distance over the previous three decades and concluded that values are stable over time. The concept of cultural distance has been criticized, however, because 'distance' is symmetrical, so that 'a Dutch firm investing in China is faced with the same cultural distance as a Chinese firm investing in the Netherlands. There is no support for such an assumption.'[90]

A study of multinational companies' (MNCs') decisions to standardize or customize (local) performance management systems found from a response sample of 97 Bulgarian and Romanian companies that overall cultural distance mattered less in customization decisions than specific cultural dimensions – power distance and masculinity – and global integration strategy.[91] Similarly, national cultural distance was found from a survey of 131 managers of subsidiaries of foreign MNCs to have less influence than organizational cultural distance on international technology transfer.[92]

In the context of international joint ventures, findings by Kaufmann and O'Neill (2007) suggested that greater cultural distance was associated with an increased probability that a marketing or supplier alliance would be formed and a lower probability that an innovation-oriented alliance would be formed.[93] In international acquisitions, Reus and Lamont (2009) found that cultural distance impeded the understandability of key capabilities that need to be transferred and also constrained communication between the acquirers and their acquired units. These factors resulted in a negative effect on acquisition performance. On the other hand, if these difficulties could be overcome, they found, acquisition performance was increased by cultural distance because, they postulated, it increased the range of learning opportunities available.[94] Finally, analysing a sample of 102 cross-border acquisitions by Dutch firms in 30 countries, Slangen (2006) found strong empirical support for the hypothesis that large differences in national culture reduced foreign acquisition performance if the acquired unit was tightly integrated into the acquirer, but that they enhanced acquisition performance if post-acquisition integration was limited.[95]

> Conceptual issues that are discussed in this section include the questions of whether 'culture' is a reification and whether intracultural behaviours can be generalized to intercultural contexts. Which behaviours to attribute to culture and which to other influences is often unclear; and many important societal groups do not exhibit the predominating characteristics of cultures. The term culture can usefully be applied in discussing ethnic and religious groups as well as nations; however, for other groups, such as those defined by gender, age, sexual orientation, social class, education and so on, the term 'subculture' may be more appropriate. Despite these and other limitations, cultural concepts are significant and understanding of cultural difference is important: cultural differences are brought to work and affect people's behaviour there. Cultures change, but deep cultures, unlike surface cultures, do not seem to be converging, and cultural and subcultural differences will continue to affect both the intra- and extra-organizational environments of people at work.

1.6 CULTURES, WORK AND ORGANIZATIONAL BEHAVIOUR

Culture has been credited with a strong influence on a society's economic prosperity.[96] Lee and Peterson (2000) argued that a society's propensity to generate independent, risk-taking, innovative, competitively aggressive and proactive entrepreneurs and firms

'South Korea relies on manufacturing for 60 to 70% of its GDP. In manufacturing industry, a military culture is strongly embedded....How this culture reveals itself can be shown by the following example: a new product is to be developed; Japan is used as a benchmark; Japan took 12 months to develop it; a target is sent down to a team to develop it within 6 months; the team accepts it as a mission and works round the clock – sacrificing personal life if necessary.

This is because "the organisation's success is our own success."

When Sony aimed at emulating Korea's prowess at execution, they studied Samsung but concluded that they could not copy it because they lack the military culture.'

Source: interview with a South Korean executive, author's research

depended on its cultural foundation. Culture strongly influenced how entrepreneurial people are, although economic, political–legal and social factors (also influenced by culture) moderated the relationship.[97] Muzychenko (2006) asserted that culture influences the cognition and behaviour of international entrepreneurs in identifying cross-border opportunities, as well as their competence in making related decisions.[98] Cultural differences in risk assessment may lie behind the findings of a large-scale exploratory study that national business cultures within Europe affected acquirers' beliefs about how to proceed in cross-border mergers and acquisitions. Specifically, the study found that national cultural differences affected beliefs about the value of due diligence and professional advisers in the pre-acquisition phase. By influencing how an acquirer regards target companies, the researchers suggested, these differences may have important consequences for the negotiation of deals and the subsequent management of the acquired company.[99] In marketing, cultural influences on consumers have long been recognized. 'Products are not just products: they become what they are as the result of their integration into particular contexts, i.e. by being creolized by the local socio-cultural and economic contexts.'[100]

Within organizations, culture affects behaviour at all levels. For instance, responses to Western management practices have shown that these practices can easily backfire in non-Western cultures.

'Some staff members grow cold and distant after receiving feedback on their work, and team members may clam up at meetings when asked for suggestions. A Western manager may view having subordinates participate in problem-solving to be a move towards making them feel valued, but an employee who has been taught deference to age, gender or title, might – out of respect – shy away from being honest or offering ideas, because offering suggestions to an elder or a boss might appear to them to be challenging authority. A time-conscious manager may wrongly see people whose cultures take a more relaxed view towards deadlines as being less committed to team goals, as well as less dependable, accountable and reliable. Another manager may be frustrated by an employee who nods in apparent understanding of a direction, then does not carry it out.'[101]

In addition to the above, corporate codes of ethics and corporate governance have been linked to culture. A comparison of the contents of 197 corporate codes of ethics (78 Australian, 80 Canadian and 39 Swedish) revealed that the contents of the

Australian and Canadian codes were similar but those of the Swedish codes were very different in some areas. In the view of the researchers, these differences reflected the cultural differences between Sweden and the other two countries.[102]

For most countries, the behaviour of their corporations is a subject of vital concern. They are key institutions in the generation and allocation of society's resources. Therefore distinct, complex systems of corporate governance to regulate corporate behavior have evolved. Scholars have sought to explain the diversity of these systems on a variety of grounds: the quest for economic efficiency, the existence of political constraints on financial institutions, and the differing nature of legal systems. While each of these factors has certainly been important in shaping systems of corporate governance around the world, one other significant factor that has received relatively little attention is culture. Corporate regulatory systems in both law and practice have been shaped not only by national policies, but also by the cultures of the countries concerned. Differing systems for regulating corporations, [are] based ... on strong cultural preferences.

In this way Salacuse (2003) argued that systems of corporate governance are strongly influenced by culture,[103] while Guirdham (2009) showed that the governance practices of businesses in five Asian countries were influenced by business culture.[104]

> National cultural differences have been linked to a range of economic, business and organizational concerns, including entrepreneurialism, pre-acquisition information seeking, consumer acceptance of new products, workers' responses to management approaches, corporate codes of ethics and systems of corporate governance.

1.7   THE GROWING IMPORTANCE OF INTERCULTURAL COMMUNICATION AT WORK

Interpersonal communication, which, as Section 1.1 showed, is vital for modern work effectiveness, is also the aspect of work where the impact of cultural difference is arguably most direct and experienced by most people. In the words of Khoo (1994):

'It is simply not enough for us to know how and why people differ culturally. We also need to know to what extent such differences can be generalized across situations, and especially to interactions with culturally different individuals. The need for a more global understanding of people, organizations, attitudes, norms, group processes, values and ways of operating can be enhanced by examining how people interact and transact, both among themselves as well as with culturally different individuals.'[105]

Although these remarks were addressed to intercultural researchers in particular, there seems no reason to doubt that they also apply to anyone concerned with cultural difference and its impact on work and organizations.

There is clear evidence that organizations should value skilled interpersonal communication. For instance, trust in both top management and an immediate supervisor is strongly related to the amount of information received by organizational members.[106] In turn, perceived organizational effectiveness is strongly related to trust in management. This finding remains significant across diverse organizations, industries and geographic locations. Again, a 1996 literature search reported, 'Communicated knowledge is viewed as probably the single most important source of competitive advantage into the 21st Century.' Since competitive advantage yields above normal financial performance,[107] it follows that there is a strong positive relationship between effective and efficient communication and financial performance.[108]

Parallel to, and as important as, the needs of managers for intercultural communication skills are the needs of the large numbers of service providers who interact directly with an increasingly diverse public. For example, health care organizations face demographic shifts in the patients served and their families. Ulrey and Amason (2001) found that cultural sensitivity and effective intercultural communication, besides helping patients, personally benefited health care providers by reducing their stress. Effective intercultural communication and cultural sensitivity were found to be related. Health care providers' levels of intercultural anxiety also were found to correlate inversely with effective intercultural communication.[109]

Communication at work may, however, be one of the more problematic consequences of diversity. Although diversity is 'an asset to be valued rather than a problem to be solved, ... communication can be seen to work best when people are similar, or at least on a similar wavelength,'[110] '... it should be clear that communication works better the more participants share assumptions and knowledge about the world.'[111] Research has indicated that people behave differently when they are interacting with others whom they perceive as culturally dissimilar: they ask more questions, but self-disclose less; they seek out information about dissimilarities instead of information about similarities. They are less willing to draw inferences about the attributes of people from other cultures. The researcher's conclusion was that 'people know how to get to know other people from the same culture but not from different cultures'.[112] The findings suggested that people experience intercultural contact as different, even difficult, and attempt to handle it differently. Grimes and Richard (2003) even argued that whether cultural diversity is advantageous or detrimental for organizations depends on how organization members communicate.[113]

For professionals, other service providers and interface workers, training in how to deal with people appropriately is gradually being introduced; similarly, equal opportunities awareness training is now widespread. However, most of the interpersonal skills training being provided gives little help in adjusting to the different values,

Box 1.12

A lawyer had three appointments with new clients in one morning. Judging from their names, he anticipated that the first would be a white Anglo-Saxon male, one a Bengali woman and one a French male. His prior expectations were that the communication with the first client would go most smoothly, that with the third the next most smoothly, while that with the second client, the Bengali woman, would be the most difficult.

However, these expectations were confounded. The white Anglo-Saxon male was aggressive from the beginning ('He had a chip on his shoulder against the law'), the French male was uncommunicative ('He seemed to be afraid of giving himself away'), while the Bengali woman, who was wearing a chador, was articulate, well educated and reasonable.

Source: author's research

attitudes and motives of different individuals; and most of the equal opportunities awareness training omits any serious treatment of communication. It is true that adaptation at the individual level can only be achieved through sensitivity, active listening and gaining feedback; nevertheless, awareness of cultural and subcultural difference and knowledge of how to communicate with different others is an important underpinning for such adaptation. This raises the question of how the work context affects intercultural communication. 'Work context' here refers to the fact that colleagues usually share an understanding of tasks and technical knowledge; also that their communication is influenced by their work roles and by the organizational culture. Does this work context obliterate or eliminate differences in communication and behaviour resulting from differences in backgrounds? Is it the case that: 'When social behaviour is regulated by other, less diffuse social roles, as it is in organizational settings, behaviour...primarily reflect(s) the influence of these other roles and therefore lose(s) much of its...stereotypical character?' The author who posed this question answered it in the negative from her own research findings on leadership styles: 'Nevertheless, women's leadership styles were more democratic than men's even in organization settings. This sex difference may reflect underlying differences in female and male personality or skills (e.g. women's superior social skills) or subtle differences in the status of women and men who occupy the same organizational role.'[114]

While, clearly, there are task and organizational constraints on differences in behaviour at work, the evidence that will emerge in this book confirms that such differences still obtain, are significant and need to be taken into account more than they are currently. The core competencies required of both domestic and international managers in the twenty-first century have been identified as an 'ability to balance the conflicting demands of global integration versus local responsiveness; an ability to work in teams comprised of peoples from multiple functions/disciplines, different companies, and diverse industry backgrounds; an ability to manage and/or work with peoples from diverse racial/ethnic backgrounds'.[115] These three competencies all depend on intercultural communication skills and all assume that cultural differences remain potent despite the work setting.

This point is reinforced by a second: how people communicate at work generally reflects the preferred style of one cultural or subcultural group. In Western societies, with some exceptions (such as Body Shop), the dominant style in most business organizations is that of the individualist, monochronic, universalistic male. In other societies, other modes prevail: in Hong Kong Chinese businesses, for instance, people tend to express themselves less explicitly than is usual in Western businesses. There is evidence that work and organizational effectiveness can be enhanced if more diverse communication modes operate, allowing entry and influence to the diverse values, attitudes and ideas of the diverse populations now involved. Third, large numbers of people interface with the public in the course of their work. As the behaviour of their clients, patients, students or customers may not be greatly affected by the task setting, the social and cultural influences on their co-interactors' behaviour are still likely to be paramount and need to be understood.

> The increasing diversity of domestic workforces, markets and populations, together with globalization, means that few organizations or individuals at work can afford to ignore cultural difference. For individuals to be effective at work in diverse organizations and societies or internationally, they need to be able to communicate interculturally. The work context does not suppress differences so far as to eliminate this need. Intercultural communication is difficult but achievable through awareness and skill development.

1.8 CONCLUSION

Communication can claim to be called the most important single work activity, and interpersonal communication has increased in importance with organizations' new emphasis on individuals and teams. In much of the world there has been a huge expansion in the demographic diversity of people typically met with through work in a range of roles, including as colleagues, customers, suppliers, advisers and many others. Increased demographic diversity implies increased cultural and subcultural diversity – diversity of values, identities, meanings and ways of communicating as well as beliefs, attitudes and ways of behaving. A number of conceptual issues are raised by discussions of culture, but, although there are limits to the concept's validity and scope, it seems clear that culture does influence, though it does not determine, work and communication behaviour. Culture has been linked to a range of economic, business and organizational concerns. Effectiveness in diverse organizations and societies, as well as internationally, depends, therefore, on effective intercultural communication.

QUESTIONS AND EXERCISES

1. What does 'diversity' mean to you?
2. Debate the contention from Section 1.1 that communication is the most important work activity in modern, service-oriented, team-based organizations. What other work activities might contend for this description and why?
3. Discuss the relative importance of the factors given in the text as contributing to the increased significance at work of (a) contact with different others, (b) intercultural communication.
4. The text gives two categories of benefits that diversity brings to organizations. What are they and are there others?
5. In as diverse a group of four or five people as is available, create a proforma for observing the effects of diversity on creativity in workgroups.
6. The dictionary definition of 'race' is 'group of persons or animals or plants connected by common descent'. How does this differ from the definitions of ethnicity given in this book?
7. In this text, the term 'ethnicity' is used rather than the term 'race'. What explanation may account for this?
8. Is it time to abolish the concept of ethnic minorities, as an article in *The Economist Online* argued on 22 October 2009?
9. What factors might account for the fact that women face 'harsh realities' in labour markets?
10. The text makes no distinction among the different types of diversity – national, ethnic, gender, disability, age, religion, sexual orientation, educational level, social class – in terms of their importance for work and work communication. Should it? Give reasons.
11. Box 1.3 discusses the implications for organizations of population ageing in most developed nations. How are these changes likely to affect the careers of younger workers? What skills are younger workers likely to need to work alongside or manage older workers?
12. Discuss the contention that disability is 'context-dependent'. What kinds of beliefs do people have about disability? How do these beliefs influence communication with people who have disabilities?

13. Do you agree with Hofstede (1981) that religion is not a fundamental cultural value, or with Huntington (1997), who considered it a central element of any civilization? Give your reasons.

14. It has sometimes been pointed out that what is considered 'different' now can in future be seen as more or less similar, and vice versa. Give examples of these two kinds of change.

15. Give three examples of ways in which culture appears to influence consumer purchasing behaviour.

16. Identify situations in which intercultural contact is likely to occur in the following service industries: banking, tourism and healthcare.

17. Give an example to show the effects on communication of surface-level and deep-level culture.

18. List three discourses (not including medical discourse, given in the text).

19. Consider your own cultural identity in your relationship with a person from another culture (if possible a work colleague). How does your cultural identity impact on this relationship?

20. Is diversity valued in the organization in which you work or study? Give reasons for your answer.

21. 'People know how to get to know other people from the same culture but not from different cultures.' Does this statement explain why people behave differently when communicating with culturally different others? Give your reasons.

22. The text gives a number of indicators of the importance and growth of intercultural communication at work in Europe. What are these? What others might be used if data was available?

23. In the light of the material in this chapter on how cultural change is brought about, consider the following statement. Continue the discussion of how cultural change happens:

■ The traditional strong preference of Chinese people for boy children is being altered: 'After 15 years of state-managed family planning (supported by heavy fines and forced abortions for the rebels) many young people, male and female, now claim it does not matter to them whether their only child is a boy or a girl.' (*The Economist*, 10 January 1996)

■ 'Taiwan has become an industrialized economy. Social changes occur along with economic changes....People's attitudes have changed as well. The important traditional values – authoritarian attitude, filial piety (respect for ancestors and parents), fatalism, male superiority, and conservatism (self-restraint and control) – have made way for modern values such as democratic attitudes, independence and self-reliance, progressiveness and optimism, equality of males and females and respect for personal feelings. However, filial piety is still very important' (Matsu, B. and Yeh, R.-S. (1992)); 'Taiwan management communication practices: past, present and future', a summary of a presentation by Ryh-Song Yeh at the David Lam Centre for International Communication, Pacific Region Forum on Business and Management Communication, Simon Fraser University, Harbour Centre on 23 January).

NOTES AND REFERENCES

1. Throughout this book, the term 'Asia' refers to Eastern and South Asia rather than West or Central Asia.

2. It should not, however, be thought that culture is the only important influence on communication. Many other factors influence it and both hinder and facilitate intercultural communication. Equally, in this book, culture is not regarded as 'essential' or as having 'emblematic' features that influence every member of a social system.

3. Stohl, C. (1995) *Organizational Communication: Connectedness in Action*, Thousand Oaks, CA: Sage.

4. Barnett Pearce, W. (1979) *Communication and the Human Condition*, Carbondale, IL: Southern Illinois University Press.

5. Delia, J.G. (1987) 'Communication research: a history', in Berger, C.R. and Chaffee, S.H. (eds) *Communication Science*, Newbury Park, CA: Sage.

6. See, for instance, Allen, M.W., Gotcher, M.M. and Seibert, J.H. (1993) 'A decade of organizational communication research', in Deetz, S. (ed.) *Communication Yearbook*, **16**: 252–330.

7. Sypher, B.D. and Zorn, T.E. (1986) 'Communication abilities and upward mobility: a longitudinal investigation', *Human Communication Research*, **12**: 420–31.

8. Zorn, M.T. and Violanti, M.T. (1996) 'Communication abilities and individual achievement in organizations', *Management Communication Quarterly*, **10**(2): 139–67.

9. Kline, S.L. and Ceropski, J.M. (1984) 'Person-centred communication in medical practice', in Wood, J.T. and Phillips, G.M. (eds) *Human Decision-Making*, Carbondale, IL: Southern Illinois University Press.

10. Frymier, A.B., Shulman, G.M. and Houser, M. (1996) 'The development of a learner empowerment measure', *Communication Education*, **45**: 181–99.

11. McChesnay, R.W. and Schiller, D. (2003) 'The political economy of international communications: foundations for the emerging global debate about media ownership and regulation', *United Nations Research Institute for Social Development, Technology, Business and Society Programme Paper 11*.

12. International Trade Statistics, 2009, World Trade Organization, URL: http://www.wto.org/english/res_e/statis_e/looking4_e.htm#summary, last accessed on 14 December 2010.

13. Schreiber, E.J. (1996) 'Muddles and huddles: facilitating a multicultural workforce through team management theory', *The Journal of Business Communication*, **33**: 459–73.

14. Smith, M.G. (1986) 'Pluralism, race and ethnicity in selected African countries', in Rex, J. and Mason, D. (eds) *Theories of Race and Ethnic Relations*, Cambridge, UK: Cambridge University Press.

15. Collier, M.J. and Thomas, M. (1988) 'Cultural identity: an interpretive perspective', in Kim, Y.Y. and Gudykunst, W.B. (eds) *Theories in Intercultural Communication*, Newbury Park, CA: Sage.

16. Zagefka, H. (2009) 'The concept of ethnicity in social psychological research: definitional issues', *International Journal of Intercultural Relations*, **33**(3): 228–41.

17. Acker, J. (1992) 'Gendering organizational theory', in Mills, A.J. and Tancred, P. (eds) *Gendering Organizational Analysis*, London: Sage.

18. European Commission (2009) Employment in Europe 2009: URL: http://ec.europa.eu/social/main.jsp, last accessed on 14 December 2010

19. US Census Bureau (2009) International Data Base, URL: *www.census.gov/ipc/www/idb/informationGateway.php*.

20. United Nations Economic and Social Commission for the Asia Pacific, *Statistical Yearbook* (2009).

21. UK Office for National Statistics Labour Force Survey (2009) *Self-employment among people with disabilities: evidence for Europe*.

22. Pagan, R. (2009) 'Self-employment among people with disabilities: evidence for Europe', *Disability & Society*, **24**(2): 217–29.

23. US Census Bureau, op. cit.

24. Dansby, M.R. and Knouse, S.B. (1999) 'Percentage of work-group diversity and work-group effectiveness', *Journal of Psychology*, 133: 486–95.

25. Trompenaars, F. (1993) *Riding the Waves of Culture*, London: Nicholas Brealey.

26. Cheong, Y., Kim, K. and Zheng, L. (2010) 'Advertising appeals as a reflection of culture: a cross-cultural analysis of food advertising appeals in China and the US', *Asian Journal of Communication*, **20**(1): 1–16.

27. Dawar, N., Parker, P.M. and Price, L.J. (1996) 'A cross-cultural study of interpersonal information exchange', *Journal of International Business Studies*, **27**(3): 497–516.

28. Furrer, O., Shaw-Ching, B. and Sudharshan, L.D. (2000) 'The Relationships between culture and service quality perceptions: basis for cross-cultural market segmentation and resource allocation', *Journal of Service Research*, May: 355–71.

29. Waarts, E. and Everdingen, Y.V. (2005) 'The influence of national culture on the adoption status of innovations: An empirical study of firms across Europe', *European Journal of Management*, **23**(6): 601–10.

30. Triandis, H.C. (1994) 'Cross-cultural industrial and organizational psychology', in Triandis, H.C., Dunnette, M.D. and Hough, L. (eds) *Handbook of Industrial and Organizational Psychology*, 2nd edn, **4**: 103–72, Palo Alto, CA: Consulting Psychologists Press.

31. Ferraro, G.P. (1994) *The Cultural Dimension of International Business*, 2nd edn, Englewood Cliffs, NJ: Prentice-Hall.

32. Tung, R.L. (1993) 'Managing cross-national and intra-national diversity', *Human Resource Management*, **32**(2): 18–34.

33. Schreiber 'Muddles and huddles'.

34. Pelled, L.H., Eizenhardt, K.M. and Xin, K.R. (1999) 'Exploring the black box: an analysis of work group diversity, conflict and performance', *Administrative Science Quarterly*, **44**: 1–28.

35. Tung 'Managing cross-national and intra-national diversity'.

36. Tung, R.L. (1996) 'Managing diversity for international competitiveness', Paper presented at David See-Chai Lam Centre for International Communication; Pacific Region Forum on Business and Management Communication, Simon Fraser University At Harbour Centre. URL: www.**sfu**.**ca**/davidlamcentre/forum/RTung96–12-23.html, last accessed on 14 December 2010.

37. Bartlett, C.A. and Ghoshal, S. (1989) *Managing Across Borders, The Transnational Solution*, Cambridge, MA: Harvard Business School Press.

38. Chalofsky, N.E. and Reinhart, C. (1988) *Effective Human Resource Development*, San Francisco: Jossey-Bass.

39. Naisbitt, J. and Aburdene, P. (1985) *Re-inventing the Corporation*, New York: Warner Books.

40. Savage, C.M. (1990) *5th Generation Management*, Bedford, MA: BARD Productions, Digital Press.

41. Robinson Hickman, G. and Creighton-Zollar, A. (1998) 'Diverse self-directed work teams: developing strategic initiatives for 21st century organizations', *Public Personnel Management*, **27**(2): 187–200.

42. Cooper, C.R. (1998) 'Theories linking culture and psychology: universal and community-specific processes', *Annual Review of Psychology*, **49**: 559–84.

43. Hall, B.J. (1997) 'Culture, ethics, and communication', in Casmir, F.L. (ed.) *Ethics in Intercultural and International Communication*, Mahwah, NJ: Lawrence Erlbaum Associates.

44. Triandis, H.C. (1994) 'Cross-cultural industrial and organizational psychology', in Triandis, H.C., Dunnette, M.D. and Hough, L. (eds) *Handbook of Industrial and Organizational Psychology*, 2nd edn, **4**: 103–72, Palo Alto, CA: Consulting Psychologists Press.

45. Spencer-Oatey, H. (2005) '(Im)politeness, face and perceptions of rapport: unpacking their bases and interrelationships', *Journal of Politeness Research: Language, Behaviour, Culture*, **1**(1): 95–119.

46. Schwartz, S.H. (1992) 'Universals in value content and structure: theoretical advances and empirical tests in 20 countries', *Advances in Experimental Social Psychology*, **25**: 1–66.

47. Ali, A.J. and Wahabi, R. (1995) 'Managerial value systems in Morocco', *International Studies of Management and Organization*, **25**(3): 87–96.

48. Rokeach, M. (1993) *The Nature of Human Values*, New York: Free Press.

49. Schwartz, S.H. (1999) 'Cultural value differences: Some implications for work', *Applied Psychology: An International Review*, **48**: 23–47.

50. Aldridge, M.G. (2002) 'What is the basis of American culture?' *Intercultural Communication*, 5 April. URL: http://www.immi.se/intercultural.
51. Kincaid, D.L., Yum, J.O. and Woelfel, J. (1983) 'The cultural convergence of Korean immigrants in Hawaii: an empirical test of a mathematical theory', *Quality and Quantity*, **18**: 59–78.
52. Haslett, B. (1989) 'Communication and language acquisition within a cultural context', in Ting-Toomey, S. and Korzenny, F. (eds) *Language, Communication and Culture: Current Directions*, Newbury Park, CA: Sage.
53. Burke, B.A. and Patterson-Pratt, J.R. (2002) 'Establishing understandings: teaching about culture in introductory television courses', *American Communication Journal*, **15**(2). URL: www.americancomm.org/~aca/acj/acj.html, last accessed on 14 December 2010
54. Deetz, S. and Mumby, D.K. (1990) 'Power, discourse, and the workplace: reclaiming the critical tradition', *Communication Yearbook*, **13**: 18–47.
55. Ibid.
56. Hall, S. (1997) *Introduction to Representation: Cultural Representations and Signifying Practices*, Milton Keynes, UK: Open University.
57. Foucault, M. (1982) 'The subject and power', in Dreyfus, H. and Rabinow, P. (eds) *Michel Foucault: Beyond Structuralism and Hermeneutics*, pp. 208–66. New York: Harvester Wheatsheaf.
58. Aaker, J.L., Benet-Martínez, V. and Garolera, J. (2001) 'Consumption symbols as carriers of culture: a study of Japanese and Spanish brand personality constructs', *Journal of Personality and Social Psychology*, **81**(3): 492–508.
59. Aritz, J. and Walker, R.C. (2010) 'Cognitive organization and identity maintenance in multicultural teams: A discourse analysis of decision-making meetings', *Journal of Business Communication*, **47**: 20–41.
60. Collier, M.J. and Thomas, M. (1988) 'Cultural identity and intercultural communication', in Gudykunst, W. and Ting-Toomey, S. (eds) *Culture and Interpersonal Communication*, Newbury Park, CA: Sage.
61. Ibid.
62. Chesebro, J.W. and Fuse, K. (2001) 'The development of a perceived masculinity scale', *Communication Quarterly*, **49**(3): 203–78.
63. Delmestri, G. (2006) 'Streams of inconsistent institutional influences: Middle managers as carriers of multiple identities', *Human Relations, 59: 1515–41.*
64. Gjerde, P.F. (2004) 'Culture, power and experience: towards a person-centered cultural psychology', *Human Development*, **47**:138–57.
65. Markus, H.R. and Kitayama, S. (1991) 'Culture and the self: implications for cognition, emotion, and motivation', *Psychological Review*, **98**: 224–53.
66. Hofstede, G. (1981) *Cultures and Organizations: Software of the Mind*, London: Harper Collins.
67. Hickson, D.J. and Pugh, D. (1995) *Management Worldwide: The Impact of Societal Culture on Organizations around the Globe*, London: Penguin.
68. Cai, D.A. and Donohue, W.A. (1997) 'Determinants of facework in intercultural negotiation', *Asian Journal of Communication*, **7**(1): 85–110.
69. Harpaz, I., Honig, B. and Coetsier, P. (2002) 'A cross-cultural longitudinal analysis of the meaning of work and the socialization process of career starters', *Journal of World Business*, **37**(4): 230–44.
70. Chevrier, S. (2009) 'Is national culture still relevant to management in a global context?' *International Journal of Cross Cultural Management*, **9**(2): 169–83.
71. Kim, Y.Y. (1988) 'On theorizing intercultural communication', in Kim, Y.Y. and Gudykunst, W.B. (eds) *Theories in Intercultural Communication*, Newbury Park, CA: Sage.
72. Hofstede, *Cultures and Organizations*.
73. Kampf, C. and Kastberg, P. (2005) 'Appreciating the ties that bind technical communication to culture: a dynamic model to help us understand differences in discourse structure', Professional Communication Conference 2005, IPCC, 396–403.
74. Phinney, J.S. (1996) 'When we talk about American ethnic groups, what do we mean?' *American Psychologist*, **51**(9): 918–27.

75. Huntington, S. (1997) *The Clash Of Civilizations And The Remaking of World Order*, London: Simon & Schuster.
76. Orbe, M.P. (1998) 'From the standpoint(s) of traditionally muted groups: explicating a co-cultural communication theoretical model', *Communication Theory*, 8(1): 1–26.
77. Lytle, A.L. (1994) *The Influence of Culture in Negotiation, Dissertation*. Northwestern University: Evanston, IL. Cited in Lytle and Willaby (2006) – endnote 78.
78. Lytle, A. and Willaby, H. (2006) 'Intracultural and intercultural negotiations: patterns of tactics', IACM 2006 Meetings Paper, available at SSRN: http://ssrn.com/abstract=905462
79. Pinker, S. (1994) *The Language Instinct*, London: Penguin.
80. Budhwar, P.S., Woldu, H. and Ogbonna, E. (2008) 'A comparative analysis of cultural value orientations of Indians and migrant Indians in the USA', *International Journal of Cross Cultural Management*, 8: 79–105.
81. Li, J. and Karakowsky, L. (2002) 'Cultural malleability in an East Asian context: an illustration of the relationship between government policy, national culture and firm behavior', *Administration & Society*, 34(2): 176–201.
82. Hofstede, G. (1981), op. cit.
83. Aldridge, 'What is the basis of American culture?'.
84. Norris, P. and Inglehart, R. (2008) 'Is national diversity under threat? Cosmopolitan communications and cultural convergence', Paper for presentation in Panel 38:8 'Communication and Political Support' at the Annual Meeting of the American Political Science Association, Toronto, 10.15 am, Friday 4 September 2008.
85. *Deccan Chronicle*, 8 March 2009.
86. *The Economist*, 12 November 2009.
87. Chiang, F.F.T. and Birch, T. (2007) 'The transferability of management practices: examining cross-national differences in reward preferences', *Human Relations*, 60(9): 1293–330.
88. Ford, D.L. and Ismail, K.M. (2006) 'Perceptions of effective leadership among Central Eurasian managers: a cultural convergence-divergence examination within a globalization context', *Journal of International Management* 12(2): 158–80.
89. Tregaskis, O. and Brewster, C. (2006) 'Converging or diverging? A comparative analysis of trends in contingent employment practice in Europe over a decade', *Journal of International Business Studies*, 37(1): 111–26.
90. Shenkar, O. (2001) 'Cultural distance revisited: towards a more rigorous conceptualization and measurement of cultural differences', *Journal of International Business Studies*, 32(3): 519–35.
91. Claus, L. and Hand, M.L. (2009) 'Customization decisions regarding performance management systems of multinational companies: an empirical view of Eastern European firms', *International Journal of Cross Cultural Management*, 9: 237–58.
92. Cui, A.S., Griffith, D.A., Cavusgil, S.T. and Dabic, M. (2006) 'The influence of market and cultural environmental factors on technology transfer between foreign MNCs and local subsidiaries: A Croatian illustration', *Journal of World Business*, 41(2): 100–11.
93. Kaufmann, J.B. and O'Neill, H.M. (2007) 'Do culturally distant partners choose different types of joint venture?' *Journal of World Business*, 42(4): 435–48.
94. Reus, T.H. and Lamont, B.T. (2009) 'The double-edged sword of cultural distance in international acquisitions', *Journal of International Business Studies*, 40: 1298–316.
95. Slangen, A.H.L. (2006) 'National cultural distance and initial foreign acquisition performance: the moderating effect of integration', *Journal of World Business*, 41(2): 161–70.
96. Porter, M.E. (2000) 'Attitudes, values, beliefs and the microeconomics of prosperity', in Harrison, L.E. and Huntington, S.P. (eds) *Culture Matters*, New York: Basic Books.
97. Lee, S.M. and Peterson, S.J. (2000) 'Culture, entrepreneurial orientation, and global competitiveness', *Journal of World Business*, 35(4): 401–16.
98. Muzychenko, O. (2006) 'Cross-cultural entrepreneurial competence in identifying international business opportunities', *European Journal of Management*, 26(6): 366–77.

99. Angwina, D. (2001) 'Mergers and acquisitions across European borders: national perspectives on preacquisition, due diligence and the use of professional advisers', *Journal of World Business*, **36**(1): 32–57.

100. Kragh, S.U. (2000) 'Three perspectives on intercultural marketing', in Sorensen, O.J. and Arnold, E. (eds) *Marketing and Development Challenges*, Proceedings of the 7th International Conference on Marketing and Development, Ghana.

101. House, R. and Wright, N. (1999) 'Cross cultural research on organizational leadership: a critical analysis and a proposed theory', URL: http://jonescenter.wharton.upenn.edu/papers/1999/wp99–03.pdf, last accessed on 14 December 2010.

102. Singh, J., Carasco, E., Svensson, G., Wood, G. and Callaghan, M. (2005) 'A comparative study of the contents of corporate codes of ethics in Australia, Canada and Sweden', *Journal of World Business*, **40**(1): 91–109.

103. Salacuse, J.W. (2003) 'Corporate governance, culture and convergence: corporations American style or with a European touch?' *Law & Business Review of America*, **9**: 33–62.

104. Guirdham, M. (2009) *Culture and Business in Asia*, Basingstoke, UK: Palgrave Macmillan.

105. Khoo, G. (1994) 'The role of assumptions in intercultural research and consulting: examining the interplay of culture and conflict at work', Paper given at David See-Chai Lam Centre for International Communication: Pacific Region Forum on Business and Management Communication, Simon Fraser University at Harbour Center. URL: hoshi.cic.sfu.ca/forum/, last accessed on 14 December 2010.

106. Ellis, K. and Shockley-Zalabak, P. (2001) 'Trust in top management and immediate supervisor: the relationship to satisfaction, perceived organizational effectiveness and information receiving', *Communication Quarterly*, **49**(4): 382–98.

107. Porter, M.E. (1990) *The Competitive Advantage of Nations*, New York: Free Press.

108. Meyer, G.D., Tucker, M.L. and Westerman, J.W. (1996) 'Organizational communication: development of internal strategic competitive advantage', *The Journal of Business Communication*, **33**(1): 51–69.

109. Ulrey, K.L. and Amason, P. (2001) 'Intercultural communication between patients and health care providers: an exploration of intercultural communication effectiveness, cultural sensitivity, stress and anxiety', *Health Communication*, **13**(4): 449–63.

110. Thompson, N. (2003) *Communication and Language: A Handbook of Theory and Practice*, Basingstoke: Palgrave Macmillan.

111. Scollon, R. (2000) *Intercultural Communication: A Discourse Approach*, New York: Blackwell.

112. Gudykunst, W.B. (1983) 'Similarities and differences in perceptions of initial intracultural and intercultural encounters: an exploratory investigation', *The Southern Speech Communication Journal*, **49**: 49–65.

113. Grimes, D.S. and Richard, O.C. (2003) 'Could communication form impact organizations' experience with diversity?' *The Journal of Business Communication*, **40**(1): 7–27.

114. Wanous, J.P. (1977) 'Organizational entry: newcomers moving from outside to inside', *Psychological Bulletin*, **81**: 601–18.

115. Tung,'Managing diversity for international competitiveness'

chapter two

Cultural Differences and Work

The purpose of this chapter is to describe a range of understandings of the ways in which cultures differ and then to apply these understandings to the world of work. This is essential background for effective intercultural communication at work. Section 2.1 describes the ways in which research to date has found cultures to vary: these consist of classifications of cultures based on 'values' on the one hand and high-context/low-context communication on the other. The descriptive content of these taxonomies help us to identify cross-cultural similarities and differences. Section 2.1 also describes some of the findings of a longitudinal series of surveys, The European and World Values Surveys. Section 2.2 discusses three other ways of analysing cultures – as subjective cultures, as elements of institutions and as strategic resources. Section 2.3 expands on the topic of how culture and cultural differences impact on work behaviour, a topic introduced in Chapter 1, but this time drawing on concepts and findings that have been introduced in this chapter. Section 2.4 considers the impact of culture on work organization and management. Finally, Section 2.5 shows how culture influences two key aspects of an organization's environment: the operation of networks and the presence and extent of corruption. Figure 2.1 shows the questions discussed in the sections of this chapter.

2.1 HOW CULTURES VARY

A major thrust of theorizing and research into culture has been the attempt to identify and classify similarities and differences among cultures. This section describes some of the main results of these efforts, covering taxonomies of culture-level values and dimensions: Hofstede's (1981 and 1990), Trompenaars' (1993) and Schwartz's (1999). To the extent that some of these taxonomies claim to be comprehensive, they must be alternatives. Nevertheless, it is still not known which is most valid, so they may all be learnt from and usefully applied in appropriate ways. Differences in national values are the core concept behind most findings on cultural variation. Unfortunately, such national values found by research cannot legitimately be translated to the individual level, because different individuals have different priorities on values (including the meaning and importance of work). However, the average priorities attached to different values by members of a society 'reflect the central thrust of their shared enculturation. Hence, the average priorities point to the underlying, common cultural values.'[1]

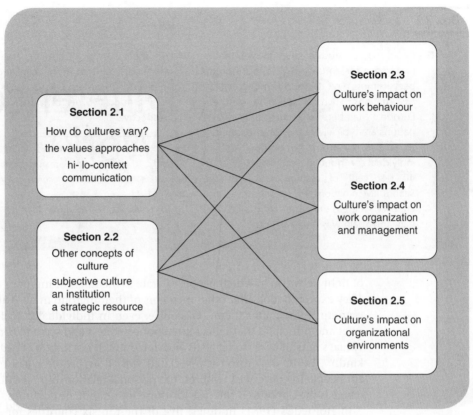

Figure 2.1   *Relations among the sections of Chapter 2*

Work by Schwartz (1992) has produced a set of 'motivational' values, some of which can be applied at the individual level.[2]

Hofstede's (1981 and 1993) culture-level values

In the late 1960s and early 1970s, Geert Hofstede undertook the most comprehensive cross-cultural study to that date, using questionnaire data from 80,000 IBM employees in 66 countries across seven occupations.[3] From this research Hofstede established four values – individualism/collectivism (IC), power distance (PD), uncertainty avoidance (UA) and masculinity/femininity (MAS) – that differ across cultures:

1. Individualism–Collectivism is defined by the extent to which individuals' behaviours are influenced and prescribed by others: individualists prefer self-sufficiency while collectivists give more recognition to their interdependent roles and their obligations to their group. Studies of social categorization and inter-group relations show that all people mentally 'group' others, using salient characteristics (i.e., those characteristics that are important to them. These range from family or work unit membership to demographic or other characteristics). The group that the categorizer feels similar to and identifies with is called the 'ingroup' and other groups are called 'outgroups'. People from all types of culture categorize others in this way, but the importance of the distinction is much greater for people from collectivist cultures. In individualist societies people primarily operate as individuals or as members of their immediate families, whereas collectivist societies are composed

Box 2.1

■ Cross-cultural studies have shown that a preference for equality with one's ingroup peers is most typically found among collectivist nations, such as those in southern Europe. Members of more individualist nations are typically keener on the freedom to receive rewards in proportion to their individual contribution. No more than 30 to 40 per cent of respondents from the Scandinavian nations (except Iceland) chose equality, whereas the pattern from Portugal, Italy and Spain was the reverse.[a]

■ To most western Germans, freedom (49 per cent) matters more than equality (35 per cent). To eastern Germans, it is the other way around (36 per cent and 51 per cent respectively).[b]

Sources: (a) Eyjolfsdottir, H.M. and Smith, P.B. (1996) 'Icelandic business and management culture', _International Studies of Management & Organization,_ 26(3): 61–73

(b) _The Economist,_ 18 September 2004

of tight networks in which people operate as members of ingroups and outgroups. They expect to look after other members of their ingroup in need and expect their ingroup to look after them. (Of course, even in individualist societies, there are rules and principles that reflect interconnectedness and serve to constrain an individual's pursuit of personal goals and outcomes. It is a matter of degree rather than kind.)[4] The IC dimension is associated with how people relate to one another. For people in collectivist cultures, the personal relationship prevails over the task, whereas the opposite is the case for those in individualist cultures.

In Hofstede's (1981) findings, five of the top six countries for scores on individualism were 'Anglo' countries – USA, Australia, Great Britain, Canada and New Zealand – with The Netherlands occupying position 5; five of the lowest in individualism (highest in collectivism) were South American and the sixth was Pakistan. Fourteen European countries clustered in the top 20 on individualism, none were in the lowest 18 and only three (Greece, Yugoslavia and Portugal) were in the middle group of 15 countries. In Asia, Japan and India were about at the mid-point on individualism–collectivism; Taiwan, Singapore, Hong Kong and China were high on collectivism; no Asian country was high on individualism.

Although the IC concept may in fact represent a number of cultural factors rather than a single trait, and has been criticized on other grounds as well, as the critique in this section will explain, it is perhaps the most important as well as the most frequently cited cultural dimension.[5] It will often recur in this book.

2. Power distance (PD) is defined by the degree of separation between people of various social statuses, or, to put it another way, the extent to which all members of a society, including the less powerful, expect and accept that power is distributed unequally. Low PD cultures endorse egalitarianism; high PD cultures endorse hierarchies. In high PD societies, relations between unequals are formal, often patron–client in format, information flow is formalized and restricted, and companies are organized in rigid vertical hierarchies. In low PD societies relations are open and informal, information flows are functional and unrestricted, and companies tend to have flat hierarchies and matrix organizations. Countries particularly high on PD were Malaysia, four South American countries and the Philippines; those particularly low on this variable were Austria, Israel, New Zealand, Ireland and

the four Scandinavian countries. Eleven European countries were in the lowest 20 on PD, only three (Yugoslavia, France and Belgium) in the top 20. In addition to Malaysia, six other Asian countries, including China, India and Singapore, were ranked in the top 20 on PD; no Asian country was in the bottom 20, while Japan, ranked 50th, was the lowest-scored Asian country on PD.

3. Uncertainty Avoidance (UA) refers to the extent to which a culture prefers to avoid ambiguity and to the way in which it resolves uncertainty. High UA cultures prefer rules and set procedures to contain the uncertainty, low UA cultures tolerate greater ambiguity and prefer more flexibility in their responses. In high UA societies, families, groups and organizations tend to be closed to outsiders, to stress compliance and obedience, to punish error and nonconformity, and to reward conformity, loyalty and attention to detail. Low UA societies tend to accept outsiders at all levels, stress personal choice and decision-making, reward initiative, team-play and risk-taking. They also stress the development of analytical skills. In low UA cultures, values include a tolerance for deviance and innovative ideas. What is different is seen as curious, as opposed to dangerous. Therefore, in low UA cultures, innovations will be looked upon more favourably than in cultures with high UA.[6]

However, cultures with similar UA levels may devote different amounts of effort and attention to reducing uncertainty by imposing laws, rules and regulations. Although Germany ranks in the middle of Hofstede's scale, the author himself gives many examples of the German inclination for orderliness; expressions such as Befehl ist Befehl ('A command is a command') or Ordnung muß sein ('There must be order') are well known internationally.[7]

Two Southern European countries (Greece and Portugal) and two South American (Guatemala and Uruguay) were highest on UA, while those lowest in this characteristic were four small nations (Singapore, Jamaica, Hong Kong and Ireland) and two Scandinavian countries. European countries differed more on uncertainty avoidance than on individualism–collectivism or power distance: six were in the highest 20 countries, seven in the next 20 and four in the lowest 13. Asian countries tended to cluster at the lower end of the rankings on UA: only Japan, at 11th,

---

Box 2.2

Client complaints had been fed back by the US sales force about the product of a software development team in India. This was a crisis and the company had to respond. The two team managers insisted that the team should work all weekend to get the problems sorted out, threatening disciplinary action against any team member who did not obey. However, when the European Managing Director went into the office on the Saturday, he found that neither of the team managers themselves were there. 'Because they are higher in the hierarchy, they don't believe that they should have to obey the same rules,' he said. 'In fact it would undermine their status if they did.'[a]

'Korean business is not hierarchical. The military culture is one where leaders go first and so are exposed to all the dangers of their followers. Team leaders in business work as hard as or harder than their team. They face the same problem as Japanese team leaders of reconciling internal harmony with an outward-facing competitiveness, but resolve it more in the direction of encouraging aggressive competitiveness.'[b]

Sources: (a) interview with an expatriate manager in India, author's research

(b) interview with a South Korean senior manager, author's research

Box 2.3

By their own account, many Chinese people operate by trial and error. For example, the Chinese managers of a French multinational company's Chinese subsidiary drew up a plan to launch a new brand in the Chinese market. 'We would recruit 200 dealers, support them with minimum back-up, find an agency, design a logo and off we go.' The French headquarters wanted 'long discussion and research' before taking action.[a]

'Poland is a country that foreigners criticize at their peril. Even the mildest mention of habitual unpunctuality, brusque telephone manners or bad roads can prompt a lengthy and emotional review

of the outside world's insensitive and ignorant attitude to the country's tragic history. ... What is rather odder is that praising Poland can go down badly too. A mild remark about the variety and excellence of the country's media or the growing strength of its private sector can be taken as being insensitive to poverty, unemployment and the inadequacy of public services, let alone the country's historical tragedies.'[b]

Sources: (a) interview with a Chinese marketing manager, Beijing, author's research
(b) _The Economist_, 11 May 2006

was in the top 20, while China, Malaysia, India and Indonesia, as well as Singapore and Hong Kong, were in the bottom 20.

4. Masculinity/Femininity (MAS) defines quality of life issues. High MAS cultures endorse assertiveness, competition and aggressive success; low MAS cultures prefer modesty, compromise and co-operative success. In high MAS societies people tend to believe that matters of material comfort, social privilege, access to power and influence, status and prestige, and the ability to consume are related to ability and that any individual who wants these benefits of society can have them. This also means they believe that people who do not have the ability, or the character, cannot and should not have them, since they are essentially a reward for hard work and success. High MAS societies tend to reward financial and material achievements with preferential social prestige and status, and even to attribute strong character and spiritual values to such high achievers.

In some low MAS societies, living in material comfort and having a high standard of living are believed to be matters of birth, luck or destiny. In some other low MAS societies, material comfort and lifestyle are considered less an indication of a person's character and value than their religious devotion, their social conscience, their intellectual or artistic abilities, their stature as a wise elder, or (and this probably applies in Scandinavia) their rights as a fellow member of a caring society. On the MAS variable, Japan was higher than any other nation, while Austria, Venezuela, Italy and Switzerland were in positions two to five; four Northern European countries were highest on the 'feminine' end of the dimension. European countries polarized on MAS, with seven countries in the top 20, nine in the bottom 20 and only one (Belgium) in the middle group. Apart from Japan, China, at 11th, was the only Asian country in the top 20 on MAS, while Vietnam and South Korea, ranked at 55–8 and 59 respectively, were the only two in the bottom 20. Hong Kong, India, Bangladesh, Malaysia, Pakistan, Singapore and Indonesia were all in the middle range of the rankings.

MAS was the only dimension on which Hofstede (1981) found significant differences between men and women, though, even then, not consistently. In the most 'feminine' countries there was no real difference, but in the most 'masculine' countries men scored 50 per cent higher than women on MAS, and correspondingly for the countries in between. Because this was the only dimension on which men and women differed, Hofstede (1981) labelled it 'masculine'/'feminine'; however, because sexism can be read into these labels, some writers have renamed its poles 'Achievement' and 'Relational' orientations.

Later, Hofstede (1993) identified a fifth cultural value – long-term or short-term time orientation: willingness to postpone 'payback' and satisfaction against wanting or needing quick returns and rewards. In the context of international joint ventures, it has been shown, the effect of long- or short-term orientation is stronger than that of any of the other dimensions of culture.[8] Hofstede's research in a smaller sample of 39 countries, China, Hong Kong, Taiwan, Japan, Vietnam and South Korea were the top six countries on long-term orientation; Brazil and Hungary were the only non-Asian countries in the top ten. Many European countries clustered in the centre of the rankings, with the Czech Republic, Spain, Great Britain and Portugal in the bottom ten.

Hofstede (1981) found that national culture explained half the variance in employees' attitudes and behaviours.[9] Hofstede (1993) reported that, although the original six European Community (EC) countries had a degree of homogeneity around individualism (with only 26 per cent of the variation seen across the worldwide samples) and power distance (with only 35 per cent of the variance), the European Union (EU) of (at the time) 12 countries, or a broader set of 18 European countries, 'explodes' into massive cultural diversity. 'Nowhere on earth does such variation exist in such a small geographical space.'[10] 'Eighty-six percent of worldwide variance on uncertainty avoidance, 82 percent of variance on masculinity–femininity, 73 percent of variance on individualism–collectivism, and 70 percent of variance across power distance is found in Europe.'[11] Although the variability Hofstede found in Asia was less, differences were found especially in two major dimensions often perceived as definitional for Asian cultures: long-term orientation and collectivism. On long-term orientation, China was the highest ranked and Pakistan the lowest, with scores of 188 and 0 respectively; even on collectivism, two major Asian countries, Japan and India, were well down the rankings.

Hofstede's (1981 and 1993) definitions and analyses of culture were not intended to be rigid categorizations of behaviour or people: the culture of a country – or any other category of people – is not a combination of properties of the 'average citizen' or 'modal personality'. One person from a culture may react in one way (such as feeling nervous), another from the same culture in another way (such as wanting rules to be respected); these would both be manifestations of a common cultural tendency to avoid uncertainty. In addition, such reactions need not be found within the same persons or in all persons from the culture, but only statistically more often in the same society. Few people fall entirely into one or the other cultural pattern, but the tendency is there.

Hofstede's work has been both supported and refuted by replication, although the majority of replications support the existence of the values. There have also been numerous applications of the values to economic and other work-related behaviours. For example, Erumban and de Jong (2006), noting that the rate of adoption of information and communication technology (ICT) diverges considerably from one country to another regardless of their income levels, found that the national culture and the ICT adoption rate of a country are closely related. They used Hofstede's dimensions and two different measures of ICT adoption, namely the average share of ICT spending in GDP across 42 countries, and numbers of computers per capita across 49 countries. Most of the Hofstede dimensions appeared important in influencing ICT adoption, although power distance and uncertainty avoidance emerged as the most important ones. The results were robust in both datasets, even after controlling for levels of education and income.[12] Individualism–collectivism and power distance were linked to four different approaches to participative decision-making: face-to-face, joint (collective), pseudo- and paternalistic participative decision-making, Sagie and Aycan (2003) found.[13] Perceptions of the relative importance of service quality features were linked to individual-level cultural dimensions, a study showed. For instance, individuals with large power distance, high collectivism, high masculinity, neutral uncertainty avoidance and short-term orientations attached most importance to service quality assurance; individuals exhibiting large power distance, medium individualism, high masculinity, low uncertainty avoidance and short-term orientations were only concerned with the tangibles associated with the service, to which they attached extremely high importance.[14] Despite this support from research, however, the values are not all-inclusive and there are additional variables that can be used: religion, gender equality, ethnocentrism and high- and low-context communication (explained in Section 2.2) are examples of national-level variables that have been used to date.

Vertical and horizontal individualism and collectivism

Some cultural researchers have considered individualism–collectivism and verticality/horizontalism, a dimension loosely related to power distance, to be orthogonal, so that their interaction yields the four cultural categories of vertical and horizontal individualism and collectivism. People in vertical cultures are understood to consider their 'self' to be different from others in social status, whereas in horizontal cultures people consider their 'self' to be more or less the same as others'.[15] Within horizontal collectivist cultures, such as Israeli kibbutz society, people see themselves as 'merged with the members of their own ingroup who are extremely similar to each other in terms of their tastes and preferences'. Vertical collectivists, while still prioritizing their group memberships, prefer to think of themselves as 'different' from other members of the ingroup. China, Korea, Singapore and India (with its caste system) exemplify vertically collectivist cultures, according to these researchers. Horizontal individualism is the cultural pattern that applies in countries where individuals consider themselves relatively independent of the ingroup but also as more or less equal in status with others. Australia, Denmark and Sweden are typical. Finally, in countries where an independent self is postulated and individuals see themselves as relatively unique and expect inequality in status, the cultural pattern is described by vertical individualism. France, Germany, the UK and the USA exemplify this cultural pattern.

These four cultural patterns have been linked to the ease or difficulty with which different kinds of knowledge are absorbed and acted on in different societies. As Chapter 9 will explain, the four cultural patterns and the interactions among them have also been linked to the ease or difficulty of international knowledge transfers within and between organizations.[16]

Trompenaars' (1993) relationships and attitudes taxonomy

For Trompenaars (1993), culture was 'often intangible and difficult to define'.[17] However, Trompenaars, like earlier researchers, generated a set of dimensions by which

Box 2.4

In Taiwan, relationships are social resources – they could even be described as business resources. The senior partner in a Taiwanese venture capital firm expressed the point in this way: 'For traditional Taiwanese businesses, mutual trust of contacts and reputation are key.'[a]

Relationship patterns in two Taipei computer companies have been shown to be influenced by Chinese traditions which 'view human emotion and orders of relationship as the basis of society. Taiwanese employees, particularly salespeople, are shown as adept at fusing functional and emotional elements to flexibly manage interpersonal relationships in complex and dynamic Taiwanese social, political, and economic contexts.'[b]

Sources: (a) Guirdham, M. (2009) *Culture and Business in Asia*, Basingstoke, UK: Palgrave Macmillan
(b) Chang, H.-C. and Holt, G.R. (1996) 'An Exploration of interpersonal relationships in two Taiwanese computer firms', *Human Relations,* **49**: 1,489–1,517

cultures can be classified. The analysis was derived partly from 15 years of training of managers, and more specifically from academic research. This research used samples from 30 countries of a minimum of 100 people with similar backgrounds and occupations. Seventy-five per cent were managers, while 25 per cent were general administrative staff from a variety of multinational companies.

Trompenaars (1993) identified three main categories and eight subcategories of cultural dimensions. They are:

1. Relationships with people:
   ■ Universalism versus particularism.
   ■ Individualism versus collectivism.
   ■ Neutrality versus emotionalism.
   ■ Specificity versus diffuseness.
   ■ Achievement versus ascription.

2. Attitudes to time:
   ■ Future versus past orientation.
   ■ Polychronic versus monochronic time.
   ■ Time as a stream or a cycle.

3. Attitudes to the environment.

Universalism and particularism

Universalism is a preference for drawing general principles and is contrasted with particularism, which is a preference for the anecdotal or itemized. For example, where one person might say, 'One of the characteristics of modern Western life is for married women with children to work,' another might say, 'It's a curious fact, but three of my friends – all married women with children – have got themselves jobs. There's Mrs X running a playgroup, Mrs Y working at the supermarket and Mrs Z training to be a solicitor.' Much of the subsequent research into this cultural dimension has come from the USA, and is influenced by American cultural preferences. However, a British management writer, Charles Handy, illustrated the principle from a personal experience:

'Particularist countries think that the relationship is more important than the contract and that a good deal requires no written contract – the particular people and the particular situation matter more than the universal rules. You can see that you could cause great offence if you got it wrong, as I once did myself, when I insisted on bringing in a lawyer to sign an agreement that my Chinese dealer had thought we had settled with a handshake over a cup of Chinese tea. That particular deal fell through. Or perhaps I should say that when I tried to apply my universal approach to that particular situation, it failed.'[18]

Individualism and collectivism

Trompenaars (1993) defined this value dimension slightly differently from Hofstede (1981), as a conflict between what each person wants as an individual and the interests of the group he or she belongs to. Individualism is 'a prime orientation to the self', collectivism is a 'prime orientation to common goals and objectives'. For Trompenaars, writing in the early 1990s, the success of the 'Five Dragons' – Japan, Hong Kong, Singapore, South Korea and Taiwan – raised 'serious questions about both the success and the inevitability of individualism'.

Neutrality and emotionalism

This dimension is about the display of feeling, rather than the level or range of emotions experienced. Trompenaars (1993) considered that emotional display is a major difference between cultures, and argued: 'There is a tendency for those with norms of emotional neutrality to dismiss anger, delight or intensity in the workplace as "unprofessional".'

Specificity and diffuseness

This distinction is based on the concept of 'life spaces'. People have different senses of what is in the public and private domains of life and of how separate these different domains should be. For example, Swiss and Japanese people do not readily invite business contacts to their home; North Americans are much freer in this respect.

Achieved and ascribed status

This is a matter of the importance attached to what a person has done or is doing (what they have achieved through their own efforts) versus their position resulting from external factors. Trompenaars (1993) disputed the Western view that ascription is inferior to achievement, arguing that some ascriptions, such as age and experience, education and professional qualifications make good sense in predicting a person's business performance.

Concepts of time

There are several ways in which concepts of time vary between cultures – time as a cycle or a sequence; past, present and future emphasis (the British emphasize the past, North Americans the future); time as a precious resource which must not be wasted versus a more leisurely approach. A major distinction is between monochronic and polychronic notions of activity: people from Anglo-Saxon cultures often find their

Box 2.5

The European manager of an offshoring operation in India found himself repeatedly invited
to his subordinates' weddings. Many of the
staff were at the age when in India it is usual
to marry, Indian weddings are prolonged and
there is a peak wedding season, for astrological

reasons, in February. The manager was forced
to find a way to refuse these invitations without
causing offence.

_____

Source: author's research

sense of order disrupted if work is not clock-regulated, if they are expected to do several
things at a time or find others around them doing several things at once. For example,
many British people would feel uncomfortable if they enter someone's office for an
appointment, are waved to a seat and smiled at while the person they have come to
see continues a telephone conversation, making notes. For an Argentinian, this would
be quite normal and acceptable.

Concepts of the environment

Is the environment to be controlled or harmonized with?

Schwartz's (1999) values approach

A different set of cultural values emerged from the work of Schwartz and his colleagues.
Based on preceding anthropology, Schwartz *et al.* (1999) theorized that three basic
issues confront societies:

1. To define the nature of the relation between the individual and the group,
2. To guarantee responsible behaviour that will preserve the social fabric, and
3. To decide the relation of humankind to the natural and social world.[19]

When a values survey was conducted among teachers and students in nearly 50
countries, Schwartz *et al.* (1999) found a set of culture-level values corresponding to
these three concerns:

1. Embeddedness versus autonomy. This value is related, but not identical, to earl-
    ier value concepts such as individualism–collectivism and autonomy/conserva-
    tism, but also contrasts maintaining the status quo with openness to change.
2. Hierarchy versus egalitarianism. Again, there is a link, this time to power dis-
    tance, but there is also a key difference. Egalitarianism calls for people to
    recognize one another as moral equals who share basic interests as human beings –
    these elements are absent from low power distance.
3. Mastery versus harmony. Mastery is similar to masculinity but does not imply
    selfishness; harmony is related to uncertainty avoidance but does not imply an
    emphasis on controlling ambiguity.

Box 2.6

X was an internal auditor for an international company. His current assignment was to audit the travel department of the company's Italian subsidiary. The department had responsibility for organizing and paying for all the travel and accommodation arrangements as well as visas for a staff of 35 international executives and sales representatives.

(1) X arrived at the time arranged but was kept waiting in an outer office for 25 minutes. When he entered, he looked somewhat pointedly at his watch. The manager of the department smiled broadly, saying, 'Ah, we have plenty of time, have we not? Would you care for a coffee?' X refused. (2) The manager, having shaken hands, moved closer to X, who felt uncomfortable and backed away. (3) X's discomfort was increased by the fact that the office seemed to be overcrowded with desks occupied by people to whom he was not introduced, while other people continuously came and went through a side door. (4) The conversation was several times interrupted by people asking the manager questions, to which he would intersperse his answers with his answers to X, who began to feel confused. The manager also often interrupted their discussion himself, to speak to a colleague about some unrelated matter, or to answer the telephone. He also seemed excited, jumping up to find a paper from his desk, and using emphatic gestures. However, X had expected the last of these: he'd heard about the Italians. (5) When they were seated, the manager asked him about his journey, and appeared to be really interested (possibly a professional interest, X thought). He asked about X's family, commented on the latest political happening in X's country and asked X about his political views. 'Next he'll be wanting to know what religion I am,' X thought. (6) X began by raising the two problem areas highlighted in his junior's preliminary audit report. One was complaints of late payment of travel expenses by expatriates working in the subsidiary; the other was numerous instances where rules had been infringed. (He did not beat about the bush in raising these matters, but came straight to the point. Afterwards, he wondered if he had seemed impolite.) (7) He suggested they deal with them in that order; the travel department manager agreed, then jumped quickly to the rules question. (8) 'You know, some of these rules, they are not practical,' he said. 'They only make work for nothing. You will agree that your colleague found no instances of dishonesty or misappropriation of funds?' X agreed – none had been found, but 'Rules are rules,' he thought.

The following helps explain the behaviour of X's Italian colleague:

(1) It is said that punctuality in Milan means 20 minutes late, in Rome 30 minutes and in Naples 45 minutes. (It is also said that a red traffic light in Milan is an instruction, in Rome a request and in Naples a decoration.)

(2) Italians have a Mediterranean sense of distance comfort – closer than most North Europeans'.

(3) Italians' sense of privacy and of how compartmentalized different aspects of life should be is less restrictive than most North Europeans' – their culture is more diffuse than the more specific North European cultures.

(4) Italians' sense of time is polychronic – they expect to do more than one thing at a time and have others around them doing several things at once; this contrasts with the monochronic sense of time in some cultures.

(5) This experience also reflects Italy's diffuse culture. Matters are openly discussed which in some cultures would be irrelevant and private in a business context.

(6) It is likely that the Italian manager will find X's bluntness impolite, especially as it follows his earlier refusal of the coffee and determination to get right down to business.

(7) Following agendas and precise sequences of dealing with matters is not the Italian way.

(8) Italians frequently bend rules and interpret agreements flexibly; this does not mean they are dishonest, only that in grey areas they see flexibility as common sense.

Based on: author's research

A set of 44 country profiles suggested the existence of broad cultural groupings of nations. These were related to geographical proximity but were also based on other factors such as shared histories, religion, levels of development and contact with other cultures. The regions to which the countries in this sample were allocated are:

- the Western European nations (high in autonomy, egalitarianism and mastery – except Italy, which was high in harmony);
- the English-speaking nations (high in mastery and autonomy, intermediate in hierarchy/egalitarianism);
- the Eastern European nations (high in harmony and conservatism, intermediate in hierarchy/egalitarianism); and
- East Asian countries (high in hierarchy and conservatism, low in harmony).

Islamic countries (high in hierarchy, conservatism, intermediate in mastery/harmony) and sub-Saharan African countries formed other groups. Thus empirical work based on Schwartz's (1999) theory yielded meaningful transnational groupings, which may correspond closely to culture.

National cultures, differentiated according to Schwartz's values taxonomy, had an influence on organizational cultures and practices and therefore on individual employees' experience of, for instance, role stress, a comparison of 21 nations found:

- Managers in nations high on mastery and hierarchy but low on harmony were more likely to report role overload. This might be the effect of their trying to 'change the world' and the overloading of subordinates being legitimated by superordinate (organizational) goals.
- Egalitarianism and intellectual autonomy had little effect on role ambiguity, although they might be expected to result from cultural willingness to change role definitions.
- Managers in nations high in hierarchy and low in harmony reported greater role conflict, even though the correlation with mastery was not significant.

Sagiv and Schwartz (2000), by reanalysing data from an earlier study of 12 nations, found the following:

- Managers in nations with cultures that emphasize harmony chose integrating rather than analysing solutions to managerial dilemmas.
- Managers in nations where embeddedness is emphasized chose payment that took into account the size of the employee's family, not just his or her work.
- Managers in nations where mastery and hierarchy are emphasized chose commitment to the organization rather than commitment to a friend.[20]

Unlike Hofstede (1981), who inferred values from respondents' answers on questions about preferred states or outcomes, Schwartz's (1999) measurement instrument asked directly about values. Whereas Hofstede's approach reduced the chance of respondents giving utopian answers that might not be reflected in their actual behaviour, but risked the chance of situational variables having a strong impact on the respondents, Schwartz's approach did the reverse: 'It does eliminate, at least potentially, the chance of situational variables having a strong impact on the respondents. On the other hand, it does open the argument that when asked about values (rather than specific out-comes) respondents may be inclined to choose a more utopian answer, which in turn may not be reflected in their actual behaviour.'[21]

Communalism

Some societies have been characterized as communalist rather than collectivist.[22] The term has been applied to countries as different in some ways as Brazil and Saudi Arabia and to Nigeria, Korea, Thailand and Jamaica. Kim (1994) found that 'family-oriented communalism has been transformed into corporate communalism in the Korean busi-ness sector', and that 'communal particularism' appeared to permeate the 'diffused, shared' systems of occupational welfare in Japan'.[23] In the words of Moemeka (1998), 'Communalism is the principle or system of social order in which, among other things, the supremacy of the community is culturally and socially entrenched, society is hier-archically ordered, life is sacrosanct, and religion is a way of life. In such a community, people are not seen as important in their own right. Each one is an integral part of the whole, and derives his or her place in the context of the community. People in a com-munalistic community are born into the community.'[24] Furthermore, another scholar explained, 'In a communalistic social order, community welfare undergirds actions. Nothing done, no matter how important and useful it is to the individual, is consid-ered good unless it has relevance for the community. ... the guiding dictum is this: "I am because we are".'[25]

Adherence to communication rules (tacit but socially sanctioned understand-ings about appropriate ways to interact in given situations) is a strict requirement. Noncompliance provokes strict social, and often economic and psychological, sanc-tions. Unlike in collectivism, where the concern of the individual is with the adaptabil-ity of the self-presentation image,[26] in communalism the concern is the authenticity of the community-presentation image.

According to the proponents of the view that distinguishes communalism from collectivism, it is communalism that is particularistic, ascription-oriented and uses high-context communication; collectivism is more like individualism on these dimensions, being universalistic and achievement-oriented and using low-context communication.

Values surveys

The European Values Survey and the World Values Survey are major empirical studies. Unlike those of the earlier researchers, they provide a longitudinal view, and allow findings on changes: surveys were undertaken in 1981, 1990, 1995, 2000, and 2006. They were designed to measure all major areas of human concern, including reli-gion, politics, economics and social life. Two dimensions, traditional/secular–rational and survival/self-expression values, explained more than 70 per cent of the cross-national variance in a factor analysis of ten indicators, and each of these dimensions was strongly correlated with large numbers of other important orientations. The trad-itional/secular–rational values dimension reflects the contrast between societies in which religion is very important and those in which it is not. Societies near the trad-itional pole emphasize the importance of parent–child ties and deference to author-ity, along with absolute standards and traditional family values, and reject divorce, abortion, euthanasia and suicide. These societies have high levels of national pride and a nationalistic outlook. Societies with secular–rational values have the opposite preferences on all of these topics. Industrialization leads to a shift from traditional

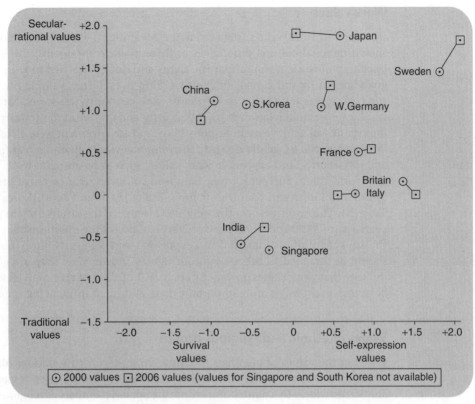

Figure 2.2   *World Values Surveys findings for five European and five Asian countries*
Source: based on the World Values Surveys, see www.worldvaluessurvey.org

values towards secular–rational values, but, as societies make a further shift towards becoming knowledge-based economies, priorities shift from survival values – an overwhelming emphasis on economic and physical security – towards self-expression values. These give high priority to environmental protection, tolerance of diversity and rising demands for participation in decision-making in economic and political life. Societies that rank high on self-expression values also tend to rank high on interpersonal trust.[27] Figure 2.2 shows levels and trends for these variables for five Asian and five European countries.

Combined values approaches

In recent years some researchers have begun to use a selection from the different values and dimensions taxonomies to study a phenomenon of interest. An example is a study of work investment and disposition to work. The study reported that time investment in work is heavier among men than women (although the gender difference is greater in masculine societies than in feminine societies); work time investment is also greater in societies where survival values are important, compared with those where self-expression values are more important, and where mastery values are high compared with those where they are low. Disposition to work, however, displays a different cross-cultural pattern: it is more common in societies where self-expression values are more important than survival values, and more common among men in masculine than in feminine societies.[28]

Work values

In regard to work values, data from the Meaning of Work Study have consistently shown national cultural differences in three major components: the importance and centrality of work, norms about the rights and duties attached to work, and the work goals sought by individuals in their working lives.[29] For example, in comparison to the USA, it was found that in Germany work centrality was lower. Meaningful work, good interpersonal relationships, job security and opportunities to learn were all more important, but achievement, responsibility and advancement were all less important.[30] Work values can be subdivided into instrumental work values, such as financial reward and job security, and expressive work values, such as meaningful work. Findings from the World Values Surveys for four European countries (France, Great Britain, Italy and Spain) and four Asian countries (China, India, Japan and South Korea) are shown in Table 2.1. The findings show the weighted average of the results for two years about ten years apart – 1990 and 1999, 2000 or 2001 – of two of the questions that contributed to the assessment of instrumental and expressive work values. Not too much importance should be attached to the selection of figures shown here: they are given merely to indicate that work values do vary by country (but stage of economic development may be as important as, or more important than, culture in influencing them.)

Values of ethnic and religious groups

Whether the values of members of ethnic minorities within nations align with those of the nation or the wider ethnic group is complex and not well researched. It probably varies widely by country and ethnic group. For members of religious groups, while common sense would suggest some important differences between their values and, for instance, those of other religious groups, no research seems to have applied to them the cultural dimensions discussed in this section.

Values of subcultures

Gender appears to have a rather limited effect on the core cultural values, except the masculine/feminine (achievement/relational) dimension, according to Hofstede's (1981) findings. Social class has been shown to affect values. Less educated, low-status employees

Table 2.1   *Factors mentioned as important in a job – four Asian and four European countries*

| Country | Important in a job: percentage mentioning | | | |
	Good pay	Good Job security	That you can achieve something	An opportunity to use initiative
China	66.4	55.7	34.2	42.8
India	89.1	81.6	64.4	58.0
Japan	81.0	70.7	60.2	43.2
South Korea	56.0	65.4	57.2	47.0
France	62.7	42.0	47.1	40.9
Great Britain	73.6	60.1	62.9	43.5
Italy	78.1	68.3	63.2	54.9
Spain	78.4	71.0	43.4	36.5

Box 2.7

When applying for something from their UK local authority (planning consent, housing benefit), members of some ethnic minorities go in person, thinking that the relationship will ease their path.[a]

A study of Vietnamese migrants to the UK ('old' first generation, second generation and 'new' first generation migrants) found differences among these groups in, for instance, the degree of collectivism practised in running the business; however it also found differences from the broader UK population in the influence of strong family loyalties. The findings emphasized the need to take account not only of intercultural differences, but also the intracultural differences that exist within different ethnic minority groups.[b]

Sources: (a) statement by a local authority staff member, author's research
(b) Bagwell, S. (2006) 'UK Vietnamese Businesses: Cultural Influences and Intracultural Differences', *Government and Policy*, **24**(1): 51–69

in various Western countries have more authoritarian values than their higher-status co-workers. These authoritarian values are manifested not only at work, but also at home. A study in the USA and Italy showed that working-class parents demanded more obedience from their children than middle-class parents.[31] The difference was larger in the USA than in Italy. However, when Hofstede (1981) divided occupations within IBM into six groups according to the level of achievement or relationship (masculine or feminine) values they reported, people in unskilled and semi-skilled occupations recorded the highest level of relationship values apart from office workers. This placed them above managers of all categories, skilled workers/technicians, professional workers and the group with the most masculine values, sales representatives.

High-context/low-context communication

Cultures can be analysed in terms of communication styles. Hall (1976) drew a distinction between high-context communication and low-context communication, and used the distinction as the basis for differentiating cultures. In high-context cultures (HCCs), people rely heavily on the overall situation to interpret messages, so that spoken messages can be ambiguous or vague. In low-context cultures (LCCs), people rely more on the explicit verbal content of messages.[32] In discussions, people in LCC cultures tend to exhibit patterns of linear thinking, shifting from information already stated to information about to be given, while HCC communication tends to exhibit circular thinking, jumping back and forth and leaving out detail.[33]

Unfortunately, there is a dearth of empirical data to identify where given countries are located on the high–low-context dimension; furthermore, 'linguistically, it is very complex to identify degrees of directness, since explicitness – implicitness, communicative strength, and bluntness-cushioning are all involved.'[34] There are, however, confirmatory findings from a small number of studies. Members of HCCs, such as Japanese people, use non-verbal cues and information about a person's background to a greater extent than members of LCCs, such as the British. Xie *et al.* (2008) showed that high-context people (HCP) comprehended non-verbal clues better than low-context people (LCP), while LCPs did the reverse.[35] Results from a 16-item survey of Chinese, Korean and US subjects showed that the three cultures differed in a way that was consistent with Hall's conceptualization. The Chinese and Korean subjects were shown to exhibit tendencies that were

Box 2.8

'One Japanese can and will guess what another one wants to say without him saying it. Western people cannot understand this. ... Japanese people will guess what other people think from a few words and accommodate, behave in a civilized way. [At work] people, including juniors, are generally attuned to reading atmosphere and context and adapting. Bosses don't quarrel openly, especially not in front of others. However, others may detect that there is hidden conflict and they will try to make it right. Acting maturely, adjusting to atmosphere used to be considered one of the most important work skills; it is becoming less common now. [But] conflict is always avoided.'[a]

In Hindi, the same word, 'kal', means either tomorrow or yesterday – literally one day away; and 'parso' means two days away – either the day after tomorrow or the day before yesterday. The precise meaning depends on the context.[b]

Sources: (a) interviews with a Japanese Finance and Accounting lecturer and a Japanese product manager from a Western multinational pharmaceutical manufacturer. Quoted in Guirdham, M. (2009) *Culture and Business in Asia*, Basingstoke, UK: Palgrave Macmillan (b) author's research

consistent with Hall's description of high-context cultures, and the American subjects were shown to exhibit tendencies that were consistent with low-context cultures.[36]

In a high-context culture, 'most of the information [to be communicated] is either in the physical context or internalized in the person, while very little is in the coded, explicit, transmitted part of the message.' In contrast, in a low-context society, 'the mass of the [communicated] information is vested in the explicit code.'[37] People in high-context cultures tend to adopt a role-oriented style. Role-oriented communication emphasizes the social roles that the participants hold. Different 'scripts' are used in different role relationships. Work meetings in Eastern countries, for instance, are usually very formal by Western standards. As a result, interactions in such meetings are impersonal and ritualistic. In contrast, people in low-context cultures use a personal style. A personal style emphasizes personal identity over social position. Because role relationships and status differences are less important, communication is less formal and often more intimate.[38] Weldon (1997) and Ting-Toomey (1988) linked conflict management behaviour to low- versus high-context communication style.[39,40] An exploratory analysis of McDonald's websites identified five different strategies by which visual communication is used to support high-context communication traits in a low-context medium.[41]

Critiques of taxonomic approaches to culture

Treatments of culture such as those of Hofstede (1981), Trompenaars (1993), Schwartz (1999) and the World Values Surveys, which provide lists of shared background characteristics such as world views, values and behavioural characteristics, have been criticized for being oversimplified, static and lacking a basis for determining whether two cultures are different. Trompenaars' (1993) work also attracts the criticism that, while his variables are intended to be a continuum, only lip service is paid to this; in reality they are treated as dichotomous. For instance, he writes of 'the ascriptive culture', although 21 out of 39 countries in his research fall between 25 per cent and 33 per cent on this measure, and of 'the achievement-oriented culture', although again 21 countries fall between 61 per cent and 70 per cent on this measure. Hofstede's (1981) work, though much admired and widely applied, has been criticized, primarily on two grounds: that it omits important values and that it is non-dynamic. The comment of Tayeb (1996) is typical of these criticisms: 'A country's culture is too vibrant and complex an entity to be simplified and described only in terms of these dimensions.'[42] According to Aldridge (2002), 'Human culture is a problem formation and problem resolution process and uses higher order abstractions via speech communication to provide for change. It is possible, for example, to have a highly individualist culture, as defined by Hofstede, but miss the variations in individualist cultures around the globe which have differing core values that may enhance or limit second order change.'[43]

Other criticisms focus on the lack of explanatory power of dimensional and 'shared values' models. Kim (1988), for instance, commented: 'When broad dimensions such as individualism–collectivism … are invoked to account for cultural differences, it is uncertain exactly how or why these differences occur. The use of culture as a post hoc explanation of observed differences does little to help us understand the underlying causes of behavior.'[44] Collier and Thomas (1988), too, criticized taxonomic conceptualizations because they do not supply answers to how many of the characteristics need to be different for there to be a cultural difference, because the fact that the characteristics vary in their impact on different cultures is ignored, and because such definitions may not capture the experience of the participants.[45]

A specific criticism made against Hofstede's account of individualism–collectivism is that research findings show that their relations can only be interpreted by a threefold categorization into individualism and two kinds of collectivism – relational and categorial (sic). The researchers behind these findings contend that relational collectivism, in which social exchange in networks determines social action and in which interests of partners are taken into consideration, should be distinguished from categorial [sic] collectivism in which a classification of groups guides social action and in which an abstract group interest is taken into consideration.[46] A further criticism of the individualism–collectivism dichotomy is implicit in the assertion of communalism[47] as set out earlier in this section, while the so-called 'collectivism' of East Asia may be better regarded as a lesser degree of individualism, rather than its conceptual opposite as an emphasis on groups.[48] This interpretation is consistent with Oyserman et al.'s (2002) finding that some East Asian cultures (Japan, Korea) did not differ from the USA in collectivism, although the USA was higher in individualism than the East Asian cultures.[49] Furthermore, experimental research found that Japanese people were less trusting and trustworthy exchange partners than cultural Chinese. 'This suggests that Japanese collectivism is based more on long-term assurance networks, whereas Chinese collectivism provides a more expansive, guanxi-based approach to building new social networks.'[50]

There is a further problem in describing cultures as discrete entities. As de Munck (2001) put it, 'A theory of culture as a discrete entity (or as homogeneous) logically implies that every member of that culture is culturally more similar to each other than they are to any one member from any other culture. But this is obviously not so. This also leads to the confusion where culture is passive and one selects from it [known as hybridization theory], at the same time culture is active and shapes the individual.'[51] Hybridization theory itself is illogical, because, if individuals select, then no two individuals are likely to select the same set of elements and everyone is going to belong to a culture (or group) of one. 'We might [also] argue that culture is a whole made out of parts such as class, religion, politics, economics, education and so forth and those similarities are limited to part similarities. But this Humpty Dumpty analogy of culture doesn't work, for if religion and the other subsystems shape individuals, then 'culture' is reduced to a category label that signals all these subsystems but has no function.' This critic concluded: 'The noun definition ignores and, in fact, hinders us from an analysis of the most constant and central aspects of culture – that it is a process and that it changes.' Unfortunately,

Box 2.9

(1) In the course of a negotiation with the Chief Financial Officer (CFO) of a company listed on the Bombay (India) stock exchange, the negotiator for an American company was startled when his opposite number, having taken a call on his mobile phone, suddenly excused himself and left the room. Another member of the Indian negotiating team explained, smiling, that the CFO had been summoned by the 'owner's' wife to assist with discussions over payments for her daughter's wedding.

(2) An applicant for a junior post in a British-owned offshore business in India had done well at his first interview and was called for a second. He had appeared very enthusiastic about getting the job and had in fact telephoned in every day following the first interview to find out whether he would be called for the second. Now he called in to say that he could not attend on the appointed day. When told that was the only day when second interviews would take place, and that those who did not attend would lose their chance, he sounded disappointed but said it was impossible.

(3) An Indian executive was well over an hour late for a middle of the day meeting with senior colleagues; the meeting's location was 20 minutes away from the office where he spent his working days. His Indian colleagues sat talking until he arrived, as he was bringing information without which no decisions could be taken. Although he had an office-supplied mobile phone, no call or message was received during this interval and he did not reply when the number was called.

(4) Perusing the accounts of the unit of a small software business he was auditing, an expatriate auditor new to India found to his surprise payments for a religious ceremony; these included fees to the Brahmin priest and payments for garlands and coconuts as well as for food. These turned out to relate to the opening of a new office.

(5) An important client waiting for confirmation of urgent travel arrangements from a Chennai travel agency which depended heavily on the client's custom did not receive the expected call at 1 pm. He waited until 1.30 pm and then phoned. When told that the person dealing with the matter was unavailable, he expostulated. 'But he has to have his lunch,' was the reply.

Explanations:

(1) Most Indian businesses are 'family-owned' and little distinction is made between serving the needs of the business and those of the owning family; in some cases the needs of the family take precedence over those of the business. This applies to financial matters as well as to the time of the employees, no matter how senior.

(2) It is quite common for Indians to consult an astrologer before any important occasion. If the job applicant had been told that the date set for the interview was inauspicious, he would consider that his chances of succeeding on that date were too low for it to be worthwhile – and more than that, to ignore the astrologer's advice might bring misfortune in other ways.

(3) Many Indians do not regard it as necessary to excuse lateness or warn those who might be affected by it. This executive might reason, 'They will know traffic is bad in the city. They will expect me to be late.' This is changing, but slowly.

(4) Developments such as the opening of a new office are usually marked by a religious ceremony in India. The accountant might well also have witnessed staff doing 'pujas' to their computers.

(5) Lunchtime breaks in Chennai are sacrosanct.

Source: author's research

de Munck (2001) was unable to propose a theory of culture that would satisfy his criteria, stating: 'At present I think we are not ready to develop a unified theory of culture, but we can develop many well-formed, midrange theories of culture that incorporate the core features: that it is shared, that it is located in the individual, and that it is learned. These features have many facets however, depending on the questions asked.'

Differing from the dominant bipolar paradigm of analysing national cultures, Fang (2005) championed a dialectical approach that sees each national culture as having a life of its own full of dynamics and paradoxes.[52] Findings by Zou et al. (2009) run counter to the perspective that cultural differences in social judgement are mediated by differences in individuals' personal values and beliefs; instead, the findings support a view that culture affects people through their perceptions of what is consensually believed. Thus, individuals who perceive that traditional views are culturally consensual (e.g., Chinese participants who believe that most of their fellows hold collectivistic values) will themselves behave and think in culturally typical ways. Participants' perceived consensus as much as participants' personal views mediated cultural differences.[53]

Greenfield (1997) discussed the limitations of using Western-made research instruments in other cultures. She pointed out that it is not defensible to take a test to other cultures where respondents have different basic assumptions about values, as the response to a question on values may not have the same importance in every culture; knowledge, as people in the various cultures may not be equally likely to know something; and communication, as the context of the test item may not have the same meaning in all the cultures.[54] Finally, the alternative view of cultures set out by DiMaggio (1997) and described in Section 2.4 below is an explicit rejection of culture as values that 'suffuse other aspects of belief, intention, and collective life'.[55]

> Values-based approaches to analysing cultures have been described. These are Hofstede's (1981 and 1993), which distinguishes individualism–collectivism, power distance, uncertainty avoidance, masculinity/femininity and long-term/short-term orientation as the primary cultural values; Trompenaars' (1993), which focuses on three primary values (relationships with people and attitudes to time and environment); and Schwartz's (1999), which considers that there are three primary values, all related to but distinct from Hofstede's – embeddedness/autonomy, hierarchy/egalitarianism and mastery/harmony. Values surveys are also described here. High-context/low-context communication differentiates according to communication style.
>
> Taxonomic approaches such as these have been criticized, especially for their static nature. Culture, it is asserted, is dynamic and constantly is being created through people's actions and communication. Such criticisms certainly have considerable force. Despite their limitations, however, taxonomic approaches have generated a large amount of empirical research and provided the most widespread increase in our awareness and understanding of cultural difference and its implications for work behaviour.

2.2 OTHER WAYS OF ANALYSING CULTURAL DIFFERENCE

In addition to the values taxonomies and high-context/low-context communication, there are three other approaches to cultural analysis underpinning the rest of this book. These approaches respectively emphasize institutions, subjective cultures and culture as a resource that people use strategically.

Subjective culture

'Subjective culture' is an approach that focuses on psychological constructs, such as beliefs, attitudes and individuals' values, although it also includes a number of sociological factors, such as norms, roles and tasks. Triandis (2002) defined subjective culture as a society's 'characteristic way of perceiving its social environment'.[56]

It 'consists of ideas about what has worked in the past and thus is worth transmitting to future generations. Language and economic, educational, political, legal, philosophical and religious systems are important elements of subjective culture. Ideas about aesthetics and how people should live with others are also important elements. Most important are unstated assumptions, standard operating procedures, and habits of sampling information from the environment.' How people categorize the world is considered to reveal much about their subjective culture, partly because it shows what they value. An example is the Greek category of 'philotimos', which is possibly unique to that culture and, indeed, more prevalent in rural districts and islands of Greece than in cities. Its literal meaning is 'friend of honour' and it can be translated as 'a person who does very frequently what family and friends expect done'.

Subjective culture theory distinguishes tight from loose cultures. In tight cultures, people are expected to behave precisely as specified by the culture's norms; in loose cultures, they have more latitude. Triandis (2002) pointed out, though, that a culture might be tight in some areas and loose in others. His example was that American culture is tight about passing bad cheques but loose about whom you choose as a roommate. Usefully, subjective culture incorporates an explanation for subcultures. They are considered to emerge 'because people share other elements, such as gender, physical type, neighbourhood, occupation, standard of living, resources, climates, and so on. For example, lawyers all over world share some elements of subjective culture. Japanese lawyers have a subculture that differs from other lawyers as well as general Japanese culture. A nation consists of thousands of cultures, but many of these cultures have common elements.'[57]

Culture as an institution

Over recent years, culture has acquired the status of a major influence on economic variables, from national economic growth to the location decisions of multinational enterprises. This status is derived from culture's position as an element in institutional theory, which holds that economic activity, business systems and organizations' decisions are constrained by the institutions of the places (generally countries) where they potentially or actually operate. Exploratory research by Guirdham (2009) suggested that one type of institution, business culture, was influential in a whole range of business decisions made in five Asian countries and so in the resulting patterns of ownership, financing, governance, organization, management and strategy.[58] Institutions are

> social structures that have attained a high degree of resilience. [They] are composed of cultural-cognitive, normative and regulative elements that, together with associated activities and resources, provide stability and meaning to social life. Institutions are transmitted by various types of carriers; these include symbolic systems, relational systems, routines, and artefacts. Institutions operate at different levels of jurisdiction, from the world system to localized interpersonal relationships. Institutions by definition connote stability but are subject to change processes, both incremental and discontinuous.[59]

The cultural-cognitive element of institutions includes traditions and taken-for-granted rules and conventions, together with preconscious widely accepted customs. The element 'equates to culture'.[60] A country's level of institutional development may have a direct effect on the composition of entrepreneurs' networks (i.e., the prevalence of strong ties – between people who are in frequent contact with one another – versus weak ties, in which contact is relatively distant and infrequent). Furthermore, both strong and weak ties may have direct, positive effects on the speed of new venture internationalization through the rationale that entrepreneurs use to draw on their social networks and drive internationalization.[61]

Culture as a strategic resource

Modern research in cognitive psychology suggests that our minds are full of images, opinions and information, untagged as to truth value, but to which we are inclined to attribute accuracy and plausibility. Research on memory reveals that information (including false information) passes into memory without being 'tagged' as to source or credibility, and that active inference is required to identify the source of the information when it is recalled. People retain (and store with a default value of 'correct') almost every image or idea with which they have come into contact. Within this perspective of cognitive psychology, culture is seen as a large 'toolkit', on which people draw to make decisions about how to behave. Different situations cue differing cultural frames or understandings; this helps explain findings that culture is fragmented across groups and inconsistent across its manifestations. People behave as if they use culture strategically. This means that individuals do not acquire a unique culture by imbibing it (and no other) through socialization. This in turn explains the capacity of individuals to participate in multiple cultural traditions, even when those traditions contain inconsistent elements.

The finding that culture is stored in memory as an indiscriminately assembled and relatively unorganized collection of odds and ends imposes a far stronger organizing burden on actors than did the earlier highly socialized view. The question, then, is how the actor organizes the information that s/he possesses. Psychological research points to two quite different mechanisms or modes of routine and deliberative cognition.

■ Routine, everyday cognition relies heavily and uncritically upon culturally available schemata – knowledge structures that represent objects or events and provide default assumptions about their characteristics, relationships and entailments under conditions of incomplete information. 'Schemata are both representations of knowledge and information-processing mechanisms. ... Much cognitive research demonstrates that schematic material dominates other material in accurate recall, in intruded recall, in recognition confidence, in recall clustering and in resistance to disconfirmation. ... Schemata also facilitate inaccurate recall when the information is schema consistent. In schematic cognition we find the mechanisms by which culture shapes and biases thought.'

   People are more likely to perceive information that is germane to existing schemata, to recall schematically embedded information more quickly and more accurately; people may falsely recall schematically embedded events that did not occur. Research on social cognition enhances our understanding of how culture constrains but does not support theories that depict culture as overwhelmingly constraining. Instead, consistent with contemporary sociological theorizing, work in psychology provides micro-foundational evidence for the efficacy of agency, or the capacity of individuals and groups to act with intention.

■ In contrast to routine (automatic) thought, psychologists noted a quite different form of cognition, which is 'explicit, verbalized, slow, and deliberate'. When sufficiently motivated, people can override programmed modes of thought to think critically and reflexively. In these circumstances, the influence of culture may be minimal.

Psychological research suggests that people shift into deliberative modes of thought relatively easily when their attention is attracted to a problem; they may also shift from automatic to deliberative cognition when they are strongly motivated to do so; finally, people shift to more deliberative modes of processing when existing schemata fail to account adequately for new stimuli. Cultural understandings may be fragmented by domain, so that, when persons or groups switch from one domain to another, their perspectives, attitudes, preferences and dispositions may change radically.[62]

According to DiMaggio (1999), it follows from this 'culture as a toolkit' perspective that large-scale cultural changes may be caused by large-scale, more-or-less simultaneous frame switches by many interdependent actors, while according to Tipton (2009), in the USA, Japan and Western Europe, 'individuals choose their own culture'.[63]

The approaches described in this section emphasize three different facets of culture.

Triandis's (1994 and 2002) subjective culture concept incorporates a large number of psychological and sociological constructs. For the most part, this approach remains at the theoretical level, having received much less testing and research than the values approaches. Nevertheless, the concepts are empirically, if unscientifically, based and have plausibility and usefulness. A second approach, which incorporates culture as a major element in the institutional framework of a country or region, is emerging and awaits further testing. Finally, a modern view that draws on the findings of cognitive psychology is that culture is a 'toolkit', a resource that people deploy strategically to make decisions, judge behaviours and govern their own behaviours; although routine, everyday transactions and interactions rely on cultural programmes, when people are motivated they can and do override cultural prescriptions.

2.3　THE IMPACT OF CULTURE ON WORK BEHAVIOUR

There is evidence for the influence of culture on employees' work centrality, preferences regarding standardization and for being challenged at work, attitudes to punctuality and deadlines, organizational commitment, justice perceptions, responses to low job satisfaction, norms, and groupwork behaviour, including conformity. For instance, countries high in uncertainty avoidance (UA) showed the greatest increases

Box 2.10

Two surveys of Belgian people's hostility to the wearing of the veil by Islamic women revealed that subtle prejudice/racism, self-enhancement and security values and anti-religious thinking predicted greater levels of anti-veil attitudes beyond the effects of other related variables such as age and political conservatism. Universalist values and spirituality predicted relatively lower levels of anti-veil attitudes.

Source: Saroglou, V., Lamkaddem, B., Van Pachterbeke, M. and Buxant, C. (2009) 'Host society's dislike of the Islamic veil: The role of subtle prejudice, values, and religion', *International Journal of Intercultural Relations*, **33**(5): 419–28

in work centrality (the importance attached to work) among young people start-ing work. The smallest increases occurred in countries high in masculinity. Again, professional employees from high power distance, high uncertainty avoidance and high-context cultures preferred greater service activity standardization across offices and geographies, whereas employees from high individualism cultures preferred less standardization.[64] Lower levels of individualism in French culture may underlie find-ings that the French found it less important to be challenged while at work than members of Anglo cultures did. Furthermore, whereas Anglo countries viewed time as a valuable commodity ('time is money'), punctuality was expected, and deadlines were to be met, in contrast, Latin Europeans, including the French, were less inclined to abide by schedules. Again, collectivism as a cultural value orientation increased employees' commitment to their organizations, and the relationship between com-mitment and outcomes is also stronger in a collectivistic context.[65] Another study found that cultural values affected individuals' commitment to their organization, supervisor and workgroup. High UA led to individuals feeling more committed to their relationship with all three; high PD led to them feeling a stronger sense that they should feel committed; high collectivism led to a stronger sense of commitment to their workgroup, though not necessarily to their supervisor or organization. A third study that used a US-developed instrument to measure 'organizational identification', a construct related to organizational commitment, in Thailand, found key differ-ences from the earlier US results. The US conceptualization of identification included employees' sense of membership, similarity and loyalty to their organization, whereas the Thai dimensions reflected life values ('pride in membership'), social values ('fit with organization'), and personal values ('comfort zone').[66]

An interesting line of research suggested that European Americans had an attitude to interpersonal conflict at work that differed from that of members of many other cul-tures. A cross-cultural experiment showed that European Americans were more likely than Koreans to join a talented team despite its likelihood of experiencing relation-ship conflict, and to take longer than the Koreans to reach a decision. The evidence suggested that this difference in behaviour was linked to the fact that, compared with Koreans, European Americans were less likely to believe that relationship conflict – but not task conflict – limits a team's ability to succeed. Given that a long series of prior research has clearly demonstrated that interpersonal conflict reduces team performance, the researchers in the present case concluded that European Americans underestimated the negative influence of relationship conflict. A possible explanation for such an attitude could be found in Protestant Relational Ideology (PRI), a distin-guishing attribute of European Americans' work style, which tends 'to give diminished importance to the relational dimension of workplace interactions'. This 'anomaly' of

Box 2.11

A US-trained Chinese senior partner in the Beijing branch of an accountancy firm com-pared the differences in work behaviour in the two countries as follows: 'You see differences in how teams operate – [in China there is] more variability within the organization, differences of style. In the USA, if the partners are away, the work can still be handled; but though the organ-ization in China has the same back-up system as in USA, things don't get done.'

Source: Guirdham, M. (2009) *Culture and Business in Asia*, Basingstoke, UK: Palgrave Macmillan

European American attitudes (it does not apply outside the work context) has been shown by sociological, historical and psychological research to be linked to the beliefs and practices of the founding Protestant communities of European American society. Over time, beliefs about the importance of restricting relational concerns while working were secularized and incorporated into the contemporary ethos of European American culture.[67]

There are cross-national differences in perceptions of distributive justice (fairness in differences in rewards in relation to the status and work contribution of those involved). There are marked variations in perceptions of distributive justice across Europe. Employees in Belgium, France, Greece, Portugal and Spain tended to prefer equality-based pay policies that rewarded group-level effort and efficiency. In contrast, Danish, German, Irish and British employees preferred equitable pay policies. In many European organizations, it is expected that top pay levels should not exceed 12 to 15 times the average pay level. By comparison, in North American organizations, an individual deal may create multiples of over 100.

The behavioural responses to low job satisfaction of participants in Hong Kong and New Zealand were influenced by collectivism/individualism. Whether individuals responded to low job satisfaction with exit, voice, loyalty or neglect was affected by their collectivism or individualism, while this cultural variable also moderated the effect of quality of job alternatives and job satisfaction on exit and loyalty, and of quality of job alternatives on voice.[68]

Table 2.2 shows how different cultural values can affect the norms applied to work behaviour. In some cultures, however, normative pressures may operate in a different manner. In Spain, researchers have found a higher incidence of 'perverse norms' than in Anglo countries. Perverse norms are norms that are agreed to exist but are rarely enforced. Within a system of perverse norms, authority figures may maintain control by determining when norms will be enforced and when they will not.[69] Behaviour during groupwork is also influenced by culture, as Table 2.3 shows. However, while individualists are likely to behave in the same competitive way in most groups, collectivists may behave differently in different groups. In principle, in groups composed of their ingroup, co-operativeness will predominate; in those composed of their outgroups, they may be more inclined to compete or, in the case of conflict arising, to 'uncharacteristically' confront. The level of majority influence on group minorities appeared to depend on their cultural propensity toward collectivism (or individualism) a cross-cultural experiment found. Majority influence on collectivistic group minorities was manifested more strongly than that on individualistic group minorities. This applied in both culturally

Table 2.2   *Effect of cultural values on work norms*

Cultural values	Work norms
High power distance	Penalties for breaches apply more to lower members; higher ones are 'above the law'; norms are imposed by leaders rather than emerging by consensus.
High masculinity (achievement)	Adherence to norms is more enforced in more punitive ways than in feminine cultures.
High uncertainty avoidance	Norms are more rigid – there is less scope for different interpretations than in low uncertainty avoidance cultures.
High collectivism	Norms concerned with loyalty to the group are emphasized; there are different norms for ingroup versus outgroup members.

Table 2.3   *Effects of cultural values on groupwork*

Effect of	High/long	Low/short
Power distance	Difficulty in working in an unchaired or unsupervised group	Lack of deference to authority
Uncertainty avoidance	Preference for agendas and sticking to them, structured discussion, clear outcomes, minutes	Preference for informality
Masculinity (achievement)	Task orientation dominant	Maintenance orientation dominant
Individualism	Competitive atmosphere	Co-operative atmosphere
Time orientation	Exploration of all issues before seeking a decision	Sense of urgency, pressure for closure

homogeneous and culturally heterogeneous groups. Moreover, group minorities behaved consistently in the way that conformed to their cultural norms and beliefs regardless of the degree of group diversity and the national culture of the majorities.[70]

Basic aspects of group performance, such as productivity and conformity, differ substantially by culture. In groups, people may tend to work less hard, partly because their effort is less likely to bring them personal reward than it is when they work independently. This tendency is known as social loafing. However, in China, Israel and Japan, social loafing is not only absent but is significantly reversed. In studies in China and Israel, subjects who endorsed collectivist values worked harder in group settings than individually. This finding contrasts with the findings on social loafing found in Western societies. Again, a meta-analysis of 133 replications of the Asch conformity study (which found that people tend to agree with the judgement of a group even when it contradicts what they can see in front of them), found that conformity was even higher among those with high scores on the collectivist pole of Hofstede's (1981) individualism–collectivism value dimension.

Perhaps equally important as a population's work behaviour in existing organizations is its tendency to start new organizations, in other words its entrepreneurialism. A 2002 analysis of the findings of 21 empirical studies that examined the association between national cultural characteristics and aggregate measures of entrepreneurship found some evidence that broad cultural characteristics were associated with national levels of entrepreneurship, but these relationships were not consistent over time. National rates of innovation were positively correlated with individualism, negatively with uncertainty avoidance. Findings on power distance and national rates of innovation were contradictory.

Need for approval, perceived instrumentality of wealth, communitarianism, need for personal development, need for independence and need for escape are all motives associated with individual entrepreneurialism; the importance of these motives varies systematically across cultures. The same systematic cross-cultural variation applies also to need for recognition of achievement, learning and development, and roles. On the other hand, one study found that entrepreneurs across several cultures scored high in power distance, individualism and masculinity and low in uncertainty avoidance, suggesting that entrepreneurialism is a trait with universal features. Contrastingly, another study found that entrepreneurial traits (internal locus of control, risk-taking and high energy levels) decreased as cultural distance from the US increased. Entrepreneurship within organizations in the form of corporate venturing, strategic renewal, and spin-offs for ideas generated within organizations was linked to uncertainty avoidance in a finding that it is positively associated with a preference for joint ventures and greenfield sites over acquisitions as an entry mode. A follow-up study found positive linear relationships between entrepreneurship and an external orientation, an organizational cultural orientation toward decentralization, and a long- versus short-term orientation.[71]

Finally, intra-organizational entrepreneurialism, in the form of product or process championing styles, has been linked to culture: styles that appeal to group norms were linked to low individualism; styles that emphasize monitoring strategies to high power distance; styles that adhere to rules and procedures to uncertainty avoidance. A preference for licensing over foreign direct investment was linked to low uncertainty avoidance, as were preferences for network facilitator, transformational leadership, organizational maverick and organizational buffer types of championing roles.[72]

In the management literature it has been common to assume that demographic variables, such as age and gender, are universally linked to work behaviour. This has not been directly investigated.[73] In fact, there is some indirect contrary evidence. In China, unlike the West, researchers found, demographic variables such as age and gender had no direct effect on an individual's commitment to the organization. Under the influence of traditional Chinese culture, including 'personalism' and '*guanxi*' (connections), Chinese employees behaved differently from their Western counterparts.[74] Pelled (1996) pointed out that there are cultural differences in the significance of particular demographic factors; for instance, age and gender play especially significant roles in Mexican culture. In addition, some demographic categories vary cross-nationally: Mexican workplaces typically lack some of the ethnic categories present in US workforces (e.g., African American and Asian) while other ethnic distinctions (i.e., between Mestizo, Amerindian and White people) are important in the Latin American culture.[75] Ofori-Dankwa and Lane (2000) argued that demographic diversity and value similarity (congruence) are not opposed but interact to determine how co-operative or competitive the relations between individuals and groups in an organization will be.[76]

The influence of culture on the intrapersonal factors and processes underlying work behaviour will be discussed in Chapter 4.

> A range of differences in work behaviour, including commitment, the operation of norms, and behaviour during groupwork are related to culture. Links between differences in work behaviour and subcultural differences have not been extensively studied.

2.4 THE IMPACT OF CULTURE ON WORK ORGANIZATION AND MANAGEMENT

Culture has a strong influence on the structures, processes and predominant managerial styles of organizations in different societies. For example, in a culture that is high on measures of uncertainty, formalization and centralization are prominent features of organizational structure; decision-making authority, responsibility and communication are distributed according to a hierarchical pattern; and the climate is reserved. In a low UA culture, on the other hand, the structure is informal and decentralized; decision-making authority and all that goes with it is widely distributed; and an open climate of discussion and bargaining prevails. Organizational structures and work roles, organizational cultures, decision-making processes, employment relationships, perceptions of managerial effectiveness, task versus relationships orientation of managers, managers' roles and styles, and managerial beliefs are among features of organization and management that may be influenced by culture.

Organizational structures and work roles

A review of the literature concerned with French, British and American work practices found a number of differences based on PD, UA and individualism. French managers typically viewed organizations as a formal pyramid of differentiated levels of power, and thought that success stemmed from their ability to 'work the system' by managing power relationships effectively. Early attempts to transfer Management by Objectives (MBO) to France were unsuccessful because the idea of supervisor and subordinate jointly reaching decisions about the subordinate's performance was inconsistent with the importance of hierarchy in French organizations. In France, typically only the supervisor or manager has power, so MBO meant that subordinates were held responsible for goals without having the power to achieve those goals. Similarly, the ideas of matrix management are quite inconsistent with the way French managers view authority: 'How can someone take orders from two bosses?' In contrast, British managers hold a less hierarchical view of organizations; they see them primarily as a network of relationships between individuals who get things done by influencing each other through communication and negotiation. These differences are attributed to higher French cultural PD. Higher French UA is reflected in their being less willing to show trust, allow participation in decisions and share information than people from Anglo countries (British and Americans). French managers have been found to be preoccupied with absolute accuracy for all control indicators and less concerned about what the data implies. Schneider and DeMeyer (1991) found that the French, more than those from Anglo countries, viewed strategic issues as threats instead of as opportunities.[77]

Work roles are extensively affected by cultural values: high PD leads to steep hierarchies and narrow spans of control (and vice versa for low power distance); high UA to strict adherence to job descriptions and formality (and vice versa for low UA); individualism to an emphasis on personal responsibility; collectivism to an emphasis on group responsibility; high achievement orientation to prioritizing task completion; high relationship orientation to concern with maintenance.

Organizational cultures

Organizational cultures can be analysed in a variety of ways, such as externally versus internally driven and as task- or people-focused. Hofstede (1981) identified six dimensions closely related to his concepts of culture: The six are:

1. Process-oriented versus results-oriented cultures. Process-oriented work cultures emphasize technical and bureaucratic routines; results-oriented cultures focus on outcomes.
2. Job-oriented versus employee-oriented cultures.
3. Professional versus parochial cultures. This distinction corresponds to an older one between individuals with a cosmopolitan outlook and those with a local outlook.
4. Open system versus closed system cultures. Here the reference is to how openly the organization communicates both internally and externally, and to how easily it admits outsiders and newcomers. Hofstede (1981) found that the Danish organizations he studied were more open than the Dutch. This was the only difference found between organizational cultures in the two countries.
5. Tightly versus loosely controlled cultures. The difference here concerns the degree of formality and punctuality required of staff. Whether an organization's culture

is tightly or loosely controlled is partly a function of its technology – banks, for example, are more tightly controlled than advertising agencies – but some variation occurs within the same technology.

6. Pragmatic versus normative cultures. Pragmatic cultures have flexible ways of dealing with the environment, especially customers; rigid cultures do not. The distinction reflects the organization's degree of customer orientation.[78]

Some other researchers have applied the societal cultural dimensions, such as individualism–collectivism, directly to organizational cultures. Research into the direct effects of national cultures on organizational cultures has, however, produced conflicting results. An assessment of the cultures of an American, a Japanese and a Taiwanese bank, as well as an American bank operating in Taiwan, confirmed that organizational cultures differed as a result of the impact of national cultures.[79] The GLOBE (Global Leadership and Organizational Behavior Effectiveness) study of culture, organizations and leadership found support across 62 societies for the proposition that 'societal cultural values and practices affect organizational culture and practices' both directly and through affecting leadership practices.[80] On the other hand, Gerhart (2009) found from a review of the literature that most of the variance in organizational cultures is not explained by country and that, of the variance that is explained by country, only a minority is due to national culture differences.[81] In addition, Vertinsky et al. (1990) suggested that the norms on which organizational culture was based were subject to a process of globalization that reduced cross-cultural and national differences. These authors, however, acknowledged that some norms of organizational design and management reflected national culture values and were resistant to change and convergence.[82] Diversity and organizational cultures in combination affect work-based communication, conflict, creativity and productivity, a study found:

■ Diverse co-workers in collectivist organizations communicated more by memos and less by face-to-face interaction compared with both non-diverse co-workers in collectivist organizations and diverse co-workers in individualist organizations. When people were more different from their co-workers they were more reluctant to interact in person. Unfortunately, sending memos may be less effective than face-to-face interactions for conveying information and resolving problems.

■ No more conflict was found between demographically different than demographically similar co-workers. Also, in an organizational culture that emphasized collective goals, demographically different co-workers were more likely to find conflict beneficial. Workers in individualist organizational cultures were more likely both to experience conflict (probably because their goals and values differed more from each other's) and to find it harmful.

■ Dissimilar people in collectivist organizational cultures had the highest creative output. This finding suggests that creativity emerges from the combination of (1) access to a larger set of novel ideas afforded by more diverse members and (2) trust that novel ideas will be used for the benefit of the collective.

■ While similar people were significantly more productive in individualist than collectivist organizational cultures, dissimilar people were equally productive across the two kinds of culture. They were also more productive than similar co-workers, although less likely to interact. This may be partly explained by whether the co-workers' interaction was task-related or social. Dissimilar co-workers may have focused more consistently on tasks, because they may have had fewer other topics in common to discuss with one another. However, diverse people may have a wider variety of ideas to share and debate during their interaction, allowing them to realize greater returns for the time invested. Unfortunately, interaction among dissimilar people, while perhaps the most beneficial, also appears to be the most difficult to cultivate.[83]

The effect of national cultures on organizational cultures can make it difficult for organizational cultures to cross geographical boundaries. Individuals tend to select and to be selected by organizations with values similar to their own. 'Goodness of fit' with the organizational culture is important to an individual's commitment, satisfaction, productivity and longevity with an organization. It may also affect attitudes to work communication. In Italy, it was found that people who did not agree with how success appeared to be defined in the organization (who may have a poor 'fit' with the organizational culture) were dissatisfied with their own ability to send messages to management, in contrast with those who agreed with how success was defined.[84]

Decision-making processes

Linked to differences in organizational structures are differences in how decisions are made. These vary widely across cultures. 'In Western societies, decisions are made on the basis of input from those involved. Or, they gather individual preferences and democratically vote on the solution. In cultures with greater hierarchies, group members assume an authority will decide and they are only to enact the decision, not to have input or take responsibility. Of course, this is hard to assess since the criteria for success in relationship-based cultures is very different from those in material- or success-based cultures. Not only do the processes differ, the basis for evaluation of alternatives and the outcome also differ.'[85] In this respect Japan must count as 'Western'. There, decision-making is by consensus.

Perceptions of managerial effectiveness

Across Europe, there are marked differences in the skills, qualities and competencies that are perceived to be central to performance and the consequent expectations of managers. Assumptions about what makes a good manager are all influenced by national culture. For instance, 'While Anglo-Saxon managers emphasize the need for interpersonal skills and job visibility, being labelled "high potential" is the most important criterion for French managers (reflecting the elitist management development systems), and having a creative mind is the most important indicator for German managers.'[86]

Task versus relationships orientation of managers

A comparison of Nordic, Latin-European and Hungarian managers' management styles found the strongest task orientation in Latin Europe, whereas the most intense employee orientation was found in the Nordic countries. Latin-European managers scored lower on consideration, 'as their cultures seem to support a more authoritarian manager who decides without any negotiation with his or her subordinates.'[87] Task behaviour in the study was further analysed, showing that Nordic managers emphasized planning and order, whereas Latin-European managers relied on goals, information and supervision behaviour. 'This seems to be indicative of the more authoritarian character of Latin-European managers, while Nordic managers plan more beforehand and communicate more with their subordinates.' In terms of relations to employees, Nordic managers were considerate. They relied on their subordinates, supported them, allowed them to make decisions and showed regard for them as individuals. Latin-European managers created 'an atmosphere free of conflict', probably by using direct supervision and clear rules and principles. Power seemed to be more centralized in Latin-European organizations. 'Managers have the knowledge and make the decisions. There are no negotiations and therefore there is a low conflict level in their organizations. Latin-European managers seem to have much more of the boss-oriented mentality in their organizations: the boss is the head of the organization and does not expect ideas and support from the lower levels.'[88]

Managers' roles and styles

Research has pointed to significant national differences in managers' roles and styles. The cultural definition of a manager's role contributes to his or her structuring activities, whether alone or with peers, and to the tendency to invite or disregard subordinates' input.[89] For instance, a general management survey on perceptions of national management style was given to 707 managers representing diverse industries from the USA (156), Indonesia (177), Malaysia (192) and Thailand (182). It found significant differences in formality of structures and controls, individual versus team development, employee involvement in setting goals and the appraisal process, intrinsic versus extrinsic rewards and frequency of feedback.[90]

Box 2.12

X was a newly appointed manager in an international Swedish engineering firm. X was not Swedish, unlike most of his subordinates. One came to see him in early March, (1) without an appointment. She opened with his first name, (2) then said, 'I need some time off – about two weeks, in June, to revise for my exams.' (3) Her tone, though polite, appeared to imply that the request was routine and would be granted automatically. X was surprised and pointed out that June was a peak workload period. It would be difficult for her to be spared. (4) Given her previous attitude, he expected her to argue back, but instead she said, 'That's a problem, I can see. How can we get round it?'

Intrigued by this unexpectedly co-operative approach, X suggested that he could re-arrange the unit's holiday schedule, so she could take some of her six weeks holiday in late May/early June – he would speak to Johann about swopping with her. She looked startled, (5) was quiet for a long time, (6) then said, 'Holiday schedules can only be re-arranged following extensive consultation and discussion among the whole team and with the agreement of all those affected.'

The responses of the subordinate in this manager–subordinate interaction may be explained as follows:

(1) Swedish culture is egalitarian (low in power distance), which is reflected in a lack of formality in forms of address within organizations.

(2) Swedish spoken style tends towards the direct or blunt, though not extremely.

(3) Workers' rights for time off in Sweden are more extensive than in some other countries.

(4) Swedish conversational rules encourage brainstorming and working things out co-operatively.

(5) Swedes are more comfortable with silence than some other people.

(6) Many decisions that in some countries would be the prerogative of management are taken by consensus in Sweden.

Based on: author's research

In addition to these national differences, there are well-researched differences between women and men as managers. To a greater extent than men, Finnish studies found, women tended to encourage their subordinates to use their abilities fully and to cut through bureaucratic red tape. They did this by facilitating informal contacts between leaders and workers, introducing new working methods and training, disseminating information and taking workers' views into consideration.[91] A meta-analysis of 370 studies compared men's and women's leadership styles and concluded: 'The strongest evidence...for a sex difference in leadership style occurred on the tendency for women to adopt a more democratic or participative style and for men to adopt a more autocratic or directive style....92 per cent of the available comparisons went in the direction of more democratic behaviour from women than men.'[92] This difference was attributed to women's greater interpersonal skills and cognitive complexity.

Managerial beliefs

Culture and managerial beliefs have been linked since the early studies of Haire *et al.* (1966).[93] Their survey of 3,500 managers in 14 countries around the world found that about 28 per cent of the variance in managerial beliefs about participation and the capacity of their subordinates to participate effectively could be accounted for by nationality alone. The countries could be grouped, on the basis of the managers' responses, into four clusters: Nordic-European, Latin-European, Anglo-American and developing countries. A later study of Australian managers supported a cultural explanation of these findings by demonstrating the similarity of their leadership beliefs to those in the Anglo-American group.[94] Another study across 12 countries linked managers' goals, preferences for taking risks, pragmatism, interpersonal competence, effective intelligence, emotional stability and leadership style to national cultures.[95] However, studies in Greece and five developing countries showed 'a low level of industrialization' to be such a potent explanatory variable as to offset the effects of cultural diversity. The researchers commented that national culture seemed to have more explanatory power for mature industrialized countries.[96]

Employment relationships

Many practices that are valued and widely applied in the USA, the UK and Canada are seen as far less important in Italy, Japan and Korea and positively devalued in France and Germany. These practices include pay systems that promote performance, wide spans of control that promote delayering, the eradication of specialized and directed work forces, reliance on flexible cross-functional teams, the promotion of employee empowerment and involvement, an emphasis on management development, the analysis of individual performance, rewards for business productivity gains, and the sharing of benefits, risks and costs with the workforce.[97]

> In this section, the impact of culture at work has been considered in terms of its effects on organizational structures and work roles, organizational cultures, decision-making processes, perceptions of managerial effectiveness, task versus relationships orientation of managers, management roles and styles, managerial beliefs and employment relationships. In all these areas research has found some differences that can be attributed to culture, although debates continue regarding, for instance, the impact of culture on organizational culture.

2.5 THE IMPACT OF CULTURE ON ORGANIZATIONAL ENVIRONMENTS

Social and economic institutions not only include culture, but are themselves affected by culture. As was explained earlier in this chapter, institutions consist of normative and regulative elements as well as cultural-cognitive elements. Normative elements are purposely constructed and include authority systems and roles that occur in response to what is consciously perceived as necessary and proper to direct the behaviour of individuals and organizations. The rules of professions such as accountants and lawyers are examples of normative institutions. The regulative elements of a country's institutions include laws, regulations and codified government policies.[98] These normative and regulative institutions are a significant part of any organization's environment, embracing government, law, politics and so on; they are heavily influenced by culture.[99] Furthermore, culture has been linked to countries' business systems,[100] to national patterns of business ownership, financing and governance[101] and to nations' levels of civil society and social capital.[102] These huge topics are outside the scope of this book, but the impact of culture on two aspects of organizational environments that are influenced by culture and impact directly on work communication are considered: these are networks and corruption.

Networks

The term 'network' usually refers to a loose organization of non-state actors characterized by voluntary, reciprocal and horizontal patterns of communication and exchange.[103] The central argument of network theory is that actors, such as organizations, are embedded in networks of interconnected social relationships that offer opportunities for, and constraints on, behaviour. Culture has a strong influence on how dense and connected such networks are. A replication in Israel of a study of Californian social networks found that the Israeli networks were denser than the American equivalents.[104] Culture, local social and business organizations and institutional arrangements have been shown to be critical in explaining the formation of inter-organizational networks both in the United States and abroad. Scott (1995 and 2001) showed that the different forms of inter-firm relations in Britain, France, and Germany could be traced to their distinct patterns of historical development. Much of the institutional research on inter-firm structures in East Asia, such as that of Whitley (1992), has accounted for variations in network structures by focusing on cultural, political and historical contexts.[105] Business cultures have been linked to the dense and highly interconnected phenomenon of business groups in East Asia.[106]

According to the theory of structural holes,[107] networks inherently contain social capital, a competitive advantage enjoyed by members of the network. The advantage is conceptualized as structure standing as proxy for information, based on the fact that people cluster into groups as a result of interaction opportunities that arise in the places where people meet, the neighbourhoods they live in, the organizations they join, the projects they take part in. Communication is both more frequent and more influential within than between such groups, so that people develop a common view of history, similar views of proper opinion and behaviour, similar views of how to move into the future. 'What was once explicit knowledge interpretable by anyone becomes tacit knowledge meaningful only to insiders. Over time, the tacit knowledge becomes more complex, harder to move to outsiders or for outsiders to access. It becomes "sticky".'[108]

Box 2.13

A Western procurement manager for an American firm exporting leather goods through Hong Kong found that members of the procurement unit routinely obtained supplies through their *guanxi* network instead of following company procedures of obtaining three quotes or, for larger amounts, by tender. When she raised the issue with them, they replied that they could always get a better deal through their contacts.

Source: author's research

This tears holes in the flow of information between groups. These holes in the social structure of communication, or more simply 'structural holes', are missing relations that inhibit the information flow between people.

Structural holes theory distinguishes two network sources of advantage: brokerage and closure. These are forms of social capital inasmuch as they originate, evolve and decay as a function of the surrounding network. Closure is about staying on your side of a structural hole. It is about the benefits of protection from variation in opinion and behaviour, protection afforded by focusing on connections with your own kind. Structural holes prevent people from being overwhelmed by the diversity of knowledge on offer; they also enable organizations to effect control at lower cost. Brokerage is about the benefits of exposure to variation in opinion and behaviour by building connections across structural holes. 'In business, network brokerage provides people, product, process and market enhancements to grow the business; closure provides labour, management and speed efficiencies that cut costs. Connecting across more holes means more exposure, which provides a vision advantage in selecting earlier between alternative ways to go, synthesising new ways to go, framing a proposal to be attractive to needed supporters and detecting potential supporters. ... Network brokers enjoy more positive evaluations than their peers, higher compensation and faster promotions.'[109] (But there are costs in wasted time because not all new ideas are any good.)

Burt (1992) put it succinctly: 'Brokerage is about coordinating people whom it would be valuable, but risky, to trust. Closure is about making it safe to trust. The key to creating value is to put the two together. Bridging a structural hole can create value, but delivering value requires the closed network of a cohesive team around the bridge.'[110] However, Xiao and Tsui (2007) found that brokers do not fit with the collectivistic values of China. Further, the more an organization possesses a clan-like, high-commitment culture, the more detrimental are structural holes for employees' career achievements such as salary or bonus, even after controlling for a host of other factors that may influence these career outcomes. In high-commitment organizations, the 'integrators' who bring people together to fill structural holes enjoy greater career benefits.[111]

Networks occur within as well as between organizations, and there is evidence that national culture influences social network patterns within organizations. For example, French employees preferred weak links at work, whereas Japanese workers tend to form strong, multiplex ties.[112] Given the Japanese group orientation to decision-making, as opposed to the individualistic emphasis in the United States as a whole, it is not surprising that density and interconnectedness are greater in Japanese companies. *Guanxi*, the sophisticated version of networking that operates in China, functions within as well as between organizations.[113]

Corruption

In anecdotal terms the link between culture and corruption (often defined as the illegal use of public office for private gain) is so strong that the term 'culture of corruption' has gained currency. 'Culture of corruption' is seen by some as a consequence, by others as a cause of corruption. Others have linked corruption to wider cultural values and factors: Jorge Nef (2001), for example, pointed to a range of cultural attributes in Latin America to account for the region's corruption, including particularism (within the inner circle), formalism (a double standard), role expectation of dispensing favours, corporatism, authoritarianism, and even centralism.[114] The view here is that the culture of corruption feeds corrupt behaviour rather than fostering behaviour ensuring good governance. The research findings in this area are few, however. One study found that uncertainty avoidance moderated the relationship between economic adversity and corruption, whereas power distance and uncertainty avoidance were positively associated with corruption. Another found that Hofstede's cultural dimension variables together with national wealth, national religion and a construct labelled 'personality at the national level', which included variables such as introversion–extraversion and conscientiousness, did have an effect on corruption in 54 countries.[115]

Corruption is higher among countries split among several language or ethnic groups.[116] The reason is that most such countries are those where patronage of friends and relatives is higher because relationships are more personalized. In those countries, doing favours for friends and relatives is generally considered a moral obligation, not corruption. Again, in countries where gift exchange is a norm in business transactions, public officials often consider that receiving 'gifts' from those whom they can favour is acceptable. Finally, loyalty to a clan, a kingship or a family is of utmost importance in some societies and leads to hiring associated or related others even at the expense of the common good.[117]

Box 2.14

Under the heading, 'The global crackdown on corporate bribery: governments around the world are making life difficult for corrupt firms', *The Economist* of 12 November 2009 reported on a series of record fines imposed on businesses that bribed government officials and others in order to obtain contracts. These punishments included the following: 'In February American courts fined KBR, a construction firm, and Halliburton, its former parent, $579m over bribes paid to obtain contracts in Nigeria. Last year they hit Siemens, a German conglomerate, with an $800m fine– the biggest to date. The German authorities also fined Siemens a similar amount.

That case has helped spur more zealous pursuit of corporate bribery in Europe, says Richard Dean of Baker & McKenzie, another law firm. In September British prosecutors secured their first big conviction, of Mabey & Johnson, a bridge-building company, over bribery of foreign government officials. But prosecutors are still weighing politically charged allegations of bribery involving BAE Systems, a defence contractor, and foreign officials. The British government says its proposed new law will close several loopholes and make prosecutions easier.'

Source: The Economist, 12 November 2009

A public goods game experiment conducted between Indians (from a culture high in corruption according to Transparency International) and Swedes (from a low-corruption culture) supported the contention that the higher the level of trust in a country the less corrupt it will be. Average contributions were significantly larger in Sweden, implying a higher level of trust and co-operation in Sweden than in India.[118] Since, as Chapter 4 shows, research has established a number of links between trust and culture, this finding reinforces the argument for a cultural basis to corruption.

2.6 CONCLUSION

Differences in people's behaviour, including their communication behaviour, which may result from diversity, have been analysed in terms of culture. This chapter described and analysed the elements and dimensions that are considered to be the core components of culture. The chapter opened by pointing out that cultures represent central tendencies. In general, individual members of a culture are likely to act consistently with these findings, but not everyone will do so and even those who do will not always do so.

The first section of the chapter outlined three values approaches to cultural difference; these which provide taxonomies of cultural values. To varying but considerable degrees, these values are believed to influence taken-for-granted thinking processes. Hofstede (1981), in a telling phrase, has called culture 'software of the mind'. Section 2.1 also explained how high-context/ low-context communication can differentiate cultures. The next section described other approaches to culture: these are subjective culture, culture as an institution and culture as a strategic resource. All these different understandings of culture and cultural difference underlie the rest of this book. The chapter then returned to the subjects of culture and work, and discussed work behaviour, management and organization, organizational networks and corruption in the light of the understandings of culture introduced in the chapter.

QUESTIONS AND EXERCISES

1. Discuss the cultural values that may be reflected in the examples in Box 1.9 and in the following passages:

    'A Belgian research analyst who worked for a UK research organization in London said: 'In my country only people with good qualifications in statistics or economics would be employed in this kind of work. As a result, they would be demanding about the quality of the data and statistics that they would agree to use, which might sometimes mean that they could not give the client companies the sort of information they need. Here, most researchers are arts graduates, with rather weak statistical backgrounds. As a result, they are flexible about data, and willing to provide client companies with answers to their questions, based, perhaps, on small samples.'

    Based on: Interview, author's research

    'If Eskimos have dozens of words for snow, Germans have as many for bureaucracy. As an example of ridiculous rules: a tailor (who) had to put up a sign saying "fire extinguisher" next to (guess what) her fire extinguisher, to produce a thick folder with all regulations relevant to her business, to raise her work table by ten centimetres, to buy a special emergency kit, and to check if her only employee was allergic to nickel – at a cost of 400 euros. Germany is, in short, one of the most rule-bound countries in the world.'

Source: The Economist, 11 October 2003

2. What might explain the different values of West and East Germans on freedom and equality described in Box 2.1?

3. Which of the following are strongly influenced, influenced or not influenced by culture? Give reasons.

   ■ how people think
   ■ their loyalties
   ■ what they believe (such as in religion or politics)
   ■ what they find moving (emotions)
   ■ how they behave (such as childrearing practices)
   ■ work motives
   ■ ambitions

4. 'Until the financial crisis [of late 2008] struck, successive French governments had been reducing their involvement in business. The state sold majority stakes in big firms such as France Telecom in the 1990s and early 2000s, and let those firms still largely in government hands, such as Electricité de France (EDF), take a more market-oriented approach. But the crisis has prompted a creeping return to an earlier tradition. "The tide was going in one direction for years–even the socialists privatized, we had less political interference and more financial savvy," says an investment banker in Paris, "but now we're stepping backwards." To be sure, intervention is newly in style in several countries, with governments around the world taking stakes in banks and America's taking charge of two carmakers. But as might be expected, France is going further.' (From *The Economist,* 30 December 2009). How far might cultural values help explain French statism?

5. Research in Germany (D), United Kingdom (UK) and France (F) found the following characteristics for organizations in those countries. Look up the findings of Hofstede's research for cultural values in the three countries, then discuss the extent to which the organizational characteristics shown may be related to the cultural values of the countries concerned.

	Low	Medium	High
Tallness of hierarchy	D	UK	F
Functional differentiation	D	UK	F
Share of white-collar employees	D	UK	F
Supervisory span of control	D	UK	F
Administrative and commercial personnel/workers	D	UK	F
Authority positions/white-collar workers	UK	D	F
Authority positions/white-collar workers	UK	D	F

Based on: Sorge, A. (1995) 'Cross-national differences in personnel and organization', in Harzing, A.W. and Ruysseveldt, J.V. (eds) International Human Resource Management, London: Sage.

6. Complete the following questionnaire on your own culture.

People in my group (culture) generally tend to:	Strongly agree	Agree	Neither agree nor disagree	Disagree	Strongly disagree
1. describe their experiences					
2. relate stories or anecdotes					
3. generalize					
4. give examples or particular instances when enunciating a principle					
5. speak in abstract terms					
6. feel personally responsible for their own success or failure					
7. have many friendships and relationships outside their families					
8. show emotion freely					
9. think showing emotion in the workplace is unprofessional					
10. talk about their feelings					
11. have most of their friendships from among their colleagues					
12. try to mix work and pleasure					
13. be respected for being wealthy					
14. think that people should be judged on their achievements alone					
15. believe in promotion by seniority					
16. think that time is money					
17. try always to be on time, even if it means risking offending someone by rushing them					
18. care about relaxation					
19. be more interested in the past than in the future					
20. think a lot about their future plans					

See Appendix for scoring and interpretation of this questionnaire

7. Explain the distinction between high-context and low-context communication cultures, with examples.

8. In *The Language Instinct* (1994) p. 251, the linguist S. Pinker stated that the difference between two cultures generally correlates with how long ago they separated.[119] Find examples to support or refute this statement.

9. What, if anything, justifies treating culture as an 'institution'? If it is justifiable so to treat it, what differentiates culture as an institution from other institutions?

10. Tipton (2009) is quoted as arguing that people in Japan, the USA and Western Europe now 'choose their own culture'.[120] In the light of the material in this chapter, discuss this proposition. Are there limits to such choices? If so, what are they?

11. The following questions were used in research into cultural difference. What aspects of culture do you think they were trying to access?

- You have just come from a secret meeting of a board of directors of a certain company. You have a close friend who will be ruined unless he can get out of the market before the board's decision becomes known. You happen to be having dinner at your friend's home this evening. What right does your friend have to expect you to tip him off?

- Which of the following describes a company?
   (a) A system designed to perform functions and tasks in an efficient way: People are hired to fulfil these functions with the help of machines and other equipment. They are paid for the tasks they perform. *Or*
   (b) A group of people working together: The people have social relations with other people and with the organization. The functioning is dependent on these relations.

- Which of the following do you agree with?
   (a) A company should take into account the size of the employee's family. The company is responsible for the extra compensation per child.
   (b) An employee should be paid on the basis of the work he [sic] is doing for the company. Therefore, the company does not have to take into account the employee's family.

Source: Hampden-Turner, C. and Trompenaars, A. (1993) *The Seven Cultures of Capitalism*, Garden City, NY: Doubleday

12. Role Play 1: conduct a market research interview between a Western, individualist, low power distance, low-context communication interviewer and an Asian, collectivist, high power distance, high-context communication interviewee.

Role Play 2: reverse the roles in Role Play 1.

Role Play 3: conduct a selection interview between an interviewer from a diffuse culture in which status is achieved, and an interviewee from a specific culture in which status is ascribed.

Role Play 4: reverse the roles in Role Play 3.

Role Play 5: conduct a negotiation between one party from a particularist culture in which emotional display is accepted and another party from a universalist culture in which emotional display is not tolerated.

Role Play 6: reverse the roles in Role Play 5.

Note: There should be prior agreement on the topics for these role plays – for instance, the product in Role Plays 1 and 2, the job vacancy in Role Plays 3 and 4, and the matter being negotiated (price, for example) in Role Plays 5 and 6. Use one or preferably two observers to notice and record points in the role plays at which cultural difference may be affecting the course of the interaction. Then discuss these points in the group and in class debriefings.

13. Which cultural values might be reflected in the European behaviours described in the following passage?

'As Americans, I think we often lose track of time, because we're too busy making money for a giant corporation, or defending "Big Business", or doing some other activity that will someday appear meaningless. In Europe, as I observed, things just move slower. People have more time for their lives, their families, and their selves. It's almost amazing to understand what people in our country are willing to give up for their job, and how the Europeans view that so vastly differently. ... One thing we seemed to find over and over again is that [in Europe] businesses are run on the schedules of the owners. When the owner of a business wants to eat lunch, he does so without thinking, even if that means closing his shop for an hour or two. Not only is this an accepted practice, it's conventional.'

Source: Required paper written to receive credit from the Haworth College of Business for Study Abroad experience. URL: godzilla.hcob.wmich.edu/~s8rich/391.html

14. Choose a colleague from a country other than your own. How much do you know about people from his or her country (hereinafter X)? Complete the following test and then discuss your answers with your colleague.

	True	False
In face-to-face communication, people from X stand closer together than people do from your own culture.		
People from X place a very high value on an individual's initiative and achievement.		
Citizens of X value obedience to authority and typically will not disagree with someone in a higher position of power.		
When people from X communicate, they use words that are clear and direct, allowing for no ambiguities.		
People from X need formal rules, absolute truths and conformity.		
People from X tend to avoid conflict and competition and seek consensus.		
In X gender roles are highly differentiated.		
People from X tend to do one thing at a time. They take time commitments very seriously and adhere closely to plans.		
People from X commonly sympathize with the weak and believe that nurturing individuals is more important than material success.		

15. Working with a partner from a different cultural (ethnic, national or religious) background, identify some core and peripheral values from your respective cultures. Discuss the reasons for and the implications of any differences in your lists.

16. Interview someone (several people, if possible) whose culture is different from your own on power distance, masculinity/femininity (achievement), uncertainty avoidance or individualism–collectivism. Discuss such matters as attitudes to work, spending and saving money, spending and using time, family, relationships and friends.

17. Interview at least two people from different backgrounds about (a) the importance and centrality of work, (b) norms about the rights and duties attached to work or (c) their work goals. Then devise a questionnaire to test for these values.

18. What might account for the finding of the European Values Survey that the data 'show higher levels overall and wider cross-country differences for expressive than instrumental work values'?

19. Research has shown that social class affects individuals' work values. Would you expect demographic differences, whether based on ethnicity, gender, age, disability, religion or sexual orientation, to affect work values? If so, explain how. If not, give your reasons.

20. Individual A is ready to begin his presentation at the exact time when the meeting was scheduled to start. He talks a long time before he suggests what he's recommending and provides less detail than Individual B would like. What could Individual B learn from the dimensions of Hall's (1959), Hofstede's (1981), and Trompenaars' (1993) that might help him accept this behaviour without being irritated by it?

21. An Indian said of his fellow Indians, '[They are] always playing social roles, doing drama, never asserting their own personality. Indians can bend with the wind, fit in and suppress their own opinions.' If this description is correct, what does it imply about whether Indians are individualist, collectivist or communalist?

22. Using the analytical base supplied in Section 2.3, examine organizational commitment, work norms, groupwork behaviour and intrapreneurialism in an organization known to you in order to determine what cultural values they imply.

23. Using the analytical base supplied in Section 2.4, examine organizational structures and work roles, organizational cultures, decision-making processes, employment relationships, perceptions of managerial effectiveness, task versus relationships orientation of managers, management roles and styles and managerial beliefs in an organization known to you in order to determine what cultural values they imply.

24. How would you describe the culture of the organization in which you work (or study)?

25. Recent years have seen a trend for organizations to develop and emphasize their 'organizational culture' in order to unite their employees and co-ordinate their approaches at a deeper level than that achieved by plans and strategies. Discuss the implications of Chapter 2 for this process.

26. Explain why collectivist values might 'not fit' with brokerage.

27. What are the implications of the reports in Box 2.14 for the link between culture and corruption? (Before answering this question, look up the Transparency International ratings of the USA, Germany and Britain.)

NOTES AND REFERENCES

1. Hofstede, G. (1981) *Cultures and Organizations: Software of the Mind*, London: Harper Collins, p. 31.
2. Sagiv, L. and Schwartz, S.H. (2000) 'A new look at national cultures: illustrative applications to role stress and managerial behavior', in Ashkanasy, N.N., Wilderom, C. and Peterson, M.F. (eds) *The Handbook of Organizational Culture and Climate*, Newbury Park, CA: Sage, pp. 417–36.
3. Hofstede, *Cultures and Organizations*.
4. Earley, P.C. and Gibson, C.B. (1998) 'Taking stock in our progress on individualism–collectivism: 100 years of solidarity and community', *Journal of Management*, **24**(3): 265–304.
5. Bazerman, M.H., Curhan, J.R., Moore, D.A. and Valley, K.L. (2000) 'Negotiation', *Annual Review of Psychology*, **51**: 279–314.

6. Maitland, C. (1998) 'Global diffusion of interactive networks: the impact of culture', *Electronic Journal of Communication*, **8**(3): URL: http://www.cios.org/www/ejc/v8n398.htm, last accessed 22 December 2010.

7. Barkema, H.G. and Vermeulen, F. (1997) 'What differences in the cultural backgrounds of partners are detrimental for international joint ventures?', *Journal of International Business Studies*, **28**(4): 845–64.

8. Alkhazraji, K.M., Gardner, W.M. III, Martin, J.S. and Paolillo, J.G.P. (1997) 'The acculturation of immigrants to US organizations: the case of Muslim employees', *Management Communication Quarterly*, **11**(2): 217–65.

9. Hofstede, G. (1993) 'Cultural constraints in management theories', *Academy of Management Executive*, **7**(1): 81–94.

10. Sparrow, P.R. (1998) 'Reappraising psychological contracting: lessons for the field of human resource development from cross-cultural and occupational psychology research', *International Studies of Management and Organization*, **28**(1): 30–63.

11. Maitland, 'Global diffusion of interactive networks'.

12. Erumban, A.A. and de Jong, S.B. (2006) 'Cross-country differences in ICT adoption: A consequence of culture?' *Journal of World Business*, **41**(4): 302–14.

13. Sagie, A. and Aycan, Z. (2003) 'A cross-cultural analysis of participative decision-making in organizations', *Human Relations*, **56**: 453–73.

14. Furrer, O., Shaw-Ching, B. and Sudharshan, L.D. (2000) 'The relationships between culture and service quality perceptions: basis for cross-cultural market segmentation and resource allocation', *Journal of Service Research*, May: 355–71.

15. Bhawuk, D.P.S. (2001) 'Evolution of culture assimilators: toward theory based assimilators', *International Journal of Intercultural Relations*, **25**(2): 141–64.

16. Bhagat, R.S., Kedia, B.L., Harveston, P.D. and Triandis, H.C. (2002) 'Cultural variations in the cross-border transfer of organizational knowledge: an integrative framework', *Academy of Management Review*, **27**(2): 204–21.

17. Trompenaars, F. (1993) *Riding the Waves of Culture: Understanding Cultural Diversity in Business*, London: Nicholas Brealey.

18. Handy, C., Trompenaars, F. and Hampden Turner, C. (2000) 'The Handy guide to the gurus of management, Episode 13 – Fons Trompenaars and Charles Hampden Turner'. http://www.bbc.co.uk/worldservice/learningenglish/work/handy/transcripts/trompenaarsturner.pdf.

19. Schwartz, S.H. (1999) 'Cultural value differences: Some implications for work', *Applied Psychology: An International Review*, **48**: 23–47.

20. Sagiv and Schwartz, 'A new look at national cultures'.

21. Dahl, S. (2004) 'Intercultural research: the current state of knowledge', *Middlesex University Discussion Paper No. 26*. Available at SSRN: http://ssrn.com/abstract=658202.

22. Moemeka, A.A. (1998) 'Communalism as a fundamental dimension of culture', *Journal of Communication*, **48**: 118–41.

23. Kim, U.M. (1994) 'Significance of paternalism and communalism in the occupational welfare system of Korean firms: a national survey', in Kim, U., Triandis, H., Kagitcibasi, C., Choi, S. and Yoon, G. (eds) *Individualism and Collectivism: Theory, Method; and Applications*, London: Sage.

24. Ibid.

25. Mbiti, J.S. (1969) *African Religions and Philosophy*, London: Heinemann.

26. Gudykunst, W. and Ting-Toomey, S. (eds) 'Introduction', *Culture and Interpersonal Communication*, Newbury Park, CA: Sage.

27. Inglehart, R. and Welzel, C. (2005) *Modernization, Cultural Change and Democracy*, New York: Cambridge University Press.

28. Snir, R. and Harpaz, I. (2009) 'Cross-cultural differences concerning heavy work investment', *Cross-Cultural Research*, **43**(4): 309–19.

29. England, G.W. (1995) 'National work meanings and patterns: Constraints on managerial action', in Jackson, T. (ed.) *Cross-Cultural Management*, Oxford: Butterworth-Heinemann.

30. Lingnan, O.S. (2003) 'Job stress and job performance among employees in Hong Kong: the Role of Chinese work values and organizational commitment', *International Journal of Psychology*, **38**(6): 337–47.

31. Kohn, M.L. (1969) *Class and Conformity: A Study in Values*, Homewood, Illinois: Dorsey Press.
32. Hall, E.T. (1976) *Beyond Culture*, New York: Doubleday.
33. Würtz, E. (2005) 'A cross-cultural analysis of websites from high-context cultures and low-context cultures', *Journal of Computer-Mediated Communication*, **11**(1): 13.
34. Dahl, 'Intercultural research'.
35. Xie, A., Rau, P.P.L., Tseng, Y., Su, H. and Chen Z. (2008) 'Cross-cultural influence on communication effectiveness and user interface design', *International Journal of Intercultural Relations*, **33**(1): 11–20.
36. Kim, D., Pan, Y. and Park, H.S. (1998) 'High- versus low-context culture: A comparison of Chinese, Korean, and American cultures', *Psychology and Marketing*, **15**(6): 507–21.
37. Ibid.
38. Okabe, R. (1983) 'Cultural assumptions of East and West: Japan and the United States', in Gudykunst, W. (ed.) *Inter-cultural Communication Theory*, Beverley Hills, CA: Sage.
39. Weldon, E. (1997) 'Inter-cultural interaction and conflict management in US–Chinese joint ventures', in Stewart, S. (ed.) *Advances in Chinese Industrial Organization*, Vol. 4, Greenwich, CT: JAI Press.
40. Ting-Toomey, S. (1988) 'Intercultural conflict styles: a face-negotiation theory', in Kim, Y.Y. and Gudykunst, W.B. (eds) *Theories in Intercultural Communication*, Newbury Park, CA: Sage.
41. Würtz, 'A cross-cultural analysis of websites from high-context cultures and low-context cultures'.
42. Tayeb, M.H. (1996) *The Management of a Multicultural Workforce*, England: John Wiley.
43. Aldridge, M.G. (2002) 'What is the basis of American culture?' *Intercultural Communication*, 5 April. URL: http://www.immi.se/intercultural.
44. Kim, Y.Y. (1988) 'On theorizing intercultural communication', in Kim, Y.Y. and Gudykunst, W.B. (eds) *Theories in Intercultural Communication*, Newbury Park, CA: Sage.
45. Collier, M.J. and Thomas, M. (1988) 'Cultural identity and intercultural communication', in Gudykunst, W. and Ting-Toomey, S. (eds) *Culture and Interpersonal Communication*, Newbury Park, CA: Sage.
46. Brewer, M.B. and Chen, Y.-R. (2007) 'Where (who) are collectives in collectivism? Toward conceptual clarification of individualism and collectivism', *Psychological Review*, **114**(1): 133–51.
47. Moemeka, 'Communalism as a fundamental dimension of culture'.
48. Kashima, Y., Kashima, E., Chiu, C.-Y., Farsides, T., Gelfand, M., Hong, Y.-Y., Kim, U. Strack, F. and Wer. L. (2005) 'Culture, essentialism, and agency: Are individuals universally believed to be more real entities than groups?', *European Journal of Social Psychology*, **35**: 147–69.
49. Oyserman, D., Coon, H.M. and Kemmelmeier, M. (2002) 'Rethinking individualism and collectivism: Evaluation of theoretical assumptions and meta-analyses', *Psychological Bulletin*, **128**(1): 3–72.
50. Takahashi, C., Yamagishi, T., Liu, J.H., Wang, F., Lin, Y. and Yu, S. (2008) 'The intercultural trust paradigm: studying joint cultural interaction and social exchange in real time over the Internet', *International Journal of Intercultural Relations*, **32**(3): 215–28.
51. de Munck, V. (2001) 'In the belly of the beast: two theories of culture and why they dominate the social sciences (Pt. 2)', *Cross-cultural Psychology Bulletin*, **35**(3): 5–14.
52. Fang, T. (2005) 'From "Onion" to "Ocean": paradox and change in national cultures', *International Studies of Management and Organization*, **35**(4): 71–90.
53. Zou, X., Tam, K-P, Morris, M., Lee. S-L., Lau, I.Y-M and Chiu, C-Y. (2009) 'Culture as common sense: perceived consensus vs. personal beliefs as mechanisms of cultural influence', *Journal of Personality and Social Psychology*, **97**(4): 579–97.
54. Greenfield, P.M. (1997) 'You can't take it with you. Why ability assessments don't cross cultures', *American Psychologist*, **52**(10): 1115–24.
55. DiMaggio, P. (1997) 'Culture and cognition', *Annual Review of Sociology*, **23**: 263–88.
56. Triandis, H.C. (2002) 'Subjective culture', in Lonner, W.J., Dinnel, D.L., Hayes, S.A. and Sattler, D.N. (eds) *Online Readings in Psychology and Culture* (unit 15, chapter 1). URL: http://www.wwu.edu/culture, last accessed 22 December 2010.
57. Ibid.
58. Guirdham, M. (2009) *Culture and Business in Asia*, Basingstoke, UK: Palgrave Macmillan.

59. Scott, W.R. (1995 and 2001) *Institutions and Organizations*, Thousand Oaks, CA: Sage.
60. Ahlstrom, D. and Bruton, G.D. (2002) 'An institutional perspective on the role of culture in shaping strategic actions by technology-focused entrepreneurial firms in China', *Entrepreneurship: Theory and Practice*, **26**(4): 53–69.
61. Kiss, A.M. and Danis, W.M. (2008) 'Country institutional context, social networks, and new venture internationalization speed', *European Journal of Management*, **26**(6): 388–99.
62. DiMaggio, 'Culture and cognition'.
63. Tipton, F.B. (2009) 'Modeling national identities and cultural change: the Western European, Japanese, and United States experiences compared', *International Journal of Cross Cultural Management*, **9**(2): 145–68.
64. Newburry, W. and Yakova, N. (2006) 'Standardization preferences: a function of national culture, work interdependence and local embeddedness', *Journal of International Business Studies*, **37**: 44–60.
65. Felfe, J., Yan, W. and Six, B. (2008) 'The impact of individualism-collectivism on commitment and its influence on organizational citizenship behaviour and turnover in three countries', *International Journal of Cross Cultural Management*, **8**: 211–37.
66. Maneerat, N., Hale, C.L. and Singhal, A. (2005) 'The communication glue that binds employees to an organization: a study of organizational identification in two Thai organizations', *Asian Journal of Communication*, **15**(2): 188–214.
67. Neuman, E.J., Sanchez-Burks, J., Ybarra, O., Park, H. and Goh, K. (2004) 'Is team harmony necessary for success? Cultural beliefs about conflict and team performance', *Ross School of Business Paper No. 909*. URL: http://ssrn.com/abstract=901775.
68. Thomas, D.C. and Au, K. (2002) 'The effect of cultural differences on behavioral responses to low job satisfaction', *Journal of International Business Studies*, **33**: 309–26.
69. Fernandez Dols, J.P. (1992) 'Procesos escabrosos en psicologia social: el concepto de norma perverse', *Revue Psicologica Sociologica*, **7**: 243–5.
70. Zhang, D., Lowry, P.B., Zhou, L. and Fu, X. (2007). 'The impact of individualism-collectivism, social presence, and group diversity on group decision making under majority influence', *Journal of Management Information Systems*, **23**(4): 53–8.
71. Zahra, S.A., Hayton, J.C. and Salvato, C. (2004) 'Entrepreneurship in family vs. non-family firms: A resource-based analysis of the effect of organizational culture', *Entrepreneurship: Theory and Practice*, **28**(4): 363–81.
72. Hayton, J.C., George, G. and Zahra, S.A. (2002) 'National culture and entrepreneurship: A review of behavioral research', *Entrepreneurship: Theory and Practice*, **26**(4): 33–52.
73. Carroll, G.R. and Harrison, J.R. (1998) 'Organizational demography and culture: insights from a formal model and simulation', *Administrative Science Quarterly*, **43**: 637–67.
74. Chen, Z.X. and Francesco, A.M. (2000) 'Employee demography, organizational commitment and turnover intentions in China: do cultural differences matter?', *Human Relations*, **53**(6): 869–87.
75. Pelled, L.H. (1996) 'Relational demography and perceptions of group conflict and performance: a field investigation', *International Journal of Conflict Management*, **7**: 230–46.
76. Ofori-Dankwa, J. and Lane, R.W. (2000) 'Four approaches to cultural diversity: implications for teaching at institutions of higher education', *Teaching in Higher Education* [Electronic database], **5**(4), Ipswich, MA: Academic Search Elite.
77. Schneider, S.C. and De Meyer, A. (1991) 'Interpreting and responding to strategic issues: the impact of national culture', *Strategic Management Journal*, **12**: 307–20.
78. Hofstede, *Cultures and Organizations*.
79. Lee, M. and Barnett, G.A. (1997) 'A symbols-and-meaning approach to the organizational cultures of banks in the United States, Japan and Taiwan', *Communication Research*, **24**(4): 394–412.
80. House, J.H. and Javidan, M. (2004) 'Overview of Globe', in House, R.J., Hanges, P.J., Javidan, M. Dorfman, P.W. and Gupta, V. (eds) *Culture, Leadership, and Organizations: The GLOBE Study of 62 Societies*, Thousand Oaks, CA: Sage.
81. Gerhart, B. (2009) 'How much does national culture constrain organizational culture?', *Management and Organization Review*, **5**(2): 241–59.

82. Vertinsky, I., Lee, K-H., Tse, D.K. and Wehrung, D.A. (1990) 'Organizational design and management norms: a comparative study of managers' perceptions in the People's Republic of China, Hong Kong and Canada', *Journal of Management*, **16**(4): 99–110.

83. Chatman, J.A. (1998) 'Being different yet feeling similar: the influence of demographic composition and organizational culture on work processes and outcomes', *Administrative Science Quarterly*, **43**: 749–80.

84. Hofstede, *Cultures and Organizations*.

85. Olson, G.M. and Olson, J.S. (2000) 'Distance matters', *Human Computer Interaction*, **15**(2–3): 139–78.

86. Sparrow, 'Reappraising psychological contracting'.

87. Arvonen, J. and Lindell, M. (1996) 'The Nordic management style in a European context', *International Studies of Management and Organization*, **26**(3): 73–93.

88. Ibid.

89. Ali, A.J. (1993) 'Decision-making style, individualism and attitudes toward risk of Arab executives', *International Studies of Management and Organization*, **23**(3): 53–74.

90. Vance, C.M., McClaine, S.R., Boje, D.M. and Stage, D. (1992) 'An examination of the transferability of traditional performance appraisal principles across cultural boundaries', *Management International Review*, **32**: 313–26.

91. Hanninen-Salmelin, E. and Petajanieme, T. (1994) 'Women managers: the case of Finland', in Adler, N.J. and Izraeli, D.N. (eds) *Competitive Frontiers*, Cambridge, MA: Basil Blackwell.

92. Eagly, A.H. and Johnson, B.T. (1990) 'Gender and leadership style: a meta-analysis', *Psychological Bulletin*, **108**(2): 233–56.

93. Haire, M., Ghiselli, E.E. and Porter, L.W. (1966) *Managerial Thinking: An International Study*, New York: Wiley.

94. Bass, B.M. (1981) 'Leadership in different cultures', in Bass, B.M. (ed.) *Stogdill's Handbook of Leadership*, New York: Free Press.

95. Kozan, M.K. (1993) 'Cultural and industrialization level influences on leadership attitudes for Turkish managers', *International Studies of Management and Organization*, **23**(3): 7–18.

96. Morley, D.D., Shockley-Zalabak, P. and Cesaria, R. (1997) 'Organizational communication and culture: a study of 10 Italian high-technology companies', *The Journal of Business Communication*, **34**: 252–66.

97. Sparrow, 'Reappraising psychological contracting'.

98. Scott, W.R. (1995 and 2001) *Institutions and Organizations*, Thousand Oaks, CA: Sage.

99. Khan, P.W. (2000) *The Cultural Study of Law: Reconstructing Legal Scholarship*, Chicago: University of Chicago Press.

100. Whitley, R. (1992) *Business Systems in East Asia: Firms, Markets and Societies*, London: Sage Publishing.

101. Guirdham, *Culture and Business in Asia*.

102. Putnam, R.D. (2007) 'E Pluribus Unum: Diversity and Community in the Twenty-first Century: The 2006 Johan Skytte Prize Lecture', *Scandinavian Political Studies*, **30**(2): 137–174.

103. Alkoby, A. (2008) 'Global networks and international environmental lawmaking: a discourse approach', *Chicago Journal of International Law*, **8**(2). Available at SSRN: http://ssrn.com/abstract=1095019

104. Fischer, C.S. and Shavit, Y. (1995) 'National differences in network density: Israel and the United States social networks', *Administrative Science Quarterly*, **17**(2): 129–45.

105. Whitley op. cit. and Brass, D.J., Galaskiewicz, J., Greve, H.R. and Tsai, W. (2004) 'Taking stock of networks and organizations: A multilevel perspective', *Academy of Management Journal*, **47**(6): 795–817.

106. Guirdham, *Culture and Business in Asia*.

107. Burt, R.S. (2009) *Neighbour Networks: Competitive Advantage Local and Personal*, Oxford, UK: Oxford University Press.

108. von Hippel, E. (1994). '"Sticky information" and the locus of problem solving: implications for innovation', *Management Science*, **40**(4): 429–39.

109. Xiao, Z. and Tsui, A.S. (2007) 'When brokers may not work: The cultural contingency of social capital in Chinese high-tech firms', *Administrative Science Quarterly*, **52**(1): 1–31.

110. Burt, R.S. (1992) *Structural Holes: The Social Structure of Competition*, Cambridge, MA: Harvard University Press.

111. Xiao, op. cit.

112. Monge, P.R. and Eisenberg, F.M. (1987) 'Emergent communication networks', in Jablin, F.M., Putman, L.L., Roberts, K.H. and Porter, L.W. (eds) *Handbook of Organizational Communication: An Interdisciplinary Perspective*, Newbury Park, CA: Sage.

113. Guirdham, *Culture and Business in Asia*.

114. Nef, J. (2003) 'Government corruption in Latin America', in Caiden, G.E., Jabbra, J.G. and Dwivedi, O.P. (eds) *Where Corruption Lives*, VA: Kumarian Press, pp. 159–174.

115. Connelly, B.S. and Ones, D.S. (2008) 'The personality of corruption: a national-level analysis', *Cross-Cultural Research*, **42**(4): 353–65.

116. Mauro, P. (1995) '*Corruption and Growth*', *Quarterly Journal of Economics*, **110**(3): 681–712.

117. Ghazanfar, S.M. and May, K.S. (2000) 'Third World corruption: a brief survey of the issues', *The Journal of Social, Political, and Economic Studies*, **25**(3): 351–69.

118. Ahmed, A.M. and Salas, O. (2008) 'Trust in India and Sweden: an experimental examination of the Fukuyama conjecture', *Cross-Cultural Research*, **42**(4): 420–9.

119. Pinker, S. (1994) *The Language Instinct*, London: Allen Lane, The Penguin Press.

120. Tipton, F.B. (2009) 'Modeling national identities and cultural change: the Western European, Japanese, and United States experiences compared', *International Journal of Cross Cultural Management*, **9**(2), 145–68.

chapter three

Culture and Communication

There are certainly more similarities than differences between human beings from different groups, and this applies to their ways of communicating as much as to anything. Nevertheless, the differences are significant and do affect communication between different groups of people. Chapter 2 discussed ways of analysing how cultures differ and how these analyses can be applied to groups that differ by nationality, ethnicity and religion and in part to groups that differ by gender, age, (dis)ability, sexual orientation, education, social class or profession. In the next two chapters, the discussion is extended into how differences of background affect individuals' communication behaviour at work. Subcultural differences are considered alongside cultural differences. Chapter 3 concerns the overt communication behaviour of individuals; Chapter 4 looks at behavioural factors and processes underlying how we communicate. (The relation between Chapters 3 and 4 is shown in Figure 3.1.)

This chapter begins with a brief note on communication as a subject, encompassing definitions and the question of universals versus cultural specifics in communication. It takes the introduction given in Section 1.1 a stage further. Section 3.2 covers, broadly, some aspects of communication that may differ from (sub)culture to (sub)culture, in order to alert readers to recognize them when they occur. Section 3.3 gives more detail on what research has so far taught us about the communication differences and similarities of different cultures, ethnicities, genders and so on.

3.1 A BRIEF NOTE ON COMMUNICATION

One definition of communication would be 'message exchange between two or more participants which is characterized by the intentional, conscious (at some level of awareness) use of mutually intelligible symbol systems'.[1] This definition excludes the possibility of communication without conscious intent and so is not universally accepted: habits and emotions are generally regarded as sources of communication that do not involve conscious intention. Sarbaugh (1988) preferred to define communication as the process of using signs and symbols that elicit meanings in another person or persons for whatever intent, or even without conscious intent, on the part of the person producing the symbols or signs.[2]

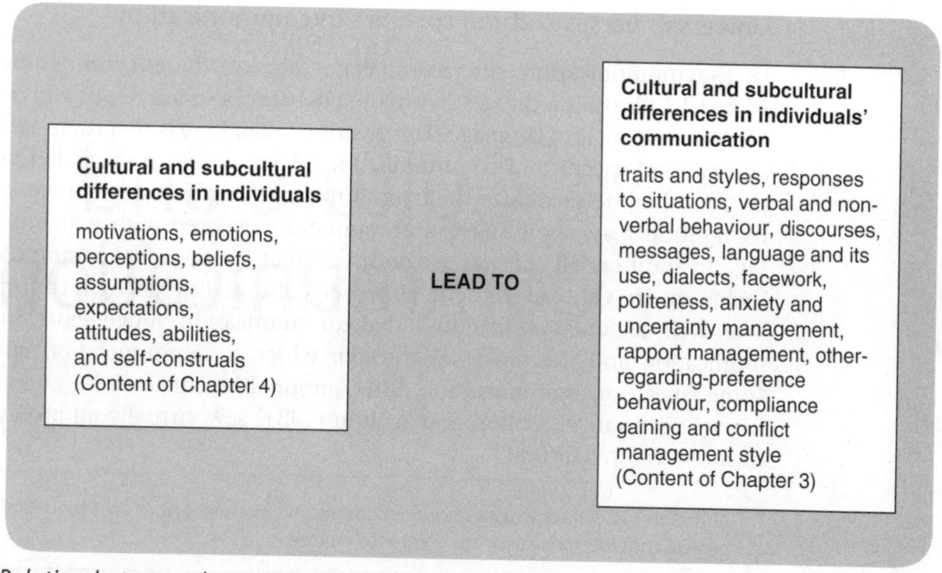

Figure 3.1   *Relation between the contents of Chapters 3 and 4*

Note: Feedback from interlocutors leads to modifications, but these effects are not covered in these chapters

Box 3.1

One website asserted the following in 1996:

1. A language must have rules.
2. Languages must have basic units, which have their own meaning. For spoken language, these are the words; phrases with a meaning that cannot be deduced from the basic units that make them can also be regarded as basic units.
3. Most of the messages are combinations of several words, according to some rules (grammar).
4. The basic structure of most messages is association of some object with attribute or effect.
5. The rules of combinations are expressed by one of: meaning of the words, word order, word modifications, special words and modification of words by adding something.
6. Semantic information is normally used whenever it is available to decide about the appropriate combination.
7. Word order is used for simple and frequently used features of the grammar.
8. The grammar has to allow combining any message with more information.
9. The main bulk of words mean either an object, an attribute, an action or an effect.
10. The language must have tools to make identification of objects efficient.
11. The language must have a way to signify repeated reference to the same object.
12. Languages are far from optimum.[a]

A blog posted in January 2010 urged to the contrary: 'It seems that there might be nothing really "universal" about human language.' However, it went on to ask, 'What about human communication?...In all types of human communication, both verbal and non-verbal, a significant contrast is established between narrative/descriptive and imperative contents.' This blog led to further suggestions from other bloggers: that negatives and questions are also essential to human communication.[b]

The debate no doubt continues.

Sources: (a) http://human-brain.org/language.html, last accessed 22 December 2010

(b) http://languagecontinuity.blogspot.com/2010/01/universals-of-human-communication.html

Universals versus cultural specifics in communication

Do the communication patterns and behaviours of different groups differ significantly? As Box 3.1 illustrates, there is an ongoing debate about universals and non-universals in communication and language. The position taken here is that there are both universals and cultural specifics in communication.[3] Some research suggests that humans may be 'pre-wired' to recognize the communicative importance of language. This 'innate' recognition may, some suggest, account for the speed with which children learn to talk. In addition, all cultures use both verbal and non-verbal communication systems, including dress and adornment. However, cultural differences in communication have been well documented in non-verbal communication, judgements, inter-group communication and the processes through which a communication episode develops. Some aspects of communication differ among different subcultures, as opposed to cultures. For instance, Scollon and Scollon (1981) saw virtually all professional communication as intercultural.[4]

> Although a wide range of categories of communication behaviour are found in all cultures, their precise content may vary from culture to culture.

3.2 DIFFERENT COMMUNICATION PRACTICES

This section introduces differences in the ways in which the functions of communication are carried out in different cultures and subcultures. Illustrating the importance of this section for organizations is a finding that internal communication was identified as the HRM (human resource management) practice most sensitive to cultural difference in a study that analysed data from 19 countries (Australia, Austria, Denmark, Finland, France, former East Germany, former West Germany, Greece, Ireland, Israel, Italy, Japan, The Netherlands, Portugal, Spain, Sweden, Switzerland, Turkey and UK). (The HRM practice least sensitive to cultural influences was found to be rewards and benefits.)[5] The aspects of communication where (sub)cultural differences are identified in this section include the following: communication traits and styles, how situations are interpreted and responded to, messages, codes, verbal and non-verbal communication, communication rules, conversational constraints, information-seeking, facework, politeness, rapport management, anxiety and uncertainty management, other-regarding-preference behaviour, compliance gaining and conflict management. The section ends with a critique. Figure 3.2 depicts the relations among the factors discussed in this section.

Communication traits

Early attempts to analyse behavioural phenomena (leadership is one example) have often included trait theories. This is also true for communication. A trait is a tendency to behave in a certain way, in the judgement of the self or others. Four sets of communication traits are especially important in an intercultural work context – rhetorical sensitivity, relational attunement, assertiveness and argumentativeness.

Rhetorical sensitivity

The trait of adapting messages to audiences is termed rhetorical sensitivity. People differ in how far they use sensitivity and care in adjusting what they say to allow for the knowledge, ability level, mood or beliefs of the listener.[6] Some people express themselves without adjusting to others (these speakers are 'rhetorically insensitive'); others (the

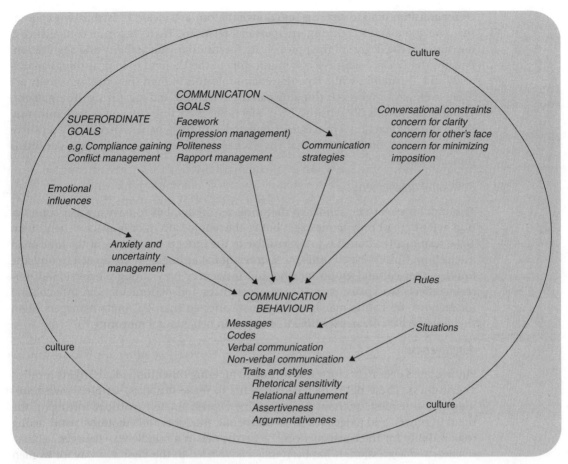

Figure 3.2   *Factors that influence communication behaviour*

'rhetorically reflective') mould themselves completely to what they perceive as likely to please others; rhetorically sensitive people adopt an intermediate way, showing concern for themselves, others and the situation. Most people use all three types of communication but show a tendency to use one more than the others, so displaying a rhetorical trait. Findings on cultural differences in rhetorical sensitivity include some that are unexpected. When a test for rhetorical sensitivity was conducted on 316 Thai and 182 US American students, US Americans displayed significantly higher levels of rhetorical sensitivity than the Thais. This finding was contrary to prior expectations based on the belief that the highest Thai cultural values are associated with social harmony.[7] Research among nurses found age-related and other subcultural differences. Nurses under the age of 35 and those with more education were more rhetorically sensitive, those over 55 more rhetorically reflective. Registered nurses were the most rhetorically insensitive. However, another study found that rhetorically sensitive communicators tended to be non-differentiated by gender role. The suggestion was made that there is a need for an examination of 'currently held conceptualizations of gender roles'.[8]

Going beyond such comparisons, Okabe (2007) argued that American and Japanese conceptualizations of rhetorical competence and sensitivity differed. Among the differences noted were these: the US prototype of rhetorically competent communicators is that they consciously use symbols to create understanding and to form, strengthen or change an attitude in their audience, whereas rhetorically competent Japanese communicators tend to view the function of rhetoric as a means of establishing consensual agreement and smoothing interpersonal relations. Their rhetorical competence is measured by the degree of their propensity for intuition, adaptability and aggregation. Equally, rhetorically sensitive communicators of the US tend to look at things analytically and disparately, while Japanese communicators of high rhetorical sensitivity are likely to employ a synthetic thinking pattern in framing and organizing the argument. Thirdly, the rhetorically sensitive US model is one of 'acting out' and is predominantly linear and unidirectional in nature, compared with the Japanese rhetorically sensitive communicators' presumption that the exchange between two interacting persons is primarily circular.[9]

Relational attunement

This trait appears to be similar to rhetorical sensitivity, but to have a wider connotation, referring not only to messages but to the whole pattern of interactive behaviour. To be relationally attuned is to be sensitive to the other person's state at the time of an interaction. Culture-based differences in relational attunement are argued to underlie findings that cultural group membership influences how strongly behavioural mirroring affects workplace participants' experiences and performances in intercultural interactions. US Latino managers were more affected than US Anglo managers when their interlocutor, in an experiment, engaged in behavioural mirroring.[10]

Assertiveness

Putting one's own rights forward without hampering other individuals' rights is called assertiveness. These rights include the rights to make mistakes, set one's own priorities, refuse requests without feeling guilty, express oneself (without infringing the rights of others) and judge one's own behaviour, thoughts and emotions, while taking responsibility for the consequences.[11] Assertiveness is a middle way between submissiveness and aggression. It has been much advocated in the West as a way for women and members of ethnic minorities to communicate, especially with people who are prejudiced against them or who for other reasons are inclined to 'put them down'. It can be effective. However, in reality rights are not separable from the society in which someone communicates. Assertiveness is therefore culture-related – what is assertive in one society is aggressive in another.[12] A study found that people from both English-speaking and continental European cultures were higher than East Asian cultures in self-perceived assertiveness. The English-speaking culture means and the continental European culture means, however, were not significantly different on assertiveness. Perhaps unsurprisingly, Chinese men were more assertive than Chinese women.[13]

Research evidence across a number of disciplines and fields has shown that women can encounter both social and financial backlash when they behave assertively, for example, by asking for resources at the bargaining table. This backlash appears to be most evident when a gender stereotype that prescribes communal, nurturing behaviour by women is activated. In situations in which this female stereotype was suppressed, for instance when resources were so plentiful that a request was not threatening to the respondent, when the female was described as being of high status, or when women were acting as advocates for others (and so indirectly fulfilling their 'nurturing' role), backlash against assertive female behaviour was attenuated.[14]

Argumentativeness

Willingness to engage in constructive persuasive debate is called argumentativeness.[15] It is a trait that managers have been shown to value in subordinates. However,

Kim *et al.* (2001) suggested that argumentativeness is a form of verbal aggression. It is acceptable in US culture because the attack is directed against an 'object' – the matter under discussion – rather than a person, but this distinction is probably neither understood nor accepted in other cultures. Research by Kim *et al.* (2001) showed that individualism increased argumentativeness.[16] (Other research found that aggression within organizations was related to ethnic group and within ethnic group to gender.[17]) Conversely, research found no differences in argumentativeness between ethnic groups in the USA. The groups tested included African Americans, Asian Americans, Hispanics and European Americans.[18] When over 900 adults from Taiwan, Hong Kong and China participated in a study to ascertain the relationship between traditional Chinese value orientations and argumentativeness, it was found that Taiwanese people were located on the low end whereas people in Mainland China were at the high end of being argumentative. People in Mainland China perceived 'being argumentative' more positively than both those from Hong Kong and those from Taiwan. Mainland Chinese perceived argument as a relatively positive and constructive action, and several traditional value orientations contributed to argumentative tendencies.[19]

Communicator style

For some psychologists, a bundle of traits is called a personality; the equivalent for communication theorists is communicator style. Style theorists believe that individuals have dominant styles. Style variables that have been researched include being friendly, relaxed, contentious, attentive, precise, animated, open, dominant, impression-leaving and having a positive communicator image. Communicator style is partly individual, partly influenced by social background. The environment plays an important part in the development of an individual's 'communication personality', which thus can be expected to vary among cultures and subcultures.[20] Female supervisors' communicator styles were perceived as placing more emphasis on interpersonal relations than those of male supervisors.[21] On the other hand, a US study found that male and female managers in two organizations demonstrated similar communicator styles in their staff meetings.[22]

Box 3.2

During China's Cultural Revolution, Britain's Ambassador to Beijing, Sir Percy Cradock, 'was asked by the [Red] Guards, as they beat him round his back and shoulders, to cry "Long Live Chairman Mao!" He refused, "and fortunately the demand was not pressed." Forced to bow his head in the ritual kowtow, he kept trying to raise it. He was asked afterwards why he could not make just one small gesture of obeisance. He replied, with that opaque courtesy beloved of both Chinese officials and Whitehall mandarins, that it could not be done.

He was a figure who might have been at home in the Middle Kingdom, where professional scholar-officials, with the equivalent of his double starred firsts in English and law from Cambridge, kept the vast realm ticking like clockwork. Like them he was low-key but razor-sharp, happy to let ministers have their say first, but with an impish glint in his eye, or a slow steepling of his fingers, that showed he had instantly grasped the danger, or the absurdity, of a situation.

His regret was that he could not always lead others to grasp it too; that they could not learn to see things from the Chinese point of view.'

Source: The Economist, 11 February 2010

Communication situations

Somewhat contrary to the underlying premise of trait and style theories, there is evidence that the meanings attached to both verbal and non-verbal forms of communication are partly determined by the situation in which they are produced. A communication situation is the entire communication event, including the participants, the setting and the activities taking place. According to situation theorists, people normally adjust their communication behaviour for the situation.

There are cultural differences in how people interpret situations. 'Two people socialized to different cultures may react to a situation differently because of differences in internalized conceptions of the content of the situation, of what is normal, what is appropriate and so on.'[23] For instance, in some cultures a funeral is seen as a joyful and not a sorrowful occasion. The work context, too, is a situation, or, rather, a large number of different situations with some shared characteristics, such as the norm of focusing on the task. The fact that work communication is different from social or other behaviour applies cross-culturally, although how it differs varies from one (sub) culture to another.

Messages

Only messages can be sent and received; meanings cannot be transmitted. This means that senders of messages must encode their meanings into symbols, choosing those that are likely to be familiar to their audience. Receivers, equally, have to decode messages and have to recreate their meaning, often by inference. These facts create scope for miscommunication: for instance, there is no way for Person A to be certain that Person B means the same by 'blue' as they do. Much speech is elliptical: in ordinary work conversation Person A is quite likely to say, 'Bring me the blue folder, please,' even if there are several blue folders, so long as s/he has some reason to think that the person s/he is addressing will be able to infer which blue folder s/he means.

Applying a five-stage model of communication as consisting of constructing and transmitting, acquiring, interpreting and responding to messages, Gibson and Manuel (2003) suggested that cultural differences in communication are most evident during the first two stages of constructing and transmitting messages. These differences, they suggested, are often reconciled during the last three phases of acquisition, interpretation and response. In encoding messages, communicators 'choose' between an implicit style that obscures any unpleasantness or excessively positive positioning and an explicit style that conveys the message directly, even when it is unpleasant. People from collectivist cultures are more likely than those from individualist cultures to adopt an implicit style. Second, in contrast to communicators from high-context cultures, 'Communicators from low context cultures will tend to utilize external sources of information more often than internal sources when constructing messages.' Third, messages are affected by cultural differences in the extent to which rational material based on facts is preferred versus material based on intuition and personal perspective. In the transmission phase, use of formal or more informal communication channels is influenced by the attitudes towards hierarchy in the communicator's culture.[24] Figure 3.3 depicts this model in a diagram.

Recently, attention has turned to micro-messages. These are small, often non-verbal and unconscious messages that we constantly send and receive. Micro-messages can be either positive or negative. Some examples in everyday interactions include winking to show understanding, glancing at a watch while someone is speaking to show boredom,

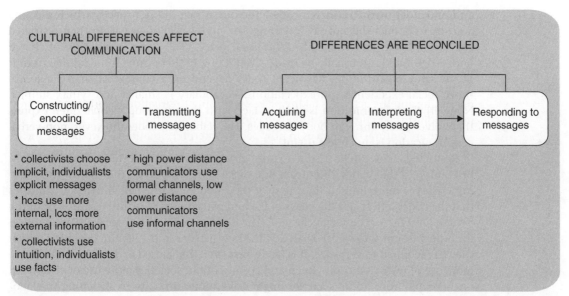

Figure 3.3 *A five-stage communication model showing the impact of culture at the different stages*

Based on: Gibson, C.B. and Manuel, J. (2003) 'Building trust: effective multi-cultural communication processes in virtual teams', in Gibson, C.B. and Cohen, S.G. (eds) Virtual Teams that Work: Creating Conditions for Virtual Team Effectiveness, San Francisco, CA: Jossey-Bass

Box 3.3

'Unlike in the USA, where asking a single question will elicit ample information from a salesperson or office clerk, in France a question is understood in a narrow way, with the assumption that you know everything else there is to know about the topic. ...

Relying purely on the answer to one question in France is the best way to have a miserable time. Here is a very recent illustration: One of my clients went alone to get information about the status of a performing artist who wants to work in France. There are actually two options for this artist, yet this client was only told about one because his question did not directly ask for information about other options.'

Source: Taquet, J., 'What's in a question?: A cross-cultural perspective', JB Intercultural Consulting, URL: www.culture-at-work.com

or leaning forward during conversation with a colleague to show attentiveness. In a routine ten-minute conversation, two people will send each other, on average, between 40 and 100 micro-messages. Micro-messages sometimes contradict spoken messages, as when a prejudiced person says that s/he regards everyone present as equal but in practice repeatedly interrupts the speech of minority members. As micro-messages are less under conscious control, they differ more by culture and subculture.

Codes

A distinction can be drawn between restricted and elaborated communication codes. As the names imply, restricted codes explicate less fully than elaborated codes do. For example, if someone approached a colleague in an office corridor the conversation might run like this: 'Where's the meeting?' The answer might be a nod. Both questioner and responder used a restricted code – the questioner did not specify which meeting and the responder did not say anything: the nod was enough within their restricted code to indicate something like 'The usual place.' The same assumption of shared knowledge could not usually be made, even if one of them came from a different unit of the same organization. Restricted codes depend on a context of shared assumptions, social experience and expectations. Vocabulary is smaller and syntax simpler. Non-verbal communication is vital; in fact, with their ingroup, people often express themselves solely through body language. For elaborated codes, however, non-verbal communication is much less useful.

Restricted codes can be used to express group membership. A study of social class in Britain found that codes differ from one social class to another: the code of the working classes is more limited than that of the middle classes. This difference indicates that the codes reflect specific views of life and perceptions of reality resulting from the diverse lifestyles of the social classes.[25] The difference lies in the speakers' assumption (or otherwise) of knowledge shared with their listener and thus the degree to which they feel required to verbalize. It is likely, however, that closed or 'local' societies make more use of restricted codes, open and cosmopolitan societies more use of elaborated ones. People from 'local' societies might have more difficulty in switching to elaborated codes when they meet outsiders.

There is an obvious parallel between the 'elaborated/restricted code' distinction and Hall's (1976) high-context/low-context communication distinction (described in Chapter 2), although the code concept is more fluid – the same people might use the restricted code among their familiars and the elaborated code with strangers.

Verbal communication

Verbal behaviour (speech and writing) is particularly good for communicating information and intentions, less useful for communicating relationships and feelings. Communicating verbally requires the use of spoken or written language, in which conventions vary, as Box 3.4 illustrates. Cultural differences in verbal behaviour are highlighted by the concept of a speech community, which is central to the discipline of socio-linguistics. A speech community is based on several core components. Some of these components are considered to be: a common form of socialization, regular interaction during which norms are established and reinforced, a shared body of words to mean certain things and a certain type of verbal behaviour. All these combine to create a feeling of belonging (however loosely) and exclusivity (insiders understand the meaning of what is said but outsiders may not).[26]

Paralinguistics is the term for behaviours such as turn-taking, voice tone, speed of speech and length of time that one speaker speaks; these, it has been shown, vary cross-culturally. People from collectivistic cultures distribute their turns and speaking time more evenly than those from individualistic cultures. Paralinguistics are used to reinforce and communicate identity as a group member. Speech style and accent are

---

Box 3.4

The Hindi language has no equivalents of the English verbs 'to have', 'to possess', 'to own', etc. 'We have a white car' is expressed in Hindi as 'Hamare pas ek safed ghari hai' – 'A white car is ours'.

Source: author's research

the main paralinguistic vehicles performing this function, as exemplified in the difference between middle-class and working-class speech in British English.[27]

Language

'Encounters between expatriates and local employees of a Danish subsidiary in England showed that competition for resources and recognition made their interactions into negotiations in which language differences seemed to affect the formation of social identities among organization members.'[28] As this finding shows, language differences can lead to work colleagues dividing into language-based groups and competing with one another.

Since international business has now largely adopted English as a lingua franca, a large number of people at work are effectively bi- or multi-language speakers. The language choices of these speakers may reveal which cultural influence is currently affecting them, while language switching may reveal a change of cultural influence. Du-Babcock (1999) showed that in decision-making meetings people whose first language was Cantonese and whose second language was English acted in some ways differently according to the language in which the meeting was conducted. Although ideas, volume and context level were similar in both situations, statistical analysis revealed differences in turn-taking frequency, length of spoken time per turn, amount of felt information exchange, and degree of felt influence. When the meeting was conducted in Cantonese, the pattern of the discussion was spiral; when it took place in English, decisions were reached by a sequence of linear processes.[29]

Later research by Du-Babcock (2003) suggested that second-language proficiency 'is likely a contributing factor that affects the topic management of Chinese bilinguals when participating in Cantonese and English meetings'; nevertheless, the point seemed confirmed that culture and language are intertwined, so that native speakers of Cantonese (a language mainly used in a high-context communication culture) will approximate more closely to a low-context communication culture when speaking English, a language embedded in such a culture.[30] Chen and Jackson (2008) found empirical support for the idea that individuals both intentionally and inadvertently disclose how they accentuate task concerns (task co-ordination/engagement) and express relational concerns (personal struggle and/or accountability) through their use of language(s). The language used, they contended, influences individuals to perceive and recognize the intention of task or relational concerns. A change of language produces a change of cognitive behaviour; it can also signal a need. For instance, when multinational company members who are capable of managing both lingua franca and their mother language feel ignored or isolated from task collaboration, they may use, choose or switch to a high-context language or increase multiple language cues to disclose their wish for engagement.[31]

In most languages there are dialects that reflect ethnic, regional and other differences. Dialects employ different pronunciation, vocabulary and grammatical structures. To linguists, the word 'dialect' refers to a way of speaking a language, and not to an incorrect way of speaking a language. While all dialects of a given language are linguistically legitimate, some achieve social prestige. In literate, economically developed societies, the dialect spoken by those with the most formal education, socio-economic status and political power tends to acquire the greatest social prestige. Typically, it becomes the standard dialect for the culture, for writing and education. Standard dialects also provide a medium that persons from different linguistic backgrounds use to communicate with one another. However, there are many kinds of non-standard dialect. These include those tied to social class and educational level. Other aspects of verbal communication that differ cross-(sub)culturally include discourses, speech acts and conversational constraints. These are explained later in this section.

Non-verbal communication

Non-verbal communication (NVC) such as gestures, facial expressions and posture has some characteristics which make it different from verbal communication.[32] For instance, the meaning of some NVC is universal; it is harder to control, so that emotion, for example, 'leaks out' through NVC; it is also 'the major contributor to communication of "affect" in messages'[33] and can convey some meanings more accurately than words: as Becker *et al.* (2000) explained, gestures are used in group design projects to characterize concrete aspects of the design, such as size and shape. 'Anyone who has sat through a face-to-face design meeting in which many ideas are generated and debated knows that gestures are as common as words.' Depending on the kind of entity that is being designed, participants may use gestures, simulate the use of the design, emphasize their verbally stated points about the design, point to drawings or lists, and in many other ways use their body in the space around them to communicate about the design.[34]

Non-verbal behaviour is used to reinforce and communicate identity as a group member. In the West, high-level executives walk quickly along office corridors to convey the importance and urgency of their work; in Asia, they walk slowly to express dignity. People who misread these symbols may behave inappropriately – they may fail, for instance, to give the chief executive his or her due, or they may dress in an inappropriate style that will lead insiders to see them as outsiders.

Many (sub)cultural differences in non-verbal behaviour have been recorded. Examples include the following:

■ For Americans, forming a circle with thumb and forefinger signals 'OK'; it means 'zero' or worthless in France, money in Japan, and calling someone a very bad name in Germany; putting the shod feet on the table is a (male) American gesture which is offensive to nearly every other country around the globe.

■ For some groups, touching another person is proscribed. These groups include the people of China, Indonesia, Japan, the Philippines, Thailand, Australia, England, Germany, The Netherlands, Norway, Scotland, America, India and Pakistan. Contact groups (who use 'touch' with less inhibition) include the people of Iraq, Kuwait, Saudi Arabia, Syria, the United Arab Republic, Bolivia, Cuba, Ecuador, El Salvador, Mexico, Paraguay, Peru, Puerto Rico, Venezuela, France, Italy and Turkey.

■ Numerous conventions govern handshakes in different countries: in India, where a 'namaste' with palms pressed together and fingers pointing upwards is the traditional greeting, men should not proffer a hand to a woman unless she does so first. In China, the handshake is often accompanied by a slight bow. 'Shaking hands is important in Madagascar. To omit this little ceremony can be construed as a deliberate insult.'[35] The Russian handshake is firm almost to the point of being bone-breaking and eye contact is maintained; the French handshake is rather gentle.

■ Research has shown that demeanour varies by gender. Demeanour consists primarily of non-verbal and paralinguistic behaviours, and is controlled in part by status within a group. It creates and perpetuates status inequalities and beliefs about unequal abilities. It also affects the influence an individual exerts in a group and how credible an impression s/he makes. An autocratic demeanour on the part of a leader reduces group members' satisfaction, while behaving simply 'as the boss'

Box 3.5

'You can watch it in a restaurant in the evening [in Tokyo]. Six or seven salary men will be dining at a round table. Within a minute, you can tell who is the senior guy by the way all the others are silent if he even starts to open his mouth and the way they laugh at his jokes. The younger ones, the rookies, will never speak at all unless spoken to. If the younger shows enough respect, the older will say, 'Let us speak frankly,' but the younger still knows he mustn't. No first names are ever used at work; occasionally the rookies will be given a nickname. In this so-called socialising after work, now that I am getting older, senior, I no longer have to keep offering food and drink to seniors.'

Source: A Japanese manager quoted in Guirdham, M. (2009) *Culture and Business in Asia*, Basingstoke, UK: Palgrave Macmillan

usually increases satisfaction. This research also showed that the demeanour of those involved affects the definitions that people apply to a situation (for instance, whether it is a crisis or a routine event) and so affects their response.[36]

Rules

Communication is governed by rules, which can vary (sub)culturally. Communication requires people to co-operate, which they do partly by following rules. People generally use rules to interpret what they see and hear (rules of meaning) and then act on the basis of their interpretations. They employ rules of action to decide what kind of action, in this case communication action, is appropriate. In the West, co-operation is achieved by following the rules or maxims of quality (being truthful), quantity (providing enough but not too much information), relevance and manner (not being obscure, disorganized or ambiguous).[37] Communication rules, like other rules, are affected by cultural values. For example, people from collectivist cultures follow a maxim of seeking harmony and may not depend so heavily on the maxim of quality (truthfulness).

Rules also govern speech acts. To speak is to perform an act. Speech is not just used to designate or describe something; it actually *does* something. Speakers do not speak only to give information: they may have a range of intentions.[38] Speech acts, with their associated intentions, may be stating, questioning, commanding, promising or one of a number of other possibilities. If a speech act is successful, the receiver will understand the speaker's intention. If, for example, when Person A asks a question, the receiver, Person B, only understands the words, but not that A intended to ask a question, B is unlikely to give an answer. In this case, A's speech act will not have been a successful one.

Understanding what the speaker's intentions are in saying something is crucial to a receiver. For instance, if a colleague says something like 'The post has arrived,' the literal meaning is easily understood by decoding, but the receiver needs to know *why* the speaker made this announcement. What was the intention behind saying this? It might simply be a desire to impart the information, but usually the speaker intends to communicate more. In the example above, it might be that the speaker wants the receiver to go to the post room to collect the post, or that s/he wants them to know that s/he has been to the post room. Receivers will need to know which of the possible communicative intentions apply or they will miss the full meaning of the message. To decide, they will draw on a set of assumptions that they use to understand their experience. These assumptions are likely to vary cross-culturally, as Chapter 4 will show.

Speech Act Theory identifies what it takes to make a successful speech act, that is, to have an intention understood. There are guidelines on how to use speech to accomplish a particular intention – for instance, if A wants something, s/he makes a request, and does it in a form which B will understand to obligate him/her either to grant it or to turn it down. Therefore, when speakers perform a speech act, they must follow rules and those rules must be known to and be understood by receivers, if they are to communicate successfully. Speech Act theory also explains how people use intentions to structure communication. It is probable that, in all cultures, to speak is to perform an act and that to be successful the communicative intention behind the act must be understood by the receiver. However, both intentions and the forms required to communicate them may be culture-specific and hard for outsiders to comprehend. For instance, in some societies, for a guest to praise a host's possession usually obliges the host to offer it as a gift; it is assumed that the guest's intention is to ask for it. Without prior knowledge, Westerners would not understand that implication of praise.

There are also rules for discourses. A discourse refers to the ways in which language is used in a particular social context. There are (sub)cultural differences in the rules for general discourse. These rules govern topics of conversation, types of anecdotes, sequences of the elements of a story or account and amounts of speech to use. They also cover how to open and close conversations, take turns during conversations, interrupt, use silence or laughter as communication devices, interject humour at appropriate times and use non-verbal behaviour.[39] In addition to the cultural differences in these discourse rules, every culture can be shown to consist of a number of internal, intersecting and overlapping discourse systems, such as those of different age groups, ethnic groups, genders, social classes and professions. For instance, many teenagers use media-derived personal idioms, partly in order to identify with other teenagers.

An analysis of interviews with and documents from Indian and Israeli business partners suggested that local discourse systems played a major role in their business communication. The findings included the following:

- Indians' faxes were 2.7 times longer than Israelis'. They included declarations of solidarity, such as 'On long-term and uninterrupted relationship with concrete and sound foundations, let us build our joint empire,' and long paragraphs with no numbers. Negatives, such as a refusal to go to Israel, were expressed indirectly.
- The Israelis commented on the Indian communications: 'Every sentence has two extra degrees of freedom. You can never hold or grasp something. Words have double or triple meaning.' The Indians' comment on the Israeli communication style was that it was aggressive, lacked flexibility, style, patience and human orientation.
- Israelis used 'dugri' discourse, which emphasizes faithful projection of one's own feelings, often producing a forceful and confrontational tone; the Indians used Indian English, which is formal, poetic and inefficient, and requires long, indirect sentences to be polite.

Although there are cultural differences in power distance and uncertainty avoidance between Indians and Israelis, which may be reflected in their discourse systems, it is the difference in those discourse systems themselves that is most noticeable in these findings. This means they conflict with the culture-as-shared-values approach, which portrays culture as having a global influence on people's communication behaviour. That approach has been criticized for failing to explain variations within a culture or variations between cultures that share a broad value. Complexity and variation in communication patterns are often ignored.[40]

The culture-in-context approach (also known as the discourse/practice approach), in contrast to the culture-as-shared-values approach, builds on the premise that different groups use different discourses. It also treats individuals as active participants (agents) – they make pragmatic choices, decisions and calculations. Thus the discourse/practice approach emphasizes individuals' communication choices, particularly as such choices are shaped by the various discourse systems to which the individual belongs. In support of this view, some research showed that businesspeople did not fully conform to one cultural code, but instead adapted to specific situations (sometimes the Indians and Israelis adopted versions of the other culture's style); that negotiators from different cultural backgrounds modified their behaviour in intercultural, as opposed to intracultural, interactions; that negotiators tended to match the other's bargaining strategies; and that body movement and language were co-ordinated.[41]

Conversational constraints

Conversational constraints (CCs) are criteria for selecting conversational strategies. Three CCs are commonly identified: concern for clarity, concern for minimizing threats to the hearer's face and concern for minimizing imposition. The concerns are linked to interaction goals. Concern for clarity is linked to the goal of getting one's own way. Concern for minimizing threats to the hearer's face and minimizing imposition are both linked to the goal of avoiding hurting the hearer's feelings. Each interaction goal/CC pair is also linked to a choice of conversational strategy, particularly the choice between direct and indirect forms, as shown in Figure 3.4.[42] Later versions of CC theory added two more concerns: for avoiding negative evaluation by the hearer and for effectiveness.

CC theory is relevant to cultural differences in communication behaviour because it makes links between individuals' self-construals (described in Chapter 4), their needs, psychological make-up and choice of communication strategy. For instance,

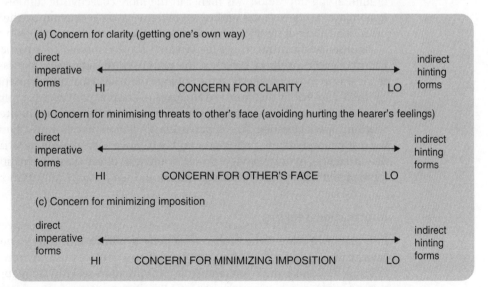

Figure 3.4   *Conversational constraints, interaction goals and choice of conversational strategy*

Based on: Kim, M.-S., Hunter, J.E., Miyahara, A., Horvath, A., Bresnahan, M. and Yoon, H. (1996) 'Individual- vs. culture-level dimensions of individualism and collectivism: effects on preferred conversational styles', *Communication Monographs*, **63**: 29–49

Box 3.6

'When presenting a privatization proposal to Turkish government officials, one issue is whether to give a balanced view, referring to potential problems, or not. Generally, Turkish history and culture predispose them to believe that any problems referred to are the tip of a very large iceberg and will actually prove fatal to the project. They are not used to working through problems; instead their experience is that problems cause failure. It makes it difficult to follow banking prudence nostrums – you do not know what to say that would make them realize you are being prudent without triggering alarm bells.'

Source: interview with an investment banker, author's research

psychological masculinity leads to concern for clarity; psychological femininity leads to concern for others' face.

A study undertaken with 972 undergraduates studying in Korea, Japan, Hawaii and mainland USA found the following: culture-level individualism correlated positively with concern for clarity and promoting one's own goals in communication but not with the relational constraints of concern for minimizing threats to the hearer's face, for minimizing imposition or for avoiding negative evaluation by the hearer. In contrast, the results for culture-level collectivism were the reverse. In both cases, the researchers found that a mediating cultural variable – an independent or interdependent self-construal – was operating.[43] A later study posed one of six questions about hypothetical 'request' situations to each of 892 undergraduates in Korea, Hawaii and mainland USA, and asked them to rate the perceived importance of each conversational constraint in that situation. The results indicated that the perceived importance of clarity was higher in the more individualistic cultures, while the perceived importance of avoiding hurting the hearer's feelings and of minimizing imposition was higher in the more collectivistic cultures. The perceived importance of effectiveness and of avoiding negative evaluation by the hearer, on the other hand, did not significantly differ across the three cultural groups.[44]

Another study within the same research project showed that participants' gender had no significant direct effect on the perceived importance of any of the CCs. This result was found consistently across all four societies researched. The finding seems to contradict assertions that men use language to assert a 'position of dominance' by coming directly to the point (clarity), whereas women use language to create and maintain relationships of closeness. The apparent contradiction may, however, be related more to the distinction between preferences and behaviour; many researchers have found gender differences in verbal styles (power, politeness, directness) but this still leaves room for men and women to be relatively similar in their *preferred* conversational styles.[45]

Information-seeking

Information-seeking is the process or activity by which individuals attempt to obtain information in order to understand, predict and control their environment, increase task mastery and reduce role ambiguity. Information-seeking facilitates communication by reducing uncertainty and errors based on misinformation. There are cultural differences in information-seeking behaviours, which correspond to the high-context/low-context communication distinction explained in Chapter 2. Communicators from high-context culture (HCCs) are more cautious in initial encounters, use more

Box 3.7

'In a Chinese company, if a manager writes a report, he or she must always put, right at the start, that senior managers or other departments shared in the achievement of his or her department.'[a]

A UK retailing company was running a competition to find the 'best' sales assistant in each store. The method was to get customers to give feedback on their instore experience; participating customers had a chance of winning a prize. The method of entry was printed on the receipt. One store manager received two separate complaints about one assistant. On investigating it was discovered that she was writing the words 'Strongly Agree' on each receipt and telling the customers to mark their feedback questionnaire in this way. Had they complied, this would have resulted in her gaining top marks in the competition. The sales assistant was from a collectivist country.[b]

Sources: (a) interview with a Chinese expatriate manager in London: author's research

(b) interview with a retail branch manager in London: author's research

subtle behaviours, make more assumptions about but also ask more questions about a stranger's background. They are also more confident in making attributions about the 'causes' of another person's behaviour. Communicators from low-context cultures (LCCs) rely more on verbal expressiveness and are more likely to use interrogation and self-disclosure.[46]

Facework

Face is the 'positive social value people assume for themselves, the image they try to project to the public'.[47] Although face concerns are universal, the meaning and enactment of face are heavily culture-dependent. Face is 'grounded in the webs of interpersonal and sociocultural variability'.[48] Because the relative importance of the self and the group differ in individualist and collectivist cultures, the characteristics of an appropriate face and the nature of facework also differ. In a collectivist culture, facework is used to present the self as an appropriate member of the social network, and people are expected to help others maintain a similarly appropriate face. In contrast, in an individualist society, facework focuses more on maintaining one's own personal identity, with less interest in helping others maintain theirs.[49] The concept of face and its elements has been further analysed in terms of a combination of two theories of culture: individualism – collectivism and high-context/low-context communication.[50] These variables influence the following:

- whether the person's sense of identity is 'I' or 'we';
- whether the primary face concern is for the self or the other;
- the relative importance of negative or positive face need;
- whether the style used is controlling, confrontational and oriented towards solving 'problems' or obliging, conflict-avoiding and oriented towards maintaining positive feelings;
- whether the person's communicative strategy is competitive or co-operative;
- whether the person's mode of expression, speech acts and non-verbal behaviour are usually direct or indirect.[51] Table 3.1 gives a summary of the differences in these constructs in LCCs (low-context cultures) and HCCs (high-context cultures).

Table 3.1   *A summary of low-context and high-context face negotiation processes*

Key constructs of 'face'	Individualist, low-context communication cultures	Collectivist, high-context communication cultures
Identity	Emphasis on 'I' identity	Emphasis on 'We' identity
Concern	Self-face concern	Other-face concern
Need	Autonomy, dissociation, negative-face need	Inclusion, association, positive-face need
Style	Controlling or confrontation and solution-oriented styles	Obliging or avoidance and effective-oriented styles
Strategy	Distributive or competitive	Integrative or collaborative
Mode	Direct	Indirect
Speech acts	Direct	Indirect
Non-verbal acts	Individualist non-verbal acts, direct emotional expression	Contextualistic non-verbal acts (role-oriented), indirect emotional expression

Based on: Ting-Toomey, S. (1998) 'Intercultural conflict styles: a face-negotiation theory', in Kim, Y. and Gudykunst, W. (eds) *Theories in Intercultural Communication*, Newbury Park, CA: Sage; and Ting-Toomey, S., Gao, G., Trubisky, P., Yang, Z. Kim, H., Lin, S.L. and Nishida, T. (1991) 'Culture, face maintanance, and styles of handling interpersonal conflict: a study in five cultures', *The International Journal of Conflict Management*, **2**: 275–96.

Some facework researchers have included at least one cultural difference variable in their models. A six-country study (in Chile, Hong Kong, Israel, Japan, Sweden and the United States) showed that uncertainty avoidance influenced the choice among ritualistic, harmonious, and aggressive facework strategies in an embarrassing situation.[52] In Japan, a collectivist culture, people are exposed to face loss from both excessive humility (seen as lack of dignity) and excessive claims to dignity (seen as arrogance). They strive to remain in an intermediate zone in which face can be maintained (see Figure 3.5).[53]

Strategies to protect 'own face' in a collectivist culture include the following:

- asking someone else to transmit a message
- talking to a third person in the intended hearer's presence
- acting as if a delegate – 'pretending' to be a messenger from a third person
- not expressing wishes explicitly, but expecting the other person to understand
- corresponding by letter or email, so avoiding meeting face-to-face.

All these strategies are available to and used by people in a range of cultures, but people from collectivist cultures use them more often. Equally, strategies to protect one's own face and threaten the other's face, such as self-praise or arrogance, are more common in highly individualist cultures. They also occur in collectivist cultures, but are disapproved of and regarded as antisocial.

Politeness

Politeness theory is an extension of the concept of facework. Some speakers do not seem to aim to construct their messages in the most efficient way, contrary to rule theories. Instead, speakers are often guided by the requirements of politeness. According to politeness theory, there is a relationship between a speaker's face concerns, perceived threats to face and the ways in which a speaker will express a request, explanation, disagreement or any other verbal communication.[54] All communication risks a threat to the faces of either the speaker or the hearer or both. This is because all people

HUMILITY		DIGNITY
Face loss (seen as lacking in dignity)	Face maintenance	Face loss (seen as arrogant)

Figure 3.5   *Face maintenance in Japan*

Based on: Lebra, T.S. (1971) 'The social mechanism of guilt and shame: the Japanese case', *Anthropological Quarterly*, **44**(4): 241–55

Box 3.8

In a study of apologizing, Koreans and Americans showed a greater discrepancy between themselves and their estimate of most people in their own culture than Chinese participants did. On the other hand, although people from all three cultures felt a greater obligation to apologize to a stranger than to a friend, both Americans and Chinese showed a greater discrepancy than Koreans did.

_____

Source: Guan, X., Sun-Park, H. and Lee, H.E. (2009) 'Cross-cultural differences in apology', *International Journal of Intercultural Relations*, **33**(1): 32–45

---

have two conflicting desires: for other people's approval (positive face need) and yet to be independent of others and their approval (negative face need). Different kinds of communication, such as requests or apologies, are intrinsically more or less threatening to either the speaker's or the hearer's face. Threat is also increased by three factors: how much the communication imposes on the hearer (asking for directions is less of an imposition than asking for a loan); the status relations between the speaker and hearer (a schoolmaster is more threatened by a pupil's disagreeing with him than the reverse); and how well the speaker and hearer know one another (knowing one another well reduces threat). Politeness theory defines politeness in communication as the attempt by the speaker to minimize or reduce the threat to the hearer's face, and postulates that the more intrinsically threatening the situation, the more polite the speaker will be.

There are national, ethnic and gender differences in concepts of politeness, the amount of politeness that people use, the influence of content versus relationship concerns on politeness, and the politeness of direct and indirect forms. For instance, Japanese people generally follow different sets of politeness norms from North Americans, including showing a higher level of deference to older people. Politeness is a rule of appropriate behaviour in different ethnic groups across the USA, but the particular behaviours that are defined as polite vary.[55] Again, some women have a pattern of politeness behaviours that is different from men's and can lead to an image of less intelligence. Women have 'learned the language of apology'. Unfortunately, these linguistic politeness patterns can negatively affect credibility and suggest uncertainty in the speaker and triviality in the subject matter.[56] In contrast to North American communication norms, avoiding obscurity or ambiguity (the maxim of manner) is not an expectation in cultures with different value orientations. For example, Koreans do not often use negative responses like 'No', or 'I disagree with you'. Instead they are likely to say, 'I agree with you in principle, but...' or 'I sympathise with you, but...' Koreans' collectivist values and consequent sense of politeness prevent directness of negative communication.[57]

Rapport management

One important function of communication is the effective management of relationships of all kinds, including work relationships. In contrast with some linguists' focus on facework and politeness, scholars concerned with rapport management maintain that linguistic politeness is just one of the resources available for managing relationships. It should be studied within the situated social psychological context in which it occurs. It is therefore important to consider the motivational concerns underlying the management of relations.

Rapport management theorists suggest that face has two interrelated aspects:

1. Quality face: people have a fundamental desire for others to evaluate them positively in terms of their personal qualities, such as competence, abilities or appearance.
2. Social identity face: people have a fundamental desire for others to acknowledge and uphold their social identities or roles, for instance as group leaders, valued customers or close friends.

Similarly, rapport management theorists suggest that people have 'fundamental beliefs' that they possess certain 'sociality rights'. These rights have two interrelated aspects:

1. Equity rights: people have a 'fundamental belief' that they are entitled to personal consideration from others, so that they are treated fairly: that they are not unduly imposed upon or unfairly ordered about, that they are not taken advantage of or exploited, and that they receive the benefits to which they are entitled.
2. Association rights: people have a fundamental belief that they are entitled to association with others that is in keeping with the type of relationship that they have with them. People feel, for example, that they are entitled to an appropriate amount of conversational interaction and social chitchat with others (that they are not ignored on the one hand, but not overwhelmed on the other). These association rights also relate to the extent to which people share concerns, feelings and interests. Naturally, what counts as 'an appropriate amount' depends on the nature of the relationship, as well as on personal preferences, but also on sociocultural norms.

As can be seen, rapport management is conceptualized as having two motivational sources: concerns over face and concerns over sociality rights. Sociality rights are not treated as face issues, because sometimes an infringement of sociality rights may simply lead to annoyance or irritation, rather than to a sense of face threat or loss. Similarly, a request for help, which in politeness theory would be regarded as a face-threatening act, may not in fact be regarded as an infringement or threat at all. On the contrary, it may be regarded either as a boost to quality face, since the request shows trust in the other person's qualities, or simply as an acknowledgement of association rights. The notion of sociality rights relates partly to the concept of negative face but is not synonymous with it: it is broader in scope and is not limited to autonomy-imposition issues.[58] People's perceptions of the level of rapport in an interaction are affected by their behavioural expectations, face sensitivities, and interactional wants (what they hope to get from the interaction). Negative rapport perceptions can lead to conflictual interpersonal relations, while positive rapport perceptions can generate interpersonal harmony. Rapport perceptions are dynamic, changing during the course of the interaction.[59]

There is evidence for cross-cultural differences in rapport management. A study compared the preferences of Greeks and Germans for attending to the relationship aspect of communication in telephone conversations. It found that Greeks seemed to prefer an exchange of phatic utterances like greetings (which maximize the relational and minimize the informational content of talk), before coming to the reason for calling. Germans opted for a more direct path to the main section of the call. Greeks used more redundancy in closing telephone calls than Germans did, making the closing process more extended. In Greek calls, the decision to end the call was negotiated. In German calls, common ground was invoked.[60] (Common ground among interacting individuals is defined as the sum of their mutual, common or joint knowledge, beliefs and suppositions.[61]) A study showed that one vehicle through which rapport is communicated in workplace interactions is behavioural mirroring, and that such co-ordination is affected by culture (Latinos mirror more than Anglos), though not by gender.[62]

Anxiety and uncertainty management (AUM)

AUM theory assumes that the very process of interacting can cause individuals to experience anxiety and uncertainty, especially in a first meeting with strangers. Because these psychological experiences cause discomfort, people attempt to reduce their impact through communication. They do this especially if the strangers will be encountered in future and can provide rewards. Most importantly, uncertainty and anxiety are aroused and people attempt to reduce them when strangers act in a deviant fashion from the perspective of the individual's own culture or subculture. Thus cultural differences in behaviour are central to AUM theory. Uncertainty and anxiety are related to a range of communication behaviours: how much communication occurs between people, their non-verbal affiliative expressiveness (the degree to which they show warmth to one another by body language such as smiling, eye contact or touching), their level of information-seeking, reciprocity, liking and how intimately they communicate.

Reciprocity, similarity and liking are also related to uncertainty. (In general each of these relations are inverse – thus, the greater the amount of communication and the higher the similarity, the lower the uncertainty. However, information-seeking is higher in the presence of high uncertainty.) People adopt one of three general strategies for reducing uncertainty: a passive strategy (doing nothing in the hope that as time passes things will become clearer); an active strategy (finding out as much as possible from outside sources); and an interactive strategy (seeking out opportunities to interact with people about whom uncertainty exists and using those occasions to obtain as much information as possible).[63] Core elements of AUM theory are the concepts of the stranger, initial encounters, uncertainty and anxiety.

■ Strangers are people who are different because they are members of other groups. When strangers act in a way that is deviant in terms of an individual's own culture, the individual experiences uncertainty and anxiety, especially when those strangers will be encountered in future or can provide rewards.

■ Initial encounters, by definition, are between strangers. Culture forms an implicit theory (about the rules being followed and the 'game' being played) that individuals use to guide their behaviour and interpret others' behaviour. Much culturally influenced behaviour is habitual and therefore not 'conscious'.[64] The matter is different, though, in the initial stages of intercultural communication. When interacting with a stranger, individuals become aware that the stranger does not share their own implicit theory about the rules or the game. Therefore they become more conscious of that implicit theory. The result is that interactions between strangers take place at high levels of behavioural awareness.

■ Uncertainty is of two distinct types: not being able to predict what strangers' attitudes, feelings, beliefs, values and behaviour will be and not being able to explain why they behave in the way they do. When uncertainty is too high for comfort, people will either try to reduce it by gaining information or end the interaction. When uncertainty is too low for comfort, people may be too bored to act effectively.

■ Anxiety refers to the feeling of being uneasy, tense, worried or apprehensive about what might happen. This is an affective (emotional) response, whereas uncertainty is a cognitive (thought process) one. Anxiety is usually based on people's negative expectations, such as that their self-concepts will be damaged or that they will be negatively evaluated. When anxiety is too high for comfort, people either avoid encounters or their attention is distracted from the communication. Then they rely on information like stereotypes to predict other people's behaviour, and therefore may misinterpret it. When anxiety is too low, people may not care what happens in the interaction, not pay attention and miss important cues.

Support for the existence of uncertainty reduction as part of the dynamic of interaction with strangers has come from research which showed that it applies to both low-context communication and high-context communication cultures,[65] friendship relations across cultures,[66] interactions between Blacks and Whites in the USA,[67] and inter-ethnic communication generally in the USA.[68] A study of Japanese and Caucasian subjects found, as AUM would predict, that ethnicity, stage of relationship, shared networks and ethnolinguistic identity strength influenced how much interlocutors self-disclosed, how many questions they asked, whether their body language expressed affiliation, whether they saw one another as similar and how confident they were in making attributions about the causes of different others' behaviour, using both high- and low-context measures.[69]

A number of hypotheses based on AUM theory relate anxiety or uncertainty to cultural dimensions. These include:

■ An increase in collectivism will produce a decrease in uncertainty in outgroup communication relative to ingroup communication.

■ An increase in uncertainty avoidance will produce an increase in anxiety and a decrease in inter-group adaptation and effectiveness.

■ An increase in the strength of ethnolinguistic identities leads to an increase in confidence but also an increase in anxiety, though only when members of the outgroup are perceived as typical and ethnic status is activated.[70]

AUM theory has been criticized for being static and for taking the individual interactor, rather than the dyad or group, as the unit of analysis. However, because behavioural contagion is known to be particularly common when one party is anxious, the theory has the potential to be interactive and dynamic. AUM theory has also been crit-icized for assuming that uncertainty will always produce anxiety.[71] These critics further suggest that it would be more appropriate to focus on communication and uncertainty management. To better explain these processes, they argue, answers are needed to questions about the experience and meaning of uncertainty, the role of appraisal and emotion in uncertainty management, and the range of behavioural and psychological responses to uncertainty. However, the fact that these criticisms imply a reduced role for anxiety management means that they may be considered an error by those who appreciate the emotional as well as the cognitive aspects of intercultural interaction. In any case, AUM's focus on initial interactions and the early stages of acquaintanceship makes it valuable for understanding those aspects of intercultural work communica-tion that involve meeting strangers, such as opening interviews between professionals and clients or international negotiations.

Other-regarding preference behaviours

It has been argued that other-regarding preferences (ORPs) such as trust, reciprocity and altruism are integral elements in economic transactions between companies, between consumers and retailers, between employers and employees, and in deter-mining economic performance. Trust has been shown to have a positive influence on the economic performance of corporations, reciprocity helps explain the persistence of co-operative actions in the absence of immediate incentives to co-operate and has been shown to increase the set of enforceable contracts and help markets to achieve efficiency gains, while altruism, in which the consumption by others appears posi-tively as an argument in an individual's utility function, has been linked to helping behaviour in the workplace. Buchan *et al.* (2006) found in an experiment that there were variations in the proportion of trust-, reciprocity- or altruism-based behaviours shown by participants from four different countries. Chinese participants sent and returned more ORPs than their counterparts from other countries. They also exhibited no bias towards their ingroup (and in fact the US participants exhibited the greatest ingroup bias, exceeding not only China but Japan and Korea as well.)[72] This finding, which, in the words of Buchan *et al.* (2006), 'does not line up neatly with any exist-ing theory', may suggest that ingroup biases in collectivist cultures are only evident among naturally occurring groups in society, not among the kind of experimentally conducted temporary groups used for this and other studies.

Compliance gaining

An important purpose for which communication is used at work is to influence. Influencing ranges from the relatively weak effect of getting others to re-evaluate how they think about something to the relatively strong effect of gaining their compliance to doing something. Communication methods for getting other people to comply may correspond to cultural values. One study found that in the USA giving reasons and explanations were favoured over threats or moral pressure. These preferences were probably linked to values of individual autonomy. In contrast, in Colombia, which has a collectivist culture, *confianza* (which means the degree of trust and closeness in a relationship, plus responsibility for others) interacted with acceptance of authority. This meant that in some relationships it was acceptable for one party to 'command' the other. This could allow the use of threats and moral pressure and remove the need to give explanations. In other words, individualism – collectivism may influence compliance-gaining methods.[73]

Compliance gaining with subordinates means using persuasion to influence them to do what they are directed to do and to convince them that the task is worth doing. Such communication is common between superiors and key subordinates. Research suggests that US and European managers use mainly reasoning and friendliness, as opposed to sanctions, bargaining or appeals to higher authority. The probable reasons are that such appeals avoid making superior – subordinate interactions more risky and help both superiors and subordinates to attain their goals. What applies to Japanese managers? Findings based on three samples of 14, 13 and 41 Japanese managers were that reasoning was the most used strategy. However, when Japanese managers saw themselves as permanent employees they resorted more to the use of assertiveness: they frequently set deadlines for key subordinates, told them that they must comply and reminded them repeatedly. Permanently employed Japanese managers also made more use of loyalty appeals, even when the subordinates were temporary workers.[74]

A study of the effectiveness of various ways of gaining compliance compared Dutch, Turkish and Moroccan groups. It found that, across all groups, high source expertise was the most effective way of gaining compliance – there were no significant cross-cultural differences for this finding; in cases of low source expertise, however, Moroccan and Turkish people were more compliant than Dutch people, regardless of the compliance-gaining strategy used.[75]

Conflict management

Conflict is the 'perceived and/or actual incompatibility of values, expectations, processes, or outcomes between two or more parties over substantive and/or relational issues'.[76] According to Triandis (2000), cultures differ on a number of aspects of conflict communication. For instance, in the West, the structure of messages is likely to be 'Fact 1, fact 2, generalization, conclusion'; in other cultures the conclusion may be stated first, followed by facts that fit the conclusion. This structure permits deviations from a straight line. Another difference is between universalist and particularist cultures: universalists expect all facts to 'fit in' with a position; particularists may feel this is unnecessary. Third, there is a cultural difference between those, like Westerners, who use abstractive communication and those others who use associative communication, for whom the importance of symbols is greater. Conflict intensity, also, may vary as a function of culture because the value attached to a goal is influenced by subjective culture. What one culture may perceive as a major conflict may be quite minor in another.[77] Because on the surface work-related conflict focuses on substantive issues, not relational and image issues, face negotiation has implications for how people manage conflict. Ting-Toomey and Kurogi (1998) argued that culturally competent facework is a critical aspect of conflict management.[78]

A useful distinction can be drawn between simplex relationships, which are confined to a single interest – for instance, that between a doctor and patient – and multiplex relationships, which serve many interests, such as economic, kinship and shared leisure time interests.[79] Because of the significant interdependence involved in a multiplex relationship, continuation of the relationship is very important to the well-being of the participants. In cultures and societies where multiplex relationships predominate, there is likely to be a preference for conflict resolution procedures that allow compromises, so that the relationship can continue smoothly. Examples of such conflict resolution procedures include negotiation and mediation. Societies where simplex relationships are more common, on the other hand, tend to prefer adjudication or arbitration, which lead to win – lose settlements. This might help account for the fact that, in 1976, the USA had 18 lawyers per 1,000 people, West Germany four, France two and Japan one. Simplex relationship-oriented societies also tend to prefer adversarial adjudication, where the contending parties compete to make their case, rather than investigative adjudication, where a third party (magistrate or judge) investigates as well as judges.

A number of cross-cultural studies of negotiation-related behaviour have provided evidence that members of individualist cultures are more likely to handle conflicts directly through competition and problem-solving, whereas members of collectivist cultures are more likely to handle conflict in indirect ways that attempt to preserve the relationship.[80] A study of the conflict style of Vietnamese refugees concluded that they are part of a collectivist (as opposed to individualist), high-context (rather than low-context) culture, which often desires to avoid conflict. In a 1994 conflict situation in Louisville, Kentucky, USA, the Vietnamese conflict-avoiding style aided a defusing of tensions.[81] Yugoslavians (collectivists by Hofstede's measures) and Japanese prefer collaboration or compromise in handling a conflict, North Americans prefer competition.[82] Greeks, who by European standards are relatively collectivist, treat their ingroup as a source of protection and social insurance, but are more suspicious of and competitive with outgroup members, such as strangers. This ingroup – outgroup aspect of collectivism affects conflict: for instance, Chinese people are more likely to sue a stranger and less likely to sue a friend than North Americans are.

Cultural collectivism also influences business conflict resolution: a study showed that Japanese managers perceived the level of trust to be higher when an American partner requested a mutual conferral to resolve disputes rather than binding arbitration. However, collectivism, as exemplified in the Chinese preference for 'harmony', does not mean that Chinese people literally avoid conflict at all costs. Fieldwork studies have shown that 'co-operative conflict' occurs in Chinese organizations. Furthermore, experiments showed that Chinese people valued and used conflict to explore issues, make effective decisions and strengthen relationships. Co-operative conflict in China contributed to effective teamwork, quality service and leadership. Co-operative conflict was achieved through the protagonists communicating that they wanted to manage the conflict for mutual benefit rather than to win at the other's expense.[83]

Conflict management styles have also been linked to other cultural variables. First, people from feminine cultures, such as the Dutch, have been shown to prefer harmony-enhancing conflict resolution procedures (such as mediation and negotiation) to confrontational procedures (such as threats and accusations). This preference was stronger among the Dutch than among Canadians, who score high on masculinity. Second, members of high power distance cultures (the Philippines, Venezuela, India, France, Belgium) had fewer conflicts with their superiors and were more likely to have superiors intervene in settling their conflicts than members of low power distance cultures (Denmark, Israel, Austria). Third, members of low-context communication cultures (USA, Germany, Scandinavia, Switzerland) were found to communicate more directly and to have different communication goals in conflict than members of high-context communication cultures (Japan, China, Korea, Vietnam).

Avoidance styles of conflict management are more common in collectivist than individualist cultures. Kim and Leung (2000) proposed a model that suggests that collectivists' tendency to avoid conflict can be explained by their desire to preserve relational harmony and by their motivation to save others' faces.[84] From research among 85 managers and employees in six State Owned Enterprises in South China, Tjosvold and Sun (2002) found other motivations that drive conflict avoidance in collectivist cultures.

Outflanking (trying to work round the opponent in conflict) can arise from a combination of co-operative goals and fear of revenge. Results were interpreted as indicating that, among collectivists, avoiding conflict reaffirms existing strong relationships.[85]

A meta-analysis of studies of five methods of conflict handling at work based on Blake and Mouton's (1964) *The Managerial Grid*, Houston, TX: Gulf Publishing – smoothing, withdrawing, compromising, problem-solving and forcing methods – was conducted to provide a clearer overall picture for the variables of culture (individualistic versus collectivistic), gender and organizational role (superior, subordinate and peer). Based on 123 paired comparisons within 36 empirical studies, the results of the meta-analysis indicated: (1) individualistic cultures chose forcing as a conflict style more than collectivistic cultures; (2) collectivistic cultures preferred the styles of withdrawing, compromising, and problem-solving more than individualistic cultures; (3) in individualistic cultures, compromising was endorsed more frequently by females; (4) females were more likely to endorse the use of compromising than males, regardless of culture; (5) males were more likely to report using forcing than females in individualistic cultures; and (6) with regard to organizational role, males were more likely than females to choose a forcing style with their superiors.[86]

Critique

Although the purpose of this section is to note cultural variations in ways of communicating, the concepts and theories underpinning it derive mainly from a tradition that sees the individual human mind as the independent locus for processing information and for generating and understanding messages. This individualist cognitive approach was dominant in Western social science during the twentieth century, but it can be challenged both in social science generally and in the study of communication, which is essentially something that happens between people and so cannot be explained solely from the perspective of the individual mind.

> (Sub)cultural differences have been found for communication traits, styles and situations. Process-based analyses of communication refer to the exchange of messages and the creation of meaning by assigning signs or interpreting messages. There are (sub)cultural differences in which signs are used and what they refer to. Both verbal and non-verbal signs and their referents can vary. Users of spoken or written languages form different speech communities. The language used may itself influence the cultural preferences of communicators during interactions: language and culture are intertwined.
>
> Communication rules for achieving the necessary co-operation, for speech acts and for discourses can also differ. Conversational constraints, which link to interaction goals, have been found to vary between masculine/feminine and individualist – collectivist cultures. (Sub)cultural differences have been found in information-seeking, expressing and understanding intentions, facework, politeness, rapport management, anxiety and uncertainty management, the sending and return of other-regarding preferences and in two specific types of interaction, compliance gaining and conflict management. These differences partly reflect the cultural values differences described in Chapter 2, but in some cases appear to be independent variables. Apart from 'high-context/ low-context', we do not as yet have a taxonomy of (sub)cultural differences in communication itself.

3.3 (SUB)CULTURAL COMMUNICATION

To varying degrees, as the previous section began to show, many aspects of how people communicate are affected by culture. This section gives a breakdown of communication similarities and differences by national culture, ethnicity, gender, age and disability, religion and social class. The communication of marginalized groups and professional, business and organizational discourses are also discussed.

National culture and communication

National cultural values play an important part in determining the general tone of communication. For instance, within individualism, it is the individual's responsibility to 'say what's on his or her mind' if s/he expects to be attended to or understood: 'For a person oriented toward the independent construal of self, the general tone of social interaction may concern the expression of his or her own needs and rights.'[87] In individualist cultures, too, highly verbal people are perceived positively because they are more successful at establishing identity. However, the value attached to being talkative varies cross-culturally. The benefit of low verbal output among collectivists comes from being understood without putting one's meaning on record. Understanding is seen, not as the result of putting meaning into words, but rather as the greater understanding of shared perspectives, expectations and intimacy.[88] The cultural values of individualism – collectivism, power distance, masculinity/femininity and uncertainty avoidance can be used to predict and explain differences between communicator styles in different countries. A study by Gudykunst *et al.* (1996)[89] explored this question and found the following:

- Individualism–collectivism had both a direct effect on communicator styles and an indirect effect that was mediated through self-construals and values. Gudykunst *et al.* (1996) found that independent self-construals and individualist values mediated thividualism – collectivism had both a direct effect on communicator styles and an ie influence of cultural individualism – collectivism on the use of low-context communication, while interdependent self-construals and collectivist values mediated the influence of cultural individualism – collectivism on the use of high-context communication.
- High power distance in general inhibited direct communication, leading to lower levels of disclosure, openness and informality than in low power distance cultures. At work, high power distance led to greater differences according to who was communicating with whom: between managers and subordinates, the above points apply and were reinforced, with subordinates' style conveying deference and managers' condescension or paternalism. On the other hand, between co-workers low down in the hierarchy, it could lead to high levels of informality, with joking, teasing and a private language, as the low level of responsibility required of these workers encouraged a playful or childish approach.
- Cultures with strong achievement (masculine) values, such as Austria, Venezuela and the Republic of Ireland, tended to use more assertive and competitive forms of communication than cultures with more relational (feminine) values, such as Sweden, Norway and The Netherlands. Japan, which ranks first on the achievement values index, was an exception, possibly because the strength of collectivism in the culture outweighs even the powerful achievement value.
- High uncertainty avoidance cultures, such as those of Greece, Portugal and the Latin American countries, are cultures where communicator styles were more expressive. 'They are the places where people talk with their hands, where it is socially acceptable to raise one's voice, to show one's emotions, to pound the table.'[90,91] Conversely, countries known for their low-key style of communication,

such as Great Britain, Singapore and the Nordic countries, are also low in uncertainty avoidance.

Gudykunst *et al.* (1996) concluded that culture influences communication both directly, guided by cultural norms and rules, and indirectly, through self-construals and values that influence individuals' styles of communication. Table 3.2 summarizes the findings. Other influences of national culture have been found in communication rules, and the value placed on control, affiliation, content and relationship in communication.

■ Communication rules, like other rules, are affected by cultural values. For example, Americans self-disclosed (told others about themselves) more than Europeans, who, in turn, self-disclosed more than Asians. In business transactions, Americans generally tolerated open discussion of errors and accepted criticism of performance, while Koreans did not. Again, Americans differentiated criticism of a person from criticism of that person's actions, while Koreans viewed criticism as personal and face-threatening.[92]

■ There are differences in the relative value placed by different national cultures on control, affiliation, content and relationship in communication. Japanese culture, for instance, places a very high value on communicating subtle aspects of feeling and relationship and a much lower value on communicating information.

Most Japanese people also believe that the most important things cannot be communicated in language. Most Western cultures, despite some recent shifts, are the opposite. Not only do they emphasize communicating content at the expense of relationship, but they tend to treat what cannot be expressed in language as not worth attending to. (Women from Western cultures, though, are closer to the Japanese in this respect.)

■ In some cultures communication is normally used for negotiation, whereas in other cultures it is normally used for ratification. In some societies relationships are thought of as spontaneously created by individuals and communication is used to negotiate those relationships; in other societies relationships are thought of as predetermined and set – here communication ratifies pre-existing relationships. In business negotiations, Asians, who follow the ratification model, may

Table 3.2   Relations among different cultural values and communication styles

Cultural values	Communication styles	Comment
High-certainty avoidance	Expressive	
Low-certainty avoidance	Low key	
High masculinity (achievement)	Assertive, competitive	Except among Japanese
High feminity (relationships)	Supportive; co-operative	
High power distance	High formality; low disclosure and openness	This applies to manager – subordinate interactions; depends on power balance
Low power distance	Low formality; high disclosure and openness	
High individualism	Competitive	Mediated by self-construals
High collectivism	Co-operative with in-group	Mediated by self-construals

state their positions less extremely if they feel that not to do so would disrupt the harmony of the relationship; Westerners may assume that each party has in mind only achieving their own best advantage and may state their positions strongly as a negotiating ploy.

A comparison of US and Japanese communication is instructive because they perhaps represent polar extremes; communication in most European countries is located at varying points in between. The USA is a country formed by immigrants and is multicultural, despite past attempts to encourage assimilation. Japan, which was entirely closed to the outside world for centuries, is recognized as ethnically and culturally more homogeneous than any other major country in the world. These differences affect their preferred communication styles. The USA is 'a nation made up of ethnically diverse people who must work and live together. Reliance upon symbolic coding of experience has become a necessary survival skill'. For them, language is *the* mode of communication. For the Japanese, it is *a* mode of communication.

The Japanese prefer a style that employs assumptions about the opinions and feelings of their compatriots. (In Bernstein's (1971) terms, they use the restricted code.) The concept of *enryo* translates into a hesitancy about speaking frankly and immediately, which carries the risk of being thought brash. Japanese people are comfortable with silence, which has multiple meanings – for instance, showing respect by waiting for a senior to speak first. In Japan, the form of an event or communication is as important as its content. There are rituals for events, such as leavers' parties, which would be mainly informal in the USA. There are set phrases for apologies, excuses, requests and so on. For North Americans, interaction formats, especially at work, are persuasive, quantitative and pragmatic; in contrast, for Japanese, they are harmonizing, holistic and process-oriented. North Americans expect that each party, whether an individual or a small group representative, will state its own point of view and attempt to persuade the other party or parties. Japanese people aim to avoid distinguishing individual views or clarifying where differences lie. People are as likely to change their views out of respect or empathy as by responding to logical arguments. The receiver has as much responsibility for understanding what is said as the speaker has for making him/herself clear. Japanese people tend to give feedback non-verbally rather than by asking questions or in other verbal ways. Arguments written by 239 Japanese respondents were significantly more indirect and succinct than those written by their 90 US counterparts.[93]

National culture and language usage

A culture's preferred communication style is reflected in its use of language. Thus, in cultures where the preferred style is direct (i.e., speakers reveal their intentions through explicit verbal communication), the language used features judgemental adjectives, directives, oppositions, negations, questions and references to quantity; these are less used in cultures whose preferred style is indirect. A preference for succinctness or elaborateness affects how many intensifying adverbs, dependent clauses, sentence initial adverbials ('Well ...') and negations are used. Person-centred versus role-centred communication style preferences are reflected in the number of 'I' references, judgemental adjectives, oppositions and negations. Finally, the proportion of references to quantity, place, emotion, oppositions and negations reflect whether the cultural preference is for instrumental communication (which is oriented to the sender's goals) or affective communication (which is oriented to the relationship with the receiver).[94]

Box 3.9

In Chinese and Hindi, the word for 'please' is seldom used. In fact, the closer you are to someone you communicate with the less likely you would be to use 'please' because the word sounds distant and formal in both languages. In Australian culture 'please' is one of the most used words, to friends and family members as well as to strangers. However, the fact that Chinese and North Indians are not used to the word 'please' of course does not mean they are not polite. There is a language problem. In Hindi 'Bato' is an unsoftened imperative meaning 'Sit,' whereas 'Bataie' means 'Please sit'. When Chinese speak Chinese they use many 'functional words' to soften the tone of their speech. These functional words include particles such as *ya, la, ma* and so on which do not have any semantic meaning except to soften the tone of speaking. *Ni zuo shenme* would be a formal or impolite way of saying 'What do you do?' or 'What are you doing?' whereas *Ni zuo shenme ya* would be warmer and softer. However, these kind of particles and constructions are very difficult to translate into English.

Sources: Gao, M.C.F. (2000) 'Influences of native culture and language on intercultural communication: the case of PRC student immigrants in Australia', *Intercultural Communication*, 4: 33–53
Author's research

Thus, cultural styles are reflected in language features. At the same time, the language used and the communicators' language competency affect both the content and style of communication, which builds culture. Some languages give speakers easier access than others to particular personal and sociocultural ideas; these in turn relate to or influence message content. For example, English gives ready access to business concepts. Russian supplies fewer of these; Russian speakers often use loan words from English for business concepts. On specialized topics people who are bilingual may use the language that gives them better access to relevant concepts. For instance, some speakers of English-as-a-second-language use English for professional speaking and writing because this is the language in which they received training and learned professional concepts.[95] Beyond this, individuals at different language proficiency levels communicate very differently. In meetings, low-proficiency second-language speakers contribute fewer ideas than do fluent second-language speakers or first-language speakers.[96] It is sometimes difficult to distinguish between what is cultural and what is linguistic.

The problem of language is most obvious when people speak different languages. Many terms are untranslatable, because the underlying concepts differ; for example, the fact that the Bulgarian word closest to 'ambitious' never carries a negative loading, as it does in the English term 'ambitious schemer'. Loan words can be a particular problem: for instance, in Kazakhstan the loan word 'executive' refers only to the Chief Executive.

Differences in meaning can be just as significant, however, when each culture uses the 'same' language. 'Momentarily' in British English means 'for a moment', while in American English it means 'in a moment', so that an air stewardess might say: 'We'll be landing momentarily.' This would have a very strange sound in British ears. 'Scheme' and 'collaborate' carry negative implications in US English, but not in British. If a British native tells her American friend to put the bags in the boot, the American may not know that she means her to place the luggage in the trunk of the car. While this is an obvious example, it does remind us that objects, events, experiences and feelings have a particular name solely because a community of people have arbitrarily decided so to name them.[97]

Box 3.10

The following cultural variations in language use are well established:

- Japanese people can speak to one another using a selection of many different address forms to indicate explicitly any one of a whole range of relationships – for example, intimate, familiar, neutral, polite, deferential or authoritative. This illustrates the hierarchy and ceremony of interpersonal relationships in the society.
- English people, when speaking, continually use the words *please* and *thank you* in their conversations, and often avoid direct statements. English language and behaviour aim to avoid offending or alienating the other person. The result can be, however, that people from other cultures, like Spain, suspect that they are insincere.
- The Indian language Hindi has separate words for: my sister's husband (*behnoi*), my

husband's elder brother (*jait*), my husband's younger brother (*deva*), and my husband's sister's husband (*nandoya*). Kinship vocabulary is an indication of the nature of the more significant family relations in a culture. The single word *brother-in-law* in English indicates that one behaves similarly towards all the men in those different kinship statuses. The variety of words in Hindi indicates that each of these categories of people is treated differently.

- Greeks, too, have many different words for various family relationships and relatives that are very important in their large and extended families. Many of these words cannot be directly translated into English, as there is no exact word equivalent or in some cases there is not even an approximate word equivalent.

National culture and non-verbal behaviour

Some non-verbal behaviours differ across culture groups – for example, voice tone. Latinos tend to vary their tone a great deal, East Asians tend to favour monotony, while Anglo-Saxons are in between. There are also differences in the way different culture groups sequence their communication. Anglo-Saxons, for example, tend to follow without overlapping (interrupting is rude); Latinos to overlap; and East Asians to leave silence gaps. Long breaks in speaking are usual and acceptable between Finns, and are not mistaken for turn-taking signals.[98]

There are universal features: there is always some norm to regulate non-verbal features of social interaction; bowing, where it is used, always signifies submission; similarly, smiling is a universal sign of wanting to appease another. The meaning of most non-verbal behaviours, however, varies: head nodding and shaking, hissing and spitting, though having the same meaning in many cultures, all have different meanings in at least some – for instance, spitting is a sign of affection among the Masai of East Africa.

Facial expression, which has been shown to be linked to emotion, has both an innate and a cultural basis; culture modifies innate emotional expression in three ways:

- The event that gives rise to the emotion has a different meaning (a funeral could be an occasion of sorrow or joy).
- The reaction to emotions is affected (expressions of anger may not be shown because the person has been culturally induced to suppress anger).
- 'Display rules', such as those which make losers in competitions act as 'good losers', vary across cultures.[99]

Nevertheless, there is growing evidence that the facial expression of emotions can be judged accurately across cultures.[100]

Proxemics, the study of the way in which people use space as a part of interpersonal communication, recognizes that 'people of different cultures do have different ways in which they relate to one another spatially.'[101] It is well known that Arabs stand 'very close' when conversing. In fact, Arabs and Europeans differ on distance, facing, touching, loudness and eye contact.

National cultures and assertiveness, facework and rapport management

There are differences in the value that people from different backgrounds place on communication behaviours such as assertiveness. For example, American and Japanese people appear to have differing attitudes towards being assertive. One study found that American subjects rated assertive behaviour more highly and as more competent than Japanese subjects did. Japanese subjects discriminated more between ingroup and outgroup members in their attitudes towards being assertive. They rated assertive behaviour more highly when performed by ingroup members than by outgroup members.[102]

A study that investigated face and facework during conflicts across four national cultures, China, Germany, Japan and the USA, found the following:

- Self-construals had the strongest effects on face concerns and facework. Independence was positively associated with self-face and dominating facework; interdependence was positively associated with other- and mutual-face and integrating and avoiding facework.
- Power distance had small, positive effects on all face concerns and on avoiding and dominating facework.
- Individualist, small power distance cultures had less other-face concern and avoiding facework, and more dominating facework than collectivist, large power distance cultures.
- Germans had more self- and mutual-face concerns and used defending more than North Americans.
- Chinese had more self-face concern and involved a third party more than Japanese.
- Relational closeness and status had only small effects on face concerns and facework behaviour.[103]

Box 3.11

'Working with people in Russia, I'm struck by how they often reflect for several seconds before answering a question. Often they will not answer it and will not even refer to it. This is due to two factors, I was told. First they don't want to say an incorrect or inaccurate thing, so it's culturally better to say nothing, and they are accustomed to people considering their responses before replying. Second, to show yourself as too eager, or to state an incorrect fact in front of your superiors, was (and maybe in some places, still is) dangerous. I had to teach them how to give a quick answer, even if it was to say that they needed more information, but could give a reply later.'

Source: e-mail from a financial expert, author's research

These findings, and those of earlier research,[104] suggest that culture influences face-work. However, observation and analysis of rapport management in meetings between the representatives of a British host company and a visiting Chinese business delegation showed that both parties, not just the (collectivist) Chinese, were strongly influenced by group rather than individual face concerns. The British were concerned about the company's reputation: 'They wanted the visitors to learn more about their company, and to go back to China with a deep and positive impression, firstly of the company and secondly of Britain. Similarly, the Chinese delegation presented themselves as a group, and was concerned about the group's face and the reputation of Chinese people in general. "You just tell him. Is it so easy to bully us Chinese, so easy to fool us?" Equally, both parties were more concerned with "own face" than "other face".' The researchers concluded that, in different types of interactions and different cultural settings, different kinds of face and sociality rights may arise.[105]

National culture and work communication

There is evidence for cultural effects on business communication, despite the 'universal' focus on the work. For instance, according to a study of complaint letters, US and Korean business writers prefer different structures and styles. The majority of the letters written by the US managers in this study followed the 'direct' pattern: identification of the problem, discussion of relevant information, request for action, and a buffer, with the buffer representing an optional move. Only a small proportion of the Korean letters followed the US model, despite the fact that they were written in English to conduct business with US companies. Instead, the standard Korean pattern was indirect: most led with relevant information about the problem before identifying the problem itself. This kind of delay often requires the reader to absorb details, sometimes relevant and sometimes not, before discovering the problem.[106]

In contrast to North American methods, Japanese people use common sense more than 'quantification' in management. For instance, instead of checklists, they use discussions and making resolutions to 'do better'. Information is shared with 'appropriate others', who also participate in making decisions, so that a sense of group involvement results. Making decisions takes longer, but implementation is more certain and often quicker. As an interviewee told the author, 'The Japanese are not good at doing deals. One reason is that consensus is essential. There is a longer approval cycle. A negotiator will have only limited discretion and when he or she refers back, it is not to one individual with more discretion but to make sure everybody is well informed and approves the deal.'[107] There is a preference for face-to-face contact, rather than by email, memo or telephone. Japanese offices are usually open plan, allowing day-to-day awareness of others' non-verbal behaviour and its context, which allows them to be interpreted more effectively.

Within Europe, differences have been found in the models of business communication used by people from different national cultures, based on different assumptions about relations and communication between a boss and subordinates. Marked differences in conversation rules were found among Finnish, Swedish and Austrian students of business. Finnish conversation rules encourage observation and reflection before speaking on important, controversial issues. Finns are often more likely to speak openly in one-on-one situations than in a group situation. They try to avoid open conflict and seek consensus via a strategy of listening and observing before speaking. This strategy can also lead to a polite, silent approach that avoids confrontation but leaves core controversial opinions unstated. In contrast, the Swedish and Austrian students in

Box 3.12

A Polish engineer called in a British international salesman to help interpret an American manual for a machine. The problem was the term 'stickup point'. The British salesman had never heard of it and could not make it out from the context. When he got back to England, he telephoned the company and was told the phrase meant 'point of maximum deflection'; it came from the fact that the meter needle would 'stick' in the 'up' position at that point. The US engineer was mystified that its meaning was not obvious.

The present author received an email from an Indian training client which included the following: 'Let me know a tentative plan from your end, including the commercials, so that we start our sales pitch.' On asking an Indian colleague whether the request was for her to create TV commercials, she received the following reply: 'About the mail, I think what is meant is that they would like the following details from you: your tentative calendar (arrival, proposed dates for the program etc); your commercial fee (what the client will have to pay you per batch/whole program or however you would like to price this); minimum and maximum number of participants per batch you would like; number of batches (if there are larger numbers, you may need to look at multiple batches).'

Sources: author's research

the study communicated according to conversation rules that encourage brainstorming. Their goal was to get a variety of views on the table and to use polite verbalization and phrasing of opinions when talking about problems and seeking consensus. They pursued strategies for talking around the problem with the goal of getting closer to a consensus without directly addressing a controversial issue.[108]

According to Aycan (2002), in many developing countries, the pattern of communication in organizations is indirect, non-assertive, non-confrontational and usually directed downwards in terms of hierarchy. There is strong preference for face-to-face communication in business dealings. The context determines the way in which information is coded and understood. As such, there is room for subjective interpretation of the content and intent of the message.[109]

Ethnicity and communication

Only a small amount of communication research has so far focused on the communication behaviours of people from different ethnic backgrounds within the same general culture, despite language being the most salient feature of ethnicity in symbolic terms.[110] What evidence there is suggests that people from different ethnic backgrounds use different communication behaviours. For example, differences have been found in information requesting strategies. Second, differences have been found between the conversational improvement strategies (CISs) used by African and European Americans (AAs and EAs respectively). CISs are used after 'failure' events, such as interactions not running smoothly or expectations being violated. AAs self-reported as more likely to use active and mutual CISs, especially 'other orientation – involving the other person more, having patience with the other person or focusing on them' and 'avoidance – not bringing up unpleasant topics'. EAs, in contrast, said they were more likely to use passive strategies that put the onus on the other person, such as 'giving in, apologizing or agreeing'.[111]

Ethnic differences in conveying and interpreting positive and negative messages have been found. A comparison of encoding and decoding of messages by Australian nationals found that positive messages by Australian and Italian men were decoded less accurately than positive messages by British men. On negative and neutral messages, Italian male speakers were decoded less accurately than Australian and British male speakers. There were fewer differences for female speakers. These results suggested that decoding and encoding were influenced by both social skills and attitudes towards the other interactors.[112]

Gender and communication

There is continuing debate about how differently men and women communicate. Most recent scholarship argues that women and men are more similar than different, but that the differences that do exist between men and women are enough to make a difference in how they create and interpret messages as well as in how they are evaluated as communicators. Within marriage, women and men have similar conceptions of friendships, social support, language use, intimacy, responses to anger, sadness and jealousy, encoding and decoding non-verbal deception and how to maintain conversations. In much communication research, being female or male explains less than five per cent of the variance in communication. However, gender differences are found in smiling and non-verbal sensitivity, flirting behaviours, marital conflict communication, especially the demand – withdraw pattern, and everyday conversational topics.[113]

There are gender differences in the basic message transmission and reception processes. Women are slightly better decoders of affect (feelings and attitudes) and considerably better encoders, especially with strangers.[114] A study showed that, overall, positive messages were decoded worst and negative messages best; but men were worse on both positive and negative messages. Brain imaging research conducted at the Indiana University School of Medicine found that men listened with only one side of their brains, while women used both. A majority of the men showed activity exclusively in the temporal lobe on the left side of the brain, which is associated with listening and speech. The majority of women showed activity in the temporal lobe on both sides of the brain, although predominantly on the left. The right temporal lobe is associated with non-language listening, such as to voice tone. Women often soften their messages by adopting linguistic practices such as using tag questions (for instance, 'That's a good idea, don't you think?') and qualifiers (like 'perhaps', or 'might' instead of 'should'). Gender differences in speaking appear easy to recognize: a study found that people were extremely successful at identifying the gender of speakers from short pieces of written-down talk that lacked any reference to the gender of the speaker. Socio-economic status and other personal characteristics of the listeners had almost no impact on respondents' ability to identify the gender of the speakers. The authors commented: '[The fact] that respondents should be able to recognize gender from such short excerpts, transcribed and out of context, suggests that distinct male and female voices exist and can be heard.' However, recognition of gender varied dramatically for some of the extracts, suggesting that some talk may not be gendered.[115] This may be because gender is not always important, but 'waxes and wanes in the organization of group life'.[116]

In 1975, research was published that seemed to show that men interrupted their female conversation partners more than they interrupted other men. Women interrupted speakers of either gender less than men did. (Interruption is 'a device for exercising power and control in conversation' because it involves 'violations of speakers' turns at talk'.) However, a 1998 meta-analysis of 43 published studies indicated that men were more likely than women to initiate interruptions, but only to a slight extent. This effect was higher, though, in the case of intrusive interruptions as opposed to supportive interruptions. Intrusive interruptions occurred more often in unstructured talk, which suggests that work-related conversations may be less prone to male attempts to dominate.[117]

One summary view of gender differences in language use is that women use language on a more co-operative basis – they are concerned with 'connectedness'. For instance, Carter (2002) found from extended interview and journal data with nine mid-career women that their professional development was created and sustained largely through talk. This talk achieved transformative learning – learning that significantly revised beliefs, attitudes and values, and not just with instrumental, performance-based learning. Instead of analytical, point – counterpoint discussions, the women professionals' conversations were often highly personal and self-disclosing.[118] Men, contrastingly, tend to focus on using language to gain status or establish territory.[119]

Politeness theory research shows that women are more likely than men to use a form that minimizes the threat to the hearer's face. They may:

- Give their orders as requests, such as 'Please would you mind finishing this letter first?'
- Make their statements sound provisional by using qualifiers.
- Use tag questions, as in 'I think we need to call a meeting, don't we?'
- Use disclaimers – 'I may be wrong, but …'
- Use supportive rather than powerful vocabulary.

One researcher has found that use of politeness of these kinds can lead to some women being rated as less intelligent and less well-informed than other people, including other women who do not use them. It is difficult, however, to know whether use of polite forms 'causes' these attributions, because men who use them are not similarly downgraded.[120] There may be a halo effect from the gender of the polite speaker, in the same way as some occupations, such as teaching, have been downgraded in social estimation because they are largely women's occupations.

Some women use body language to express submissiveness. They may take up less physical space in relation to their size than men, hover in the background or lower their eyes when looked at instead of making eye contact. Women managers, in contrast, sometimes show their understanding of the subcultural meaning of non-verbal behaviour by dressing in a masculine way or decorating their offices in a neutral 'sexless' manner.

A review of research on interpersonal conflict and anger shows that women and men do not consistently behave in ways indicated by traditional sex stereotypes. Actual behaviour shows that, if anything, women are more competitive than men, that men have a tendency to avoid conflict and that, except for crying, both genders express anger in the same ways. This applies particularly in private life. In public and social domains, such as work, expectations based on sex stereotypes are stronger and more constraining, while power differences between the genders can also lead to differences in the behaviour of men and women. For instance, one study found indications that females sent less information to supervisors and experienced less information overload than males.[121]

There are several different kinds of explanation for gender differences in communication. One is based on findings that the genders' language style preferences parallel those that distinguish national cultures, that is, direct versus indirect, succinct versus elaborate, personal versus contextual, and instrumental versus affective. This might suggest that women and men differ culturally along the lines of individualism – collectivism, for example, though no conclusive studies have been done. Tannen (1990) also argued that gender differences can best be observed from a cross-cultural approach, one that does not assume that differences arise from men's efforts to dominate women.[122] Instead, masculine and feminine styles of discourse are viewed as two distinct cultural dialects rather than as inferior or superior ways of speaking.[123] While some scholars do not believe that identifying gendered communication styles is important or even appropriate,[124] others, such as Tannen (1990), believe that ignoring those differences is riskier than naming them.

Are women less assertive than men at work? There is some evidence that, compared with male managers, women managers are more inclined to ingratiate; less likely to focus on the importance of their jobs to the organization and society; less likely to claim success, but more likely to report low performance expectations and make attributions to lack of ability; and four times less likely to report that they would move directly to coercive tactics if faced with a non-compliant subordinate. Research has shown that men talk more than women do in formal versus informal tasks and more in public versus private communication. While most members of same-sex task teams produced similar amounts of verbal output, in mixed-sex teams the men produced more than the women. In public, for instance, men spoke for a greater length of time, and men's speech was more on the task, while women's was more reinforcing. Men tended to hold the floor for long periods, so that they dominated and prevented others from speaking. This dominance also implies higher social status and suggests that men believed themselves more competent to complete the tasks or to discuss the issues at hand than were women. Men used a more adversarial style in discussions, while women were likely to ask more questions.[125] (Despite all the above, men perceive women as dominating a discussion even when they contribute as little as 30 per cent of the talk. One explanation is that men think it is the 'natural order of things' for women to contribute significantly less to a group discussion than their male counterparts do. It is, however, possible that women *let* men take more of the air time and that this behaviour reflects their self-perceived lower status – subordinates do the same for managers.) Other findings, though, suggest that both male and female managers displayed 'masculine' characteristics. The environment in a typical organization may socialize women into behaving like 'honorary men'.[126]

Whatever the causes, both stereotype-based impressions of, and actual differences in, ways of communicating tend to be to women's disadvantage at work. For instance, research shows that how credible an individual is judged to be is influenced not only by his/her status and expertise but also by speech style and vocal and facial qualities linked to gender.[127] Women's linguistic styles affected evaluators' attributions of truthfulness, guilt, deception and dominance. A further effect is to render women 'silent'. In those discourses that are more highly valued in society (religious, political, legal, scientific and poetic discourses) women's voices are heard less often than men's.

Communication of older people and those with disabilities

How some older people and some people with disabilities communicate is affected by both intrinsic and externally provoked factors. The clearest communication effects of intrinsic disability occur in people with a hearing impairment. Generally, communicators who are born with a hearing impairment speak with low fluency and mispronunciations; they also have difficulty in controlling how loudly they speak. People who are hard of hearing commonly repeat what has already been uttered and interrupt others

Box 3.13

A study showed that similarity in age influences the likelihood of technical communication between co-workers, but not all that strongly. In a study of a 92-member technical project group, the coefficient of determination between age similarity and communication with other project members was 0.18.

Source: Zengler, T. and Lawrence, B. (1989) 'Organizational demography: the different effects of age and tenure distributions on technical communication', *Academy of Management Journal*, **32**: 331–50

because they do not hear them talking. Some adults who become deaf later in life have difficulty adjusting to their deafness, but a few studies show that many late-deafened people can communicate perfectly well.[128] The intrinsic effects of ageing on other communication abilities are also variable. Though there is little evidence for changes in communication abilities and practices among people below the age of 60, there is some for progressive changes after that age, although there are wide variations from individual to individual. With age, working-memory capacity and processing speed decline in normal adults. This may lead to them having more difficulty in interpreting complex syntax. In addition, older adults have more problems than younger adults in retrieving proper names. This normal, age-related name-retrieval problem can lead interlocutors wrongly to infer more cognitive disability than simply forgetting a name. Also, some older individuals have been shown to be quite insensitive to the needs and concerns of their younger conversational partners; to introduce embarrassing self-disclosures; and to talk excessively with a lack of focus on the general content of the conversation. However, these findings all relate to private-life situations and we have no evidence on whether the same communication problems arise with older people who are at work.

Whatever the intrinsic communication situation of some older people and those with disabilities, they are likely to be affected by the way they are addressed. It has been shown that messages to negatively stereotyped older adults are shorter, less complex and more demeaning in tone. There is clear evidence that patronizing talk from younger individuals to older adults is common. It is likely that being spoken to in these ways affects how older adults communicate.[129] However, except among older people with less education, negative social experiences do not adversely affect older adults' ability to function.[130] The responses of people with disabilities to how others speak to them include shorter interactions, decreased eye contact and low verbal immediacy.[131] These are ways of avoiding communication.

Gaze is influenced by the stereotypes and prejudices about disabled people. People with visible disabilities can be made to feel worthless, unattractive and stressed by how others look at them. This happens especially in the medical context (some doctors perform 'public stripping'), but also within everyday social interaction. When one person in an interaction has a visible impairment the other person gains privileged information and therefore power.[132] According to Morris (1991), 'It is not only physical limitations that restrict us to our homes and those whom we know. It is the knowledge that each entry into the public world will be dominated by stares, by condescension, by pity and by hostility.'[133] People whose disability is invisible may fear 'exposure'.

Religion and communication

Are there differences that may be relevant at work in the communication behaviours of religious and non-religious people and between adherents of different religions? It might be expected that religious people would be unlikely to use blasphemy, perhaps less likely than others to use swear words generally, and possibly be more easily offended by others who do. One study found differences between religious groups in both communication behaviour and the factors underlying it. It found major differences between two denominations – Protestant and Catholic Christians in Northern Ireland – on measures of group identification, self-disclosure, attraction, trust and outgroup contact; on verbal and non-verbal behaviour when speaking with people from the other denominations; and on attitudes and experiences. Such differences imply that there may be a 'religious effect' on communication behaviour generally.[134] Another study found partial support for a relationship between a 'quest' religious orientation and an attentive communicator style, although no more general relationship between religious orientation and communicator style was found.[135]

Communication by religious people about religion has certain characteristics: it cannot be expressed in non-figurative ways, it identifies metaphysical referents that can be grasped but not defined, and it is metaphorical. The metaphors that communicators use become fraught with moral and ethical repercussions, as in the use of war metaphors by Christians.[136] Clearly, this is a long way from the usual discourses of business or management. However, we do not know to what extent people can be 'diglossal' between religious and other ways of communicating or to what extent they may 'interpret' from one to the other before speaking or responding.[137] Some religious groups emphasize spontaneity in prayer, which may carry over to other discourses.[138]

Social class and communication

Many working-class people, particularly those from mainly oral cultures, tend to prefer a speaking style that presumes knowledge shared with the audience, 'shows' rather than 'tells' and implies linkages among a wide range of topics, which need not be presented chronologically. In working-class environments, 'people simply talk and do not have to prove everything that they say.'[139] Systematic studies show that middle-class speakers tend to talk more, use more varied vocabulary and employ more varied grammatical constructions than working-class speakers. There is evidence that class differences in communication exist also on the non-verbal level – appearing already in pre-school age children; middle-class children are less affected than working-class children by whether an instruction is spoken in a positive, neutral or negative tone of voice. However, the notion that in some (sub)cultures language is more simple or primitive is probably wrong. The basic structuring principles on which language is founded appear to be universal, and most linguists now assume that languages do not differ greatly in their underlying structures or in their formal characteristics. In all languages, sentences are hierarchically structured and their interrelationships are equally complex. The same applies to the language of people of different socio-economic status or ethnicity – the rules for constructing sentences are of equal difficulty and complexity in all cases.

Marginalized groups

There is a body of theory and research, termed co-cultural communication, which asserts that in interactions between minority or marginalized group members and those from dominant groups the communication of those from the subordinate group has particular features. Examples of the 25 or more strategies identified in the research range from emphasizing commonalities (focusing on human similarities while downplaying or ignoring cultural differences) to sabotaging others (undermining the ability of dominant group members to take full advantage of their privilege inherent in dominant structures). 'The ongoing research, termed co-cultural theory, explores the common patterns of communication both across and within these different marginalized groups.'[140] Six factors have been identified as central to the co-cultural communication process. These are preferred outcome, field of experience, abilities, situation, perceived costs and rewards, and communication approach. These factors are always present but their roles may vary greatly from one co-cultural interaction to another.

Professional, business and organizational discourses and their reception

Professionals, such as doctors and lawyers, business executives in particular industries and company employees often use vocabulary, phrases and ways of speaking that are unknown to outsiders. These discourses may be the most efficient ways of talking about what are specialist areas, but they also have the effect of reinforcing the speaker's group membership and of excluding people who are not members of the group.

A study in two multinational accounting firms found that the work socialization of trainee accountants led to their professional identities and discourse prioritizing 'the client'. As a result, the authors suggested, management control, friends, family and the profit motive were all 'written out' of the accountants' professional discourse.[141] In certain roles, such as that of clergy, 'immediacy' is important in the evaluation of the role holder. From qualitative research, eight categories of immediacy have been identified: personal interest in the 'client' (parishioner) and its opposite, expressing appreciation for commendable work and its opposite, inclusion and exclusion, unexpected role behaviour and support for personal contributions.[142]

The communication expectations of those with whom professionals deal probably reflect those professionals' usual culturally influenced discourses. A study found that there were both similarities and differences in US and Hong Kong Chinese patients' expectations of communications from medical staff. The main similarities were expectations of task competence, technical competence and information-seeking; important differences were that the US patients looked for friendliness from receptionists and nurses and socio-emotional support from physicians; the Chinese patients did not expect these from their communications with medical staff.[143]

> For most classifications of people, at least some significant differences have been found in their ways of communicating. For the most researched classifications, those of national culture and gender, the significant differences are numerous.

3.4 CONCLUSION

This chapter has been concerned with cultural and subcultural differences in how we communicate. Although there are still large gaps in our knowledge, enough has been found through research to suggest that there are important differences in communication behaviour among groups. Communication states, traits and styles, responses to situations, verbal and non-verbal communication, discourses, messages, language and how it is used, dialects, information-seeking facework, politeness, anxiety and uncertainty management, rapport management, amount of other-regarding preference behaviour messages and conflict management styles all reveal such differences. At least some of the differences in these aspects of communication occur between different national cultural groups, ethnic groups, genders, religious groups, social classes, age groups, people with and without specific disabilities, professions, businesses and organizations. It is too soon to be able to say precisely which differences are to be found between which kinds of groups or whether all such differences will be found eventually between all kinds of groups. It is also likely that group membership is not determinate, whatever its influence. Individual and situational variations will sometimes override or compensate for group differences. However, we do know that effective intercultural communication depends on being aware of possible group differences in ways of communicating.

QUESTIONS AND EXERCISES

1. Discuss in a culturally mixed group whether the communication 'universals' given in Box 3.1 really are universal and consider whether there are others not listed.
2. Discuss ways in which cultural and subcultural differences in rhetorical sensitivity, relational attunement, assertiveness and argumentativeness might affect intercultural communication at work.
3. Create an Observer's Proforma from the dimensions of rhetorical sensitivity given in Section 3.2. Then complete the Proforma during and after observing two colleagues performing one of the following role plays:

   - A student complaining to his/her professor about the grade for an assignment
   - A sales manager communicating a highly ambitious sales target to a commission-only salesman

   Both parties to this role play should be observed, so two observers, each with a Proforma, are needed. Rhetorical sensitivity is about adaptation of communication to an interlocutor; it is therefore necessary that the role plays should continue for at least ten minutes.

4. In a mixed-culture group, discuss the meaning of and attitudes to 'argumentativeness' in the different cultures represented, in the light of the material given in the text.
5. Create an Observer's Proforma from the communicator style variables given in the text plus any others that you consider relevant. Use the Proforma during and after observing colleagues performing one of the role plays in Question 3 (or others from elsewhere in this book). Observe and compare colleagues from different groups (cultures, ethnicities, genders, age groups and so on).

6. Which of the following, if any, apply to people's responses to situations?

   (a) They adjust their goals if the situation requires it.
   (b) They evaluate others differently in different situations.
   (c) They use more energy and time to communicate according to the situation.
   (d) They pursue strategies to achieve their interaction goals.

7. Explain in your own words the key differences between the culture-as-shared-values approach and the culture-in-context (or discourse/practice) approach to communication.

8. How may cultural differences affect how different situations impact on communication behaviour? Give at least one work-related example.

9. Give two work-related examples of restricted codes that might be used in your culture. Then 'translate' them into elaborated code equivalents.

10. In which of the following circumstances, if any, are restricted codes used?

    (a) in routine situations in which conventional 'goals' and plans are 'given' to actors in closed societies;
    (b) when people want to express group membership rather than individual differences;
    (c) when speakers expect marked differences from those with whom they are interacting;
    (d) when there are marked differences of status among interactors.

11. Add as many examples as possible to the list of cultural or subcultural variations in non-verbal behaviour given in the text. Try to find at least one example of each of the following: posture, gesture, gaze, eye contact, facial expression.

12. Enact the following role play: You are a Western senior manager of the Indian manufacturing subsidiary of a French MNC. The annual 360 degree appraisal round has just been completed. A senior Indian team leader, whose skills and expertise are extremely important to the business, has received a very good, though not perfect, appraisal (his lack of experience in leading large teams is showing). You are aware that he will be expecting a substantial salary increase and hoping for a promotion. Your duty is to tell him that, partly owing to the economic climate, he will receive a below-inflation salary increase and no promotion.
    Now enact the same situation with a Japanese senior manager and an Indian subordinate.

13. Discuss the implications (preferably in a work-related context) of the cultural difference that people from some collectivist cultures depend on seeking harmony to achieve the co-operation needed for communication, whereas people from individualist cultures depend on truthfulness. How can intercultural communicators adjust for these differences?

14. The text gives an example of a culture-specific speech act. The example given relates to some societies' obligations on a host to give away possessions that a guest praises. Find other examples.

15. The following are extracts from business complaint letters: (a) 'You have charged us the wrong amount'; 'Please send us a replacement at your earliest convenience'; (b) 'It appears that there is a discrepancy in the invoice compared with the estimate'; 'We would like to request that you consider replacing this item'. Compare (a) and (b) in terms of clarity, effect on the supplier – customer relationship and overall effectiveness. How far do you think your evaluation is related to your culture?

16. What cultural influences might be affecting the two behaviours described in Box 3.7?

17. Using the material given in the text on information-seeking by high- and low-context communicators, analyse which of these types of communicator applies to people you meet for the first time in the near future.

18. Complete the questionnaire.

When managers ask subordinates to do something they should	Strongly agree	Agree	Neither agree nor disagree	Disagree	Strongly disagree
1. Explain the reason for the request and its objective merits					
2. Aim to create a favourable impression, relying on friendliness					
3. Use loyalty appeals					
4. Employ a forceful manner, making demands and setting deadlines					

See the Appendix for guidance on how to score and interpret this questionnaire.

19. How would you most naturally express the following in speaking to a subordinate?
    ■ A criticism of their work
    ■ Bad news about their hoped-for promotion
    ■ An order to do a piece of work
    ■ A compliment on their work
    ■ An apology
    ■ Acceptance of a compliment
    ■ Accepting an offer to work late
    ■ A promise

    Compare your answers with colleagues from a different culture or subculture.

20. Why do you think that AUM theory predicts that an increase in collectivism will produce a decrease in uncertainty in outgroup communication relative to ingroup communication?

21. In a mixed cultural or subcultural group, discuss the contention of rapport management theory that people are as much concerned with their 'rights' in interactions as with their 'face'.

22. You have been a probationary, entry-level employee in a company for the past six months. As a result of a recent personnel rearrangement, Mr Power, an executive from another department, was transferred in as your new boss. Mr Power put many extra duties on you, including personal matters, as soon as he arrived. For example, he asks you to purchase gifts for his family, to pick up his laundry and to buy lunch for him. You are upset about this extra work but so far you follow your boss's orders. He evaluates your work performances; you do not want to upset him. If you do not keep a good relationship with him, your promotion, salary, annual bonus, even job may be in jeopardy.

    Which of the following would be your preferred way of dealing with this situation? Compare your answer with that of as many people as possible from other countries or of different genders.

    1. I would tell Mr Power's supervisor about the problem and ask him to call a meeting between the three of us to discuss the situation
    2. I would tell Mr Power directly that these are NOT my duties
    3. I would talk to my boss for some benefits for doing the extra work – e.g., free time to do his shopping

4. I would still follow his orders but make tiny mistakes so that after a time he will not ask me any more
5. I would file a request with Mr Power's supervisor for a transfer to another department
6. I would continue to follow his requests and do nothing to change the situation.

Question based on: T.J. Knutson, V.R. Smith (Ref. 7)

23. Complete the following questionnaire:

When conflicts arise at work, people from my culture tend to:	Strongly disagree	Disagree	Neither agree nor disagree	Agree	Strongly agree
1. Seek a compromise					
2. Try to get a third party to adjudicate or arbitrate					
3. Try to bring all their concerns out in the open so that issues can be resolved					
4. Collaborate with their colleagues to come up with decisions acceptable to all					
5. Try to win					
6. Try to work with colleagues for a proper understanding of the problem					
7. Try to get a third party to mediate					
8. Place more emphasis on preserving the relationship than on winning					

See the Appendix for guidance on how to score and interpret this questionnaire.

24. What explanation would you suggest for Gudykunst *et al.* (1998)'s finding that uncertainty avoidance is correlated with the expressiveness of a culture's communication style?
25. How might Americans' willingness to self-disclose and their tolerance of criticism in business (by comparison to Koreans') be related to the cultural factors described in Chapter 2?
26. Explain why language can be seen as the 'gateway' to culture.
27. Find examples of terms that are untranslatable into English, either from your own language or by interviewing a native speaker of another language.
28. Tannen (1990) argued that gender differences in communication are based in women's lower power-orientation. How good an explanation do you think this is for the differences described in Section 3.3?

NOTES AND REFERENCES

1. Hewstone, M., Stroebe, W., Codol, J.P. and Stephenson, G.M. (eds) (1988) *Introduction to Social Psychology*, Oxford: Basil Blackwell.

2. Sarbaugh, L.E. (1988) 'A taxonomic approach to intercultural communication', in Kim, Y.Y. and Gudykunst, W.B. (eds) *Theories in Intercultural Communication*, Newbury Park, CA: Sage.

3. Haslett, B. (1989) 'Communication and language acquisition within a cultural context', in Ting-Toomey, S. and Korzenny, F. (eds) *Language, Communication and Culture: Current Directions*, Newbury Park, CA: Sage.

4. Scollon, R. and Scollon, S. (1981) *Narrative, Literacy and Face in Interethnic Communication*, Norwood, NJ: Ablex Publishing Corporation.

5. Papalexandris, N. and Panayotopoulou, L. (2004) 'Exploring the mutual interaction of societal culture and human resource management practices: Evidence from 19 countries', *Employee Relations*, **26**(5): 495–509.

6. Hart, R.P. and Burks, D.M. (1972) 'Rhetorical sensitivity and social interaction', *Speech Monographs*, **39**: 75–91.

7. Knutson, T.J., Smith, V.R. and Han, P.C. (2002) 'A comparison of Taiwanese and American samples on rhetorical sensitivity and conflict style', in Chen, G.-M. and Ma, R. (eds) *Chinese Conflict Management and Resolution*, Greenwood Publishing Group.

8. House, J.H. and Javidan, M. (2004) 'Overview of Globe', in House, R.J., Hanges, P.J., Javidan, M., Dorfman, P.W. and Gupta, V. (eds) *Culture, Leadership, and Organizations: The GLOBE Study of 62 Societies*, Thousand Oaks, CA: Sage.

9. Okabe, R. (2007) 'The concept of rhetorical competence and sensitivity revisited: From western and eastern perspectives', *China Media Research*, **3**(4): 74–81.

10. Sanchez-Burks, J. and Blount, S. (2006) 'Unpacking rapport: the role of behavioral co-ordination and culture in workplace interviews', *Ross School of Business Paper No. 911*. Available at SSRN: http://ssrn.com/abstract=901778, last accessed on 22 December 2010.

11. Langrish, S. (1981) 'Assertive training', in Cooper, C.L. (ed.) *Improving Interpersonal Relations: Some Approaches to Social Skills Training*, London: Gower.

12. Ibid.

13. Anderson, C.M., Martin, M.M., Zhong, M. and Wesst, D. (1997) 'Reliability, separation of factors, and sex differences on the assertiveness-responsiveness measure: A Chinese sample', *Communication Research Reports*, **14**(1): 58–64.

14. Tinsley, C.H., Cheldelin, S.I., Schneider, A.K. and Amanatullah, E.T. (2009) 'Women at the bargaining table: pitfalls and prospects', *Negotiation Journal*, **25**: 233–43, *Marquette Law School Legal Studies Paper No. 09–19*. Available at SSRN: http://ssrn.com/abstract=1397699.

15. Waldron, V.R. (1999) 'Communication practices of followers, members, and proteges: the case of upward influence tactics', *Communication Yearbook*, **22**: 251–99.

16. Kim, M.-S., Aune, K.S., Hunter, J.E., Kim, H.-J. and Kim, J.-S. (2001) 'The effect of culture and self-construals on predispositions toward verbal communication', *Human Communication Research*, **27**(3): 382–408.

17. Galin, A. and Avraham, S. (2009) 'A Cross-cultural perspective on aggressiveness in the workplace: a comparison between Jews and Arabs in Israel', *Cross-Cultural Research*, **43**(1): 30–45.

18. Schullery, N.M. (1998) 'The optimum level of argumentativeness for employed women', *The Journal of Business Communication*, **35**: 346–67.

19. Chen, L. and Yeh, J. B. (2004) 'Traditional value orientations and argumentativeness: A study of Mainland, Hong Kong and Taiwan Chinese', Paper presented at the annual meeting of the International Communication Association, New Orleans Sheraton, New Orleans, LA, URL: http://www.allacademic.com/meta/p113433_index.html.

20. Horvath, C.W. (1995) 'Biological origins of communicator style', *Communication Quarterly*, **43**: 394–407.

21. Hanninen-Salmelin, E. and Petajanieme, T. (1994) 'Women managers: the case of Finland', in Adler, N.J. and Izraeli, D.N. (eds) *Competitive Frontiers*, Cambridge, MA: Basil Blackwell.

22. Birdsall, P. (1980) 'A comparative analysis of male and female managerial communication style in two organizations', *Journal of Vocational Behavior*, **16**(2):183–96.

23. Hall, E.T. (1976) *Beyond Culture*, New York: Doubleday.

24. Gibson, C.B. and Manuel, J. (2003) 'Building trust: effective multi-cultural communication processes in virtual teams', in Gibson, C.B. and Cohen, S.G. (eds) *Virtual Teams That Work: Creating Conditions for Virtual team Effectiveness*, San Francisco, CA: Jossey-Bass.

25. Bernstein, B. (1971) *Class, Codes and Control: Theoretical Studies Toward a Sociology of Language*, London: Routledge and Kegan Paul.

26. Trudgill, P. (1983) (revision of 1974 edition) *Sociolinguistics: An Introduction to Language and Society*, Harmondsworth, Middlesex: Penguin Books.

27. Du-Babcock, B. (2003) 'A comparative analysis of individual communication processes in small group behavior between homogeneous and heterogeneous groups', Proceedings of the 2003 Association for Business Communication Annual Convention, URL: http://www.businesscommunication.org/conventionsNew/ProceedingsNew/2003New/PDF/41ABC03.pdf, last accessed on 22 December 2010.

28. Lauring, J. (2008) 'Rethinking social identity theory in international encounters: language use as a negotiated object for identity making', *International Journal of Cross Cultural Management*, **8**: 343–61.

29. Du-Babcock, B. (1999) 'Topic management and turn taking in professional communications: first- versus second-language strategies', *Management Communication Quarterly*, **12**(4): 544–74.

30. Du-Babcock, 'A comparative analysis of individual communication processes'.

31. Chen, C.Y. and Jackson, P.R. (2008) 'Lingua Franca, communication and knowledge transfer in MNEs'. Available at SSRN: http://ssrn.com/abstract=1374684.

32. Harrison, R. (1974) *Beyond Words: An Introduction to Nonverbal Communication*, Englewood Cliffs, NJ: Prentice-Hall.

33. Gallois, C. and Callan, V.J. (1986) 'Decoding emotional messages: influence of ethnicity, sex, message type and channel', *Journal of Personality and Social Psychology*, **51**(4): 755–62.

34. Becker, M.M., Olson, J.S. and Olson, G.M. (2000) 'How does radical collocation help a team succeed?' Proceedings of the 2000 ACM Conference on Computer supported Cooperative work, Philadelphia, Pennsylvania, United States, 339–46.

35. Murphy, D. (1985) *Muddling Through in Madagascar*, London: Century Press.

36. Rashotte, L.S. (2002) 'What does that smile mean? The meaning of nonverbal behaviors in social interaction', *Social Psychology Quarterly*, **65**(1): 92–102.

37. Grice, H.P. (1975) 'Logic and conversation', in Cole, P. and Morgan, J. (eds) *Syntax and Semantics 3*, New York: Academic Press.

38. Searle, J. (1969) *Speech Acts: An Essay in the Philosophy of Language*, Cambridge: Cambridge University Press.

39. Van Dijk, T.A. (ed.) (1997) *Discourse as Structure and Process: Discourse Studies, A Multidisciplinary Introduction*, Vol. 1, London: Sage.

40. Ibid.

41. Kim, M.-S., Hunter, J.E., Miyahara, A., Horvath, A., Bresnahan, M. and Yoon, H. (1996) 'Individual- vs. culture-level dimensions of individualism and collectivism: effects on preferred conversational styles', *Communication Monographs*, **63**: 29–49.

42. Ibid.

43. Kim, M.-S., and Wilson, S.R. (1994) 'A cross-cultural comparison of implicit theories of requesting', *Communication Monographs*, **61**: 210–35.

44. Kim, M.-S. (2006) 'Cross-cultural comparisons of the perceived importance of conversational constraints', *Human Communication Research*, **21**(1):128–51.

45. Kim *et al.* 'Individual- vs. culture-level dimensions of individualism and collectivism'.

46. Baldwin, J.R. and Hunt, S.K. (2002) 'Information-seeking behavior in intercultural and intergroup communication', *Human Communication Research*, **28**(2): 272–86.

47. Goffman, E. (1959) *The Presentation of Self in Everyday Life*, Garden City, NY: Doubleday.

48. Ting-Toomey, S. (1988) 'A face negotiation theory', in Kim, Y.Y. and Gudykunst, W. (eds) *Theories in Intercultural Communication*, Newbury Park, CA: Sage.

49. Katriel, T. (1991) *Communal Webs: Communication and Culture in Contemporary Israel*, Albany: SUNY Press.

50. Ting-Toomey, S., Gao, G., Trubisky, P., Yang, Z., Kim, H., Lin, S.L. and Nishida, T. (1991) 'Culture, face maintenance, and styles of handling interpersonal conflict: a study in five cultures', *The International Journal of Conflict Management*, **2**: 275–96.

51. Ibid.

52. Merkin, R.S. (2006) 'Uncertainty avoidance and facework: A test of the Hofstede model', *International Journal of Intercultural Relations*, **30**(2): 213–28.

53. Lebra, T. (1971) 'The social mechanism of guilt and shame: the Japanese case', *Anthropological Quarterly*, **44**(4): 241–55.

54. Brown, P. and Levinson, S.C. (1978) 'Universals in language usage: politeness phenomena', in Goody, E.N. (ed.) *Questions and Politeness: Strategies in Social Interaction*, Cambridge, Cambridge University Press.

55. Collier, M.J. (1989) 'Cultural and intercultural communication competence: current approaches and directions', *International Journal of Intercultural Relations*, **13**: 287–302.

56. Stewart, C.M., Shields, S.F. and Sen, N. (1998) 'Diversity in on-line discussions: A Study of cultural and gender differences in Listservs', *Electronic Journal of Communication*, **8**(3/4).

57. Kim, *et al.*, 'Individual- vs. culture-level dimensions of individualism and collectivism'.

58. Spencer-Oatey, H. (2002) 'Managing rapport in talk: using rapport sensitive incidents to explore the motivational concerns underlying the management of relations', *Journal of Pragmatics*, **34**: 529–45.

59. Spencer-Oatey, H. (2005) '(Im)politeness, face and perceptions of rapport: unpacking their bases and interrelationships,' *Journal of Politeness Research: Language, Behaviour, Culture*, **1**(1): 95–119.

60. Pavlidou, T.-S. (2000) 'Telephone conversations in Greek and German: attending to the relationship aspect of communication', in Spencer-Oatey, H. (ed.) *Culturally Speaking: Managing Rapport Through Talk Across Cultures*, London: Continuum.

61. Clark, H. (1996) *Using Language*, Cambridge, UK: Cambridge University Press.

62. Sanchez-Burks and Blount, 'Unpacking rapport'.

63. Berger, C.R. and Calabrese, R.J. (1975) 'Some explorations in initial interactions and beyond', *Human Communication Research*, **1**: 99–112. See also: Berger, C.R. (1987) 'Communicating under uncertainty', in Roloff, M.E. and Miller, G.R. (eds) *Interpersonal Processes*, Newbury Park, CA: Sage.

64. Baldwin, R. and Hunt, S.K. (2002) 'Information-seeking behavior in intercultural and intergroup communication', *Human Communication Research*, **28**(2): 272–86.

65. Ibid.

66. Gudykunst, W.B., Yang, S.M. and Nishida, T. (1985) 'A cross-cultural test of uncertainty reduction theory: comparisons of acquaintance, friend and dating relationships in Japan, Korea and the US', *Human Communication Research*, **11**: 407–55.

67. Gudykunst, W.B. and Hammer, M.R. (1988) 'Strangers and hosts: an uncertainty reduction based theory of intercultural adaptation', in Kim, Y.Y. and Gudykunst, W.B. (eds) *Intercultural Adaptation*, Newbury Park, CA: Sage.

68. Gudykunst, W.B., Nishida, T. and Chua, E. (1986) 'Uncertainty reduction in Japanese–North American dyads', *Communication Research Reports*, **3**: 39–46.

69. Gudykunst, W.B., Sodetani, L.L. and Sonoda, K.T. (1987) 'Uncertainty reduction in Japanese–American/Caucasian relationships in Hawaii', *Western Journal of Speech Communication*, **51**(3): 256–78.

70. Gudykunst, W.B. (1988) 'Uncertainty and anxiety', in Kim, Y.Y. and Gudykunst, W.B. (eds), *Theories in Intercultural Communication*, Newbury Park, CA: Sage.

71. Brashers, D.A. (2001) 'Communication and uncertainty management', *Journal of Communication*, **51**: 477–97.

72. Buchan, N. R., Johnson, E.J. and Croson, R.T.A. (2006) 'Let's get personal: An international examination of the influence of communication, culture and social distance on other regarding preferences', *Journal of Economic Behavior & Organization*, **60**: 373–98.

73. Fitch, K.L. (1994) 'A cross-cultural study of directive sequences and some implications for compliance-gaining research', *Communication Monographs*, **61**: 185–209.

74. Sullivan, J. and Taylor, S. (1991) 'A Cross-cultural test of compliance-gaining theory', *Management Communication Quarterly*, **5**(2): 220–39.
75. Schouten, B.C. (2008) 'Compliance behavior and the role of ethnic background, source expertise, self-construals and values', *International Journal of Intercultural Relations*, **32**(6): 515–23.
76. Oetzel, J.G., Ting-Toomey, S., Yokochi, Y., Masumoto, T. and Takai, J. (2000) 'A typology of facework behaviors in conflicts with best friends and relative strangers', *Communication Quarterly*, **48**(4): 397–419.
77. Triandis, H. (2000) 'Culture and conflict', *International Journal of Psychology*, **35**(2): 145–52.
78. Ting-Toomey, S. and Kurogi, A. (1998) 'Facework competence in intercultural conflict: an updated face-negotiation theory', *International Journal of Intercultural Relations*, **22**: 187–225.
79. Gluckman, M. (1954) *The Judicial Process Among the Barotse of Northern Rhodesia*, Manchester: University Press for the Rhodes-Livingston Institute.
80. Bazerman, M.H., Curhan, J.R., Moore, D.A. and Valley, K.L. (2000) 'Negotiation', *Annual Review of Psychology*, **51**: 279–314.
81. D'Silva, M.U. and Whyte, L.O. (1998) 'Cultural differences in conflict styles: Vietnamese refugees and established residents', *Howard Journal of Communications*, **9**(1): 57–68.
82. Cushman, D.P. and King, S.S. (1999) *Continuously Improving an Organization's Performance: High-speed Management*, Albany, NY: SUNY Press.
83. Tjosvold, D., Hui, C. and Law, K.S. (2001) 'Constructive conflict in China: cooperative conflict as a bridge between East and West', *Journal of World Business*, **36**(2): 166–83.
84. Kim, M.-S. and Leung, T. (2000) 'A multicultural view of conflict management styles: review and critical synthesis', *Communication Yearbook*, **23**: 227–69.
85. Tjosvold, D. and Sun, H.F. (2002) 'Understanding conflict avoidance: Relationship, motivations, actions, and consequences', *International Journal of Conflict*, **13**(2): 146–64.
86. Holta, J.L. and De Voreb, C.J. (2005) 'Culture, gender, organizational role and styles of conflict resolution: a meta-analysis', *International Journal of Intercultural Relations*, **29**(2): 165–96.
87. Thompson, N. (2003) *Communication and Language: A Handbook of Theory and Practice*, Basingstoke: Palgrave Macmillan.
88. Kim, M.-S. (2001), op. cit.
89. Gudykunst, W.B., Matsumoto, Y., Ting-Toomey, S., Nishida, T., Kim, S. and Heyman, S. (1996) 'The influence of cultural individualism–collectivism, self-construals and individual values on communication styles across cultures', *Human Communication Research*, **22**: 507–34.
90. Hofstede, G. (1991) *Cultures and Organizations: Software of the Mind*, London: McGraw Hill.
91. Park, M.Y., Dillon, W.T. and Mitchell, K.L. (1998) 'Korean business letters: strategies for effective complaints in cross-cultural communication', *The Journal of Business Communication*, **35**: 328–45.
92. Ramsey, S.J. (1998) 'Interactions between North Americans and Japanese: considerations of communication style', in Bennett, M.J. (ed.) *Basic Concepts of Intercultural Communication: Selected Readings*, Maine: Intercultural Press.
93. Suzuki, S. (2010) 'Forms of written arguments: a comparison between Japan and the United States', *International Journal of Intercultural Relations*, article in press, March.
94. Armstrong, G.B. and Kaplowitz, S.A. (2001) 'Sociolinguistic inference and intercultural coorientation: a Bayesian model of communicative competence in intercultural interaction', *Human Communication Research*, **27**(3): 350–81.
95. Babcock, R.D. and Du-Babcock, B. (2001) 'Language-based communication zones in international business communication', *The Journal of Business Communication*, **38**: 372–412.
96. Park, *et al.*, 'Korean business letters'.
97. Samovar, L.A. and Porter, R.E. (1985) 'Introduction', in Samovar, L.A. and Porter, R.E. (eds) *Intercultural Communication: A Reader*, 4th edn, Belmont, CA: Wadsworth.
98. Kirra, K.M. (2000) 'Finns in interaction with non-Finns: problematic phenomena perceived as critical incidents', *Intercultural Communication*, **4**: 109–23.

99. Ekman, P. and Friesen, W.V. (1968) 'Nonverbal behaviour in psychotherapy research', in Schlein, J.M. (ed.) *Research in Psychotherapy*, Vol. 3, Washington, DC: American Psychological Association.

100. Matsumoto, D., Olide, A., Schug, J., Willingham, B. and Callan, M. (2009) 'Cross-cultural judgments of spontaneous facial expressions of emotion', *Journal of Nonverbal Behaviour*, **33**(4): 213–38.

101. Birdwhistell, R. (1970) *Kinesics and Context*, Philadelphia: University of Pennsylvania Press.

102. Singhal, A. and Motoko, N. (1993) 'Assertiveness as communication competence: a comparison of the communication styles of American and Japanese students', *Asian Journal of Communication*, **3**(1): 1–18.

103. Oetzel, J., Ting-Toomey, S., Masumoto, T., Yokochi, Y., Pan, X., Takai, J. and Wilcox, R. (2001) 'Face and facework in conflict: a cross-cultural comparison of China, Germany, Japan, and the United States', *Communication Monographs*, **68**(3): 235–58.

104. Ting-Toomey and Kurogi, 'Facework competence in intercultural conflict'.

105. Spencer-Oatey, H. and Xing, J. (2000) 'A problematic Chinese business visit to Britain', in Spencer-Oatey, H. (ed.) *Culturally Speaking*, London: Continuum.

106. Park *et al.*, 'Korean business letters'.

107. Guirdham, M. (2009) *Culture and Business in Asia*, Basingstoke, UK: Palgrave Macmillan.

108. Auer-Rizzi, W. and Berry, M. (2000) 'Business vs. cultural frames of reference in group decision making: interactions among Austrian, Finnish, and Swedish business students', *The Journal of Business Communication*, **37**(3): 264–92.

109. Aycan, Z. (2002) 'Leadership and teamwork in developing countries: challenges and opportunities', in Lonner, W.J., Dinnel, D.L., Hayes, S.A. and Sattler, D.N. (eds) *Online Readings in Psychology and Culture* (unit 15, chapter 8), URL: http://orpc.iaccp.org/, last accessed on 22 December 2010.

110. Thompson, *Communication and Language*.

111. Martin, J.N., Hecht, M.L. and Larkey, L.K. (1994) 'Conversational improvement strategies for interethnic communication: African American and European American perspectives', *Communication Monographs*, **61**(3): 236–55.

112. Gallois, and Callan, 'Decoding emotional messages'.

113. Canary, D.J. and Dindia, K. (eds) (1998) *Sex Differences and Similarities in Communication: Critical Essays and Empirical Investigations of Sex and Gender in Interaction*, Mahwah, NJ: Lawrence Erlbaum Associates.

114. Hall, *Beyond Culture*.

115. Wolfinger, N.H. and Rabow, A. (1997) 'The different voices of gender: social recognition', *Current Research in Social Psychology*, **2**(6): 50–65.

116. Thorne, B. (1993) *Gender Play: Girls and Boys in School*, New Jersey: Rutgers.

117. Anderson, K.J. (1998) 'Meta-analyses of gender effects on conversational interruption: who, what, when, where, and how', *Sex Roles: A Journal of Research*, **39**(3): 225–52.

118. Carter, T.J. (2002) 'The importance of talk to midcareer women's development: a collaborative inquiry', *The Journal of Business Communication*, **39**(1): 55–91.

119. Tannen, D. (1990) *You Just Don't Understand: Women and Men in Communication*, p. 42, New York: William Morrow.

120. Colwill, N. and Sztaba, T.I. (1986) 'Organizational genderlect: the problem of two different languages', *Business Quarterly*, **3**: 64–6.

121. Allen, D.G. and Griffeth, R.W. (1997) 'Vertical and lateral information processing: the effects of gender, employee classification level, and media richness on communication and work outcomes', *Human Relations*, **50**: 1,239–60.

122. Tannen, *You Just Don't Understand*.

123. Mulac, A., Bradac, J.J. and Gibbons, P. (2001) 'Empirical support for the gender-as-culture hypothesis: an intercultural analysis of male/female language differences', *Human Communication Research*, **27**(1): 121–52.

124. Romaine, S. (1999) *Communicating Gender*, Mahwah, NJ: Erlbaum.

125. Stewart, *et al.*, 'Diversity in on-line discussions'.

126. Gardner, W.L. III, Van Eck Peluchette, J. and Clinebell, S.K. (1994) 'Valuing women in management: an impression management perspective of gender diversity', *Management Communication Quarterly*, **8**(2): 115–64.

127. Robinson, K.A. (1998) 'Gender and truthfulness in daily life situations', *Sex Roles: A Journal of Research*, **38**(9): 821–31.

128. McIntosh, A. (2000) 'When the deaf and the hearing interact: communication features, relationships, and disability issues', in Braithwaite, D.O. and Thompson, T.L. (eds) *Handbook of Communication and People with Disabilities: Research and Application*, New York: Lawrence Erlbaum.

129. Nussbaum, J.F. and Baringer, D.K. (2000) 'Message production across the life span: communication and aging', *Communication Theory*, **10**(2): 200–9.

130. Krause, N. and Shaw, B.A. (2002) 'Negative interaction and changes in functional disability during late life', *Journal of Social and Personal Relationships*, **19**(3): 339–60.

131. Fox, S.A., Giles, H., Orbe, M.P. and Bourhis, R.Y. (2000) 'Interability communication: theoretical perspectives', in Braithwaite, D.O. and Thompson, T.L. (eds) *Handbook of Communication and People with Disabilities: Research and Application*, New York: Lawrence Erlbaum.

132. Reeve, D. (2002) 'Negotiating psycho-emotional dimensions of disability and their influence on identity constructions', *Disability and Society*, **17**(5): 493–508.

133. Morris, J. (1991) *Pride Against Prejudice: Transforming Attitudes to Disability*, London: Women's Press.

134. Dickson, D.A., Hargie, O.D.W. and Rainey, S. (2000) 'Communication and relational development between Catholic and Protestant students in Northern Ireland', *Australian Journal of Communication*, **27**(1): 67–82.

135. Baesler, E.J. (1994) 'Religious orientation, persuasion, and communicator style', *The Journal of Communication and Religion*, **17**(2): 61–72.

136. Hostetler, M.J. (1997) 'Rethinking the war metaphor in religious rhetoric: Burke, Black, and Berrigan's "Glimmer of Light"', *The Journal of Communication and Religion*, **20**(1): 49–60.

137. Lessl, T.M. (1993) 'Toward a definition of religious communication: scientific and religious uses of evolution', *The Journal of Communication and Religion*, **16**(2): 127–38.

138. Bland, D. (1990) 'Patterns of spontaneous rhetoric: ways of praying among the charismatic bible temple community', *The Journal of Communication and Religion*, **13**(1): 1–11.

139. Hoyt, S.K. (1999) 'Mentoring with class: connections between social class and developmental relationships in the Academy', in Murrell, A.J., Crosby, F.J. and Ely, A.J. (eds) *Mentoring Dilemmas: Developmental Relationships within Multicultural Organizations*, Mahwah, NJ: Lawrence Erlbaum.

140. Orbe, M.P. (1998) 'From the standpoint(s) of traditionally muted groups: explicating a cocultural communication theoretical model', *Communication Theory*, **8**(1): 1–26.

141. Anderson-Gough, F., Grey, C. and Robson, K. (2000) 'In the name of the client: the service ethic in two professional services firms', *Human Relations*, **53**(9): 1,151–74.

142. Pruitt, W., Koermer, C. and Goldstein, M. (1995) 'How the clergy conveys immediacy to parishioners: an exploratory qualitative study', *The Journal of Communication and Religion*, **18**(1): 35–47.

143. Anderson, C.M. (2001) 'Communication in the medical interview team: an analysis of patients' stories in the United States and Hong Kong', *The Howard Journal of Communications*, **12**(1): 61–72.

chapter four

How Culture Affects Behaviour

Communication, from one point of view, is only a particular form of behaviour. This means that we can increase our understanding of how people communicate by learning more about the influences on their behaviour. There are two ways of doing this. One method is to examine the 'internal factors' (actually constructs), which help explain and may even help predict what people do; Section 4.1 describes these internal constructs. The other is to consider the processes that people go through before and while they are communicating; these processes are covered in Section 4.2. In this book there is no space to introduce these vast subjects (but readers are recommended to follow them up: some relevant books are listed in 'Further Reading'). Instead the focus is on how cultural differences are reflected in these constructs and processes that underlie communication. Chapter 3 argued that there are both universals and culture-specifics in communication; the same applies to the constructs and processes described in this chapter, despite the emphasis here on differences.

4.1 INTERNAL FACTORS

The internal factors covered in this section are motivations, emotions, perceptions, beliefs, assumptions, expectations, attitudes, and the 'self', which covers personality, identity, self-construals and self-esteem. Ethics and morality, which promote some behaviours and act as a restraint on others, are also covered here. The relationships among these variables are shown in Figure 4.1. Perceptions embody an awareness of the environment, both physical and social; beliefs are cognitions to which people attach a degree of credence; assumptions are taken-for-granted beliefs; and expectations are beliefs about the future. Values, and how culture affects them, were described in Chapters 1 and 2.

Motives

Motives are internal responses to needs. They result from inherited drives acting on felt needs. Needs are states of physical or psychological disturbance or discomfort. Needs, then, are conceived as being experienced by the individuals who have them

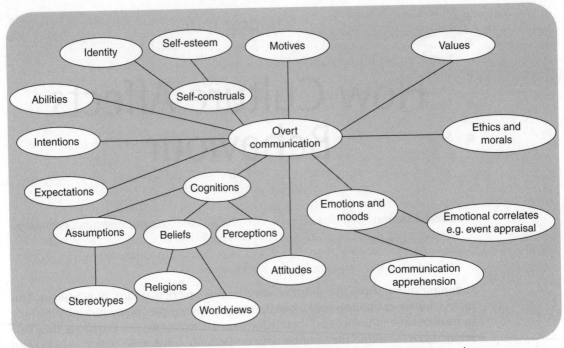

Figure 4.1   *Factors in work communication behaviour that may differ across cultures*

as discomfort or pain, and, with drives, as motivating them to change their condition. Some needs are biological: for food, sex, rest. Others are learned: for esteem, power, self-fulfilment. Others – for security and affection – are intermediate between the learned and the biological needs. Recognizing the needs that we and other people are attempting to satisfy helps in understanding our and their actions better.

At work, motivation and differences in motivational patterns have long been associated with a whole range of outcomes, from productivity to job satisfaction and employee turnover. In a communication context, motivation is a central concept in influencing processes, as well as explaining much about how and why people communicate. Most current theories of motivation originated in the USA and are now being criticized for being culture-specific. For example, it has been argued that the needs for power, esteem and achievement, which feature strongly in Western motivational theories, are not found in all cultures. Achievement, which means individual achievement, may be a motive limited to individualist cultures; similarly, the need for power may not motivate many people in a high power distance culture, such as Malaysia's, where most people accept that they have a 'preordained' position in a social hierarchy. Aycan (2002) suggested that, in developing countries, work motivations differ from Western models in the following ways:

■ The importance of relationships and networking is 'one of the most salient cultural characteristics' – overriding rules and procedures in every aspect of social, political and economic life; acting loyally and to preserve harmony, together with ingroup status, determine who gets organizational benefits.
■ Work is perceived as a duty done in the service of the family and work achievements are valued as enhancing family status. Work is less important than family,

and family reasons are normal excuses for absence. Many organizations are 'families', with paternalistic superior–subordinate relations.

■ Job performance is less valued than good interpersonal relations at work. An intention to do well is as important as goal achievement.

■ Individuals have a low sense of control, self-reliance may be distrusted as disloyalty, and fatalism can lead to low initiative taking.

■ Preserving face is very important, resulting in problems in both giving and receiving feedback.

■ People respect 'authority' rather than rules – a position that is a prescribed norm in Islam and Confucianism. 'Some paradoxical dualities exist in the superior–subordinate relationship. First, there is high respect but also high affection towards the superior. As such, there is an element of both love and fear in this relationship. Second, being an ingroup member, the superior is considered as 'one of us', but, being a person with higher status, s/he is 'unlike us'. Third, superiors have close relationships with their subordinates and are involved in all aspects of their lives, but this does not translate to an informal 'friendship' relationship. Instead, the subordinate–superior relationship is formal and distant.[1]

Research has examined the effects on the structure and strength of achievement motivation of individualist and collectivist cultural orientations. The strength of achievement motivation varied markedly across US, Dutch, Israeli, Hungarian and Japanese samples.[2] Respondents from the USA, a highly individualist culture, demonstrated the strongest tendencies for personal achievement. Respondents from the more collectivist cultures of Japan and Hungary showed the lowest levels of achievement motive. They had a tendency to avoid individual tasks or obligations that involved personal responsibility.

In the literature on culture and work motivation, organizational loyalty or commitment (OC) is a major concern. It has been shown that different cultures conceptualize OC differently. In the USA, for instance, dedication, obligation, integrity and determination emerged as the primary themes, reflecting high individualism. In contrast, four of the five themes from the Japanese sample reflected collectivism: connection, membership, responsibility and co-operation.[3] In Islamic countries, according to a study of 474 employees from 30 organizations in the United Arab Emirates, the Islamic work ethic promotes individuals' commitment to their organization – an effect that might be less clear for the Protestant work ethic, though no comparison was made.[4]

Differences in communication motives are attracting research attention. One such study investigated the communication motives of different ethnic groups. It first identified issues that African Americans (AAs) find relevant to satisfaction in inter-ethnic encounters. These issues were as follows:

■ Acceptance (a feeling of being accepted and respected by the other party)
■ Expressiveness (unrestricted communication of thoughts and feelings)
■ Understanding (interactors feel their meaning is shared)
■ Negative stereotyping
■ Goal attainment (objectives are met through conversation)
■ Powerlessness (AAs feel controlled, manipulated and trapped)
■ Relaxation (feeling relaxed with one's own self-presentation)
■ Relational solidarity (a feeling of closeness or bonding)
■ Shared world view (identity of perspectives or values)

Later research found that powerlessness, relaxation and shared world view were most salient to AAs. In contrast, identity, goal attainment and relational solidarity were most salient to European Americans (EAs). In low-intimacy relationships, such as those at work, authenticity and relational solidarity were most important for EAs, and understanding (task concern), stereotyping and shared world view were most salient for AAs. Both groups emphasized acceptance in low-intimacy relationships, such as those experienced at work.[5]

Regarding subcultures, motivational differences between the genders may have been exaggerated. In research into 1,001 adolescents, girls were not found to have lower achievement orientations than boys. On the other hand, a review of research into women's and men's professional communication found that women's communication motivations were more affiliative and less power-oriented than men's. In a study of age effects on motivation in the German workforce, measures of personal initiative were examined as a function of age, in combination with other demographic and work characteristics. Overall initiative tended to be greater among older people. Initiative in job behaviour showed no significant age differences among male employees, but a negative age-pattern was found for both men's and women's initiative in educational activities.[6]

Emotions

Emotions are feelings. They are linked to needs and motives. For example, a person who is experiencing the emotion of hate may be motivated to seek relief by acts intended to harm another. Emotions have been defined as: 'first and foremost, modes of relating to the environment: states of readiness for engaging, or not engaging, in interaction with that environment'. Aspects of that engagement include: 'modifying inter-individual interactions ... regulating the balance of power ... determining general patterns of social interaction and ... motivating social cohesion'.[7] In the work environment, therefore, communicators must take (sub)cultural variations in emotions into account.

Even in complex situations, such as work-related initial intercultural encounters, feelings generally affect behaviour, although thoughts modify the effect. For instance, it has been shown that, when the situation is complex, being in a positive mood triggers more confident, direct interpersonal behaviours than being in a negative mood. Again, during complex negotiations, people in a positive mood had more ambitious goals and higher expectations and bargained in a more co-operative and integrative way, leading to greater success, compared with people in a negative mood.[8]

It has been shown that six basic kinds of emotion are perceived by most people: love, happiness, surprise, anger, sadness and fear. This finding has been replicated across diverse cultures and age groups. Although the experience of basic moods and emotions tends to be universal, their expression and correlates may have both universal and culture-specific elements.[9] In regard to expression, 'Classic research revealed that the intended emotions in posed expressions were recognised by members of many different cultural groups at rates better than predicted by random guessing. However, recent research has also documented evidence for an in-group advantage, meaning that people are generally more accurate at judging emotions when the emotions are expressed by members of their own cultural group rather than by members of a different cultural group.'[10]

Among the 'correlates' of emotions are antecedent events (which trigger feelings), event categorization (e.g., as humiliating or flattering), appraisal of the event according to its category (e.g., humiliation as harmful, flattery as pleasant), physiological reaction (like sweating or blushing), action readiness (to run, to leave the room), emotional behaviour (like insulting vengeful speech or crying) and regulation (people can either inhibit or enhance responses). A review article reported that both cultural similarities and differences have been found for nearly all these correlates of emotions. For example, appraisal includes evaluating how controllable the outcome of the event seems and what causes it. These elements of appraisal seem to be universal, but the weight placed on the different elements varies across cultures. The importance of certain emotions also varies across cultures. Variations in cultural collectivism or individualism seem to explain these differences.[11]

People conceptualize emotion differently – in the West, emotion is usually considered separate from reason, whereas the Eastern ideal is that emotion is a part of reasoning. This difference influences how people deal with their emotional experiences. In one study, directors from 48 separate factories in the People's Republic of China said they experienced intense pleasant and unpleasant emotions as a result of social, moral and material/economic conditions. Some directors expressed these emotions in culturally conforming ways, using reason to understand them; others vented or suppressed them, contrary to their cultural norm. The study concluded that those directors who used culturally conforming methods dealt with their emotions better.[12] Another study showed that African Americans self-reported different behaviours as revealing that they felt shy from those reported by White Americans; this implies that behaviours displaying shyness feelings may be culture-specific.[13] Finally, a cross-cultural comparison of the implications of self-disclosure found differences in the Eastern and Western concepts of 'sincerity'.[14]

Subculturally, there are findings of emotional differences between genders and between people with different types of disability. Women managers may be more responsive to emotional issues than men, as shown in Table 4.1. Deaf and hard-of-hearing technical professionals may develop emotional barriers to face-to-face communication. For example, a deaf man who worked as a systems analyst for Procter & Gamble said he was still learning to work on projects as part of a team. 'I grew up with a strong preference for solitary activities. This has been one of my greatest challenges.'[15]

Communication apprehension

Unsurprisingly, perhaps, the major negative effect of fear of communicating, or communication apprehension (CA), is on communication, although it also affects job satisfaction. Individuals who are high in communication apprehension – whether about speaking or listening – are likely to be less willing to listen than others are and to be poor communicators.[16] For instance, CA reduces people's tendency to talk to doctors or seek out health information, though it does not affect health-related behaviours such as taking exercise, going to health fairs or using tobacco.[17] CA may be culturally induced: Swedish children were found to be more apprehensive than North American children and older children (ages 9–11) more apprehensive than younger.[18] A comparison of

Table 4.1   *Gender differences in the emotional responsiveness of managers*

Emphasis in interpersonal relationships	Women housing managers	Men housing managers
With own team	Understanding of people; sensitivity; care for individual feelings and development; rich perception of human beings	Support own team; look after their interests; defend them to the hilt
With clients	Empathy; relationships; understanding of different needs	Can use pressure groups

Based on: Sparrow, J. and Rigg, C. (1993) 'Job analysis: selecting for the masculine approach to management', *Selection and Development Review*, **9**(2): 5–8

Korean, Hawaiian and US students found that high CA (and low argumentativeness) may be a function of culture-level collectivism.[19]

However, there is evidence that who suffers from communication fear, and when, is not stereotypical. The results of one study indicated that Middle Eastern and European subjects in the USA reported levels of apprehension well *below* statistical norms previously established by US subjects, while Asian and Latin American subjects reported levels just slightly below those norms when communicating in their native languages. All groups indicated that CA was more of a problem when speaking in English, with Asians and Latin Americans reporting the highest levels. Women were slightly more apprehensive overall when communicating in either language, but women in the Latin American sample reported less apprehension than men in every context except public speaking. Neither the subjects' number of years speaking English nor the length of time living in the USA correlated with CA.[20] CA in a first language is a much better predictor of apprehension in a second language than is self-perceived competence in that second language.

Thus, if CA is culturally induced, it nevertheless varies between subgroups. CA is probably personal, though affected by (sub)culture. Among Chinese college students in Taiwan, individuals who held more independent views of the self and who received more encouragement from their teachers to speak up were less likely to be high in CA, though family communication patterns were not shown to have any effect.[21] Women were found to be higher in CA (men are higher in shyness), but it was suggested that this might be linked to cultural norms and stereotypes about gender rather than biological sex. It was not related to self-perceived competence in speaking a language.[22]

Some individuals are apprehensive about communicating with members of other ethnic groups specifically, rather than in general. Such individuals are more likely to be ethnocentric. Inter-ethnic communication apprehension (IECA) affects whether and how people attempt to maintain relations with people from other ethnic groups. High IECAs are less likely than low IECAs to use strategies to maintain inter-ethnic relations. These strategies include performing duties and sharing responsibilities (task), emphasizing common affiliations (networking), being optimistic, cheerful and uncritical (positivity), directly discussing the relationship (openness) and stressing the desire to remain in the relationship (assurance). High IECAs may in fact *be* less willing to remain in inter-ethnic relationships, and that may be why they use so few relation maintenance strategies.[23]

Scholarship on CA has been criticized as biased by the individualist assumption that communication 'approach' is more desirable than communication 'avoidance'. While it is accepted that extreme forms of communication avoidance and lack of verbal assertiveness can be a handicap in any culture, the view that communication avoidance is solely a deficiency is linked to the Western ethnocentric preoccupation with the self.[24]

Emotional intelligence

Emotional intelligence (EI – also referred to as EQ) is a factor now widely considered to affect work behaviour,[25] and has been linked to leadership (especially transformational leadership), effectiveness in teams, and interviewee performance in interviews.[26] It has been defined as the 'accurate appraisal and expression of emotions in oneself and others and the regulation of emotion in a way that enhances living', and as 'the ability to be aware of one's own feelings, be aware of others' feelings, to differentiate among them, and to use the information to guide one's thinking and behaviour'.[27] Emotional intelligence appears to be distinct from, but positively related to, other intelligences; it is an individual difference, wherein some people are more endowed, and others are less so; it develops over a person's lifespan and can be enhanced through training; and it involves, at least in part, a person's ability to identify and to perceive emotion (in the self and in others), as well as possession of the skills to subsequently understand and manage those emotions successfully.[28]

The research so far on EI is extremely limited. EI is 'a multidimensional skill – not an isolated or simple ability – encompassing a range of constructs with complex relationships to each other'. Few of these constructs have been rigorously researched in a cross-cultural setting. One study, however, used measures of self-awareness, self-regulation, motivation, empathy and social skills as the constructs comprising EI and tested their interrelationships and their links to supervisor–subordinate conflict management across seven countries. The findings are shown in Table 4.2. As the researchers noted, there were many limitations on the study to prevent its findings being generalized; nevertheless, it does point to some cultural differences in the constructs making up EI and to the relationships between those constructs and conflict management.[29] Subsequently, Sharma *et al.* (2009) reported that a comparison of German and Indian factor structures composing EI, including perception of emotions, managing own emotions, managing others' emotions and utilization of emotions, showed differences, not all of which could be accounted for by individualism–collectivism, on which, they considered, the two countries' cultures differed most markedly.[30]

Table 4.2 Relations among constructs comprising EI and supervisor-subordinate conflict management across seven countries

	Bangladesh	Hong Kong and Macao	Greece	Portugal	China	South Africa	USA
Self-awareness linked to self-regulation and social skills	yes	yes	yes	yes	no	yes	yes
Self-regulation linked to social skills	yes	yes	not significant	yes	yes	yes	yes
Self-regulation linked to empathy	yes	yes	yes	no	no	no	yes
Motivation* linked to empathy	yes	no	yes	yes	no	yes	yes
Motivation linked to social skills	yes	yes	no	yes	no	no	yes
Motivation linked to a problem-solving style of conflict management	yes	yes	yes	yes	yes	yes	yes
Motivation linked to a bargaining style of conflict management	no	no	no	no	no	no	yes

* defined as the ability to remain focused on goals despite setbacks, to operate from hope of success rather than fear of failure, delay gratification and accept change to attain goals.

Based on: Rahim, M.A. and Psenicka, C. (2002) 'A model of emotional intelligence and conflict management strategies: a study in seven countries', *The International Journal of Organizational Analysis*, **10**(4): 302–26.

Box 4.1

Where the American people see only two options (something is either true or false), French people see three options: true, somewhat true, and false, and they expect the second to be the most common. I have always had problems explaining this to my American clients who get into difficult situations because of this phenomenon.

Source: Taquet, J., 'Is it lying?: A cross-cultural perspective', *JB Intercultural Consulting.* URL: www.culture-at-work.com/lyingxc.html, *last accessed on 22 December 2010*

Box 4.2

■ Where some White males perceive a hierarchical structure open to talent and energy, people from ethnic minorities, women and people with disabilities often perceive a glass ceiling. For instance, in the Netherlands, in a diverse organization, ethnic minority employees experienced less person-related communication at work and perceived higher levels of unequal treatment of minorities than ethnic majority employees.[a]

■ Americans scored significantly higher than Israelis on a Protestant ethic scale, but were consistently more deterministic in their interpersonal perceptions than Israelis when asked to rate on the basis of past information, the probabilities of a person being at present a 'mental patient' or a 'successful businessman'.[b]

■ A country's relative size, in combination with linguistic similarity, predicts the likelihood of people from one country perceiving another as less sympathetic, more arrogant and less similar to themselves. These findings come from research into Dutch/German, Belgian/French and Dutch-Belgian versus French-Belgian attitudes towards Holland.[c]

Sources: (a) Dinsbach, A.A., Feij, J.A. and de Vries, R.E. (2007) 'The role of communication content in an ethnically diverse organization', *International Journal of Intercultural Relations,* **31**(6): 725–45

(b) Goitein, B. and Rotenberg, M. (1977) 'Protestantism and retrospective labeling: a cross-cultural study in person perception', *Human Relations, ***30***: 487–97

(c) van Oudenhoven, J.P., Askevis-Leherpeux, F., Hannover, B., Jaarsma, R. and Dardenne, B. (2002) 'Asymmetrical international attitudes', *European Journal of Social Psychology,* **32**(2): 275–89

Perceptions

Some writers on culture, especially those concerned with culture and management, place perceptions centrally in their analysis of how culture affects individuals' behaviour. For example, according to Johansson (1994), culture 'serves to highlight certain aspects of a situation and downplay others. It frames reality as observed and interpreted, and provides behavioral rules as a guide for acting on it. Culture involves behavioral constraints imposed by society. This suggests that culture is a strong determinant of observed behavior.'[31] Robinson (1997) agreed with the centrality of culture in perception, arguing that culture 'lies at the very roots of perception'.[32] Box 4.2 gives some examples of how work-related perceptions can vary with culture.

Cultural influences on social perceptions are of particular interest for this book. People from different cultures exhibited 'dramatic and consequential differences' in constructing social meaning – that is, in their perceptions of the meaning of interpersonal behaviour, according to research by Menon *et al.* (2000).[33] The particular study looked at the effect of creating 'need for closure' by increasing the time pressure on people to make attributions of what caused others to act as they did. Previously, it had been thought that a universal information-processing strategy would apply under increased time pressure, leading people to attribute more behaviour to the observed actor's personal dispositions and less to their situation. However, although this research found this predicted pattern among North Americans, among Chinese people the need for closure increased attributions not to personal, but to group, dispositions. This finding is consistent with past findings that North American and Chinese attributors had different implicit social theories. North Americans conceived of individuals as autonomous agents; Chinese conceived of groups as autonomous.

It is worth noting that these findings do not mean that individuals' social perceptions are rigidly determined by their culture. Instead they are guided by it only when it is activated – as in the case of heightened need for closure. Additionally, individuals may have other tools for understanding the social world in addition to their 'native' cultural theory. For instance, bicultural people may have developed 'foreign' cultural meaning systems that may be activated to guide their social perceptions.

The group they identify with, the perceived person's communication style, the perceiver's social identity and the situation all affect how people perceive one another. For instance, men are more likely to be evaluated more highly than women in ambiguous situations or in the presence of competent women, women in 'male' contexts or women who behave in ways that are incongruent with their sex-roles. These biases result in women managers often being perceived as less committed to the organization than their male counterparts are. Because commitment is linked to lower absenteeism, lower turnover rates and increased intention to stay with the firm, negative perceptions of women's commitment may be linked to their lower rates of pay and career progress. These biases apply less in clear-cut situations, for example where quality of performance is obvious, than in more ambiguous cases.

Two factors can combine to shape evaluations of commitment. First, single female managers and male and female managers with families evaluate traditional behaviours differently from their single or childless married counterparts, even when controlling for the specific behaviour described and the individual characteristics of the actor. Second, work group gender demographics shape managers' beliefs to the degree that managers conform to the beliefs of the majority. Thus, the more numerically male-dominated the work group, the more likely it is that traditional indicators of commitment, such as working long hours, will be used.[34]

Which particular social perceptions are activated also depends on the situation. A survey of 284 American executives affected by foreign or domestic acquisition of their company investigated their perceptions of (organizational) cultural differences, system changes in the acquired company, acquisition negotiations, executives' reasons for staying or leaving after the acquisition and post-acquisition outcomes for the organization. It was found that the executives' perceptions differed significantly in all five areas according to whether the executive was involved in a foreign or domestic acquisition.[35] Finally, cross-culturally similar perceptions can lead to different reactions. Vigoda (2001) found no significant differences between British and Israeli civil servants' perceived levels of organizational politics. Despite this, the British reacted with significantly higher intentions of leaving the organization, lower levels of loyalty and job satisfaction and a stronger sense that their expectations had not been met.[36]

Beliefs

Belief systems 'help people perceive, interpret, and predict events (e.g., predicting whether people will succeed or fail) and select courses of action (e.g., deciding whether to help a victim of misfortune.)'[37] Belief systems represented by everyday sayings have been related to different levels of prejudice towards a variety of socially stigmatized groups, including racial minorities, gay men and lesbians, 'overweight' persons and women. It has been argued that a taxonomy of beliefs that vary cross-culturally would 'help to move the field beyond its excessive reliance on values'. Cross-cultural variation has been demonstrated in core beliefs about how the world works, locus of control, belief in a just or unjust world, religion, and beliefs about work.

Core belief systems

Six fundamental belief systems about how the world works have been identified and shown to vary from culture to culture. According to Bond and Smith (1996), these dimensions of beliefs, along which countries may be arrayed, overlap only moderately with measures of values for the same countries.[38] This may mean that they have the potential to be used as a different or additional way of analysing culture. These belief systems are authoritarianism, social dominance orientation, Protestant work ethic, humanitarianism–egalitarianism, beliefs about the malleability of human attributes and beliefs about diversity.[39]

- Authoritarianism has been defined as consisting of three factors: submission to society's established authorities, holding to conventions that they seemingly endorse, and support for aggression towards people who break society's rules or conventions. Cross-cultural studies have shown that some people in many cultures score high on authoritarianism (Canada, Ghana, Russia, South Africa, USA included), though in varying numbers. For instance, a greater proportion of people high in authoritarianism was found in the USA than in Russia.
- Social dominance orientation (SDO) refers to the belief in and support for a natural hierarchy among individuals and groups. SDO has been validated in the USA, Canada, Taiwan, Israel and China, but its expression varied across cultures. In the USA, people who strongly agreed with SDO blamed people in low-status positions (such as poverty) for their misfortunes. However, in Taiwan, people who strongly agreed with SDO tended to believe that people's misfortunes were due to forces outside themselves. Agreeing with SDO predicted a tendency to justify inequality in the culturally endorsed manner. There were also within-culture variations in levels of SDO; in general, people in higher status positions were more likely to agree strongly with SDO, although their level of support depended on the context and situation.[40] One study found that men supported SDO more than women and that this varied little with culture, situation or context.
- The Protestant work ethic (PWE) is an individualist belief system that stresses successful outcomes for anyone who works hard, and attributes failure to personal factors such as lack of effort and weakness of character. Tests of PWE beliefs among university students in 13 nations (including India, Germany, USA and Zimbabwe), found that, in general, wealthy countries were less likely to endorse PWE beliefs than countries that were not wealthy. This may be because striving for success is more necessary and useful in poorer societies. The research also found a strong

correlation between PWE scores and power distance scores. Of the three European countries in the sample, Great Britain and Germany ranked low on most measures of PWE, whereas Greece ranked much higher.[41]

■ Humanitarianism–egalitarianism (H–E) is a belief in and support for equality, social justice and concern for others. It is a belief central to relationship-oriented cultures, such as Norway's, but has also been referred to as an aspect of a US core value, despite that country's high masculinity (achievement) rating.

■ Beliefs about the malleability of human attributes refer to beliefs about whether people can change in their human qualities, such as morality, personality and intelligence. Opposing views on malleability have been found in different cultures (USA, Hong Kong and France).

■ Beliefs about diversity itself. These are positive or negative attitudes towards ethnic diversity, other specified ethnic groups and women's equality. These beliefs correlated with levels of awareness of racial privilege. Diversity beliefs were also correlated with ethnicity and gender – in sum, with the position of the belief holder's group in society, although the relationship was far from one to one.

Locus of control

Locus of control scale is a set of beliefs about what controls the outcomes of an individual's actions. In particular they concern whether factors internal or external to the individual have more influence. Locus of control beliefs are important in predicting individual behaviour. They are closely related to cultural differences in individuals' experiences of control, harmony and submission to their environment. Studies have reported a number of mean differences between country samples in locus of control scores; for instance, Oriental Asians, particularly Japanese, consistently showed higher external locus of control scores than North American Caucasians. A study in 43 countries found three different dimensions related to locus of control, which varied cross-culturally as follows:

■ Eastern European countries endorsed harmony with the environment; most other countries endorsed mastery of the environment.

■ Cultural collectivism and power distance predicted low scores on internal locus of control.

■ Four Asian countries endorsed items asserting the role of luck or chance in life, but without an implication of failure. An East German sample produced an extreme negative measure on this dimension.[42]

Belief in a just or unjust world

Rank ordered 'just world' belief and 'unjust world' belief scores from 12 countries (1,700 psychology students) correlated significantly with power distance and individualism. Few sex differences were found within each society, but, within societies, richer and more powerful individuals were more likely to believe in a just world. However, belief in a just world and belief in an unjust world are independent variables, not highly negatively correlated. This made it possible for a wealth-polarized country, India, to rank first in both belief in a just world and belief in an unjust world. Of three European countries in the sample, Great Britain and Germany ranked far lower in terms of just world beliefs than Greece.[43]

Religion

Religious belief is clearly a strong influence on behaviour, although different religions do not differentiate greatly in what they judge to be virtues. Written documents from Confucianism and Taoism (China), Buddhism and Hinduism (South Asia), Athenian philosophy, Judaism, Christianity, and Islam (the West), converged on six virtues: courage, justice, humanity, temperance, wisdom and transcendence. The effects of religious belief on communication have already been introduced in Chapter 3. Research has shown that communal identity and a sense of the importance of community, institution and hierarchy were strong among religious groups such as Roman Catholics in Australia. These beliefs were reinforced by ritual, story and the variety of social rituals that accompany such events as first communion.[44]

Religion's influence on behaviour is seen at work as elsewhere, affecting moral judgements, attitudes to wealth and ways of gaining it, such as earning interest on capital, among other factors. Most religions view work in a positive light. When data from 44,030 individuals in 39 countries were used to test the influence of religion on work values, they showed that Buddhism, Hinduism and Islam (but not Christianity) had a positive influence on extrinsic work values, while all four religions showed a positive relationship with intrinsic work values. (However, those who reported no religions affiliation also viewed work values positively.)[45] Muslims believe that work is a means of worshipping God; thus, in contrast to the PWE, which places a high value on most work whatever its content, Islamic religious belief affects attitudes to the content of work. For example, producing or selling alcohol or working in 'usurious' occupations, such as Western-style banking, are prohibited. In addition, Islam provides a complete set of guidelines for conducting economies in accordance with Islamic teachings, specifying how to deal with such problems as unemployment and inflation.[46,47]

A study of 277 Muslim immigrants to the USA found that acculturation to US organizational practices was related to different factors from those that affected acculturation in private and/or social lives. Willingness to acculturate to the US national culture was promoted by collectivism (presumably because collectivists try to harmonize with the surrounding culture), and affected by religious beliefs and practices (the stronger and more active their religious beliefs, the more individuals clung to their national culture), gender, education (male and more educated respondents were more willing to integrate) and years lived in the USA. Factors influencing acceptance of US organizational cultures, however, included acculturation to the US national culture but also how much discrepancy in work cultures the person perceived. Despite this, acculturation to US organizational cultures still occurred more readily: most were more inclined to retain their original national culture for their private lives but accepted US organizational cultures. More educated Muslims perceived greater discrepancies between the US and 'own country' organizational cultures; other demographic variables, collectivism and degree of religiosity were unrelated to this variable.[48]

Work-related beliefs

In addition to other beliefs, people also, of course, hold beliefs that are more specifically related to their work. Beliefs about what is important can affect which of the stimuli bombarding managers and others at work are attended to; beliefs about causal relations can affect choice of strategy or action. One cross-cultural analysis found significant differences in beliefs about money, business ethics, corporate social responsibility and *guanxi* among youths in two Asian economies – Hong Kong and Singapore – from those in two Western economies – Canada and Hawaii.[49] 'Western' Christians (Australian) and non-Western Buddhists (Sri Lankan) reportedly had similar perceptions about the meaning of work, except that Sri Lankans seemed to be more strongly committed to hard work and did not endorse the belief that hard work leads to success as enthusiastically as Australians did.[50]

Against these findings of a link between national culture and work-related beliefs, however, a study in five Hungarian firms with Anglo-Saxon or Western management found that factors such as national culture, functional area, education, age, rank and gender had relatively little influence on beliefs about company strategy compared with the factor of whether or not an individual was located in a unit favourably affected by that strategy.[51] In fact, there is no conclusive evidence on any relationship between national-cultural background and beliefs about strategic issues. One study, for example, found a positive relationship between national culture and the expressed preferences of US and Japanese managers towards various generic strategies; another, on the other hand, failed to find a relationship between the perceived importance of strategic goals and the national culture of managers.

As far as subcultural variation in beliefs is concerned, the issue is far from clear-cut. In most cases, members of different subcultures within a culture share the same core beliefs. Some feminist scholars, however, have described the female world view as significantly different from the male world view. Gilligan (1982), arguing from a psychological perspective, stated that female identity revolves around interconnectedness and relationship. Conversely, 'Male identity stresses separation and independence.'[52] These ways in which concepts of social relationships (and their accompanying communication patterns) differ between genders are argued to be parallel to gender differences in world view. Certainly, there is some evidence that, cross-culturally, males are consistently higher on social dominance orientation than females, reflecting status and power differences between males and females across cultures. Among professional women, having an internal locus of control is negatively linked to perceptions of role ambiguity, role overload and nonparticipation in the workplace. Both male and female workers with higher externality scores report higher levels of career dissatisfaction and illness.[53] Gender-based world views may be reflected in basic work-related beliefs such as those about requesting a higher salary. Women's salary requests and outcomes are lower than men's, and it has been shown that this is linked to their beliefs about requesting a higher salary.[54] Opposing views on human malleability have been found across age groups (elementary school, middle school and college). A study of 292 Russian managers' beliefs found, together with many similarities among responding groups, some differences depending upon managerial level, age and gender. These differing beliefs included those relating to humanistic belief systems and work ethics.[55]

Assumptions

Assumptions are taken-for-granted, unquestioned beliefs. This 'knowledge', which people in different cultures and subcultures take for granted, is extensive. It affects their behaviour, including their communicative behaviour, in many ways. It influences surface culture, as well as rituals, status differentials and values, including:

- Roles – what is done and not done by people in various categories, such as male/female, supervisor/subordinate, teacher/student.
- Work – how much emphasis is placed on social interaction versus task completion; how supervisors treat subordinates.

- Time – how late a person can be without apologizing; whether it is more important to be on time for the next appointment or to complete the business at hand.
- Space – when a person will feel that their 'territory' has been invaded; how acceptable open-plan offices are; how many people can get into a lift before they feel crowded.

Writing specifically in a work context, Schein (1992) actually defined culture in terms of assumptions: 'I am defining culture as the set of shared, taken-for-granted implicit assumptions that a group holds and that determines how it perceives, thinks about and reacts to its various environments.'[56] Norms are one manifestation of these assumptions, but it is important to remember that behind the norms lies this deeper taken-for-granted set of assumptions that most members of a culture never question or examine.

Assumptions undoubtedly affect behaviour and are hard to detect, sometimes even by the person holding them. At work, relevant assumptions include those held by managers about their subordinates' work motivations, those that negotiators hold about their opponents and those that people hold about the members of other social groups. For instance, assumptions about the stereotypical characteristics of women (emotional, sensitive, nurturing and interdependent) and men (independent, dominant, emotionally inhibited and goal-directed) are strong unspoken influences on their relative treatment in terms of job segregation and career advancement. Three sets of assumptions that are especially important for intercultural communication are agency, ethnocentrism and stereotypes.

Agency

Agentic social beings are goal-directed, carry out actions in pursuit of goals, are responsible for their actions, and may potentially be praised or blamed for their actions. Cultural differences arise in whether or not groups, as opposed to individuals only, are perceived as agentic. In three East Asian cultures (Hong Kong, Japan and Korea), an equal level of agency was conferred on both individuals and groups, but in three English-speaking cultures (Australia, UK and USA) and two continental European cultures (Belgium and Germany) the individual person was seen to be more agentic than groups. The English-speaking version of individualism placed still more emphasis on the agency of the individual than the continental European version.[57] Differences in assumptions as fundamental as this to attributions of, for instance, responsibility and blame must clearly influence work communication.

Ethnocentrism

A biased set of assumptions in favour of one's own ethnic group has been given the label ethnocentrism. To some degree, biases in favour of people's own in-group and in opposition to outgroups are 'natural'. There are studies that show that people from all cultures:

- Think of what goes on in their own culture as natural and correct and what goes on in other cultures as not natural or not correct;
- Perceive their own customs as universally valid;
- Believe their own norms, roles and values are correct, particularly as concerns their own immediate ingroup or subculture;

■ Favour and co-operate with ingroup members while feeling hostile towards out-groups.[58]

These points apply most strongly, however, where the members of a social group-ing are concentrated and in day-to-day contact with other members (as in the case of, say, the Greek–Cypriot community in areas of London), even if the grouping is subordinate and low in attractiveness. It applies less strongly where the members of a subordinate social grouping are spread out among the members of the dominant social grouping.

Ethnocentrism is rewarded in interactions within an ethnic group: high ethnocen-trics are more likely to conform to its norms, roles and values and therefore to be accepted. A work-based task-group study found that ethnocentrism varied, depend-ing on whether respondents were reporting on task aspects or relationship aspects of their inter-group dynamics. In some conditions groups even seemed to minimize or invert their usual ethnocentric tendencies. Over allocation of resources, groups mini-mized their advantage or emphasized their disadvantage – in 'marked contrast to the usual ingroup–outgroup pattern in which groups see themselves favorably and others unfavorably'.[59] An obvious explanation of this last behaviour, however, is that the groups were motivated to lower the favourability of their self-perceptions in order to try to obtain more resources.

Stereotypes

A stereotype is a stable set of beliefs or preconceived ideas that the members of a group share about the characteristics of a group of people. The concept of stereotype has gradually lost its earlier sense of irrationality and prejudice. Instead, stereotyping is now considered an ordinary cognitive process in which people categorize in order to avoid information 'overload'. There is much evidence that people apply stereotypes to form complex images of others from first impressions. For instance, when 80 students guessed the attitudes of several people whose pictures they were shown, it was found that they expected men to have conservative attitudes on child discipline, feminism, immigration and homosexuality, while women were expected to be conservative on religion. Attractiveness was linked to liberalism, age to conservatism. The research also revealed that the participants used sub-stereotypes: the age and attractiveness of the target modified the impression based purely on gender.[60]

People are more likely to create stereotypes of members of different groups from themselves. Stereotypes also tend to favour ingroups. Outgroup members are believed to be less attractive, capable, trustworthy, honest, co-operative and deserving than in-group members. As a result, people behave differently towards outgroup mem-bers. Because stereotypes are constructed socially, group discussion makes members' stereotypes more extreme.[61] A Dutch study showed that participants' stereotypes were 'domain-specific' – for instance, they varied according to whether people were think-ing of an ethnic outgroup as neighbours, colleagues, classmates or (marital) partners. The study also showed that how much social distance people imposed as a result of stereotypes varied according to the particular attributions in the stereotype – for instance, traditionalism, deviancy or low education/dark skin. (Imposing or main-taining social distance refers to avoiding intimacy or spending time with another person.[62])

Demonstrations that stereotypes affect behaviour include showing that people whose concept of rudeness was primed interrupted the experimenter more quickly

Box 4.3

- An Indian woman doctor, who lived for many years in the Middle East and worked extensively with colleagues from different countries in that area, said: 'Iraqis and Palestinians are very hard working; Syrians are clever and they do work hard but more because there is so much competition there than because it comes naturally; Bengalis and Bangladeshis are not motivated to work hard. They don't seem to want to improve themselves.'[a]

- 'On the positive side, Germans often see Americans as friendly, open, resourceful, energetic, innovative, and, in general, capable in business…[with] greater freedom, generally happier, …more productive and creative than many other people…; [and having] opportunities to succeed.…[Americans find Germans] highly disciplined, well educated, neat and orderly, …systematic, well organized, meticulous, …efficient…Some Americans find them hard to get to know – not unfriendly, but reserved. On the negative side, …Germans are [seen by Americans as] pushy in service lines…and often insensitive to the feelings of others.'[b]

- Research into Black–White communication stereotypes found that Whites saw Black communication as argumentative, emotional, aggressive, straightforward, critical,

sensitive, ostentatious, defiant, hostile, open, responsive and intelligent. Blacks saw White communication as demanding, manipulative, organized, rude, critical, aggressive, arrogant, boastful, hostile, ignorant, deceptive and noisy.[c]

- In the former Yugoslavia, negative stereotypes of women included regarding them as inefficient, not competent in politics and management, less self-confident than men, less successful in making public speeches, more interested in practical matters (schooling, medical care), and as preferring to spend more time on housekeeping and taking care of others. These stereotypes reflected and supported structural inequalities.[d]

Sources: (a) author's research
(b) Hall, E.T. and Hall, M.R. (1990) *Understanding Cultural Differences: Germans, French, and Americans*, Yarmouth, ME: Intercultural Press
(c) Leonard, R. and Locke, D. (1993) 'Communication stereotypes: is interracial communication possible?', *Journal of Black Studies*, **23**(3): 332–43
(d) Kavcic, B. (1994) 'Women in management: The former Yugoslavia', in Adler, N.J. and Izraeli, D.N. (eds) *Competitive Frontiers*, MA: Blackwell

and frequently than did people primed with polite-related stimuli; people for whom an elderly stereotype was primed walked more slowly down the hallway when leaving the experiment than did those from a control group, showing that even their self-concept could be stereotypically primed; and participants for whom a negative African American stereotype was primed reacted with more hostility to a vexatious request from the African American experimenter than those for whom a positive stereotype was primed. Stereotypical beliefs significantly affected respondents' attitudes towards the training, promotion and retention of older workers, their willingness to work with older workers and their support for positive discrimination.[63]

Other research, however, challenges the idea that implicit biases are automatically and invariantly activated when perceivers come into contact with members of stigmatized groups. For instance, people self-completing race attitude questionnaires showed less race bias when the experimenters were Black than when they were White.[64] Moreover, stereotypes are not continually affecting attitudes and behaviour. For example, when research subjects watched a video of a member of a group about which they had stereotypes, these were first activated (after 15 seconds), then dissipated (after 12 minutes). They were reactivated when the person portrayed expressed disagreement with the research subjects' own view on a court judgement.[65]

Stereotypes of subgroups can be quite specific. For instance, when British listeners gave their social evaluations of audiotaped voices, they upgraded standard accented speakers on competence-related traits but downgraded them on solidarity, regardless of age. Older speakers were perceived as less hesitant but more benevolent than younger speakers. Older-sounding standard speakers were judged most competent, older-sounding non-standard speakers least competent. Slow-talking younger speakers were most downgraded on competence.[66] However, people tend to overestimate the degree to which they themselves are perceived as different – that is, the extent to which they are stereotyped. This has been demonstrated for stereotypes of and by women, business students and students from different geographical regions.[67]

Stereotypes of subgroups show both similarity and difference from culture to culture. A widespread stereotype of people with disabilities is that they can be easily offended and highly sensitive about their disability, and can communicate anger and resentment. Similarly, an examination of sex stereotypes in 30 countries concluded that there is substantial agreement among cultures concerning the psychological characteristics differentially associated with men and women. The stereotypes were scored for activity, strength and favourability of affective meaning. The content of the male stereotype turned out to be more active and stronger in affective meaning, but not any more favourable. However, stronger male stereotypes, that is, a greater attribution of active, strong characteristics to males than to females, were found in cultures with lower levels of literacy and socioeconomic development and with a lower proportion of women enrolled in college.[68] Another study also found cultural differences in stereotypes, in this case of older workers. Compared to a Hong Kong sample, UK respondents saw older workers as more effective but less adaptable. The study also found age-related effects on age stereotypes: older respondents reported positive stereotypes of older people, although not for work effectiveness in the case of older supervisors.[69]

Some stereotypes are positive. Many, though, are negative: for instance, when working-class individuals do not use middle-class speech, they are stereotyped as unintelligent, uneducated and possibly lazy.[70] Other stereotypes may be positive in some contexts but negative in others. For example, stereotypes that are shared by many people about gender differences have men as high in instrumental traits such as aggressiveness and independence, and women as possessing expressive traits such as sensitivity, nurturance and tactfulness. Women's stereotypical traits may well be positively regarded in the context of friendship or the home, but they are generally regarded negatively in the context of work, especially higher-level executive or managerial work.

Because assumptions, including ethnocentrism and stereotypes, are both powerful and inaccessible to self-awareness, they are key variables in encounters. This applies particularly to assumptions about outgroup members, such as unconsciously held stereotypes. There is evidence that one party's assumptions can change the reality for both parties, that 'interpersonal beliefs actively guide social interaction, creating a social world that fits the expectations of the actors. Actors engaged in social interaction behave as if their beliefs about the others are true, and their targets, in turn, tend to act in ways that verify these beliefs. In negotiations, too, the parties, through their belief systems, create the interaction and its outcomes. Negotiators can, and do, "change the game"'.[71]

Box 4.4

A woman member of a minority ethnic group was being interviewed about her claim to housing benefit. The officer asked her to describe her circumstances. She replied with a long story about the difficult behaviour of her child, her husband's being out of work, her own poor health and the failures of the (private) landlord to deal with problems in her flat. The officer thought she was being evasive. He interrupted her – 'I didn't mean that, I meant your financial circumstances. How much money do you have coming in each week?' The woman was silent.

Comment

The woman from a collectivist ethnic minority expected the officer to take all her circumstances and problems into account; the officer, mindful of the rules, wanted to know only the pertinent facts. The (high power distance) woman was perhaps silenced by her respect for the officer's authority, though it is unlikely she either understood or accepted the reason for his demands. She might expect sympathy for her 'failed' family and appreciation of her modest silence under what she could experience as an attack.

Based on: author's research

Box 4.5

A British-owned start-up in India was expanding very fast, planning to increase its head count from 450 to 900 in a single year. This entailed renting new premises. After an exhaustive search, suitable offices were located. It was in an older part of town, not in the new 'high-tech' area, but the building was brand new and better equipped. When the news was given out, however, there were strong objections from some of the staff: journeys to work would be longer (though in fact over half the staff affected by the move lived nearer the new offices than the old ones), there were inadequate lifts (there were only two but the offices were on the second and third floors and most staff were in their twenties), there was insufficient car parking.

The British Managing Director's reaction was as follows: 'This is about expectations and status. Expectations here are high on both sides: people work very long hours for relatively low pay and are quite prepared to interrupt holidays for work reasons. In return they expect transport to work, subsidised food in the canteen, and so on, but above all they want to work for a company that gives them prestige in the eyes of their families and friends. The problem with the new offices is simply that they are not in a prestige area.'

Source: author's research

Expectations

Expectations are beliefs about how people do and should behave and more particularly how they themselves should be treated. In interactions they apply to both verbal and non-verbal behaviour. They influence how people interpret and evaluate what others say and do during interactions; when they are violated, people react, often with negative evaluations of the violator.[72] On the other hand, they may also be changed (co-constructed) during the interaction.[73]

Expectations about both work and communication behaviour are influenced by national-cultural differences in values. For instance, individualism influences expectations, commitment and behavioural decision-making patterns. Individualism is reflected in the desire to avoid submission to authority figures as well as a preference for doing things in one's own way. Less individualistic people have a longer-range view and are more willing to take advice.[74] Cultural values concerning, for instance, the relative importance of self-respect and harmonious work relationships are reflected in both life and personal goals, such as the centrality of work. They are also reinforced by social cues – that is, by information imparted by co-workers and work groups. These cues shape employees' judgments about standards of behaviour and how individuals interpret the actions and communications of others at work, including those perceived as representing the organization. In high-individualism countries, such as the UK, Italy, Belgium and France, individuals expect others to display self-respect. In collectivist countries, such as Japan, Taiwan, and Portugal, people expect others to place more emphasis on harmonious relationships and the maintenance of face.

Power distance also plays a role in how individuals interpret organizational actions and standards of behaviour. In high power distance societies such as Spain, Italy, France, Belgium, Greece, Portugal and Turkey, employees expect power within institutions to be distributed unequally and authority to be centralized. It is accepted that power holders will negotiate special privileges for themselves. In contrast, in low power distance countries such as Denmark, Norway, Sweden, the UK, the Netherlands, Germany and Finland, a more democratic contracting style may be expected.

The expectations a person has about the behaviour of people from another culture are related to all of the following:

- How much they know about that culture;
- What they believe and what their attitude is to that culture;
- Stereotypes of individuals from that culture;
- Their own self-concept (e.g., as 'proud to be British' or as 'a citizen of the world');
- Whether they have roles which require interfacing with people from the other culture;
- Previous experience of people from the other culture;
- Perceptions of their own and the others' relative status.[75]

Differences in the definition of honesty may be among the important differences in behavioural expectations of parties in intercultural transactions. Two societies may have the same degree of honesty but may nevertheless define differently the components of honest or of cheating behaviour. Debates about comparative corruption indicate how definitions of honest and dishonest behaviour may vary between societies. Differences in the definition of honesty may mean that people from one society believe that they are being cheated when the other party is behaving honestly by their own code of conduct. This distinction may distort the perception of compliance with contracts or agreements, which of course is fundamental to the relationship between the two parties.[76]

Subcultural variations in expectations are shown by research which found that physician and patient groups had different role expectations of themselves and one another, and that age differences affected role expectations in both groups.[77] Other research showed that professional nurses in psychiatric wards were more likely to respond therapeutically to violent patient behaviour directed against staff if they perceived the behaviour as arbitrary rather than intended. In other words, their professional role created expectations about patient behaviour that were different from those most people would have about others' behaviour, and, if the expectations were not fulfilled, their response was affected.[78]

Religion can affect gender role expectations. A study of religious television's depiction of family life suggested that the role of women expected in mainstream American religious groups might be more conservative than in secular life. It might also be becoming increasingly traditional. Women were found to be under-represented and portrayed in minor roles typically associated with the household. Only infrequently did they initiate interaction with other people.[79]

Expectations influence supervisor–subordinate relations. When 'normal' expectations are contravened, as when the supervisor is from an ethnic minority and the subordinate is from the dominant majority, problems arise. When supervisors and subordinates were demographically similar, a study showed, the subordinates' behaviour outside their roles was favourably affected, probably because similarity creates attraction. Basic task performance was not affected, however. When supervisors and subordinates were dissimilar in ways consistent with social cultural norms (for instance, when the supervisor was a man and the subordinate a woman), both basic task performance and subordinate behaviour outside the task were positively affected.[80]

Attitudes

Attitudes are a combination of beliefs and affect. 'Affect' means 'enduring positive or negative evaluations about some person, object or issue'. Attitudes received a great deal of attention from psychologists when it was believed that they had a strong influence on behaviour – so strong that a person's behaviour could be predicted from knowing their attitude. It eventually became clear, however, that looking for a direct attitude–behaviour link was not likely to be fruitful. Instead, efforts have been directed at establishing links between the following:

- Attitudes to performing a behaviour and performing it (e.g., attitudes to working abroad and actually seeking such an assignment);
- Attitudes to a target person or object and acting accordingly (e.g., attitudes to an overseas job offer and accepting it);
- Attitudes to the context and acting accordingly (e.g., attitudes to a country and seeking to work there);
- Attitudes to time and using it for a particular purpose (e.g., attitudes to one's career and taking a year out to gain international experience).

All four attitudes might need to be favourable before the relevant action is performed, or one might outweigh all the others.[81]

It has been shown, in the context of prejudice, that people may not be fully aware of their attitudes. A study found that, although the explicit (self-reported) attitudes of Whites predicted their own assessments of their verbal behaviour towards Blacks relative to Whites, observers' assessments of their non-verbal behaviour and bias conflicted with these explicit attitudes. Instead, the Whites' implicit attitudes, assessed by reactions to primary stimuli such as schematic faces, predicted the observers' assessments.[82]

Racial attitudes mediated European Americans' display of interaction involvement: Whites with positive racial attitudes displayed more signs of interaction involvement than African Americans did, but European Americans with negative racial attitudes showed less involvement than African Americans. African Americans showed awareness of the 'mixed messages conveyed through involvement and stress and the role of these cues as reflections of racial attitudes'.[83]

Box 4.6

Shifts in national attitudes to democracy, freedom and religion are likely as the proportion of people who qualify as members of the 'global middle class' increases, research has found. Compared with the poor, the middle classes are more likely to endorse democracy, favour freedom of speech over other freedoms such as freedom from crime and violence, and downplay the centrality of religion in their lives. Although globally there are exceptions to this last difference (the USA is both rich and religious), within countries the middle class is less likely to endorse religion. This applies to a variety of faiths. One-third of the middle class in predominantly Catholic Mexico said religion was very important to them, while about half (48 per cent) of poorer Mexicans expressed this opinion. Similar gaps exist in largely Hindu India (middle class – 60 per cent very important; lower income – 72 per cent). In Malaysia, which is majority Muslim but has significant Buddhist, Christian and Hindu minorities, 60 per cent of the middle class said religion was very important to them compared with 86 per cent of those with lower incomes.

The global middle class is also less likely to believe that faith is essential for morality.

Source: Pew Research Center's Pew Global Attitudes Project 02.12.09, URL: http://pewglobal.org/middle-class, accessed on 22 December 2010

Subcultural differences in important work-related attitudes have been reported. In state-owned enterprises in China, older employees (described as first generation) scored higher on ratings of loyalty, security and even bureaucracy, though both first and second generations expressed a desire to maintain harmony and reduce inequality.[84] Of course, inter-generational differences may be particularly marked where a major environmental shift, such as the Chinese embrace of capitalism in 1979, has occurred.

Trust

Trust is a positive attitude towards another person, assumed voluntarily in order to cope with relational uncertainty. It involves accepting vulnerability, in conjunction with expecting that another's actions will not be harmful. In interactions, trust influences levels of disclosure, openness and formality on the part of speakers and willingness to listen, believe and be persuaded on the part of receivers. Trust has been shown to promote open and influential information exchange, reduce transaction costs, negotiation costs and conflict, and improve performance in inter-organizational collaborations.[85]

There is a theory that high mutual trust is linked to economic prosperity and varies from country to country accordingly.[86] However, findings from the World Values Survey do not bear this theory out; instead a cultural influence seems to be operating. In Denmark, Sweden, Finland and The Netherlands people do indeed have high mutual trust and, as expected, economic prosperity is generally high. But, although France, Belgium and Iceland are also prosperous, their people have much less mutual trust. (The same applies to Luxembourg, the most prosperous country in Europe, which does not have the highest score in terms of mutual trust.) Again, although Eastern European countries are considerably less prosperous than Western European countries, in a few cases the degree of mutual trust is just as high as in many prosperous Western European countries. The figures have changed little over time. Although the trend in most countries is towards a decline in trust, the change is only a few percentage points.[87]

Culture influences the relative importance that people attach to different aspects of trust. Findings from a comparative survey of 153 Mexican and 177 US subjects showed that people from individualist cultures valued most the willingness to trust an agent from outside one's group to act on one's behalf, while setting limits to trust. In contrast, people from collectivist cultures most valued setting the level of trust according to the relationship.[88] Power distance is another cultural variable that influences willingness to trust, while gender is a subcultural influence. From hypothesis-testing research on a sample of Hong Kong employees, it was found that, compared with high power distance individuals, those low in power distance were more likely to link trust in their supervisor and belief that their employing organization was fulfilling its contractual obligations to whether they thought decisions were reached and carried out in a fair way. Similarly, men were more likely than women to believe their employing organization was fulfilling its contract with them only if they perceived those in authority as acting fairly.[89]

Intentions

Intentions are mental plans of action. They are more closely linked to behaviour than attitudes, though the relationship is still far from one-to-one. Because people are usually aware of their intentions, these are relatively controllable. In addition, as Chapter 3 showed, it is vital to effective communication for receivers to correctly understand speakers' communicative intentions. Intentional actions, it has been suggested, are less strongly influenced by culture than routine, habitual ones or those driven by emotion. However, people usually overestimate how deliberate others' actions are, thus underestimating the influence of culture on others' behaviour.

Personality

Personality traits are tendencies to show consistent patterns of thoughts, feelings and actions. The Five-Factor Model (FFM) is a taxonomy of personality traits, consisting of neuroticism (N), extraversion (E), openness to experience (O), agreeableness (A) and conscientiousness (C). Studies comparing the mean levels of personality traits across cultures show systematic patterns, but there may be additional personality factors specific to individual cultures, and some factors may be of greater or less importance in different cultures. For example, individual differences in openness to experience may be of little consequence in traditional cultures where life's options are severely limited. In the words of Bond and Smith (1996),

'Studies of implicit personality theory in any language studied to date indicate that a five-factor model can describe the organization of perceived personality. The apparent universality of the broad categories of extraversion, agreeableness, conscientiousness, emotional stability, and openness to experience may arise from their importance in directing universal types of social behaviors such as association, subordination, and formality. Within the general framework of this model, culture exercises its influence by accentuating certain of the Big Five dimensions over others. In free-response trait descriptions of themselves or of others, Chinese, for example, use the category of conscientiousness more often and use the category of agreeableness less often than do Americans. Moreover, the rated importance of each of the five categories varies among cultural groups, and these categories are differentially weighted in guiding social behavior.'[90]

There is evidence that personality traits vary across subcultures. They may, for instance, be age-related: studies in the USA found noticeable changes in the mean level of all five factors between adolescence and about age 30. 'N, E, and O decline, whereas A and C increase. After age 30, the same trends are seen, but at a much slower pace: in terms of personality traits, 30-year-olds resemble 70-year-olds more than 20-year-olds.' Data from Germany, Italy, Portugal, Croatia, South Korea, Estonia, Russia, Japan, Spain, Britain, Turkey and the Czech Republic showed patterns of age differences very similar to those seen in the USA.[91]

Personality traits may also be influenced by gender. Using a different taxonomy of personality traits, a study of gender differences across 16 countries found that women scored higher than men in anxiety, vulnerability, straightforwardness and openness to aesthetics; men scored higher in (claimed) competence, assertiveness, excitement-seeking and openness to ideas. However, the same study found evidence for cultural differences in the size of gender differences. Contrary to expectations, the greatest gender differences in traits like assertiveness were found in modern European countries and the least in traditional cultures (like South Korea). A possible explanation is that, in countries where women are expected to be subservient, they attribute their low assertiveness to their role as a woman rather than their traits. Contrastingly, European women who are equally low in assertiveness identify it as a part of their own personality.[92]

Adorno (1991) found that Church members, especially Catholics, in the USA were more authoritarian than those with no religion; fundamentalists – whether Hindu, Muslim, Jew or Christian – were the most authoritarian. In addition, dogmatism – being rigid in thinking, intolerant of ambiguity and unable to deal with new information – was highest among members of strict churches (American Catholics and Southern Baptists), lowest among non-believers.[93] On the other hand, Argyle (2000) recorded that religion was not much related to the general personality variables known to psychologists, such as extraversion or neuroticism.[94]

Identity and self-construals

In some schools of thought, identity, or selfhood, has emerged to replace the concept of personality. Identity is not seen as a fixed, enduring characteristic of the individual, or as a collection of psychological factors unaffected by wider social concerns. Identity theorists emphasize the social (and cultural) dimensions of identity and the fluid or changing nature of identity over time.[95] Though not synonymous, self-construals and identity are closely related. Self-construals are our mental representations of ourselves, derived, at least in part, reflexively – that is, by interpreting how others seem, from their communication with us, to perceive us. Compared with self-construals, identity is usually considered to include a more affective element and to be associated with group membership; as a result, we all have multiple identities – mother, wife, lawyer, French national and so on.

For communication theorists, cultural identification, such as that which causes someone to identify as French, is a process that happens in a constantly changing socio-economic environment and which is also affected by contact with other cultures. Cultural identities are negotiated, co-created, reinforced and challenged through communication. Whereas social psychological perspectives view identity as a characteristic of the person and the self as centred in social roles and social practices, a communication perspective views identity as something that emerges when messages are exchanged between persons. Throughout life, cultural identities are emergent, not created or completed.

According to Thompson (2003), culture shapes self-construals through giving meaning to experience. However, he noted, 'we are constrained, not only by the range of possibilities which culture offers – that is, by the variety of symbolic representations – but also by social relations'.[96] An approach to national-cultural differences based in cultural psychology argues that individualists have independent self-construals: their mental representations of the self are separate from those they have of others. In contrast, for collectivists, self-construals are fundamentally interdependent. Others are, in effect, considered part of the self. In individualist models, the self 'comprises a unique, bounded configuration of internal attributes, such as preferences, traits, abilities, motives, values and rights, and behaves primarily as a consequence of these internal attributes'.[97] For people with independent self-construals, then, although other people are crucial in maintaining the sense of self and also function as standards of comparison and sources of appraisal, the persistent concern in communicating is to express internal attributes. Against this, people from collectivist cultures are usually more strongly aware of the nature of their relationship to others and of maintaining reciprocity within those relationships. People with interdependent self-construals, such as the Japanese, may have less clarity about their selves than people with independent self-construals, such as Canadians.[98] It is, however, possible to have both interdependent and independent components in the self-construal. (They are orthogonal constructs, not a single bipolar one.)[99]

Both within and across cultures, individuals with predominantly interdependent self-construals have been found to be more aware of the status of the source of a communication, more influenced by the perceived fairness of a procedure, less inclined to perceive their in-group as homogeneous, more inclined to use hint strategies, more easily embarrassed and more easily affected by emotional contagion than individuals with independent self-construals. Furthermore, the relative amount of attitude change resulting from persuasive communication by a high-status source was significantly larger for those with interdependent self-construals than for those with independent self-construals.[100] Another cross-cultural study built on previous research, which showed that, if people thought the procedure by which the outcome of a social exchange was decided was fair, they were less influenced in assessing it by whether the outcome was in their favour or not. For example, if a performance appraisal was thought to be based on a fair procedure, workers would be less aggrieved by an unfavourable appraisal. The cross-cultural study showed that this applied even more to people with interdependent self-construals than to people with independent self-construals.[101] Finally, a direct link was found between self-construals and ways of communicating. In making a request, individuals high in interdependence were more likely to use hint strategies on the first and second attempt, while independent individuals were more likely to use direct strategies. However, when non-compliance was high, both interdependent and independent individuals used direct strategies.[102]

Continent-wide or even national cultures may be too broad to define identities or self-construals, which some research shows to vary by subculture and by environmental factors such as politics. A study found that Chinese self-construals varied across age, gender and urban–rural residence and were also influenced by the changing political, economic and sociocultural context in China. Again, Martin and Nakayama (1997) argued: 'Ethnic identity is having a sense of belonging to a particular group and knowing something about the shared experience of the group. For some [US] residents, ethnicity is a specific and relevant construct and for others it is a vague concept.'[103] Ethnic identity is a complex cluster of factors that define the extent and type of involvement with one's ethnic group. It differs both qualitatively and quantitatively among ethnic group members; two individuals who belong to the same group may differ widely on their identification with the group and their commitment to it. They may differ in how salient the group is for them and in what it means subjectively. Furthermore, ethnic identity can vary within one individual over time. The psychological correlates of ethnicity are likely to differ depending on the quality of this identity. However, although the implications of ethnicity vary widely across individuals, ethnicity is 'a highly salient and meaningful construct'.[104]

Ethnic identities ascribed to an individual by others can create 'treacherous cross-currents' that have to be negotiated. When there is no alternative to an ascribed ethnic identity, inter-group conflict can easily arise. One alternative is a creative synthesizing of local identities. University students in Hong Kong, for example, perceived themselves as similar to but distinct from typical Hong Kong Chinese. They ascribed to themselves elements of a valued Western identity in equal measure to their Hong Kong identity.[105] This creative synthesizing of local identities provides an escape. The identifications achieved by individuals, rather than ascribed to them by others, then become the basis for various forms of inter-group behaviour, such as linguistic differentiation and styles of conflict management.[106]

Gender is fundamental to most people's identity. In all cultures, men and women differ in their self-reports of masculine and feminine characteristics, although the gender difference is typically less than that reflected in gender stereotypes.[107] In the West, women may be more like people from collectivist cultures than Western men are, having more interdependent self-construals. Cross and Madison (1997) argued: 'Many gender differences in cognition, motivation, emotion and social behavior may be explained in terms of men's and women's different self-construals.'[108] For US women, but not for men, a positive relationship has been found between self-esteem and motives that favour acting in friendly or helpful ways. Self-enhancement strategies used by US men often involved boasting and exaggeration of their abilities, operating with a 'false uniqueness' bias – the false belief that one's own abilities are exceptional – and over-estimating their performances against objective standards. In contrast, US women were more likely to adjust their self-enhancement strategies for the feelings of others. For instance, women students with high grade-point averages were more likely to take into account the assessments received by their interlocutors before talking about their own grades. US women also responded more to feedback than US men did. This finding has also been interpreted in terms of their having more interdependent self-construals. On the other hand, women's greater responsiveness to feedback may be because they have lower self-esteem, rather than being directly linked to their self-construals. The fact that women have lower status than men may lower their self-confidence, leading them, among other things, to place a low valuation on their own opinion of themselves and to be more responsive than men to others' evaluations.[109]

Significant differences have been found in how accurately men and women perform the following:

- Estimate their own intelligence;
- Evaluate their productivity;
- Evaluate their performance at finding a route and on tests of sports trivia and knowledge of politics;
- Report prior grades;
- Judge their own attractiveness.

Europe-wide only three in 100 Europeans put 'Europe' first as the place they identify with. Many people, it seems, do not identify with 'Europe' because of the lack of continuity down the generations, shared memories, symbols etc. People identify with their immediate surroundings, the town or city (49 per cent), province (13 per cent) or country (28 per cent) where they live. This general low figure does not, however, mean that people reject Europe. Only around 8 per cent of Europeans overall feel they belong least of all to Europe.[a]

Typically, Muslims, and Arabians in particular hold two sets of identity: one, immediate, social and spatially particular; the other, historical, cultural and global.[b]

Sources: (a) Halman, L. and Kerkhofs, J. (2001) *The European Values Study: Selected results.* URL: www.romir.ru/eng/research/01_2001/europeanvalues, last accessed on 22 December 2010
(b) Ali, A. J. (1993) 'Decision-making style, individualism and attitudes toward risk of Arab executives', *International Studies of Management & Organization*, **23**(3): 53–74

In almost all cases, women underestimate themselves. Replicating an earlier study, Beyer (1998) found that women expected to perform worse, judged themselves as having performed worse and wrongly remembered that they had performed worse (showed a greater negative recall bias) on tests of masculine knowledge (such as American football). There were, however, no significant differences in men's and women's expectations, judgements and recall of performance on tests of 'feminine' knowledge (of film and TV stars and fashion) or neutral tests of common knowledge, character detection, practical questions and anagrams. 'This emphasizes that females' inaccurate self-perceptions are highly task specific rather than generalized'.[110]

Social class often enters into identity. Hoyt (1999) found that high-flying working-class individuals entering middle-class environments can feel stress and feelings of incompetence, because of a lack of 'cultural necessities', that is, the speech, manners, clothing and experiences of the middle class. Such individuals may be 'conflicted'. One said, 'Part of our identity was middle class while another part remained back in the working class world of our roots.'[111] According to Huntington (1997), religions give people identity by positing a basic distinction between believers and non-believers, between a superior in-group and a different and inferior outgroup.[112] People with disabilities, however, have been shown to have self-construals not significantly different from those of others, contrary to stereotypes. A study of 177 students registered with a university's disabled service and 160 other students found that students with and without disability tended to rate each other in a stereotypical manner. Students with disabilities were seen as more conscientious and cultured than were students without disabilities, whereas students without disabilities were seen as more extraverted and emotionally stable than students with disabilities. When the students rated themselves, however, no such differences emerged between the groups with and without disabilities.[113]

Personal characteristics may affect the level of cultural identity exhibited. People with high levels of national identification have been shown to be more likely to display the individualist or collectivist characteristics associated with their national culture than people with low levels of national identification.[114] Kim and Leung (2000) criticized the conceptualization of individualism and collectivism as polar opposites, arguing that a person can simultaneously maintain high independent and interdependent construals, that self-construals are dynamic, not fixed – they vary with context and over time – and that there is an increasing incidence of bicultural people. Asian students are higher than Americans on interdependent scales but not lower on independence. Kim and Leung (2000) saw 'biculturals' as having the most fully developed self-construals, 'independents' as having underdeveloped interdependence construals and 'interdependents' as having underdeveloped independence construals. They also suggested there is a fourth category, 'marginals', who have underdevelopment of both construals.[115]

Huntington (1997) argued that everyone has multiple identities that may compete with or reinforce each other: identities of kinship, occupation, culture, institution, territory, education, party, ideology and others. In the contemporary world, he argued, cultural identification is dramatically increasing in importance compared with other dimensions of identity. This is the result of social/economic modernization. At the individual level, dislocation and alienation create the need for more meaningful identities; at the societal level, the enhanced capabilities and power of non-Western societies stimulate the revitalization of indigenous identities and culture. Identity at any level – personal, tribal, racial, civilizational – can only be defined in relation to an 'other', a different person, tribe, race or civilization. The intra-civilizational 'us' and the extra-civilizational 'them' is a constant in human history. These differences in intra- and extra-civilizational behaviour stem from feelings of superiority (and occasionally inferiority) towards people who are perceived as being very different. Other sources are fear of and lack of trust in such people, difficulty of communication with them as a result of differences in language and what is considered civil behaviour, and lack of familiarity with the assumptions, motivations, social relationships and social practices of other people.[116]

There is an ongoing debate about how relevant self-construals and cultural identities are at work. One study suggests that they are relevant, but to differing degrees. Homogeneous work groups that differed from other homogeneous groups in terms of ethnicity and gender were found to vary significantly in how far cultural identity was articulated, whether ethnicity, gender or religion was the most salient identity, whether the focus was on the in-group or the outgroup and whether the references were positive or negative. However, discourses of separateness, narrowly defined identity and inequality were common.[117] Another study suggested that identities at work were affective (emotion-based) and could be measured on dimensions of 'niceness', powerfulness and liveliness. The study found that German managers and subordinates, constrained to behave according to the prescriptions of their American employing company (prescriptions which corresponded to American cultural norms), both had to adjust substantially and lost status. When the managers' affective identities were measured, they reflected substantially lower levels of niceness and powerfulness. 'This redefinition shows that he [sic] had lost any basis for corporate leadership', according to the author. Managers experienced identity problems when following culture-centric behaviour prescriptions instead of using the affective meaning of their professional identities as guidance for their behaviour.[118]

The concepts of self-construal and identity have attracted criticism. Varela et al. (1991) criticized the whole concept of a 'self' as a Western myth, arguing that, when people look inside themselves for a fixed, unitary self, no such animal can be found. Instead, they find that who they are is completely bound up with and relative to their environment. The inability to catch one's self with a self-perception, to separate the self from the world, can lead to anxiety, restlessness and self-grasping.[119]

Self-esteem

It has been asserted that culture influences the perceived gap between our actual self and our ideal self, and so decides how we evaluate our self-esteem. This implies that self-esteem is a cultural creation. The evidence, however, is somewhat conflicting. On the one hand, Farh *et al.* (1991) found cultural differences in self-esteem strongly reflected when they investigated modesty bias among Taiwanese and Western workers. Modesty bias means that subjects give self-ratings of work performance that are lower than supervisors' ratings; Western workers' self-ratings of performance are usually higher than ratings obtained from supervisors – they do not exhibit modesty bias. Farh *et al.* (1991) found that Taiwanese workers did exhibit modesty bias.[120] Their findings were explained in terms of broad cultural differences between Taiwanese and Western workers. On the other hand, a replication study using data from several organizations in mainland China showed leniency in self-ratings – that is self-ratings higher than supervisor or peer ratings – which suggests that broad cultural factors may not fully explain the reported modesty bias.[121] However, measures of self-esteem used in cross-cultural comparisons are often based on individual attributes rather than group attributes. Cross-cultural comparisons may therefore miss differences in self-evaluation derived from a person's 'collective identity'. Thus findings on whether people from certain cultural groups are more socially modest or internally depressed may be premature.[122]

Ethics and morality

It is likely that the possession of a moral code of some sort is universal. 'People are motivated to think of themselves as ethical [sic], and rate themselves as more ethical than the average person. When people do engage in ethically questionable behaviour, they often justify it as self-defence.'[123] However, since moral codes generally reflect values, which, as Chapter 2 showed, vary quite fundamentally across cultures, it is

---

Box 4.8

North Africans in France used a range of rhetorical tools for rebutting French racism, probably to prevent it damaging their self-esteem:

- They claimed that people of all races, nations and religions are equal. Moral rules are emphasized: 'Whether black or white, if they don't do evil, they are OK.'
- They demonstrated cultural similarities between the French and Moroccans, Tunisians, Algerians or Kabyles, using historical and sociocultural evidence.
- They argued that they personally conform to what they perceive to be universal moral criteria highly valued by the host (French) society. This distances the individual from the race/nation/religion in order to show that the group to which s/he belongs does not necessarily define a person.

- They demonstrated the superiority of Muslims (or their own national group) to the French – embracing an Islamic moral universalism: 'In France, old people are badly treated and their children don't come to see them. In contrast, in our country. ...'
- They explained racism by the characteristics of the racist (e.g. lack of experience of members of ethnic minorities). Only a small number of North Africans in France use this rhetoric.

Source: Lamont, M., Morning, A. and Mooney, M. (2002) 'Particular universalisms: North African immigrants respond to French racism', *Ethnic and Racial Studies*, **25**(3): 390–414.

not surprising that researchers have found cultural differences in morality. It has been argued that business ethical standards are unique to each culture, as a result of the combination of institutional, organizational and personal factors, all of which are based on the 'social foundation' of national culture.[124] The 'trial-and-error process of actual business activity' and personal interaction with other people both play an important role in the way moral reasoning is formed within civil society. Business and its underlying ethical principles of trust and co-operation in the context of civil society are captured in the notion of business as a 'mediating' institution. 'Mediating institutions break down an individual's interaction with the rest of the world into more manageable personal interaction with other human beings.'[125]

A study that compared Indian and American moral choices found cross-cultural differences in the priority given to interpersonal responsibilities relative to justice considerations. More Indians than Americans gave priority to interpersonal responsibilities. This difference was greater in non-life-threatening situations. Americans emphasized the potential harm involved in the choice situation rather than the 'uncaringness' involved in the choice; Indians did the opposite. (Unexpectedly, the various cross-cultural differences were not more marked in older than younger people.) Indians categorized their choice of the interpersonal option in moral terms; the minority of Americans who chose the interpersonal alternative categorized it in personal rather than moral terms.[126] A comparison of beliefs about distributive justice found differences between Hong Kong and Indonesia. Hong Kong respondents perceived that the use of merit as a basis for distributing resources was fairer and more principled than the use of need; Indonesian respondents, in contrast, saw the use of need as fairer than the use of merit. (Both groups, however, perceived that the allocator who favoured the needy was nicer and acted more out of concern for others.[127]) Another study found cultural variation in the acceptability of most kinds of lies, although there was cross-cultural agreement that lies perceived as told for malicious or self-benefiting purposes were unacceptable.[128] Examples of moral standards of individual cultures include Ali's (1995) finding that, in the Arab world, not only is bribery widespread but political elites encourage it, believing that the more customary the corruption, the more valid their system. 'In July 1992, I visited Jordan and found that, even in a religious court, the clerk openly asked for a bribe (he called it "Ikrameh"). In Syria, it is impossible to get a request processed in any government agency without paying bribes.'[129]

There is empirical support for moral beliefs about business being related to cultural difference. A ten-nation study found that collectivism–individualism and uncertainty avoidance helped explain national differences in judgements of the 'ethicality' of decision items – the particular items were concerned with relations with external stakeholders, the corporation and the group.[130] Another study showed that whether individuals in organizations are aware of an issue being a moral one is decided in part by their perceiving a social consensus that an issue is ethically problematic. This finding supports the idea that sociocultural influences affect individuals' moral beliefs.[131] When survey data were gathered from 252 full-time employees working in the collectivist country of Taiwan and the individualist country of the United States of America, results indicated that employees from Taiwan were more likely to indicate they would make an unethical decision that benefits the organization and less likely to openly question an unethical practice by their organization.[132] On the other hand, there is evidence that Chinese employees are more likely to report the unethical acts of peers within their organization than Canadians are.[133]

On the level of corporate ethics, an exploration of the discourse and practice of corporate social responsibility (CSR) in France showed how a country's cultural, socio-economic and legal traditions influenced the way ideas were raised, the kinds of questions considered relevant, and the sorts of solutions conceived as desirable and possible.[134] Another study tested the hypothesis that corporate social responsibility (CSR) practice varies considerably among Asian countries and that this variation is explained by stage of development, a factor only indirectly related to culture. The study's findings led to the conclusion, however, that CSR does vary considerably among Asian countries, but that this variation is not explained by development but by factors in the respective national business systems, which are more closely related to culture.[135] A 'complex interaction' of considerations, including cultural and social factors, but also historical development, legal system, corporate governance model, political system and economic development, 'provides the context' for corporate governance and business ethics in each of four Asian countries – Australia, China, Singapore, and India. The result is 'different orientations to stakeholder management and integrity behavior in the boardroom and executives' offices'. The authors concluded that 'the human capacity to protect diversity and enshrine regional and local interests seems likely to inhibit rapid change.'[136]

In regard to subcultures, a study of 3,000 students in the USA found that female survey participants were slightly but significantly more ethically inclined than male survey participants, and survey participants who reported being very religious were slightly but significantly more ethically inclined than survey participants who were less religious.[137] Perhaps the best resolution of this issue of cultural differences in ethics is that of Argyle.[138] Different societies and religions have arrived at similar moral ideas, such as advocating love, compassion and forgiveness. The application of these ideas in society, however, has varied greatly with the circumstances of life at different times.

> Values, motivations, emotions, perceptions, beliefs, assumptions, expectations, attitudes, intentions and the 'self' are affected by many individual factors. These range from genetic make-up to school environment during upbringing, from the innate element in intelligence to experiences at work. In particular, though, they are affected by the way people have been taught by their culture to look at the world. Other influences are people's societal positions, which are affected by such factors as their gender, age, (dis)ability, social class and so on. In turn, these psychological factors affect individuals' communicative styles, emphases (content versus relationship, control, affiliation), strategies and ways of using language. All these differences can affect both work behaviour generally and work communication in particular.

4.2 SOCIAL COGNITION PROCESSES

Important among the constructs described in Section 4.1 are cognitive constructs such as perceptions, beliefs, assumptions, expectations, attitudes and intentions. This section concerns the processes that produce these cognitive constructs. Cognitive processes receive, select, transform and organize information, construct representations of reality and build knowledge. Many activities are involved, including perceiving, learning, memorizing, thinking and verbalizing. These processes continuously influence one another. They are subject to a number of distorting influences. They do not directly predict particular communication behaviours such as reciprocity or defensiveness, but do so indirectly by their influence on thoughts. The emphasis in this section is on how these processes themselves may vary cross-culturally and how they may lead to differences in the resulting constructs and behaviours.

Social perceiving

People are exposed to more complex and varied information than they can process. They therefore use a number of devices to reduce the mental work involved. These devices include selective attention, limited arousal, categorization and simplification. Culture influences these processes. For example, there are cultural differences in how likely it is that someone 'samples' – that is, is aware of and seeks information on – the verbal content of communication more than its non-verbal accompaniments, such as voice tone or gesture. Again, people in some cultures tend to sample influences internal to individuals, such as attitudes or beliefs, more than externals, such as social influences or roles. Others do the reverse.[139] These differences are also, necessarily, some of the sources of bias in social perception. This was demonstrated when holders of the belief that traits are unalterable consistently displayed greater attention to and recognition of consistent information about another person, whereas holders of a belief that people's traits change incrementally paid more attention to inconsistent information about that person. Thus, beliefs can lead to processing that supports or limits stereotype maintenance.[140]

The process that introduces most cultural difference into social perceiving, however, is attribution. This term refers to deciding, often subconsciously, whether it is another person's disposition or their situation that causes their observed behaviour. People make attributions in order to predict future events, exercise control and gain understanding. For example, in order to decide whom to make redundant, a sales manager may need to decide whether a salesperson's poor sales record is the result of his or her incompetence and laziness or of market conditions. There are different kinds of personal attributions, and these differ cross-culturally. Some cultures give greater weight to ascribed attributes of persons, such as ethnicity, and others to achieved attributes, such as attitudes or past performance.

Several types of attribution bias have been well documented. Of these, one has been most clearly demonstrated to vary cross-culturally. This is the self-serving bias, or tendency for someone to attribute successful outcomes of their own actions to themselves and unsuccessful outcomes to the situation. According to the theory of self-esteem in attribution, self-serving bias helps to protect self-esteem; the extent of the need for such protection depends partly on cultural factors. The self-serving bias occurs in most cultures, but more frequently in North American and some European individuals than in Japanese, Indians, Asians or southern Europeans.[141] A study showed that Finns used self-serving bias less than Americans. In comparison to the Americans, the Finns were less likely to attribute good outcomes to internal, stable and global factors, pointing to a difference between the two Western cultures. Another study found that Dutch subjects made attributions similar to the Finns'. These findings suggest that some Western societies may exhibit more collectivist patterns of self-serving bias than originally presumed from studies of mainly Americans.[142]

Attribution processes in non-Western cultures may be 'context-dependent and occasion-bound'.[143] Their attributional logic may be less personal. Accordingly, members of non-Western cultures are more likely to make external or situational attributions than to believe that others' behaviours are consistent with internal factors such as attitudes.[144] Attribution research has found a strong bias towards attributing male, rather than female, gender to a gender-unspecified individual, even when no descriptive pronouns (such as he or she) are used.[145] Girls tend to attribute their own failure in mathematics or science to a learned-helpless orientation more than boys do.[146] At work, there is bias in attributions of managers' success – women's being more often attributed to the situation, men's more to personal qualities.[147] Attributions of blame for sexual harassment at work are also biased. Men allocate more blame overall than women, and specifically more to the target of the harassment.[148] Gender also influences attributions and emotions in helping contexts – men perceive themselves as having more responsibility and become angrier.[149] In laboratory research, people tend to offer different explanations for the same level of performance, depending on the gender of the performer. Women's success tends to be attributed more strongly than men's to high effort, luck or the ease of the task, but their failure to lack of ability. However, a field test of gender effects on managers' attributions for the performance of their direct subordinates found that employees of both genders in the main attributed both their successes and their failures to personal responsibility. They were seen to succeed mainly because of their ability and because they worked hard; they were seen to fail chiefly because of limitations in the same two areas. The managers' own gender was unrelated to how they attributed the performance of their staff. In this study, unlike in laboratory studies, there was no support for the hypothesis that the performance of female employees would be explained differently and less favourably than that of men.[150]

Religious orientation has some effect on attributions. A Swedish study found that religious participants preferred secular attributions, especially when assessing the causes of failure. People with high extrinsic religious orientation (who view religion instrumentally and as one of many influences on life) were most likely to make different attributions depending on the topic.[151]

Thinking

Several aspects of mental processes may differ between cultures. These include categorizing, logic style, learning style and problem-solving processes.

Categorizing

How people classify or differentiate other people, things or issues is not 'natural', but rather learned, mainly through communication. The complexity of the categories in a child's cognitive system increases as the child gains experience. In mature individuals it varies – some people differentiate more finely than others and most people differentiate more finely on subjects they are interested in or knowledgeable about. Because the categories that people use are learned, not 'natural', they are culturally influenced. For example, English uses the word 'aunt' to mean both 'mother's sister' and 'father's sister'. Other cultures distinguish between the two. Chinese has different words for 'older brother' and 'younger brother', as age is an important indicator of status. 'Categorizing is a fundamental and natural human activity. It is the way we come to know the world.' As a result, 'any attempt to eliminate bias by attempting to eliminate the perception of differences is doomed to failure.' More subtle categorical distinctions bring stereotypes closer to reality. To increase accuracy, people should make more, not fewer, distinctions. For instance, Europeans and Americans should divide Japanese people into male and female, rather than see both genders in terms of the same national stereotype.[152]

Logic style

Western logic emphasizes atomistic analysis, dichotomization, deduction and induction from empirical data by an accepted set of procedures and abstractions. There are variations within Western cultures on which of these is more emphasized. According to Maletzke (1996), Anglo-Saxon thought patterns are predominantly inductive, Latin American and Russian thought patterns are predominantly deductive. Whereas inductive thinking aims to derive theoretical concepts from individual cases, deductive thinking aims to interpret individual cases within previously derived theoretical concepts. Argumentation and more general communication styles will be quite different in the two approaches, Maletzke (1996) contended. Western logic systems as a whole, however, can be contrasted with those of Eastern cultures. In these, again with internal variations, holism and intuition predominate, together with an emphasis on seeing the relationships between the external and internal world.[153]

Learning style

While the capacity to learn from experience is clearly universal, there are (sub)cultural differences in what is learnt, how it is learnt and the degree to which mature adults remain open to such learning. Joy and Kolb (2009) found that a significant portion of the variance in the preference for abstract conceptualization as against reflective observation was explained by culture, gender, level of education and area of specialization. The variability in preference for active experimentation over reflective observation, however, was accounted for by age and area of specialization; the impact of culture on this preference was only marginally significant. On cultural dimensions, Joy and Kolb (2009) found, individuals tended to have a more abstract learning style in countries that were high in a combination of in-group collectivism, institutional collectivism, uncertainty avoidance, future orientation and gender egalitarianism. Individuals may have a more reflective learning style in countries that are high in a combination of in-group collectivism, uncertainty avoidance and assertiveness.[154]

Problem-solving processes

How people work and their preferences for certain actions or solutions to work-related issues are affected by how they approach obtaining information and manipulating it and by their approach to problem-solving. There is evidence that these processes, which are known together as cognitive style, are affected in turn by cultural influences. There is also evidence that people with different cognitive styles experience difficulties in communicating with one another. These interaction problems can lead to conflict. A study of Canadian and Japanese cognitive styles found differences: Canadians were found to have a tendency to seek fast decisions and to rush to closure on data collection. The Japanese were found to resist fast decision-making because of a preference for obtaining large amounts of information.[155]

> There are (sub)cultural differences in how people perceive, including what they notice about other people and to what causes they attribute others' behaviour. (Sub)cultural differences also affect how people categorize as well as their preferred styles of logic, learning and problem-solving. These differences affect how they interact at work with culturally different others.

4.3   CONCLUSION

The purpose of this chapter has been to deepen and widen the analysis of (sub)cultural similarities and differences in ways of communicating that were discussed in Chapter 3. To achieve this, it has explored psychological constructs and processes underlying overt communication behaviour. The chapter has shown that individuals' values, motivations, emotions, perceptions, beliefs, assumptions, expectations, attitudes, abilities and even their sense of 'self' differ from group to group. How individuals perceive other people and how they think also differ according to their (sub) culture. However, other factors than group memberships, including individual heredity, interact with these group effects to influence behaviour.

QUESTIONS AND EXERCISES

1. What would make a psychological construct 'universal'? How can universal psychological constructs differ from culture to culture?

2. Consider the differences between male and female housing managers' approaches to interpersonal relations with their staff and clients, shown in Table 4.1. How would you expect these differences to affect their work?

3. In the study of how Chinese managers deal with emotional issues at work (Ref. 12), they identified the best processes as: (a) to pay attention to or recognize the seriousness of the disruption; (b) to divert attention and thinking away from the disruption; (c) to calm unpleasant inner feelings, either privately or in connection with others; (d) either to maintain or to calm pleasant emotions; (e) to keep up their employees' pleasant emotions; (f) to come to a better understanding of problems and possible solutions by thinking and feeling through them; (g) to learn from emotional experiences so that pleasant ones can be sustained and unpleasant ones can be avoided in future. How would these processes differ from those most likely to be used by managers in your own culture? Where there are differences, which would you expect to be more effective in your own culture and why?

4. The text describes six 'fundamental belief systems about how the world works'. These are authoritarianism, social dominance orientation, Protestant work ethic, humanitarianism–egalitarianism, beliefs about the malleability of human attributes and beliefs about diversity. Other 'core' beliefs include locus of control and belief in a just or unjust world. Discuss possible reasons why such belief systems vary cross-culturally. Would you expect such belief systems to show less variability within than between cultures? Give your reasons.

5. Why might males generally agree more strongly with SDO than females?

6. What groups of people are most likely to benefit from the belief systems that are most widespread in their society?

7. Discuss the contention that 'the "trial-and-error process of actual business activity" and personal interaction with other people play an important role' in honing moral reasoning.

8. Research more consistently shows a relationship of national culture to beliefs about aspects of organization, such as worker participation, than to strategy. Why might this be?

9. In the light of the findings on agency given in the text, role play a sales targeting meeting between a sales manager from Australia and a sales representative from Japan.

10. What is ethnocentrism? How does it differ from stereotyping? How can it affect work behaviour?

11. An ethnic minority householder went into the local authority offices to complain that a large item of furniture left for collection was not picked up with the rest of their rubbish.

   He spoke to the receptionist. The item (a double bed) had to be picked up that day or it would affect arrangements for a cultural celebration. The receptionist tried to explain to him that special arrangements had to be made with the council for the removal of large items and that a standard charge was levied. (Coincidentally, neighbours had phoned to complain that this large item had been left outside the house in question.) During the discussion it emerged that the householder had offered the refuse men money to remove the item. He was angry because they declined. Now he wanted to negotiate a price for the item to be picked up. He asked if it would be cheaper if he put it in the street. The receptionist was young and female, the householder male and older. He wondered if she had enough authority to make decisions – was he being palmed off? He demanded to speak with the manager (whom he assumed to be male). In turn, the receptionist wondered if he was sexist – she could not understand why it was so important that the item was moved that day. She also wondered if the offer of money to the refuse men was an attempt at a bribe.

Analyse the factors influencing the behaviour of the participants in this scene. The case may also be used as the basis for a role play.

12. What factors influence the expectations that a person has about the communication behaviour of someone from another culture?

13. A newly appointed senior manager complained to the CEO of a medium-sized business in a North European country about a series of issues with the staff of his unit: lack of commitment, poor discipline, etc. The newly appointed manager was from Southern Europe. His/her expertise was extremely important to the company's future development and was also rare; the company was fortunate to attract him/her, after a long search. The CEO, who knew that this unit had an excellent performance record (the company judges by results), referred the matter to you, the HR manager. What factors do you consider in deciding how to deal with this issue?

14. Complete the table from the material in the text or other sources:

(Sub)cultural differences that influence expectations	Expectations that may be influenced
Individualism	Desire to avoid submission to authority figures

15. What is trust? What aspects of communication does it influence? How does trust vary (a) in different economies and (b) between individualist and collectivist cultures?

16. In a mixed (sub)culture group, discuss the contention of Varela (1991) (Ref. 119) that, when people look inside themselves for a fixed, unitary self, no such animal can be found. Instead, they find that who they are is completely bound up with and relative to their environment.

17. What is the core difference between a communication perspective on identity and a social psychological perspective?

18. Draw an identity map for yourself. Compare yours with a colleague and discuss the reasons for the differences.

19. Find examples additional to those given in the text of cultural or subcultural differences in the following aspects of the thinking processes: categorizing, logic style, learning style and problem-solving.

NOTES AND REFERENCES

1. Aycan, Z. (2002) 'Leadership and teamwork in developing countries: Challenges and opportunities', in Lonner, W.J., Dinnel, D.L., Hayes, S.A. and Sattler, D.N. (eds) *Online Readings in Psychology and Culture* (Unit 15, Chapter 4). URL: http://orpc.iaccp.org/, last accessed on 22 December 2010.
2. Sagie, A., Elizur, D. and Yamauchi, H. (1996) 'The structure and strength of achievement motivation: a cross-cultural comparison', *Journal of Organizational Behavior*, **17**(5): 431–44.
3. Guzley, R.M., Araki, F. and Chalmers, L.E. (1998) 'Cross-cultural perspectives of commitment: individualism and collectivism as a framework for conceptualization', *Southern Communication Journal*, **64**(1): 1–19.
4. Yousef, D.A. (2000) 'Organizational commitment as a mediator of the relationship between Islamic work ethic and attitudes toward organizational change', *Human Relations*, **53**(4): 513–39.
5. Martin, J.N., Hecht, M.L., Moore, S. and Larkey, L.K. (2001) 'African American conversational improvement strategies for interethnic communication', *Howard Journal of Communication*, **12**: 1–27.
6. Warr, P. and Fay, D. (2001) 'Age and personal initiative at work', *European Journal of Work and Organizational Psychology*, **10**(3): 343–53.
7. Frijda, N.H. and Mesquita, B. (1994) 'The social roles and functions of emotions', in Kitayama, S. and Markus, H.R. (eds) *Emotion and Culture: Empirical Studies of Mutual Influence*, Washington, DC: American Psychological Association, pp. 51–87.
8. Forgas, J.P. and Vargas, P. (1998) 'Affect and behavior inhibition: the mediating role of cognitive processing strategies', *Psychological Inquiry*, **9**(3): 205–10.
9. George, J.M., Gonzalez, J.A. and Jones, G.R. (1998) 'The role of affect in cross-cultural negotiations', *Journal of International Business Studies*, **29**(4): 749–72.
10. Elfenbein, H.A. and Ambady, N. (2002) 'Universals and cultural differences in recognizing emotions: a meta-analysis', *Psychological Bulletin*, **128**(2): 208–35.
11. Mesquita, B. and Frijda, N.H. (1992) 'Cultural variations in emotions: a review', *Psychological Bulletin*, **112**(2): 179–204.
12. Krone, K.J., Chen, L., Sloan, D.K. and Gallant, L.M. (1997) 'Managerial emotionality in Chinese factories', *Management Communication Quarterly*, **11**(1): 6–50.
13. Cutspec, P. and Goering, E.M. (1988) 'Acknowledging cultural diversity: perceptions of shyness within the black culture', *Howard Journal of Communications*, **1**(1): 75–87.
14. Wolfson, K. and Pearce, W.B. (1983) 'A cross-cultural comparison of the implications of self disclosure on conversational logics', *Communication Quarterly*, **31**(3): 249–56.
15. McKee Ranger, L. (2002) 'Communication is key for deaf and hard of hearing technical pros', *Diversity/Careers Professional*, Oct/Nov. URL:http://www.diversitycarrers.com/ articles/pro/octnov02/fod_com_deaf.htm
16. Roberts, C.V. and Vinson, L. (1998) 'Relationship among willingness to listen, receiver apprehension, communication apprehension, communication competence, and dogmatism', *International Journal of Listening*, **12**: 40–56.
17. Booth-Butterfield, S., Chory, R. and Beynon, W. (1997) 'Communication apprehension and health communication and behaviors', *Communication Quarterly*, **45**(3): 235–50.
18. Watson, A.K., Monroe, E.E. and Atterstrom, H. (1989) 'Comparison of communication apprehension across cultures: American and Swedish children', *Communication Quarterly*, **37**(1): 67–76.
19. Kim, M.-S., Aune, K.S., Hunter, J.E., Kim, H.-J. and Kim, J.-S. (2001) 'The effect of culture and self-construals on predispositions toward verbal communication', *Human Communication Research*, **27**(3): 382–408.

20. Allen, M. and Bourhis, J. (1996) 'The relationship of communication apprehension to communication behavior: a meta-analysis', *Communication Quarterly* **44**(2): 214–26.
21. Hsu, C.-F. (2002) 'The influence of self-construals, family and teacher communication patterns on communication apprehension among college students in Taiwan', *Communication Reports*, **15**(2): 123–32.
22. McCroskey, J.C., Fayer, J.M. and Richmond, V.P. (1985) 'Don't speak to me in English: communication in Puerto Rico', *Communication Quarterly*, **33**(3): 185–92.
23. Toale, M.C. and McCroskey, J.C. (2001) 'Ethnocentrism and trait communication apprehension as predictors of interethnic communication apprehension and use of relational maintenance strategies in interethnic communication', *Communication Quarterly*, **49**(1): 70–83.
24. Kim, M.-S. (1999) 'Cross-cultural perspectives on motivations of verbal communication: Review, critique, and a theoretical framework', *Communication Yearbook*, **22**: 51–89.
25. Goleman, D. (1998) *Working with Emotional Intelligence*, New York: Bantam Books.
26. Ashkanasy, N. M. and Daus, C. S. (2005) 'Rumors of the death of emotional intelligence in organizational behavior are vastly exaggerated', *Journal of Organizational Behavior*, **26**: 441–52.
27. Mayer, J.D., DiPaolo, M. and Salovey, P. (1990) 'Perceiving affective content in ambiguous visual stimuli: A component of emotional intelligence', *Journal of Personality Assessment*, **54**: 772–81.
28. Ashkanasy, op. cit.
29. Rahim, M.A. and Psenicka, C. (2002) 'A model of emotional intelligence and conflict management strategies: a study in seven countries', *The International Journal of Organizational Analysis*, **10**(4): 302–26.
30. Sharma, P., Tam, J.L.M. and Kim, N. (2009) 'Demystifying intercultural service encounters: toward a comprehensive conceptual framework', *Journal of Service Research*, **12**: 227–42.
31. Johansson, J.K. (1994) 'Cultural understanding as managerial skill: Japan, North America and Europe', Presentation made at the David See-Chai Lam Centre for International Communication – Pacific Region Forum on Business and Management Communication, Simon Fraser University at Harbour Centre. URL:http://www.cic.sfu.ca/forum
32. Robinson, S. (1997) 'Intercultural management: the art of resolving and avoiding conflicts between cultures', AIESEC Global Theme Conference: Learning and Acting for a Shared Future. URL:http//www.eye.ch/~gtc97/intercul.html
33. Menon, T., Chi-yue, C., Morris, M.W. and Hong, Y.Y. (2000) 'Motivated cultural cognition: the impact of implicit cultural theories on dispositional attribution varies as a function of the need for closure', *Journal of Personality and Social Psychology*, **78**(2): 247–59.
34. Porter, D.M., Jr. (2001) 'Gender differences in managers' conceptions and perceptions of commitment to the organization', *Sex Roles: A Journal of Research*, **45**(5/6): 375–98.
35. Krug, J.A. and Nigh, D. (2001) 'Executive perceptions in foreign and domestic acquisitions: an analysis of foreign ownership and its effect on executive fate', *Journal of World Business*, **36**(1): 85–105.
36. Vigoda, E. (2001) 'Reactions to organizational politics: a cross-cultural examination in Israel and Britain', *Human Relations*, **54**(11): 1,483–1,518.
37 Bond, M.H. and Smith, P.B. (1996) 'Cross-cultural social and organizational psychology', *Annual Review of Psychology*, **47**: 205–35.
38. Ibid.
39. West, T. and Levy, S.R. (2002) 'Background belief systems and prejudice', in Lonner, W.J., Dinnel, D.L., Hayes, S.A. and Sattler, D.N. (eds) *Online Readings in Psychology and Culture* (unit 15, chapter 4). URL: http://orpc.iaccp.org/, last accessed on 22 December 2010.
40. Sidanius, J., Levin, S., Liu, J. and Pratto, F. (2000) 'Social dominance orientation, antiegalitarianism and the political psychology of gender; an extension and cross-cultural replication', *European Journal of Social Psychology*, **30**: 41–67.
41. Furnham, A., Bond, M.H., Heaven, P., Hilton, D., Lobel T., Masters, J., Payne, M., Rajamanikam, R., Stacey, B., Daalen, H.V. (1993) 'A comparison of Protestant work ethic beliefs in thirteen nations', *Journal of Social Psychology*, **133**: 185–97.
42. Smith, P.B., Trompenaars, F. and Dugan, S. (1995) 'The Rotter locus of control scale in 43 countries: a test of cultural relativity', *International Journal of Psychology*, **30**: 377–400.

43. Furnham *et al.*, 'A comparison of Protestant work ethic beliefs in thirteen nations'.
44. Greeley, A. (1990) *The Catholic Myth,* New York: Macmillan.
45. Parboteeah, K.P., Paik, Y. and Cullen, J. (2009) 'Religious groups and work values,' *International Journal of Cross Cultural Management,* **9**(1): 51–67.
46. Alkhazraji, K.M., Gardner III, W.L., Martin, J.S. and Paolillo, J.G.P. (1997) 'The acculturation of immigrants to US organizations: the case of Muslim employees', *Management Communication Quarterly,* **11**(2): 217–65.
47. Stewart, R.A. and Roach, K.D. (1993) 'Argumentativeness, religious orientation, and reactions to argument situations involving religious versus nonreligious issues', *Communication Quarterly,* **41**(1): 26–39.
48. Alkhazraji *et al.*, 'The acculturation of immigrants to US organizations'.
49. Swee, H.A. (2000) 'The power of money: a cross-cultural analysis of business-related beliefs', *Journal of World Business,* **35**(1): 43–60.
50. Niles, F.S. (1999) 'Toward a cross-cultural understanding of work-related beliefs', *Human Relations,* **52**: 855–67.
51. Markoczy, L. (2000) 'National culture and strategic change in belief formation', *Journal of International Business Studies,* **31**(3): 417–42.
52. Gilligan, C. (1982) *In a Different Voice: Psychological Theory and Women's Development,* Cambridge, MA: Harvard University Press.
53. Gianakos, I. (2002) 'Predictors of coping with work stress: the influences of sex, gender role, social desirability, and locus of control', *Sex Roles: A Journal of Research,* **42**: 1059–79.
54. Barron, L. (2003) 'Ask and you shall receive? Gender differences in negotiators' beliefs about requests for a higher salary', *Human Relations,* **56**(6): 635–62.
55. Puffer, S.M., McCarthy, D.J. and Naumov, A.I. (1997) 'Russian managers' beliefs about work: beyond the stereotypes', *Journal of World Business,* **32**(3): 258–76.
56. Schein, E.H. (1992) *Organizational Culture and Leadership* (2nd edn), San Francisco, CA: Jossey-Bass.
57. Kashima, Y., Kashima, E., Chiu, C.-Y., Farsides, T., Gelfand, M., Hong, Y.-Y., Kim, U., Strack, F. and Wer. L. (2005) 'Culture, essentialism, and agency: Are individuals universally believed to be more real entities than groups?', *European Journal of Social Psychology,* **35**: 147–69.
58. Triandis, H.C. (1990) 'Theoretical concepts that are applicable to the analysis of ethnocentrism', in Brislin, R.W. (ed.) *Applied Cross-Cultural Psychology,* Newbury Park, CA: Sage.
59. Alderfer, C.P. and Smith, K.K. (1982) 'Studying intergroup relations embedded in organizations', *Administrative Science Quarterly,* **27**: 5–65.
60. Grat, M.J., Button, C.J., Hannah, T.E. and Ross, A.S. (2002) 'Uncovering the multidimensional nature of stereotype inferences: a within-participants' study of gender, age and physical attractiveness', *Current Research in Social Psychology,* **8**: 2. URL:http://www. uiowa. edu/~grpproc/crisp/crisp.html
61. Brauer, M., Judd, C.M. and Jacquelin, V. (2001) 'The communication of social stereotypes: the Effects of group discussion and information distribution on stereotypic appraisals', *Journal of Personality and Social Psychology,* **81**(3): 463–75.
62. Hagendoorn, L. and Kleinpenning, G. (1991) 'The contribution of domain-specific stereotypes to ethnic social distance', *British Journal of Social Psychology,* **30**: 63–78.
63. Chiu, W.C.K., Chan, A.W., Snape, E. and Redman, T. (2001) 'Age stereotypes and discriminatory attitudes towards older workers: an East-West comparison', *Human Relations,* **54**(5): 629–62.
64. Devine, P.G. (2001) 'Implicit prejudice and stereotyping: how automatic are they?', *Journal of Personality and Social Psychology,* **81**(5): 757–9.
65. Kunda, Z., Davies, P.G., Adams, B.D. and Spencer, S.J. (2002) 'The dynamic time course of stereotype activation: activation, dissipation, and resurrection', *Journal of Personality and Social Psychology,* **82**(3): 283–99.
66. Giles, H., Henwood, K., Coupland, D., Harriman, J. and Coupland, J. (1992) 'Language attitudes and cognitive mediation', *Human Communication Research,* **18**(4): 500–27.

67. Rettew, D.C., Billman, D. and Davis, R.A. (1993) 'Inaccurate perceptions of the amount others stereotype: estimates about stereotypes of one's own group and other groups', *Basic and Applied Social Psychology*, **14**: 121–42.

68. Best, D.L. and Williams, J.E. (1994) 'Masculinity/femininity in the self and ideal selfdescriptions of university students in fourteen countries', in Bouvy, A.M., van de Vijver, F.J.R., Boski, P. and Schmitz, P. (eds) *Journeys into Cross-Cultural Psychology*, Amsterdam: Swets & Zeitlinger.

69. Chiu *et al.*, 'Age stereotypes and discriminatory attitudes towards older workers'.

70. Hoyt, S.K. (1999) 'Mentoring with class: connections between social class and developmental relationships in the Academy', in Murrell, A.J., Crosby, F.J. and Ely, R.J. (eds) *Mentoring Dilemmas: Developmental Relationships within Multicultural Organizations*, Hillsdale, NJ: Lawrence Erlbaum.

71. Williams, J.E. and Best, D. (1990) *Sex and Psyche: Gender and Self Viewed Cross-Culturally*, Newbury Park, CA: Sage.

72. Burgoon, J.K. and Le Poire, B.A. (1993) 'Effects of communication expectancies, actual communication and expectancy disconfirmation evaluations of communicators and their communication behavior', *Human Communication Research*, **20**(1): 67–96.

73. Ducharme, D. and Bernard, R. (2001) 'Communication breakdowns: an exploration of contextualization in native and non-native speakers of French', *Journal of Pragmatics*, **33**: 825–47.

74. Ali, A.J. (1993) 'Decision-making style, individualism and attitudes toward risk of Arab executives', *International Studies of Management and Organization*, **23**(3): 53–74.

75. Berger, C.R. and Zelditch, M. (1985) *Status, Rewards and Influence*, San Francisco: Jossey-Bass.

76. Thompson, A.G. (1996) 'Compliance with agreements in cross-cultural transactions: some analytical issues', *Journal of International Business Studies*, **27**(2): 375–90.

77. Cichon, E.J. and Masterson, J.T. (1993) 'Physician-patient communication: Mutual role expectations', *Communication Quarterly*, **41**(4): 477–89.

78. Apel, D. and Yoram, B.-T. (1996) 'Nursing staff responses to violent events in closed psychiatric wards: a comparison between attributional and cognitive neo-associanistic analyses', *British Journal of Social Psychology*, **35**: 509–21.

79. Abelman, R. (1991) 'The depiction of women in religious television', *The Journal of Communication and Religion*, **14**(2): 1–14.

80. Tsui, A.S., Porter, L.W. and Egan, T.D. (2002) 'When both similarities and dissimilarities matter: extending the concept of relational demography', *Human Relations*, **55**(8): 899–930.

81. Ajzen, L. (1991) 'The theory of planned behaviour: some unresolved issues', *Organizational Behavior and Human Decision Processes*, **50**: 179–211.

82. Dovidio, J.F., Kawakkami, K. and Gaertner, S.L. (2002) 'Implicit and explicit prejudice and interracial interaction', *Journal of Personality and Social Psychology*, **82**(1): 62–8.

83. Ickes, W. (1984) 'Compositions in black and whites: determinants of interaction in interracial dyads', *Journal of Personality and Social Psychology*, **47**: 330–41.

84. Liu, S. (2003) 'Cultures within culture: unity and diversity of two generations of employees in state-owned enterprises', *Human Relations*, **56**: 387–417.

85. Gibson, C.B. and Manuel, J. (2003) 'Building trust: effective multi-cultural communication processes in virtual teams', in Gibson, C.B. and Cohen, S.G. (eds) *Virtual Teams That Work: Creating Conditions for Virtual team Effectiveness*, San Francisco, CA: Jossey-Bass.

86. Fukuyama, F. (1995) *Trust: The Social Virtues and the Creation of Prosperity*, New York: Free Press.

87. Halman, L. and Kerkhofs, J. (2001) *The European Values Study: Selected Results*. URL:www. romir.ru/eng/research/01_2001/european-values.htm, last accessed on 22 December 2010.

88. Nicol, D. (1994) 'Trust: critical and cultural', URL: http://blue.temple.edu/~eastern/nicol. html

89. Lee, C., Madan, P. and Law, K. (2000) 'Power distance, gender and organizational justice', *Journal of Management*, **26**(4): 685–704.

90. Bond and Smith, 'Cross-cultural social and organizational psychology'.
91. McCrae, R.R. (2002) 'Cross-cultural research on the five-factor model of personality', in Lonner, W.J., Dinnel, D.L., Hayes, S.A. and Sattler, D.N. (eds) *Online Readings in Psychology and Culture* (unit 6, chapter 1). URL: http://orpc.iaccp.org/, last accessed on 22 December 2010.
92. Ibid.
93. Adorno, T.W. (1991), *The Culture Industry: Selected Essays on Mass Culture*, London: Routledge.
94. Argyle, M. (2000) *Psychology and Religion: An Introduction*, London: Routledge.
95. Thompson, N. (2003) *Communication and Language: A Handbook of Theory and Practice*, Basingstoke: Palgrave Macmillan.
96. Ibid.
97. Markus, R.H. and Kitayama, S. (1994) 'A collective fear of the collective: implications for selves and theories of selves', *Personality and Social Psychology Bulletin*, **20**(5): 568–79.
98. Abramson, N.R., Lane, H.W., Nagai, H. and Takagi, H. (1993) 'A comparison of Canadian and Japanese cognitive styles: implications for management interaction', *Journal of International Business Studies*, **24**(3): 515–87.
99. Singelis, T.M. (1994) 'The measurement of independent and interdependent self-construals', *Personality and Social Psychology Bulletin*, **20**: 580–91.
100. Tasaki, K., Kim, M.-S. and Miller, M.D. (1999) 'The effects of social status on cognitive elaboration and post-message attitude: focusing on self-construals', *Communication Quarterly*, **47**(2): 196–214.
101. Brockner, J. (2000) 'Culture and procedural fairness: when the effects of what you do depend on how you do it', *Administrative Science Quarterly*, **45**: 138–59.
102. Kim, M.-S., Shin, H.-C. and Cai, D. (1998) 'Cultural influences on the preferred forms of requesting and re-requesting', *Communication Monographs*, **65**(1): 47–66.
103. Martin, J.N. and Nakayama, T. (1997) *Intercultural Communication in Contexts*, Mountainview, CA: Mayfield Publishing Company.
104. Phinney, J.S. (1996) 'When we talk about American ethnic groups, what do we mean?' *American Psychologist*, **51**: 918–27.
105. Weinreich, P., Luk, C. and Bond, M.H. (1994) 'Ethnic identity: identification with other cultures, self-esteem and identity confusion', International Conference on Immigration, Language Acquisition and Patterns of Social Integration, Jerusalem.
106. Ting-Toomey, S. (1988) 'Intercultural conflict styles: a face-negotiation theory', in Kim, Y.Y. and Gudykunst, W.B. (eds) *Theories in Intercultural Communication*, Newbury Park, CA: Sage.
107. Best and Williams, 'Masculinity/feminity in the self'.
108. Cross, S.E. and Madison, L. (1997) 'Models of the self: self-construals and gender', *Psychological Bulletin*, **122**(1): 5–37.
109. Roberts, T.-A. (1991) 'Gender and the influence of evaluations on self-assessments in achievement settings', *Psychological Bulletin*, **109**(2): 297–308.
110. Beyer, S. (1998) 'Gender differences in self-perception and negative recall biases', *Sex Roles: A Research Journal*, **38**: 103–33.
111. Hoyt, 'Mentoring with class'.
112. Huntington, S.P. (1997) *The Clash of Civilizations and The Remaking of World Order*, London: Simon & Schuster.
113. Kelly, A.E., Sedlacek, W.E. and Scales, W.R. (1994) 'How college students with and without disabilities perceive themselves and each other', *Journal of Counseling and Development*, **73**: 178–82.
114. Jetten, J., Postmes, T. and McAuliffe, B.J. (2002) 'We're all individuals: group norms of individualism and collectivism, levels of identification and identity threat', *European Journal of Social Psychology*, **32**(2): 189–207.
115. Kim, M.-S. and Leung, T. (2000) 'A multicultural view of conflict management styles: review and critical synthesis', *Communication Yearbook*, **23**: 227–69.

116. Huntington, *The Clash of Civilizations*.
117. Lind, R.A. (2001) 'The relevance of cultural identity: relying upon foundations of race and gender as laypeople plan a newscast', *Journalism and Communication Monographs*, **3**(3): 113–45.
118. Schneider, A. (2002) 'Behaviour prescriptions versus professional identities in multicultural corporations: a cross-cultural computer simulation', *Organization Studies*, **23**(1): 105–32.
119. Varela, F., Thompson, E. and Rosch, E. (1991) *The Embodied Mind*, Cambridge, MA: MIT Press.
120. Farh, J.L., Dobbins, G.H. and Cheng, B. (1991) 'Cultural relativity in action: a comparison of self-ratings made by Chinese and US workers', *Personnel Psychology*, **44**: 129–47.
121. Yu, J. and Murphy, K.R. (1993) 'Modesty bias in self-ratings of performance: a test of the cultural relativity hypothesis', *Personnel Psychology*, **46**: 357–73.
122. Bond and Smith, 'Cross-cultural social and organizational psychology'.
123. Bazerman, M.H., Curhan, J.R., Moore, D.A. and Valley, K.L. (2000) 'Negotiation', *Annual Review of Psychology*, **51**: 279–314.
124. Stajkovic, A.J. and Luthans, F. (1997) 'Business ethics across cultures: a social cognitive model', *Journal of World Business*, **32**(1): 17–34.
125. Kazakov, A.Y., Taylor, T.C. and Thompson, M. (1997) 'Business ethics and civil society in Russia', *International Studies of Management and Organization*, **27**(1): 5–18.
126. Miller, J.G. and Bersoff, D.M. (1992) 'Culture and moral judgment: how are conflicts between justice and interpersonal responsibilities resolved?', *Journal of Personality and Social Psychology*, **62**(4): 541–54.
127. Murphy-Berman, V. and Berman, J.J. (2002) 'Cross-cultural differences in perceptions of distributive justice', *Journal of Cross-Cultural Psychology*, **33**(2): 157–170.
128. Seiter, J.S., Bruschke, J. and Bai, C. (2002) 'The acceptability of deception as a function of perceivers' culture, deceiver's intention, and deceiver-deceived relationship', *Western Journal of Communication*, **66**(2): 158–180.
129. Ali, A.J. (1995) 'Cultural discontinuity and Arab management thought', *International Studies of Management and Organization*, **25**(3): 7–30.
130. Jackson, T. (2001) 'Cultural values and management ethics: a 10-nation study', *Human Relations*, **54**(10): 1,267–1,302.
131. Butterfield, K.D., Treviño, L.K. and Weaver, G.R. (2000) 'Moral awareness in business organizations: influences of issue-related and social context factors', *Human Relations*, **53**(7): 981–1,018.
132. Sims, R.L. (2009) 'Collective versus individualist national cultures: comparing Taiwan and U.S. employee attitudes toward unethical business practices', Business & Society, **48**(1): 39–59.
133. Zhuang, J., Thomas, S. and Miller, D.L. (2005) 'Examining culture's effect on whistle-blowing and peer reporting', Business & Society, **44**: 462–86.
134. Antal, A.B. and Sobczak, A. (2007) 'Corporate social responsibility in France: a mix of national traditions and international influences', Business & Society, **46**: 9–32.
135. Chapple, W. and Moon, J. (2005) 'Corporate social responsibility (CSR) in Asia: a seven-country study of CSR web site reporting', Business & Society, **44**: 415–41.
136. Kimber, D. and Lipton, P. (2005) 'Corporate governance and business ethics in the Asia-Pacific region', *Business & Society*, **44**: 178–210.
137. Albaum, G. and Peterson, R.S. (2006) 'Ethical attitudes of future business leaders: do they vary by gender and religiosity?' *Business & Society*, **45**: 300–21.
138. Argyle, *Psychology and Religion*.
139. Triandis, H. (2000) 'Culture and conflict', *International Journal of Psychology*, **35**(2): 145–52.
140. Plaks, J.E., Stroessner, S.J., Dweck, C.S. and Sherman, J.W. (2001) 'Person theories and attention allocation: preferences for stereotypic versus counterstereotypic information', *Journal of Personality and Social Psychology*, **80**(6): 876–93.
141. Chandler, T.A., Shama, D.D., Wolf, F.M. and Planchard, S.K. (1981) 'Multiattributional causality for social affiliation across five cross-national samples', *Journal of Psychology*, **107**: 219–29.

142. Nurmi, J. (1992) 'Cross-cultural differences in self-serving bias: responses to the attribu-tional style questionnaire by American and Finnish students', *Journal of Social Psychology*, **132**(1): 69–76.

143. Shweder, R.A. and Bourne, E.J. (1982) 'Does the concept of the person vary cross-culturally?' in Marsella, M.J. and White, G.M. (eds) *Cultural Conceptions of Mental Health and Therapy*, Dordrecht: Reidel, pp. 97–137.

144. Morris, M.W. and Peng, K.P. (1994) 'Culture and cause: American and Chinese attributions for social and physical events', *Journal of Personality and Social Psychology*, **67**: 949–71.

145. Merritt, R.D. and Kok, C.J. (1995) 'Attribution of gender to a gender-unspecified individual: an evaluation of the "people = male" hypothesis', *Sex Roles: A Journal of Research*, **33**: 145–57.

146. Peckham, P. and Ryckman, D.B. (1987) 'Gender differences in attributions for success and failure situations across subject areas', *Journal of Educational Research*, **81**(2): 120–5.

147. Martin, L.R. and Morgan, S. (1995) 'Middle managers in banking: an investigation of gen-der differences in behavior, demographics, and productivity', *Quarterly Journal of Business and Economics*, **34**(1): 55–68.

148. De Judicibus, M. and Mccabe, M.P. (2001) 'Blaming the target of sexual harassment: impact of gender role, sexist attitudes, and work role', *Sex Roles: A Journal of Research*, **41**: 401–17.

149. Macgeorge, E.L. (2003) 'Gender differences in attributions and emotions in helping con-texts', *Sex Roles: A Journal of Research*, **48**(3): 175–82.

150. Rosenthal, P. (1996) 'Gender and managers' causal attributions for subordinate perform-ance: a field story', *Sex Roles: A Journal of Research*, **34**: 121–36.

151. Hovemyr, M. (1998) 'The attribution of success and failure as related to different patterns of religious orientation', *International Journal for the Psychology of Religion*, **8**(2): 107–24.

152. Kashima, Y. and Triandis, H.C. (1986) 'The self-serving bias in attributions as a coping strat-egy: a cross-cultural study', *Journal of Cross-Cultural Psychology*, **17**(1): 83–97.

153. Maletzke, G. (1996). *Interkulturelle Kommunikation: zur Interaktion zwischen Menschen*. Opladen: Westdeutscher.

154. Joy, S. and Kolb, D.A. (2009) 'Are there cultural differences in learning style?' *International Journal of Intercultural Relations*, **33**(1): 69–85.

155. Abramson *et al.*, 'A comparison of Canadian and Japanese cognitive styles'.

Intercultural Communication at Work

chapter five

Barriers to Intercultural Communication

Common experience teaches that communication is flawed and can lead to misunderstanding and even conflict. Communication theorists generally take it as given that communication can never be perfect.[1] There are many sources of miscommunication. They include 'noise', in the technical sense of interference, whether physical or psychological, which prevents messages being received; poor encoding by the sender; distortion by the medium; and selection, inaccurate decoding, distorted interpretation and indiscriminate categorization by the receiver. The two-way nature of face-to-face communication creates possibilities for reducing miscommunication by feedback (the sender can find out how well the receiver is understanding and responding). However, it also imposes demanding time pressure on each receiver in turn to respond, so reducing opportunities for thinking through what they say.

In the case of people from different backgrounds, there are some additional sources of miscommunication. For people who do not take cultural difference into account there is the impediment commented on by Trompenaars (1993): 'Without awareness of the nature of the differences between cultures, we tend to measure others against our own cultural standards. An early and sometimes painful lesson is that all cultures have their own, perfectly consistent but different, logics.'[2] Cultural 'imprisonment' can lead to arrogance, cultural imperialism and an uncritical dependence on one way of thinking.

In this book, the term 'miscommunication' is used broadly, even to cover cases where communication is intended but none occurs – as when B hears what A says but ignores it and pretends not to hear. This broad definition means that miscommunication includes at least all the following cases:

- Communication is intended but none occurs.
- The receiver makes no sense of the message.
- The receiver misunderstands the message – the speaker's meaning and the receiver's understanding of the meaning are different.
- The speaker's communicative intention (to ask a question, make a request, make a promise, etc.) is not understood.
- Information imparted by the speaker, which s/he intended to have believed, is not believed.
- An attempt to persuade fails.

■ An attempt to exert power fails.
■ A communication is understood but provokes unintended conflict.

So broad a use of 'miscommunication' extends its usual definition, but allows it to refer to all cases where barriers to communication are effective. However, this does not mean that all cases of disagreement, for example, constitute miscommunication: a process of working through disagreement can increase understanding.

Section 5.1 describes those sources of miscommunication that are 'universal' barriers, but that apply with particular force in intercultural situations. Section 5.2 describes prejudice, discrimination and harassment and discusses their negative consequences for individuals, organizations and work communication. Section 5.3 describes those obstacles arising from the fact that, as the previous two chapters showed, differences of background, whether cultural or subcultural, ethnic, gender-based or based on some other distinction, do affect how people communicate. There is, however, still some debate about whether such differences actually do create barriers to communication, and if so how. This chapter will attempt an answer to this question; it will argue that they do and try to show how. Section 5.4 builds on the analysis of cultural differences in the factors and processes underlying behaviour to consider how those differences can create barriers to intercultural communication. Section 5.5 introduces two specifically work-related types of barrier – heterogeneity of work groups and task-related conflict. Section 5.6 considers the possible barriers to intercultural communication created by negative or weak organizational policies regarding diversity, and the contrariwise effect of strong positive policies.

5.1 'UNIVERSAL' BARRIERS

As the introduction to this chapter stated, some barriers apply to all or most communication, but create particular problems in intercultural communication. This section discusses two such barriers: the general problem of inter-group communication and stereotyping.

The general problem of inter-group communication

Modern work generally involves meeting or working with individuals from different ethnic backgrounds, socio-economic classes, age groups, occupational categories and so forth. In these encounters, people may communicate with each other not just or even mainly as individuals with unique temperaments and personalities but to a considerable extent as undifferentiated representatives of social groups. For example, Person A might deal with Person B as a 'Polish Catholic lawyer' or 'White male doctor' and Person B might deal with Person A as a 'Welsh Protestant client' or an 'Afro-Caribbean woman nurse'. (When people respond to one another primarily in terms of their group membership, the terms 'inter-group encounter' and 'inter-group communication' apply even if only two people are present.) This tendency to emphasize group membership is especially strong at initial meetings with 'strangers', which here means anyone who is believed to lack understanding of the social world inhabited by members of the other person's or people's in-group.

Whether people do or do not treat an encounter as inter-group usually depends on the four factors shown in Figure 5.1. Recognizing that someone's ethnicity, religion or gender is different can lead to an interaction being treated as inter-group. It may not, however, if the individual's personal attitudes or the subject of the interaction make

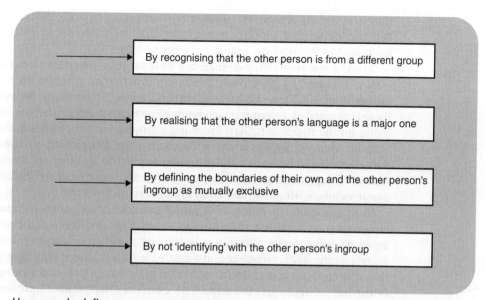

By recognising that the other person is from a different group

By realising that the other person's language is a major one

By defining the boundaries of their own and the other person's ingroup as mutually exclusive

By not 'identifying' with the other person's ingroup

Figure 5.1 *How people define an encounter as inter-group*

Based on: Rogers, E. and Kincaid, D. (1981) *Communication Networks: Toward a New Paradigm for Research*, NY: Free Press

group memberships seem irrelevant. For example, perceived religious difference might have no bearing on a discussion of software capability. A second factor is whether the other person's language is perceived as a major one; if not, as in the case of English-speaking people interacting with Welsh-speaking people, the English might not treat the encounter as inter-group (but the Welsh might). Third, where people draw their in-group boundaries varies from person to person and occasion to occasion. A French person might, on some occasions, perceive his or her in-group as 'European' and so not regard an encounter with a German as inter-group. Finally, an individual may disregard social group differences if s/he perceives the status of the other person's in-group as high and identifies with it or perceives an overlap in social categories ('You may be an English businesswoman, but, like me, you are a woman.'). Where none of these exceptions applies, awareness that the other person is from a different major group usually leads to the encounter being treated as inter-group.

Outgroup co-variation effect and in-group favouritism

Part of the explanation for treating strangers as group members rather than individuals is the 'outgroup co-variation effect'. People generally see their outgroups as less variable (more similar) along single characteristics, such as intelligence or cleanliness, than their in-group. They may also be affected by inter-group bias – a tendency to see members of their in-group more favourably than members of outgroups. Inter-group bias is a complex phenomenon. For example, people without disabilities tend to display more bias towards people with disabilities than the latter do toward the former. The former are also more likely to be derogatory about people with disabilities than vice versa. In contrast, following a rewarding interaction experience with a member of a 'no disability' outgroup, people with disabilities display an evaluative bias in favour of, and identify with, the 'no disability' outgroup. An explanation can be found in social identity theory, which states that people identify more strongly with groups that they find socially rewarding.[3] Inter-group bias occurs so easily that it is common even between 'minimalist' groups – where individuals are randomly allocated to groups and know that that is how the groups have been formed.[4]

It has been shown that people from a wide range of categories favour their in-group. It may be caused by individuals' needs to simplify their complex environment (need for cognitive economy) and for self-enhancement.[5] However, so far as the second of these is concerned, recent research tends to contradict this prediction. No support was found for the hypothesis that, following a group's showing in-group favouritism in a particular domain, such as artistic ability, individual group members' self-esteem in that domain would increase. A similar finding applied to members of a religious group – American Baptists. One possible explanation for these negative findings is that the group members felt guilty about having shown favouritism.[6]

How legitimate members of a group consider their status in relation to other groups profoundly affects their inter-group attitudes, emotions and behaviour. If their ingroup's status seems illegitimately low, its members experience higher perceived relative deprivation, prejudice and a desire for social change; they may engage in realistic and/or social competition, collective protest or action and inter-group conflict. Perceiving an ingroup's status to be illegitimately high leads to pro-social instead of discriminatory attitudes and action tendencies. This has been found among White South Africans towards Black South Africans and West Germans towards East Germans. The perceived legitimacy of an outgroup's status seems to be related to how far the outgroup members conform to prototypical norms. When Germans were asked whether they thought that Turkey was entitled to become a member of the European Union (EU), the more they thought Germany was relatively more prototypical for Europe than Turkey, the less they thought Turkey was entitled to membership in the EU.[7]

It has been shown that how people evaluate an ingroup's standing on an ability dimension is based partly on performance outcomes of an in-group in comparison with an outgroup and partly on circumstances related to their performance. Thus, when people know their in-group is disadvantaged, there is an increase (1) in their beliefs that together they can improve their performance, (2) in their individual effort on behalf of the in-group and (3) in their tendency to hinder the future performance of an outgroup.[8]

Social distance

The degree of felt closeness to other participants in an interaction, such as a negotiation, is called social distance. It is acknowledged to have a profound influence on individual decisions and helps to explain individual economic decisions that bear social consequences. It was previously treated as universal, but results from a 2006 study demonstrated differences between countries regarding the effect of social distance. Cultural orientation at the individual level demonstrated clear differences in the responsiveness of individually versus collectively oriented participants to the manipulation of social distance.[9]

Effects of inter-group problems

Communicating with others as representatives of their groups can create barriers and complications in at least the following ways:

- People's group membership is not always obvious: identifying it is often a creative process in which linguistic 'work' must be done and group membership must be inferred. There is scope for making errors during this process.

■ Interpersonal factors cannot be ignored in inter-group encounters, so both group and personal factors must be handled, creating complexity.

■ Inter-group communication involves at least one of the individuals present being regarded as a 'stranger'. Interactions with strangers can create anxiety and often are experienced by both parties as a series of crises.[10]

■ As Chapter 4 showed, people attribute other people's behaviour to their disposition or their situation. When they treat an encounter as 'inter-group', they commonly use their knowledge of the group to 'decide' their attributions. This increases the likelihood that they will attribute different others' behaviour to their disposition as opposed to their situation, and will possibly judge it more harshly.[11] In addition, they may not know much about the 'culture' (beliefs, attitudes and so on) of the different other's group, leading them to make false attributions or, if they are aware of the problem, to make limited and provisional attributions that inhibit openness.[12]

■ Ethnocentrism is readily activated in inter-group encounters, leading to hostility towards the different others.

■ Criticism from outsiders provokes high levels of defensiveness and inter-group suspicion, leading to rejecting the truth of the comments. In contrast, criticism from in-group members is tolerated 'surprisingly well', and is seen to be more legitimate and constructive than outgroup criticism. Positive comments are received from outsiders as well as from insiders, suggesting that the effect of outsiders' criticism is not due to general outgroup negative bias.[13]

■ Inter-group relations are more competitive and discordant than relations between interacting individuals; this is particularly so when the people involved depend on one another. Highly interdependent research subjects endorse threat more and acceptance of others' demands less to a relatively greater degree in an inter-group as opposed to an inter-individual conflict.

These sources of potential miscommunication are summarized in Figure 5.2.

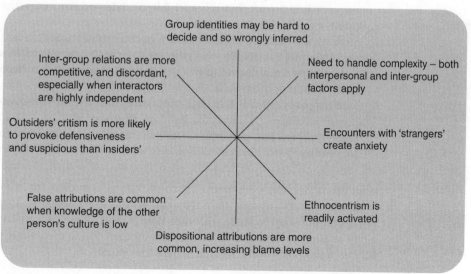

Figure 5.2   *Factors increasing the amount of poor communication in inter-group encounters*

Box 5.1

A Chinese woman banker looking for work in London was often interviewed for jobs on the strength of her cv but then failed the selection interviews. On one occasion she was asked why she had left her previous job. Her answer was 'A new woman manager was appointed and she did not like me.' The interviewers' report was that she had excellent banking expertise but lacked 'competencies'.

Source: author's research

Stereotyping

Stereotypes were explained in Chapter 4. Stereotyping, though a natural and necessary process, can distort communication. It may lead people to base their messages, their ways of transmitting them and their reception of them on false assumptions.

These distortions arise in at least the following five ways:

1. Stereotypes can influence how information is processed. More favourable information is remembered about those of whom the stereotype is positive, less favourable about those of whom it is negative; for instance, someone who has a stereotype of Scottish people as 'mean' is likely not to notice or quickly to forget if a Scottish person shows generosity.
2. Objectively, there is often more variation within groups than between them. This applies even to fundamental cultural values, and still more to more superficial characteristics such as 'meanness'. Stereotyping, though, leads to individuality being overlooked.
3. Stereotypes create expectations about 'others', and individual others often feel a pressure to confirm these expectations. It may seem unlikely that Scottish people will try to confirm expectations that they are mean, though it can happen; but research has shown that schoolchildren underperform if teachers expect less of them because of their background.
4. Stereotypes constrain others' patterns of communication. Conventions and politeness may prevent people who perceive they are being treated in accordance with a stereotype from disputing it. Even if they do react, this is likely to disrupt the conversation or discussion.
5. Stereotypes create self-fulfilling prophecies in the form of stereotype-confirming communication. A clear example is the way that, as Chapter 3 showed, some women use 'powerless' ways of speaking to conform to stereotypes of femininity.[14]

In addition, negative stereotypes can contribute to prejudice. For instance, 76 per cent of African Americans said they felt that Whites are insensitive to people and that Whites do not want to share with non-Whites, and 79 per cent that Whites see themselves as superior and able to boss others around. These communication stereotypes may be 'a key piece of the interracial relations puzzle'.[15]

Contributory causes and effects of two 'universal' sources of miscommunication were discussed. Dealing with other people as 'representatives' or typical members of their group leads to in-group favouritism and inter-group negative bias. Stereotypes distort communication when they lead people to base their messages, their ways of transmitting them and their reception of them on false assumptions. These distortions occur most often in communication between members of different societal groups.

5.2   PREJUDICE AND DISCRIMINATION

Prejudice, discrimination and harassment not only 'deafen' their perpetrators to communication from the groups against which they are prejudiced or against which they practise discrimination, but cause members of those groups and other unprejudiced people to close down or distort their communication with the perpetrators.

Prejudice

Prejudice is a thoughtless, derogatory attitude or set of attitudes towards all or most of the members of a group. Although the term can refer to a positive bias, in modern usage prejudice usually refers to an irrationally unfavourable or hostile attitude. It includes racism, sexism, homophobia and ageism. Religious prejudice, too, can be as potent and thoughtless as any of these. Prejudice gives rise to myths, such as that some dialects or accents indicate lower intelligence. From a linguistic point of view, all languages and dialects are complex, sophisticated sets of systems and it makes little or no sense to argue that one is 'superior' to another.

One major strand in approaches to the origins of prejudice is to view it as a personality trait linked to authoritarianism (measured by an 'F' – for Fascist – scale) resulting from early socialization. However, a cross-cultural study of prejudice in South Africa and the United States showed that racists in those countries did not necessarily have high levels of authoritarianism.[16] Furthermore, individual-level explanations of extreme prejudice fail to account for its widespread incidence in some societies. For these reasons, sociocultural factors are now considered better at explaining prejudice. Research into how prejudice operates is beginning to reveal some unexpected aspects. For example, people seem to be more, not less, willing to act in a prejudiced way after they have, for instance, disagreed with blatantly sexist statements or made a job selection in favour of a member of a group against whom there is a widespread prejudice, such as a Muslim in Southern France. They might then reject a woman for a stereotypically male job or reject a member of a minority group for a job stereotypically suited to majority members. This behaviour may occur because they feel they have previously established their moral credentials and so act according to their prejudices.[17]

Ethnic prejudice

Between 1990 and 2000 most countries of Europe saw a decrease in ethnic prejudice, as measured by the percentages stating that they would not want members of another race as neighbours. In Eastern Europe, the decreases were generally significant.[18]

Although most people in Western countries would no longer explicitly deny ethnic equality, however, they might instead exhibit 'aversive racism'. This is defined in terms of feelings of discomfort and uneasiness that motivate people to avoid ethnic outgroups and maintain social distance from them.[19] A Swedish study found that classical (overt or direct) racial prejudice and modern (covert or subtle) racial prejudice are distinct. It showed that a scale to measure modern prejudice distinguished both between native Swedes and immigrants and between men and women, the former in each case being more prejudiced in the modern sense. In contrast, a scale to measure classical prejudice found few differences between the pairs.[20] Another piece of research found that white French subjects showed significantly different psychophysiological responses, such as change of heartbeat rate, to pictures of outgroup members (Arabs) as against in-group members (other white French). This applied even though, when self-report measures were used, the subjects did not exhibit anti-Arab prejudice.[21]

In a work context, findings from interviews with 219 ethnic minority and majority employees and managers, divided over 15 Dutch organizations, were that ethnic differences as such did not necessarily affect inter-ethnic relations in a work setting, but did so only when they were meaningful to individuals or within a particular context. Examples of 'meaningful' conditions included those where ethnic differences were perceived to affect people's sense of achievement (e.g., work goals), their sense of belonging (e.g., unity of the group), and their sense of equality (e.g., procedural justice). Such problems were reported more often when ethnic differences were associated with other types of diversity, such as information diversity and value diversity, than when the differences related to ethnicity alone.[22]

Box 5.2

X is a manager in a UK Local Authority. He was interviewing an applicant for a post in the Authority's Committee Section. The job description calls for a person with strong organizational and communication skills, who is excellent at meeting deadlines, has or is able to develop a detailed knowledge of procedures and constitutions and is prepared to work in the evenings. The interviewee was from an ethnic minority and was older than the interviewer.

During the interview, an observer recorded differences in body language and eye contact – the manager sat well forward in his seat with his body slanted towards the interviewee and made considerable use of gesture; he maintained a steady gaze directed at the interviewee; throughout he spoke loudly, clearly and fast.

The interviewee, in contrast, sat still, with hands folded, and appeared to back gradually away from the interviewer. She looked down at the space between them, and spoke quietly and slowly, though clearly.

The interviewee appeared uncomfortable with detailed questions. More than once she proffered CV and qualifications certificates, but the manager would not take them or look at them.

Questions included asking whether she would be able to fulfil the long hours and evening working sometimes required and asking what her written English is like. The observer read into the manager's conduct that he is making assumptions like 'Aren't your lot a bit laid back?' and that foreign qualifications are of less value than those of his own country.

Source: author's research

Box 5.3

A woman expatriate working for an international consultancy in China said she had experienced 'difficult work relationships with the Chinese, especially with men over 35, regardless of whether they have overseas experience. They will not address any of my suggestions, long telephone calls show no progress, they never contact me; there is virtually no communication. I have been told they have a comfort hierarchy and foreign women are at the bottom of it, just below young Chinese women.'

Source: Guirdham, M. (2009) *Culture and Business in Asia,* Basingstoke, UK: Palgrave Macmillan

Prejudice against other subgroups

There is evidence of gender prejudice. A meta-analysis of research in which actual performance indicators were equalized between men and women found an overall tendency to favour male leaders. Although the bias was slight, it was real. It was larger in the following conditions:

- Where the woman leader's style corresponded to male stereotypes (that is, was not interpersonal and participative);
- For roles usually occupied by men as against those occupied equally by both sexes or where the sex distribution was unknown;
- In some organizational contexts, such as sports and athletics coaching or business and manufacturing. The evaluation of male business managers was generally slightly more favourable than that of female business managers;
- Men were more likely to devalue women than women were. Women were largely neutral.[23]

Religious belief has been linked to prejudice. Members of Christian churches are usually more racially prejudiced towards Jews and Blacks than non-members, although in Holland church members are less prejudiced than others against immigrants. Intrinsics – the 'uncritically orthodox' as opposed to those with multiple motivations for religiosity – are less racially prejudiced but are prejudiced against homosexuals. High correlations have been found between prejudice and measures of fundamentalism, not only for populations of Christians but also for Jews, Moslems and Hindus.[24]

Perceptions of prejudice are themselves often biased. There is a tendency to believe that certain groups (such as older White male managers) are prejudiced or that its victims are members of certain groups (such as Bangladeshi women). That is, perceptions of prejudice are influenced by expectations about who is typically prejudiced about whom.[25] In an interview with the author, the Personnel Director of a major UK car manufacturer said: 'We find that the stereotypes of who will be prejudiced are often wrong. We tend to think that it will be the older males, especially from the engineering or factory side, that will be most biased. Often, though, it's the "young Turks" – mostly graduates – in Sales and Marketing. I think perhaps they see them – the women – as rivals, in a way the older ones don't.' False suspicions of prejudice can create communication problems in a wide range of organizational, work, social and educational settings.

Box 5.4

- 'My supervisor always refers to my co-workers and myself as "girls" or "ladies". As in "Good night, ladies (or girls)"'[a]
- 40 interviews with Lithuanian gays and lesbians found the following:

Most respondents attempted to enact the accepted norms of masculinity and femininity at work by controlling their appearance, dress, gestures and informal communication. One said: 'I accepted myself but I had to pretend sometimes... For instance, to invent stories about my adventures with women [at work], etc.' Another observed: 'You must constantly play the [heterosexual] role in your family and at work.' Some gays and lesbians experienced constant verbal violence, insults and ridicule directed towards them.

It was easier for homosexual men to affirm their identity in female-dominated areas, since women were less homophobic and more accepting of gays and lesbians than men.

There was growing distance among them and colleagues after their coming out. In the words of one, 'This communication [at work] took place as if I didn't exist, as if I did not participate in this party [of my co-workers]. And you felt some kind of silent, passive but nonetheless rejection...' Direct or formal discrimination was infrequent. However, some instances of this discrimination, namely the obstruction of promotion and firing from their jobs, occurred among the respondents. One gay man had to leave a couple of his previous jobs because his co-workers found out that he was gay. Despite being gay or lesbian themselves, a large proportion of the respondents did not consider indirect discrimination such as jokes about gays and lesbians as 'discriminatory.'[b]

Sources: (a) posted on 28 July 2009, URL: http://www.ehow.com/how_9433_be-politically-correct.html

(b) Tereškinas, A. 'Open and safe at work? Between uncomfortable privacy and undecided homophobic public', URL: www.ilga-europe.org/.../EQUAL per cent20Lithuania per cent20presentation per cent20in per cent20Sofija.ppt

Discrimination

Discrimination is a widespread part of the context of work communication. All minority groups, including people with disabilities, religious minorities, homosexuals and older people as well as ethnic minorities and women, are affected by prejudice and discrimination both at work and in society more generally. Discrimination is any situation in which a group or individual is treated unfavourably on the basis of arbitrary grounds, especially prejudice. Discrimination is a manifestation of prejudice that is often institutionalized and pervasive throughout an organization. Discrimination seriously reduces minority groups' chances of obtaining employment, equal earnings and promotion.

Discrimination against ethnic minorities

Despite extensive legal protection against discrimination in many countries, one problem that continues to affect ethnic minorities is indirect discrimination: selection criteria, for instance, are applied equally to everyone but disproportionately affect members of particular groups. 'Many of the ordinary, routine aspects of the recruitment market and the labour market may give rise to indirect discrimination – for example, the notion that candidates must "fit in". If selectors hold stereotypes of minority ethnic groups which mean they do not "fit in", indirect discrimination follows.'[26] Changing work patterns only add to this – Asian women workers are recognized as loyal, hard-working and uncomplaining; but new labour demands are for flexibility, ability to exercise initiative and responsibility for checking one's own work. There is often an assumption that, just because Asian women workers are the former, they cannot be the latter.

One definition of indirect discrimination on grounds of ethnic or national origin is that it occurs when a person, X, applies to another person, Y, a provision, criterion or practice which X applies to everyone; and the provision, criterion or practice puts (or would put) people from Y's ethnic or national origin at a particular disadvantage; and the provision, criterion or practice puts Y personally at a disadvantage; and X cannot show that the provision, criterion or practice is a proportionate means of achieving a legitimate aim. Examples of provisions, criteria or practices that might be indirectly discriminatory include the following: 'A firm's policy of filling senior management positions internally, from a pool of senior and middle managers, most of whom are white'; 'A word-of-mouth recruitment policy in a European firm where the majority of the workforce are Asian'; service provisions such as 'A bank requires applicants for a loan to be registered on the electoral roll, so that it can carry out credit checks. This may discriminate indirectly against non-citizens who are not eligible to vote'; 'If the proportion of qualifying people from an ethnic minority group who receive meals-on-wheels (a service provided by the local government) is smaller than persons who are not of that racial group'; 'If the proportion of potholes in the road filled in an ethnic

---

Box 5.5

'Europe's attitudes to Gypsies are both ignorant and prejudiced. Time to do better. At least 6m Gypsies, or Roma, live in Europe, most of them in former communist countries or scattered around the Mediterranean. ... The treatment of these Gypsies is perhaps the most important civil-rights issue in Europe. ... In Hungary and the Czech Republic, where they make up around 3 per cent of the population, Gypsies have been among the biggest losers in the past ten years. Unemployment rates for Gypsies run at 70 per cent and above. A study in Ostrava, an industrial city in the Czech Republic, found that a Gypsy child was 23 times more likely to be placed in a school for the mentally retarded than a white Czech child, even when of normal intelligence. The best such a child can hope for is a career as a cleaner. In Hungary Gypsy children are banned, in some schools, from the 'whites only' cafeteria and gym. Across Central Europe, Gypsies are the prime target of neo-Nazi thugs.

The Czech and Hungarian governments, and many citizens too, are committed to improving matters. In merely recognizing the problem, they are already doing better than EU countries such as Spain, Italy and especially Greece.'[a]

10 Common Basic Principles on Roma inclusion aim at guiding the EU institutions and Member States, candidate and potential candidate countries when they design and implement new policies or activities. They represent a legally non-binding declaration. However, by referring to the Principles in the Council conclusions, Member States have shown their commitment to base future initiatives on these principles.[b]

Sources: (a) *The Economist,* 10 May 2001

(b) *Principles annexed by Employment and Social Affairs Ministers of the EU countries on 8 June 2009, to their Conclusions on the inclusion of the Roma.* URL: http://ec.europa.eu/social/main.jsp?catId=761&langId=en

minority area is lower than that in a non-ethnic minority area'. Indirect discrimination can arise through lack of monitoring, rather than intention.[27]

Discrimination against women

Recent evidence for direct discrimination against women is less explicit than that for discrimination against some ethnic groups, although the statistical story told in Section 1.2, combined with the evidence of women's suitability for modern employment and management, are strong pointers. In addition, there are undoubtedly sectors, such as the insurance industry, where prejudice and discrimination are overt. It may, though, be indirect discrimination that is currently having more damaging effects on women at work. Indirect discrimination ranges from the lack of family-friendly policies in many organizations to the gendering of organizations. 'Family-friendly policies' is the term for the provision of childcare (and eldercare) resources and facilities, such as workplace nurseries, part-time, flexi-time, work-at-home, job sharing, compressed work weeks, extended lunch breaks, and maternity and parenting leave. However, many European employers, including very large employers of women, provide few, if any, of these benefits. Even where they exist, their value is limited. First, there is a widespread belief that the use of leaves and flexible working arrangements involves sacrificing career advancement, at least in the short term, and perhaps permanently. Second, it has been shown that an individual's immediate supervisor or manager affects how much work–family conflict individuals experience, and whether they fear negative effects at work from using family-friendly policies. Attitudes of such supervisors and managers are key and may often be unsupportive. A study in an insurance business found that supervisors often sent 'mixed messages' about work and family when implementing family-friendly policies amidst organizational constraints such as frequent deadlines and a team-based culture. These constraints often called for supervisors to make 'judgement calls' about work–family programme implementation, which they made while at the same time trying not to set a precedent they might regret. Third, research has shown that family-friendly resources are more likely to be available to senior and non-minority staff, which means they may actually reinforce the glass ceiling.[28]

Organizational gendering refers to the existence and persistence of a male-dominant organizational culture and climate that occur through four distinct but interrelated processes:

1. The construction of gender divisions, with men almost always in the highest positions of organizational power;
2. The construction of symbols and images that explain, express or reinforce those divisions, such as language, dress and media image;
3. The gendered components of individual identity and presentation of self; and
4. The demands for 'gender-appropriate' behaviour and attitudes.[29]

One explanation for the gendering of organizations is that 'the suppression of sexuality is one of the first tasks the bureaucracy sets itself.'[30] This suppression occurs in order to try to control the interferences and disruptions to the 'ideal functioning of the organization' caused by sexuality, procreation and emotions. There is a view that women working in bureaucracies will alter them in a significant way, but others argue that it is more likely that women will become co-opted – that is, will function like men in order to operate effectively at senior levels.[31] Despite their progress in the last 30 years of the twentieth century, women as a group are still comparatively in low-power positions at work. In the words of Colwill (1995), 'The lack of women in management is an issue, not of education and training, but of power. Time, patience and women's self-improvement do not appear to be the solution. The solution, in fact, is similar to the problem: power.'[32]

Discrimination against people with disabilities

Until the second half of the twentieth century, it was rarely recognized that, apart from their specific impairment, people with disabilities have the same needs, abilities and interests as the mainstream population. For many people with disabilities, the greatest handicap has been the image of them as a 'breed apart' who have often been pitied, ignored or placed in institutions that offered mere custodial care.[33] In Europe (but not in Asia) this situation has improved. People with disabilities are, as Section 1.2 showed, a significant part of the active workforce. Despite this, they continue to face discrimination. For example, a 2002 study found that most UK employers were aware of governing legislation, most gave positive statements of intent to meet their legal obligations, but that little use was made of government schemes to promote and assist employment of disabled people.[34] Organizations are often frightened of the cost of employing people with disabilities. However, a US analysis of more than 10,000 disabled employees showed that 31 per cent of their hirings required no added cost for special training or facilities, 50 per cent were under $50 and 69 per cent cost less than $500. Only 1 per cent cost over $5,000. Studies show that building a new facility that is accessible adds only one half of 1 per cent to the building's cost.

Another UK study found significant differences in the levels of satisfaction with their working conditions between men and women with disabilities. Only 43 per cent of men with a long-term illness or disability affecting their daily lives were extremely, very or fairly satisfied with physical working conditions, hours of work and amount of variety, and a slightly higher 50 per cent with relationships with management; only 29 per cent were satisfied with departmental management and attention paid to suggestions. In contrast, 85 per cent, 87 per cent and 82 per cent respectively of women with disabilities were extremely, very or fairly satisfied with physical working conditions, hours of work and amount of variety, 81 per cent with relationships with management, 64 per cent with departmental management and 67 per cent with attention paid to suggestions.[35] It is not clear whether these differences are due to different treatment of men and women with disabilities or other causes.

Discrimination based on age

Ageism, a term originating in about 1970, is discrimination against people, usually older people, on the grounds of their age. Ageism has been blamed for people ageing poorly in Western societies. Discrimination directed against older people leads to higher redundancy rates among older employees and difficulty for anyone over 50, or in some cases 40, in obtaining employment following redundancy. Age prejudice is largely a problem of individualist Western cultures – in collectivist cultures elderly people are usually highly respected and their contribution is acknowledged. Fear of growing old among the young and middle-aged is a powerful factor in ageism. Age discrimination affects women particularly, as it reduces career prospects for women returning to work after childrearing. As Section 1.2 noted, however, demographic changes in the West may soon reduce the practical impact of ageism on older workers' job prospects, but this will not necessarily reduce discrimination where employers are in a position to discriminate.

Discrimination against homosexuals

In Europe (but, again, not really in Asia), there is a widespread shift towards eliminating overt discrimination and reducing hidden discrimination against homosexuals. There are four factors promoting this favourable change: scientific evidence of homosexuality as innate, an around-the-world development of a middle class, a category into which many gays fall, democratization – democratic societies are more permissive – and the use of the Internet for global information-sharing and resistance to oppression.[36] Despite such favourable trends, there are many persisting bastions of discrimination against homosexuals, including religious institutions and the armed forces. Moreover, although gay men appear to be empowered to self-identify as professionals in 'gay-friendly' work contexts, even within gay-friendly organizational settings (such as a UK National Health Service Trust), for gays to fashion a professional identity involves negotiation and struggle. Professional norms and discourses assume that heterosexuality is normal and treat sexuality and professionalism as polar opposites.[37]

Discrimination based on religion

Some of the discrimination affecting 'minority groups' is so accepted that even liberal members of the dominant (sub)culture are barely aware of it. For instance, many European societies provide a double bind for people from religious backgrounds other than the dominant Christian one, so far as accommodating their religious practices is concerned. The working week is built around the practice of Sunday worship, even though in some countries the majority of the population takes no active part, while the secular tone means that organizations and individual managers often underestimate the priority which people from religious backgrounds give to having time free for worship. For Moslems being able to attend a mosque on Fridays, for Hindus time free for festivals and ceremonials, for Jews being home before sunset on Fridays are considerations which they are often forced to trade off against earnings or career.

Harassment and workplace bullying

Dictionaries define harassment as 'vexing by repeated attacks'.[38] A European study found the incidence of experiencing workplace bullying to be equal for men and women, at a reported 20 per cent of respondents, but for women it was more likely to be sexual harassment by co-workers and for men more likely to be bullying by supervisors as well as co-workers. Poor social climate was a significant predictor for both genders, and both experienced feelings of stress, poor mental health and lowered job satisfaction as a consequence.[39] Danish research indicates that it is not necessarily the quantity of the negative acts that causes the change in behaviour, but the fact of being exposed to such acts at all.[40] In Britain, few differences were found for the experience of self-reported bullying between workers, supervisors, middle or senior managers. Workers and supervisors were more frequently exposed to negative acts, such as derogatory or exclusionary behaviour, than managers, who more often reported exposure to extreme work pressure. Women managers, however, were subjected to negative acts.[41] Research in a large telecommunications call centre showed

Box 5.6

A BBC programme in January 2010 included an interview of and discussion among three Indian women members of the Indian dalit (formerly 'outcaste') community. The topic was caste prejudice and discrimination in modern Britain. The women asserted that discrimination was common in cases where a caste Indian had power – for instance of appointment or promotion – over a dalit Indian. This occurred, for example, in the National Health Service. They said that caste – or 'outcaste' – status was easy to read by other Indians from names, family locations in India or mannerisms. They added that in some ways the problem was now worse in Britain than in India where the law prohibited such discrimination and there was affirmative action for the 'scheduled' castes. In Britain the government had refused to extend discrimination law to the matter, saying the evidence was not strong enough.[a]

Banning the burqa: 'For people raised outside the Gulf or Afghanistan, dealing with somebody whose facial expressions are hidden is uncomfortable. Unlike the headscarf, the burqa appears, in itself, to be a restraint on female freedom and also symbolises what many Europeans see as the repression that women can suffer in Islam. And although many, and probably most, Muslim women wear the headscarf out of choice, some tell the police that they were forced to wear the burqa against their will.

Nor do democracies give absolute rights to citizens to wear what they like....People cannot, in most countries, walk the streets naked. And Europeans clearly favour a ban. A recent poll found that a majority backed one in France (70 per cent), Spain (65 per cent), Italy (63 per cent), Britain (57 per cent) and Germany (50 per cent). In America, with its stronger culture of religious freedom, only a minority (33 per cent) was in favour.

Yet the very values which Europeans feel are threatened by the burqa demand that they oppose a ban. Liberal societies should let people wear what they want unless there is a strong argument otherwise. And, in this case, the three arguments for a ban – security, sexual equality and secularism – do not stand up.'[b]

Sources: (a) Woman's Hour, BBC Radio 4, January 2010
(b) *The Economist*, 15 May 2010

that employees used the term 'bullying' to describe difficult work situations, which they saw as imposed by the organization, as well as the oppressive behaviour of individuals. The authors commented: 'This additional narrative brings issues of power and politics in organizations to the fore.'[42]

Definitions of what constitutes sexual harassment depend on gender, with women consistently defining more experiences as harassing than men. The differences in definition create comparability problems for studies of harassment incidence; however, there seems little doubt that it is widespread in the workplace. Research into the problem of sexual harassment has tended to focus on harassment that occurs within overt power relationships, for example, bosses and employees, teachers and students, doctors and patients, lawyers and clients. However, sexual harassment often occurs between peers – persons whose relationship is not based on an overt power or status differential. One study found that sexual harassment was pervasive in terms of the numbers of females and males who had been victims/targets of peer sexual harassment, the relationship of the harassers to their victims, the settings in which harassment occurred, and the verbal and non-verbal behaviours communicated.[43]

Many feminists regard sexual harassment as a patriarchal control strategy used by men to keep women 'in their place': men are seen as intentionally or unintentionally reducing women employees to sexualized beings. In addition, feminists assert, men often subscribe to a 'male sexual drive discourse' in which their sexuality is treated as 'incontinent', 'out of their own control' and essentially biologically driven.

The effects of prejudice, discrimination and harassment at work

The direct effects of prejudice are mainly discrimination and harassment. Both of these, in addition to their negative effects on individuals and organizations, are intrinsically barriers to communication, but so is prejudice itself, even when it is not overt. Prejudiced people distort and misread communication from those about whom they hold prejudiced views. On the other side, people who become aware of others' prejudices about themselves or others are likely to reduce communication with them or to develop negative attitudes to the prejudiced individual's opinions in general, regardless of how soundly based those other opinions may be.

Prejudice is often displayed in negative micro-messages. These are subtle, semi-conscious, devaluing messages, which discourage and impair performance, possibly leading to damaged self-esteem and withdrawal. For example, negative micro-messages (micro-inequities) can occur within a team when a manager or a colleague communicates different messages to people, usually linked to a difference between them such as ethnicity, gender, age, sexual orientation, social class or final educational level. Micro-messages can affect such things as employee productivity, morale, absenteeism and turnover – all critical to the success of a company. Negative micro-messages can cause employees to withdraw, complain, question their own abilities, be absent from work frequently and possibly leave; conversely, positive micro-messages can encourage employees to excel in their work, commit to the company, and feel motivated. Individuals who belong to groups that have been historically excluded and devalued because of their difference may have stronger reactions to micro-inequities.[44,45]

Past experience of prejudice naturally affects the response of members of minority groups to communications they receive at work. Excuses, apologies and explanations, which are collectively called 'social accounts', may be counterproductive when used by members of dominant groups with members of minority groups. In areas such as negative pay decisions and layoffs, researchers have found that a well-constructed account that explains what happened and why can reduce perceptions of injustice and anger. However, social accounts may be ineffective when used by White managers to Black subordinates. The pattern of responses across four studies demonstrated a 'persistent injustice effect'. Black employees had more experience than White with unjust acts; they reported higher levels of both past and expected future injustices, and greater mistrust. This experience of 'persistent injustice' may account for the findings that a social account reduced perceived injustice less for Black respondents observing Black than White victims or than for White respondents observing either Black or White victims. Black respondents observing Black victims, when there was higher racial identification or higher levels of personal experience with injustice, were similarly less influenced by social accounts. The same applied when Black respondents observed Black victims hurt by White harm-doers. Black respondents also perceived higher initial levels of injustice, disapproval and intentionality when observing Black victims hurt by White harm-doers. These findings are consistent with earlier studies that found that social accounts were less effective at diminishing perceptions of injustice for union officials and female managers when the hypothetical victim was a member of their in-group. When there is a persistent injustice effect, it is likely to be invisible to a manager, who has given what on the surface may be received as a successful excuse, apology or explanation. As a result, ' "solutions" end up being partial and temporary, and the conflicts get driven underground, to incubate and surface again at some other time, in some other form.'[46]

As the introduction to this section stated, discrimination negatively affects minority groups' chances of obtaining employment, equal earnings and promotion. For instance, a naturalistic field experiment examined the responses of recruitment agencies to unsolicited resumés from native-born and immigrant candidates in the technology sector in New Zealand. The findings revealed that immigrant candidates with equivalent educational and occupational experience were significantly less likely to be contacted for further information and significantly more likely to have contact terminated than native-born candidates.[47] Discrimination and harassment create barriers that go beyond the immediate situation, putting fear, resentment and even hatred into intercultural relations wherever they are experienced or heard about. Understanding and knowing about this is essential background for communicating across barriers created by difference. Without such understanding and knowledge, there can be no possibility of the awareness of sensitive issues, which, as Chapter 6 will show, is vital. The effects of discrimination on work communication depend partly, however, on how negative behaviours of one group towards another are interpreted. It has been found that the more members of low-status groups endorse the ideology of individual mobility, the less likely they are to attribute negative outcomes from higher-status group members to discrimination. Conversely, the more members of high-status groups endorse this same ideology, the more likely they are to attribute negative outcomes from low-status group members to discrimination.[48]

Within organizations, in addition to the consequences of direct and indirect discrimination, harassment and bullying, there may be glass ceilings and walls – invisible but impermeable barriers. These limit how far members of minorities may be promoted, segregate people into separate spheres and create status differences. In general, glass ceilings and walls in the workplace reflect the conditions of the wider society. Writers on race comment on 'the silencing of the importance of race in organizations', and ask, 'why so much attention [has] been given to race and ethnicity outside of organizations and why so little inside?'[49] Feminist writers argue that organizations are gendered, embedding the values, attitudes and norms of one gender, usually the male. It is possible to view gender and other classifications as something organizations 'do', rather than as a natural attribute of people. In some organizations, the relations between men and women doing similar 'male' jobs are defined by practices based on a 'symbolic' order which places women below men in the hierarchy. The result is rules and rituals which create and recreate ambiguity in the expectations of how women workers should behave.[50]

'Glass walls', or job segregation, keep women and minority men out of some functional areas (e.g., manufacturing) and locked into others (e.g., human resource management). Usually, the areas from which minorities are excluded are the ones most likely to lead to the top of the organizations; they may even be those of which experience is essential to get there. For example, in a multinational company a woman or ethnic minority man may be less likely than members of the majority group to get an overseas posting, but international experience may be a requirement for a job at Board level; or, in an industrial marketing company, where a period of experience as a sales representative is regarded as basic for promotion above a certain level, women graduate trainees may not be allowed to gain such experience – theoretically, for their protection. A UK study found that senior posts to which women were promoted tended to be 'dangerous': those where the risks of failure were higher.[51]

As significant a problem for intercultural work communication as blatant discrimination is now caused by 'micro-inequities', which can occur wherever people are perceived as different. These include Caucasians in a Japanese-owned company, African Americans in a white firm, women in a traditionally male environment and Roman Catholics in a traditionally Protestant environment. Micro-inequities 'include exclusion from informal peer support, networking, and mentoring; restricted information and a lack of feedback from supervisors and co-workers; inadequate or inaccurate performance appraisals by supervisors or work groups; and inequitable delegation of tasks.... One of the main things blacks complained about...was the withholding of information by white supervisors. Time and time again, they recounted how...their counterparts were given the whole picture.' Blacks were given jobs to 'prove their competence'; Whites were given learning experiences. Because they often encountered stereotypes, Blacks tended to be more aware than Whites of how others might perceive and evaluate their behaviours. This perception might inhibit open communication within a variety of formal contexts (e.g., team meetings, job interviews or sales consultations). Low report rates mean little: it has been shown that members of stigmatized groups are less likely to report an experience as discriminatory in the presence of a member of a non-stigmatized group than in private.[52]

Racial dynamics also affect mentoring activities, often inhibiting authentic collaboration in cross-racial relationships.[53] Gender discrimination, too, is now often created and sustained more by communication micropractices than by overt discrimination. Women interviewed by Hatcher (2000), particularly those from financial institutions, spoke eloquently of the ways in which they were excluded from organizational life. The topics of conversation, including the omission of topics such as parenting responsibilities, the styles of communication, the policing of female sexuality through the repression of involvement in banter, or the turning of the male gaze onto female bodies through innuendo and game-playing, all contributed to the performance of gender in organizations.[54]

US data suggest that 50 per cent of women will be harassed at some time in their working lives; consequences include job loss, decreased morale, absenteeism, decreased job satisfaction and damage to interpersonal relationships at work, as well as negative effects on psychological and physical health.[55] A wide range of people – not just women – are affected by harassment. The victims of bullying, as well as some sexual harassment, are more often men than is generally acknowledged. For women, however, the psychodynamics of sexual harassment maintain an unequal power structure between the sexes, forcing women to comply with traditional sex roles. The findings from an Australian study suggest that organizational culture and environment influence respondents' attitudes to sexually harassing behaviour.[56]

The Changing Legal Framework

Despite a backlash in some countries (for instance in Uganda regarding homosexuality in 2010) and persistent conservatism in others (for instance in Saudi Arabia regarding women), in many countries, including Europe and some Asian countries, changing societal expectations in the late twentieth and early twenty-first centuries brought significant changes to the legal framework on discrimination. Specifically, these changed expectations were that the frontiers of equality law expanded to cover

Box 5.7

On 1 January 2005, a new immigration law came into effect that altered the legal method of immigration to Germany. The introduction of the new immigration law meant that Germany for the first time ever acknowledged itself to be an 'immigration country'. Although the practical changes to the immigration procedures were relatively minor, new immigration categories for highly skilled professionals and scientists were introduced to attract valuable professionals for the German labour market, but the labour market remained closed for unskilled workers.

Amendments to the Act took effect on 28 August 2007. These amendments included provisions to implement 11 EU directives on residence and asylum rules, to prevent sham or forced marriages, to enhance internal security, to implement decisions of the German Conference of Interior Ministers on nationality law, to facilitate the immigration of company founders and, above all, provisions to foster the integration of legal immigrants.

Source: Wikipedia 10 March 2010 URL: http://en.wikipedia.org/wiki/Immigration_to_Germany, last accessed on 23 December 2010

disability, sexual orientation, religion and age, and that, whereas the early aim was to achieve a 'colour blind', gender-neutral world, now the aim was for a merit-based world and for diversity. Modern legal positions, it was argued, should be based on four platforms:

1. Redressing disadvantage (equality of results). Promoting respect for dignity (which has whatever content people choose to give
2. it; the EU human rights legislation attacks stigma, stereotyping and denigration).
3. Affirming community identities (change is needed in the public 'space', not in the individual).
4. Facilitating full participation in society.

Early attempts to achieve equality through law consisted of banning direct discrimination (for instance, skin colour was to be irrelevant in appointing 'alike' people); this was found to be a flawed paradigm. There is difficulty in establishing what counts as alike. (For instance, it could be argued that, if women are seen as irrational, they are intrinsically unlike men.) These early attempts led to a requirement that minority groups conform to a white male norm of behaviour. This showed that equal treatment can entrench inequality – it led to indirect discrimination. Instead there was a need to equalize the starting points. The later view is that authorities and employers should equip people to be able to use their opportunities and that business demands should be screened for fairness. Although it can be argued that the law has a limited capacity to protect individuals who suffer subtle discrimination, such as excluding minority members from information networks, it can also be argued that the law has an educative function and that it can place positive duties on employers to support minorities.

Despite the extensive European legal framework governing the treatment of minorities, however, the position of minorities in regard to work in many countries is by no means acceptable, pointing to the fact that organizations in many cases are evading the law. As Glastra *et al.* (1998) stated, in connection with The Netherlands,

'Equity policies have far less salience in smaller firms...Such firms often lack the human resources capacity to address legal requirements...while they may feel much more dependent on a stable workforce. Hence it might not be very realistic to expect them to follow the example set by larger corporations.'[57] In addition, Green (2005) noted a substantial gap in existing legal discourse, where work culture was more frequently seen as a matter of business prerogative than one of antidiscrimination concern.[58]

> Some kinds of prejudice may be diminishing but still are widely prevalent and lead to transmitting negative micro-messages. Discrimination, too, persists everywhere, including in Europe, although in some places more than others, and in different countries is directed mainly against different groups. Indirect discrimination and micro-inequities may be more common than blatant discrimination. Harassment and workplace bullying are also widespread. Experience of prejudice, discrimination or harassment naturally affects the responses of members of minority groups. The consequences for both individuals and organizations are seen in ill-health and high absentee and attrition rates as well as in communication breakdowns that impair performance. Changes to the legal framework in some countries, such as those of the EU, give some hope for improvement.

5.3 DIFFERENT COMMUNICATION PRACTICES AS BARRIERS

Cultural differences affect intercultural encounters, usually by leading to misunderstanding or conflict, at both the individual and the group level. At the individual level interpersonal misunderstanding and conflict can arise as different values, beliefs or world views are manifested in communication behaviours and as culture creates differing expectations and differing styles or patterns of speech. Section 5.5 considers these individual-level sources of communication problems. At the group level, inter-group processes can be triggered by, for instance, an individual's non-verbal behaviour or ways of speaking which stereotypically represent a group.[59] This section aims to show how variations in the way particular communication functions are performed, described in Chapter 3, Section 2, can lead to misunderstanding and even conflict in intercultural encounters. The practices covered include encoding and decoding of messages, language ambiguity, inferences, elaborated codes, the topic–comment structure of a communication, social knowledge, relevance, face issues, politeness, non-verbal behaviour, high-context low-context communication, detecting deceptions, communication strategies, conflict management and the functions talk is used for.

Encoding and decoding of messages

Intercultural communicators often have problems both in encoding their own messages so that they can be understood by the other party and in accurately decoding what the other party says. Bias increases this difficulty. Gallois and Callan (1986) considered that the results of their study of message decoding in Australia, described in Chapter 3, revealed that the negative attitudes of Anglo-Australians to Italian men are reflected in the difficulty they have in decoding these speakers when the Italian voice and accent are present. They concluded that the listener's own goals and perception of the context as threatening may have led to an overall distortion of the speaker's messages.[60]

Language ambiguity

Language is fundamentally ambiguous,[61] giving rise to much confusion, especially for non-native speakers. For instance, in English, there is nothing in the words themselves to say: 'This is the important point.' That emphasis is supplied by the expectations each speaker has that the other speaker will use language in the same way that s/he does. In the case of English this means they have to grasp the subtle English use of voice modulation. For example, questions can be expressed as statements spoken in a rising voice pitch, as in 'So you went to the bank this morning.' This is a statement if spoken in a level pitch and a question if spoken in a rising pitch. Because we have no choice but to draw inferences about meaning, when language is ambiguous we rely on two main sources: (1) the language a speaker has used and (2) our knowledge about the world. A statement like, 'There is a man at the door,' *could* mean 'There is a man sitting on the doorstep playing the guitar.' However, we are likely to discount this in favour of assuming it to mean 'There is a man at the door waiting to be let in,' or a similar statement. In other words, we are likely to assume, unless a speaker states otherwise, that the obvious common-sense assumption is correct. However, what constitutes 'common sense' varies across cultures. In fact, even within interactions by native speakers of the 'same' language from different cultures, such as speakers of British and American English, there are at least four categories of language differences that have the potential to confuse. The four categories are: (1) the same expression with differences in style, connotation, and/or frequency; (2) the same expression with one or more shared and different meanings; (3) the same expression with completely different meanings; and (4) different expressions with the same shared meaning.[62]

Box 5.8

The following are examples of ambiguity in English:

My son has grown another foot; visiting relatives can be boring; vegetarians don't know how good meat tastes; I saw the man with the binoculars.

The following examples are from newspaper headlines:

The judge sentenced the killer to die in the electric chair for the second time.

Dr. Tackett Gives Talk on Moon.

No one was injured in the blast, which was attributed to the build-up of gas by one town official.

The summary of information contains totals of the number of students broken down by sex, marital status and age.[a]

Other examples include:

On a packet of soya milk: There are many more delicious products from Alpro; why don't you try them?

Overheard in a lift: 'I want the porter to turn off the TV thing; I don't want to see people.'

(Actually he meant he only wanted an audio entry phone, not a video one).

On a poster advertisement: The less you pay to travel, the more you have to spend when you get there.[b]

Sources: (a) Pinker, S. (1994) *The Language Instinct*, London: Allen Lane, The Penguin Press

(b) author's research

Inferences

There are subtleties of language use that enable receivers of messages spoken in their native language to draw accurate inferences about the speakers' meanings. These subtleties will tend to escape non-native speakers. Equally, the other source of inference, knowledge of the 'world', may be defective when the speaker is from another culture, as the two participants' 'worlds' will be influenced by their culture. For example, Kotani (2002) noted that native English speakers assume that 'I'm sorry' means 'I admit responsibility,' and that the words closely represent the speaker's feeling; conversely, Japanese speakers mean 'I acknowledge that you have suffered,' and there can be low correspondence between the words and the feeling. This may lead to English speakers judging Japanese people insincere.[63] Misunderstanding also arises interculturally because of misinterpreting the 'cues' used to decide what kind of language event is occurring. Expectations about how conversational exchanges should develop, appropriate ways of speaking and the interpersonal relations and speaking rights of those involved are based on these cues, which may be missed or misread by people from outside the culture.[64] Differences in what aspects of a communication receivers 'sample' (e.g., attitudes or roles) also 'have profound implications for the probability of conflict and the type of conflict that will develop between individuals and groups'.[65]

Elaborated codes

When people realize that they are interacting with someone from a different background, they usually adapt their discourse by using elaborated rather than restricted codes.[66] This adaptation is necessary, but can mean that intercultural encounters are marked by formality. This formality slows the pace at which relationships develop, while people from some (sub)cultures, such as the North Americans, find it unfriendly. In addition, the requirements for adapting to the elaborated code place heavy demands on people's communication resources. On the other hand, what a person from one culture overhears in a discussion between two people from a different culture using a restricted code can be mystifying or misleading.

The topic–comment structure of a communication

Speakers may either give the context of what they want to say first and then their main point, or vice versa. Topic–comment order varies between cultures and this can cause confusion, especially in languages like English that (unlike Japanese, for instance) have no semantic way of marking the main subject. Research in a major East Asian city studied situations that could be considered to require professional communication. It found that, among people from North American / European cultures, it was usual to put the comment, main point or suggested action first and then give the topic, background or reason. People from Asian cultural backgrounds did the reverse: they put the topic, background or reason first and then their main point, comment or the action they were suggesting.[67] For example, a North American might say, 'We could announce price cuts on 100 items for the next three months – we'd run a big press campaign and an in-store sales promotion, try to get lots of publicity [suggested action]. That way we'd really cut the ground out from under our competitors with their selective weekly price cuts [reason].' An Asian listener, expecting to hear the reason for any action first, might find this abrupt, or might interpret the opening sentence as the reason and become confused. By contrast, an Asian speaker would be more likely to say, 'Our competitors are launching a campaign of weekly price cuts. This could have very serious consequences for our sales and market share [reason]. We could look at announcing price cuts on 100 items for the next three months... [suggested action].' A North American listener might grow impatient, especially if the reasons were elaborated, as they might well be. The North American might then be inattentive when the Asian speaker reached the point of proposing action.

Social knowledge

Intercultural communicators, even those with high technical understanding of the other culture's language, will often be hampered by lack of social knowledge. For instance, they might not know the definitions and boundaries of situations that are well understood in the other culture, the precise nature of role relationships occurring in those situations or the linguistic and non-verbal codes to use.[68] Errors result when people impose the social rules of their own (sub)culture in a situation where the social rules of another (sub)culture would be more appropriate. One type occurs when a speech strategy is employed that is inappropriate for the language being spoken: for instance, speaking loudly and forcefully in Japanese. Another type involves getting the balance between talk and silence wrong for the culture. On the other hand, attempting to adapt to the perceived needs of the person being spoken to can itself produce problems – for instance, using a simplified 'foreigner talk' register, as the Japanese often do, even when the person they are addressing is highly competent in the language, limits discussion as well as possibly giving offence.

Relevance

Interlocutors have to decide which is the relevant intention out of various possibilities that might underlie a communication. In intercultural situations, however, using relevance to decide another person's intention can create problems. The speaker may have a limited ability to make their intention correspond to the beliefs most likely to be relevant to the receiver. For instance, in the example given in Box 3.6, a Western banker explained that in dealing with Turkish officials he had difficulty in conveying an intention to be 'properly and prudentially' cautious because of not knowing what beliefs would be relevant to them in the situation at issue.

Face issues

In uncertain situations, which may threaten their sense of their identity, people experience problems with facework. In uncertain situations, active facework is needed. The parties engage in two kinds of facework: those concerned with their own face and those with the other party's face.[69] Important work meetings, negotiations or interviews, which involve meeting people from another culture for the first time, are examples of uncertain situations. Culture influences people's use of facework and which kind of facework they will more often select. For instance, people from one culture may choose strategies that avoid face issues while people from another culture select strategies that defend their face. Non-alignment or misalignment of facework strategies can lead to miscommunication – the people who are interacting misread each other's signals and so respond inappropriately. This can lead to spiralling conflict.

Politeness

Another source of intercultural communication problems arises from the miscommunication of politeness. As Ambady *et al.* (1996) speculated in their conclusion to research about cultural differences in politeness strategies, 'Perhaps many misunderstandings that occur between cultures are due to the miscommunication of politeness.'[70] What constitutes a face-threatening act varies cross-culturally. For instance, making a request is generally a less face-threatening act for North Americans (as shown by their dictum 'Always ask') than to many British people. Some intercultural miscommunication is produced by directness and indirectness in certain situations involving greetings, farewells, compliments and negative observations. Directness perceived positively is called 'honesty'. However, if it is negatively perceived it quickly becomes 'rudeness'. Indirectness perceived positively is regarded as 'politeness' or 'friendliness', but if perceived negatively is seen as 'superficiality' or 'insincerity'. This issue has been found to affect communication between North Americans and Germans. North Americans often show politeness through behaviours and language perceived as 'friendliness', while Germans show it through what they might label 'respect'. Many Germans stress 'honesty' in encounters, while many North Americans wish to maintain an agreeable attitude and do not want to disappoint their interlocutors. Thus, when they meet, if they are expecting behaviour from the others that they find in their own cultures, North Americans and Germans often do not have their expectations met and they become disappointed in the members of the other culture.[71]

Non-verbal behaviour

Variations in the meaning of non-verbal behaviours lead to misinterpretation:

Kinesics:	Asians in general tend to smile or laugh more readily than Westerners when they feel difficulty or embarrassment. Westerners then misinterpret this as normal pleasure or agreement and the source of difficulty is missed.
Proxemics:	Hall (1959) put forward the notion of a 'space bubble' in which each individual moves and feels comfortable. The size of this space bubble varies by culture: Arabs and Latin Americans feel comfortable with a smaller space bubble than Anglos. This leads them to stand closer, creating discomfort for an interacting Anglo, who may move backwards, thus giving an impression of unfriendliness to the Arab. Responses to perceived invasion of space have been shown to differ between men and women. While men may respond aggressively, women tend to yield space rather than challenge the intruder.
Speed of delivery:	Faster speakers almost always evaluate slower speakers negatively. Thus Europeans and people from the Northern USA often wrongly regard people from the Southern states of the USA, whose culture inculcates slow speech, as slow-thinking.[72]
Speech styles:	Language and communication norms among young African American males, particularly those of lower socio-economic status, are related, at least in part, to their higher rate of disciplinary problems and special education placements. Speaking ethnically

based English vernaculars and the use of urban argots can be seen by such youths as markers of masculinity and defiance of White standards, but it 'virtually guarantees' academic problems and, sometimes, social problems by conflicting with the school's communication norms.[73]

Communicator style: A study examined the role that culture plays in communication distortion by using observation and interviewing techniques to gather data while applicants from West Africa and Westerners applied for a visa. The results suggested that speech patterns, body posture, eye contact, information disclosure and verbal aggression are interpreted differently depending on culture, which leads to communication distortion.[74]

Communication traits and styles

Differences in, for instance, argumentativeness can also create communication barriers. For instance, the point has already been made that there are cultural differences in what counts as assertiveness and the value attached to it. Using a level of assertiveness that is appropriate in one culture with interactors from another will probably be seen as aggression or, on the other hand, over-submissiveness.

High-context communication (HCC) and low-context communication (LCC)

Misunderstanding arises easily between users of HCC and LCC. When a speaker uses HCC, the problem for LCC receivers is literally to grasp their meaning: so much is left unsaid and they are not attuned to the implicatures and inferences being used, or to the extensive use of non-verbal communication. Indirectness and an emphasis on relationship data compound the problem. When the speaker uses LCC, the problem for HCC receivers is less to grasp their overt meaning than to avoid over-interpreting and seeing inferences that may not be present. They may also be affronted by directness or the 'brutality' of the concentration on hard content; or simply suffer from information overload.

Detecting deceptions

Three types of assessment are generally used to decide whether a speaker is telling the truth: whether the speaker's non-verbal behaviour breaches common expectations, whether the message being communicated is plausible and how nervous the speaker is. People from a different background can misread all these indicators. When Americans and Jordanians were videotaped while telling lies and truths and other Americans and Jordanians watched the resulting videotapes and made lie detection judgments, results showed similar patterns of lie detection within each of the two cultures but no lie detection across cultures. In both the US and Jordan, people who 'breached common expectations' by avoiding eye contact and pausing in the middle of speaking were judged to be deceptive, but despite this no lie detection occurred across cultures.[75] Another cross-cultural study, however, found that the type of lie affected overall detection rates: they were better than chance (50 per cent) for 'emotional' lies and below it for non-emotional lies.[76]

Communication strategies

Differences of communication strategy can produce conflict, especially between members of different subcultures. For example, in discussions with men, women's communication strategies often express the subordinate, non-aggressive role allocated to women, but this can be misleading. Soft-spoken women who use multiple hesitations and tag questions may nevertheless be highly determined and power-oriented; they may be deliberately, and even successfully, adopting a 'feminine' style or they may lack awareness of their own style and so miscommunicate their attitudes or intentions. Communication strategies that impede real communication may, however, reflect the interactors' real intentions or attitudes, and these may be culturally induced. For instance, a study of group encounters between Israeli Jews and Palestinians highlighted how the participants pursued their rhetorical goals in ways that frustrated dialogue. These ways included using symbols of ethnic identity to support a case in argument, unquestioned assumptions by each side that forestalled progress, and various argumentative strategies (e.g., question asking, collaboration argument, limited topical space).[77] Similarly, among individuals in a financial services company operating in the UK and in Mumbai, India, cultural ascriptions were used to justify certain existing patterns of behaviour and to foreclose discussion of alternatives. Respondents 'mobilized discourses of culture and cultural difference to describe and justify this positioning, with particular reference to "the language barrier", work ethics and notions of competence'.[78]

Conflict management

Cultural differences in how conflict is usually conducted may increase the difficulty of resolving intercultural conflicts. Triandis (2000) pointed out that conflict is greater when two cultures are very different than when they are similar. The degree of difference is called cultural distance, which is a function of language, social structure (e.g., family structure) and religion, among other factors.[79]

Functions of talk

The functions to which talk is put can differ between groups, at least in emphasis, and so create misunderstanding. One function is to distribute control of the interaction; another is to determine the level of affiliation. Some women see talk as the essence of a relationship, while some men use talk to exert control, preserve independence and enhance status.

> Encoding and decoding of messages, language ambiguity, inferences, elaborated codes, the topic–comment structure of a communication, social knowledge, relevance, face issues, politeness, non-verbal behaviour, high-context/low-context communication, detecting deceptions, communication strategies, conflict management and the functions talk is used for are all communication practices that may be influenced by culture and so prone to create intercultural misunderstanding.

5.4   (SUB)CULTURAL COMMUNICATION BARRIERS

This section aims to show how the (sub)cultural differences in ways of communicating described in Section 3.3 can create barriers to intercultural communication. National, ethnic, gender and social class differences in how people speak and interact can lead to them being perceived as disorganized or poor thinkers or as being insulting. A survey found that respondents perceived the following dimensions of communication as problematic in their interactions with people of other nationalities: lack of language proficiency, transfer of mother tongue patterns into a foreign language, mistaking a concept to mean the same in the other culture as in their own, use of a concept unfamiliar in the other person's culture, words taken too literally or personally, use of directness or indirectness, use of directness or indirectness in criticism, self-presentation, acceptance of an offer or invitation, choice of topic, register or form of address perceived as unexpected or inappropriate, turn-taking perceived as difficult, back-channelling perceived as unexpected or negative, use of silence perceived as excessive or insufficient, eye contact, smiles, gestures misinterpreted (e.g., wrongly seen as inviting intimacy), use of space perceived as unexpected, territoriality behaviour and attitudes to time perceived as negative or unexpected, treating the other person on the basis of stereotyped views, gender attitudes and behaviour perceived as negative or unexpected, and power distance orientation perceived as negative or unexpected. Example comments from the respondents included the following: 'I expected everybody to listen to what I had to say. This was not the case but the Italians interrupted me in what I considered to be a harsh way and started all to give their own opinion in chorus.' 'We were sitting in a bus on an excursion with our group when she asked me if I shaved my legs. I was surprised at the question as I considered it all too personal to be asked in a public place.' 'An American fellow passenger kept asking too personal matters such as whether I was married and why I was not married.'[80] The respondents to this survey were Finnish, but it seems likely that many of their categories of perceptions would be common to members of other nationalities.

Subcultural as well as national differences create problems. For instance, in the UK, schoolchildren of Afro-Caribbean ethnic origin, and elsewhere in Europe children of Algerian, Turkish or Indonesian ethnicity, display differences from the majority in dialect, frequency of interruption, storytelling and conversational rules. These differences have resulted in lower performance expectations from teachers, excessive speech or language therapy placements, and communication differences being treated as discipline problems. For the children themselves, their treatment often results in lowered self-expectations and a tendency to see the school climate as negative. Gender differences in ways of talking and non-verbal behaviour can also cause problems: the male sex may be seen as powerful and decisive and the female as submissive and indecisive. Tannen (2001) argued: 'Communication between men and women can be like cross cultural communication, prey to a clash of conversational styles.'[81]

Disability is a major source of communication barriers. For instance, this applies to communicators with a hearing disability. Even in ideal conditions, skilled lip-readers accurately interpret less than 50 per cent of what is being said. The late-deafened communicator, especially, has a difficult time adapting to new communication strategies. People talking to communicators who are hard of hearing may not have the skills to repair communication breakdowns, leaving both parties dissatisfied with the communication encounter.[82] Problems persist even when efforts are made to overcome them. A deaf man who developed software for a big company could speak and lip-read, but said: 'I lose a lot of information, which leads to misunderstandings. I prefer written means to be sure I'm getting the full message.'[83]

For other kinds of disability, the communication problem usually arises because of the behaviours of an interlocutor without disabilities. Within the first few interactions with such an interlocutor, people with disabilities must often manage or fend off requests for information and invasions of privacy in an attempt to retain individuality and control. At the same time they have to try to build relationships. If uncertainty about the disability is not reduced, it often has a negative impact on interability relationships, including premature termination of the relationship.[84]

A three-tier model of intercultural communication consists of the intrapersonal, interpersonal and systemic. At the intrapersonal level, social demands, such as the one to treat people with disabilities with kindness, might be in conflict with others, such as to treat them as equals. This paradox constrains interability interactions, especially those between strangers. At the interpersonal level, people without disabilities, operating with stereotypes, may be unclear as to what constitutes appropriate behaviour (e.g., to help or not to help). This leads them to constrain their behaviour. At the systemic level, which concerns power relations, people without disabilities, who have the upper hand in conversations, may misconstrue statements made by people with disabilities and guide behaviour in a way that supports negative stereotypes. A study had female confederates (trained to use a wheelchair) either feign a disability or remain visibly non-disabled when interacting with a non-disabled respondent. The study found that the non-disabled respondents sought more information and were more aware of behaviour from the non-disabled confederate than from the apparently disabled confederate. The results showed that less positive predicted outcomes led to less information-seeking behaviour.[85]

> This section has shown that differences of background, whether cultural or subcultural, ethnic, gender-based or based on some other distinction, not only affect how people communicate but can also be a serious cause of miscommunication.

5.5   BEHAVIOURAL BARRIERS

All of the underlying psychological factors, which, as Chapters 2 and 4 showed, vary cross-culturally, are capable of leading to behaviours that disturb effective intercultural communication. These include values, motives, emotions, beliefs, assumptions, expectations, intentions and self-construals. The processes of social perception and thinking are similarly vulnerable.

Values

Between people from different sides of these cultural divides, communication can be inhibited by non-acceptance of the others' values. For example, the attempt of someone with high power from a high power distance society to receive the attentions 'due' to their status will grate on people from more egalitarian communities. On the other hand, people from low power distance cultures can also cause difficulties when they work in high power distance societies. For instance, university lecturers in Central Europe regarded the egalitarianism between students and staff that is now usual in British universities as damaging the learning process by undermining their authority. Both deep and surface cultural values can be problematic in intercultural communication: deep culture because communication which conflicts with others' values is very likely to be misunderstood, rejected and found offensive; surface culture because it determines matters such as what is polite and what is not. For example, in the West to proffer the wrong hand for a handshake is a mere error; to do so in Arab countries is a grave offence against manners. Sometimes the problem is one of false interpretation: the examples in Box 5.8 illustrate such a case. At other times, there are genuine differences in values that, when accurately communicated, create negative responses. It is probable that differences in education and upbringing between the French and British (both of which may be rooted in differences in their cultural levels of uncertainty avoidance) do lead at least some of the people of these two nations to approach issues differently. It is also quite possible that both have low tolerance for the other's approach.

Universalism and particularism, as Chapter 2 explained, contrast a preference for drawing general principles with a preference for anecdotes or lists of specific items. People who think and speak in universal modes can underrate the quality of thinking of those who think and speak particularistically. Conversely, particularistic thinkers can regard universalistic thinkers as 'academic' and out of touch with the real world. In both cases, these attitudes lead to poor listening – a lack of serious attention and consideration of the views being expressed or the information being imparted. When these attitudes to others are transmitted, often unintentionally, to the person to whom they apply, a natural reaction for them is to withdraw, reducing the amount of communication they offer, or to get angry. Either reaction can lead to a breach in communication. Again, people from specific cultures, with their small areas of privacy clearly separated from public life, have considerable freedom for direct speech. This may result in 'insulting' people from diffuse cultures, for whom the principle of losing

Box 5.9

An apartment block in the new financial district of London had residents and leaseholders (owners) from all round the world in addition to the British: Chinese, Americans, French, Indians, Italians, Nigerians and others. In a two-year period the following intercultural incidents occurred:

1. A resident asked a neighbour the meaning of a Japanese term she had come across. She had been told by the porter that that neighbour was Japanese. 'We are Chinese, I cannot help you,' the neighbour said, clearly offended.

2. A newly arrived American couple invited all the residents to a 'get-to-know-you' party. People attended and the conversation was lively. The gesture was appreciated. Soon thereafter, however, the American woman put herself forward to be Chair of the Residents' Association Board. This was seen as presumptuous in someone newly arrived and the party was reinterpreted as a political ploy.

3. A French accountant was elected to the Board. She noticed that a small invoice had been paid twice and demanded a thorough investigation going back some years. It was suggested by the other Board members that this was a one-off error, since no others had been found in a sample. When her request was refused, she sent an open letter to all the leaseholders. She found herself unpopular and eventually resigned from the Board.

4. An American resident put in charge of the Christmas decorations arranged for the traditional natural Christmas tree in the lobby to be replaced by an artificial one supplied by a local building firm. A notice stating that this was given by the builder stood at the foot of the tree. There was a saving to the Residents' Association finances, but some of the British residents were offended and found the new arrangement 'tawdry'.

Source: author's research

face is 'what happens when something is made public which people perceive as being private'. The importance of avoiding loss of face is the reason why in diffuse cultures so much more time is taken to get to the point: it is necessary to avoid private confrontation because it is impossible for participants not to take things personally. Many similar examples could be cited to show how differences in core values lead to miscommunication, broadly defined.

Several of the core cultural values have the property of constituting barriers to communication in themselves, regardless of whether intercultural communication is at issue. For example, if everyone were an extreme individualist, one might predict a world of poor communication – individualists show low concern for 'other face'; if all were collectivists, one could predict poor communication and conflict between groups. Collectivists erect barriers to communication with outgroup members, regardless of whether those outgroup members are themselves collectivists or not. People in high power distance cultures erect barriers against those in a different power position from themselves, although their communication with those in a similar power position to their own may be enhanced, because similarity fosters liking, acceptance and persuasibility. High uncertainty avoidance leads to reluctance to engage in uncertain communication situations regardless of whether they are with culturally different people. High masculinity as a trait (as opposed to a value) has been shown to correlate with low ability to 'read' others' emotional states or to express emotion; it seems probable that the equivalent value tends to lead to similar communication deficiencies.

Inter-ethnic differences in values were revealed by American research as a reason why inter-ethnic conversation was often unsatisfying and did not go smoothly. African Americans' core values include sharing (which endorses the in-group, reflects collectivism and implies bonding), uniqueness (individuality), positivity (emotional vitality), realism ('tellin' it like it is') and assertiveness. European Americans prioritize the individual, the right to choose, the self, traditional social roles, being honest, sharing and communication. Even where the labels were the same, they were understood differently: for European Americans 'sharing' meant sharing opinions, not bonding; honesty meant expressing one's true understanding rather than realism; their 'self' implied less interpersonal connectedness than African Americans' 'uniqueness' implied.[86]

Motives

The differences, reported in Chapter 4, in the communication motives of the genders may reduce the chances that either side will find their communication satisfying.[87]

Emotions

As Chapter 2 revealed, Trompenaars (1993) contended that the amount of visible display of emotion is a major difference between cultures.[88] These differences in culturally inculcated rules for emotional display can create severe difficulties for participants in intercultural encounters. The English, with their famous 'stiff upper lip', have traditionally been embarrassed, to the point where their ability to empathize or sympathize was subverted, by the more demonstrative displays of affection and grief shown by Mediterranean people. The same applies to subcultures – men in Western cultures often fear the 'emotionalism' of women (and so take the route of avoidance) although the gender differences here may be more closely related to culturally induced differences in what it is legitimate to display than to the real level of emotion. In addition

Box 5.10

'It has been shown that cancer patients are generally willing to address their emotional and psychosocial functioning. Physicians, on the other hand, are often inadequately trained in communication skills, which may lead to distancing and avoidance in discussing emotionally difficult communications with cancer patients. Although recognition of psychological distress is a crucial aspect of patient care, oncologists often fail to detect general distress in patients and ask few questions regarding patients' psychological health.

Discrepancies found between physician-rated satisfaction and patient satisfaction indicate that physicians often perceive patients' affective responses inaccurately.'

Source: Zachariae, R., Pedersen, C.G., Jensen, B., Ehrnrooth, E., Rossen, P.B. and von der Maase, H. (2003) 'Association of perceived physician communication style with patient satisfaction, distress, cancer-related self-efficacy, and perceived control over the disease', *British Journal of Cancer*, **88**(5): 658–65

to the obstacles created by these cultural differences, the intercultural encounter itself often gives rise to emotions that can create further barriers. For example, in international negotiations, 'increasingly negative' emotional reactions can cause ill will, harm the negotiation process and even bring it to an end. 'In negotiations between Japanese and US negotiators, the latter may be prone to experiencing frustration and the former may be prone to experiencing anxiety. The anxiety of the Japanese negotiators results in increasing frustration on the part of the US negotiators, leading to a vicious circle of increasingly negative feelings.'[89] Again, in encounters between people with and people without disabilities, anxiety, as well as negative stereotypes and expectations, affects both parties and leads to miscommunication.

Communication fear or apprehension (CA), which was described in Chapter 4, impedes communication. Individuals who experience CA ask few questions during the first minute of an interaction, engage in high levels of self-disclosure and are considered less competent by their communication partners. 'Individuals who experience high levels of CA are high in global uncertainty and lack expertise when playing out acquaintance scenarios.'[90] Intercultural communication apprehension (ICA) is often objectively unjustified. On structured communication tasks, inter-ethnic dyads (e.g., a French Canadian with an English Canadian) were just as efficient at communicating with each other as intra-ethnic dyads (e.g., a French Canadian with a French Canadian). Likewise, in the unstructured situation of a free interaction, mixed-ethnicity pairs showed the same pattern of conversational topics, did not take longer to begin communicating and did not talk less than same-ethnicity pairs. Yet, despite this evidence that inter-ethnic communication can be as successful as intra-ethnic communication, it has been found that not only did subjects enter these inter-group encounters with negative expectations but they also left them with an unfavourable impression of what had been achieved. Such negative expectations no doubt serve as an important deterrent to future inter-group interaction.

Emotional discomfort can arise in intercultural encounters from other causes:

1. Disconfirmed expectations: being upset not because a situation is bad, in and of itself, but rather because it is not what was expected.
2. A frustrated desire to belong – not being part of the 'ingroup' of a culture; always feeling like an outsider. This feeling can be provoked by physical difference – being

tall and fair among people who are short and dark – or the perceived attitudes of the culture's members.

3. Ambiguity – by not being sure what is 'going on' or how to interpret events.

4. Confrontation with one's own prejudices: in being socialized into their own culture, people learn to categorize people as 'like me' and 'not like me', and develop ways of treating people in those two groups differently. In another culture, where all or a majority of people are 'not like me', they have to rethink how they treat other people. Sometimes they may be dismayed to find themselves prejudiced.

5. Awareness of inadequacy: anxiety is caused by not knowing whether a given behaviour is appropriate, what is safe, how to negotiate a situation and so on.[91]

(Some of these points relate particularly to sojourning.)

Other common negative emotions in intercultural situations include a need to be dependent or a feeling of being overwhelmed and a need to withdraw. It is not, of course, the emotion itself that constitutes a communication barrier: it is how the individual responds to that emotion. If his/her response is withdrawal or aggressiveness, communication is impeded. Having strong emotional reactions to intercultural situations is normal, and one of the skills of becoming interculturally competent is learning how to deal with such emotions in productive ways.

Beliefs

Probably more disagreement arises over differences in conscious beliefs than anything else. Disagreement should not be confused with miscommunication, even on a broad view. However, to the degree that conflict can be taken as a measure of miscommunication, the amount of conflict prevailing throughout history and still raging today around issues of religion is an indication of how this kind of beliefs produces barriers. Huntington (1997) argued that intercultural conflicts centring on beliefs are perhaps the most intractable of all. While ideological differences can at least be debated, and differences in material interests negotiated, core beliefs are not negotiable or even discussable. 'Hindus and Muslims are unlikely to resolve the issue of whether a temple or a mosque should be built at Ayodhya by building both, or neither, or a syncretic building that is both a mosque and a temple. Similarly, neither French authorities nor Muslim parents are likely to accept a compromise which would allow schoolgirls to wear Muslim dress every other day during the school year. Cultural questions like these involve a yes or no, zero-sum choice.'[92]

Chapter 4 described a set of beliefs, consisting of authoritarianism, social dominance orientation, Protestant work ethic, humanitarianism–egalitarianism, beliefs about the malleability of human attributes and beliefs about diversity. These belief systems are linked to prejudice, which, as Section 2 of this chapter showed, distorts and damages communication. Social dominance orientation (SDO) is associated with negative attitudes towards policies that promote equality across gender, social class, ethnic or racial groups, and sexual orientation, and towards the groups that would benefit from such policies. In North America, people who agree with SDO are more likely to agree with sexism, racism, and ethnocentrism (seeing one's own culture as superior) than people who agree with authoritarianism. Following directly from beliefs that people who are stigmatized are responsible for their lesser outcomes, people who agree with the Protestant work ethic (PWE) in the USA tend to dislike overweight persons and to be prejudiced toward racial minorities. A belief in the PWE has been positively associated with behavioural measures of prejudice, including, in Australia, opposition to public assistance programmes and, instead, support for 'tough-minded' solutions to the problem of unemployment, such as restricting immigration and reducing unemployment benefits. The other three beliefs systems, humanitarianism–egalitarianism, positive beliefs about the malleability of human attributes and positive beliefs about diversity, are linked to low levels of prejudice. For instance, holders of these beliefs tend to attribute Blacks' negative outcomes, such as experiencing discrimination, to causes located outside the individual, believe that society, rather than the individual, should change to improve those outcomes, agree less strongly with stereotypes of ethnic and occupational groups, and less readily form extreme trait judgements of novel (unfamiliar) groups.[93]

Assumptions

Making false assumptions based on the situation in someone's own culture can lead to impeding communication through giving or taking offence by, for example, not giving deference where it is expected or expecting it where it will not be granted. Who is important, whom it would be useful to get to know and who is to be respected may be different in one culture than it is in another. A religious leader may be more important in one culture, someone with wealth in another. In one culture Black people may be the 'insiders', in another it may be South Asians. People who are insiders in their own culture, due to their economic, professional or educational status, may be outsiders in another culture, because their skills are not important there, or because of ethnicity or gender, or simply because they are from another culture and can never be fully accepted in the host culture.

Expectations

Violations of expectations, including role and norm expectations, often lead to people evaluating the violator negatively. People have expectations about both the verbal and the non-verbal behaviour of others, based on social (cultural) norms, previous experience with the situation and, where applicable, previous experience of the other person. These expectations refer both to how they think others do behave and to how they think others should behave. However, as norms for behaviour vary from social group to social group, these expectations are often violated in intercultural encounters. For instance, in the European American middle-class subculture of the USA, 'one expects normal speakers to be reasonably [sic] fluent and coherent in their discourse, to refrain from erratic movements or emotional outbursts and to adhere to politeness norms'.[94] What counts as reasonable fluency and coherence, erratic movement, emotional outburst or politeness varies considerably from one culture (and subculture) to another, so European American middle-class people interacting with many other groups in the world are likely to have their expectations violated. Insofar as fear of violations of expectations means that people expect interactions with people from outside their own social circle to be more costly in terms of effort than rewarding in terms of social gain, people may be more inclined to avoid such interactions.[95]

Intentions

Inferring the intentions of a speaker, which, as Chapter 3 showed, is crucial to communication, is highly problematic for receivers from another culture. Some of the problems have already been pointed out in the discussion of language ambiguity.

Box 5.11

'Manager [Bob]

"Elliot was diagnosed with schizophrenia about eight years ago. He seems stable on his medication and confident that he can monitor his symptoms reasonably well. He lives alone in a flat with support from his parents who live nearby. Elliot started working part-time at Merrinvale Enterprises nearly two years ago. Although his attendance is a problem – he only gets to work about 50 per cent of the time – he works very well on the days he is there. The productivity and quality standards he achieves are way above average."

From Fran's notebook

"We have 200,000 seed pots to process for Mallard's this week – huge job – and I was relying on Elliot being here to get it done. He's the only one capable of operating the labelling device at the level we need. He wasn't in yesterday and he's missing again today.

I've had words with Bob over it. We should not be putting up with Elliot. He just comes in whenever it suits him, never mind what we have to do. Anyone else would have got the sack a year ago." '

Source: Effective workplace communication with employees with psychiatric disability. URL: http://www.fahcsia.gov.au/sa/disability/pubs/documents/consumertrainingsupportproducts/employers/psychiatric_disability/sec10.htm

Self-construals

A final factor is the different self-construals held by people from different cultures. This applies particularly to people from individualist and collectivist cultures. It means that each group is likely to make false assumptions about members of the other group. For instance, 'Asians will possibly overestimate a Westerner's concern about his [sic] group's response to an issue, while a Westerner is likely to assume a greater degree of independence on the part of an Asian with whom he is negotiating.'[96]

Social perception and thinking

The processes of social perceiving and of thinking are also subject to difficulties and errors particular to inter-group and intercultural encounters. The increased tendency to make errors when making inter-group attributions was noted in Chapter 4. Categorization is another error-prone process; there is evidence that some people categorize narrowly, and some of them, as well as some others, categorize rigidly. Narrow categorizers group together only cases that are closely similar on a particular criterion: for instance, a narrow categorizer might apply the label 'manager' only to people who are responsible for the work of others. Broad categorizers, in contrast, allow more cases to fit into the same category by using an increased number of criteria. Thus, broad categorizers might count as managers people who manage budgets or brands as well as those who manage people. Both narrow and broad categorizers might be flexible or rigid categorizers, willing or unwilling to shift their category 'definitions' on receiving new information. There is, though, a tendency for rigidity and narrowness to go together. Rigidity and narrowness, especially when combined, create obstacles to intercultural communication by leading people to overemphasize differences and ignore similarities and by reducing their willingness to search for appropriate interpretations of different others' behaviour. Finally, (sub)cultural differences in logic style, learning style and problem-solving, such as those described in Chapter 4, obviously impede mutual understanding.

This section has been concerned with how the behavioural factors and processes underlying communication behaviour can contribute to miscommunication between people from different groups. To date, most attention has been paid to the barriers created by different values, by emotions, especially fear, and by the violation of expectations.

5.6 WORK-SPECIFIC BARRIERS

In the work context, a number of additional issues arise to limit intercultural communication effectiveness. For example, organizational cultures of blame and defensiveness reduce internal communication effectiveness, while different organizational cultures within merged organizations can lead to a breakdown of intra-organizational communication.[97] Two areas have attracted particular attention: (1) the effects of the heterogeneity of problem-solving and task groups and (2) task-related conflict.

Heterogeneity of work groups

Because organizations are increasingly moving to team-based job design, communication within both task groups and decision-making groups is increasingly important. This has led to research being undertaken into the effects of heterogeneity in work groups on how well people working in them communicate and on related matters such as their creativity. A study of 20 actual work units with 79 respondents suggested that heterogeneity is associated with lower levels of groups' social integration. This, in turn, is associated with higher staff turnover. The study focused on age heterogeneity. It found that group members more distant in age are the ones likely to leave. 'Individuals in an age-heterogeneous [work] group have higher turnover rates as do individuals distant in age from an otherwise homogeneous group.' One possible explanation comes from an earlier finding that, after controlling for an individual's demographic characteristics, the greater the difference in superior–subordinate dyads, in terms of age, education, race and sex, the lower the supervisor's rating of the subordinate's effectiveness and the higher the subordinate's role ambiguity. If subordinates experience 'prejudiced' assessments when they are in a mixed work group or when they are different in background from their supervisor, they may decide that the easiest solution is to leave.[98]

Task-related conflict

There is clear evidence for poor work relations in intercultural situations. For instance, studies of Chinese–American joint ventures reported the following:

- '[Chinese] workers...evaluated Chinese managers by a simple standard: whoever quarrelled with Americans the most aggressively would be considered comrade in arms, and whoever co-operated with the Americans would be nicknamed 'Er Gui Zi' (fake foreigners).'[99]
- 'American managers complained that the Chinese did not recognize the importance of deadlines and schedules; that the Chinese were not proactive and would not take risks; that the Communist party representative at the firm often had more power than the Chinese managers; and that the hardship of working in China was a chronic stressor, which exacerbated inter-cultural conflict. The Chinese managers complained that Americans did not try to understand and

Box 5.12

X was attending a meeting of the French subsidiary of the global organization he worked for. He was acting as the representative of another subsidiary in a discussion of the basis on which his company would supply the French company with components.

The meeting was formally convened by the Chairman [sic], then the French company's Purchasing Director began describing X's company's offer in negative terms. (1) X interrupted, addressing the last speaker directly, not through the Chair. X explained the rationale for his company's offer. (2) The next speaker said, 'Chairman, I'm afraid I must disagree with X. Just because we have received a concessionary price, it does not follow that we should accept delivery delays. These matters are not directly connected.' (3) X thought they would never get to the point of stating their demands. 'Analysis paralysis', he thought. (4) However, when they finally did say what they wanted, he felt trapped – they had constructed so powerful a rationale to support their demands that it was difficult to find any weakness where their position could be attacked. (5) X found the outcome of the meeting unsatisfactory – nothing had been decided. (6) Though probing continuously for his company's aims and objectives, the French negotiators had sidestepped every effort on his part to get them to reveal theirs. (7) At times, the discussion had seemed more like an intellectual exercise than a business meeting.

The following help explain the barriers which led to X finding the meeting unsatisfactory:

(1) X's interruption, and especially his lack of formality in not going through the Chair, would be regarded as a serious breach of etiquette in many French organizations.

(2) French negotiators often concentrate on weaknesses in the other party's logic, rather than on 'getting to yes' by building areas of agreement.

(3) French use of logic can lead to extensive analysis of all matters under discussion.

(4) Instead of a process of making initial offers and concession-making, French negotiators' demands often follow a careful build-up of supporting rationale, which can be very powerful.

(5) Important decisions are rarely taken in meetings.

(6) The French do not regard disclosure of business information as a mutual win–win matter, but as a competitive win–lose 'game'.

(7) Prolonged discussion allows French negotiators to grasp their opponents' weaknesses.

Based on: author's research

learn from the Chinese; that the American management style was too abrupt; that Americans failed to recognize the importance of relationships; and that they overemphasized the importance of formal rules and regulations. "The atmosphere [at Beijing Jeep] became so tense that even the most trivial business dealings between the American and Chinese became bogged down in charges and countercharges." '[100]

Larkey (1996) proposed that there are five dimensions of interaction in culturally diverse groups at work.[101] Being dimensions, they have positive as well as negative poles, but it is the negative poles that are most often associated with workforce diversity. The dimensions are inclusion/exclusion, convergence/divergence, conforming/varied ideation, understanding/misunderstanding and positive/negative evaluation:

- Exclusion in the workplace is the practice of marginalizing members of certain groups by limiting contact and restricting entry into certain job arenas. The related communication behaviours include simple exclusion from conversations. This is done by avoidance or starting conversations only when selected individuals are absent or by non-verbally or linguistically excluding outsiders who are present. Other exclusions are changes in the content of information, especially to exclude individuals from job-related information, either deliberately or by the assumption that they are not appropriate recipients, the use of privileged forms of discourse and exclusion from the normative expectations.

- Convergence/divergence is a concept already introduced in Chapter 4 (and to be further explained in Chapter 6). Convergent communication means adjusting ways of speaking (such as style, dialect, rules and primary language choice) to match those of a partner perceived as different or to show a wish for affiliation; divergence is adherence to one's own way in spite of perceived differences. It is open to individuals in diverse work groups to diverge deliberately in order to increase social distance.

- Conforming ideation means suppressing divergent points of view and converging towards normative views in decision-making; varied ideation is the reverse. A climate of conforming ideation is likely to lead to suppressing the views of minorities.

- Misunderstanding here means the mismatching of expectations and meanings for people in interaction. Both employees and managers are predisposed to interpret the communication of others according to specific culture-based expectations. For instance, views of what makes a good leader or a good employee may vary substantially, leading to misinterpretations of the behaviour of individuals in those roles. Among the resulting communication practices are complaints of inappropriate responses or expectations.

- Negative evaluations can be explained by perceptions of ingroup/outgroup membership and associated responses to social identity, reinforced by stereotyping (the communication of even positive stereotype beliefs may elicit negative responses from those being categorized). The resulting behaviours include harassment, overt statements of negative stereotyping and stories with negative implications.

Figure 5.3 shows the relations between cultural diversity in groups and the above five communication practices.

5.7 (SOME) ORGANIZATIONAL CULTURES AND CLIMATES

Organizations and their managers are generally highly conscious of the disadvantages of diversity. They are aware of the difficulties involved in reaching agreement, standardizing procedures and working in parallel on aspects of a project when individuals from a range of cultural or subcultural backgrounds are involved. For many organizations the cost of diversity is highly visible. It includes the negative reactions

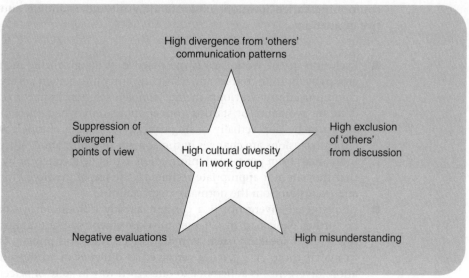

Figure 5.3   *Sources of miscommunication and conflict in diverse work groups*

to diversity in the workplace by some employees. Indeed, the main diversity goal of many organizations might be described as to minimize the costs diversity entails. In other companies, 'Diversity programs are not usually seen as critical to the survival of the company, even though statements are made about markets and bottom lines. No one in the organization is likely to lose his or her job if they don't "value" diversity the way they could if the production of goods and the selling of goods and services are not improved. Thus, diversity can be seen as a discretionary activity to be postponed when more pressing situations are faced.'[102] Furthermore, a negative trend for diversity support has been noted in recent years: employers have increasingly turned to 'employee fit' as a formal job requirement and have retreated from detailed bureaucratic structures in ways that place heightened importance on social relations. 'These structural moves raise new concerns about workplace equality, for they strengthen demands to conform with prevailing work culture by making social relations more crucial to an individual's employment success.'[103] Poor organizational support for diversity impedes intercultural communication.

The Hofstede (1981) classification of organizational cultures described in Chapter 2 has significance for the likely impact of the culture on diversity within the organization and so on the barriers to intercultural communication within it. Because process-oriented cultures cannot tolerate a range of approaches, they may well support diversity less well than the alternative results-oriented cultures, which can accept different approaches provided the results are satisfactory. Organizations with job-oriented cultures assume a narrower responsibility for employees' well-being than those with employee-oriented cultures. Obviously, in organizations with a diverse workforce a job-oriented culture is less likely to ensure that all individuals have opportunities for advancement. A parochial organizational culture is likely to be linked with a degree of xenophobia or distrust of outsiders. Such distrust can make diversity costly because of the amount that existing employees must adapt. Closed systems cultures are likely to be less accessible to minorities than open systems cultures as well as less capable of benefiting from the increased sensitivity to the environment which diversity makes possible. Tightly controlled cultures are less able than loosely controlled cultures to tolerate the behavioural differences which come with diversity; tightly controlled cultures require all individuals to conform to a single model. Since flexibility is both a necessary condition for and an outcome of diversity, normative cultures are less well adapted to benefit from it than pragmatic cultures are.[104]

In most organizations, at present, one culture is dominant. In the UK organization Body Shop, the dominant culture is that of white liberal women, which favours 'feminine' values, such as care for the environment and the support of equal opportunities. This is exceptional, however: the pervasiveness of the masculine culture in most Western organizations has been noted by a number of researchers: the expectations of this workplace culture are masculine heterosexual. These expectations create difficulties for gay people as well as for heterosexual women. This culture is reinforced through joking, which often has a focus round three rules of sexuality: the ideal, typical, real man, definitions of males as not-female and the normality of heterosexuality. Men's continuing domination of the most powerful positions in most organizations results in a widespread emphasis on power and control over people, resources, environments and events as the only path to corporate success; worse, in the late twentieth century, in many organizations abrasiveness and macho approaches like working extremely long hours came to be valued for themselves. While the end of the 1990s saw the pendulum swing to some degree against this, performance evaluations in many British and North American companies continued to be heavily based on personal power and control.[105]

Organizations with a strong dominant culture force those from the 'minority' cultures (who may or may not be in a numerical minority) to adjust their behaviour to accommodate it. Worse, they may not even be able to admit to having values that conflict with those of the dominant group. This not only creates stressful internal conflict for those individuals, but sets up a climate in which creativity is hampered, because too many points of view are inhibited, thus ruling out the conditions favourable to creativity. Such a climate may also be one in which the damage done by groupthink (or lack of challenge to majority views) can most readily occur. Moreover, as Schreiber (1996) noted, such organizations curb productivity because workers 'who assimilate are denied the ability to express their genuine selves in the workplace. ... People who

---

Box 5.13

A study in the UK plant of a German MNC (multi-national company) found that managers sometimes ignored the real impact of local ethnic diversity, focusing instead on inter-management conflicts. The neglect of the underlying issue contributed to problems with employee morale; it also conflicted with the German company's attempts to promote a global corporate culture.

However, where diversity was recognized, more success followed.

Source: Moore, F. and Rees, C. (2008) 'Culture against cohesion: global corporate strategy and employee diversity in the UK plant of a German MNC', *Employee Relations*, **30**(2): 176–89

must spend significant amounts of energy coping with an alien environment have less energy left to do their jobs'.[106]

> The cultures of the organization or organizations for which communicators work may create a climate which can impact adversely on their communication.

5.8　CONCLUSION

This chapter was concerned with sources of intercultural miscommunication. These barriers are real in their consequences and seem often to have their greatest effect for not being perceived. When they are recognized, people often try to overcome them, and often succeed. Cultural and subcultural differences in the ways in which people from different backgrounds communicate, as well as in the intra-individual factors and processes underlying their behaviour, were shown to create these intercultural barriers to communication. Behaviours such as ingroup/outgroup differentiation, stereotyping, prejudice, discrimination and harassment also construct communication barriers. Work-specific barriers include heterogeneity of work groups and task-related conflict; some organizational cultures are impediments to effective intercultural communication. These barriers create misunderstandings between individuals, whether in the roles of colleagues, professionals and their clients or suppliers and their customers. These misunderstandings often result in emotional distress and reduced performance. Other consequences are that heterogeneous work groups, while potentially more creative, take longer to perform well and are more likely to break down, and that transnational negotiations and business operations can be fraught with conflict. The next chapter shows how these barriers can be overcome and how effective intercultural communication can be achieved.

Box 5.14

Some scholars dispute the idea that intercultural communication is a special kind of communication in which misunderstandings arise because the participants do not share meanings and communication practices. Instead, they argue, all communication requires interactors to go through a process to establish common ground. Misunderstandings are part of that process. 'Existing research on intercultural misunderstandings usually explain them as caused by culturally different conventions…here misunderstanding is understood as part of the process of constructing a discursive interculture.'[a]
Contrary to expectations, one study has produced results which suggest that 'in a world of globalization and international perspectives, an intercultural context may cue people to co-operate rather than compete.' The findings were that the intercultural context in a negotiation was associated neither with higher national social identity nor with lower reciprocity.[b]

Source: (a) Koole, T. and ten Thije, J.D. (2001) 'The reconstruction of intercultural discourse: methodological considerations', *Journal of Pragmatics*, **33**: 571–87.
(b) Traavik, L.E.M. (2007) 'Reciprocating concessions in intercultural and intracultural contexts', *IACM 2007 Meetings Paper* Available at SSRN: http://ssrn.com/abstract=1100608. (Last accessed 23.12.2010)

QUESTIONS AND EXERCISES

1. The text gives examples of how differences in communication practices can lead to misunderstanding and even conflict in intercultural encounters. Collect a list of other examples.

2. List four ways in which stereotypes can distort inter-group communication.

3. What might be influencing the actions of the participants in the following confrontation? What behaviours might improve their communication? 'A woman Council officer responsible for parks met with a local Residents' Group representative. The representative was young, male and from an ethnic minority. His Group had been petitioning the Council to double the resources for patrolling and clearing up in their local park, claiming that drug users' needles were often left lying about. From the start, he seemed intemperately angry to the officer. He stood too close, looked intently in her eyes and spoke loudly. Gradually she responded by getting angry too. It ended in a shouting match.'

4. **Role 1:** You are a fund manager for a Western sustainable ethical investment fund. You are to interview the Head of Mergers and Acquisitions for one of the companies in which your fund invests. The company itself makes solar panels and is located in Asia. You suspect that their due diligence processes for mergers and acquisitions are not adequate to ensure that your fund's principles of sustainability and environmental protection are being adhered to.

   Note: In your country's culture communication is low-context, while power distance and uncertainty avoidance are low and individualism is high.

   Role 2: You are the Head of Mergers and Acquisitions for an Asian company which makes solar panels. A fund manager for a Western investment fund has arranged to interview you about your mergers and acquisitions strategy and processes. The fund holds only 1 per cent of your company's shares.

   Note: In your country's culture communication is high-context, while power distance and uncertainty avoidance are low and individualism is high.

   Role play this interview.

5. Give examples to clarify the distinction between prejudice, discrimination and harassment.

6. Box 5.6, quoting from *The Economist*, asserts that 'the three arguments for a ban [on women wearing the burqa] – security, sexual equality and secularism – do not stand up.' Discuss.

7. Discuss the extent to which an organization known to you is 'gendered'.

8. Discuss the contention that sexual harassment is a patriarchal control strategy used by men to keep women 'in their place'.

9. The European Communities Council Directive intended to establish a general framework for equal treatment in employment and vocational training permits 'positive action' measures, which prevent or compensate for disadvantages. Positive action, especially positive discrimination, is controversial. Discuss its advantages and disadvantages.

10. The early aim of equality law was to achieve a 'colour blind', gender-neutral world. Give reasons that would explain why that aim has changed.

11. Currently, the aim of equality law is to support a merit-based world and diversity. How effective would you expect to be the four platforms on which, it is suggested, law with these aims should be based?

12. Give three examples of positive and three of negative micro-messages.

13. Video any of the role plays provided in this book, watch it closely and record any instances of micro-messages. Distinguish positive from negative micro-messages.

14. Discuss the findings on direct (overt) and subtle (covert) racism given in the text. What consequences for work behaviour would you predict from the substitution of covert for overt prejudice?

15. Referring to a story about a ban on gays in the Armed Forces, a columnist for *The Times* of London, himself openly gay, wrote: 'If prejudice among soldiers runs so deep and wide, it should be respected.' Do you agree? Why or why not?

16. What conclusions do you draw from the meta-analysis of research into prejudice directed against women managers and leaders described in Section 5.2?

17. Discuss the item in Box 5.3. What may it tell us about the nature of prejudice?

18. Explain the persistent injustice effect. How might it be overcome in a work context?

19. The text gives a list of 23 dimensions of communication that Finns perceive as problematic in their communication with non-Finns. How many of those dimensions do you perceive as problematic in your communication with people of nationalities other than your own? Which are most important? Are there any others not in the Finns' list?

20. Devise a questionnaire to test whether respondents are more concerned about 'control' or 'affiliation' in communication and administer it to a sample of equal numbers of men and women.

21. Reword the following to put the topic, background or reason first and the main point, suggested action or comment second: 'You take the ring road to go to the factory.' Reword the following to put the main point, suggested action or comment first and the topic, background or reason second: 'Because of difficulties in transit which have led to delivery delays and increases in packaging costs which are beyond our control, we have been forced to reconsider our pricing policy, leading to a new price structure from 1st November.'

22. Give an example of misalignment of facework strategies.

23. Give examples showing how the behaviour of non-disabled people can reinforce stereotypes of disabled people.

24. Discuss the challenges people with disabilities face in asserting a positive identity in inter-ability situations.

25. How does viewing a person with a disability as atypical because he or she does not act in a stereotypical way help to keep stereotypes intact?

26. Give examples of how communication between people from different cultures can be inhibited or distorted by non-acceptance of the others' core values.

27. Give examples of how cultural differences in the following antecedents of communication can create barriers:
    - the self
    - conscious beliefs
    - assumptions
    - display of feeling

28. 'My phone company has, yet again, sent me a faulty bill. I have made more than half a dozen attempts to get it corrected in the past few weeks but these appear to have fallen on deaf ears. I pick up the phone, dial the familiar customer service number to lodge yet another complaint. After listening to a barrage of tape-message torture and punching several clicks finally a customer service representative arrives on the line. He speaks with a foreign accent and is clearly following a script – there is no spontaneity. Before I can explain my complaint he insists on taking me through a set of questions – the so-called "confirmation of identity" – and then as soon

as I have stated the issue puts me on "hold" to listen to the telecom service jingle, in which I have no interest whatsoever.'

    (a) What emotions am 'I' likely to be experiencing at that time? What thoughts am 'I' likely to be thinking?

The customer service representative returns.

    (b) Visualize and write down or role play the conversation that follows, assuming that 'I' am not skilled in intercultural communication. How would 'I' feel afterwards?

29. Assume you are facilitating a mixed-ethnicity, mixed-gender, mixed-age group of software designers to articulate the competencies they require for the ambitious fourfold growth envisaged by their company. The discussions are animated, the participants deeply engaged. Midway through the discussion there is an impasse. The group appears to be stuck with multiple, contrarian views held by its different members. What barriers to intercultural communication might account for this difficulty the group is experiencing? What should the facilitator do to end the logjam in this situation?

30. A Consultant has a junior colleague who has persistently failed to complete a simple task of documentation, despite repeatedly promising to do it. The junior is intelligent and understands the work required, is quite competent and does not have an excessive workload.

    (a) Assume the junior colleague is a woman and the Consultant an older man; or
    (b) Assume the junior colleague is a man and the Consultant an older woman.

In both cases, assume the Consultant's intercultural communication skills are weak. Visualize and write down or role play his/her discussion with the junior colleague.

31. In discussing the effects of beliefs on intercultural communication, Kincaid (1987) wrote: 'Absolute certainty renders communication inoperable.' Discuss this contention in relation to the material on core beliefs and prejudice in the text.[107]

32. What are the implications of the following finding for Black/White relations at work? In a study with a full inter-group design, Black and White participants rated Black and White racial groups. Members of both groups underestimated how favourably their own group was rated by members of their respective outgroup (Krueger, J. (1996). 'Personal beliefs and cultural stereotypes about racial characteristics', *Journal of Personality and Social Psychology*, **71**: 536–48).

33. '[Inter-group] conflict, despite appearances, still leads to inter-group influence.' Discuss this statement.

34. Discuss the criticism given in Box 5.15 of the view that misunderstandings arise because participants do not share meanings and communication practices.

NOTES AND REFERENCES

1. Burke, K. (1966) *Language as Symbolic Action*, Berkeley, CA: University of California Press.
2. Trompenaars, F. (1993) *Riding the Waves of Culture*, London: Nicholas Brealey.
3. Guimond, S., Dif, S. and Aupy, A. (2002) 'Social identity, relative group status and intergroup attitudes: when favourable outcomes change intergroup relations for the worse', *European Journal of Social Psychology*, **32**(6): 739–60.
4. Ashburn-Nardo, L., Voils, C.I. and Monteith, M.J. (2001) 'Implicit associations as the seeds of intergroup bias: how easily do they take root?', *Journal of Personality and Social Psychology*, **81**(5): 789–99.
5. Stangor, C. and Thompson, E.P. (2002) 'Needs for cognitive economy and self-enhancement as unique predictors of intergroup attitudes', *European Journal of Social Psychology*, **32**: 563–75.

6. Hunter, J.A. (2003) 'Ingroup favoring allocations and domain-specific self-esteem in the minimal group setting', *Current Research in Social Psychology*, **8**(13): 177–87.

7. Weber, U., Mummendey, A. and Waldzus, S. (2002) 'Perceived legitimacy of intergroup status differences: its prediction by relative ingroup prototypicality', *European Journal of Social Psychology*, **32**: 449–70.

8. Ouwerkerk, J.W. and Ellemers, N. (2002) 'The benefits of being disadvantaged: performance-related circumstances and consequences of intergroup comparisons', *European Journal of Social Psychology*, **32**: 73–91.

9. Buchan, N.R., Johnson, E.J. and Croson, R.T.A. (2006) 'Let's get personal: An international examination of the influence of communication, culture and social distance on other regarding preferences', *Journal of Economic Behavior & Organization*, **60**: 373–98.

10. Wiemann, J.M. and Giles, H. (1988) 'Interpersonal communication', in Hewstone, M., Stroebe, W., Codol, J.-P. and Stephenson, G.M. (eds) *Introduction to Psychology*, Oxford: Blackwell.

11. Hewstone, M. and Jaspars, J. (1984) 'Social dimensions of attributions', in Tajfel, H. (ed.) *The Social Dimension vol. 2.*, Cambridge: Cambridge University Press.

12. Detweiler, R. (1975) 'On inferring the intentions of a person from another culture', *Journal of Personality*, **43**: 591–611.

13. Hornsey, M.J., Oppes, T. and Svennsson, A. (2002) ' "It's ok if we say it, but you can't": responses to inter-group and intragroup criticism', *European Journal of Social Psychology*, **32**: 293–307.

14. Hewstone, M. and Giles, H. (1986) 'Social groups and social stereotypes in inter-group communication: review and model of inter-group communication breakdown', in Gudykunst, W.B. (ed.) *Inter-group Communication*, London: Edward Arnold.

15. Leonard, R., and Locke, D. (1993) 'Communication stereotypes: is interracial communication possible?', *Journal of Black Studies*, **23**(3): 332–43.

16. Pettigrew, T.F. (1958) 'Personality and sociocultural factors in inter-group attitudes: a crossnational comparison', *Journal of Conflict Resolution*, **2**: 29–42.

17. Monin, B. and Miller, D.T. (2001) 'Moral credentials and the expression of prejudice', *Journal of Personality and Social Psychology*, **81**(1): 33–43.

18. Halman, L. and Kerkhofs, J. (2001) *The European Values Study: Selected Results.* URL: www.romir.ru/eng/research/01_2001/european-values.htm, last accessed on 22 December 2010.

19. Hagendoorn, L. and Kleinpenning, G. (1991) 'The contribution of domain-specific stereotypes to ethnic social distance', *British Journal of Social Psychology*, **30**: 63–78.

20. Akrami, N., Ekehammar, E. and Araya, T. (2000) 'Classical and modern racial prejudice: a study of attitudes toward immigrants in Sweden', *European Journal of Social Psychology*, **30**: 521–32.

21. Dambrun, M., Desprès, G. and Guimond, S. (2003) 'On the multifaceted nature of prejudice: psychophysiological responses to ingroup and outgroup ethnic stimuli', *Current Research in Social Psychology*, **8**: 187–206.

22. Schaafsma, J. (2008) 'Interethnic relations at work: Examining ethnic minority and majority members' experiences in The Netherlands', *International Journal of Intercultural Relations*, **32**(5): 453–65.

23. Eagly, A.H., Makhujani, M.G. and Klonsky, B.G. (1992) 'Gender and the evaluation of leaders: a meta-analysis', *Psychological Bulletin*, **111**: 3–22.

24. Argyle, M. (2000) *Psychology and Religion: An Introduction*, London: Routledge.

25. Inman, M.L., and Baron, R.S. (1996) 'Influence of prototypes on perceptions of prejudice', *Journal of Personality and Social Psychology*, **70**: 727–39.

26. Noon, M. (1993) 'Racial discrimination in speculative applications: evidence from the UK's top 100 firms', *Human Resource Management Journal*, **3**(4): 35–47.

27. [UK] Regulations implementing the Race Relations Act 1976 (Amendment) 2003.

28. Farley-Lucas, B.S. (2000) 'Communicating the (in)visibility of motherhood: Family talk and the ties to motherhood with/in the workplace', *Electronic Journal of Communication*, 10. URL: http://www.cios.org/getfile/farley V10n3400.
29. Acker, J. (1992) 'Gendering organisational theory', in Mills, A.J. and Tancred, P. (eds) *Gendering Organisational Analysis*, London: Sage.
30. Burrell, G. (1984) 'Sex and organizational analysis', *Organization Studies*, **5**: 97–118.
31. Colgan, F. and Ledwith, S. (1996) 'Women as organizational change agents', in Colgan, F. and Ledwith, S. (eds) *Women in Organizations*, Basingstoke: Macmillan.
32. Colwill, N.L. (1995) 'Women in management: power and powerlessness', in Vinnicombe, S. and Colwill, N.L. (eds) *The Essence of Women in Management*, Hemel Hempstead: Prentice Hall.
33. Bram, L.L. and Dickey, N.H. (1993) 'Disabled people', *Funk and Wagnalls Encyclopaedia*, Cleveland, OH: World Almanac Education.
34. Stevens, G.R. (2002) 'Employers' perceptions and practice in the employability of disabled people; a survey of companies in south east UK', *Disability and Society*, **17**(7): 779–96.
35. McLean, J. (2002) 'Employees with long term illnesses or disabilities in the UK social services workforce', *Disability and Society*, **18**(1): 51–70.
36. *The Economist*, 6 January 1996.
37. Rumens, N. and Kerfoot, D. (2009) 'Gay men at work: (re)constructing the self as professional', *Human Relations*, **62**: 763–86.
38. Grimshaw, J. (1999) *Employment and Health: Psychosocial Stress in the Workplace*, London: The British Library.
39. Vartia, M. and Hyyti, J. (2002) 'Gender differences in workplace bullying among prison officers', *European Journal of Work and Organizational Psychology*, **111**: 113–26.
40. Hogh, A. and Dofradottir, A. (2001) 'Coping with bullying in the workplace', *European Journal of Work and Organizational Psychology*, **10**(4): 485–95.
41. Hoel, H., Cooper, C.L. and Faragher, B. (2001) 'The experience of bullying in Great Britain: the impact of organizational status', *European Journal of Work and Organizational Psychology*, **10**(4): 443–46.
42. Liefooghe, A.P.D. and MacKenzie Davey, K. (2001) 'Accounts of workplace bullying: the role of the organization', *European Journal of Work and Organizational Psychology*, **10**(4): 375–92.
43. Ivy, D.K. and Hamlet, S. (1996) 'College students and sexual dynamics: two studies of peer sexual harassment', *Communication Education*, **45**: 149–66.
44. Stangor, C., Swim, J.K., Van Allen, K.L. and Sechrist, G.B. (2002) 'Reporting discrimination in public and private contexts', *Journal of Personality and Social Psychology*, **82**(1): 69–74.
45. Wanguri, D.M. (1996) 'Diversity, perceptions of equity and communicative openness in the workplace', *The Journal of Business Communication*, **33**: 443–57.
46. Davidson, M. and Friedman, R.A. (1998) 'When excuses don't work: the persistent injustice effect among Black managers', *Administrative Science Quarterly*, **43**: 154–83.
47. Ward, C. and Masgoret, A.-M. (2007) 'Immigrant entry into the workforce: a research note from New Zealand', *International Journal of Intercultural Relations*, **31**(4): 525–30.
48. Major, B., Gramzow, R.H., McCoy, S.K., Levin, S., Schmader, T. and Sidanius, J. (2002) 'Perceiving personal discrimination: the role of group status and legitimizing ideology', *Journal of Personality and Social Psychology*, **82**(3): 269–82.
49. Alderfer, C.P. and Smith, K.K. (1988) 'Studying inter-group relations embedded in organizations', *Administrative Science Quarterly*, **27**: 5–65.
50. Gherardi, S. and Poggio, B. (2001) 'Creating and recreating gender order in organizations', *Journal of World Business*, **36**(3): 245–59.
51. *The Times*, 9 September 2004.
52. Stangor *et al.*, 'Reporting discrimination in public and private contexts'.
53. Wanguri, 'Diversity, perceptions of equity and communicative openness in the workplace'.

54. Hatcher, C. (2000) 'Making the visible invisible: constructing gender through organizational microRpractices', *Electronic Journal of Communication*, **10**(1 and 2). URL: www.cios.org/www/tocs/AJC/0192.htm.
55. Grimshaw, *'Employment and Health'*.
56. Ivy and Hamlet, 'College students and sexual dynamics'.
57. Glastra, F., Schedler, P. and Kats, E. (1998) 'Employment equity policies in Canada and the Netherlands: enhancing minority employment between public controversy and market initiative', *Policy and Politics*, **26**(2): 163–76.
58. Green, T. (2005) 'Work culture and discrimination', *California Law Review*, **93**. Available at SSRN: http://ssrn.com/abstract=655302, last accessed on 23 December 2010.
59. Larkey, L.K. (1996) 'The development and validation of the workforce diversity questionnaire', *Management Communication Quarterly*, **9**(3): 296–337.
60. Gallois, C. and Callan, V.J. (1986) 'Decoding emotional messages: influence of ethnicity, sex, message type and channel', *Journal of Personality and Social Psychology*, **51**(4): 755–62.
61. Sperber, D. and Wilson, D. (1986) *Relevance: Communication and Cognition*, Cambridge, MA: Harvard University Press.
62. Scott, J.C. (2000) 'Differences in American and British vocabulary: implications for international business communication', *Business Communication Quarterly*, **63**(4): 27–39.
63. Kotani, M. (2002) 'Expressing gratitude and indebtedness: Japanese speakers' use of "I'm sorry" in English conversation', *Research on Language and Social Interaction*, **35**(1): 39–72.
64. Thompson, N. (2003) *Communication and Language: A Handbook of Theory and Practice*, Basingstoke: Palgrave Macmillan.
65. Triandis, H.C. (2000) 'Culture and conflict', *International Journal of Psychology*, **35**(2): 145–52.
66. Bernstein, B. (1971) *Class, Codes and Control*, St Albans: Paladin.
67. Yum, J.O. (1987) 'Asian perspectives on communication', in Kincaid, D. (ed.) *Communication Theory: Eastern and Western Perspectives*, New York: Academic Press.
68. Armstrong, G.B. and Kaplowitz, S.A. (2001) 'Sociolinguistic inference and intercultural coorientation: a Bayesian model of communicative competence in intercultural interaction', *Human Communication Research*, **27**(3): 350–81.
69. Ting-Toomey, S. (1988) 'Intercultural conflict styles: A face-negotiation theory', in Kim, Y.Y. and Gudykunst, W.B. (eds) *Theories in Intercultural Communication*, Newbury Park, CA: Sage.
70. Ambady, N., Koo, J., Lee, F. and Rosenthal, R. (1996) 'More than words: linguistic and nonlinguistic politeness in two cultures', *Journal of Personality and Social Psychology*, **70**: 996–1,011.
71. Wierzbicka, A. (1991) *Cross-Cultural Pragmatics: The Semantics of Human Interaction*, Berlin: Mouton de Gruyter.
72. Hall, E.T. (1959) *The Silent Language*, New York: Doubleday.
73. CNORSE 'Cross-cultural communication: an essential dimension of effective education'. URL: http://www.nwrel.org/cnorse/index.html, last accessed on 23 December 2010.
74. Olaniran, B.A. and Williams, D.E. (1995) 'Communication distortion: an intercultural lesson from the visa application process', *Communication Quarterly*, **43**(2): 225–40.
75. Bond, C.F. Jr, Adnan, O., Adnan, M. and Bonser, R.N. (1990) 'Lie detection across cultures', *Journal of Nonverbal Behaviour*, **14**(3): 189–204.
76. Warren, G., Schertler, E. and Bull, P. (2009) 'Detecting deception from emotional and unemotional cues', *Journal of Nonverbal Behaviour*, **33**(1): 59–69.
77. Maoz, I. and Ellis, D.G. (2001) 'Going to ground: argument in Israeli–Jewish and Palestinian encounter groups', *Research on Language and Social Interaction*, **34**(4): 399–419.
78. *Cohen, L. and El-Sawad, A. (2007) 'Lived experiences of offshoring: An examination of UK and Indian financial service employees' accounts of themselves and one another', Human Relations, 60(8): 1,235–62.*

79. Triandis, 'Culture and conflict'.
80. Kirra, K.M. (2000) 'Finns in interaction with non-Finns: problematic phenomena perceived as critical incidents', *Intercultural Communication*, **4**: 109–23.
81. Tannen, D. (2001) *You Just Don't Understand: Men and Women in Conversation*, New York: Quill.
82. McIntosh, A. (2000) 'When the deaf and the hearing interact: communication features, relationships, and disability issues', in Braithwaite, D.O. and Thompson, T.L. (eds) *Handbook of Communication and People with Disabilities: Research and Application*, New York: Lawrence Erlbaum.
83. Ranger, L.M. (2002) 'Communication is key for deaf and hard of hearing technical pros', *Diversity/Careers Professional*, Oct/Nov. URL: http://www.diversitycareers.com/
84. Fox, S.A., Giles, H., Orbe, M.P. and Bourhis, R.Y. (2000) 'Interability communication: theoretical perspectives', in Braithwaite, D.O. and Thompson, T.L. (eds) *Handbook of Communication and People with Disabilities: Research and Application*, New York: Lawrence Erlbaum.
85. Ibid.
86. Martin, J.N., Hecht, M.L. and Larkey, L.K. (1994) 'Conversation improvement strategies for interethnic communication: African-American and European-American perspectives', *Communication Monographs*, **61**(3): 236–55.
87. Hecht, M.L., Larkey, L. and Johnson, J. (1992) 'African American and European American perceptions of problematic issues in interethnic communication effectiveness', *Human Communication Research*, **19**: 209–36.
88. Trompenaars, *Riding the Waves of Culture*.
89. George, J.M., Gonzalez, J.A. and Jones, G.R. (1998) 'The role of affect in cross-cultural negotiations', *Journal of International Business Studies*, **29**(4): 749–72.
90. Douglas, W. (1991) 'Expectations about initial interaction: an examination of the effects of global uncertainty', *Human Communication Research*, **17**: 355–84.
91. Brislin, R., Cushner, K., Cherrie, C. and Yong, M. (1986) *Intercultural Interactions*, Beverly Hills, CA: Sage.
92. Huntington, S. (1997) *The Clash Of Civilizations And The Remaking of World Order*, London: Simon & Schuster.
93. West, T. and Levy, S. R. (2002) 'Background belief systems and prejudice', in Lonner, W.J., Dinnel, D.L., Hayes, S.A. and Sattler, D.N. (eds), *Online Readings in Psychology and Culture*. URL: http://www.wwu.edu/~culture, last accessed on 23 December 2010.
94. Burgoon, J. and Hale, J. (1988) 'Nonverbal expectancy violations', *Communication Monographs*, **55**: 58–79.
95. Hoyle, R., Pinkley, R. and Insko, C. (1989) 'Perceptions of social behavior', *Personality and Social Psychology Bulletin*, **15**: 365–76.
96. Yum, 'Asian perspectives on communication'.
97. Thompson, *Communication and Language*.
98. O'Reilly III, C.A., Caldwell, D.R. and Barnett, W.P. (1989) 'Work group demography, social integration and turnover', *Administrative Science Quarterly*, **34**: 21–37.
99. Grub, P.D. and Lin, J.H. (1991) *Foreign Direct Investment in China*, New York: Quorum Books.
100. Mann, J. (1989) *Beijing Jeep: The Short, Unhappy Romance of American Business in China*, New York: Simon and Schuster.
101. Larkey, 'The development and validation of the workforce diversity questionnaire'.
102. Muir, C. (1996) 'Workplace readiness for communicating diversity', *The Journal of Business Communication*, **33**: 475–84.
103. Green, 'Work culture and discrimination'.
104. Hofstede, G. (1981) *Cultures and Organizations: Software of the Mind*, London: Harper Collins.

105. Collinson, D.L. and Hearn, J. (1996) 'Breaking the silence; on men, masculinities and managements', in Collinson, D.L. and Hearn, J. (eds) *Men as Managers, Managers as Men: Critical Perspectives on Men, Masculinities and Managements,* London: Sage.
106. Schreiber, E.J. (1996) 'Muddles and huddles: facilitating a multicultural workforce through team management theory', *The Journal of Business Communication,* **33**: 459–73.
107. Kincaid, D.L. (1987) 'The convergence theory of communication, self-organization and cultural evolution', in Kincaid, D.H. (ed.) *Communication Theory: Eastern and Western Perspectives,* New York: Academic Press.

chapter six

Communicating Interculturally

Chapter 5 discussed barriers to intercultural communication. That people are aware of these barriers is shown by a study that found that native speakers of American English who interacted with non-native speakers perceived interaction as more difficult than did their counterparts who interacted with other native speakers. They also had more thoughts showing confusion, but also more thoughts focused on the partner and fewer on the content of the conversation, more focus on understanding the other's message, less on clarifying their own message and less on displaying their own involvement.[1] Many of these responses to being aware of barriers may improve intercultural communication, although others impede it.

This chapter focuses on how intercultural encounters can be made more effective. Section 6.1 covers inclusive language, Section 6.2 discusses ethical issues in intercultural communication, Section 6.3 describes effective intercultural communication behaviours and Section 6.4 analyses effective intercultural communication processes, many of which are interactive and mutual. It also offers a critique of theoretical approaches to intercultural communication. The final section, 6.5, is an examination of what effectiveness means in an intercultural communication context.

Box 6.1

Digh (2001) reported that, to get messages across, American companies are now providing 'Ads in Spanish, TV commercials featuring people with disabilities, marketing messages using cross-generational icons such as Britney Spears and Bob Dole. ..."There's no longer one solution or message that will work for everyone," says Myrna Marofsky, President of ProGroup Inc., a diversity consulting firm. "For example," she says, "if a company wants to tell employees something about health benefits, human resources should consider not what's easiest, but what would make the value of health benefits clear to all the cultures represented in your workplace."'

Source: Digh, P. (2001) 'One style doesn't fit all: to get your message across to diverse groups within your workforce, send it in various ways – each version tailored to their distinct needs', *HR Magazine*, November

6.1 INCLUSIVE LANGUAGE

None of the ways of overcoming intercultural communication barriers described later in this chapter is likely to work if, whether unintentionally or out of a perverse or misguided intention not to be 'politically correct', biased language is used. Biased language has been shown to affect adversely the self-image of members of the group excluded or negatively portrayed. There is, therefore, a strong argument from social justice (equal opportunity) for avoiding it. In addition, biased language naturally provokes resentment among members of negatively portrayed groups, which contributes to social disharmony and disrupts intercultural communication. For instance, as research among French women managers showed, they disliked 'compliments concerning their physical appearance.... In the workplace, women managers wanted to be recognized for their abilities. The French language allows a job title to indicate the gender of the person holding the job, but most women managers chose to use the masculine form rather than the feminine form of their professional title, especially on their visiting cards.'[2]

Non-inclusive language reinforces barriers that prevent all members of an organization or society from participating fully in its work; it also undermines policies aimed at diversity. Non-inclusive language is of three main kinds:

1. Using generic masculine words or titles to refer to all persons.
2. Using terms or expressions that reinforce inappropriate, outdated or demeaning attitudes or assumptions about persons or groups. These may be based on age, disability, ethnicity, gender, national origin, religion or sexual orientation.
3. Misusing stereotypes, which too often represent an oversimplified opinion, subjective attitude or uncritical judgment. They become particularly offensive and demeaning when used to make assumptions about the intellectual, moral, social or physical capabilities of an individual or a group. Neither individuals' demographic and other characteristics, nor their group membership, should be mentioned, unless it is specifically relevant to the topic being discussed. (Inclusive language aims to respect the wishes of the group to or about whom the communication is taking place.[3])

In addition to these general points, care should be taken over terms for people's ethnicity, gender, age group, type of disability and sexual orientation. Ethnicity is a social and political phenomenon, and, as such, its categories are not fixed. As society changes, so do the labelling conventions that define groups. Within broadly drawn groups, individual members may not agree about which term they feel best defines them. In the UK, 'White' and 'Black' (sometimes distinguishing 'Black Caribbean' and 'Black African') are current; Indian, Pakistani and Bangladeshi are generally used specifically, though 'Asian' also occurs. Interestingly, the equivalents of terms such as 'Black American' or 'Asian American' – for example, 'Black Briton' or 'Asian Briton' – are not current, which perhaps points to a lack of inclusiveness in British social attitudes. On the other hand, the term 'people of colour', which is widely used in the USA, ceased to be acceptable in the UK in the mid-1990s. Referring to members of both genders by traditional terms such as 'man' and 'mankind' and the masculine pronouns 'he', 'him' and 'his' has two costs: ambiguity and exclusion. Using these terms requires the listener or reader to decide whether the reference really does include women as well as men. More seriously, studies have shown that girls and women do feel excluded by this usage. Feeling excluded from history books, policy statements, professional titles and the like can have a powerful impact on the self-image and aspirations of women. Stereotyping by gender often takes the form of assigning complementary and opposing characteristics to men and women, such as active/passive, strong/weak and rational/emotional. In these formulations, it is usually the characteristic associated with masculinity that is viewed as more positive and desirable, at least in a work context. Men and women should be treated primarily as people, and not as members of different genders. Their shared humanity and common attributes should be stressed. Neither gender should be stereotyped. Both men and women should be represented as whole human beings with human strengths and weaknesses, not masculine and feminine ones.

Using ageist language shows ignorance of the fact that, in many countries, people are living longer in good health. Just as some people in their twenties and thirties are not as vigorous as others of their age, people in their sixties and seventies differ greatly in their physical health and abilities. Expressions such as 'Even at 75, x can do y' or 'Octogenarian w still does y' are ageist; even describing someone as 'old' depends on a judgement which may be prejudiced. At the other end of the scale, young men and women should not be referred to as 'boys' and 'girls'. Giving the age of individuals in reports, as newspapers do (especially for women), reinforces ageism (and sexism). Unless age is the topic being written or spoken about, it is generally preferable not to refer to it.

People with disabilities prefer that others focus on their individuality, not their disability, unless, of course, it is the topic that is being written or spoken about. The terms 'handicapped', 'not able-bodied', 'physically challenged', and 'differently abled' are also discouraged, and so is the article 'the' with an adjective (e.g., 'the deaf') to describe people with disabilities. The preferred usage, 'people with disabilities' ('people who are deaf'), stresses the essential humanity of individuals and avoids objectification. Alternatively, the term 'disabled people' ('deaf people') may be acceptable, but still defines people as disabled first and people second. It is important to be careful not to imply that people with disabilities are to be pitied, feared or ignored, or that they are always somehow more heroic, courageous, patient or 'special' than others. The term 'abnormal' (or 'normal' in contrast) should never be used.

Sexuality is now generally regarded as determined early in life. As a rule, it cannot be changed. Thus, 'sexual orientation' is a more accurate term to describe a person's sexuality than 'sexual preference' or 'choice'. The clinical term 'homosexual' may be appropriate in certain contexts, but generally the terms 'gay men', 'lesbians' and 'gay people' are preferable. The euphemisms 'lifestyle' or 'alternative lifestyle' should be avoided, because gay people, like heterosexuals, have a variety of lifestyles. The term 'domestic partner' is being used increasingly to refer to the person with whom one shares a household on a permanent basis, whether married or not.

Although during conversation finding the acceptable term for members of a group may be tricky, it becomes easier with practice. Where possible, use the term preferred by members of the group themselves. When speaking about any group or individual, emphasize accomplishments and deeds, and concentrate on the person's essential humanity, not on characteristics such as ethnicity, gender or age.

Box 6.2

'Many people with psychiatric disability feel insecure and pessimistic about life. This sense of insecurity may be demonstrated in negative attitudes: they find it hard to believe they can do anything positive, or that anything good can happen. Help promote a more positive outlook by actively supporting the employee to see any positives and achieve even the smallest target. For example, if Martina says, '*I couldn't do the catalogue job,*' reply with, '*You read so quickly and accurately, you can sort the catalogues faster than anyone else. You got distracted though – that's not your fault.*' Provide frequent feedback.

... Social relationships are often severely disrupted by mental illness and the skills involved in building these relationships can be impaired. This takes effort and the person recovering from an illness needs to be encouraged wherever possible to practise these skills. Provide support and coaching to employees to assist them to learn the skills of social interaction.'

Source: Effective workplace communication with employees with psychiatric disability. URL: http://www.fahcsia. gov.au/sa/disability/pubs/documents/consumertrainingsupportproducts/employers/psychiatric_disability/ sec10.htm

6.2   ETHICAL ISSUES

Intercultural business ethics addresses moral issues that emerge when the norms and values of stakeholders, including employees, reflect cultural differences in the way described in Chapter 4. For example, while Western cultures tend to turn moral issues into issues of conscience or law, this might not be the case in other cultures. Ethical relativism claims that there is no culture-free, universal morality and therefore no way of ranking moral views and practices as more or less right, at least across cultures. Ethical relativism runs counter to assumed cultural superiority (or ethnocentrism) and to top-down morality. However, ethical relativism has been criticized on grounds such as the following:

- Obvious empirical differences of moral beliefs and practices do not prove that they are all right.
- Even though some practices that vary from place to place are justifiable, surrender of principles in the face of disagreement hurts integrity.
- Disagreement about judgements does not necessarily prove disagreement about the principles upon which such judgements are based.
- Relativism can confuse behaviour and analysis rather than enlighten them.
- There is no moral-free space, although there are many moral grey zones.

These arguments suggest that ethical dilemmas arising in intercultural work communication cannot be evaded by a resort to ethical relativism. What is needed (and sufficient), according to Brinkmann (2002), is an intercultural consensus about an ethical minimum. Ethics integrates people by seeking a consensus around good principles and procedures.[4] The communication ethics approach of Habermas (1998) suggests, as a principle, fair and open communication among all the stakeholders affected, in order to build a consensus.[5] However, individual conscience, cultures' differing moral customs and positive law vary more than minimum ethics.

Box 6.3

A British executive working in India found that there was a conflict between his environmental values and the expectations of his staff. Concern for the planet meant that, instead of owning a car and having a driver, as would be expected for someone in his senior position, he normally went to work by auto-rickshaw (a means of transport that does not add greatly to global warming) and only used a car occasionally. This was consistent with company policy, but he found that it was seen as undermining the status of staff working for the company, even though he made no attempt to impose a similar set of values on them.

Source: interview with an expatriate manager, India, author's research

Brinkmann (2002) proposed the following model, described as a 'virtuous (but vulnerable) circle of delaying judgement and transcending ethical relativism'. If a moral conflict or dilemma is faced in an intercultural setting, intercultural communication, ideally, could contribute with (1) unprejudiced, non-ethnocentric description and interpretation and with (2) tools for communication and barrier reduction, while ethics would focus (3) on moral and value conflicts and (4) on possibilities for solutions, preferably consensus-building. Such an interdisciplinary mix of competencies could then (5) reach a preliminary minimum consensus, a first step towards transcending ethical relativism and (6) produce positive examples and experiences for future situations. Such idealism, that is, a virtuous circle, is self-reinforcing once it works, but is also vulnerable, that is, can fail or even turn into a vicious circle.[6]

Deetz *et al.* (1997) considered that the international business situation poses unique and complex issues of ethics and responsibility. Only a stakeholder approach to organization, combined with 'adequate' conceptions of communication and micro-practices of negotiation, could lead to ethical daily practices in modern organizations. Because the organization is part of the community, the values and ethical standards of the community should be both represented and considered. The problem is to give the minority or marginalized stakeholders a sufficient 'voice' or representation so that their views are reflected. Deetz *et al.* (1997) argued that to increase the 'voice' of multiple stakeholders in organizations that are intrinsically biased against weaker stakeholders, such as the surrounding community, requires four changes. These are:

1. An end to the fixing of roles (e.g., by the division of labour) and to the suppression or ignoring of the complexity of people's identities and aspirations. These identities include those such as being a parent, citizen or softball player as well as an employee or customer.
2. Ending the limits imposed on discussion by rules and authority relations; such limits make stakeholders unequal in power.
3. Opening information production activities to stakeholder discussion: in most cases the information available to stakeholders is manufactured by management groups and is both limited and skewed.
4. Ensuring that discussion focuses on ends rather than means.[7]

Many of the intercultural communication skills given later in this chapter, including empathy and tolerance for ambiguity, may be seen as indicators of individual cultural relativism, which means trying to understand different others according to their own frame of reference. It should be distinguished from ethical relativism, but may be considered an interculturally ethical stance. Hall (1997) added the point that 'ethical efforts to assist others must include a deep concern for the value systems of others involved in the process....It means that we should be concerned about others' dignity, rights, values and concerns as much as we are about our own. Of course, such an attitude can also result in applauding the learning and growth processes of individuals and nations as their intercultural and international communication efforts become more effective, more caring, and their judgments of situations and people more adequate.'[8]

> Ethical issues are among the most problematic in intercultural work. Ethical relativism, which evades ethical issues by the contention that no moral system is better than any other, appears to be logically flawed. Consensus building by fair and open communication based on cultural relativism, finding a way to increase the power and voice of weaker stakeholders and having a deep concern for others' value systems are among the suggested ways to achieve ethical intercultural work communication.

6.3 INTERCULTURAL COMMUNICATION BEHAVIOURS

Many factors may affect the success or failure of intercultural communication. Some of these are not within a person's immediate control – for instance, their status in the eyes of the person with whom they are interacting or the prejudices of other participants. However, the person's own behaviour during the interaction impacts very directly and is within their control. This section looks at behaviours that help intercultural communication. It begins with skills that improve intercultural understanding of others' communication. Skills for effective intercultural self-presentation follow. Next the section deals with general traits for intercultural effectiveness. The last set of behaviours covered is the application of skills to particular situations.

Enhanced intercultural understanding of others

A first stage in skilled communication behaviour is to understand the values, motives, beliefs, attitudes and intentions of an interlocutor. As Figure 6.1 suggests, some factors that influence behaviour are relatively easy to perceive; others are more difficult. In an intercultural context, both interpersonal and intercultural understandings are needed. The skills involved include increasing intercultural social perceptiveness, unlearning and learning, accurately predicting others' behaviour and responses, tolerating ambiguity, being non-judgemental, being mindful and developing positive expectations about intercultural encounters.

Intercultural social perceptiveness

To perceive accurately in intercultural contexts, communicators need awareness of their own and others' cultural sensitivities, of the context and of perceptual barriers.

■ Some trainers in intercultural communication now consider that working to enhance self-awareness is the most essential preparation for working in another

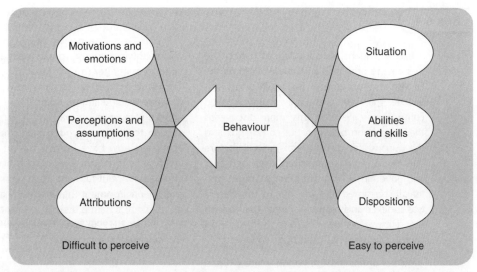

Figure 6.1   *Ease and difficulty of perceiving factors influencing others' behaviour at work*

culture as a sojourner or on international assignments. Most people remain unaware that their own behaviours, attitudes and beliefs are culture-specific, unless they are exposed to at least one other culture. Therefore, a first step towards better intercultural understanding is to seek out such exposure at work or at leisure. Learning from such experiences then needs to be enhanced and speeded up by reflective observation, either alone or in discussion. The purpose is to understand one's own stereotypes, prejudices, ethnocentrism, values and attitudes as much as or more than those of others.

■ It is easy, when ignorant of the sensitivities of another culture, not only to set up barriers to good communication but also to cause serious offence. The problem is how to develop cultural awareness in order to avoid such problems. Studying the culture of the people with whom we interact in order to know what sensitivities they are likely to have is one possible solution. However, many people face the problem that they interact with people from a wide range of cultures and subcultures. For instance, if the computer teacher quoted in Box 6.4 worked in a central London University, she might find in her classes people from several different European, African and Asian nations, from several different British ethnic and religious minority religious groups (e.g., Bangladeshi, Indian, Pakistani, Afro-Caribbean, Jewish, Muslim, Sikh, Roman Catholic, Church of England), plus, of course, of different genders, sexual orientations and levels of physical ability. In addition, often the answer to the question 'How can I learn about culture X?' is the discouraging information that there is no comprehensive book (or list) available about culture X. There is, anyway, no substitute for experience in gaining knowledge of other cultures. However, realistically, few service providers are likely to be able to visit all the countries represented among their students, patients or clients or even to get well acquainted with all the ethnic or religious groups so represented. There is no easy solution, but there are some principles that can be applied:

1. The best, and most neglected, source of information on a culture is people from that culture. Often they can be met in the course of work. Setting aside time to talk with as many of them as possible about the sensitivities inculcated

Box 6.4

'I had a student from an African nation. He was having problems with understanding the English and computer terms. I paired him with another man who was a jolly soul who loved computers. One day this man discovered the connection between the commands and the purpose for giving them in DOS [before Windows]. He was so excited, I reached over and gave him a hug. The poor man got hysterical, screamed and ran out of the class. I was shocked and his partner went to check on him. He was crying so hard in the hall, and I couldn't figure what I had done so wrong.

Moral of the story: A young white woman hugged him. That was a death sentence in his home town. A young woman touched him, he had to marry her (me) or I would be shamed. Yicks, his partner, calmed him down, told him no one would kill him, I didn't have to marry him and everything was o.k. It wasn't a fun lesson to learn, the young man dropped my course. I now have learned the art of praise without a touch, or just a touch of hands. A hard lesson, but fair when you work in a university environment that has many cultures.'

Source: Frazier, J. (1996) *Stories from a computer teacher.* URL: frazier@ccit.arizona.eduää

through their culture is an excellent use of time. Most will be willing to help someone who explains that they want to understand more out of respect and to avoid giving offence. If the people concerned are clients, patients, advisers, customers or suppliers it may be necessary to arrange a special time for the discussion; with colleagues, opportunities may arise naturally in the course of the work.

2. The following points should be kept in mind:
   – First-hand experience is necessary to understand many subtleties of any culture.
   – What is logical and important in a particular culture may seem irrational and unimportant to an outsider.
   – In describing another culture, people tend to stress the differences and overlook the similarities; in contrast, in interacting with people from another culture, they tend to assume more similarity than actually exists.
   – Stereotyping may be inevitable among those who lack frequent contact with another culture, but an understanding of the limited truth of stereotypes is essential.
   – Personal observations of others about another culture should not be taken as objective evidence.
   – Many subcultures often exist within a single ethnic or language group, religion or nationality. These subcultures are differentiated by education, age, gender, socio-economic status, education, and exposure to other cultures. Highly educated people of a given cultural group are less likely to reveal indigenous language and communication patterns than less educated persons.
   – All cultures have internal variations.
   – Cultures are continually evolving. Understanding another culture is a continuous process.
   – To best understand a culture, one should understand the language of that culture.[9]

Box 6.5

X was a visiting official from the international parent organization of the Hungarian Business Association, which was holding a presentation and reception for members to meet a VIP. The Hungarian President of the Association spoke first. X had agreed with him beforehand that he would convey a 'message' about the Association's mission. (1) The President began by telling several funny anecdotes. It was clear that the audience enjoyed these. Then he began to get quite emotional, even melancholy, and philosophical. (2) After a while, X began to feel that the agreed 'message' was not going to be conveyed. (3) During the networking at the reception after the presentations, X found, as she had before, that, while the Hungarian men were very courteous to her (one even attempted to kiss her hand!), (4) they dominated the conversation in a series of unstoppable monologues and she had difficulty getting any chance to speak. (5) When she did manage to make herself heard, though, she was careful to open with a couple of sentences in praise of Hungary and its cultural heritage. After that, things became easier. (6) Nevertheless, as soon as the topic turned to Association business, she found that her interlocutors quickly confronted her with a series of problems. It would be wrong, she thought, to describe them as complaints – they were presented just as problems – but there was no attempt to identify solutions. (7) Instead, there seemed to be an expectation that finding ways round the problems was up to someone else.

The following cultural knowledge would help the visiting official to understand better:

(1) Hungarians are great raconteurs and equate fluency with intelligence.
(2) As they develop their arguments, Hungarians may become emotional and philosophical more than logical, and so it is easy for non-Hungarians to lose the thread. This does not seem to be a problem for Hungarian members of audiences themselves, though.
(3) 'Old-fashioned' courtesy towards women is still common in Hungary.
(4) Hungarian conversational rules do not require equality in turn-taking (often several people will speak at once). This increases the tendency for men to dominate conversations.
(5) Small talk usually precedes business; displaying a knowledge and appreciation of things Hungarian is an accepted, even expected, form of compliment.
(6) Possibly as a residue of communism (or of subjection under the Austro-Hungarian Empire), some Hungarians display a kind of fatalistic pessimism, which recognizes problems but has no expectation that they will be put right and certainly no sense that they themselves can put them right.

Based on: author's research

■ Communication takes place within a context that fundamentally affects the knowledge needed by participants.[10] Therefore, they need awareness of contexts. A context has at least four dimensions, each of which can magnify, reduce or have neutral impact on how aware the participants are of their cultural differences.

1. Power and status. These exert an influence over whose cultural preferences are accepted and in some cases who controls the discussion. A British study showed that, in contact between White and Black people, the White person typically controls access to valued resources that the Black person needs or wants.[11]

2. Cultural assumptions defining the 'rules of the game'. For example, in a high power distance culture, a subordinate from a low power distance culture would

be probably be frustrated by the restraints on free speech in talking to a manager. This would probably not bother a subordinate from the high power distance culture.

3. Attitudes, based on personal experiences.
4. The role the participants assign to the immediate encounter. For instance, if two colleagues of different sexes, ethnicity and professional status were discussing why a photocopier broke down, their awareness of their cultural differences would probably be low. It would be higher, though, if they were negotiating with one another over the pay of one of them.

An appreciation of the context of an encounter is a useful tool in increasing intercultural effectiveness. Intercultural encounters have distinctive characteristics and texture, according to their context: for instance, tourism encounters, unlike some others, essentially celebrate, rather than try to overcome or pacify, the experience of cultural difference. When Western tourists tell stories of bargaining in 'native' stores, they are relating their enjoyment of the, to them, unusual experience. International trade, diplomacy and scholarly exchanges are other examples of encounters with their own distinctive characteristics and texture. All these contexts 'create differences in the expectations of the parties to encounters and the requirements for effective communication'.[12] In work encounters the nature of the task also has a strong contextual influence.

Another contextual factor influencing intercultural encounters is how well the participants know one another – how often they have met. Initial encounters are generally the most difficult. Not surprisingly, the influence of cultural norms and stereotypes diminishes as people get to know one another. Therefore, being able to communicate successfully when the level of cultural dissimilarity is high is most important on first acquaintance or in formal settings. (These contexts, of course, occur often at work.) Work contexts can sometimes reduce intercultural communication difficulties, however, because, where both parties concentrate on the task, the near-universalism of 'technology' (in its broadest sense) creates a bridge. Unfortunately, though, there has often been an over-reliance on this factor, with resulting poor work relations between people from different cultures.

■ Being aware of stumbling blocks can help in avoiding them, so interactors need awareness of perceptual barriers to intercultural communication. Intercultural communication is improved by learning not to assume that others have the same values and attitudes, by becoming more sensitive to differences in others' verbal and non-verbal language, more aware of societal preconceptions and stereotypes that portray other groups from our own as 'different', or, in the case of the other gender, as 'opposite', and by reducing the tendency to evaluate another's culture as inferior.

Box 6.6

Low perceived similarity in cultural values with other employees was found to be negative for employee identification with their organization and work team. When a strong intercultural group climate was in place, however, employees still reported high levels of identification with the organization *despite* low perceived similarity in cultural values.

Source: Luijters, K., van der Zee, K.I. and Otten, S. (1998) 'Cultural diversity in organizations: enhancing identification by valuing differences', *Cross-Cultural Research*, **32**(1): 154–63

Unlearning and learning

Increasing all the forms of awareness just described is really a matter of unlearning and learning. Unlearning may often be a necessary preliminary to improving social perception: it means being freed from past attitudes, preconceptions, prejudices and expectations in order to absorb new ideas and information. Unlearning is, of course, learning by another name; but it is a difficult type of learning because it involves a change in self-organization – in the self-construal. Such changes are threatening and tend to be resisted.

Learning (and hence unlearning) is easier when the subject matter is perceived as having relevance for someone's own goals. Therefore learning about cultural difference and intercultural communication comes more easily just before an important meeting with someone from a different background or before an overseas journey. In addition, when external threats are at a minimum, learning that is threatening to the self is more easily perceived and assimilated, because there is a limit to the level of threat to the self that most people can tolerate.[13]

The following behaviours also facilitate learning:

- Activity – much significant learning is acquired by doing.
- Active learning, in which the learner drives and steers the process, works better than passive learning.
- Self-initiated learning which involves the whole person – feelings as well as intellect – is the most lasting and pervasive.
- Formative evaluation by the learner is more helpful than summative evaluation by others. If learners can assess, somewhat objectively, their own progress, strengths and weaknesses as they go along, they will gain independence, creativity and self-reliance as well as knowledge.
- Learning how to learn through a continuous openness to experience and incorporation into oneself of the process of change is of crucial importance.

Predicting others' behaviour and responses accurately

Predictive skill is needed to guide choices of communication strategy, to avoid giving offence inadvertently and to keep the flow of discussion smooth. Without necessarily being aware of doing so, all communicators predict others' responses repeatedly during interactions. Often, however, their predictions are inaccurate. This is especially likely if they are members of a dominant subculture interacting with members of a 'minority' subculture, as they may receive little feedback about their communication

---

Box 6.7

A research study found the following. 'Blacks reported more discussion about racial issues, both within their own group and outside it, than Whites did....Members of the minority group are forced to deal with intergroup issues and to come to grips with their relationships in intergroup terms. Members of the majority group can overlook group forces and can attempt to explain their relationships mainly in terms of the individuals involved.'

Source: Alderfer, C.P. and Smith, K.K. (1982) 'Studying intergroup relations embedded in organizations', *Administrative Science Quarterly*, **27**: 5–65

performances, especially if they as individuals are in positions of power. Fear or a wish to ingratiate may lead minority group members to conceal negative responses. Even aside from people in dominant positions, though, everyone relies on stereotypes and rules based on past experience to predict others' responses. These necessary simplifications often produce inaccuracy.

Predicting others' responses more accurately depends on the following:

- Obtaining as much information as possible both before and during interactions,
- Becoming more aware of sensitive issues, language and non-verbal behaviour,
- Examining and modifying stereotypes, implicit theories and rules, and
- Encouraging others to give us feedback.

Tolerating ambiguity

People who tolerate ambiguity can control their feelings in situations where it is unclear what is happening, why, or what the outcome is likely to be. Tolerating ambiguity involves managing the feelings associated with unpredictability: it is not suggested that discomfort or other negative feelings should not be experienced when confronted with uncertain situations, but that both those feelings and their display can be controlled. Individuals with a high tolerance for ambiguity are more inclined to seek out 'objective' information, which means that their intercultural behaviour is more likely to be based on a realistic appreciation. People with lower tolerance for ambiguity tend to seek supportive rather than objective information – that is, in order to feel less psychological discomfort they select and distort incoming information.

Behaviours that support being or becoming tolerant of ambiguity include:

- Delaying the decision on how to approach a new person or situation until as much information as possible has been gained by observation,
- Having flexible short-term aspirations or goals (for instance, not being fixated on achieving a particular goal in the present encounter – being willing to try again at a later date if necessary),
- Using trial and error rather than the same formula until what works becomes clear,
- Consciously relaxing muscles, especially those in the back and neck,
- Avoiding tense behaviours such as frowning, growling, pacing, sounding exasperated, clenching teeth, fidgeting, talking fast or pounding anything (remembering that how someone behaves affects how they feel as much as the reverse), and
- Projecting confidence to oneself through positive messages: 'I feel confident, I can handle this, and I feel relaxed.'

Other traits related to being tolerant of ambiguity are uncertainty-orientation and field independence. Uncertainty-oriented individuals seek information more than certainty-oriented individuals. People whose sense of self is not too much affected by their environment experience less stress on entering a new culture than field dependents, who are strongly affected by their environment.[14]

Being non-judgemental

Judging others' behaviour or others as people, especially early in initial meetings, risks making errors of judgement, especially because it increases reliance on stereotypes. As a result, it can lead to basing one's own behaviour on false premises. It also leads to communicating to interlocutors the fact that they are being judged, which can lead them to have negative attitudes to the speaker. Behaviours that support and communicate a non-judgemental perspective include:

- Withholding preconceived opinions – asking, not telling;
- Framing questions openly rather than in a closed way: 'What do you think?' or 'What do you mean by...?', rather than 'Do you think X?', or 'Is this what you mean?';
- Soliciting feelings specifically: 'How do you feel about...?'
- Asking questions to find out explanations of others' behaviour that may be deep-seated in their values or culture;
- When expressing views, making it clear that it is understood that they are only opinions with which other people may disagree;
- Acknowledging different values, beliefs and perceptions as valid;
- Listening openly;
- Listening to another's view without interrupting or criticizing;
- Acknowledging the other's point of view as valid: 'I see what you mean';
- Providing reassurance: 'Don't worry – this won't be taken as agreement';
- Avoiding calling a view which is disagreed with bad or wrong;
- Sorting 'objective' facts from more subjective feelings, perceptions and stereotypes;
- Avoiding over-generalizations, and
- Making statements in a form that acknowledges one's own subjectivity, such as 'I feel uneasy when Mr Ling does not appear to react to what I am saying', rather than generalizing or laying claims to objectivity, as in 'Chinese people are hard to read'.

Being mindful

To correct the tendency to misinterpret others' behaviour, people need to become more aware of their own mental processes – more 'mindful'. Mindfulness means tuning in consciously to habituated mental scripts; mindlessness is the rigid reliance on old categories, whereas mindfulness means the continual creation of new ones. Mindfulness carries a certain degree of existential vulnerability (openness). As shown in Figure 6.2, it occupies an intermediate zone between uncaringness and monitored constraint – between not caring about learning or improving and an inhibited caution that is defensive and closed to new ideas. Mindfulness includes creating new categories, being open to new information and being aware of more than one perspective.[15]

The concept of mindfulness as just described is intrapersonal; it has, however, been extended to include shared mindfulness, which emphasizes communication and has been defined as: 'a state of mindfulness achieved conjointly, whereby, in communicative interaction, the individuals involved are in an active state of attending, responding, and perceiving information correctly.' As a result, 'they are continually updating, attuned, and open to incoming data that are unexpected, disconfirming, improbable, implicit, and/or contested.'[16] From a study of interactions among pilots during crises in the cockpit, Krieger (2005) deduced the following as the behaviours most closely related to whether or not a state of shared mindfulness arises: effective decision-making was related to reasoning from a positive perspective; using a kaleidoscopic perspective, speaking thoughts and feelings aloud, precisely,

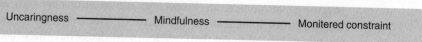

Figure 6.2 *The mindfulness continuum*

and conditionally, and acknowledging communication substantively. The following behaviours either significantly hindered or precluded the formation of shared mindfulness in an interaction: precognitive commitment, non-positive reasoning strategies and overt dominance.[17]

Having positive expectations about intercultural encounters

People's expectations influence their ability to understand different others. The attitudes someone has about a particular other (sub)culture or other (sub)cultures in general create expectations about experiences in interactions with different others. The stereotypes someone has about people also affect expectations. Someone who is open to other (sub)cultures, with a positive attitude towards the specific (sub)culture, and has positive stereotypes about the people of the (sub)culture will probably have positive expectations about their experiences, and vice versa. Negative attitudes and stereotypes create negative expectations. Negative expectations, in turn, tend to create self-fulfilling prophecies; that is, leading to interpreting the behaviour of members of the other (sub)cultures negatively and therefore to having negative experiences. On the other hand, expectations transferred without mindfulness from the 'own' culture are particularly likely to be violated. These are further reasons for avoiding, or at least postponing, evaluating the behaviour of 'different other' people.

These pointers are based on Expectations States Theory, whose core idea is the influence of expectations, which were introduced in Chapter 4, on behaviour in interactions. People 'choose among various communication strategies on the basis of predictions about how the person receiving the message will respond'.[18] Three types of information are used in making predictions: cultural, social (roles and group memberships) and personal. (North Americans use more personal than social information; the Japanese do the reverse.) We saw in Chapter 4 that the expectations people have about how others will respond to what they say strongly influence their communication behaviour. Chapter 5 showed how communication barriers can arise when expectations are violated. Expectations themselves are a function of knowledge, beliefs and attitudes, stereotypes, self-conceptions, roles, prior interaction and status characteristics.[19] Figure 6.3 shows the relationships among these variables. The knowledge referred to in the model is mainly knowledge of the group to which people who are being met for the first time are thought to belong. When a person meets 'strangers' without any previous knowledge of the strangers' group, s/he predicts how they will behave by watching and listening to what they do and say. These observations are, of course, selective, and the impressions gained are influenced by the individual's own cultural framework. Those observed and interpreted behaviours are then treated as 'typical' and inferences are drawn from the impressions.

The need to make inferences is greater when dealing with people who are unfamiliar; this can lead to extreme predictions and expectations. The more knowledge people have beforehand about the other group, the less they are inclined to over-interpret small samples of behaviour, such as are observed on first meeting. Thus, prior knowledge affects expectations and so behaviour. If this knowledge is accurate, the effect is likely to be beneficial. If, however, they have false beliefs or the 'knowledge' consists of simplified and inaccurate stereotypes, the resulting expectations can distort behaviour with adverse effects on communication. Videotaped conversations between 46 US students and confederates from India showed significant differences in the Americans' communication behaviour depending on their previous knowledge or beliefs about India.[20]

People employ one or more of three strategies for gaining information about another group. One is a passive strategy such as watching TV (which is the strategy most likely

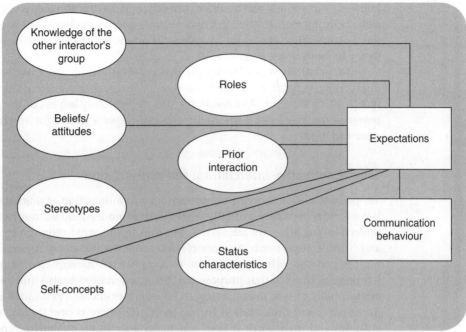

Figure 6.3   *Expectations states theory: factors influencing expectations and behaviour in intercultural encounters*

Box 6.8

Surprisingly, indirect contact (having an ingroup friend who has an outgroup friend) reduces prejudice at levels comparable to those of direct contact (having an outgroup friend yourself). A large probability survey of German adults found that both direct and indirect contact were negatively related to prejudices against foreigners and Muslims living in Germany.

Source: Pettigrew, T.F., Christ, O., Wagner, U. and Stellmacher, J. (2007) 'Direct and indirect intergroup contact effects on prejudice: A normative interpretation', *International Journal of Intercultural Relations*, **31**(4): 411–25

to lead to over-reliance on stereotypes), or observing directly but without interacting. The second is an active strategy of asking others from their own group about the other (sub)culture, and the third is an interactive strategy of meeting members of the other (sub)culture, asking them questions, self-disclosing and trying to detect deceptions. This last sounds on the surface like the best information-gathering strategy, and it can be. However, to gain accurate information, contacts with other (sub)culture members must be made under conditions that do not increase prejudice.

Status is widely used in all cultures as input to the expectations individuals form about others with whom they will interact. In general, a wider range of behaviour is expected and tolerated from a high-status person than others. Status is assessed from external factors (e.g., ethnicity, sex, attractiveness, education and occupation) and expressive cues (e.g., dialect, eye contact, speech styles and skin colour) or indicative cues (such as someone's statement that they grew up in Mexico). Although these factors are used in all cultures to assess status, they are not used in identical ways. In Japan, professional position is so important that people need to know it in order to know how to address one another correctly, and an introductory exchange of business cards is de rigueur. In the USA, in contrast, questions directed at ascertaining someone's professional status can be rude, and physical attractiveness is often a key status factor for both sexes, even at work.

In Expectations States Theory predictions about others' responses serve as the main intervening variable between behaviour in intercultural encounters and a range of independent variables. As a result, the theory inevitably leaves out the possibly equally powerful variables put forward in other theories – goals, for instance, or episode representations.

Skills for effective intercultural self-presentation

Self-presentation is as essential a process for communication as is understanding others. It is essential because we usually need others to understand us, not just in the sense of understanding what we are saying, but also in the sense required by our association and consideration needs, as rapport management scholars assert (see Chapter 3). If we want to persuade others or get them to comply with our requests, we need appropriate self-presentation for that purpose too. Self-presentation is also unavoidable. Whether intentionally or not, every person in an interaction conveys an impression to others. An effective self-presentation in the sense used here is one that accurately conveys attitudes and intentions. It does not necessarily imply making a 'good impression'. However, if the objective in an interaction is to achieve effective intercultural communication, it helps if the attitudes and intentions conveyed are positive rather than negative. The skills required to achieve an effective intercultural impression include language choice, following appropriate conversational rules, achieving clarity, adjusting for non-routine interactions, showing empathy, communicating a relationship as well as a task orientation, communicating appropriate assertiveness, being a resourceful communicator and sharing information.

Language choice

People usually appreciate it when an interlocutor speaks their language. However, when one person speaks the other's language well but the reverse is not true, using the language best understood by both parties increases understanding. Sometimes, though, partial bilingual communicators may in fact be more effective, as their encoded blunt or 'rude' messages are more likely to be tolerated and attributed to their language deficiencies than would be the case for full bilinguals or native speakers. Silence and pauses in conversation are normal and accepted parts of communication between partial bilinguals, so they can use breaks in the conversation flow strategically, even in situations where they could process information faster and send messages sooner. For instance, they may use pauses to avoid introducing unproductive and destructive comments into conversations and to provide breaks for reflection. However, while the norms of some languages, such as Chinese and Japanese, mean that such silences do not cause anxiety, the same might not be true for some Westerners.

Language choice has implications for the nature of the relationships that bilingual speakers develop and for whether they are included in informal communication channels. Bilingual expatriates who choose to use their own language remain outsiders and so are less likely to be sanctioned for not following the country's customs and social norms. By choosing the host country language, however, they become insiders, develop closer interpersonal relationships with colleagues and have more access to 'soft' information.[21]

Following communication rules

As Chapter 3 explained, communication requires people to co-operate, which they do, in part, by following conversational rules. Schwarz (1994) suggested the following lists of requirements for speakers and receivers. Speakers should:

- Take the receiver's characteristics into account,
- Be coherent and comprehensible,
- Give neither too much nor too little information,
- Be relevant,
- Produce a message that is appropriate to the context, the circumstances and the communicative purpose,
- Convey the truth as they see it, and
- Assume that the receiver is trying, as much as possible, to follow the rules of communication.

Receivers should:

- Take the speaker's characteristics into account,
- Determine the speaker's communicative intent or purpose,
- Take the context and circumstances into account,
- Pay attention to the message and be prepared to receive it, and
- Try to understand the message and provide feedback, when possible, to the speaker concerning their understanding of the message.[22]

In intercultural communication both speakers and receivers need also to allow for cultural differences in communication rules. Learning what those cultural differences are is another aspect of developing cultural awareness.

Achieving clarity

Communicating clearly is often, though not always, an important communication objective, especially in work-based situations where the requirements of the task demand it. For instance, for a doctor, important though it is to communicate empathy and concern for relationship, clarity is even more important because of the importance of accuracy in diagnosis and in patients' following of instructions.

The distinction between restricted and elaborated codes, referred to in Chapter 3, is relevant to how clarity is achieved in intercultural communication. In communication with people who are familiar, language use goes on largely at a level below consciousness, with varying degrees of effectiveness; with new acquaintances or people from different backgrounds, however, effectiveness depends on heightened consciousness of how language is being used. This need for high awareness applies widely in work situations. When speakers expect marked differences from other people with whom they are interacting, they both do and should use more formal language, that is, the elaborated code, instead of the restricted code that they use when they can assume that the receiver will understand their assumptions.[23] An expectation of marked difference leads the speaker to express fully those meanings that are expected to be misunderstood. In other words, these meanings have to be put into words rather precisely to make them available to the receiver. Therefore elaborated codes require a large vocabulary and complex syntax, though not too large and complex for the receiver to understand.

Clear communication requires the following actions:

■ Stating points concisely and precisely,
■ Adjusting to the other person's level of understanding without being demeaning,
■ Simplifying language,
■ Explaining or avoiding jargon,
■ Where possible and acceptable, using the idiom of the other (sub)culture,
■ Avoiding slang,
■ Slowing down (but not speaking louder),
■ Starting from where the other person is 'at',
■ Using progressive approximations,
■ Dividing explanations into smaller, more specific units,
■ Repeating in alternative ways,
■ Getting the other person to ask questions,
■ Giving short answers – stopping after a partial reply and waiting for their response, and
■ Checking understanding to ensure messages are communicated clearly and completely: for example, by asking 'Am I being clear?', 'Will you say it back to me in your own words?', 'Let me show you what I mean', 'Why don't you give it a try now?'

Adjusting for non-routine interactions

In non-routine contexts, people cannot achieve their communication goals by just applying cultural rules, conventions and codes. Instead they need to use person-centred messages.[24] Person-centred messages recognize other people's perspectives and explain the reasons for requests or orders in terms of the other's perspective. To construct person-centred messages, speakers first use open questioning to obtain information about

---

Box 6.9

'A review of the literature suggests that patient-centred approaches generally are associated with greater satisfaction, compliance, feelings of being understood, and resolution of patient concerns. Patient-centred interactions have been defined as those in which the patient's point of view is actively sought by the physician, which implies that the physician behaves in a manner that facilitates the patient to express himself, and that the patient feels free to speak openly and ask questions. There is compelling evidence demonstrating that better physician–patient relationships are associated with improved health outcomes, including greater symptom resolution, reduced stress, lower blood pressure in hypertensive patients, lower blood glucose levels in diabetics, and better postoperative pain control with reduced use of analgesics.'

Source: Zachariae, R., Pedersen, C.G., Jensen, B., Ehrnrooth, E., Rossen, P.B. and von der Maase, H. (2003) 'Association of perceived physician communication style with patient satisfaction, distress, cancer-related self-efficacy, and perceived control over the disease', *British Journal of Cancer*, **88**(5): 658–65; internal references omitted

the other's attitudes, beliefs and values. They then take others' attitudes and beliefs into consideration and acknowledge them when appropriate. Person-centred messages demand more thought from the communicator. They have, though, been shown to be more effective in gaining others' compliance. Since intercultural encounters are often non-routine, communicators should expect to use more inquiry, less advocacy and more attempts to see and acknowledge the other's point of view and emotions than they do in routine situations.

These suggestions are based on the constructivist approach. Much current social science research uses a metaphor of 'person-as-a-naive-scientist', attempting to make sense of his/her world; the constructivist approach, on the other hand, argues that, when people are interacting, their inferences and behaviour are aimed at accomplishing goals. When they respond to each other, they typically are less concerned with understanding why others behave as they do than with understanding the immediate implications of what others do and say for their ability to achieve their own goal(s). These goals differ and may include personal goals or goals brought into being by the situation. Often the goal is simply to respond appropriately and keep the conversation on track. In routine situations, communication is dominated by conventional goals and plans 'given' to the interactors. For instance, at the end of routine work meetings, people discuss and decide the date of the next meeting without thinking about why or how. It is in such situations that the influence of culture and cultural differences on communication is most obvious. Thus, in a high power distance culture, the forward engagements of the most senior person present will be the deciding factor on the date of the next meeting; in a more egalitarian culture, a gap will be sought in everyone's diary. However, because these conventions are so well known, people entering into intercultural communication often are unaware that the conventions of the other culture may be different. Therefore, the influence of culture on communication may be least recognized, as well as strongest, not in initial interactions but in later stages of work relationships. This conflicts with most other views of the influence of the stage of relationship.

Constructivism offers a partial explanation for individuals' motivations within intercultural interactions, although, being goal-based, it is a highly cognitive one, which leaves 'needs theories' out of account. It also provides little explanation for why people enter such encounters in the first place or how their motives in entering interactions relate to their goals within them.

Showing empathy

Being empathic means accurately understanding the thoughts and motivations of another person in an interaction and putting oneself in their place when making a judgement about them. It does not necessarily mean agreeing with them or sympathizing with them – only really trying to understand them. Total empathy with another person is probably impossible, even when both are from the same culture and subculture. However, most people's communication with others would be more successful if they could increase their ability to empathize and, equally importantly, if they could convey to their interlocutor an intention to empathize.

To communicate empathy involves the following actions:

- Asking open-ended questions, such as 'What was the experience like for you when...?',
- Listening actively,

- Paraphrasing the other person's words (e.g., 'What I think I hear you saying is ...', 'Is this what you mean?') to check for understanding and to show a sincere attempt to understand,
- Checking out verbal and non-verbal cues to find out what another is feeling: 'I sense you are feeling... angry... sad... glad... afraid. Am I reading you correctly?', and
- Paying attention to any of one's own non-verbal messages that may make another person uncomfortable; and mirroring elements of the other person's body language, tone and pace, when appropriate.

Communicating a relationship as well as a task orientation

People from individualist cultures, especially men, are at risk of provoking a culture clash if they act with people from collectivist cultures according to what may be their usual priority of getting on with the task 'regardless'. It is well known that Arabs and other Middle-Easterners prefer to do business by building a relationship and then, when trust has been established, proceeding to the negotiation or discussion. The same applies to people of many other nationalities and ethnicities. Equally, men who wish to move away from the position in which their dominance imposes a style that may be inimical to their women colleagues, clients or patients and/or counterproductive for the organization should try to increase the amount of 'relationship' orientation they communicate at work.

Methods include:

- Remembering people's names and small details about them learnt unobtrusively or by asking,
- Using their names according to their culture (e.g., patronymic first),
- Initiating conversations on non-work topics,
- Being sensitive to nuances,
- Reciprocating acts of consideration,
- Using humour appropriately and with care,
- Finding common ground with counterparts,
- Supporting others' communication,
- Bringing others in to discussions,
- Thanking others for their work or contribution,
- Praising above-standard work (in public or private according to the other person's culture), and
- Where appropriate giving candid feedback (in private).

Communicating appropriate assertiveness

Chapter 3 made the point that assertiveness, while fundamentally desirable as a communication attribute, is a variable; the level appropriate in one culture appears as aggression or submission in others. There is a matter of judgement here. Some people may be unwilling to compromise their own assertiveness level even if they are aware that the other person is likely to regard their behaviour as aggressive or submissive. However, the optimal intercultural communication approach is to seek the appropriate level of assertiveness for the culture of the person being interacted with.

Being a resourceful communicator

Communication resourcefulness is the knowledge and ability to apply cognitive, affective (emotional) and behavioural resources appropriately, effectively and creatively in diverse interactive situations.[25] Like other forms of resourcefulness, it is related to approaching new situations as learning opportunities.

- Whether someone thinks of an intercultural encounter as an opportunity or as an anxiety-ridden event has a profound influence on how they approach interactions with strangers. Being secure in one's own cultural identity and not feeling threatened by another person's different cultural identity allows a person to approach an encounter as an opportunity to learn. If one person conveys a sense of identity security it tends to evoke the sense of security in the other, and vice versa.
- The emotions of an intercultural encounter are either ego-focused or other-focused, or more often some combination of the two. Culture plays a major role concerning the emotional meanings and reactions attached to encounters. For individualists, ego-focused emotions are most common: they are concerned with 'justice' and revolve around conflicting claims which are seen as able to be resolved by invoking impartial rules, principles or standards. Conversely, other-focused emotions, most commonly experienced by collectivists, revolve around issues of relationships. In both cases, demands are made on the individual's affective resourcefulness (which is similar to emotional intelligence) to resolve emotional issues.
- To deal with the diverse identity needs of different persons in different situations, intercultural interactors need the behavioural resourcefulness to develop a wide range of verbal and non-verbal repertoires. Being responsive to strangers and open to learning from them are other aspects of behavioural resourcefulness.

Thus, to become a more resourceful intercultural communicator, there are three aspects to work on:

- Regarding intercultural encounters as opportunities to affirm one's own and endorse other people's identities rather than as sources of anxiety.
- Achieving an acceptable and appropriate balance between 'ego' concerns and 'other' concerns in interactions. This also means achieving a good balance between relying on principles, rules and procedures for guidance and regulation of the encounter, and on the other hand relying on trust and caring – a relationship approach. Highly individualist, achievement-oriented people are often deficient in the 'other' dimension of affective resourcefulness and should attempt to shift in that direction; other groups, including many women, may gain in affective resourcefulness by more emphasis on their own needs and on principles rather than feelings.
- Developing a wide range of verbal and non-verbal repertoires to deal with the diverse identity needs of different persons in different situations. Another key theme is behavioural adaptation and flexibility.[26]

Sharing information

A study has shown that by sharing information individuals can create more favourable impressions among colleagues from whom they are demographically different and who negatively stereotype them as outgroup members. Such information sharing comes more naturally to extraverts and to high self-monitors, described next, but is

Box 6.10

'In a major city in Siberia I was training about 40 local administration employees to give presentations to potential providers of finance. I asked them what laws the region had to support new enterprises. No one said a word. I suggested to them that they all knew this information and told them I was now going to act like an international financier. I packed up my papers and stomped out of the room, muttering that I had wasted my time. I then returned and listed five major benefits that their recent law gave to local and foreign investors. I also stated that any international financier would find out such information in advance (I had found it from a website) and would expect the people working to promote business to both know the law and explain how it actually worked. "Silence is not an option." One person in the audience called out, "You didn't tell us silence wasn't an option."

Soviet ways led to people finding that keeping silent was the safest option. Such a response is likely in any currently or formerly authoritarian society and needs to be anticipated.'

Source: email from a financial expert; author's research

available to all. When others' impressions of them are more positive, the study showed, demographically different people performed better, were more satisfied and reported higher levels of social integration, no matter how different they were from their work colleagues.[27]

General traits for intercultural effectiveness

Self-monitoring, dealing with intercultural communication emotions and cultural relativism and biculturalism are the traits that support intercultural effectiveness.

Self-monitoring

The habit of self-observation and analysis is known as self-monitoring. There is substantial research evidence that it has positive effects on intercultural communication. High self-monitors are better able to do all the following:

■ Discover appropriate behaviour in new situations,
■ Have control over their emotional reactions,
■ Create the impressions they wish,
■ Modify their behaviour to changes in social situations,
■ Make more confident and extreme attributions,
■ Seek out information about others with whom they anticipate interacting, and
■ Initiate and regulate conversations more.[28]

They also have a greater need to talk, and are more likely to be leaders. This applies to both genders.

Dealing with intercultural communication emotions

Because people's behaviour is affected by their moods and emotions as well as by their thoughts, attitudes and values, intercultural interactors need to take moods and emotions into account. Chapter 5 described some sources of negative emotions that can arise during intercultural encounters. These emotions include anxiety and communication fear. Moreover, individuals' previous experience in interactions with a particular other party or with people from a related group is likely to evoke thoughts about the past experiences, to which positive or negative emotions may be attached. These evoked emotions have the potential to influence the emotions that are experienced during the current interaction.

Although there are situations where it is desirable to increase the level of anxiety felt during an interaction, in intercultural interactions, particularly with strangers, it will more often be appropriate to lower harmfully high anxiety levels.[29] There are three main reasons: fear will make interaction unpleasant or painful, it will make it difficult to concentrate enough to behave in a skilled way and it will communicate itself to interlocutors. Ability to manage anxiety and communication fear should mainly be developed away from interaction itself, through introspection, observation and the following practices:

■ Identifying, as precisely as possible, situations that give rise to communication fear;

■ Observing, carefully, from memory if possible and from future interactions as they take place, just how, if at all, past expectations were proved wrong (the fear usually originates in past experiences of disconfirmation of expectations);

■ Taking equally careful note of when expectations were confirmed (there is a tendency to notice our failures but not our successes, which undermines confidence unnecessarily); and

■ Checking that, when a situation requiring communication gives rise to apprehensiveness in future, the problem is not caused by over-generalizing. Communication situations have multiple aspects: two people may be from different continents, but both may be mothers; the discussion may be about accounts, which make a person nervous, but with fellow-students to whom they can talk without fear on other subjects. Instead of concentrating on the difficulties, it is more effective to concentrate on the emotionally easy aspects.[30]

Cultural relativism and biculturalism

Achieving real and ethical intercultural communication requires cultural relativism. This involves a shift away from a position in which the norms, roles, values and behaviours into which a person was socialized are seen as uniquely valid. Instead, the person sees others' norms, roles, values and behaviours as equally valid in themselves, possibly beneficial, and eligible for adoption. Unfortunately, this shift is difficult to achieve: following norms into which one was socialized is reflexive and requires little effort; not following them, or following others, is non-reflexive and requires substantial effort. The key skill required is mindfulness, which, with practice, can become habitual.

Biculturalism goes beyond this and involves accepting role-taking as part of the human condition, avoiding stylized verbal behaviour, being willing to accept the strain of adaptation, being well aware of conversational constraints and showing flexibility in conversational adaptation.[31] There are, however, individual differences in whether biculturals see their two cultures as oppositional or compatible. It is easier for people who see their two cultures as compatible to switch between culturally different interpretive lenses or frames. For example, they may make external attributions in the Chinese cultural manner after Chinese primes and internal attributions after American primes.

Applications of skills to particular situations

Situations calling for both general and specific intercultural skills to be applied include inter-ability communication, avoiding and proscribing harassing or discriminatory behaviour, coping with others' harassment, bullying, prejudice or discrimination, subverting the suppression of motherhood in the workplace and helping change others' stereotypes about outgroup members.

Inter-ability communication

Relying on broad 'disability knowledge' is not enough in interactions with a particular person with a disability. Implying that another person cannot enact any role outside his or her 'disabled' identity threatens both their fellowship and their competence face. Instead, the following can help develop inter-ability relationships:

- Notice cues that help to reveal others' preferred identities instead of relying on one's own impression.
- Emphasize personal, not (sub)cultural identities.
- Treat people and relationships as unique, not as representatives of any category.
- Anticipate face needs and learn to overcome face threats by including the other person and respecting his or her abilities. When face threats do occur, apologize.
- Be aware that it may take several interactions to achieve effective inter-ability communication.[32]

Disclosing a disability, its type and cause, can reduce tension and uncertainty so that the initial focus on the disability will recede and the individual, not the disability, will become the focus. This strategy has the drawback, however, that it disregards the needs and feelings of the person with a disability and makes them responsible for disclosure. Both parties prefer the other to take the initiative, but, since the privacy issue most concerns the person with a disability, it is important that the decision to disclose information remains theirs.[33] As the examples in Box 6.11 show, in practice people with disabilities are often the ones who do undertake the roles of enabling communication and of educating or training people without disabilities to achieve inter-ability communication.

Avoiding and proscribing harassment and discriminatory behaviour

Any kind of harassing or discriminatory behaviour is not only wrong and unacceptable in itself, it also creates barriers to communication, not only with its victims but also with all who perceive and condemn it. Although these subjects have been covered in Chapters 3 and 5, they are so important that a reminder at this point is worthwhile. Some perpetrators of harassment, especially sexual harassment, do not always understand that what they do is harassment. Not all harassment at work is done by men to women, although the majority is. The main kinds of sexual harassment are (1) non-verbal (e.g., pin-ups, leering, whistling and suggestive gestures), (2) physical (unnecessary touching), (3) verbal (unwelcome sexual advances, propositions or innuendo), (4) intimidation (offensive or superfluous comments about dress, appearance or performance), and (5) sexual blackmail.[34] While awareness of some of these behaviours as harassment has increased and most men avoid them, others continue to be a problem.

People accused of harassment are generally rated more credible, more likeable, more dedicated and more competent when they accept responsibility, rather than when they

Box 6.11

A man whose hearing was impaired worked on satellite technology at Walgreens (a US pharmacy chain). He explained: 'If words fail I try body language, writing or typing…. It's a matter of perseverance to prove to the hearing that my deafness will not interfere with my work. But in this age of advancing communication technology the barriers are diminishing quickly.'

A woman who was deaf and worked in consumer documentation at Microsoft used a hearing aid to help her use her residual hearing. 'I read lips and speak fairly well', she said, 'I've learned how to put people at ease. And of course many discussions are conducted through e-mail or IM [instant messaging].'

A development engineer in the design automation group of Eastman Kodak's R&D [Research and Development] engineering technology centre said, 'I try to educate my co-workers on how

they can help me understand them. Keep your hands away from your mouth, face me when you talk, and e-mail me or stop by my office rather than call or leave voice mail'. He added, 'I have reaped the benefits of…interacting with people who have an understanding of deafness.'

The availability manager for global Web applications in IT for IBM wore two hearing aids and heard quite well with their help, but found that unusual speech patterns and phone conversations could be a challenge. She coped by not being shy about asking people to repeat things she might have missed.

Source: Ranger, L.M. (2002) 'Communication is key for deaf and hard of hearing technical pros', *Diversity/Careers Professional*, Oct/Nov. URL: http://www.diversitycareers.com/articles/pro/octnov02/fod_com_deaf.htm

rely on excuses or denials. Excuses lead to more warnings, punishments and advice for the accused; denials prompt respondents to study the matter further or refer the entire incident higher up.[35]

Coping with others' harassment, bullying, prejudice or discrimination

Sexist, racist and other prejudiced behaviours are not the fault of the victims. Responsibility for preventing them and putting them right belongs primarily to the perpetrators and secondarily to any relevant managers, organizations or institutions. Despite this, victims do often need to handle them in order not to be damaged emotionally or in their ability to communicate and maintain relationships at work. There are both positive and negative coping strategies for dealing with work stress, however caused. Positive (control-related) coping styles include help-seeking (which involves actively pursuing consultations with others in the work situation, publicly announcing decisions about what should be done, and undertaking policy changes to prevent future problems), positive thinking and direct action (devoting more time and energy to do what is expected, using more effective planning methods, and working harder and longer hours). A study found that high scores on gender identity roles, whether masculine or feminine, were linked to positive coping styles. Low scores on gender identity were associated with the escape-related coping styles of alcohol use and avoidance/resignation. High masculinity, but not high femininity, was linked to help-seeking scores. 'Such activities seem to require certain levels of assertiveness and analytical decision-making skills, traits more descriptive of a masculine rather than feminine gender role.' (These findings relate to gender role, which was more closely linked than biological sex to ways of coping with work stress.) Having an internal locus of control increased people's tendency to use help-seeking and positive, direct action coping strategies; an external orientation, that either powerful other people or chance controls what happens, increased the tendency to use escape-related strategies. Older workers are less likely to avoid or resign themselves to workplace stressors. This finding is consistent with other research that finds older workers exhibit a greater sense of being in control and more accurate self-appraisals; these may result from their longer experience with effective coping behaviours.[36] Suggestions for how women and other 'minority' groups can learn to cope with others' damaging behaviours include the following:

- Having one's own clear parameters and consistent commitment to fair treatment,
- Judging when to 'let it go' and when to react strongly,
- Recognizing allies in the oppressing categories,
- Getting a mentor,
- Getting better qualifications and experience than the 'competition', and
- Accepting the need to prove oneself over and over.

A German study found that most victims started with constructive conflict-solving strategies, changed their strategies several times but, regrettably, ended with trying to leave the organization. The unsuccessful victims, in their fight for justice, often contributed to the escalation of the bullying conflict. On the other hand, successful copers (those victims who believed that their situation at work had improved as a result of their coping efforts) less often fought back with similar means, less often used avoidance behaviour such as absenteeism, and were better at recognizing and avoiding escalating behaviour.[37]

Subverting the suppression of motherhood in the workplace

Gendered and discriminatory organizational practices can coerce women into disguising their commitments as mothers. These practices include pervasive assumptions that working mothers are less reliable, less committed or less professional than their childless colleagues. A qualitative study found that women interpreted supervisory patterns and interactions and often decided to edit ties to motherhood, express their 'public' and 'private' identities differently and operate self-surveillance and control. However, most also engaged in family talk and 'bring children to work' through conversation.[38]

Helping change others' stereotypes about outgroup members

In order to promote a good atmosphere for intercultural communication in an organization, there can be a need to influence co-members of an ingroup to change their stereotypes of other (sub)cultural groups. Research has shown that members of an attractive ingroup can help shift stereotypes held by other members. A study reported in the *British Journal of Social Psychology* discussed referent information influence. This is the motivation individuals have to agree with (i.e., share the beliefs of) other members of a group, where their social identity as a group member is salient. In these circumstances, people expect to agree with the other group member. When disagreement occurs, they may be motivated to reduce the subjective uncertainty that arises from disagreement with people with whom they expect to agree. Then they may change their views in one of three ways. They may recategorize the disagreeing ingroup members as an outgroup (e.g., as in 'My sister Mary works with Asian women and she says they are not nearly as submissive as people think but Mary's always had some peculiar ideas – she's not like the rest of our family'); attribute the disagreement to perceived relevant difference in the stimulus situation (e.g., as in 'My sister Mary works with Asian women and she says they are not nearly as submissive as people think – but she's talking about the ones who've been brought up in the West – they're different'; or alter them to become consistent with other ingroup members (e.g., by shifting their own stereotypes – as in 'My sister Mary works with Asian women and she says they are not nearly as submissive as people think – she could be right').[39] If the ingroup member's stereotype about an outgroup is a positive one, this last response to disagreement could be beneficial.

Another approach is based on attribution theory. Counter-stereotypic behaviour by one member of an outgroup often fails to change outgroup stereotypes because it can be dismissed as an exception to the rule. Thus, for instance, Mrs Thatcher's behaviour as UK Prime Minister failed to change many men's stereotypes of women because they chose to regard her as an 'honorary man', that is, not a typical woman. However, a study has shown that the impact of an individual outgroup member's behaviour on stereotypes can be increased. This happens if two conditions apply: the behaviour is attributed to a stable internal cause such as personality, rather than to an external cause, such as 'luck' or an unstable internal cause such as mood; and the outgroup member is seen as typical, because in other ways their behaviour is similar to the behaviour of many members of the outgroup. Thus, by dressing in a feminine way to confirm male stereotypes of women but consistently making the 'hard' decisions, women managers increase their chances of shifting their male colleagues' stereotypes of women. Unfortunately, though, negative beliefs are often more resistant to change than positive ones.[40]

> A wide range of behaviours and traits can contribute positively towards achieving effective intercultural communication. They include skills that enhance intercultural understanding of others, skills for effective intercultural self-presentation, general traits for intercultural effectiveness and applications of skills to particular situations such as inter-ability communication. Some of these fall into the category of 'self-management'; others are directed at reassuring interlocutors of having good intentions and a desire to establish good relations.

6.4 INTERCULTURAL COMMUNICATION PROCESSES

This section discusses processes that increase intercultural communication effectiveness; most of them require both parties to co-operate. These processes are grounding, communication accommodation, adapting in initial intercultural encounters, developing shared representations of intercultural episodes, appreciative inquiry, managing uncertainty and anxiety in intercultural encounters, conflict resolution, mutual conversational improvement strategies, developing a 'third culture' perspective and CQ (cultural intelligence) talk.

Grounding

In attempting to speak so as to be understood, speakers make assumptions about the common ground they share with their interlocutors. Each time they are understood

Box 6.12

The following example of grounding occurred during an interview in English between an immigration lawyer and her Chinese client:

Lawyer: 'Another option would be to switch into another category, like the "Highly Skilled Migrant Programme". Do you understand?'

Client: 'Do you mean, instead of getting my employer to support my application for permanent residence?'

Lawyer: 'Yes. It's a points system – so many for a degree, so many for relevant experience. You have to have enough points.'

Client: 'Do you get points for professional qualifications?'

Lawyer: 'Yes.'

Client: 'So that might be better for me?'

Lawyer: 'It's another option.'

Client: 'Yes, I'll have to decide which is best.'

Lawyer: 'Yes.'

Source: observed by author, author's research

and each time they understand what the other person says, the common ground is extended, so that 'in orderly discourse, common ground is cumulative'.[41] This process by which people establish and continuously update their shared understanding in conversations is called grounding. It occurs naturally, but can be enhanced by asking and answering questions or by one party anticipating the other's information needs and supplying them without being asked. In either case, unsuccessful grounding can occur if the information supplier does not correctly understand the other person's needs; however, a process of 'successive approximations' can be successful. The more intercultural pairs ground, the better they communicate. It has been suggested, however, that they are less inclined to ground than monocultural pairs, although one study found the contrary.

A study that analysed authentic spoken data revealed that common ground more often comes to be established between two persons through shared beliefs than through mutual knowledge. Shared beliefs are held to be true by virtue of indirect information or experience as a result of a prior discussion and interaction with another individual concerning the same belief. In contrast, mutual knowledge is held to be true by direct experience of both parties.[42]

Communication accommodation

When two or more people are communicating face-to-face, they often adjust features of their speech or behaviour, including accent, speed, loudness, vocabulary, grammar, voice tone or gestures. Sometimes they adjust in a way that makes their communication more like the other person's (converging), sometimes to make it more unlike (diverging). Diverging usually accentuates a person's own group membership. Converging and diverging are probably strategies to signal communicators' attitudes towards one other. They may converge to gain approval or identify. They may diverge to differentiate themselves from their interlocutor.[43] Communication accommodation theory (CAT) identifies factors that influence whether people try to converge or diverge; it is illustrated in Figure 6.4.

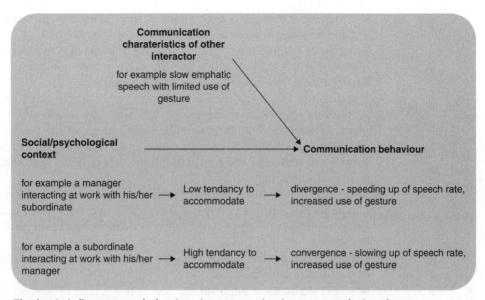

Figure 6.4 *The basic influences on behaviour in communication accomodation theory*

Based on: Gallois, C., Franklyn-Stokes, A., Giles, H. and Coupland, N. (1998) 'Communication accommodation in intercultural encounters' in Kim, Y.Y. and Gudykunst, W.B. (eds) *Theories in Intercultural Communication*, Newbury Park, CA: Sage.

According to CAT, people from different cultures (or groups) can increase their ability to communicate with one another by converging through a process of attuning.[44] Attuning consists of:

- Using increasingly similar phrasing and vocabulary, formality levels and non-verbal behaviour,
- Sharing the choice of topic, taking turns to speak and listen, responding to what others say and supporting others' 'face',
- Minimizing interruptions, corrections and evaluations,
- Adjusting speech rate, loudness, framing and focusing moves to maximize ease of understanding for the partner.

Other important CAT processes include the following:

1. Learning when to expect people to behave more in inter-group terms and more in accordance with their norms; being more careful about breaches of norms. This means learning to:
   - Realize when an interaction is likely to involve status issues,
   - Recognize people who are highly dependent on their group and those whose sense of solidarity with their group is high,
   - Recognize people who feel that they or their group are disadvantaged and be aware of its implications (see Section 5.1),
   - Distinguish members of dominant and subordinate groups and know how that status is likely to affect their behaviour (see Section 5.1),

- ■ Treat initial encounters as occasions when people will be particularly conscious of and behaving in accordance with their group memberships.
2. Being aware that the long-term motivations of interactors to build relationships or otherwise will affect how much they are likely to accommodate.
3. Paying attention to others' needs and behaviours.
4. Noticing how much attention interlocutors pay to others' needs and behaviours.
5. Monitoring interlocutors' communication strategies to identify them as convergence, divergence or maintenance; becoming aware of the possibility of using a wider range of strategies than are normally used; trying to gain the level of personal control that will allow using an appropriate strategy rather than simply adopting a strategy unthinkingly.
6. Being sensitive to the other party's evaluations of one's own interactive behaviour as accommodative or not and attributable to oneself, one's situation or one's group; monitoring one's own equivalent evaluations and ensuring they are soundly based.
7. If interlocutors are converging, being aware that that probably implies one or more of the following on their part:
   - ■ They desire social approval,
   - ■ They perceive the 'costs' of attuning as lower than the perceived rewards,
   - ■ They desire to meet the perceived communication needs of their interlocutor(s),
   - ■ They desire a mutual self-presentation and equal-status role relations.
8. Similarly, the presence of these factors suggests that attuning can be expected.
9. If interlocutors are diverging, being aware that that probably implies that they desire:
   - ■ To communicate a contrastive self- or group-image,
   - ■ To dissociate personally from their interlocutors or their definition of the situation,
   - ■ To signal differences from their interlocutors in experience, knowledge, intellectual capability or communicator style,
   - ■ To achieve or maintain a high-status role.
10. Knowing the counter-intuitive findings on people's use of interaction strategies – for instance, that people from collectivist cultures may use politeness to create social distance.[45]

Adapting in initial intercultural encounters

Adaptation Theory complements communication accommodation concepts. It is concerned with the conditions under which individuals who are interacting interculturally make more or less effort to adapt; in particular it concerns how responsibility for adapting is allocated between two participants. Adaptation is regarded as a burden that the participants will assume equally or differentially according to their relative power in the interaction or their relative dependence on it for desired outcomes. Adaptations are the changes that individuals make in their emotions, thoughts, sense of identity and communication behaviour as they interact in a new cultural environment. The extent and nature of the adaptation depend on their motivation.

People are more likely to adapt when they have a goal in an interaction, as opposed to merely engaging in a casual conversation. If the goal is shared: if, for instance, both are team members who will benefit from a good team performance, both participants will adapt; if only one participant has a goal that will be served by adaptation, then only that person will adapt. Goals arise from needs for co-operation, participation or

Box 6.13

'We had a couple of communications and then we decided we needed to get out to the suppliers and show them we are one company...And what would happen is that first we would brief each other and then we would drive and spend a couple of hours talking in the car...He sees things in a similar manner, the same strengths, the same opportunities, so I can have confidence and trust in this guy.'

Source: spoken comment quoted in: Han O. (2007) 'Situated knowledge: a practice-based view on intercultural interaction', *The Academy of Management Proceedings* URL: aom.metapress.com/index/j2m4544071706055.pdf, last accessed 21 January 2011.

agreement in such areas as commerce, manufacturing, defence, education, science, technology, politics, agriculture, medicine, the arts and scholarly research. When one person adapts ineffectually, the other participant will respond by invoking culture-based beliefs about difference. So, if a European in negotiation with someone from China suddenly starts 'stone-walling', in a clumsy attempt to adopt what s/he regards as Chinese negotiating style, the Chinese person might ascribe the behaviour to Western deviousness, if that is part of his or her culture-based belief about Europeans. Adaptation is disrupted when culture-based beliefs are invoked. If they are not, other impediments, such as status differences, are more likely to be overcome.

Adaptation Theory concerns first-time encounters. These are less predictable than later meetings and their outcomes often determine whether there will be further contact. In first-time encounters, the theory states, people will probe one another's beliefs, especially those related to the task or purpose of the meeting, in order to identify areas of agreement or disagreement. An important outcome of this process is reinforcement or modification of prior cultural stereotypes. This learning will become a cognitive resource for future encounters. Whether such learning proves to be positive or negative for such future encounters depends on how closely 'strangers' met in future conform to the stereotype. Experience does not necessarily increase competence in intercultural communication, although it has the potential for doing so. Also important is self-examination. Adaptation involves confronting not only the 'other', but also the self. In this process, the personal cultural stereotype is reinforced or modified, and this learning also becomes part of the background of the individual's future intercultural encounters.[46]

The implications of this theory for improving intercultural communication are that it is beneficial to:

■ Realize that both participants may be wrongly diagnosing the intercultural situation. This could happen if they both wrongly identify the culture of the different other person. It could also occur if they have incomplete or inaccurate knowledge of the cultural stereotype with which the other has been correctly identified or how closely the individual actually conforms to the stereotype.
■ Expect beliefs to be probed for areas of agreement and disagreement; understand the importance of agreement for building relationships.
■ Anticipate that how either party sees the interaction will affect whether they will take on, reject or intend to share the 'burden' of adaptation. They are likely to adapt their own communication behaviour more than they expect of the other party in the following circumstances: if they see the encounter as purposeful, its

goals as shared, the benefit as mutual or theirs, the 'territory' as the other's and their power and status as lower than the other's. If any of the above conditions do not apply, they are likely to adapt less than they expect of the other.

- Understand that adaptation itself is likely to change the attitudes and perceptions of adapters, both about the other party and their culture and about themselves and their own culture.
- Avoid invoking culturally based beliefs which may conflict with the other person's.

To speed progress with the task it is beneficial for each party to:

- Offer more functional adaptive behaviour; if there is inequality in adaptive behaviour to shift towards parity (i.e., assume more of the 'burden' than would be 'natural').
- Expect the major beneficiary of task completion to take responsibility for accelerating adaptive behaviour.
- Disregard differences of status or territory that are to their advantage; or invoke them to increase the amount of adaptation the other party will supply.[47]

Appreciative Inquiry

This approach appears to have originated in a 1987 book called *Research in Organizational Change and Development*, which contained a chapter called 'Appreciative inquiry in organizational life', by David L. Cooperrider and Suresh Srivastava (1987).[48] Essentially, according to its advocates, the approach is based in the definitions of the two terms in its title: appreciate and inquire. To appreciate is to value: it refers to the act of recognizing the best in people or the world around us, affirming past and present strengths, successes and potentials, perceiving those things that give life (health, vitality, excellence) to living systems. A second meaning is to increase in value, as when an investment has appreciated in value. To inquire is to undertake the act of exploration and discovery or to ask questions; it involves being open to seeing new potentials and possibilities.

The theoretical underpinning of Appreciative Inquiry (AI) is social constructionism – the theory that humans co-create reality, for instance by telling stories and through conversations (particularly inquiry) that continuously create new images, actions and realities. AI is intended to substitute an appreciative process for conventional problem-solving processes. The differences are set out in Table 6.1. The present author has not

Table 6.1   *A comparison of conventional problem-solving processes and AI processes*

Conventional problem-solving processes	AI processes
Define the problem	Search for solutions that already exist
Fix what's broken	Amplify what's working
Underlying grammar is of problems, symptoms, causes, solutions, action plans, interventions	New grammar of the true, good, empowering
Focus on decay	Focus on life-giving forces
Learn from our mistakes	Learn from what works
Slow. Takes a lot of positive emotion to bring about real change	Expands vision; creates energy fast
Can lead to a 'blame' culture	Assumes others are sources of capacity and imagination

Based on: a seminar given by Harish Rainchandani of Potentia in Hyderabad, India, 17/18 February 2010

been able to locate any research that applies AI to intercultural situations, but the approach seems capable of being used effectively in such contexts.

Developing shared representations of intercultural episodes

Intercultural communication is made more effective when the participants think of interactions in similar ways. 'For interaction to succeed, participants must essentially agree in their social situation definition.'[49] It has been argued that members of a given culture or subculture have a 'shared, implicit cognitive representation of inter-action episodes'. These representations cover assessments of the episode's intimacy, involvement and friendliness; the importance of task- versus relationship-orienta-tion; participants' own self-confidence and anxiety levels; their positive or negative evaluation of each encounter. These representations, which are influenced by cul-tural values such as individualism–collectivism and achievement/relationship, usu-ally differ from those held by members of different cultures.[50] For instance, research among Chinese and Australian subjects found that Chinese subjects perceived epi-sodes mainly in terms of communal values, power distance and usefulness, rather than pleasantness. Australians were more aware of competitiveness and individual-ism. Age, sex and personality also predicted how social episodes were seen in both cultures, but the pattern of such links was culture-specific. Other research included a comparative study of students and housewives. This study showed that, for house-wives, episodes were mainly thought of in terms of intimacy and friendliness, self-confidence and positive or negative evaluation. Results are not given for students, but it is implied that they were different.[51] A comparative study of university Faculty, research students and other staff showed that decreasing status was associated with an increasing role for anxiety in episode perceptions; involvement was a criterion used mainly by Faculty; and students were least evaluative but placed the greatest importance on task-orientation.

The greater the differences between how communicators think about interaction episodes, the harder it is for them to understand one another. Thus these cultural and subcultural differences can create barriers, although at work factors such as common technical expertise favour intercultural understanding. These barriers can be overcome by understanding how people from a different culture think about interactions and so coming to have 'shared representations' of interaction episodes. Two other factors can assist: thinking about interactions in more complex ways and being generally socially skilled. A study compared more successful and cohesive with less successful and cohe-sive student teams. The more cohesive teams had more complex episode representa-tions, based on three dimensions, friendliness, intimacy and activity, than the more fragmented teams, which had two-dimensional representations, based only on evalu-ation and friendliness. It has been shown that how someone thinks about encounters is related to social skill. Highly socially skilled individuals see episodes more in terms of evaluation and intensity, while less socially skilled persons are primarily affected by anxiety in their mental representations of social episodes.

Managing anxiety and uncertainty in intercultural encounters

To adapt successfully to working with different others, individuals need to manage the levels of uncertainty they experience about others' behaviour and the anxiety they feel about interacting with different others. This means that they must be able to understand the different others (manage uncertainty) and to manage their emotional reaction to the differences (control anxiety).[52] They may also be able to help the other party manage uncertainty and anxiety and so to interact more effectively. Several factors contribute towards people's ability to manage uncertainty and anxiety.

These factors include:

- Knowledge of the other's culture or subculture – for instance, its communication rules and behavioural norms;
- Open, flexible and accurate stereotypes;
- Positive attitudes towards the other (sub)culture and its members;
- Intimate and rewarding contact with members of the other (sub)culture;
- Perceiving similarities between their own (sub)culture and the (sub)culture of the different others;
- Sharing communication networks with members of the (sub)culture;
- A positive cultural identity (when a person's cultural identity is negative, the insecurity and anxiety stimulated by intercultural contact will seem greater, perhaps too great, leading to avoidance); and
- A demeanour that may help shift other participants' definition of a situation from 'difficult interaction with strangers', which would tend to be an anxiety-provoking definition that would lead to heavy reliance on stereotypes, to a more relaxed one where individual characteristics can be taken into account. Research has shown that the demeanour of those involved in a situation affects the definitions that people create for situations (for instance, whether it is a crisis or a routine event) and so how people respond to the situation.[53] By decreasing uncertainty and anxiety, a relaxed demeanour may allow people to adapt more and be more effective in intercultural communication.

Managing uncertainty and anxiety in intercultural encounters requires the skills to make accurate predictions, tolerate ambiguity, be mindful, empathize, self-monitor and adapt behaviour through cultural relativism and biculturalism. Competence in a second language, which need not necessarily be used in the interaction, also reduces anxiety. These skills, with some suggestions on how to develop them, were described in Section 6.3.

This guidance on factors and skills for reducing uncertainty and anxiety in intercultural encounters comes from Anxiety/Uncertainty Management (AUM) theory, which was introduced in Chapter 3. Effective communication occurs when levels of uncertainty and anxiety are optimal – intermediate between too high and too low. However, in interactions with strangers, both are normally too high for effective communication. In these cases, effective intercultural communication depends on controlling anxiety through tension-reducing behaviour and reducing uncertainty by information seeking. In intercultural as against intracultural interactions, information seeking involves more interrogation, self-disclosure and non-verbal affiliative expressiveness, but there

---

Box 6.14

'Intergroup contact is an important predictor of reduced social distance even after demographics and media and broader intergroup dynamics are taken into account.'

Source: Ata, A., Bastian, B. and Lusher, D. (2009) 'Intergroup contact in context: the mediating role of social norms and group-based perceptions on the contact–prejudice link', *International Journal of Intercultural Relations*, **33**(6): 498–506

is no increase in how many direct questions are asked. Self-monitoring, attributional confidence and attraction are related to how much information seeking takes place in an interaction.[54]

Conflict resolution

'Dispute settlement is already no easy task. ... With the addition of cultural barriers, cross-cultural negotiation may seem next to impossible.'[55] The cultural barriers consist not only of differences in beliefs and values, such as were described in Chapter 4, or of ways of communicating, as recounted in Chapter 3, but also of models of conflict resolution itself. Low-context cultures, with their 'enlightenment-based rationalism', attempt to resolve disputes by a 'means-end rationality', an emphasis on technical ways to break problems down into their component parts and a guiding ethic which is 'instrumental and manipulative'. In contrast, high-context cultures attempt dispute resolution through adaptation and eschewing dichotomous either/or possibilities. For moral conflict management, it is widely agreed, following Habermas, that there is no alternative to 'fair and open intercultural communication'.[56] Unfortunately, however, it is precisely in an intercultural setting that, according to some researchers, open communication is least likely. Whereas similarity encourages people to adopt a co-operative, integrative approach, lack of cultural similarity is a significant factor in explaining reliance on a legalistic strategy. The feeling of a lack of common ground may lead to a higher level of perceived behavioural uncertainty and so to reliance on legal mechanisms for resolving conflicts.

Conflict resolution with open problem-solving and compromising is widely advocated to enable participants to escape from deadlock situations. In international joint ventures, for instance, both partners need to adopt a give-and-take attitude in resolving disagreements.[57] Critics suggest, though, that conflict and instability are not anomalous or uncharacteristic, but inevitable; therefore the aim should be for resolutions that 'privilege instability and difference within a more stable whole'. Any positions, standpoints or solutions should always be understood as subject to being revised, changed, deleted or replaced. Most methods rely too much on linear logic, quasi-legalistic approaches and formalism that 'undermine other discourses (e.g., based on needs, differences, multicultural diverse voices, etc.) and possibly more liberating narrative constructions.'[58]

Two approaches that attempt to answer these criticisms respectively emphasize sources of conflict that stem from frustrated needs and the mental processes of the disputants. Needs, as opposed to interests, are universal.[59] Needs also differ from interests in other important ways. First, they are non-negotiable. People will not trade away their identity or their security. Identity and security are so necessary to all human satisfaction that people will do almost anything, even things that violate fundamental norms or diminish their ability to attain their interests, in an effort to obtain their basic needs. Second, needs are usually not mutually exclusive. While interests may be structured in such a way that only one side can get what it wants, needs are usually mutually supporting. Insecurity tends to breed aggression against others; security allows one to leave others alone. Similarly, if one's own identity is secure, there is no need to threaten another's sense of identity. If a group's identity is denied, however, it is likely to respond by asserting its identity against that of the opposing group(s).

A second approach emphasizes the mental processes of the disputants. One important aspect is how the parties perceive their situation, as opposed to how it might appear to an independent observer. Second, especially where some participants are

Box 6.15

Sense-making is a concept introduced by Karl Weick (1995, 2002). Its properties, he suggested, include the following:

Meaning is extracted from past experience and used to formulate meaningful actions in the future; sense-making is social. We make sense of things while in conversation with others, while reading communications from others, and while exchanging ideas with others. Sense-making requires talking, interaction, conversation, argument and dialogue with others. Sense-making is focused on extracted cues; the cues we extract from situations tend to be simple and familiar and are crucial for their ability to get us moving.* Sense-making is driven by plausibility rather than accuracy. Looking for what is plausible in the complex, confusing world in which we live is often of more practical help than finding accuracy. Totally accurate perception is not needed, which is a good thing because it is seldom achieved.

Source: Weick, K.E. (1995) _Sense-making in Organizations,_ Thousand Oaks, CA: Sage

Weick, K.E. (2000) _Making Sense of the Organization,_ Malden, MA: Blackwell Publishers

*We may miss important cues that others may see and be able to bring to our attention

'subaltern voices', such as those of women or ethnic minorities, the complexities of people's group identities must be allowed for. 'It is fundamentally important for all participants in a conflict to be heard and understood.' These understandings underpin an approach that aims for conflict transformation rather than dispute settlement. It sees conflict as both caused by and causing changes in relationships. 'Destructive interaction patterns need to be transformed into positive or constructive relationships and interactions ... development of empowerment and mutual recognition, along with interdependence, justice, forgiveness, and reconciliation.' One technique is 'dialogue' in which small groups of people who hold opposing views on highly divisive and emotional issues are brought together to have a 'new kind of conversation'. Dialogue does not always lead to settlement, but may produce a transformation in the way the conflict is pursued.[60]

A third possibility also makes the parties' perceptions a central issue but builds on practices observed as being used in work-related conflicts, both intra- and intercultural. This is the use of third parties, not as mediators or for other forms of intervention but as 'sense-makers'. Volkema _et al._ (1996) recorded finding that encounters with third parties (e.g., co-workers, friends, family) were common responses to perceived incompatibilities of interests at work. Emotional, cognitive and behavioural sense-making are components of these encounters. Support for this 'natural' behaviour, either explicitly through the provision of counsellors or by encouragement and exhortation, may have the potential to reduce such conflicts.[61]

Conversational improvement strategies

To repair communication failures, people say they use one or more conversational improvement strategies:

- Asserting a point of view: being more persuasive, expressing disagreement, arguing one's point of view,
- Open-mindedness: being less judgemental, not dismissing ideas or opinions, letting the other person express their own opinion,

- Avoidance: not bringing up unpleasant topics,
- Giving in: apologizing, agreeing,
- Interaction management: more talking, listening, turn taking, questioning, exploring topics on the part of both,
- Other-orientation: involving the other person more, having patience with other person, focusing on them.

Respondents also mention a seventh 'strategy', acceptance that nothing can be done; it seems unlikely, however, that this strategy will actually repair failures.[62]

Creating a 'third culture' perspective through cultural awareness

Cultural awareness consists of three types of awareness:

- General cultural awareness is composed of cultural sensitivity, empathy, mindfulness and competence, with their respective nuances;
- Cultural self-awareness consists of being aware of the way one's life has been shaped by one's own culture, conscious of one's own values and biases and their effects on the way one engages in intercultural interactions. Cultural self-awareness implies the necessity of becoming comfortable with cultural differences and sensitivity to circumstances.

General cultural awareness and cultural self-awareness are foundational for the third level of cultural awareness:

- Situation-specific awareness or the ability to judge a cultural situation accurately from both one's own and the other's cultural viewpoint.

Box 6.16

A Building Control Officer (BCO) for a UK Local Authority visited a householder to explain that the extension the householder built on to his house did not comply with the Building Regulations and that he needed to make alterations. (1) The householder came from an ethnic minority community, (2) and (3) about an hour into the discussion, it emerged that the householder had used a family member as architect. (4) The householder was inclined to use expansive gestures and 'shout'.

In this example, differences in culture and communication styles are likely to lead to violations of expectations, with the negative consequences described in Chapter 5. The following guidance might help resolve the conflict:

(1) The householder is probably a collectivist and so answerable to a 'constituency' of extended family.

(2) The BCO should aim for tolerance for ambiguity in the early stages of the discussion and not fall into the trap of judging indirectness as deviousness.

(3) The involvement of a family member as architect may make the householder more sensitive about what he sees as an accusation of incompetence on the architect's part: to him, family pride is at stake.

(4) The BCO should bear in mind that vivid emotional display is common in some cultures and is not necessarily aggressive.

The BCO needs to stick to the point that the rules apply to everybody. A possible resolution of the conflict is for the BCO to speak to the architect (as intermediary); this would fit well with some cultures that often use third parties in such cases.

Based on: author's research

The three types of awareness together enable a third culture perspective, which has seven characteristics: open-mindedness toward new ideas and experiences, the ability to empathize with people from other cultures, accuracy in perceiving differences and similarities between the sojourner's own culture and the host culture, an attitude of being non-judgemental, being an astute, non-critical observer of one's own and of other people's behaviour, the ability to establish meaningful relationships with people in the host culture, and low levels of ethnocentricity.[63] Analysis of documents from a Mexican company that operated on both sides of the US–Mexico border and communicated in both English and Spanish suggested that a 'third culture' approach to business communication was emerging there. Letters, proposals and invoices showed that professionals on that border were adopting, and adapting to, shared communicative standards and practices in business communication.[64]

CQ talk

Earley and Ang (2003) introduced the concept of CQ, or cultural intelligence. Originally intended to relate to individuals' ability to adapt to a host culture as sojourners, it has been adopted for a wider range of uses in subsequent research. CQ is 'a person's capability to adapt effectively to new cultural contexts'. CQ has four components: (1) cognition or knowledge of one's self, environment, information handling, and thinking processes; (2) metacognition, or one's ability to piece together the available information to form a coherent picture; (3) motivation, or one's desire to engage the new environment given one's values and expectations; (4) behaviour, or the enactment of communication by both verbal and non-verbal means in social situations. Performing the fourth of these effectively demands a large behavioural repertoire of verbal and non-verbal responses to draw on in a particular situation; but also the cognitive capability and the motivation to acquire and use such a repertoire.[65] Confirmation of the relations between the constructs was found from three substantive studies (N=794) in field and educational development settings across two national contexts, the USA and Singapore. These 'demonstrated a consistent pattern of relationships where metacognitive CQ and cognitive CQ predicted cultural judgment and decision making; motivational CQ and behavioural CQ predicted cultural adaptation; and metacognitive CQ and behavioural CQ predicted task performance.'[66]

Rogers (2008) proposed that benefits flow to intercultural communication from CQ talk, or 'an individual's deliberate verbal and nonverbal behavior during an evolving interaction to find out what needs to be learned interculturally'. Examples of CQ talk could include, 'In our meetings we usually handle several major items. Would you prefer to look at these one at a time?' (to find out whether the preferences of a monochronic or polychronic culture apply), or, 'Can we make a decision now or do you need to consult with upper management?' (to explore whether high or low power-distance values are in play).[67]

Critique

It would be wrong to create the impression that intercultural communication theories are non-problematic. Jehn and Weldon (1992), for example, criticized the ethnocentric assumption that Western theories can be applied in any culture. Although their criticism focused on conflict management theories in particular, there is every reason to believe that it applies equally to the intercultural communication theories discussed here. They wrote: 'The problem centers on the way that conflict management behavior is conceptualized, and the way it is measured in studies of cross-cultural differences. In each case, a theory of conflict management behavior developed in the West is adopted. These theories focus on dimensions that differentiate strategies of conflict management. ... These (Western-originated) dimensions of conflict management behavior are then linked to dimensions of cultural variability.'[68] These shortcomings, they argued, suggest that research based on these theories provides little useful information. To produce useful information, Western-based measures must be discarded. Instead, an inductive search must be conducted for etic dimensions (outsiders' descriptions of what people do and why they do it, developed using the methods of linguistics and anthropology) and emic constructs (what people themselves relate about what they do and why they do it). Discovering true etics allows meaningful comparisons across cultures on a set of common dimensions, and the discovery of emics contributes to a full understanding of each culture.

Other difficulties with these theories are the fact that they are partial, and yet each theory stands alone as if its proponents believed it to be a complete account. Little effort has so far been made to integrate them and, with limited exceptions, insights from other theorists' and researchers' work are not incorporated. However, this defect is probably characteristic of a young and vigorous subject area in the social sciences, and, while it reduces the immediate value of the work, it may well be productive for the further development of the field.

In addition, there are some obvious gaps in the variables covered. With the exception of accounts of intercultural competence based on Earley and Ang's (2003) account of cultural intelligence,[69] which includes several aspects of motivation, including self-efficacy expectations, goal setting, and self-concept/-evaluation through identity, and the possible exception of CAT, accounts of motivation – why some people and not others are motivated to achieve effective intercultural communication – are weak or lacking; in one case, motivational analysis is reduced to the proposition that 'length of sojourn' is the key underlying variable (see Chapter 7). Little attempt has been made so far to draw on motivational theories from psychology and social psychology.

More surprisingly, perhaps, there is a lack of recognition of cultural difference in some of the theories. With the partial exception of AUM Theory, they are silent on such questions as whether collectivists are more or less likely than individualists, those high in power distance than those low in power distance, universalists than particularists to perceive interactions in terms of cultural identity, to have their expectations violated, to adapt and so on. (It is true that one of the reported pieces of research on CAT relates part of the theory to cultural variability, but the theory *per se* does not do this.) Equally, only Cultural Identity Theory presents cultural difference as in any way a dependent variable, affected by the process of intercultural interaction. There is clearly potential for including cultural differences in the various models by a fairly simple logic, but the work has not yet been done, or not yet been published.

Reducing intercultural misunderstandings and increasing the ease and effectiveness of intercultural communication can be attained by grounding (mutual interactive checking for understanding), accommodating to the interlocutor's communication style, being willing to assume a more than equal share of the adaptation 'burden', developing shared representations of intercultural episodes, using appreciative inquiry, managing anxiety and uncertainty, conflict resolution techniques, conversational improvement strategies, creating a 'third culture' perspective through cultural awareness and CQ talk. Intercultural communication theories can be criticized for being Western-centric, partial and static.

6.5 INTERCULTURAL COMMUNICATION EFFECTIVENESS

Clearly any prescriptive work on communication needs a framework that allows an examination of whether or not any particular piece of communication or episode has been effective. Communication studies should aim to explain what works and what does not work in various situations; behaviour that is typical may not be effective. The framework offered by the communications literature is mainly in terms of communication competence. Competence implies being adequate to preserve a relationship within a desired definition, such as a 'good' working relationship, but not necessarily to do more than that. Perfect communication is probably unattainable.

Communication theorists' understandings of communication competence, not surprisingly, vary according to their understanding of communication itself.

- For linguistic pragmatists, communication competence includes a capacity for using language. However, situations do not all make identical demands on language, so competence must be evaluated in terms of some particular social circumstance. Communication requires both linguistic knowledge (for instance, participants must attach similar meanings to the messages transmitted) and non-linguistic knowledge. A minimal requirement for competence is that the individual is being co-operative – that is, makes his or her contributions as and when needed, according to the purposes of the interaction.[70]

- Communication competence can be measured either situationally or dispositionally. That is, it can be seen as particular to a given encounter or as a property of an individual. Cupach and Spitzberg (1983) showed that these are separate variables.[71] They also found that situational measures of competence predicted 'feel-good' reactions after an encounter better than dispositional measures.

- Cognitive communication theorists define competence in terms of the mental processes required to achieve effective and efficient communication. Duran and Spitzberg (1995) found the following mental processes linked to communication competence:
  1. Planning (thinking before a conversation what people might be going to talk about, mentally practising what to say, during a conversation thinking about what topic to discuss next);
  2. Modelling (watching who is talking to whom when first entering a new situation, trying to 'size up' the event; generally, studying people and being aware of people's interests);
  3. Presence (during a conversation being aware of when a topic is 'going nowhere', of when it is time to change the topic and paying attention to how others are reacting to what is said);
  4. Reflecting (after a conversation thinking about your performance and how to improve it and about what the other person thought of you);
  5. Consequence (thinking generally about how others might interpret what you say and how what you say may affect others).[72]

  Mindfulness, which was explained in Section 6.3, is another view on how communication competence is achieved, which also focuses on individual mental processes.

- Writers on communication strategy argue that competence is grounded in rational efficiency, rather than just effectiveness; that 'Given a desired end, one is to choose that action which most effectively, and at least cost, attains the end.'[73] In other words, both inputs and outputs must be considered in assessing communication strategies. Effectiveness is an 'output' consideration; it focuses on the results of strategy used and not on what effort or other resources it takes to employ a strategy. Conversely, efficiency focuses on both inputs and outputs; it considers the effort and resources that are used to achieve a given result.

■ There is an alternative view of communication competence: that it consists, not in the attributes or performance of an individual, but in a given relationship.[74] According to this view, an individual may be socially skilled, but only particular communication relationships will be competent. This is because even the most skilled individual will certainly experience some failures of communication, and even the most unskilled will certainly experience some successes when they find people with whom they are congruent. This assertion receives some support from the research cited earlier, which found that situational factors prevailed over individuals' dispositions. However, the term 'effectiveness' can still be used for analysis of communication relationships, 'competence' and 'skill' for the performance of each of the participating individuals.

Understandings of *intercultural* communication competence (ICC) and effectiveness also vary according to different theoretical perspectives.[75]

■ In AUM theory effective communication means that participants attach similar meanings to the messages transmitted. (The importance of this factor is shown by research that found that, when Black and White people interacted in public meetings, they often assigned different meanings to the matters under discussion. However, they tended to believe that the meanings they assigned were the same, and on this basis ascribed negative motives to the other group.[76]) Effective intercultural communication also requires that individuals from one culture can attribute others' behaviour to causes, whether situation or personal or group disposition, that are the same as those of a native of the other's culture under the same conditions.

■ The facework approach to intercultural communication competence is a developmental model with four stages:

Stage 1 – unconscious incompetence: the individual is fundamentally ignorant both cognitively and behaviourally;

Stage 2 – conscious incompetence: the individual understands the behaviour issues but cannot deal with them; so, for example, an interlocutor may be aware that there are too many awkward pauses and silences but not be able to correct this;

Stage 3 – conscious competence: the individual cognitively understands communication differences between cultures and is conscious of facework;

Stage 4 – unconscious competence: this is the final, fully effective stage. As with driving a car or swimming, at a certain point it becomes spontaneous and natural. Adjustment and adaptation occur without conscious effort.[77]

Satisfaction with an intercultural encounter can be one measure of its effectiveness. A study found that the level of satisfaction expressed by participants in initial intercultural encounters was linked to three factors: perceptions of how well-synchronized the conversation was, how difficult it was and how much common ground there was.[78]

■ Chen (1988) provided a set of intercultural communication competence measures, which are shown in Figure 6.5.[79]

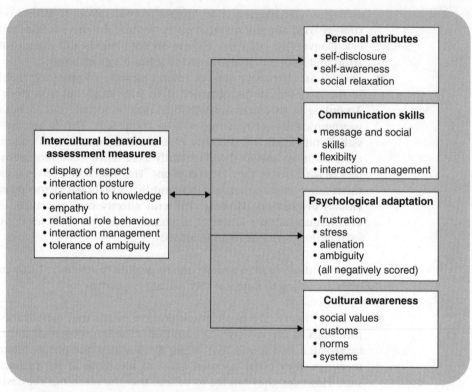

Figure 6.5   *Intercultural communication competence measures*

Based on: Chen, G.M. (1998) 'Relationship of the dimensions of intercultural communication competence'. Paper presented at the 79th Annual Meeting of the Eastern Communication Association, Baltimore MD

■ Building on earlier theoretical and empirical work, a multidimensional model of ICC proposed and tested in 2005 found that knowledge and motivation were identified as important components of ICC. Additions to a multidimensional definition of ICC included listening skills, prior cross-cultural experiences, having a global outlook as opposed to an ethnocentric one, and an other-centred style of communication.[80]

In a work context, international business managers identified the following seven dimensions of communication competence as predictors of the success of international and intercultural business management.[81] These predictors were confirmed by other empirical studies.[82]

1. How appropriately individuals adapt to new or ambiguous situations, acquire new learning and perform according to the standards and practices of the host society. Those who are unwilling or slow to adapt to new situations may have many problems in intercultural business interactions.
2. The ability to show respect and positive regard for another person in interpersonal and intercultural relations. Respect is conveyed in a variety of ways – through eye contact, body posture, voice tone, voice pitch and general displays of interest. Showing respect is a very important managerial skill for international business success.

3. The ability to understand others' situations and feelings through giving and receiving feedback or empathy.

4. Interaction management, including negotiation of topics discussed, turn taking, entering and exiting episodes and handling topical development smoothly. Holding negotiations, conducting meetings, communicating decisions and making presentations are important for international business management.

5. The ability to respond to others in a descriptive and non-judgemental way. Judgement, evaluation and appraisal are major barriers to interpersonal communication. Withholding judgement is important in international business management.

6. Having the flexibility to explain things to different people in different situations in order to reach the same results. Research findings showed that maintaining flexibility in explanations predicted culture awareness and effectiveness in intercultural communication.[83] A survey indicated that the Vice Presidents of international business corporations perceived maintaining flexibility as an important skill for international business success.[84]

7. The ability to perform both relationship and task roles and to avoid self-centred roles. In intercultural interaction, developing a working relationship is the basis on which two parties can facilitate task roles. Without a good working relationship, business cannot be conducted between two parties.

There are cultural variations in what counts as communication competence and effectiveness, whether intercultural or not. Using low-context communication in a high-context culture counts as incompetent – too many words, too little use of silence; the reverse is also true – in a low-context culture, high-context communication may be seen as inarticulate and hesitant. Indirectness is ineffective where directness is the rule and vice versa. An emphasis on relationship data is seen as 'soft' where content data is usually predominant (and, as the case of women illustrates, it also conveys a lack of authority and assertiveness); an emphasis on content data in a (sub)cultural milieu that prefers an emphasis on relationship data may be seen as an incompetent lack of subtlety and refinement. Cultural variations mean that the skills, such as tolerance of ambiguity, and the processes, such as uncertainty reduction, which have been tested and argued to be generalizable may not be universally effective. Flexibility, respect, openness, confidence or self-control may reflect a Western cultural bias on individualism or low social distance.[85]

Some results have suggested a challenge to traditional intercultural competence criteria. The type of situation and the other participants within the situation may be more powerful determining factors than the particular intercultural communication competence traits possessed by individuals. Trait criteria are considered of 'limited value in differentiating between the actual behaviour *in situ* of culturally different persons'. For instance, the situation of firing an employee elicited communication behaviour judged less competent than that for promotion or selection, regardless of the culture or gender of the stimulus person.[86] A second challenge has been made to intercultural competence approaches (here called cross-cultural competence or CC) in the context of international business on the grounds that they focus too much on the knowledge, skills and attributes that appear to be its antecedents, resulting in a gap between 'knowing' and 'doing'. A model is put forward instead that claims to explain how CC is nurtured in individuals, linked to the concept of cultural intelligence. The model follows Earley and Ang (2003) in adding the cognitive aspects of knowledge acquisition (which they called metacognition) to Hofstede (2001)'s culture-general knowledge (a focus on awareness and knowledge of cultural differences) and culture-specific knowledge (a focus on specific knowledge about another culture).[87] Metacognition provides insights into three aspects of the knowledge acquisition process:

1. 'person' aspects – intra-individual, inter-individual or universal;
2. task variables – the nature of the information required;
3. strategy variables – the procedures for using the acquired knowledge.[88]

The model adds in personal skills such as abilities and aptitudes, personal attributes such as values, beliefs, norms, personality traits such as flexibility, perseverance, self-efficacy, etc. and two moderating external factors: institutional ethnocentrism (where a multi-national company imposes its home culture way of working on its affiliates abroad) and cultural distance. Personal skills and cultural knowledge are depicted as influenced by behavioural learning and cross-cultural training, while, even in the presence of CC, international business failures may result from external factors in the environment and internal factors in the firm.[89]

> Approaches to communication and intercultural communication competence and effectiveness include both stage models and lists of dimensions. Definitions vary with the theoretical perspective of the definer.

6.6 A NOTE ON INTERCULTURAL WORK COMMUNICATION

Underlying the various models and concepts in this chapter is an assumption that people from different backgrounds who interact at work (both within and between organizations) import their own cultural values, beliefs, practices and so on, and then adapt to enable intercultural communication to take place. The effectiveness of their intercultural communication depends on how effectively one or both or all adapt. This view has been challenged by researchers within the sense-making perspective, who assert that within international organizations culture itself is negotiated. When semi-structured interviews undertaken in a German–Japanese joint venture were analysed, the results showed that 'aggregate models of cultural difference are useful only to the extent that they serve as latent conceptual anchors guiding individuals' cultural responses to events.' Instead, 'organizational events and issue domains served as points of departure for cultural negotiations.'[90] Varner (2000), too, argued that intercultural business communication is a unique construct, which is different from intercultural medical or intercultural religious communication (although they too are unique constructs in their own right).[91]

Much of the research on cultural difference has been undertaken in or applied to business contexts. Hofstede's (1981) research was undertaken using data from employees from a multinational; Hofstede and Hofstede (2005) discussed the implications of the broad values dimensions for intercultural encounters in international business organizations.[92] Hampden-Turner and Trompenaars (1993) modified and applied Hofstede's (1981) dimensions to comment on the impact of culture on business and to provide tips that help managers communicate amidst cultural differences.[93] Schwartz (1999) suggested that his theory of universal values may be applied to study societal norms about working and work and its centrality.[94] Earley and Ang (2003) included two chapters on work environments, and the enactment of communication (or behaviour) was a central construct in their theory.[95] Hall's (1976) high- and low-context model has been widely used to explain differing communication styles in business.[96] At this point, however, no clear distinction has been empirically established between intercultural work communication and intercultural communication in general.

6.7 CONCLUSION

The main psychological constructs, individual-level processes and interactive processes described in this chapter are set out in Figure 6.6. Despite the criticisms given in Section 6.4, the intercultural communication theories and research presented in this chapter collectively have carried our understanding a considerable way forward. Many of them also have the benefit of being readily applied in practice.

The techniques and approaches suggested in this chapter present individuals with a more complex interactional task than they may have understood to be necessary. However, it may be that such individuals have been living in a 'fool's paradise' in which lack of understanding, offence and even hostility went unrecognized; or that they have been imposing their 'definition of the situation' as members of a dominant group in an undemocratic and damaging way. There is an investment of energy and commitment needed to move through the stages of unconscious and conscious incompetence to first conscious, then ultimately unconscious competence, but there are both ethical and instrumental reasons for making that investment. Ethically, attempts to create a level playing field for members of minorities can be pointless if they are excluded or undermined by unskilled communication. Instrumentally, appropriate intercultural

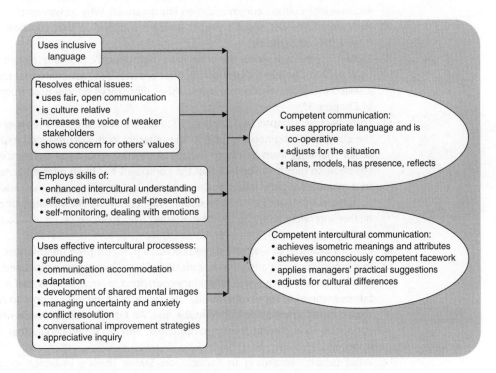

Figure 6.6   *Effective intercultural communication*

communication can help organizations win goodwill, attract the best talent, gain government business, do business with people from 'other' (sub)cultures, and have good industrial relations. For individuals, intercultural communication skills are an essential tool for providing services to, working as colleagues with or doing business with people from backgrounds different from the individual's own.

QUESTIONS AND EXERCISES

1. Give inclusive alternatives to the following non-inclusive terms: businessman, chairman, clergyman, fellow worker, fireman, forefathers, foreman, freshman, layman, mankind, manpower, man-made, postman, poetess, spokesman, stewardess, suffragette, workman, gentleman's agreement, man on the street, straw man, right-hand man.

2. How realistic do you consider the various proposals for ethical intercultural work communication? Give your reasons.

3. Give an example of a cultural norm that you have which might be reviewed in the interest of cultural relativism. Explain your reasons.

4. Explain how intercultural social perceptiveness can be improved by the four kinds of awareness described in the book.

5. Suppose that in two days' time you will meet an important potential client from a country that you know little about. What steps could you take to enable yourself to predict more accurately his or her expectations, attitudes, behaviours and responses?

6. The text states: 'An appreciation of the context of an encounter is a useful tool in increasing intercultural effectiveness.' What assumptions underlie this statement? Discuss how far such assumptions are justified.

7. Can being aware of perceptual barriers to intercultural communication really help to increase intercultural communication effectiveness? Why or why not?

8. How might you set about trying to unlearn a prejudice that you have about people from a different culture?

9. Explain in your own words the behaviours that support becoming tolerant of ambiguity.

10. Look back at Chapter 5 Question 30. Now answer Q (b) assuming that the consultant is a skilled intercultural communicator. What differences do you note from your answers in Chapter 5?

11. Look back at Chapter 4 Question 13. Assume that the HR manager suspects that the complaint originates in part in the different culturally induced expectations of a senior manager from Southern Europe about the amount of deference subordinates will show to him/her. The fact that the complaint has been referred across by the CEO to a manager slightly lower in the company's status hierarchy may add to the newly appointed manager's emotional upset. How could the HR manager deal skilfully with his/her interview with the senior manager? This exercise could also form the basis of a role play.

12. Give an example to illustrate three processes that comprise mindfulness.

13. In a group, discuss a crisis that is understood by all members (a rapid and extreme drop in sales, an extremely large budgetary overspend, a large peak in staff attrition rates, a takeover threat or some other crisis). The purpose of the discussion is to reach a state of shared mindfulness as described in the text. An Observer should note what behaviours conducive to achieving shared mindfulness, and what behaviours that might impede it, occur.

14. What factors, according to Expectation States Theory, influence expectations and behaviour in intercultural encounters?

15. How can expectations of people from another (sub)culture be made both more supportive of intercultural communication effectiveness and less subject to violations?

16. Apply the principles of Appreciative Inquiry to conduct an environmental audit of an operation of an organization with which you are familiar, or to carry out a disciplinary interview with a subordinate who has consistently breached the company's punctuality rules.

17. Discuss Schwarz's (1994) list of communication rules for speakers to follow. Would they be appropriate for someone communicating with a person from your culture? Give reasons.

18. Consult a friend or confidant(e) about a work-related problem you are facing; the purpose of the consultation is 'sense-making'; to help you understand what is happening and your own responses to the situation.

19. How can a relationship orientation be communicated? Does it conflict with getting the job done? Give your reasons.

20. An ethnic minority member of staff approached a manager with a request for extended leave to visit family abroad. S/he asked for a month off work to visit family and participate in a wedding/cultural celebration. S/he had two weeks of paid holiday unused and would expect to take the remainder of the time as unpaid leave. The manager found the request inconvenient, because its timing coincided with a peak workload period. The manager also feared that, if this staff member were allowed this extra time off, all the other staff would want the same.

    (a) How should the manager respond?
    (b) Role play the meeting between the manager and the staff member.

21. How might individualist, achievement-oriented interlocutors need to adjust their behaviour in order to increase their affective resourcefulness?

22. A male asylum seeker entered an office and went straight up to a female receptionist. It was her task to understand what the issues were and to contact the appropriate officer for an interview. The asylum seeker arrived without an appointment, wanted to see someone straight away and seemed to behave aggressively. He jumped the queue, and demanded to see 'a professional'. The receptionist had experience of people from this asylum seeker's country and knew that they are normally polite in the old-fashioned sense. It was possible that his perceived lack of courtesy had some underlying cause.
    Nevertheless, she gradually became annoyed.

    (a) How could the receptionist resolve the tension in this situation?
    (b) Role play the encounter between the receptionist and the asylum seeker.

23. Discuss ways of improving your communication with people with disabilities. Should your strategy vary according to the type of disability? Give reasons.

24. Discuss ways for members of minority groups to cope with others' prejudice, discrimination or harassment.

25. With a colleague from another culture, practise grounding in order to understand how a given business activity, such as advertising, or work activity, such as manager–labour negotiations, differ in their culture from yours.

26. List five implications of Adaptation Theory that point to behaviours, expectations and understandings that are beneficial to intercultural communication and speeding progress with the task.

27. How can an interactor develop greater social skill by following the precepts of Episode Representation theory?

28. Re-examine Question 5 in Chapter 1 and answer it in the light of the knowledge you now have of cultural differences in communication and of effective and ineffective intercultural communication.

NOTES AND REFERENCES

1. Chen, I. (2003) 'Conversation orientation and cognitive processes: a comparison of U.S. students in initial interaction with native- versus non-native-speaking partners', *Human Communication Research*, **29**: 182–209.
2. Serdjénian, E. (1994) 'Women managers in France', in Adler, N.J. and Izraeli, D.N. (eds) *Competitive Frontiers*, Cambridge, MA: Blackwell.
3. This section is developed from The Human Relations Code of the University of Maryland at College Park. URL: http://www.inform.umd.edu/Student/Diversity_Resources, last accessed on 23 December 2010.
4. Brinkmann, J. (2002) 'Business ethics and intercultural communication: exploring the overlap between two academic fields', *Intercultural Communication*, 5. URL: http://www.immi.se/intercultural/nr5/abstract5.htm#brinkman
5. Habermas, J. (1998) *On the Pragmatics of Communication*, Cambridge, MA: MIT Press.
6. Brinkmann, 'Business ethics and intercultural communication'.
7. Deetz, S., Cohen, D. and Edley, P.P. (1997) 'Toward a dialogic ethic in the context of international business organization', in Casmir, F.L. (ed.) *Ethics in Intercultural and International Communication*, Mahwah, NJ: Lawrence Erlbaum Associates.
8. Hall, B.J. (1997) 'Culture, ethics, and communication', in Casmir, F.L. (ed.) *Ethics in Intercultural and International Communication*, Mahwah, NJ: Lawrence Erlbaum Associates.
9. Gudykunst, W. and Kim, Y.Y. (1997) *Communicating With Strangers: An Approach to Intercultural Communication*, 3rd edn, Boston, MA: McGraw-Hill.
10. Katriel, T. (1989) 'From "context" to "contexts" in intercultural communication research', in Ting-Toomey, S. and Korzenny, F. (eds) *Language, Communication and Culture: Current Directions*, Newbury Park, CA: Sage.
11. Mason, D. (1995) *Race and Ethnicity in Modern Britain*, Oxford: Oxford University Press.
12. Katriel, 'From "context" to "contexts" in intercultural communication research'.
13. Rogers, K. (1951) *Client-centred Therapy*, London: Constable.
14. Gudykunst, W.B. (1988) 'Uncertainty and anxiety', in Kim, Y.Y. and Gudykunst, W.B. (eds) *Theories in Intercultural Communication*, Newbury Park, CA: Sage.
15. Langer, E. (1989) *Mindfulness*, Reading, MA: Addison-Wesley.
16. Krieger, J.L. (2005) 'Shared mindfulness in cockpit crisis situations: an exploratory analysis', *The Journal of Business Communication*, **42**(2): 135–67.
17. Ibid.
18. Burgoon, J.K. and Le Poire, B.A. (1993) 'Effects of communication expectancies, actual communication and expectancy disconfirmation evaluations of communicators and their communication behavior', *Human Communication Research*, **20**(1): 67–96.
19. Manusov, V. and Hegde, R. (1993) 'Communicative outcomes of stereotype-based expectancies: An observational study of cross-cultural dyads', *Communication Quarterly*, **41**(3): 338–54.
20. Ibid.
21. Babcock, R.D. and Du-Babcock, B. (2001) 'Language-based communication zones in international business communication', *The Journal of Business Communication*, **38**: 372–412.
22. Schwarz, N. (1994) 'Judgment in a social context: biases, shortcomings and the logic of conversation', in Zanna, M.P. (ed.) *Advances in Experimental Social Psychology*, **26**: 123–62, NY: Academic Press.
23. Berger, C.R. and Calabrese, R.J. (1975) 'Some explorations in initial interactions and beyond', *Human Communication Research*, **1**: 99–112. See also: Berger, C.R. (1987) 'Communicating

under uncertainty', in Roloff, M.E. and Miller, G.R. (eds) *Interpersonal Processes*, Newbury Park, CA: Sage.

24. Applegate, J.L. and Sypher, H.E. (1988) 'A Constructivist theory of communication and culture', in Kim, Y.Y. and Gudykunst, W.B. (eds) *Theories in Intercultural Communication*, Newbury Park, CA: Sage.

25. Ting-Toomey, S. (1989) 'Communicative resourcefulness: an identity negotiation perspective', in Asante, M.K., Gudykunst, W.B. and Newmark, E. (eds) *Handbook of International and Intercultural Communication*, Newbury Park, CA: Sage.

26. Flynn, F.J., Chatman, J. and Spataro, S.E. (2001) 'Getting to know you: The influence of personality on impressions and performance of demographically different people in organizations', *Administrative Science Quarterly*, **46**(3): 414–42.

27. Snyder, M. (1974) 'Self-monitoring of expressive behavior', *Journal of Personality and Social Psychology*, **30**: 526–37.

28. Gudykunst, 'Uncertainty and anxiety'.

29. McCroskey, J.C. (1984) 'The Communication apprehension perspective', in Daly, J.A. and McCroskey, J.C. (eds) *Avoiding Communication: Shyness, Reticence and Communication Apprehension*: pp. 13–38. Beverley Hills, CA: Sage.

30. Kim, M.-S., Hunter, J.E., Miyahara, A., Horvath, A., Bresnahan, M. and Yoon, H. (1996) 'Individual vs. culture-level dimensions of individualism and collectivism: effects on preferred conversational styles', *Communication Monographs*, **63**: 29–49.

31. Merrigan, G. (2000) 'Negotiating personal identities among people with and without identified disabilities: the role of identity management', in Braithwaite, D.O. and Thompson, T.L. (eds) *Handbook of Communication and People with Disabilities: Research and Application*, New York: Lawrence Erlbaum.

32. Fox, S.A., Giles, H., Orbe, M.P. and Bourhis, R.Y. (2000) 'Interability communication: theoretical perspectives', in Braithwaite, D.O. and Thompson, T.L. (eds) *Handbook of Communication and People with Disabilities: Research and Application*, New York: Lawrence Erlbaum.

33. Ibid.

34. The European Commission *Preventing Sexual Harassment at Work*. URL: www.un.org/womenwatch/osagi/pdf/shworkpl.pdf

35. Dunn, D. and Cody, M.J. (2000) 'Account credibility and public image: excuses, justifications, denials, and sexual harassment', *Communication Monographs*, **67**(4): 372–91.

36. Gianakos, I. (2002) 'Predictors of coping with work stress: the influences of sex, gender role, social desirability, and locus of control', *Sex Roles: A Journal of Research*, **42**: 1059–79.

37. Zapf, D. and Gross, C. (2001) 'Conflict escalation and coping with workplace bullying: a replication and extension', *European Journal of Work and Organizational Psychology*, **10**(4): 497–522.

38. Farley-Lucas, B.S. (2000) 'Communicating the (in)visibility of motherhood: family talk and the ties to motherhood within the workplace'. URL: http://www.nwrel.org/cnorse.

39. Haslam, S.A., Oakes, P.J., McGarty, C., Turner, J.C., Reynolds, K.J. and Eggins, R.A. (1996) 'Stereotyping and social influence: the mediation of stereotype applicability and sharedness by the views of ingroup and outgroup members', *British Journal of Social Psychology*, **35**: 369–97.

40. Northwest Regional Educational Laboratory: CNORSE. 'Cross cultural communication: an essential dimension of effective education'. URL: http://www.nwrel.org/cnorse.

41. Schwarz, 'Judgment in a social context'.

42. Lee, B.P.H. (2001) 'Mutual knowledge, background knowledge and shared beliefs: their roles in establishing common ground', *Journal of Pragmatics*, **33**: 21–44.

43. Giles, H. (1977) *Language, Ethnicity and Intergroup Relations*, London: Academic Press.

44. Beebe, L.M. and Giles, H. (1984) 'Speech accommodation theories: a discussion in terms of second-language acquisition', *International Journal of the Sociology of Language*, **46**: 5–32.

45. Gallois, C., Giles, H., Jones, E., Cargile, C. and Ota, H. (1995) 'Accommodating intercultural encounters: elaborations and extensions', *Intercultural Communication Theory (International and Intercultural Communication Annual)* XIX: 115–46, Thousand Oaks, CA: Sage.

46. Ellingsworth, H.W. (1988) 'A theory of adaptation in intercultural dyads', in Kim, Y.Y. and Gudykunst, W.B. (eds) *Theories in Intercultural Communication*, Newbury Park, CA: Sage.

47. Leodolter, R. and Leodolter, M. (1976) 'Sociolinguistic considerations on psychosocial socialization', in McCormack, W. and Wurm, S. (eds) *Language and Man*: p. 327, The Hague: Mouton.

48. Cooperrider, D.L. and Srivastva, S. (1987) 'Appreciative inquiry in organizational life', *Research in Organizational Change & Development*, 1: 129–69.

49. Forgas, J.P. (1983) 'Social skills and episode perception', *British Journal of Clinical Psychology*, 22: 26–41.

50. Forgas, J.P. (1976) 'The perception of social episodes: categorical and dimensional representations in two different social milieus', *Journal of Personality and Social Psychology*, 33: 199–209.

51. Gudykunst, 'Uncertainty and anxiety'.

52. Rashotte, L.S. (2002) 'What does that smile mean? The meaning of nonverbal behaviors in social interaction', *Social Psychology Quarterly*, 65(1): 92–102.

53. Triandis, H.C. (1980) 'Values, attitudes and interpersonal behavior', in Page, M. (ed.) *Nebraska Symposium on Motivation 1979*, 27, Lincoln: University of Nebraska Press.

54. Gudykunst, W.B., Nishida, T., Koike, H. and Shiino, N. (1986) 'The influence of language on uncertainty reduction: an exploratory study of Japanese–Japanese and Japanese–North American interactions', in McLaughlin, M. (ed.) *Communication Yearbook Vol. 9*, Beverley Hills, CA: Sage.

55. Leung, K. (1997) 'Negotiation and reward associations across cultures', in Earley, P.C. (ed.) *New Perspectives on International Industrial/Organizational Psychology*, San Francisco, CA: Jossey-Bass.

56. Brinkmann, 'Business ethics and intercultural communication'.

57. Lin, X. and Germain, R. (1998) 'Sustaining satisfactory joint venture relationships: the role of conflict resolution strategy', *Journal of International Business Studies*, 29(1): 197–214.

58. Lederach, J.P. (1995) *Preparing for Peace: Conflict Transformation Across Cultures*, Syracuse: Syracuse University Press.

59. Burton, J.W. (1996) *Conflict Resolution: Its Language and Processes*, Maryland: Scarecrow Press.

60. Lederach, *Preparing for Peace*.

61. Volkema, R.J., Farquhar, K. and Bergmann, T.J. (1996) 'Third-party sensemaking in interpersonal conflicts at work: a theoretical framework', *Human Relations*, 49(11): 1437–54.

62. Martin, J.N., Hecht, M.L. and Larkey, L.K. (1994) 'Conversational improvement strategies for interethnic communication: African American and European American perspectives', *Communication Monographs*, 61(3): 236–55.

63. Hammer, M.R., Gudykunst, W.B. and Wiseman, R.L. (1978) 'Dimensions of intercultural effectiveness: An exploratory study', *International Journal of Intercultural Relations*, 2(4), 382–93.

64. Ortiz, L.A. (2005) 'The emerging hybrid discourse of business communication in a Mexican-U.S. border region', *Journal of Business Communication*, 42(1): 28–50.

65. Earley, P.C. and Ang, S. (2003) *Cultural Intelligence: Individual Interactions Across Cultures*, Stanford, CA: Stanford Business Books.

66. Ang, S., Van Dyne, L., Koh, C.K.S., Ng, K.Y., Templer, K.J., Tay, C. and Chandrasekar, N.A. (2007) 'Cultural intelligence: Its measurement and effects on cultural judgment and decision making, cultural adaptation, and task performance', *Management and Organization Review*, 3: 335–71.

67. Rogers, P.S. (2008) 'The challenge of behavioral CQ: What might dialogue tell us?', in Ang, S. and Van Dyne, L. (eds) *Handbook on Cultural intelligence: Theory, Measurement and Applications*, New York: M E Sharpe, Inc.

68. Jehn, K. and Weldon, E. (1992) 'A comparative study of managerial attitudes toward conflict in the United States and the People's Republic of China: issues of theory and measurement', *Annual Meeting of the Academy of Management 1992*, Las Vegas, NV.

69. Earley and Ang, *Cultural Intelligence.*

70. Banks, S. (1989) 'Power pronouns and the language of intercultural understanding', in Ting-Toomey, S.F.K. (ed.) *Language, Communication and Culture*, pp. 180–98, Newbury Park, CA: Sage.

71. Cupach, W.R. and Spitzberg, B.H. (1983) 'Trait versus state: a comparison of dispositional and situational measures of interpersonal communication competence', *Western Journal of Speech Communication*, **47**(4): 364–77.

72. Duran, R.L. and Spitzberg, B.H. (1995) 'Toward the development and validation of a measure of cognitive communication competence', *Communication Quarterly*, **4**: 259–75.

73. Kim, Y.Y. (1991) 'Intercultural communication competence: a systems-theoretic view', in Ting-Toomey, S. and Korzenny, F. (eds) *International and Intercultural Communication Annual*, pp. 259–75, Newbury Park, CA: Sage.

74. Wiemann, J.M. and Giles, H. (1988) 'Interpersonal communication', in Hewstone, M., Stroebe, W., Codol, J.P. and Stephenson, G.M. (eds) *Introduction to Social Psychology*, Oxford: Basil Blackwell.

75. Collier, M.J. and Thomas, M. (1988) 'Cultural identity: an interpretive perspective', in Kim, Y.Y. and Gudykunst, W.B. (eds) *Theories in Intercultural Communication*, Newbury Park, CA: Sage.

76. Kochman, T. (1983) *Black and White: Styles in Conflict*, Urbana, IL: University of Illinois Press.

77. Matsu, B. and Ting-Toomey, S. (1992) 'Cross-Cultural Face-Negotiation: An Analytical Overview', Paper presented at the David See-Chai Lam Centre for International Communication Pacific Region Forum on Business and Management Communication, URL: http://www.cic.sfu.ca/forum/ting-too.html. Accessed 23.12.2010.

78. Chen, L. (2002) 'Perceptions of intercultural interaction and communication satisfaction: a study on initial encounters', *Communication Reports*, **15**(2): 133–47.

79. Chen, G.M. (1988) 'Relationships of the dimensions of intercultural competence', paper presented at the 79th Annual Meeting of the Eastern Communication Association, Baltimore, MD, USA.

80. Arasaratnam, L.A. and Doerfel, M.L. (2005) 'Intercultural communication competence: Identifying key components from multicultural perspectives', *International Journal of Intercultural Relations*, **29**(2): 137–63.

81. Kealey, D.J. (1989) 'A study of cross-cultural effectiveness: theoretical issues, practical applications', *International Journal of Intercultural Relations*, **13**: 387–428.

82. Zhao, J.J. and Ober, S. (1991) 'Communication skills needed by US international business persons', *Delta Pi Epsilon Journal*, **33**: 52–60.

83. Ruben, B.D. and Kealey, D.J. (1979) 'Behavioral assessment of communication competency and the prediction of cross-cultural adaptation', *International Journal of Intercultural Relations*, **3**: 15–47.

84. Zhao and Ober, Communication skills needed by US international business persons'.

85. Collier, M.J. (1989) 'Cultural and intercultural communication competence: current approaches and directions', *International Journal of Intercultural Relations*, **13**: 287–302.

86. Dinges, N.G. and Lieberman, D.A. (1989) 'Intercultural communication competence: coping with stressful work situations', *International Journal of Intercultural Relations*, **13**: 371–85.

87. Hofstede, G. (2001) *Culture's Consequences: Comparing Values, behaviors, Institutions and Organizations Across Nations*, 2nd edn, Thousand Oaks, CA: Sage Publications.

88. Earley, *Cultural Intelligence.*

89. Johnson, J.P., Lenartowicz, T. and Apud, S. (2006) 'Cross-cultural competence in international business: toward a definition and a model', *Journal of International Business Studies*, **37**: 525–43.

90. Brannen, M.Y. and Salk, J.E. (2000) 'Partnering across borders: Negotiating organizational culture in a German-Japanese joint venture', *Human Relations*, **53**: 451–87.

91. Varner, I.L. (2000) 'The theoretical foundation for intercultural business communication: a conceptual model', *Journal of Business Communication*, **37**(1): 39–57.

92. Hofstede, G. and Hofstede, G.J. (2004) *Cultures and Organizations: Software of the Mind: Intercultural Cooperation and Its Importance for Survival*, New York: McGraw-Hill.

93. Hampden-Turner, C. and Trompenaars, A. (1993) *The Seven Cultures of Capitalism*, Garden City, NY: Doubleday.

94. Schwartz, S.H. (1999) 'Cultural value differences: Some implications for work', *Applied Psychology: An International Review*, **48**: 23–47.

95. Earley, *Cultural Intelligence*.

96. Hall, E.T. (1976) *Beyond Culture*, NewYork: Doubleday.

Extensions and Applications

chapter seven

Skills for Working Abroad

Increasing numbers of people have opportunities to take on international assignments or become expatriates working and living in a foreign country. For business managers and other staff these opportunities arise from factors such as increasing international competition and the resulting need to market products worldwide, international merger and acquisition activity and new market access opportunities (for instance in Eastern Europe and in Asia). Globalization of telecommunications, the rapidly increasing prevalence of the English language and specific developments such as the Erasmus programme of the European Union have created similar international opportunities for a wide range of non-business personnel, from students to doctors, footballers to musicians. Young people, particularly, have shown themselves eager to seize these opportunities for international experience. However, any international assignment poses challenges in terms of adaptive capabilities and cultural sensitivity; longer-term assignments require the person to cope with culture shock and the processes of sojourner adaptation as well as dealing with new roles and responsibilities in an unfamiliar context.

This chapter is concerned with how people who are working abroad can learn to cope with and in their new cultural environment. A past perspective was that the greater the cultural distance between the host country culture and the expatriate's home culture, the less easy adaptation will be; a new perspective, however, is that cultural similarity is less important than personal fit: the ability of the individual to adapt.[1]

Clearly, all encounters taking place in an overseas host culture occur in a different context from those with different others in the 'home' country. Equally clearly, overseas visitors staying for a few days before returning home or moving on to another country are in a different situation from sojourners – people who are staying for at least a month in another country, either for work or study. (Immigrants are in a different situation again; this book does not cover most issues confronting immigrants.) Therefore the chapter considers first the needs of all visitors who go to another country to work: Section 7.1 addresses the knowledge and skills needed. Section 7.2 covers the additional skills needed by sojourners. The material given in Chapter 6 is, of course, just as relevant and important to the subject of this chapter.

7.1 CULTURAL ORIENTATION SKILLS

Working internationally, whether on a short- or long-term basis, gives rise to problems of mutual understanding and appropriate self-presentation. Experiencing these difficulties can be stressful for the individuals concerned. Organizational responses to the consequent needs of the individuals whom they send abroad to work are often inadequate – training and preparation systems are generally poor.

In the words of Belay (1993), 'Physical interconnectedness and interdependence among cultures and nations has reached a much higher level of development than the awareness and competency required from both individuals and institutions to handle this new reality positively.'[2] These words remained true long after he wrote them. Working successfully internationally depends on being able to cope in another country's culture, and this in turn depends on being adequately oriented to its culture, resolving ethical issues that may arise in a foreign culture and dealing with the negative emotions and stress aroused by the foreign culture.

Orienting to another culture

Orienting to another country's culture depends on understanding the self as a cultural being (i.e., being aware of one's own cultural identity), knowledge of the culture and its language, stereotypes of and attitudes towards people in the other culture and being able to suspend evaluation of other people's behaviour.

■ Self-awareness overcomes the dangers of cultural self-imprisonment, which were pointed out in Chapter 5. Cultural self-awareness includes being aware that usual approaches may be inappropriate.

■ Knowledge of the host culture is needed to work out how people in the culture interpret and evaluate their own behaviour. For example, in Western countries, people greet each other with a handshake (and there are rules for what constitutes an appropriate handshake). In Japan, people generally do not shake hands. Rather, they bow (and there are rules as to what constitutes an appropriate bow). Although they are different behaviours, both shaking hands and bowing perform the same function, greeting another person. In another case, people may engage in the same behaviour, but use different rules. To illustrate, people may shake hands, but the rules for shaking hands appropriately may differ – in some cultures two hands are used. Knowing specific similarities and differences such as these is essential for knowing in detail how to behave. Knowledge of general cultural similarities and differences, such as whether another culture is collectivist or individualist, particularist or universalist, is also vital: it is needed for accurately interpreting the behaviour of people in another country.

There are several ways of gaining knowledge of the host culture and its language. These include reading books or articles, watching TV programmes or films, talking to people who have had extended contact with people from the other culture or talking directly to people from the other culture. Other ways of gaining information are by observing the members of the other culture interacting among themselves and by observing their behaviour when interacting with them. One of the best ways to learn about people in other cultures is to study their language. 'Without understanding some of the host language, it is not possible to understand their behaviour.'[3] This does not necessarily mean speaking the language fluently; however, the more of the language is understood, the more the culture can be understood. Also, host nationals usually take making an effort to speak the language as a positive sign. It increases their desire to get acquainted.

Box 7.1

(1) The consultant knocked, then immediately entered the manager's office, without waiting for a 'Come in.' (2) He was wearing a smart new sweater. (3) He held out his hand and said, 'Hi, Werner, how are you doing?' The manager looked somewhat cold, but shook hands and said, 'Good morning, Dr X.' (4) X moved forward to a comfortable conversational distance. Werner backed away. They sat down. (5) X said, 'You got my message, telling you I'd be late?' Werner replied, still coldly, 'I'm afraid not.' 'That's odd, I spoke to Heidi myself.' (6) 'Ah,' Werner said, 'that explains it, Heidi does not take messages; she does not even work in this department.' (7) The meeting, which was to settle the terms of the next stage of the consultancy project, dragged on and on, going over all the finest details. (8) X grew impatient. 'Let's cut to the issue, shall we? This could take all day.' The atmosphere grew even cooler. (9) X tried to lighten the atmosphere with a joke. Werner did not even smile. 'Can't we tie this up here?' X pleaded. (10) The manager looked shocked. 'I cannot make that level of decision. I will have to report to my Director.' (11) 'We have experienced some difficulty with your company's performance, Dr X. I think you were given a report on the lack of precision in the initial findings, I might even say the lack of grasp of how important parts of our systems work. We would have expected this to be addressed and responded to in detail before proceeding to negotiate on the next phase.' (12) 'But your overall assessment of our work was "satisfactory", wasn't it, and implementing the recommendations has brought cost savings, just as we said it would?' X replied. Werner responded: 'That is true, but that could have been mere good luck. It is difficult for us to have confidence for the future when you do not seem to have put in the work to really understand our operations in depth.' X tried to defend his own and his colleagues' work. (They had followed the time-saving consultancy 'formula' successfully applied in many American and European companies – but he was not going to tell Werner Schmidt that.) (13) However, the manager had every detail of the consultancy's promotional brochure at his fingertips, and firmly but politely refuted X's arguments point by point. X ended by subsiding into silence.

The responses of X's German client can be explained as follows:

(1) Entering a German manager's office without waiting to be invited in is a breach of manners and an invasion of the strong German sense of privacy. To enter without knocking would be unthinkable.

(2) Business attire in Germany is formal – suits, not smart sweaters.

(3) Manners are also formal – titles are used, first names are not, greetings are formal.

(4) Germans' spatial comfort distance is even greater than most North Europeans'.

(5) Punctuality is very important in German culture. Time is one of the 'principal ways of organizing life'.

(6) Most large German organizations are hierarchical and highly departmentalized. There is little lateral communication between departments.

(7) Germans see command of detail as one of their strengths, linked to their belief that they are more efficient than other people.

(8) The German manager may take impatience over a thorough examination of the project as a sign of lack of seriousness and thoroughness in the consultant's organization.

(9) Germans regard jokes as inappropriate while doing business. In addition, like that of many nations, Germans' sense of humour is quite specific – X's joke may not have seemed funny to the manager.

(10) Unlike the French, Germans are willing to make decisions in meetings, but hierarchy sets firm limits on the discretion of individual managers at different levels.

(11) Germans regard open criticism of weaknesses as acceptable, even helpful. They regard themselves as having very high standards of performance and are critical when others seem to have lower standards. They expect apologies and, in a business context, compensation for failures.

(12) Germans require their business partners to be as thorough as they are themselves.

(13) Germans' method of arguing relies on absolute command of the facts – it can be very powerful.

Source: based on the author's research

Two major factors that affect the amount and type of knowledge that people obtain about another culture they visit either short- or long-term are the nature of the contacts they have with that people in the culture and their motivation to adjust to the other culture. The second of these is related to their attitudes to other cultures in general and the one they are visiting in particular.

■ Appropriate attitudes are vital to working effectively abroad. 'Once there is respect for different points of view as equally valid, there can develop a genuine desire to create new ways of working together. So long as individuals only accept the validity of their own view of the world, international working becomes a battle to get the French to follow the systems or to explain again to the Chinese that you are working to a deadline.'[4] The culture's own way of working probably represents the best way of doing things within a particular cultural context.

Respect towards the other culture is one necessary attitude; another is respect for the individuals with whom one interacts. These two attitudes can sometimes be lacking in, for instance, expatriates working in the former Soviet countries; the obvious deficiencies of some of the systems that operate are translated into a broad disrespect for the entire culture and all its people, as in 'They have no initiative,' or 'They can all be bribed.' Such attitudes communicate themselves to the people among whom the expatriate is living and working. Naturally, they elicit responses that make the expatriate's life more difficult and thus more stressful.

It is also important to be willing to change one's own attitudes, sometimes in quite fundamental areas. One example is attitudes towards what constitutes success or failure; for instance, in the situation quoted in Box 7.2, the conference, seen as a failure by the UK organizer, was regarded as a success by the Hungarians, who understood its purpose not as networking (reasonably enough, since that had not been explicitly stated) but as informing. The participants had learnt about the programme with which the conference was concerned; they had demonstrated their interest by seizing on all the brochures and by making follow-up enquiries by telephone.

Box 7.2

A conference in Hungary, jointly organized by UK and Hungarian staff, had the following features.

Ninety-three invitations were sent out, only six replies were received by the start of the conference, and 72 people attended. The Hungarian staff said: 'Hungarian people have a bad habit: they do not reply to invitations.'

The conference was intended as a participative workshop. The Hungarian staff, in charge of on-the-ground arrangements, scheduled six presentations an hour for four hours, with no time allowed for questions. This was to be followed by a one-hour 'discussion period'. The venue was the most formal room in the city's largest hotel; the seating was arranged round tables forming a huge hollow square. When the discussion period arrived (an hour later than scheduled) it was impossible to rearrange the room for group work, and, in plenary, discussion was stilted and consisted only of questions and comments addressed to the Chair. The conference was ended sharply at six o'clock because, a Hungarian said, 'Hungarians always want to rush off home.'

The UK organizer felt the workshop had been 'hijacked' and had failed to fulfil its main purpose, which was networking. However, it had been impossible to insist on other arrangements, because the local people were obviously trying so hard according to their own preconceptions.

Source: author's research

■ Describing others' behaviour before evaluating generally leads to understanding; evaluating prematurely leads to misunderstanding. There is a 'natural' human tendency to evaluate others' behaviour. Such evaluation, however, is generally based on an individual's own cultural standards. Using personal cultural standards to evaluate others' behaviour often makes it harder to understand them fully. To understand others, what is needed is first to describe what is observed; next, to look at alternative interpretations of the behaviour and then to try to work out which interpretation is most appropriate in the other culture. (To do this the knowledge gained about the other culture is needed.) Only then is it possible to evaluate the behaviour, and even then the major reason for doing so is if it is necessary to take a decision on whether or not to engage in it personally. Suspending judgement of others until the cultural logic behind their behaviour is understood is critical to making good decisions on how to react and behave towards them in various situations.

A review of the literature suggested that cultural knowledge, cross-cultural understanding and a number of intercultural behavioural skills and situational variables are important for good intercultural relations.[5] Sojourners and short-stay international visitors alike should focus on three areas of objectives:

1. Behaviour objectives: to act in accordance with another culture's norms, or to create new 'third culture' patterns which incorporate elements of both home and host cultures.
2. Skills objectives, including communication and group process skills and skills of coping with cultural differences. Some personal qualities, such as openness, flexibility, a sense of humour and pluralistic values and attitudes, are also helpful.
3. Knowledge objectives, which should be focused on the following:

   ■ Realistic expectations of the target culture(s), of which the most important are those that involve different attributions or interpretations of behaviour.
   ■ Information about roles and role relationships. This may be more useful than information about, for instance, economic, political and educational systems.
   ■ What problems to expect. Anticipating problems of the kind quoted in Box 7.3 comes with experience; other people's reported experiences can also be relevant, provided that the possibility of bias is borne in mind.

In an overseas host culture, there is a need for both specific knowledge of the kinds given in Boxes 7.2 and 7.3 and the more general understanding of cultural difference and similarity derived from the kinds of analysis presented in Chapters 2, 3 and 4.

Resolving ethical issues

There can be a dilemma over how far to accommodate to another culture when issues of principle are involved. For instance, although Japanese women are often highly educated, they are not widely accepted in the higher echelons of the corporate world. To send a woman, however senior, to negotiate in Japan is likely to prejudice the outcome. Yet for many Western organizations it is unthinkable to deny a woman such an assignment just on the grounds of her gender. Again, to some people from collectivist cultures, what is morally condemned as nepotism in the West is a moral obligation;

Box 7.3

'As Europeans have become more environmentally conscious, it has become more difficult for them to live comfortably in countries like India – probably in the developing world generally. Many of the people in these countries whom one meets or works with as an expat are tasting the fruits of growth for the first time. They are avid consumers and seem to care little for environmental values. They will buy the biggest car they can afford (an SUV for a family of three in a built-up area), never use public transport or walk if they can avoid it, use twice as many free supermarket plastic bags as they need, run the subsidized air conditioning when Europeans feel fine with a fan and so on. At seminars I have seen huge piles of small plastic bottles of mineral water demolished while a large container (with a tap) of the same stuff was being ignored.

All these behaviours are upsetting, but you have to ask yourself what right have we, who have for so long been damaging the planet, to criticize or try to change them, who up to now have had so little?'

Source: interview with an expatriate manager, India, author's research

Box 7.4

The Human Resources Manager for an American bank branch in Taipei, Taiwan, discovered that during his own temporary absence his Taiwanese colleague had bypassed the bank's appointment procedures and had appointed his nephew to a junior post. When confronted, the colleague, who was otherwise a most valuable member of staff, did not defend himself – in fact remained largely silent – but the American could see that underneath he felt he had done nothing wrong.

Source: author's research

they might criticize someone who refused to promote a relative as being one 'who does not even help his own family'.

In cases such as these, changing one's own attitudes, however desirable from the point of view of intercultural communication, may present not only psychological problems but also ethical or philosophical ones. One of the most difficult aspects of sojourning for work is trying to behave ethically when in another culture, particularly if that culture has values that are different from one's own. An 'honest' business person in a culture where bribes are routine, a teetotaller whose Russian hosts bring out a bottle of vodka to celebrate his/her arrival, or a vegetarian for whom they bring out caviar – such instances create real tensions between the need to be polite and the ethical need to adhere to one's own values. In addition, the elements of culture are interconnected; if someone thinks one element of a culture should be resisted or changed, they need to consider whether it can be changed or resisted in isolation.

Dealing with negative emotions and stress provoked by overseas encounters

Negative emotions are usually heightened when intercultural encounters occur outside one's own country as part of an international assignment or sojourn. Anxiety and stress are natural reactions to interacting intensively with members of other cultures or to living in another culture. Everyone experiences them to some degree. How well someone adjusts depends on how they cope with the stress and anxiety, not on whether they experience them. Anxiety and stress, therefore, are not 'bad' in and of themselves. In fact, anxiety provoked by unexpected reactions can serve as a cue that something is not right, and so stimulate ideas about how to adjust. There are many ways to cope with the anxiety and stress of an overseas assignment. 'Fighting' the other culture and looking down on its members, or 'taking flight' and interacting only with other members of one's own culture, are both harmful. The most successful way to cope is to try to be flexible. This means adjusting behaviour to the situation by first observing the way things are done in the culture, keeping in mind that not all members of the host culture behave in the same way. There can be tremendous variation in acceptable behaviour within a culture. These variations may occur because of education, age, social status, gender or individual differences. Armed with knowledge of how things are done in the host culture, new behaviours can be tried out; then the degree to which they were successful and enjoyable should be reflected on. Based upon reflection, a decision is made on whether or not to continue the new behaviour or try something different.

Equally, the same ways of coping used in the home culture to deal with anxiety and stress can generally be used in another culture. Ways that help include formal and informal relaxation techniques, exercise, talking to a friend about the problems, temporarily leaving the stressful situation, using humour and ensuring that you have at least one 'comfort zone' – one area of life that is continuous with your previous existence. Taking tranquillizers or other drugs, drinking too much coffee or coke, or eating, smoking and drinking alcohol too often usually do more harm than good. Creativity in solving adjustment problems is also valuable. Other approaches to coping with stress were described in Section 6.3.

> How people deal with working internationally ranges from functional ways, which include adjusting behaviour to the situation, to dysfunctional ways, which include 'fighting' the other culture. Knowledge of the other culture, having appropriate attitudes, such as respect towards the other culture, describing others' behaviour before evaluating it, self-awareness, resolving ethical issues such as how far to accommodate to another culture, and coping with negative emotions and stress are all needed for success in working internationally.

7.2 SOJOURNING

Sojourners are people who:

- Grew up in (had their 'primary socialization' in) one culture and moved, temporarily, but for at least a month, into another;
- Depend to some extent on the host environment for meeting their personal and social needs; and
- Are engaged in firsthand, continuous experiences with the host environment.

The real difficulties inherent in being a sojourner are demonstrated by studies showing that 16 to 50 per cent of US expatriates failed on foreign assignments. (Failing is defined as returning to the home country before the assignment was completed successfully – therefore not counting those who failed to perform satisfactorily but still stayed on.) European and Japanese expatriates did better: 59 per cent of a European sample of organizations reported rates below 5 per cent, 38 per cent rates of 6 to 10 per cent and 3 per cent rates between 11 and 15 per cent. A study found that 70 per cent of US expatriates were

Box 7.5

'I have an English friend here who once told me: "I've travelled all over Europe, even lived in other countries there, and whenever I heard people go on about 'cultural differences' I thought...that they were just a big myth. But now, having lived in Mexico, I know exactly what the term means."

When I first arrived in Oaxaca, I was initially taken aback to have people constantly call me *guero,* a word that when most literally translated means something like "Whitey," though in terms of strength is more like "Blondie." However, I quickly learned that in Mexican culture, identifying people by their most striking physical attribute is a matter of custom and not considered to be rude.'[a]

'People at work are the same as any colleagues: guys play football and enjoy beers together, girls are gossipy and giggly. One of the biggest differences is their conservative religious outlook on life. If you are in a relationship, people expect you to get married and if you have children but are not married, it is frowned upon. Many Peruvians go to church and joggers will stop to pay their respects if they pass a statue of the Virgin Mary. Bosses are the supreme authority and they have "the power," so employees are often intimidated and won't stand up to them. Instead they complain to other colleagues.'[b]

Sources: (a) Clark, J. 'Teaching English and living in Mexico as a Mex-Pat'. URL: http://www.transitions abroad.com/publications/magazine/0501/ teaching_english_and_living_in_mexico.shtml (b) Hansen, C. 'A year living and working in Peru'. URL: http://www.transitionsabroad.com/listings/living/articles/living_and_working_in_peru.shtml

sent abroad without any cross-cultural training. Ninety per cent of their families also received no training, although the inability of the partner to adapt to the foreign environment is a very important cause of expatriate failure. Most of the US companies that did offer training provided only brief environmental summaries and some cultural and language preparation. Of the correspondents in the study's Western European sample, 69 per cent sponsored training programmes to prepare candidates for foreign assignments. (The level was about the same in Japan.) Mostly, though, training was only for people sent outside Europe or the US, plus Eastern Europe.[6]

Another factor that may have contributed to poor adjustment is that, across many countries, job knowledge and technical or managerial ability appear to be most used for selecting international assignees. This means that little attention is paid to being able to cope in an 'alien' culture. Research that sheds some light on what these factors might be studied 338 international assignees from 26 diverse countries and 45 organizations, assigned to 43 diverse countries and performing diverse jobs. International assignees were defined as individuals posted from their home office to a host country subsidiary or branch. Five factors were identified by the international assignees themselves, in the following descending order of importance:

1. Family situation.
2. Flexibility/adaptability.
3. Job knowledge and motivation.
4. Relational skills.
5. Extra-cultural openness.

Importance ratings were not influenced by job type (managerial/non-managerial status) but they were by organization type; in general, service organization personnel attached more importance to relational and psychosocial factors, perhaps because they had more contact with the local community and host country nationals. These five factors accounted for over half the variance. Family situation was consistently important across all conditions.[7] A large sample of public-sector US professionals working in comparable jobs in 156 different countries provided direct evidence that social and perceptual skill, reasoning ability, and adjustment- and achievement-orientation personality requirements are higher in expatriate assignments.[8]

Culture shock

Part of the reason for the difficulties of international sojourners is expressed in the term 'culture shock'. This refers to feelings of anxiety and tension owing to loss of familiar customs and social interactions. Put differently, culture shock is a 'cumulative and debilitating state of disorientation, one that builds slowly from each experience in which the sufferer encounters contrary ways of perceiving, doing and valuing things'.[9] 'Culture shock' can appear in a number of guises, varying from mild to severe homesickness, or feeling frustrated, to suffering alienation and isolation. These feelings can be brought on by a number of things, including the language barrier, loneliness, difficulty in penetrating the host society, not knowing how to react in a difficult situation and always being the centre of attention.

Adjusting to a relatively similar culture is often as difficult as adjusting to a 'distant' one. This may be because expatriates do not expect differences in relatively similar cultures.[10] However, Canadian research showed that people who admitted to higher levels of culture shock were the same people who were more effective on the

---

Box 7.6

Using data from 212 host country nationals (HCNs) in China, Varma *et al*. (2009) found that HCNs' perceived relationship quality with the expatriate had a significant impact on their willingness to provide assistance, both role information and social support, to expatriates. Further, relationship quality was related to perceived cultural similarity. This meant that Chinese HCNs were more willing to include Indian expatriates than US expatriates in their *guanxi*, and therefore more willing to provide the Indian expatriates with information. The assumption is that the Chinese HCNs perceived a higher degree of homophily with Indians than with North Americans.[a]

When 222 Indians (104 in the USA and 118 in India) were asked about their attitudes to US expatriates, it was found that female expatriates from the US were preferred by Indian host country nationals as co-workers significantly more than male expatriates from the US.[b]

Attitudes of Chinese workers to expatriates are influenced by the perceived trustworthiness of the expatriates. This perception helps alleviate the impact of the Chinese workers' perception of the distributive injustice involved in the large compensation gap between them and the expatriates, a perception that tends to impact negatively on their job satisfaction and organizational commitment.[c]

(a) Varma, A., Pichler, S., Budhwar, P. and Biswas, S. (2009) 'Chinese host country nationals' willingness to support expatriates: the role of collectivism, interpersonal affect and guanxi', *International Journal of Cross Cultural Management*, 9: 199–216

(b) Varma, S., Toh, S.M. and Budhwar, P. (2006) 'A new perspective on the female expatriate experience: The role of host country national categorization', *Journal of World Business*, **41**(2): 112–20

(c) Leung, K., Zhu, Y. and Ge, C. (2009) 'Compensation disparity between locals and expatriates: Moderating the effects of perceived injustice in foreign multinationals in China', *Journal of World Business*, **44**(1): 85–93

assignment. It also found that the importance of personal variables may outweigh the situation – that is, that selection may outweigh training and social support. For example, of two individuals, one found the same situation constraining, the other liberating.[11] The main characteristics consistently listed as negative factors for cultural adjustment include:

- National origin and perceived discrimination: in the USA, for instance, sojourners from African or Asian countries have more adjustment problems than Europeans do.
- Psychological depression.
- External locus of control.

The last two characteristics, depression and external locus of control, 'point to personality factors'.[12]

Common symptoms of culture shock that have been identified include irritability, loneliness, depression and rigidity. Parallel symptoms to these have been described in the 'learned helplessness' literature. Therefore, one author suggested, the application of reformulated learned helplessness to cultural adjustment can contribute to understanding culture shock.[13] Learned helplessness is a person's belief that what happens to them and the outcomes of what they do are independent of what they do and how they do it; people suffering from learned helplessness attribute negative events internally, stably and globally ('global' here means that the cause is believed to operate on a large number of things, not just one). If people suffering from learned helplessness have a bad experience, they will tend to think it is caused by them, that the cause is long-lasting and unchangeable and that the cause will make other things bad, too. Thus, an individual's use of stable/unstable, global/specific, and internal/external attributions can affect his or her adjustment to a new culture. Figure 7.1 gives a flow chart of the possible relationship between learned helplessness and culture shock.

Culture shock and the need for a painful process of cultural adjustment have been described as 'universal aspects'.[14] Individuals are commonly disoriented when undergoing a transitional experience and the accompanying stress. Realizing that what they are undergoing is 'normal' helps many individuals to tolerate stress.

Sojourner adjustment/adaptation

Despite problems of culture shock, most sojourners do eventually adjust to the point where they are coping and effective. How do they do it? Can the process be speeded

---

Box 7.7

A longitudinal study of 15 Germans in Taiwan explored the changes in their understandings of the Chinese concept of 'face' over time. The first comments on 'face' were neutral or even positive in tone and mostly concerned Chinese politeness or fear of losing face. However, a growing negative undertone was observed; in later stages 'power games' entered the picture as the German interviewees came to believe that giving, not giving or even attacking face served a purpose in interactions and were often aimed at individual advantages rather than the other person's well-being. A concern for 'face' was further seen as opposed to reaching optimal or even acceptable solutions for work-related problems.

Source: Weidemann, D. (2001) 'Learning about "face"– "subjective theories" as a construct in analysing intercultural learning processes of Germans in Taiwan', Forum: Qualitative Research, 2(3): Art. 20

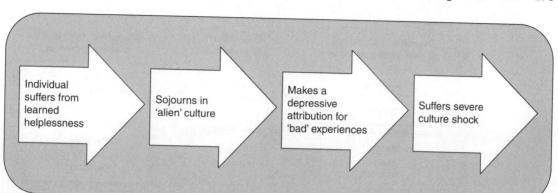

Figure 7.1   *Learned helplessness and culture shock*

up? One approach is to identify a series of stages that are usually gone through in the process of adjustment. In one such model the stages are:

1. Fascination. In the early days 'buffers' such as getting set up with accommodation prevent real contact with the host culture.
2. Hostility and aggression. As the buffers reduce, contact increases and often leads to anger towards everything and sometimes everyone in the host culture. This is a critical point where the shock can develop into rejecting the host culture.
3. Acceptance. The person then accepts the host culture as much as they can. This is never total but is sufficient to make life comfortable.
4. Adaptation. In spite of difficulties a person does his or her best to adjust to the new culture and refuses to give in to culture shock.

Motivation to adapt is the most important factor in how quickly individuals pass through these stages. Motivation to adapt depends partly on expected length of stay – the longer, the higher the motivation. Support programmes can ease the difficulties of sojourners when they first arrive. In the longer term, however, adaptation must occur primarily in the individual, not in the host society. In view of the importance of motivation, it is encouraging that a survey of expatriate managers on assignment to 59 countries revealed that the majority of expatriates viewed their international assignment as an opportunity for personal and professional development and career advancement, despite perceived deficits in corporate career management systems and a widespread scepticism that the assignment would help their careers.[15]

According to Ady (1995), sojourner adjustment is a relatively short-term, individual and time-based process that is conceptually distinct from cultural or ethnic assimilation, adaptation or intercultural communicative competence. Ady (1995) argued that adjustment occurs not 'globally' but in specific domains. There are many domains, but they can be grouped into three classes:

- task domains (employment and daily structuring tasks),
- social support domains (friendships, interaction with host nationals),
- ecology domains (physical aspects of the new environment).

In each separate domain, adjustment occurs as a function of the sojourner's judgement of how well s/he is meeting the demands of the environment and how well the environment is meeting his/her needs; total adjustment is a function of adjustment in all three domains. Figure 7.2 shows the model.

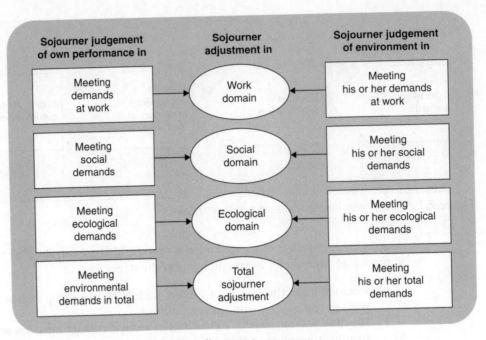

Figure 7.2 *Ady's domain model of sojourner adjustment*

Based on: Ady, J.C. (1995) 'Toward a differential demand model of sojourner adjustment', in Kim, Y.Y. (ed.) *Intercultural Communication Theory (International and Intercultural Communication Annual) XIX*, Thousand Oaks, CA: Sage.

Ady put forward four axioms concerned with sojourner adjustment:

1. It is multidimensional.
2. It varies across domains and over time; some happen more quickly than others.
3. It is experienced by sojourners as happening through a series of crises.
4. It is experienced by sojourners as non-gestalt.[16]

Ady also contended that adjustment is highly salient to sojourners. While it is going on, the problems and solutions associated with it are often central in the sojourner's consciousness.

There is a pessimistic model of sojourner adjustment, represented by an inverted U-shaped curve as illustrated in Figure 7.3, which hypothesizes that after an initial 'honeymoon' stage sojourners often become frustrated with day-to-day living and retreat to the stability and comfort of home-culture friendships.

Conversely, a more optimistic model of sojourner adaptation proposes that human beings have an inherent drive to adapt and grow; that adaptation to one's social environment occurs through communication; and that adaptation is a complex and dynamic process.[17] The process involves at least the following elements: unlearning at least some old cultural habits, learning new responses and a stress–adaptation–growth dynamic. However, sojourners go through the processes of intercultural adaptation at different rates – some adapt quickly, others more slowly, a few not at all. There are reasons for these differential rates. Some differences are related to the individual, but many, research suggests, are more closely related to the host environment: some countries and organizations are easier to fit into than others. Figure 7.4 shows the main influences.

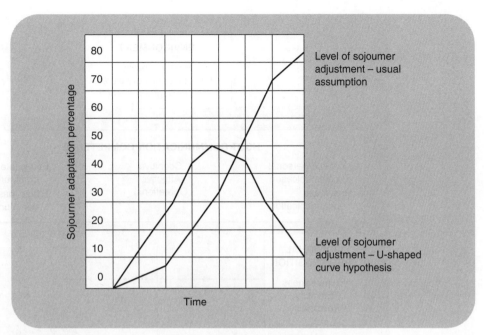

Figure 7.3   *Sojourner adjustment over time: U-shaped curve hypothesis*

A sojourner's ethnic identity is a key factor in his/her individual predisposition to adapt successfully. A strong ethnic identity tends to mean that adjustment initially occurs quite rapidly but then declines – there is an inverted U-shaped curve; a weak ethnic identity is more likely to produce a slow but steady increase in adjustment. Some empirical support for this stress–adaptation–growth model of sojourner adaptation can be found, as follows:

- Host mass communication, such as television, has been shown to help sojourners adapt.
- Extreme stress reactions in the form of escapism, neurosis and psychosis are most often seen among those whose native culture radically differs from that of the host community.
- Personality factors such as openness and strength reduce stress reactions.
- Finally, there is evidence that many employees seek out co-workers most like themselves as a way to reduce culture shock. The support of such groups helps some newcomers on the job and can promote self-esteem.[18]

Earley and Ang (2003) argued that success in global work assignments (as measured by the individual assignee's general adjustment, work performance and completion of the global assignment) is related to CQ (cultural intelligence), which was introduced in Section 6.4, but that the relationship is modified by a large set of factors. These include the individual's personality and technical managerial competence, the (level of) adjustment of any spouse and children, the cultural toughness (novelty) of the host nation, the job, and the organizational effectiveness of both the parent and the local unit organization.[19]

In a business or other work context, expatriate adjustment can often be not so much a unidirectional process of one individual adjusting to a foreign environment, but part of a process of mutual adjustment within an international team. When 11 teams of four

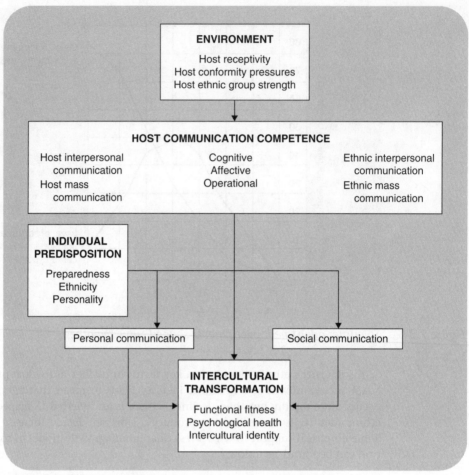

Figure 7.4　*Factors affecting sojourners' rates of intercultural adaptation*

combinations of nationalities – German–English, German–Indian, German–Japanese and German–Austrian – were examined in two German companies in a one-year longitudinal study, mechanisms of mutual adjustment were identified at the level of cognitive processes, attitudes and behaviours of team members. These adjustments were influenced by a number of external context factors such as external context factors which created power relationships. These factors created power relationships between the members of the different nationalities in the team, and the power relationships in turn had a major influence on the direction of adjustment.[20]

Acculturation

Acculturation is the establishment of an 'intercultural identity' for an immigrant, sojourner or international assignee who successfully integrates into a new environment. Intercultural identity is achieved when an individual grows beyond his/her original culture and encompasses a new culture, gaining additional insight into both cultures in the process.[21] It involves understanding the norms and values, and adopting salient reference groups, of the host society. Acculturation and acquiring

Box 7.8

A study of 52 international female managers who had worked in Asia found that they were overwhelmingly successful. Most of these women were the first female expatriates to be sent abroad to the role; only 10 per cent followed another woman into the international position. Therefore, no rules or role models existed. The decision process leading a company to send a female manager to Asia could be described as one of mutual education between management and the employee. The following is a quote by a US female manager based in Hong Kong: 'It doesn't make any difference if you are blue, green, purple, or a frog. If you have the best product at the best price, they'll buy.' US female expatriates were viewed first as Gaijinî (foreigners), then as women.

Source: Adler, N.J. (1994) 'Competitive frontiers: women managing across borders', in Adler, N.J. and Izraeli, D.N. (eds) *Competitive Frontiers: Women Managers in a Global Economy*, Cambridge, MA: Blackwell

an intercultural identity presuppose that the visitor's simplified view of the host society is replaced with a more realistic, more complex view. Competence in the language of the host country, being highly motivated to achieve acculturation and having access to interpersonal and mass communication experiences are the three factors which have most bearing on gaining more realistic perceptions of the host country.

Acculturation is a stress-inducing process. Face-to-face interviews with over 2,000 Asian immigrants to the USA found that the strongest predictors of acculturative stress were the level of the individual's English language proficiency and native language proficiency (lower proficiency meant more stress), discrimination, family cohesion and the context of migration.[22] It has been argued, however, that additional stress might result in faster and more effective acculturation. For example, Canadians in Kenya 'who would ultimately be the most effective in adapting to a new culture underwent the most intense culture shock during the transition period'. When stress is extreme, 'human plasticity' is activated to form the person more fully into a more complete intercultural identity: in longer stays (those of immigrants, for instance), initial high stress levels result in more complete acculturation, an earlier adoption of an intercultural identity and lower stress levels eventually.[23] Other evidence to support this acculturation model has been found.[24] Studies of international students showed that those students with the most host-national contact also showed the most adaptation, that 'psychological stress is found in individuals who attempt to integrate' and that longer stays result in more acculturation. It was also found that language ability was correlated to feeling at ease and satisfied with an international student experience. Evidence that initial stress can lead to eventual acculturation was found in studies of the spouses of international students. Among such spouses, stress was widespread. 'Initial feelings of sadness, loneliness, self-doubt, confusion, and frustration were present in their descriptions of the first weeks and months of the sojourn.'[25] Language difficulties made this initial stress worse. However, a 'positive change of mood usually happened within the first 3–6 months from arrival', thus confirming the view that in time 'strangers become increasingly proficient in managing their life activities in the host society.'[26]

Conversely, there is some evidence that successful exchange student experiences are more related to expectations than to acculturation. Sojourners consistently reported that expectations were met or positively violated. This may mean that the value of stress to acculturation has been overstated, as well as the value of acculturation to a successful experience. 'The notion of self-fulfilling prophecy accounts for the similarity between expectations and fulfilment of these expectations.'[27] In Anxiety/Uncertainty Management theory, anxiety and the resulting stress are expected to drive sojourning individuals towards uncertainty reduction and eventual acculturation in the new culture. However, Witte (1993) considered that culture shock results in acculturation only when acculturation into the new milieu appears to be manageable. If the danger in a fear-provoking situation appears to be manageable, individuals' preferred adaptive response is to take action to reduce the danger. If the danger in a fear-provoking situation seems to be too large to handle, however, or danger reduction strategies are absent, fear reduction takes over and the danger is ignored or rationalized away. Such responses to new cultures would result in maladaptive seclusion, and not result in acculturation of the individual or the society.[28]

Cultural intelligence

It was the observation that some individual sojourners adapt better than others to their host country that led Earley and Ang (2003) to introduce the concept of cultural intelligence, or CQ, which was described in Chapter 6. CQ equips a person to distinguish behaviours produced by the culture in question from behaviours that are peculiar to particular individuals and those found in all human beings. In their surveys of 2,000 managers in 60 countries, the authors found that most managers were not equally strong in all areas of CQ. The authors devised tools that show how to identify strengths and developed training techniques to help people overcome weaknesses. They concluded that anyone reasonably alert, motivated, and poised could attain an acceptable level of CQ.[29]

Training for international assignments and sojourns

Clearly, the better prepared sojourners are for their visit to a country with a markedly different culture from their own, the more likely they are, other things being equal, to succeed in adjustment, adaptation or acculturation. The evidence on expatriate failure and distress therefore makes sojourner training of great concern. To date most training has concentrated on cultural content: how the host culture differs from the sojourner's home culture, especially on the surface. In cultural awareness models the emphasis is on cultural insight, with individual awareness an expected by-product. One type is the 'Contrast home culture' model, which aims to assist in recognizing the sojourner-to-be's own culture's values as a first step in relating across cultures and so focuses primarily on cultural filters. Usually the contrasting culture is not intended to be seen as any specific one. These so-called orientation models of sojourner adjustment have been criticized for failing to help sojourners learn and adapt once in the host country. The assumption underlying orientation models is that adaptation is primarily an intellectual process. In fact, though, emotional and behavioural adjustments give sojourners most difficulty. 'If the trainee has only learned specific bits of data and generalizations about a culture, his [sic] everyday experience with individual members of that culture will quickly invalidate a major portion of the content knowledge he has received. ... This difference between teaching for knowledge and teaching for performance and adaptation comprises the fundamental criticism of this model.'[30] Once they arrive in the host country according to Bennett (1986)[31]:

■   Trainees will be experiencing a new environment and will need to understand approaches to deriving information from new sources; they will need to categorize the information in new ways, internalize it and use it to accomplish new goals or solve new problems.

■ They will be shifting their learning environment from the classroom to an experiential environment, that of existence in another culture.

■ The experiential learning environment will be intrinsically learner-centred (i.e., it will require adjustment from the learner).

■ Sojourners will be in an environment where all cultural cues are ambiguous, if not intimidating, their language skills may not be adequate to meet their needs and they are deprived of the ordinary reinforcement routinely received in the home culture. Simulation or area training models try to allow for these considerations. They rely on reproducing situations and conditions that closely duplicate the actual overseas site and assignment. However, the drawback of these models is their cost. Opportunities to participate in a ten-week intensive residential training programme abroad are few.

Dealing with roles and responsibilities in an unfamiliar work environment

There is evidence that the work context usually provides lower levels of culture shock and an easier adjustment for the expatriate than private life. There is an 'international culture' of work which creates continuity between countries. Nevertheless, as earlier chapters of this book have shown, organizational cultures and the behaviour and expectations of colleagues, superiors and subordinates do vary cross-culturally, and the pressure may be exacerbated by the need to adjust quickly. To work successfully internationally, individuals need to form relationships with members of the host community. A survey of 232 expatriates found that those who became involved with local businesses and communities felt less role ambiguity and had higher job satisfaction and more influence within their own companies than those who did not. Their influence was based on their ability to relay local information and identify opportunities that met the needs of their company. Local experience and the diversity of social networks available affected the extent of expatriates' boundary spanning, but having previous international work experience did not have much effect.[32]

Box 7.9

An expatriate senior manager for a Western start-up business in Asia was worried. The company had taken a lease on a new building that was to provide 500 workstations for the new staff being recruited. The landlord had promised to have the building ready by the time the staff were inducted in two months' time. However, an inspection revealed that only the crude structure was in place and little work appeared to be going on. There were rumours that the landlord was in financial difficulties. Meanwhile, recruitment was continuing apace.

Responsibility within the firm for the new building was with the expatriate senior manager's subordinate, the Asian Head of Office Management, who was a host national. This person was always extremely deferential towards the expatriate senior manager. However, one day, after daily discussions about the new building problem, he turned to the expatriate manager and said: 'You delegated this responsibility to me. I promised you I would have the new building ready on time. I think you should leave it to me to get the work done as I promised.'

Source: author's research

Another study examined instrumental and expressive ties among 457 managers in a multinational enterprise (MNE). Instrumental ties arise in the performance of work and facilitate the transfer of physical, informational or financial resources. Expressive ties provide friendship and social support. The study demonstrated that managers formed strong expressive ties with peers who were from culturally closer countries and from the same status group. However, strong instrumental ties appeared to be maintained by managers with different rather than similar background characteristics. This may be because expatriate managers made a conscious effort to overcome the barriers of their cultural background and status and to work extensively with local staff. Most interactions among managers in MNEs had both instrumental and expressive aspects. For example, formal vertical reporting relationships were often complemented by informal coaching and mentoring, while friendships and informal collegiality could lead to successful teamwork in formally appointed groups.[33]

> Sojourning, which means medium-term residence in, and usually working or studying in, a foreign country, makes high demands on individuals' ability to cope. Many international 'assignees' actually fail and return home. Selection that ignores cultural adaptation potential and poor preparation and training are widely blamed for this problem.
>
> Nearly all sojourners experience culture shock. The problem is less, though, for people who speak the host country language competently, who have sojourned before and who do not suffer from learned helplessness. To adjust and adapt to a new culture and deal with culture shock, it helps to understand that it is normal and to recognize that stress can lead to adaptation and growth. The techniques for coping with stress and for experiential learning can be used to facilitate adaptation. Training and preparation need to be appropriate and effective. The work context partially reduces the effect of sojourning but may increase other pressures. Forming links to local businesses and communities provides expatriates with more job satisfaction and influence, though most obtain their social support from people from similar backgrounds. Task relationships, however, are often strongest with people from the host country.

7.3 CONCLUSION

Working internationally calls for coping skills and behavioural adjustments as well as the cultural awareness and intercultural communication skills described in previous chapters. Sojourners usually suffer from culture shock, and it helps to recognize it as a normal reaction; there are a number of models of how to achieve adaptation. These methods include unlearning at least some old cultural habits, learning new responses and growing through adaptative responses to stress, dynamic acculturation through acquiring a nuanced understanding of the host culture, developing cultural intelligence and having appropriate preparation and training. Successful adaptation allows the sojourner to deal effectively with roles and responsibilities in a culturally unfamiliar work environment.

QUESTIONS AND EXERCISES

1. Describe four factors that influence ability to cope in another culture.
2. Give examples of the following kinds of knowledge needed by sojourners and short-stay visitors to another country: (a) realistic expectations of the target culture, (b) information about roles and role relationships and (c) what problems to expect.

3. Give examples of two ethical issues that may create intercultural difficulties for people working on foreign assignments, and discuss how they may be overcome.

4. List six functional mechanisms for coping with anxiety and stress induced by intensive exposure to another culture.

5. Look back at Box 7.4. What might explain the behaviour of the American Human Resources Manager's Taiwanese colleague? How should the American deal with this issue? (This scenario could form the setting for a role play.)

6. How can international assignees overcome the tendency to avoid intercultural experiences following an unrewarding or punishing experience?

7. How would you implement the text's recommendation that it is valuable to seek some degree of match between an individual's culture and the culture of the country to which they are assigned?

8. (a) What is 'learned helplessness'? (b) How does it relate to culture shock? (c) What are the implications of this relationship/analogy for overcoming culture shock?

9. Describe the four stages of a sojourner adaptation model.

10. Discuss the contention that sojourner adjustment is a relatively short-term, individual and time-based process that is conceptually distinct from cultural or ethnic assimilation, adaptation and intercultural communicative competence.

11. Discuss the contention that sojourner adjustment occurs in different domains in different ways and at different times.

12. Discuss the contention that, during sojourner adjustment, the problems and solutions associated with it are often central in the sojourner's consciousness.

13. Discuss the contention that people cannot acquire a generic skill of adjusting to new cultural environments, but must repeat the learning process and curve with each new sojourn.

14. Explain the 'stress–adaptation–growth dynamic' theory of sojourner adaptation.

15. Which is more realistic, the U-shaped curve hypothesis or the 'stress–adaptation–growth dynamic' theory of sojourner adaptation? Give your reasons.

16. What are the outcomes of successful sojourner adaptation?

17. How does a sojourner's ethnic group identity strength affect his or her sojourner adaptation?

18. The text notes that sojourner adaptation can be a matter of mutual adjustment of the members of a team. Adjustment occurs in cognitive processes, attitudes and behaviours. Which cognitive processes, attitudes and behaviours are likely to be positive and which negative for such mutual adjustment of team members?

19. How might the four components of CQ, described in Section 6.4, help bring about an assignee's general adjustment, work performance and completion of a global assignment?

20. Explain in your own words the meaning of 'acculturation'.

21. Look back at Box 7.9. What cultural patterns might explain the behaviour of the host national's behaviour in that Box? How might the expatriate manager's cultural background be likely to affect his/her response? How *should* the expatriate manager respond?

22. The material in the text on acculturation identifies from the literature seven independent variables as leading to successful sojourner adjustment. These are: host country language competence, motivation, access to interpersonal and mass communication experiences, stress, expectations, anxiety and attributional confidence. Draw a diagram to show the relations among these variables. How would your own set differ, if at all, from these?

23. Bennett (1986, ref. 30) gave a set of four challenges faced by 'learners' in a host country. What are they?

24. Look back at Box 4.5, which describes an incident in a British start-up business in India. Write your suggestions for the way the announcement of the partial move to a new office could have been made, or role play the announcement meeting.
25. What conclusions do you draw from the examples in Box 7.6?

NOTES AND REFERENCES

1. Jun, S. and Gentry, J.W. (2005) 'An exploratory investigation of the relative importance of cultural similarity and personal fit in the selection and performance of expatriates', *Journal of World Business*, **40**(1): 1–8.
2. Belay, G. (1993) 'Toward a paradigm shift for intercultural and international communication: new research directions', *Communication Yearbook*, **16**: 437–57.
3. Gudykunst, W.B. (1983) 'Similarities and differences in perceptions of initial intracultural and intercultural encounters: an exploratory investigation', *The Southern Speech Communication Journal*, **49**: 49–65.
4. Tayeb, M.H. (1996) *The Management of a Multicultural Workforce*, Chichester: John Wiley.
5. Dinges, N. (1983) 'Intercultural competence', in Landis, D. and Brislin, R.W. (eds) *Handbook of Intercultural Training, Vol. 1*, New York: Pergamon Press.
6. Baumgarten, K. (1995) 'Training and development of international staff', in Harzing, A.-W. and Ruysseveldt, J.V. (eds) *International Human Resource Management*, London: Sage.
7. Arthur, W. Jr. and Bennett, W. Jr. (1995) 'The International assignee: the relative importance of factors perceived to contribute to success', *Personnel Psychology*, **48**: 99–114.
8. Shin, S.J., Morgeson, F.P. and Campion, M.A. (2006) 'What you do depends on where you are: understanding how domestic and expatriate work requirements depend upon the cultural context', *Journal of International Business Studies*, **38**: 64–83.
9. Schreiber, E.J. (1996) 'Muddles and huddles: facilitating a multicultural workforce through team management theory', *The Journal of Business Communication*, **33**: 459–73.
10. Shenkar, O. (2001) 'Cultural distance revisited: towards a more rigorous conceptualization and measurement of cultural differences', *Journal of International Business Studies*, **32**(3): 519–35.
11. Kealey, D.J. (1989) 'A study of cross-cultural effectiveness: theoretical issues, practical applications', *International Journal of Intercultural Relations*, **13**: 387–428.
12. Ibid.
13. Reinicke, M.J. (1986) 'Cultural adjustment of international students in the U.S.: A re-evaluation using reformulated learned helplessness' (*ERIC Document Reproduction Service No. ED 274 939*). URL: http://eric.ed.gov/ERICWebPortal/search, last accessed on 23 December 2010.
14. Martin, J. (1986) 'Training issues in cross-cultural orientation', *International Journal of Intercultural Relations*, **10**: 103–16.
15. Günter, K.S., Miller, K.N. and Tung, R.L. (2002) 'Toward the boundaryless career: a closer look at the expatriate career concept and the perceived implications of an international assignment', *Journal of World Business*, **37**(3): 216–27.
16. Ady, J.C. (1995) 'Toward a differential demand model of sojourner adjustment', in Kim, Y.Y. (ed.) *Intercultural Communication Theory (International and Intercultural Communication Annual) XIX*, Thousand Oaks, CA: Sage.
17. Kim, Y.Y. (1988) *Communication and Cross-cultural Adaptation: An Integrative Theory*, Philadelphia: Multi-Lingual Matters.
18. Schreiber, 'Muddles and huddles: facilitating a multicultural workforce through team management theory'.
19. Earley, P.C. and Ang, S. (2003) *Cultural Intelligence: Individual Interactions Across Cultures*, Stanford: Stanford Business Books.
20. Zimmermann, A. and Sparrow, P. (2007) 'Mutual adjustment processes in international teams: lessons for the study of expatriation', *International Studies of Management and Organization*, **37**(3): 65–88.

21. Kim, Y.Y. (1992) 'Development of intercultural identity', Paper presented at the annual conference of the International Communication Association, Miami FL.
22. Lueck, K. and Wilson, M. (2009) 'Acculturative stress in Asian immigrants: the impact of social and linguistic factors', *International Journal of Intercultural Relations*, **34**(1): 47–57.
23. Kim, 'Development of intercultural identity'.
24. Ward, C. and Kennedy, A. (1993) 'Psychological and socio-cultural adjustment during cross-cultural transitions: a comparison of secondary students overseas and at home', *International Journal of Psychology*, **28**(2): 129–47.
25. De Verthelyi, R.F. (1995) 'International students' spouses: invisible sojourners in the culture shock literature', *International Journal of Intercultural Relations*, **19**: 387–411.
26. Kim, Y.Y. (1988) 'Facilitating immigrant adaptation: the role of communication', in Albrecht, T. and Adelman, M. (eds) *Communicating Social Support*, pp. 192–211. Newbury Park, CA: Sage.
27. Martin, J.N., Bradford, L. and Rohrlich, B. (1995) 'Comparing pre-departure expectations and post-sojourn reports: a longitudinal study of U.S. students abroad', *International Journal of Intercultural Relations*, **19**: 87–110.
28. Witte, K. (1993) 'A theory of cognition and negative affect: extending Gudykunst and Hammer's theory of uncertainty and anxiety reduction', *International Journal of Intercultural Relations*, **17**: 197–215.
29. Earley and Ang, *Cultural Intelligence*.
30. Bennett, J.M. (1986) 'Modes of cross-cultural training: conceptualising cross-cultural training as education', *International Journal of Intercultural Relations*, **10**: 117–34.
31. Ibid.
32. Au, K.Y. and Fukuda, J. (2002) 'Boundary spanning behaviors of expatriates', *Journal of World Business*, **37**(4): 285–96.
33. Manev, I.M. and Stevenson, W.B. (2001) 'Nationality, cultural distance, and expatriate status: effects on the managerial network in a multinational enterprise', *Journal of International Business Studies*, **32**: 285–303.

chapter eight

Culture, Communication and Work Activities

Chapter 2 introduced the idea that cultural differences may be reflected in aspects of work such as roles and norms, attitudes to groupwork, manager–subordinate relations and organizational cultures. This chapter explores cultural differences in specific work activities. It also examines ways of conducting these work activities interculturally and internationally. An important caveat here is the one given in Chapter 2.5: it cannot be assumed that the intracultural processes and behaviours of a cultural group will generalize to the intercultural context.[1] The work activities covered are selection interviewing (Section 8.1), service encounters (8.2), mentoring (8.3), mediating (8.4), negotiating (8.5), working in groups and teams (8.6), and leadership and management, including giving feedback, diversity leadership and international project management (8.7). Performing these work activities effectively in an intercultural setting depends on all the knowledge, understanding and skills described in earlier chapters. The skills for enhanced intercultural understanding and effective intercultural self-presentation, together with skills of grounding, communication accommodation, adapting in initial intercultural encounters, developing shared representations of intercultural episodes, appreciative inquiry, managing uncertainty and anxiety, conflict resolution, mutual conversational improvement strategies, developing a 'third culture' perspective and CQ talk are all relevant. Table 8.1 depicts the relationship of this chapter to the earlier ones.

8.1 SELECTION INTERVIEWING

Statistics suggest that interviews are by far the most widely used tool for selecting job candidates, and are the only means for 85 to 90 per cent of companies. Although applicants' objective credentials, such as job experience or academic performance, often determine who is invited to interview, far more important in practice for hiring decisions is the candidates' performance in the interview itself.

Cultural differences in selection interviewing

(Sub)cultural differences in interviewee behaviours and responses have been widely documented:

Table 8.1   *The relationship of the sections of Chapter 8 to previous chapters*

	Selection interviewing (8.1)	Service encounters (8.2)	Mentioning (8.3)	Mediating (8.4)	Negotiating (8.5)	Groupwork & teamwork (8.6)	Leadership & management (8.7)
Diversity awareness (Ch.1)	✓	✓	✓	✓	✓	✓	✓
Cultural knowledge and awareness (Ch.2)	✓	✓	✓	✓	✓	✓	✓
How culture affects communication (Ch.3)	✓	✓	✓	✓	✓	✓	✓
How culture affects behaviour (Ch.4)	✓	✓	✓	✓	✓	✓	✓
Barifiers to intercultural communication (Ch.5)	✓	✓	✓	✓	✓	✓	✓
Effective intercultural communication (Ch.6)	✓	✓	✓	✓	✓	✓	✓
Working abroad (Ch.7)	?	?	?	?	?	?	✓

- Respondents in some cultures often discern what they perceive the interviewer wants to hear, and modify their answers to comply with this perception. This stems from various attitudes held by respondents, such as courtesy to guests (the interviewers), the desire to satisfy them so that they may leave happy, having collected the information they 'wanted', and/or a lack of trust in the interviewers. Biases also arise because the interviewee perceives the interviewer as higher in status and, in selection interviews, higher in power; this effect is stronger in high power-distance cultures.
- The assumption that the respondents are aware of the meaning and methods of questioning is often not realistic in countries where the tradition of interviewing is not well established. Therefore, the scope for misunderstanding about what is required and its purpose is wide.
- In some countries, the presence of other person(s) during the interview affects the response of the interviewee, depending on who this person is.[2]
- Different self-presentations may be related to a (sub)culture's 'social rules'. For instance, a series of findings have shown that Chinese applicants tend to defer to the interviewer (who is categorized as a superior) and to focus on the group or family, besides being averse to self-assertion.[3] Gallois and Callan (1998) pinpointed Indians' emphasis on qualifications and their modesty about skills and individual contributions. In contrast, North European interviewers tend to prefer an emphasis

on work achievements and assertiveness. Indians emphasize 'self-worth' in terms of other people's opinions of them – diplomas are authentic credentials; they want to show they can fit in rather than make their mark.[4] Similarly, a study showed that East German interviewees avoided showing disagreement with the interviewer or assertiveness. They seemed to 'orient more to the asymmetry of the encounter, whereas West Germans (interviewers as well as interviewees) seemed to play it down'. The researchers concluded: 'Eastern [German] candidates display a tendency to shift to unspecified, generalized perspectives in a variety of contexts. The ... subjective perspective is replaced by an unspecified impersonal one and that requests for an individual perspective are answered with a generalized one referring to a higher authority.'[5] As research reported in Chapter 3 found, Latino interviewees were more inclined to co-ordinate their non-verbal behaviour with that of their interlocutor than Anglos were. The findings, according to the researchers, showed the consequences of two parties adopting different relational schemas at work; one culture had a higher relational focus than the other. The consequences for interviewees can be grave, the researchers asserted, and could lead to biases in selection.[6]

Effective intercultural selection interviewing

In job interviews, equal opportunities and diversity approaches can conflict. It used to be considered that a standardized interview procedure, which eschewed discriminatory questions such as 'How would your husband feel about your doing this work?', ensured equal and therefore fair treatment. It is now recognized that some candidates may, for reasons of local knowledge or cultural background, be less able than others to answer the same 'fair' questions. Something subtler is needed, if the organization is actively seeking to achieve a diverse workforce. Both the questions and the evaluation of candidates' answers need to take differences in cultural background into account. This makes cultural awareness a priority requirement for intercultural selection interviewers, who should also be self-aware of their own tendencies to bias, stereotyping and monocultural blindness. Evidence suggests that interviewer assessments of similarity and job-related competence (person–job fit) are important factors in stimulating their overall liking and final evaluations of applicants, and that interviewees' self-presentation is the strongest influence on these assessments. From a study of 72 real taped interviews it was found that interviewers' perceptions of person–job fit were strongly influenced by candidates' self-promotion. Their non-verbal impression management influenced perceived similarity.[7] Since there are cultural differences in both non-verbal behaviour and the acceptability of self-promotion, these biases of selection interviewers can distort selection. In international selection interviews, to avoid bias the questioner must observe lexical equivalence (asking the questions so that they mean the same in two or more languages) and conceptual equivalence (the transfer of concepts from one culture to another). This requires understanding and knowledge of the local language and culture. Interviewers influenced by their own cultural rules and identity may misjudge candidates.

A more subtle bias can occur where interviewees do not conform to stereotypes. A British study found that, when selection interviewers assessed matched samples of male and female career applicants, they judged them by different criteria according to their gender. The applicants were penalized if they did not conform to gender stereotypes. Focusing on successes was very important in assessing the men but almost ignored in assessing the women; women, but not men, who self-deprecatingly took responsibility for poor performance ('I should have worked harder') were rated highly;

Box 8.1

X was interviewing Czech applicants for a graduate-level entry post with the Prague subsidiary of an international business. The applicant was neatly dressed, polite and soft-spoken. The CV showed a record of high scholastic achievement, participation in sports and leadership in student affairs. However, when it came to the 'standard' selection interview questions, although the applicant listened carefully and seemed to understand them, X found it difficult to get the kinds of answers he was used to. For example, in response to the question 'What are your greatest strengths?' the candidate hesitated, laughed, blushed, then said, 'I'm not sure. I am very interested in working for your company because it has such a good reputation.' When X pressed, saying, 'Yes, but what could you bring to our company? Why should I give the job to you instead of someone else?' the interviewee said, 'I am hardworking and I would be a loyal worker, but, of course, I'm sure all the other applicants would, too.' Asked about ambitions, the candidate replied, 'To have interesting work and to serve my country.' Asked about a hypothetical situation in which a factory production problem had led to a chaotic disruption of deliveries to customers, the candidate said, 'I would need more information before I could answer, really.' Asked about the most important factors in business success, the candidate answered, 'Solving problems creatively, being concerned for the well-being of others, being flexible.'

Based on: author's research

men were favoured for giving long answers, women for short; women who gave sideways glances, looked at the floor, cocked their heads and nodded when the interviewer talked were preferred, whereas men who faced the interviewer head on did better. Loud voice was preferred in both genders – this was the only similarity. The researcher said she hoped that the research findings would help to prevent employers from 'taking against a talented woman just because she doesn't act demurely enough'.[8] Another study showed experimentally that even selection interviewers who avoid discriminating may be biased. White undergraduate experimental subjects who acted as selection interviewers appointed Black and White applicants in equal proportion. However, a week later they recalled the Black interviewees as giving less intelligent answers, although they had actually given the same answers.[9]

Earlier in this book, it was shown how violations of expectations may disproportionately influence responses to different others. This applies to both interviewers and candidates. In the case of candidates, their expectations in an interview are likely to be influenced by the normal approach taken in their home country. 'The recruitment process is largely determined by the conventions and legislation requirements of the country in which it takes place. In Greece, the culture of recruitment and selection seems to sanction a greater degree of inquisitiveness about personal circumstances, than in the UK. Questions may be asked about family background and origins, marriage – questions which would be technically illegal and to which candidates could exercise a "right to lie" elsewhere in the [European] Community.'[10]

There are significant cultural differences in selection interviewee behaviour, especially in the aspect of self-presentation or impression management, which has been shown to unduly influence interviewers. To avoid bias, intercultural selection interviewers should be aware of and allow for cultural differences in candidates' approach to being interviewed. This applies both to the questions asked and the evaluation of the answers.

8.2 SERVICE ENCOUNTERS

For service providers, who include cashiers, food servers, bank tellers, receptionists, call centre workers, physicians, lawyers, counsellors, hairdressers, flight attendants, teachers, consultants, investment brokers, insurance brokers and more, interacting with the public either face-to-face or by telephone is a central part of their role. While in some cases their functions may include personal selling, the service provision encounter itself is distinct.

Cultural differences in service encounters

Early service quality research posited that service quality is the gap or difference between 'perceptions and expectations'.[11] Both expectations and perceptions of received service quality were found to be influenced by cultural norms, according to a study of factors in tourism consumption.[12] From a cross-cultural survey in which consumers in Quebec and Peru evaluated the quality of supermarket services, four culture value orientations were expected to account for differences in perceived service quality: individualism, collectivism, monochronic time and polychronic time. The findings on these dimensions were not clear-cut, but other clear differences were found: responsiveness of the service supplier to their requests was the most important dimension for Quebecers while tangibles associated with the service was the most important for Peruvians.[13] Other research that tested service quality perceptions and satisfaction within what is often labelled a regional culture (high-context Confucianism) concluded that even within the region 'one size does not fit all' in terms of service offerings. In this study scenarios involving dental services were used to investigate whether Asian cultures were similar enough to allow standardization of service offerings. The findings yielded significant cultural differences, with the Chinese respondents perceiving higher service quality and expressing greater customer satisfaction when performance was high and expressing less customer satisfaction when performance was low than the Japanese and Korean respondents.[14] Another study using data from China and the United States showed that the cultural congruency of benefits emphasized by the service provider affected consumers' evaluations of service quality.[15]

Cultural elements have the greatest influence when services involve a high degree of interaction between customers and service personnel. In contrast to the negative finding on cultural value orientations and relatively impersonal supermarket services given in the paragraph above, when service quality of high-interaction services was measured in terms of reliability, responsiveness, assurance, empathy and tangibles, it was found that every service quality dimension concern of consumers was influenced by every cultural value dimension. For instance, significant positive relationships were found between uncertainty avoidance and concern with responsiveness, assurance and empathy and a relatively strong negative relationship between uncertainty avoidance and tangibles (probably because tangibles do not reduce the perceived risk of the service failing). Significant negative relationships were found between power distance and the perceived importance of empathy, responsiveness and reliability. This may be because, in cultures with a large power distance, weak customers are more likely to tolerate failure from more powerful service providers. Positive relationships were, however, found between power distance and tangibles. Probably because tangibles help to maintain distance, which in such cultures is both desired and expected, they are important in the service quality evaluation process of low-power customers.[16] In the context of business-to-business relationships, a study involving 303 Spanish, German and Swedish business-to-business service customers revealed that clients from cultures with a high degree of uncertainty avoidance were less satisfied than low-uncertainty avoidant clients when, as a result of a service defect, their service expectations were not met. The finding suggests a narrower range of acceptable outcomes for high-uncertainty avoidance cultures.[17]

On subcultural differences, a study examined whether men and women respond differently to positive and negative affective displays (smiles or scowls) by the service provider in brief, mundane service encounters. In this study women were less satisfied than men with negative emotional displays during an otherwise smooth service exchange. Conversely, when there were process failures, displays of negative feelings from the service provider had a 'double whammy' impact on male participants' satisfaction ratings but less so on those of women.[18]

Effective intercultural service provision

Findings from an exploratory qualitative study showed that the intercultural competence and perceived cultural distance of the service provider influenced the purchasers' comfort levels during the interaction, their expectations regarding adequate service levels, their perceptions of the actual received service level and their satisfaction.[19] Most empirical studies on intercultural service effectiveness, however, have concerned recovery from service failures. For instance, in an (experimental) study of factors affecting recovery by the service provider following a service failure, the impact of two recovery attributes (compensation and explanation) on customers' post-recovery perceptions were examined in a cross-cultural context (East Asia versus the United States). Offering an explanation for the failure had a positive impact on customer perceptions regardless of the customer's cultural orientation, and perceived fairness was directly and cross-culturally linked to post-recovery satisfaction. On the other hand, compensation seemed to drive customers' fairness perceptions to a greater extent with American than East Asian consumers.[20]

> Expectations and perceptions of received service quality are influenced by cultural norms, especially when high levels of interpersonal contact are required for the service. Some methods of recovery from service failures, however, appear to be effective cross-culturally, though others do not.

8.3 MENTORING

Mentoring generally refers to a senior and experienced member of the staff of an organization providing information, advice and support for a junior person. Research in several private firms and public service agencies revealed seven types of mentor assistance that were particularly helpful. These were: helping a person to shift her or his mental context, listening when the mentoree had a problem, identifying mentoree feelings and verifying them, effectively confronting negative intentions or behaviour, providing appropriate information when needed, delegating authority or giving permission and encouraging exploration of options.[21] A question arises, however, over the feasibility of some of these kinds of mentor assistance in the intercultural situation.

The mentoring relationship is intended to last over an extended period. While mentoring may be particularly beneficial for women and members of minorities, by giving the kind of support that may help them overcome the obstacles caused by prejudice, there is evidence that in fact it is White males who are most often given the most practical help. A study found that, while women and members of ethnic minorities received about the same level of mentoring help as White males, it differed in type. The help given to White males was mostly instrumental (for instance, career advice or contacts) while that given to the minority groups was mostly socio-emotional. This was mainly because of who mentored whom. White male mentors gave the same kind of instrumental help to all kinds of mentorees, but mainly mentored White males. Women and members of ethnic minorities were more likely to be mentored by women or ethnic minority members, who gave predominantly socio-emotional help.[22]

Cultural differences in mentoring

Five phases of the mentoring process are influenced by cultural values, according to Murphy and Ensher (1997): (a) attraction leading to the establishment of a mentoring relationship; (b) contracting, the definition of roles and the evaluation of costs and benefits for mentor and mentoree; (c) growth in trust and sharing of information through increased contact; (d) maturation, the stabilization of the relationship through value congruence; and (e) transition, the decision to end the relationship or move it to a different level, such as informal friendship.[23]

There are cultural differences in the expectations of different ethnic groups in regard to mentoring. For instance, culturally, Asian mentor-like relationships differ from their Western counterparts in that they are much more formally hierarchical and they blur the distinction between family and social ties. Formal language and titles, deference and other forms of reverence are expected between junior and senior peers. Asian personnel may not seek guidance and nurturance actively; instead, they expect the person with the greater power to initiate this. Asian mentorees are likely to be concerned about not taking up too much of the mentor's time. As a result, they may quickly usher themselves out of the office. This fear of being a burden is detrimental to an effective mentoring relationship.[24]

In the view of Osula and Irvin (2009), individualist cultural tendencies like those found in the USA and Great Britain cause mentors generally to prefer focusing on task accomplishment, such as starting and ending meetings on time, whereas collectivism focuses on relationship building. Ingroup collectivism also affects trust between individuals. Trust is foundational to the mentoring relationship as a whole. Individualists tend to be universalistic in their willingness to trust people and give them the benefit of the doubt. Collectivists, on the other hand, tend to be particularistic, extending trust only to those from within their ingroup. Trust must be earned slowly by consistency of character and by proof of benevolence. Harmony is a key value for collectivists. Personal confrontation is normally considered rude, and communication can be very indirect. A mentoree from a collectivist country will normally not dare to contradict his or her mentor, but may express agreement that does not imply – from the mentoree's perspective – any real commitment. People from individualist countries, on the other

---

Box 8.2

There's a lot of interest in mentoring training here at the moment. There's a problem in that mentors tend to think that the way they got there is the right way for every mentoree. They don't listen and they do lecture.

Source: interview with an HRM Consultant, India, author's research

hand, believe that speaking the truth openly, even if it causes conflict, is both virtuous and healthy. While low power-distance mentors may enjoy lively interchanges and disagreements, high power distance may produce an aversion to disagreeing with a superior, which can constrain open discussion.[25]

Effective intercultural mentoring

Crosby (1999) argued that issues of trust, comfort and rapport are central to intercultural mentoring. 'Some people might more readily act as instrumental sponsors than as psychosocial confidants for someone who differs from them on important dimensions of identity. Similarly, junior people may feel more suspicious of and behave more awkwardly around senior people who differ from them than around senior people who resemble them. Because most senior people in organizations today are still ... men, insisting on the close emotional bond between a mentor and a protégé as the only vehicle for career advancement may unwittingly serve to reinforce the ... old boys' network.'[26] Mentorees from some cultural or social backgrounds need to be taught the meaning and functions of assertiveness, encouraged to ask questions and express opinions. Similarly, mentors should be educated about the meanings of silence and learn not to interpret the absence of questions and suggestions to mean that neither problems nor ambitions exist. Mentors should not dismiss or trivialize a mentoree's emphasis on race, gender or class (as by saying 'You're focusing on class too much,' or 'You're looking at this through a class lens'). Mentors should help mentorees to make contacts and to network. The mentorees may not know how to go about it (how to introduce themselves to important figures in the field, how to remind someone that they've met before). 'The oppressed learn their place very well; even the most independent of persons knows the line.'[27] Mentorees from lower social classes may not ask how to go about doing something that everyone assumes they know how to do. They will not necessarily ask, because it can be humiliating to have to ask what you 'should' already know, such as whether a gathering is in semi-formal or casual dress, how to make small talk with guest speakers or how to contact a senior manager. Mentors should be prepared to talk with mentorees about things that they assume other junior employees know.[28]

Osula and Irvin (2009) proposed that intercultural mentoring effectiveness is a function of the mentor's and the mentoree's general cultural awareness, their cultural self-awareness and their situation-specific awareness.[29] These authors also suggested the possibility of an intercultural learning agenda in which both mentoree and mentor first learn more about each other's cultural expectations before finalizing their mentoring agreement. While this awareness of the other is commonly expected (if not always delivered) in foreign situations, such as the preparation of expatriates, diplomats or missionaries for overseas postings, its relevance for domestic situations may be even more significant and affect a broad range of issues related to diversity and the work environment. Osula and Irvin (2009) further suggested the value of cultural awareness in the mentoring relationship, leading to a 'third culture' perspective, as described in Section 6.4.[30]

> Cultural differences affect mentorees' expectations of the mentoring relationship and their communication behaviour during mentoring sessions as well as the basis for trust. Intercultural mentors should allow for (sub)cultural differences in the kind of support the mentoree needs and in their willingness to ask for help.

8.4 MEDIATING

Mediation has been defined as follows: 'Efforts by parties external to an immediate conflict, with no advance commitment by the conflicting parties to accept the mediator's ideas, which seek to bring about a settlement or resolution acceptable to both sides.'[31] Third parties can get round misperceptions, perceptions of threat and miscommunication. Mediators aim to understand each party's perceptions of the other party and the situation.[32] In some (collectivist) cultures, third-party mediation is almost a standard approach to conflict resolution. Where that applies, using a mediator may be the best strategy. Carnevale and Choi (2000) suggested that in this way culture could play a positive role in the mediation of international disputes. 'Cultural ties between the mediator and one or both of the disputants can facilitate mediation by, among other things, enhancing the mediator's acceptability to the parties, and enhancing the belief that the mediator can deliver concessions and agreements. Moreover, a mediator who is closer to one side than the other can be effective in mediation, especially when the mediator acts in an even-handed manner.'[33] Data from laboratory research on mediation, as well as anecdotal evidence, supported this view.

As Chapter 3 described, there are cultural and gender-based differences in how conflicts are usually conducted, which have implications for how mediators should proceed. One study of mediation itself found gender differences: females used more clarifying and males used more controlling formulations.[34]

Effective intercultural mediation

All mediators confront three issues: the matter of impartiality, how to deal with the emotional and psychological dimensions of conflict in the mediation process and how to ensure that mediation empowers the participants rather than disempowering them.

■ Mediators must be and be seen to be impartial. Impartiality means giving equal respect to the parties involved and treating them with equal fairness. All the parties concerned need to trust the mediator. If one of the parties perceives the mediator as biased, they will probably withdraw or disrupt the process in some way. To be seen as impartial, mediators emphasize 'good process' and technical impartiality. This refers to the mediator's ability to treat all people with respect, manage the mediation process in a way that is fair and even-handed, listen deeply to what each party is saying, identify deeper emotions and needs, and, through skilful paraphrasing, determine whether each party has been adequately understood by all.
■ The emotional aspects of conflict can lead to conflicts being recycled. 'A mediation session produces an outcome. Both parties seem relieved and satisfied. A few months later, however, the same parties are in conflict again. Different issues appear on the agenda, but with strong indications that the conflict is deriving its energy from the same deep emotional storage tanks.'[35] Mediation should not be terminated once a superficial settlement is achieved. Solutions sought on the level of, for instance, pay packages and disciplinary procedures do not make anger go away. To deal with the emotional aspects of conflict, mediators need to be in touch with their own feelings and recognize their own prejudices. Training to be a mediator can therefore never be only about acquiring technical skills; it has at the same time also to be about personal growth and maturity.
■ Mediation has the potential to create greater equality in power relationships. It can empower the relatively disempowered. (This fact, however, creates a dilemma, because it is precisely its potential to equalize relationships that raises suspicions in

people who have power.) The deepest form of empowerment takes place when the knowledge and skills necessary for constructive conflict resolution are transferred in a way that enhances participants' understanding.

Successful mediation does not always result in resolving conflict. Partial success may be recognized when there is a decrease in the level of conflict intensity and an increase in useful communications between the parties, or when there is 'de-escalation in the means of struggle, negotiations that move toward an agreed-upon settlement and a settlement that contributes to an enduring resolution'.[36]

A basic assumption of much literature on international conflict, mediation and social psychology is that the process of mediation can modify the stereotypes or images that conflicting parties hold of each other; this change, it is argued, facilitates settlement. Three case studies of international conflicts found support for this assumption. The conflicts studied were the Israeli–Egyptian conflict from 1973 to 1979, the conflict between Greek and Turkish Cypriots from 1979 to 1983 and the Iran–Iraq war from 1980 to 1985. In the one case (Egypt–Israel) where resolution was reached, images did change in a way that correlated with mediation efforts over time. In the two cases (Cyprus, Iran–Iraq) where no resolution was obtained, no image change occurred.

Leading authorities on intercultural mediation advocate a non-directive approach. This approach assumes that the best solutions are produced when parties listen to each other in a new way, co-operate in generating options and jointly arrive at the preferred solution. There should be no form of coercion or manipulation by the mediators. The parties must solve their own problems, because in this way their self-respect is served and the outcome is more sustainable. The role of the mediator is, therefore, to be a facilitator of communication. The mediator's task is to enable the parties to listen to each other on a deeper level than their previous hostile attitudes allowed. A mediator must ensure that the parties have heard each other adequately, and that each has developed sufficient understanding of the other's perceptions, motivations and interests. The mediators rely heavily on their listening, paraphrasing and summarizing skills, checking continuously whether people have been correctly understood. Improved listening then leads to better mutual understanding, which strengthens the drive to reach a solution that takes the interests of all parties into consideration.

Non-directive mediation uses a basic procedure. This procedure includes the parties themselves establishing procedural ground rules, allowing ample time for digressions, ensuring uninterrupted time for each side to state their perceptions and feelings, and joint problem-solving. Non-directive mediation is highly appropriate in situations where parties need to co-operate in future because the level of interdependence is high, and especially where conflicts are fuelled by basic differences in values or world views. Under such conditions the emphasis of mediation on promoting mutual understanding and on improving relationships is to be preferred over approaches that rely on arbitration or coercion.

Culture influences the acceptability of mediation of disputes: it may be more readily accepted in collectivist than individualist cultures. In intercultural conflicts, particularly where the parties will need to co-operate in future, mediators can get round misperceptions, perceptions of threat and miscommunication. Being and being seen to be impartial, dealing effectively with participants' emotions and empowering them are key issues for mediators. To ensure that the parties understand one another, mediators need high levels of listening, paraphrasing and summarizing skills.

8.5 NEGOTIATING

Negotiation is the process by which two or more parties attempt to resolve a perceived divergence of interest.[37]

Cultural differences in negotiation

Intercultural negotiations, whether international or not, are affected by cultural differences in negotiators' behaviour, goals, communication patterns, perceptions, values and norms. Individualism–collectivism is an important dimension of these differences. For instance, a study found, Canadians negotiated by exchanging information, aiming to encourage the other side also to exchange information expeditiously; the Japanese, however, attempted to develop a smooth, harmonious relationship that would eventually facilitate consensual decision-making; exchanging information was secondary. Canadians were concerned about time efficiency; this led them to focus on points of disagreement in an attempt to resolve them. For the Japanese, taking time to create a relationship was seen as a sign of wisdom and sincerity; focusing on disagreements was disliked as undermining harmony. Canadians did not value strong interpersonal relationships in business and relied on legal contracts to define future relationships; for the Japanese, legal contracts were not acceptable substitutes for interpersonal trust. Canadians and Japanese also tended to have a different view of the purpose of negotiations. Canadians saw the goal of negotiations as to produce a binding contract that creates specific rights and obligations. The Japanese saw the goal of negotiations as to create a relationship between the two parties; the written contract is simply an expression of that relationship. What the Japanese saw as a reasonable willingness to modify a contract to reflect changes in the parties' relationship, Canadians saw as a tendency to renege. The Japanese may have perceived Canadian insistence on adherence to the original terms of the contract as distrust.[38]

Other negotiator differences are based in concepts of time, power distance or universalism/particularism. Negotiators such as North Americans and West Europeans, who hold monochronic concepts of time, are more likely to process issues sequentially and to negotiate in a highly organized fashion. In contrast, negotiators with polychronic conceptions of time, such as Asians, Africans, South Americans and Middle Easterners, are more likely to process issues simultaneously. They tend to ignore conversational turn-taking, instead speaking simultaneously and using frequent interruptions. North Americans have been shown to regard their option of ending a negotiation as a source of power, whereas Japanese think of power as based on roles (for example, buyer versus seller).[39] 'Some cultures prefer to start from agreement on general principles, while others prefer to address each issue individually. Some cultures prefer to negotiate by "building up" from an initial minimum proposal; others prefer to "build-down" from a more comprehensive opening proposal. Cultural differences also show up in the preferred pacing of negotiations and in decision-making styles.'[40]

In addition to the general differences in values and norms that have been described earlier in this book, some specifically negotiation-related norms and values differ across cultures. Salacuse (1998) gave a taxonomy based on a literature review and interviews with practitioners. It contained the following ten items:

1. Negotiating goals: contract or relationship?
2. Negotiating attitude: win/lose or win/win?
3. Personal style: formal or informal?
4. Communication: direct or indirect?
5. Sensitivity to time: high or low?
6. Emotionalism: high or low?

7. Forms of agreement: general or specific?
8. Building an agreement: bottom-up or top-down?
9. Team organization: one leader or group consensus?
10. Risk-taking: high or low?[41]

A comparison of cultural tendencies in negotiation in Finland, India, Turkey, Mexico and the USA established the utility of the Salacuse framework in identifying significant country differences in negotiation orientations both between and within cultures; these were revealed 'at a level of complexity not found in previous empirical studies'.[42]

Despite the findings on cultural difference, however, it is important not to see negotiators' behaviour as culturally determined. Negotiations 'are affected not only by culture but by contextual constraints, such as negotiator personality, organizational culture, age, prior relationship, experience, presence of interpreters, intercultural competence of the negotiators, countries' legal and economic systems, and roles'.[43] Research in which negotiation interactions were coded for information sharing, offers and distributive tactics showed that the more collectivist the orientation of a negotiation dyad, the higher its joint profit. However, culture had no direct effect on competitiveness or information exchange; it did affect the level of fixed-pie errors (the tendency to assume that one side's gain must be the other side's loss). The strongest effect found, though, was that seller collectivism had larger and more consistent effects on communication behaviour and joint profit than buyer collectivism.[44]

Box 8.3

By surveying both Pakistani negotiators and those from other cultures who regularly negotiated with Pakistanis, Rammal (2005) found that the following Pakistani cultural factors influenced intercultural negotiations with them: centralized decision-making, relationship building and attitudes to time; contrary to expectations, the findings did not confirm the need for agents, an emphasis on structured negotiations or a preference for indirect communication.

Centralized decision-making: especially when the negotiations were conducted in Pakistan, the Chief Executive Officer (CEO) took part in the negotiations, whereas in most countries their involvement took place after all or most issues had been settled by lower-level executives. This presence of the CEO reduced the number of adjournments and delays to refer back.

Relationship building: a significant majority of the Pakistani respondents stated that they took time to evaluate the other party in order to build trust and confidence. One particular respondent said: 'During the first meeting an assessment can be made of the other party regarding its seriousness to do business, the way they would like to negotiate, quality of the product, and how much mutual trust and confidence can be built.'

Attitudes to time: Pakistani negotiators expected negotiations to proceed more quickly than their Japanese counterparts, they reported, but more slowly than European or American negotiators.

Need for agents: contrary to earlier assertions, Pakistanis did not usually use agents except when dealing with countries, like Japan, where direct negotiations are unacceptably prolonged.

Structured negotiations: except for three respondents, who stated that rules were agreed upon before face-to-face negotiations began, all the respondents stated that no such rules or procedures were agreed upon.

Direct versus indirect communication: the findings on this topic were weak, no clear pattern emerging, even though this is generally considered a major difference between cultures both in negotiations and more generally.

Source: Rammal, H.G. (2005) 'International business negotiations: the case of Pakistan', *International Journal Of Commerce And Management,* **15**(2): 129–40

Effective intercultural negotiation

In experimental research, intercultural negotiators usually achieve worse joint outcomes than intracultural negotiators. A combination of power struggle, focus on self-interest and insufficient information sharing may produce this effect. However, negotiators who are motivated to search for information, and are flexible about how that search is carried out, can reach high-quality outcomes in intercultural negotiations.[45] When negotiations expose differences on culture-based norms and values, not only can conflict be triggered, but also the negotiators are likely to experience negative moods and emotions. On the other hand, when expectations in these areas match, they can lead to positive feelings helpful to the negotiation process.[46]

Negotiators have mental models of negotiations in terms of such dimensions as relationship versus task, co-operation versus winning, and emotional versus intellectual appeals. These models, or frames, often mutually influence each other, converging during the interaction. In turn, the frames affect individual and joint monetary outcomes, as well as satisfaction with the outcomes. The other party's frame influences each negotiator's behaviour. One negotiating party sends messages that communicate the frame. In return, the responding negotiator sends messages adopting, rejecting or modifying this frame. Then a short period of initial interaction solidifies the mental models of the negotiators, resulting in a script that carries through the negotiation. When the parties do not come to a common model of the interaction, the negotiation is much more likely to result in impasse or widely disparate payoffs than when a single model is shared, regardless of how the shared model defines the interaction. This communication, which supports harmonization of mental models, is a key factor in intercultural negotiation.[47]

Again, while differences between cultural 'scripts' can create conflict over procedure, differences in preferences present opportunities for compromise. For example, cultures that differ in their perceptions of risk can create value by sharing risks and benefits proportionately but asymmetrically. One side can assume more risk, and have a chance of gaining more benefit, than the other. Because of their different risk preferences, both sides gain from this. Moreover, it can be effective to balance the cultural preferences of both sides. For instance, if one party's cultural preference is to develop relationships and the other's is to exchange information, they can follow a procedure that begins by developing relationships with others, then leads to exchanging information about the topics under negotiation. Balance might also be reached by recognizing multicultural techniques of persuasion and also emphasizing the role of concessions in achieving agreement. However, there is as yet no evidence that an individual negotiator can transcend his or her own cultural background.[48]

Box 8.4

Negotiations are central to the functioning and dynamic development of the European Union. Historically, force, equilibrium or hegemony have underscored regional integration schemes in Europe, but, in contrast, the European Union is a voluntarily agreed arrangement of sovereign or semi-sovereign states that solve their conflicts by means of non-coercive negotiations. Due to its complex structure, the EU encourages the formation of networks, and negotiation is the most important vehicle for establishing and keeping these networks in operation.

Source: Pfetsch, F.R. (1998) 'Negotiating the European Union: a negotiation-network approach', *International Negotiation Journal*, 3(3): 293–317

There are cultural differences in negotiators' behaviour, goals, communication patterns, perceptions, values and norms. While these differences can lead to conflict, cultural differences in preferences present opportunities for mutually satisfying procedures and outcomes. Communication, which makes harmonization of mental models possible, is a key factor in intercultural negotiation.

8.6 WORKING IN GROUPS AND TEAMS

This section considers the effect of cultural difference and diversity both on decision-making (problem-solving) groups and on teams entrusted with carrying out a project or performing a function; it also considers how to increase intercultural groupwork and teamwork effectiveness.

Cultural differences in groupwork and teams

It is no surprise that the processes at work in complex work decision settings are influenced by cultural factors. Culture affects participants' experience of variable decision situations, how predictable the environment is and how great the level of power distance is. In turn, these variables affect how group members approach decision-making. For example, in a complex decision task, German managers used different decision-making processes from Indian managers, even though the latter worked in modern technological industries. Specifically, though both groups performed equally well, the German managers achieved their results with comparatively few but 'strong' decisions. The Indian managers achieved their results with many small steps. The researchers commented that both the 'massive' German and the 'incremental' Indian approach appear to be effective in their respective economic environments. Highly unpredictable economic environments, such as those in India, meant it made sense to start with some small steps, closely monitor the effects and then gradually increase the size of decisions in those avenues that had proved reliable. In a more predictable environment, such as the German, probable outcomes of decisions could be anticipated and there was less risk involved in making strong decisions. The German and Indian decision-making styles might also be related to cultural differences in power distance. 'Large power distance could be related to cautious and defensive decision making whereas small power distance should work in the direction of risk-taking and assertiveness.'[49] Ethnic differences within nations are also associated with behavioural differences, and these, too, affect group outcomes. Groups composed of people from collectivist ethnic backgrounds co-operated more on a choice-based dilemma task than groups composed of people from an individualist ethnic background.

As with groupwork, so with teams: in different cultural contexts, different patterns of expectations arise concerning team roles, scope, membership and objectives. At a general level, it is true, most definitions of a team are likely to include what a team does and for whom it does it, the scope of its activity, who is on the team (roles), why (the nature of membership, especially whether voluntary or compulsory), and the reason why the team exists (its goals and objectives). However, the specific content of what people mean by teamwork varies across cultures. This can be revealed by the metaphors they use. For instance, if the national context is individualistic, then sports or club metaphors are more likely to resonate than those that imply a broader activity scope. An emphasis on tight control in the culture means that a military or family metaphor is likely to resonate.[50]

Box 8.5

A network study of the management team of a 50–50 German–Japanese international joint venture found that national culture, though not statistically significant, was important in explaining patterns of relationships in the team but was less direct and deterministic than suggested by previous research.

Source: Salk, J.E. and Brannen, M.Y. (2000) 'National culture, networks, and individual influence in a multinational management team', Academy of Management Journal, 43(2): 191–202

Effective intercultural groups and teams

Given such cultural differences in approaches to group decision-making and teamwork, it is not surprising that diversity affects group and teamwork outcomes. A study found that different percentages of various diversity categories affected group effectiveness. The diversity categories were gender, ethnic minority and persons with disabilities. The measures of effectiveness were perceived commitment, overall effectiveness, satisfaction, cohesion, trust, equal opportunity climate, and quality. The gender and ethnic minority categories showed increases in perceived workgroup effectiveness at the 11–30 per cent diversity level. This implies that a low level of diversity is not only tolerated but may even be welcomed. As the mix exceeded 30 per cent, however, perceptions of group effectiveness declined, except for groups with women, which showed a slightly higher level of effectiveness up to 50 per cent diversity. Apparently, as the proportion of a minority increases in a workgroup beyond 30 per cent (50 per cent for women), there is potential for tension and conflict. (The category of persons with disabilities was an exception in which perceived performance exhibited an almost linear decline as the percentage increased without the 'blip' that other diversity subgroups manifested at 11 to 30 per cent.[51])

In terms of objective, as opposed to perceived, measures, there are findings that moderately strong demographic subgroups in teams fostered learning behaviour. 'Subgroup strength' was defined as the degree of overlap across multiple demographic characteristics. In other words, where teams included a variety of subgroups, each composed of demographically similar individuals, team learning was enhanced.[52] Another study found that the effects of national diversity on business expansion decision-making by teams were to increase how long it took to reach the decisions, the number of options considered and the attractiveness of international expansion options. Homogeneous national teams (Canadian) ranked home expansion options as significantly more attractive than nationally diverse teams did.[53]

Findings that diverse workgroups sometimes do but sometimes do not outperform homogeneous workgroups has led to theorizing and research about why. One leading explanation is that, instead of using the workgroup itself as the relevant ingroup, members of diverse workgroups treat their demographically or functionally similar co-members as their ingroup and the other members of the workgroup as outgroups. This reasoning suggests that inducing group members 'to replace cross-cutting demographic or functional categories with the inclusive workgroup boundary as the basis for social categorization will reduce the detrimental effects of intergroup biases'.[54] Another approach is to induce group members to re-evaluate their beliefs and expectations about cultural diversity itself and its role in their workgroup.[55]

Effects of different types of diversity

Noting that the previous research on the effect of cultural diversity in teams was equivocal, Stahl *et al.* (2010) examined whether the level (surface-level versus deep-level) and type (cross-national versus intranational) of cultural diversity have different effects on the process losses and gains associated with increased divergence and decreased convergence. They tested hypotheses that task complexity and aspects of the team such as its size, duration and dispersion moderated the effects of cultural diversity on teams. The test was a meta-analysis of 108 empirical studies on processes and performance in 10,632 teams. They found that cultural diversity led to process losses through task conflict and decreased social integration, but to process gains through increased creativity and satisfaction. No significant differences were, however, found for different types or levels of diversity.[56]

Other analyses of the performance effects of diversity also distinguish different types. One such differentiated values, cognitions and demeanours as types of nationality-based diversity that differentially affected group effectiveness according to the type of group task. The types of task were creative tasks such as generating strategies; computational tasks that were likely to involve rather clear-cut data collection, analysis and solution generation; and co-ordination tasks involving elaborate interaction among group members. Table 8.2 summarizes this analysis. Thus, as Table 8.2 suggests, where the task explicitly favours multinational inputs or where there are only as many nationalities or cultures represented as needed for the task, the benefits of diversity outweigh the costs. In other cases, the reverse will apply, as, for example, if a German company with substantial experience in an industry was attempting to replicate its recent success in Spain with an entry into Portugal. The management team could benefit from consisting of one or more Germans, Spaniards and Portuguese. Any additional nationalities would be beyond what is expressly needed for the task and would be a liability.[57]

A field study of diversity, conflict and performance in 92 workgroups lent support to the idea that some types of diversity may be beneficial and others harmful

Table 8.2   *Effects of type of diversity and type of group task on group effectiveness*

Type of diversity	Type of group task		
	Creative	Computational	Co-ordinative
Values	Positive – varied perspectives stimulate creativity	Neutral	Negative – can create interpersonal strains and mistrust
Cognitions	Positive – varied knowledge helps refine alternatives	Positive up to the point where all the knowledge needed for the task is available; beyond that point, neutral	Positive up to the point where the knowledge needed for the task is available; beyond that point, negative
Demeanours (e.g. punctuality norms, conversational style)	Moderately negative – can create interpersonal strains and mistrust	Weakly negative – objective nature reduces strains	Strongly negative – most affected by communication failures

Based on: Hambrick, D.C. (1998) 'When groups consist of multiple nationalities: towards a new understanding of the implications', *Organization Studies*, **19**(2): 181–206

to workgroups. Informational diversity positively influenced group performance but value diversity decreased satisfaction, intent to remain and commitment to the group. (Readers should note that in this study 'values' referred, not to cultural values, but to what group members thought the group's real task, goal, target or mission should be.)

Values differences led to task conflict – disagreements about task content, such as over what kinds of advertising to undertake. They also led to process conflicts – disagreements about delegation and resource allocation. For instance, group members who valued effectiveness (e.g., quality) were likely to have disagreements about resource allocation with group members who valued efficiency (e.g., units produced). In addition, similarity in group members' goals and values enhanced interpersonal relations within the group. Most importantly for this book, the study found that social category diversity (age and gender) positively influenced group members' satisfaction, intent to remain, perceived performance and commitment, even though it also resulted in increased conflict. This finding runs counter to both conventional wisdom and past research. One explanation seems to be that high performance leads to high morale and low task conflict rather than that low task conflict leads to high morale and high performance. Diverse groups performed better and perhaps, therefore, were more pleased with the group in which they were working. Thus, this study found that teams were more effective when their members had high information diversity and low value diversity, more efficient when their members had low value diversity and had higher morale (higher satisfaction, intent to remain and commitment) when their members had high social category diversity and low value diversity. 'It is the diversity associated with values, and not social category, that causes the biggest problems in and has the greatest potential for enhancing both workgroup performance and morale.'[58]

Informational diversity is more likely to lead to improved performance when tasks are non-routine. Again, social category diversity unexpectedly led to greater satisfaction and commitment when task interdependence was high than when it was low. It may actually be that social category diversity results in higher morale in interdependent tasks. Being able to work together successfully, even when the group is diverse with respect to age and gender composition, may result in greater morale because the group has overcome a serious challenge to its effectiveness. Further, these groups may have discovered that the social category differences were not good signals of value diversity.

Box 8.6

A contrarian view on cultural difference in workgroups is that 'cultural diversity' and 'national culture' are used by group members as discursive resources in everyday group life. Barinaga (2007) followed an international project group for over 17 months, observing how group members discussed and made sense of what went on. Findings suggested that the way members in international project groups used the 'national/cultural' discourse played a crucial role in the organization of the project. More specifically, results demonstrated that group members shaped and developed their international project in important ways by using the discourses on 'national culture' and 'cultural diversity' to excuse confusion and misunderstanding, to position themselves vis-à-vis the group, to justify decisions and to give the group a raison d'être. Actors, the researcher concluded, have and use 'space for choice' in group-life. They are not 'dopes of their culture'.

Source: Barinaga, E. (2007) 'Cultural diversity at work: "national culture" as a discourse organizing an international project group', *Human Relations*, **60**(2): 315–40

Another study explored the relations among workgroup diversity, two kinds of conflict within the group (task and emotional) and task performance. (This study concerned non-routine tasks performed by relatively newly formed groups.) In task conflict, group members disagree about task issues, including goals, key decision areas, procedures and the appropriate choice for action. In emotional conflict, group members have interpersonal clashes characterized by anger, frustration and other negative feelings. 'We suggest that job-related types of diversity largely drive task conflict.'[59]

Task conflict was positive for performance, fostering a deeper understanding of task issues and an exchange of information that facilitated problem-solving, decision-making, and the generation of ideas; functional background diversity was the key driver of task conflict, while diversity in race, gender, age and tenure within the group were related to task conflict, but not to a statistically significant degree. In contrast to task-related conflict, 'Emotional conflict is shaped by a complex web of diversity types that increase emotional conflict based on stereotyping and decrease emotional conflict based on social comparison.' Dissimilarity in ethnicity and tenure increased emotional conflict and tended to encourage heated interactions in workgroups. On the other hand, age dissimilarity decreased emotional conflict in workgroups, probably because age similarity triggers social comparison. Age is a career-related attribute, so employees tend to measure their own career progress by looking at that of co-workers in their age cohort. When age similarity in a group increases, these comparisons of career progress, which prompt jealous rivalry, often increase. This study found no effect of gender on emotional conflict in workgroups, though other studies have found important effects of gender heterogeneity on workgroup outcomes, including reduced performance on cognitive tasks, reduced cross-gender support, and increased within-gender support.[60] The study found no evidence that emotional conflict impaired performance. This may be because 'While relationship troubles cause great dissatisfaction, the conflicts may not influence work as much as expected, because the members involved in the conflicts choose to avoid working with those with whom they experience [emotional] conflict.'[61]

Environmental influences on diversity and groupwork effectiveness

The work environment plays a significant part in determining how well diverse workgroups function. An important aspect of that environment is the perspective on workforce diversity itself that predominates in the workgroup and with its manager. A study distinguished an integration-and-learning perspective (a positive attitude to including and learning from different others), an access-and-legitimacy perspective (different others should have equal rights), and a discrimination-and-fairness perspective (different others can be treated differently but with fairness). The study found that which of these perspectives predominated determined all the following:

- How well a diverse workgroup and its members functioned;
- How people expressed and managed tensions related to diversity;
- Whether members of minority groups felt respected and valued by their colleagues;
- How people interpreted the meaning of their racial identity at work.

Only the integration-and-learning perspective provided the rationale and guidance needed to achieve sustained benefits from diversity.[62]

The organizational culture is another environmental factor in how effective diverse workgroups are. A study showed that diverse co-workers in organizations with collectivist cultures communicated more by memos and less by face-to-face interaction than either diverse co-workers in organizations with individualist cultures or non-diverse co-workers in any kind of organization. Sending memos may be less effective than face-to-face meetings for conveying information and resolving problems. When people are more different from their co-workers they are more reluctant to interact in person, especially when the organizational culture promotes collectivist values. However, no more conflict was found between demographically different co-workers than between demographically similar ones. Also, in a culture that emphasized collective goals, demographically different co-workers were more likely to find conflict beneficial. Workers in individualist organizational cultures were both more likely to experience conflict (probably because their goals and values differed more from each other's) and to find it harmful.[63]

Issues of trust and conflict in multicultural teams

In diverse teams members tend to experience lower levels of trust for and from one another. This is because it is easier for them to share information and interact on the task (or sub-task) with members of their own culture than with members of the other cultural subgroups. However, if someone limits their interaction with members of other cultural subgroups, it becomes difficult for them to know that they can trust them. Thus, lower overall levels of trust result when more cultures are present. Interpersonal conflict can destroy a team. Poor communication, dominant/passive personality clashes, status and rank in the company, as well as cultural differences, can trigger interpersonal friction. Time shortages, power struggles and excessive ego investment, along with different styles and inequitable distribution of tasks, create further problems. Problems with co-ordination and motivation can make teams underperform, while lack of clear boundaries can lead to teams competing instead of co-operating with one another.[64] Moreover, a study published in 2008 found that different interpretations of teamwork and competing legitimacy claims which reflect divergent interests can lead working in teams in itself to reinforce status and power differences. The study was conducted among health professionals in operating theatres, where 'ultimately, the privileged position of surgeons and anaesthetists over nurses and operating department practitioners is legitimated and maintained.'[65]

One kind of team that is used increasingly is the temporary team, in which trust is a particular issue. Temporary teams are groups of people who are brought together to work on important, complex tasks. In these the time for trust to develop between the parties will not usually be available. Typically, such teams are dependent on other teams, but have too little time to determine whether another team has a poor past performance. As Meyerson et al. (1996) stated, in order to trust a temporary group, the members must 'wade in' as opposed to waiting until experience shows whether a team is trustworthy. To manage issues of uncertainty, risk and perceptions, temporary teams develop (or do not develop) 'swift trust'. This is an immediate trust, fostered by the common situation confronting them; it leads to the teams engaging in respectful collaborative efforts to make sense of the situation. Global (and hence intercultural) virtual teams may experience a form of 'swift' trust, but such trust appears to be very fragile and temporary, although it may lead to trusting behaviour that helps build longer-term trust.[66]

In theory, situational cues or influences, not affiliation, will shape team member decision-making preferences in temporary teams. This argument suggests that intercultural temporary teams would be relatively easily able to overcome any cultural difference problems. However, research found that both affiliation and situational characteristics appeared to influence team members. These effects appeared to operate at different points in time, with affiliation effects being stronger initially and attenuating over time, and situational effects possibly becoming more salient towards the end, perhaps partially offsetting the influence of affiliation. In more detail, the findings showed that organizational affiliation influences appeared to drive strategic decision making in early-stage responses, over the needs of the situation; outcome-based learning may have lessened the effect of affiliation in strategic decision-making over time; and, as uncertainty decreased and information about the situation increased, observed affiliation effects dissipated. These findings appear to support long-held assumptions of uncertainty avoidance perspectives driving strategic decision-making preferences in temporary groups.[67]

Other factors affecting multicultural team effectiveness

Language diversity, team composition in status terms, reward structures and the task-capability of minority members are all factors that have been shown to affect how well a multicultural team functions:

■ Language diversity. Building trust and relationships are processes that depend on language. Language diversity has been to shown to have a significant impact on socialization processes and team building, influencing both communication acts and mutual perceptions. Language-related difficulties are experienced by native speakers of the working language as well as non-native speakers.[68]

■ Status and its accompanying power differentials. This may be because of its effect on conflict. Groups and teams that contain high-status minorities tend to have less conflict than those with less powerful minority members.

■ The reward structure of the group or team. Basing rewards on the performance of individuals exacerbates competition along diversity lines within the group. Group-oriented rewards, conversely, refocus group members towards group or team effectiveness instead of personal success.

■ The task competence of subgroup members affects team building. More task-capable minorities may have higher perceived value in the group.

Ways of improving the effectiveness of multicultural teams

A range of different approaches are available for increasing the effectiveness of multicultural teams. These include radical collocation, promoting shared team mental models, applying team management theory and multicultural theory, joint brainstorming, diversity training, negotiating and using listener-adapted persuasive messages, both identifying shared values and acknowledging unique contributions, and building common ground through time spent together.

■ Companies are experimenting with putting teams into their own large rooms (an arrangement called radical collocation). A field study of six such teams, tracking their activity, attitudes, use of technology and productivity, found that radically collocated teams showed a doubling of productivity. Schedules, too, were shortened in comparison with both the industry benchmarks and the performance of past similar projects within the firm; the teams reported high satisfaction about their process and both customers and project sponsors were similarly highly satisfied. Among other reasons for these improvements were the fact that teams had easy access to each other both for co-ordination of their work and for learning, and that the work artefacts they posted on the walls remained visible to all.[69] Although this research on radical collocation does not specifically refer to intercultural teams, it seems likely that its beneficial effects would apply to such teams.

■ Recently 'team mental models' have been identified as important factors in team effectiveness. Team mental models are 'team members' shared, organized understanding and mental representation of knowledge about key elements of the team's relevant environment'. They may enhance team members' co-ordination and effectiveness in performing tasks that are complex, unpredictable, urgent and/or novel. 'Team members who share similar mental models can, theorists suggest, anticipate each other's responses and coordinate effectively when time is of the essence and opportunities for overt communication and debate are limited.' Lim and Klein (2006) found that the more similar team members' mental models were, the more they were likely to agree upon team priorities and strategies, yielding efficient task performance.[70] The obvious question that arises is whether the mental models of diverse teams are less similar to one another than those of homogeneous teams.

■ Team management theory addresses interpersonal conflicts within teams by breaking down hierarchical structures to decentralize power. A team orientation 'validates all roles through group decision-making'. All members have input and participate in role allocation. A supportive rather than competitive atmosphere encourages participation and negotiation. Non-evaluative statements like 'Let me review what I believe we've discussed so far', and using the word 'we' rather than 'you', reinforce a democratic approach rather than a judgemental, hierarchical one. In this way, it is argued, team theory supports diversity in organizations. The basic characteristics of well-functioning teams include trust, a non-judgemental atmosphere, conflict resolution and negotiation skills, goal-setting abilities and pervasive individual responsibility. These are also the requirements for success in diversity management. 'Problems in the workplace arise from exclusion, distrust, and fear. Teams counter these difficulties by creating bonds through working together towards mutually beneficial ends. Therefore, teams play an important part in restructuring the role of the individual and others in the workplace.'[71,72]

■ Another approach to building better teams from diverse groups is to apply multicultural theory, which 'promotes mutual understanding and respect for ethnic, religious, gender, class, language, and age differences.' It also promotes equal access to economic power. Applying multicultural theory implies encouraging co-operative learning through interactive activities, such as team members answering worksheets, individuals researching issues and reporting to the group, or pairs of group members researching both sides of a problem. This fosters positive interdependence, individual accountability and face-to-face problem-solving.

Other methods include:

■ Resolving problems through brainstorming techniques that allow for group resolution. These techniques should address the conflicts inherent in diversity.
■ Training group members to improve their ability to work effectively in diverse groups. For example, it has been suggested that special team-building training may be necessary, so that groups containing members with disabilities may be able to

function more effectively. Such training may involve changing not only how the members react to their fellow members with disabilities but also how each person (including those with disabilities) reacts to each other person in terms of beliefs, reactions and job performance expectations.[73]

- Techniques that increase interpersonal congruence enhance effectiveness in diverse groups. Interpersonal congruence measures the degree to which group members see others in the group as those others see themselves. People often see themselves differently from how others see them. This factor affects group effectiveness. A study showed that creative task performance, social integration and group identification were all higher and conflict was lower in diverse groups with high interpersonal congruence. When people expressed their 'unique' characteristics within the group during their first ten minutes of interaction, the high level of interpersonal congruence within the group was still benefiting group outcomes four months later.[74]

- Negotiation and persuasion are key to managing intercultural team differences. Being able to design appropriate persuasive messages in decision-making contexts and influence others in ethical ways that recognize others' perspectives is crucial. In the team-based, postmodern organization, 'adapting messages to one's listeners takes precedence over individual eloquence'.[75] In an intercultural situation, this requirement includes adapting to the cultural perspective of the other person. Research has shown that both cognitive complexity (differentiation) and having a broad definition of one's role are related to how much someone used listener-adapted persuasive messages.[76]

- Time spent together may also influence how much national differences affect a group's functioning. Newly formed multinational groups are likely to be the most vulnerable to the drawbacks of diversity, but, over time, if they survive and meet nominal performance thresholds, they develop more trust and rapport. Members come to respect and welcome the group's complementarities, overlooking (perhaps even relishing) differences in demeanour, values and so on. For this reason, training programmes for enhancing the effectiveness of multinational groups are most needed in the early stages of the group's operation. Similarly, it is at the outset of the group's work together that multinational group leaders must be the most vigilant about possible group breakdowns due to diversity.[77]

Finally, building teams out of diverse groups requires both identifying shared values among subgroups (e.g., high-quality work or orientation towards serving the customer) and also acknowledging the unique contributions of individuals. In this way, team builders can maximize the advantages of diversity, such as enhanced perspective and broader approaches, but minimize its disadvantages, such as subgroup focus, power differentials and distorted communications.

> Cultural differences affect preferred decision-making styles and expectations concerning both group- and teamwork. Thus, diversity affects group and team functioning and performance. However, the type of diversity and the nature of the group task influence what those effects will be. Trust is crucial: research in temporary teams has revealed that a kind of 'swift trust' can develop which allows the team to function without the underpinnings that trust usually requires. The work environment, especially attitudes to diversity, and the organizational culture also influence diversity's impact on group or team performance. Other factors include status differentials and reward structures. Methods such as radical collocation, training, internal negotiation and brainstorming conflict-related problems can improve performance in diverse teams.

8.7 LEADERSHIP AND MANAGEMENT

This section contains a discussion of cultural and intercultural leadership and management. It also considers three more specific aspects of leadership and management: giving feedback, diversity leadership and international project management.

Cultural differences in leadership and management

There is widespread agreement that what is expected of leaders or managers, what they may and may not do, and the influence that they have, varies considerably as a result of culture. The GLOBE (Global Leadership and Organizational Behavior Effectiveness) project, for example, found evidence for a theory that leader acceptance is an outcome of the congruence of leader behaviours with the culturally endorsed implicit leadership theory of the culture in which the leader functions. (An implicit leadership theory is a set of 'implicit beliefs, convictions and assumptions about attributes and behaviours that distinguish leaders from followers, effective leaders from ineffective leaders and moral leaders from evil leaders'.) These theories, held by individuals, not only influence who is accepted as a leader in a given culture, but also constrain, moderate and guide the exercise of leadership.[78]

There have, though, been findings of both universality and cultural specificity of various leadership and management behaviours. For instance, one study found that managers in nations of different 'cultural-industrialized' standing were all involved in the same 44 skill activities;[79] another found no difference in ratings on attributes such as innovation and commitment among Chinese and non-Chinese managers working for a Hong Kong airline;[80] a third reported that the views of middle managers from 61 societies in 58 countries on destructive versus constructive leadership profiles reflected the harshness of the thermal climate and the degree of collective wealth rather than culture, although the researchers argued that their finding 'sets limits to the cross-cultural generalizability of theories of people-oriented and task-oriented leadership'.[81] On the other hand, a comparison of preferences for participation of managers in six European countries and the USA found differences that correlated positively with power distance scores for the seven countries. Within Europe, differences in preferences, habits, languages and cultures, in other words its diversity, are recognized as the constraint within which firms (and individuals) 'must exploit European integration opportunities'.[82]

Other empirical research 'seems to show that cultural forces influence many aspects of leadership'. These aspects include what is typically required of holders of leadership positions, the degree to which leadership roles are filled by ascription or achievement, typical leader behaviour patterns, preferences for and expectations of leaders, and followers' and subordinates' reactions to different kinds of leader behaviour. Culture also affects how much managers rely on their own experience, what they expect from work teams, how far subordinates participate in decision-making, and leaders' confidence in subordinates' decisions.[83]

A survey of managers in 16 countries found that in individualist, low power distance nations managers relied more heavily on their own experience and training than they did in collectivist, high power distance countries. Further studies showed differences in how Japanese, British and American supervisors judged work teams. In Japan, supervisors judged as most effective those work teams that placed more reliance on their peers; in the USA, those that made more reference to superiors; and in Great Britain, those that showed greater self-reliance. A comparison of decision-making by British and Chinese managers found that both the national culture and the type of decision affected the degree of subordinate participation and supervisor consultation. Another study found Chinese and several other East Asian groups (but not Japanese) more confident than Americans that their decisions were correct. This may be owing to a greater propensity to select the first adequate problem solution that is identified rather than to survey a range of alternatives before deciding. These differences may be explicable in terms of variations in individualism–collectivism.[84] While Chinese supervisor-level employees and higher-level managers exhibited a positive attitude towards employee empowerment, this positive attitude was lower for empowerment than for other managerial leader behaviour sets. This finding came from a study in an organization where previously expatriate managers had introduced and practised empowerment management, so suggests a persistent concern about the practice.[85]

In the past, leadership similarities across groups of countries generated a country cluster taxonomy based on country commonalities such as language similarities. The assumption was that employees in countries with similar languages would display similar preferences regarding leadership communication. However new research using a database of 15,000 employees in 16 countries across four country clusters revealed that the country cluster taxonomy could be used to predict leadership preferences regarding empowering, coaching and supervising, but not regarding general and personal communication, review of achievement, and positive feedback in the form of making people proud. A general implication is that language similarities do not necessarily imply similar communication preferences.[86]

In the (individualistic) West in recent years there has been considerable interest in the phenomenon of charismatic leadership. Paradoxically, however, research has shown that workgroup collectivism is important for charismatic leadership to emerge. A collectivist group may place a high value on interdependence, co-operation and

Box 8.7

An assumption-matching approach, it is argued, adopts a richer description of culture than the 'values' systems – for instance, reflecting proverbs such as 'Those who criticize us correctly are our teachers', 'If God is to be blamed, so are we', 'One tree does not make a forest, but three trees do.' Taking such an approach, Thang *et al.* (2007) pointed to the varying degree of contextual fit to a Vietnamese sample of four HRM (human resource management) practices: pay for performance, multi-source feedback, involvement and empowerment, **and** self-managed work teams. Of these, pay for performance appeared most readily compatible with the Vietnamese 'backdrop' of, for instance, preference for an equity to an equality allocation norm, use of individual ranks in education, and a critical attitude to people who blame failure on

external circumstances. The other practices 'face more subtle relationship stage barriers: only when the relationship among individuals grows closer and a certain level of trust is achieved will the application of these practices become more practical, as they conflict with obstacles such as "face saving", ... low trust climates resulting from a long history of uncertainty in daily life and (in the case of self-managed work teams) the modern Vietnamese trend of increasing popularity of pursuit of personal goals.'

Source: Thang, L.C., Rowley, C., Quang, T. and Warner, M. (2007) 'To what extent can management practices be transferred between countries? The case of human resource management in Vietnam', *Journal of World Business*, **42**(1): 113–27

sharing. Thus it may not only allow a leader who embodies these values to be more effective, but also respond to such a leader's call for teamwork and focus on collective goals. In collectivist teams, control is exercised through value consensus and not through impersonal rules. Control based in value consensus may be more appropriate than impersonal rules for a charismatic leader.[87] Moreover, collectivism and power distance are highly correlated. A collectivist group that is also high in power distance may provide opportunities for an individual to take independent action that is perceived as a successful attempt to change the status quo. In turn, this may lead to the individual being perceived as a natural leader, exhibiting charismatic behaviours and possessing charismatic qualities.[88]

Smith *et al.* (1995) argued that 'sources of guidance' serve as an intermediate variable between cultural values and actual managerial behaviours. Sources of guidance include formal rules, unwritten rules, subordinates, specialists, co-workers, superiors, own experience and widespread beliefs. Participation-oriented guidance sources, such as subordinates, are most employed in nations characterized not only by high individualism but also by cultural autonomy, egalitarianism, low power distance, mastery and masculinity. These are more typical of the nations of Western Europe than North America. Conversely, reliance on superiors and rules is associated not only with collectivism but with cultural embeddedness, hierarchy, power distance, mastery and masculinity. Most of the nations of Africa are especially high on these cultural dimensions, rather than the Asian nations more typically discussed as exemplars of contrasting management practices.[89]

A comparison of management in six nations – the UK, France, Germany, the USA, Japan and an Arab country – found a number of differences.[90] These differences could be understood in terms of cultural dimensions, as follows:

- British managers were willing to 'listen' to subordinates (being low in uncertainty avoidance) and addicted to 'old boy networks' (being high in masculinity).
- French managers were high in power distance (preserved through formality) and individualism (expressed through 'intellectualism').
- North American managers were high on individualism and achievement, leading them to embrace a 'tough', results-oriented approach to manager–subordinate relations.
- Japanese managers, though high on achievement, were strongly collectivist, which produced the 'nurturing father' type of manager.
- German managers were high on uncertainty avoidance, shown in adherence to routines and procedures and in close control of subordinates, who were seen as apprentices.
- Managers in Arab countries were intermediate on all dimensions except power distance, where they were high: the distance between manager and subordinate was maintained through the high value placed on loyalty and on avoiding interpersonal conflict.

Box 8.8 gives more examples of differences in leadership and management within Europe. However, although such differences are important, there are also similarities in how Europeans manage, by comparison with managers in other parts of the world. For instance, a model of a European style of management consists of four basic characteristics: an orientation towards people, a characteristic which is mainly based on the 'social market economy' system in Europe and European business systems; internal negotiation, which deals primarily with the nature of the social dialogue within firms

Box 8.8

- Management in the UK is seen as essentially an interpersonal task, focusing on getting things done. Management is transferable from one function to another; likewise career moves. In rejecting elitism, people are seen as having primary importance as individuals. Personal experience, rather than experience codified in the national culture, forms the basis of effectiveness, so that issues of motivation, leadership and group dynamics all form a central focus of management.

- French organizations are staffed by technical experts and managed by the application of rationality. They therefore see management as an intellectually (rather than interpersonally) demanding task; job advertisements reflect this by asking for qualities of 'reception, rigueur, and l'esprit de synthese' (i.e., powers of keen observation, rigour, analysis and synthesis). Less attention is paid to 'emission' (i.e., capacity to communicate and motivate).

- German managers do not manage in general but are instead seen to manage something in particular. German and Swiss–German managers rely on formal authority and attach a high value to technical competence, functional expertise and rationality. Organizations are seen as a co-ordinated network of individuals who will make rational decisions based on their competence and knowledge. In contrast to France, management-by-objectives transferred successfully to Germany. This may be explained by the German preference for decentralization, lower emphasis on hierarchy, and acceptance of formalization of goals, time frames and measurement.

- A comparison with US culture found that Russian culture is lower in individualism, higher in power distance, uncertainty avoidance and Machiavellianism but similar in terms of masculinity (competitiveness) and dogmatism. Russians are open to ideas from outside. Younger Russians (business students) had values closer to US values than Russian managers had. Under present Russian conditions, in addition to horizontal and vertical relations, managers' so-called diagonal relations are also very important. These are the 'contacts of industrial managers with "informal" (and, sometimes, criminal) structures. For example, managers of large enterprises bribed government servants to obtain state credits. Managers of small enterprises paid "protection fees" to racketeers. These diagonal relations served, from the perspective of managers, as catalysts which increased the efficiency of official "horizontal" and "vertical" contacts.'[a]

- In Hungary, under Communism, ideological values encouraged the status quo, opposed a future orientation, equated entrepreneurship with cheating and criminal activity, and were against the desire to change and improve performance. A study found that Hungarian managers were 'friendly but not considerate, nor did they show regard for their subordinates as individuals or allow them to make decisions. Hungarian managers seem to be less sophisticated in planning routines, but nevertheless think and analyse carefully before making decisions.'[b]

- Typical organizational practices in Sweden have been summarized by the term 'pragmatism', meaning the balancing of rituals with rational choices, the rituals thus acquiring instrumental uses and the rational choices or instruments expressing important values. A series of studies conducted in leading Swedish companies concluded that Swedish managers were very sensitive to fashions and to trends that affect the metaphors and labels used for organizational ideas and ideologies. There were definite rules for introducing change, and organizational change was strongly institutionalized. This provided room for new ideas at the same time that it protected organizations from extreme swings.[c]

- Early studies found that Greek preferences concerning management style reflected Greek culture, in particular acceptance of authority and co-operative behaviour within the ingroup, rejection of authority and extreme competitiveness with the outgroup. However, more recent work suggests the Greek model of management 'is not differentiated from the Western model'. The

Box 8.8 (cont'd)

differences that do exist are considered more closely related to lack of modernization and are disappearing under the joint impact of the EU and globalization. These are differences such as concentration of power and control in the hands of top management and a lack of modern systems to support strategic decisions.[d]

Sources: (a) Hecht, L., Kovach, K. and Tongren, H.N. (1995) 'Recognizing cultural differences: key to successful US–Russian enterprises', Public Personnel Management, 24: 1–18

(b) Kovach, R.C. Jr. (1994) 'Matching assumptions to environment in the transfer of management practices: performance appraisal in Hungary', International Studies of Management & Organization, 24(4): 83–100

(c) Czarniawska-Joerges, B. (1993) 'Swedish management: modern project, postmodern implementation', International Studies of Management & Organization, 23(1): 13–27

(d) Bourantas, D. and Papadakis, V. (1996) 'Greek management: diagnosis and prognosis', International Studies of Management & Organization, 26(2): 77–95

across Europe; managing international diversity in environments and administration; and managing between extremes, which positions the European style of management between the North American and Japanese models.[91]

Some differences in leadership style are related more closely to factors other than national culture – for instance, to gender. A thematic analysis study of 30 women managers found 'surprisingly strong and similar' perceptions that men's and women's leadership communication differed along the dimensions of closed/open and intimidating/supportive. The women managers judged masculine communication to be harmful, overpowering and ineffective, but saw themselves as isolated by their values and numbers. Their most common reported ways of handling this were rejection of masculine power, self-doubt and blame, striving for competence, confrontation, isolation and resignation.[92] Managers from four Western European cultural groups perceived gender-based differences in leadership effectiveness. Some stereotypes did vary across cultures, but these stereotyping patterns were more often linked to participants' gender than to their cultural beliefs.[93] On the other hand, a large-sample study (64,000 subordinates evaluating the leadership behaviours of their direct supervisors ($N = 13,595$), representing 42 countries) found that culture had a stronger impact on leadership behaviours than gender. The results 'suggest that gender differences in managerial behavior are predominantly present in western societies'.[94]

In fact, a range of variables other than culture have been found to be relevant for leadership and management. In a study of Nordic management style, the least development-oriented managers were older than 50, while the most significant factor for task-oriented management behaviour was the manager's gender – women were more task-oriented than men. Region, the manager's age, functional tasks (e.g., production, marketing and other services) and line of business (manufacturing, service industries) also explained variations in task orientation.[95] In a sample of Belgian managers, public-organization managers were more conciliatory, tended to be more risk-averse and had a stronger belief in external control than the average business manager. The attitudes expressed by the Belgian managers also depended on both ethnicity and organizational affiliation.[96]

Cultural and subcultural differences in attitudes to leadership lead to differences in how specific managerial functions, such as performance appraisal, are performed. For

Box 8.9

A survey of 3,500 British managers found that, except at the highest echelons of companies, both men and women subordinate managers rated female bosses more highly than male. They were found to be rated more highly on the following factors, listed in order of how much more highly the women were rated: being decisive, focusing effort, being a good mentor, managing change, inspiring others, openness to ideas, encouraging change, networking, problem-solving, clear strategy, and being supportive of mistakes. On being a good delegator, accessible and honest/consistent, men and women scored equally.

Source: Alimo-Metcalfe, B. and Alban-Metcalfe, J. (2003) 'Gender and leadership: a masculine past, but a feminine future?', *Proceedings of the BPS Annual Occupational Psychology Conference*, Brighton, UK, 8–10 January

example, in the UK, performance appraisal is characterized as a joint problem-solving activity with decentralized responsibility over how individual objectives may be met. From a cultural point of view, this is not surprising. In the UK, but also in Denmark, Sweden, Norway and The Netherlands, the national culture combines low power distance with low-uncertainty avoidance. The low power distance means that the boss can be bypassed and rules bent so that the employee can get things done. The independence and self-realization of the employee is an important value. During the appraisal process, therefore, the boss may need to find out the detail of the subordinate's tasks. Moreover, because low power distance is blended with low-uncertainty avoidance, which is associated with a higher tolerance of risk and acceptance of dependencies in performance, a reliance on resourcefulness and adaptability in achieving goals and a tendency to reactive rather than proactive feedback, it is not surprising that it is legitimate to make the performance-appraisal discussion a joint problem-solving activity. In contrast, in Germany, Switzerland, Austria and Finland, the appraisal discussion is shaped by a desire to routinize goal implementation. In these countries, while power distance is still low, giving the employee an equal say, uncertainty avoidance is high. This leads to aiming for long-term forward control of goals and performance and a preference for final bureaucratic check-offs by superiors. In countries such as Portugal, Greece, Turkey, France, Belgium, Italy and Spain, uncertainty avoidance is high, bringing with it the desire for forward control, but power distance is also high. Therefore, there is an additional preference for centralized control, and a one-way direction of communication is more acceptable, under the assumption that the boss knows best and so may predetermine the 'how' of performance. Performance is seen as a duty, not a self-fulfilling activity, and face-to-face conflict is unacceptable. In any event, the boss has privileges and can bend the rules. Finally, although subordinates may be afraid to commit themselves to performance, they also expect protection from 'above'.[97]

Effective intercultural leadership and management

Tensions between managers and subordinates can arise from (sub)cultural differences in work attitudes. A case study of teamwork and management in a French–Slovenian plant uncovered friction. 'The Slovenian model, with a short power distance and a collective orientation, met the French model, where the power distance is large and individualism is common.' Whereas in French management style authority is legitimized by the hierarchical position itself, in Slovenian management style authority belongs to the person who has the expertise. Thus, from the Slovenian point of view, the hierarchical authority should be constrained and the professionalism of the individuals stimulated. From the French point of view, the hierarchical structure should be strengthened in the plant (which would actually further reinforce the workers' inertia). However, in this case, the French management was able to take into account two main characteristics of Slovenian management, the need for equality and mutual aid. They discovered, first, that varying management styles in different countries are linked to each country's culture; second, that these management styles should be respected and not dismissed as an artefact of underdevelopment. Third, they came to understand that defining the fundamental cultural references of a nation helps to anticipate the work behaviour and reactions of individuals regarding new management procedures. The better these procedures correspond to such fundamental cultural references, the better the results.[98]

Differences in work attitudes can also lead to internal conflicts for non-Western managers who are trying to apply Western management methods. Two case studies in Russian organizations suggested that participation and empowerment, as introduced in the Western literature, did not work well in Russian organizations. Explanations were found in a series of factors linked to Russian national and organizational cultures: 'the practice of vesting authority in one man [sic], tightly coupled hierarchies, lack of knowledge sharing, anti-individualism and dependence.'[99] Studies of hotel staff in Canada and the People's Republic of China showed that China's high power distance reduced the effect of empowerment on job satisfaction.[100] Studies of Turkish managers showed a discrepancy between their beliefs in favour of participative leadership and their relatively low beliefs in employees' capacity for leadership and initiative. This might be due to a conflict between their training in Western management and human relations ideology and the high value placed in traditional Turkish culture on a benevolent autocratic style of leadership. 'A dominating style in handling differences with subordinates is widespread and is perceived to be an effective method by superiors and subordinates alike.' Expressing support for participative leadership might be seen as socially desirable rather than realistic. Another possibility is that managers had a genuine belief in participative practices, but were frustrated by employees' responses. The subordinates might not yet have embraced participative-management ideology. Change efforts that bring a more comprehensive perspective and involve all interested parties from the outset may be the more appropriate strategy.[101]

When a superior and his/her subordinate have the same nationality, ethnicity and gender the quality of their relationship is often better. People who share the same demographic attributes often share beliefs and values, or at least assume that they do. People who perceive that they think alike are more likely to like one another, feel comfortable in each other's company and have more confidence in each other because they view each other as more predictable. In addition, similar backgrounds often lead to people having similar communication patterns and so communicating more effectively and with fewer misunderstandings. In the case of age similarity, however, while the above reasoning may apply, an alternative possibility is that people of similar ages will feel themselves to be in competition (this is an implication of social comparison theory) and so have less positive superior–subordinate relationships than people of different ages. 'Subordinates who are roughly equal to their supervisor in terms of age may be inclined to consider the adverse implications for their own personal career progress.' These effects interact with cultural differences. The negative association between age similarity and good subordinate–superior relationships is likely to be stronger in high power distance cultures, like that of Mexico, where it is expected that higher status goes with age. Confirming this, a study found that age similarity had negative effects on superior–subordinate relationship quality in Mexico, but not in the USA.

Again, the positive association between gender similarity and the quality of supervisor–subordinate relationships can be expected to be stronger in cultures such as that of Mexico, whose stronger patriarchal and machismo elements make female superior – male subordinate relationships more problematic. Despite this, while gender similarity had a stronger positive impact on one dimension of relationship quality – trust – in Mexico, it had a stronger positive impact on a second dimension of relationship quality – leader–member exchange, which largely involves support and understanding – in the USA. A possible explanation of this unexpected finding on leader–member exchange is that the measure was culturally biased: Mexican men would resist the idea that their relations with other men involve support and understanding. The researchers concluded: 'Overall, demographic similarity influences the quality of relationships between supervisors and subordinates but that the precise type of influence is affected by culture.'[102]

How leaders function cannot be studied independently of the group-based social context that gives their roles and qualities expression. 'Leaders and followers are transformed and energised as partners in an emerging social self-categorical relationship.'[103] Leaders must be 'one of us', exemplify what makes 'us' better than 'them' and stand up for the group. However, although cross-cultural research emphasizes that different cultural groups often have different conceptions of what leadership should entail, some attributes associated with charismatic/transformational leadership may be universally endorsed as contributing to outstanding leadership. This hypothesis was tested in 60 cultures as part of the GLOBE Research Program. The results supported the hypothesis that specific aspects of charismatic/transformational leadership are strongly and universally endorsed across cultures.[104] Similarly, cross-cultural research among Pakistani, Kazakh and Turkish business students found that two aspects of Kouzes and Posner's (2007)[105] analysis of transformational leadership were unaffected by differences in cultural dimensions: these were 'challenging the process' and 'enabling others to act'. On the other hand, 'inspiring a shared vision' and 'modeling the way' were significantly and negatively related to uncertainty avoidance, while 'encouraging the heart' was positively related to power distance. This research also found that uncertainty avoidance was significantly and negatively related to overall transformational leadership.[106] Data from 153 senior expatriate managers and 695 subordinates from companies in all 27 countries of the European Union showed that visionary–transformational leadership by senior expatriates had a direct influence on the rate of innovation adoption. This influence was unaffected by the senior expatriates' level of cultural intelligence (CQ) in the case of product–market innovation, but organizational innovation was affected by CQ.[107]

Communication plays an important role in the process by which charismatic leadership emerges. (This is consistent with the school of thought that leadership is located, observed and interpreted as a communication process.) While similar management practices 'could be effective in societies that seem different', they need to be examined for their interpretation in different countries. This is the essence of the Global Integration – Local Responsiveness framework, where global integration emphasizes consistency or standardization and local responsiveness emphasizes customization or adaptation.[108] Managers' responsiveness relates to communication style, the content of communications and use of third parties for negative feedback.[109] Globalization has created a demand for global leaders – people with the rare capacity of leading in many cultures simultaneously. Caligiuri and Tarique (2009) studied over 200 global leaders and found that highly extraverted leaders with a greater number of high contact cross-cultural leadership development experiences were the most effective on global leadership activities.[110] Next discussed is intercultural management in relation to the specific roles of giving feedback, taking responsibility for diversity and managing international projects.

Giving feedback

When Czaplewski *et al.* (2002) researched and analysed 'cross-cultural' [sic] performance feedback in multinational enterprises, they concluded the following points:

■ Employee input is essential for identifying employee strengths and weaknesses in the most effective manner, as employees are often most aware of both aspects of their work performance. To get high power distance-oriented employees to increase their upward input to their superiors, managers are recommended to ask open-ended questions that provide opportunities for voluntary answers, and to direct specific questions to an individual's area of expertise. In collectivist cultures, it is important specifically to invite the employee to respond with his/her ideas and perspectives so that harmony is preserved. To build a personal relationship and trust with subordinates calls for being polite and showing respect. Another way to build trust is to have events where managers can have friendly and informal dialogues with subordinates. In collectivist cultures, it is important to show respect to older people and those with long tenure in the company; in high power distance cultures, this applies to those with higher social status. Respect can be shown by a marked emphasis on politeness and decorum. For example, a written communication should ask such senior employees to 'consider' doing certain things and should 'request' them to do it. Saying 'You must,' or 'You are required,' is considered impolite. In addition, proper titles should be used when addressing older people.

■ It is important to match the verbal and non-verbal communication styles of other cultures. In collectivist cultures, verbal communication of work assignments, requirements and priorities should focus on how the employee relates to the group and the organization overall. In addition, feedback and recognition should be provided that establish rapport with family, friends and associates as well as other important ingroups of collectivist employees. Non-verbally, in high-context communication cultures, loud and direct oral communication is socially unacceptable. Similarly, argumentative voices and exaggerated hand gestures are frowned upon and often lead to miscommunication. Instead of making demands, it is often useful to ask 'May I ask you a question?' or 'May I make a suggestion?' It is also important to be aware of non-verbal cues. For instance, body gestures are typically more restrained than is typical in the West, in order to demonstrate one's respect for the other person.

■ In collectivist cultures critical feedback may be seen as a personal attack, especially if someone outside the individual's own workgroup delivers the feedback. For this reason managers should establish a trusting personal relationship with the subordinate before providing any negative performance feedback. Intercultural managers should also offer advice in a diplomatic and caring manner. Managers should consider beginning by apologizing for having to conduct the session, and use analogies and other indirect communication to illustrate performance concerns. Instead of direct or blunt feedback, they should use open-ended questions, silence, paraphrasing and reflecting feelings. They should seek to observe the reaction of employees closely and be willing to tolerate ambiguities as well as sometimes leaving things unsaid rather then spelling out everything clearly. Collectivist subordinates will read between the lines and understand what is being said. An intercultural manager should also consider using a third party to convey any negative feedback, or to gain a sense of the underlying issues and obtain possible responses from the subordinate before personally giving negative feedback. The reason for this is that it is acceptable for employees in collectivist cultures to provide constructive feedback to another member of their workgroup when they have established a close and trusting relationship with each other. A trusted third party can act as a buffer to help minimize conflict, explore hidden fears and preserve the relationship, face and self-esteem of the individual and the group. In addition, a respected third party can more easily serve as a mentor or ask more junior workers to contribute their views. In addition to a respected peer from the employee's team, other potential third parties are a senior employee in the company or an employee with expertise in a particular area.[111]

Diversity leadership

There are strong arguments in favour of leaders and the organizations they lead adopting goals and policies that promote diversity. These arguments include:

- the need to obey equal opportunities law;
- ethical corporate conduct, which embraces equal opportunities out of fairness;
- the business case, especially attracting and retaining the best staff both by widening the pool from which selection is made and by the attractiveness to many potential employees of diversity-promoting employers;
- building learning communities, where diversity is valued for bringing in new knowledge and perspectives;
- supplying diverse markets and user populations and attaining global competitive advantage, both of which are facilitated by having diverse groups from the (global) environment involved in decision-making.

Box 8.10

The diversity of a company's existing workforce shows its commitment to diversity, according to 16 per cent of respondents to a survey. One-third of the respondents indicated that they eliminated a company from employment consideration because of lack of gender or ethnic diversity. Among Black job applicants, 44 per cent of those surveyed reported that they had eliminated employers from consideration because of their lack of ethnic diversity. 'Research shows that companies that are the most successful in this area use creative recruitment practices, supported by a strong track record of deployment and promotion of diversity within their organizations.'[a]

A survey found that UK business employers prefer people with South East or Home Counties accents, because they expect them to be more reliable. Most disliked were the accents of large urban areas like Liverpool, possibly because these are associated with urban deprivation.[b]

Sources: (a) Leonard, B. (2001) 'Diverse workforce tends to attract more female and minority job applicants', *HR Magazine*, April

(b) BBC 11 o' clock News 29 September 2003 (Hamer, A., University of Liverpool)

There are four different approaches towards the management of diversity: the deficit approach, the discriminatory approach, assimilation and individualization.[112] A Belgian study found that instruments associated with the individualization approach are more often employed there; however, an approach found in Denmark most closely resembled assimilation, as it maintained a focus on the sameness of people, not on the value of difference or otherness. To be effective, diversity programmes must have support from the top, and managers need to set the tone for an open and receptive environment, which actively incorporates difference. To develop functional intercultural communication between different groups in the organization, managers must reward new approaches. 'By modelling bias-free language, both written and spoken, and by illustrating a genuine acceptance of different methods and manners, managers can create a work environment that will nurture and profit from diversity.'[113]

The starting point in all diversity training programmes is an analysis of the self. Most employees are unaware of their own biases, how they are formed and how they emerge in the workplace in overt and subtle ways. Thus, good multicultural managers should have an understanding of themselves, be able to communicate effectively through verbal and non-verbal messages, be respectful and empathetic and understand other cultures' 'sense of time, concept of work and basic beliefs'. Managers who lack some of these qualities can develop them through training programmes. In many ways, cultural awareness training is key. For example, managers need to learn what is offensive to other cultures in terms of grooming, dress and communication methods as well as to understand that what is perceived as 'odd' behaviour is really just different.

A commitment to respecting difference is the first step. Training that provides an understanding of the values, beliefs, customs and preferences of other groups is much more likely to enhance cultural diversity. Effective training improves skills in listening, interpersonal communication, conflict resolution and negotiation. It also explores ways to alter current assumptions and paradigms. Training methods to achieve these goals include consciousness-raising activities (to study how culture shapes perceptions as well as behaviour) and interactive activities such as role-playing, creating scenarios to illustrate stereotypes, analysing case studies and viewing films for discussion. Trainers must create an atmosphere of trust in order to handle the 'serious and deep cultural and personal conflicts, which must be voiced, acknowledged, and explored'.[114] To minimize tensions, managers should set guidelines, such as encouraging all responses, use 'I' statements, listen with respect, maintain confidentiality and avoid blaming. These guidelines resemble those for forming effective teams; consequently, companies that encourage teamwork should succeed in multicultural efforts.[115]

International project management

Case studies of international construction projects have revealed some of the major managerial issues in intercultural management. One project, to build a hospital in Saudi Arabia, was managed by a five-member team of three Swedes, one Arab and one Briton. The construction workers were Arabs and Pakistanis. In this project the main managerial issues were negotiation, conflict resolution, raising productivity and delay in raising funds. Another project, also in Saudi Arabia, was to construct a major harbour and road. The consulting engineers were from Britain and the USA, the project manager was Swedish and the workforce consisted of more than 1,000 Thais and Pakistanis; the client was Arab. Important managerial issues were to optimize labour costs by learning how to evoke pride in the workers, to give multi-skill training and to create rivalry among workgroups. In a third project, Swedish contractors undertaking construction of a hydropower plant in Thailand found that Thai workers in Thailand were less productive than those who worked abroad. A fourth case showed that the 'democratic' Swedish approach to management did not work well in a project to construct a tunnel in Hong Kong with Chinese and Swedish management and mainly Chinese engineers.

The authors of the cases concluded that the impact of culture on project management is likely to be evident from the very early days of the project. This impact is felt even before the formal process starts. For example, a project manager stationed in the Middle East (West Asia) said: 'Social relations in the Middle East are very important; if not for anything else, it is vital for getting information. In order to know very early that a project is proceeding, you must have a network of relations to be informed...they must know you and trust you as a person first, and then trust your company. It is impossible to build such interpersonal relations without cultural awareness.' Other conclusions included the following: 'Effective management of cultural diversity at project level is an art. For example, negotiation with Arabs requires a degree of patience that few Western project managers have ever had to practice. Many of the problems are solved informally, in social meetings, based on interpersonal relationships. A project manager in the Middle East said: "There exists a strong and direct positive relationship between project performance and the project management's interpersonal relations with other actors involved in the project...delays can be avoided and much time and resources saved."' Finally, the researchers noted, 'The problems associated with cultural differences between the Arabs and Swedes were found to be very sensitive. In addition to differences in religion and value and belief systems, the concepts of contract, time and planning as well as philosophies of business were found to be different in the parties' cultural context. Arabs prefer to do business based on interpersonal relationships, they do not plan for a long-term future; to them verbal and written agreements have equal value; and they are not aware of technical and practical problems. "They contract a project today and want it to be delivered yesterday", said a project manager.'[116]

A comparative study of European project groups examined the strategies project leaders used to cope with cultural diversity. Three were identified: to draw upon individual tolerance and self-control, to enter into a trial-and-error process coupled with relationship development and to capitalize on transnational corporate or professional cultures.[117] Focusing on the complexity of power project development, Kumar *et al.* (2005) argued that developers needed to follow a strategy that combined one based on formal contracts and one based on trust building. In such a combined approach, the appropriate balance between the two components shifts over the life cycle of the project. Trust building is critical at the initiation of the project, whereas complete contracting should dominate in the project implementation stage.[118]

Although some universal aspects to leadership have been found, culture affects both what is expected of leaders and their usual behaviour. Many of these effects can be linked to the cultural values described in Chapter 2. There are also subcultural influences, particularly of gender, on leadership behaviours. (Sub)cultural differences lead to differences in how specific managerial functions are performed.

Intercultural leaders must prevent differences from leading to superior–subordinate tension, by respect for subordinates' 'face'. Feedback should allow for subordinates' attitudes to criticism. There are strong arguments in favour of active diversity leadership in organizations. Diversity leadership requires top managers both to act as models, particularly with regard to how they communicate, and to instigate and strongly support diversity training. International project managers need high levels of cultural adaptability. In general, Westerners may need to pay more attention to interpersonal relationships than they do usually, and be prepared to revise their usual management methods.

8.8 CONCLUSION

This chapter has shown how cultural differences affect selection interviewing, service encounters, mentoring, mediating, negotiating, working in groups and teams, and leadership and management. It has also shown how skilled intercultural communication helps overcome the difficulties produced by these differences.

QUESTIONS AND EXERCISES

1. Explain in your own words the problems that may arise in some cultures in obtaining accurate factual information from interviews. How may these problems be overcome?

2. Give five examples of ways in which selection interviewers who are influenced by their own social rules and identity may misjudge candidates.

3. How might an interviewer who was low in cultural awareness interpret the responses of the selection candidate in Box 8.1? How might cultural knowledge lead the interviewer to interpret the responses differently?

4. Discuss the findings reported in the text about how gender stereotypes bias selection interviewers. How can this be prevented?

5. Role play a session between a mentor and a mentoree which has been called by the mentor to encourage the mentoree to think actively about his or her career. The mentor has an active orientation – that is, s/he comes from a society in which change is generally seen as progressive and beneficial. Also, people are expected to try actively to meet their desires. People are believed to make their own luck. S/he considers that when things go wrong people should accept personal responsibility, but s/he is an optimist – s/he thinks that anyone can do almost anything if they try hard enough. S/he believes that it is right for people to attempt to control nature and that technology is capable of solving all major human problems eventually, including the ones created by technology itself.

   The mentoree has a passive orientation – that is, s/he comes from a society in which change is generally seen as threatening and it is believed that it is best to 'let sleeping dogs lie'. There is a degree of fatalism in his or her make-up – s/he believes that most of what happens to people results from forces outside their control and that their best course is to adapt and coexist with those forces. People should accept their fates. People should also try to coexist with nature, not to dominate it. S/he points to environmental degradation, global warming and the risk of terrorist attacks with weapons of mass destruction as some of the negative consequences of so-called technological advance.

6. Discuss the contention that 'a mediator who is closer [culturally] to one side than the other can be effective in mediation.'

7. Do you agree that 'Successful mediation does not always result in resolving conflict'? Give your reasons.

8. Why do leading authorities advocate a non-directive approach to mediation, and what are the implications of such an approach for how mediators should act?

9. Show how the differences in Japanese and American negotiating styles reflect collectivist and individualist values, respectively.

10. Discuss the contention of Brett [Ref. 45] that in negotiations goals, power and information sharing are each linked to different cultural values.

11. Complete the questionnaire.

In my culture negotiators tend to:	Strongly agree	Agree	Neither agree nor disagree	Disagree	Strongly disagree
1. See the goal of negotiating as creating a relationship.					
2. Expect the negotiated terms of a contract to be strictly adhered to.					
3. Think a buyer has more power than a seller.					
4. Try to get as much information as possible from the other party without giving any away themselves.					
5. Deal with one issue at a time.					
6. Expect both sides to improve on their initial offers by making concessions.					
7. Aim to 'win'.					
8. Select negotiators by seniority.					

See the Appendix for guidance on how to score and interpret this questionnaire.

12. Role play a negotiation over the purchase of a plot of land on which to build a house. The vendor is aware that land prices have been rising fast in the area and has no immediate need for the money. However, he or she is high in relationship values, which means that s/he values compromise and co-operative success. In his/her society, living well in material comfort and having other high standard of living factors are believed to be matters of birth, luck or destiny. The buyer suspects that the rising prices of land in the area may be a bubble that will burst, but has a pressing need for the land and knows that in the short term there are few alternatives available. However, he/she is high in achievement values, which means that he/she endorses assertiveness, competition and aggressive success. An Observer should identify the sources of relative power in the negotiating situation and note during the negotiation to what degree cultural values affect the playing out of power positions.

13. Role play a negotiation over a 100 work station office lease, including price per square metre, redecoration, and supply and installation of new carpets and air conditioning units. The potential leaseholder's goal is a specifically-worded contract, his/her negotiating attitude is win/lose, personal style is informal, communication is direct, sensitivity to time is high and approach to negotiating is item by item. The vendor's goal is a general agreement leading to a relationship, his/her negotiating attitude is win/win, communication is indirect, sensitivity to time is low and approach to negotiating is overall. Negotiate for 30 minutes. At the end, participants record their impressions of the negotiation and discuss the reasons for any progress or lack of progress towards agreement. An Observer should identify the sources of relative power in the negotiating situation and note during the negotiation to what degree cultural values affect the playing out of power positions.

14. Role play either or both of the two negotiations described in Questions 12 and 13 with vendor and purchaser/potential leaseholder having opposed negotiating norms concerning obtaining as much information as possible from the other party without giving any away themselves, dealing with one issue at a time and expecting both sides to improve on their initial offers by making concessions.

15. Discuss the reasons why intercultural negotiators usually achieve worse joint outcomes than intracultural negotiators. How may such problems be overcome?

16. With a colleague from a different culture, compare the meaning of 'teamwork' in your respective cultures.

17. Comment on the possible reasons for the research finding given in Section 8.6 that 'A high degree of cultural diversity did appear to constrain process and performance among group members in newly formed groups (etc.)'.

18. Discuss reasons why the potential for conflict in a workgroup might increase as the percentage of ethnic minority or male members increases beyond 30 per cent. What reasons might explain the fact that the relevant percentage for women is different?

19. Discuss the research finding that dissimilar people in workgroups in collectivist organizational cultures had the highest creative output.

20. What processes might explain the finding that over time diverse workgroups become as productive as non-diverse groups?

21. The text states that differences in how Japanese, British and American supervisors judge work teams may be explicable in terms of variations in individualism–collectivism. How?

22. Draw up a list of national characteristics and factors that appear to influence variations in European styles of leadership and management, based on the material in Box 8.9 and the surrounding text.

23. Why might participation and empowerment, as advocated in Western literature, be counterproductive in some European and Asian countries?

24. Pelled et al. (1999) found that age similarity had negative effects on work relationship quality in Mexico, but not in the United States. How can this finding be explained?

25. What explains the finding that charismatic leadership is associated with collectivist values in the followers?

26. What should the diversity training of managers aim to achieve?

27. What adjustments in attitudes, expectations and communication behaviours are likely to be needed by a Western project manager working on a project in the Middle East?

NOTES AND REFERENCES

1. Doktor, R., Tung, R.L. and Von Glinow, M.A. (1991) 'Incorporating international dimensions in management theory building', Academy of Management Review, 16: 259–61.

2. Hatem, T. (1994) 'Egypt: exploring management in the Middle East', International Studies of Management and Organization, 24(1/2): 116–36.

3. Wong, I.F.H. and Phooi-Ching, L. (2000) 'Chinese cultural values and performance at job interviews: a Singapore perspective', Business Communication Quarterly, 63(1): 9–22.

4. Gallois, C. and Callan, V. (1998) Communication and Culture; A Guide for Practice, Chichester, UK: John Wiley.

5. Birkner, K. and Kern, F. (2000) 'Impression management in East and West German job interviews', in Spencer-Oatey, H. (ed.) Culturally Speaking, pp. 256–71, London: Continuum.

6. Sanchez-Burks, J. and Blount, S. (2006) 'Unpacking rapport: the role of behavioral co-ordination and culture in workplace interviews', Ross School of Business Paper No. 911. Available at SSRN: http://ssrn.com/abstract=901778.

7. Kristof-Brown, A., Barrick, M.R. and Franke, M. (2002) 'Applicant impression management: dispositional influences and consequences for recruiter perceptions of fit and similarity', *Journal of Management*, **28**(1): 27–46.

8. Rumbelow, H. (2003) 'Feminine charm is still a career girl's best bet', *The Times*, 9 January 2003.

9. Frazer, R.A. and Wiersma, U.J. (2001) 'Prejudice versus discrimination in the employment interview: we may hire equally, but our memories harbour prejudice', *Human Relations*, **54**(2): 173–92.

10. Torrington, D. (1994) *International HRM: Think Globally, Act Locally*, Hemel Hempstead, Herts: Prentice-Hall.

11. Parasuraman, Z. and Berry, L.L. (1988) 'SERVQUAL: a multiple-item scale for measuring customer perceptions of service quality', *Journal of Retailing*, 64(1): 12–40.

12. Weiermair, K. (2000) 'Tourists' perceptions towards and satisfaction with service quality in the cross-cultural service encounter; Implications for hospitality and tourism management', *Management Service Quality*, **10**(6): 397–409.

13. Espinoza, M.M. (1999) 'Assessing the cross-cultural applicability of a service quality measure: a comparative study between Quebec and Peru', *International Journal of Service Industry Management*, **10**(5): 449–68.

14. Ueltschy, L.C., Laroche, M., Zhang, M., Cho, H. and Yingwei, R. (2009) 'Is there really an Asian connection? Professional service quality perceptions and customer satisfaction', *Journal of Business Research*, **62**(10): 921–1,038.

15. Alden, D.L., He, Y. and Chen, Q. (2010) 'Service recommendations and customer evaluations in the international marketplace: cultural and situational contingencies', *Journal of Business Research*, **63**(1): 1–96.

16. Furrer, O., Shaw-Ching, B. and Sudharshan, L.D. 'The relationships between culture and service quality perceptions: basis for cross-cultural market segmentation and resource allocation', *Journal of Service Research*, **2**(4): 355–71.

17. Reimann, M., Lünemann, U.F. and Chase, R.B. (2008) 'Uncertainty avoidance as a moderator of the relationship between perceived service quality and customer satisfaction', *Journal of Service Research*, **11**: 63–73.

18. Mattila, A.S., Grandey, A.A. and Fisk, G.M. (2003) 'The interplay of gender and affective tone in service encounter satisfaction', *Journal of Service Research*, **6**: 136–43.

19. Sharma, P., Tam, J.L.M. and Kim, N. (2009) 'Demystifying intercultural service encounters: toward a comprehensive conceptual framework', *Journal of Service Research*, **12**: 227–42.

20. Mattila, A.S. and Patterson, P.G. (2004) 'Service recovery and fairness perceptions in collectivist and individualist contexts', *Journal of Service Research*, **6**: 336–46.

21. Shea, G. F. (1992) *Mentoring: A Guide to the Basics*, London: Kogan Page.

22. McGuire, G.M. (1999) 'Do race and sex affect employees' access to and help from mentors? Insights from the study of a large corporation', in Murrell, A.J., Crosby, F.J. and Ely, R.J. (eds) *Mentoring Dilemmas: Developmental Relationships within Multicultural Organizations*, Mahwah, NJ: Lawrence Erlbaum.

23. Murphy, S. and Ensher, E. (1997) 'The effects of culture on mentoring relationships: a developmental model', in Granrose, S. and Oskamp, S. (eds) *Cross-cultural Work Groups*, Thousand Oaks, CA: Sage.

24. Goto, S. (1999) 'Asian Americans and developmental relationships', in Murrell, A.J., Crosby, F.J. and Ely, R.J. (eds) *Mentoring Dilemmas: Developmental Relationships within Multicultural Organizations*, Mahwah, NJ: Lawrence Erlbaum.

25. Osula, B. and Irvin, S.M. (2009) 'Cultural awareness in intercultural mentoring: A model for enhancing mentoring relationships', *International Journal of Leadership Studies*, **5**: 37–50.

26. Crosby, F.J. (1999) 'The developing literature on developmental relationships', in Murrell, A.J., Crosby, F.J. and Ely, R.J. (eds) *Mentoring Dilemmas: Developmental Relationships within Multicultural Organizations*, Mahwah, NJ: Lawrence Erlbaum.

27. Hoyt, S.K. (1999) 'Mentoring with class: connections between social class and developmental relationships in the Academy', in Murrell, A.J., Crosby, F.J. and Ely, R.J. (eds) *Mentoring*

Dilemmas: Developmental Relationships within Multicultural Organizations, Mahwah, NJ: Lawrence Erlbaum.

28. Ibid.
29. Ibid.
30. Osula, 'Cultural awareness in intercultural mentoring: A model for enhancing mentoring relationships'.
31. Zartman, W. and Touval, S. (1996) 'International mediation in the post-Cold War era', in Crocker, C., Hampson, F. and Aall, P. (eds) *Managing Global Chaos*, Washington, DC: United States Institute of Peace Press.
32. Ayres, W.R. (1997) 'Mediating international conflicts: is image change necessary?', *Journal of Peace Research*, **34**(3): 431–47.
33. Carnevale, P.J. and Choi, D.-W. (2000) 'Culture in the mediation of international disputes', *International Journal of Psychology*, **35**(2): 105–10.
34. Wall, V.D., Jr and Dewhurst, M.L. (2007) 'Mediator gender: communication differences in resolved and unresolved mediations', *Conflict Resolution Quarterly*, **9**(1): 63–85.
35. Odendaal, A. (1998) 'Modelling mediation: evolving approaches to mediation in South Africa', *Online Journal of Peace and Conflict Resolution*, **1**(3). URL: http://www.trinstitute.Org/ojpcr/1 3tt2.htm.
36. Ibid.
37. Pruitt, D.G. (1996) 'Bargaining', in Manstead, A.S.R., Hewstone, M., Fiske, S.T., Hogg, M.A. and Semin, G.R. (eds) *The Blackwell Encyclopaedia of Social Psychology*, pp. 81–5, Oxford: Blackwell.
38. Abramson, N.R., Lane, H.W., Nagai, H. and Takagi, H. (1993) 'A comparison of Canadian and Japanese cognitive styles: implications for management interaction', *Journal of International Business Studies*, **24**: 575–88.
39. Bazerman, M.H., Curhan, J.R., Moore, D.A. and Valley, K.L. (2000) 'Negotiation', *Annual Review of Psychology*, **51**: 279–314.
40. Salacuse, J. (1991) 'Making deals in strange places: a beginner's guide to international business negotiations', in Breslin, J.W. and Rubin, J.Z. (eds) *Negotiation Theory and Practice*, Cambridge, MA: The Program on Negotiation at Harvard Law School.
41. Salacuse, J.W. (1998) 'Ten ways that culture affects negotiating style: some survey results', *Negotiation Journal*, July: 221–40.
42. Metcalf, L.E., Bird, A., Shankarmahesh, M., Aycan, Z., Larimo, J. and Valdelamar, D.D. (2006) 'Cultural tendencies in negotiation: A comparison of Finland, India, Mexico, Turkey, and the United States', *Journal of World Business*, **41**(4): 382–94.
43. Cai, D.A., Wilson, S.R. and Drake, L.E. (2000) 'Culture in the context of intercultural negotiation: individualism–collectivism and paths to integrative agreements', *Human Communication Research*, **26**(4): 591–617.
44. Ibid.
45. Brett, J.M. (2000) 'Culture and negotiation', *International Journal of Psychology*, **35**(2): 97–104.
46. George, J.M., Gonzalez, J.A. and Jones, G.R. (1998) 'The role of affect in cross-cultural negotiations', *Journal of International Business Studies*, **29**(4): 749–72.
47. Bazerman *et al.*, 'Negotiation'.
48. Ibid.
49. Strohschneider, S. (2002) 'Cultural factors in complex decision making', in Lonner, W.J., Dinnel, D.L., Hayes, S.A. and Sattler, D.N. (eds) *Online Readings in Psychology and Culture* (unit 15, chapter 8). URL: http://orpc.iaccp.org/, last accessed on 23 December 2010.
50. Gibson, C.B. and Zellmer-Bruhn, M.E. (2001) 'Metaphors and meaning: an intercultural analysis of the concept of teamwork', *Administrative Science Quarterly*, **46**: 274–303.
51. Dansby, M.R. and Knouse, S.B. (1999) 'Percentage of work-group diversity and work-group effectiveness', *Journal of Psychology*, **133**: 486–95.
52. Gibson, C.B. and Vermeulen, F. (2003) 'A healthy divide: subgroups as a stimulus for team learning behavior', *Administrative Science Quarterly*, **48**: 75–99.

53. Punnett, B.J. and Clemens, J. (1999) 'Cross-national diversity: implications for international expansion decisions', *Journal of World Business*, **34**(2): 128–38.

54. Polzer, J.T., Milton, L.P. and Swann, W.B. (2002) 'Capitalizing on diversity: interpersonal congruence in small work groups', *Administrative Science Quarterly*, **47**(2): 296–324.

55. Ely, R.J. and Thomas, D.A. (2001) 'Cultural diversity at work: the effects of diversity perspectives on work group processes and outcomes', *Administrative Science Quarterly*, **46**: 229–73.

56. Stahl, G.K., Maznevski, M.L., Voigt, A. and Jonsen, K. (2010) 'Unraveling the effects of cultural diversity in teams: a meta-analysis of research on multicultural work groups', *Journal of International Business Studies*, **41**: 690–709.

57. Ibid.

58. Jehn, K.A., Northcote, G.B. and Neale, M.A. (1999) 'Why differences make a difference: a field study of diversity, conflict and performance in workgroups', *Administrative Science Quarterly*, **44**: 741–63.

59. Pelled, L.H., Eizenhardt, K.M. and Xin, K.R. (1999) 'Exploring the black box: an analysis of work group diversity, conflict and performance', *Administrative Science Quarterly*, **44**: 1–28.

60. Pelled, L.H. (1996) 'Relational demography and perceptions of group conflict and performance: a field investigation', *International Journal of Conflict Management*, **7**: 230–46.

61. Jehn, K. and Weldon, E. (1992) 'A comparative study of managerial attitudes toward conflict in the United States and the People's Republic of China: issues of theory and measurement', *Annual Meeting of the Academy of Management 1992*, Las Vegas, NV.

62. Ely and Thomas, 'Cultural diversity at work: the effects of diversity perspectives on work group processes and outcomes'.

63. Chatman, J., Polzer, J., Barsade, S. and Neale, M. (1998) 'Being different yet feeling similar: the influence of demographic composition and organizational culture on work processes and outcomes', *Administrative Science Quarterly*, **43**(3): 668–98.

64. Coutu, D. (2009) 'How to manage your negotiating team: an interview with J. Richard Hackman', *Harvard Business Review*, September.

65. Finn, R. (2008) 'The language of teamwork: reproducing professional divisions in the operating theatre', *Human Relations*, **61**(1): 103–30.

66. Meyerson, D., Weick, K.E. and Kramer, R.M. (1996) 'Swift trust and temporary groups', in Kramer, R.M. and Tyler, T.R. (eds) *Trust in Organizations: Frontiers of Theory and Research*, Thousand Oaks, CA: Sage.

67. Drnevich, P., Ramanujam, R., Mehta, S. and Chaturvedi, A. (2009) 'Affiliation or situation: what drives strategic decision-making in crisis response?', *Journal of Managerial Issues*, **21**(2).

68. Henderson, J.K. (2005) 'Language Diversity in International Management Teams', *International Studies of Management and Organization*, **35**(1): 66–82.

69. Teasley, S.D., Covi, L., Krishnan, M.S. and Olson, J.S. (2000) 'How does radical collocation help a team succeed?' Proceedings of CSCW 2000. URL: http://portal.acm.org/citation.cfm?id=1031607.1031621.

70. Lim, B.-C. and Klein, K.J. (2006) 'Team mental models and team performance: A field study of the effects of team mental model similarity and accuracy', *Journal of Organizational Behaviour*, **27**: 403–18.

71. Schreiber, E.J. (1996) 'Muddles and huddles: facilitating a multicultural workforce through team management theory', *The Journal of Business Communication*, **33**: 459–73.

72. Hirschhorn, L. (1991) *Managing in the New Team Environment: Skills, Tools and Methods*, Lincoln, NE: Author's Choice Press.

73. Dansby and Knouse, 'Percentage of work-group diversity and work-group effectiveness'.

74. Polzer *et al.*, 'Capitalizing on diversity: interpersonal congruence in small work groups'.

75. Coopman, S.J. and Applegate, J.L. (1997) 'Social-cognitive influences on the use of persuasive message strategies among health care team members', in Eizenberg, E. and Goodall, H. (eds) *Organizational Communication: Balancing Creativity and Constraint*, 2nd edn, New York: St Martin's Press.

76. Fine, M.G. (1995) *Building Successful Multicultural Organizations*, London: Quorum Books.
77. Hambrick, D.C., Davison, S.C., Snell, S.A. and Snow, C.C. (1998) 'When groups consist of multiple nationalities: towards a new understanding of the implications', *Organization Studies,* **19**(2): 181–205.
78. House, J.H. and Javidan, M. (2004) 'Overview of Globe', in House, R.J., Hanges, P.J., Javidan, M., Dorfman, P.W. and Gupta, V. (eds) *Culture, Leadership, and Organizations: The GLOBE Study of 62 Societies*, Thousand Oaks, CA: Sage.
79. Lubatkin, M.H., Ndiaye, M. and Vengroff, R. (1997) 'The nature of managerial work in developing countries; a limited test of the universalist hypothesis', *Journal of International Business Strategy,* **28**(4): 711–33.
80. Furnham, A. and Stringfield, P. (1993) 'Personality and occupational behavior: Myers-Briggs Type indicator correlates of managerial practices in two cultures', *Human Relations,* **46**: 827–44.
81. Van de Vliert, E. and Einarsen, S. (2008) 'Cultural construals of destructive versus constructive leadership in major world niches', *International Journal of Cross Cultural Management,* **8**: 275–95.
82. Boone, P.F. and van Den Bosch, F.A.J. (1996) 'Discerning a key characteristic of a European style of management: managing the tension between integration opportunities and the constraining diversity in Europe', *International Studies of Management and Organization,* **26**(3): 109–27.
83. House, R., Wright, N. and Aditya, R.N. (1999) 'Cross cultural research on organizational leadership: a critical analysis and a proposed theory', *Working Paper of the Reginald H. Jones Center,* The Wharton School University of Pennsylvania WP 99–03A 48.
84. Bond, M.H. and Smith, P.B. (1996) 'Cross-cultural social and organizational psychology', *Annual Review of Psychology,* **47**: 205–35.
85. Littrell, R.F. (2007) 'Influences on employee preferences for empowerment practices by the "ideal manager" in China', *International Journal of Intercultural Relations,* **31**(1): 87–110.
86. Zander, L. (2005) 'Communication and country clusters: A study of language and leadership preferences', *International Studies of Management and Organization,* **35**(1): 83–103.
87. Triandis, H.C., McCusker, C., Betancourt, H., Iwao, S., Leung, K., Salazar, J.M., Setiadi, B., Sinha, J.B.P., Touzard, H., and Zaleski, Z. (1993) 'An etic-emic analysis of individualism and collectivism', *Journal of Cross Cultural Psychology,* **24**: 366–83.
88. Pillai, R. and Meindl, J.R. (1998) 'Context and charisma: a "meso" level examination of the relationship of organic structure, collectivism, and crisis to charismatic leadership', *Journal of Management,* **24**(5): 643–71.
89. Smith, P.B., Trompenaars, F. and Dugan, S. (1995) 'The Rotter locus of control scale in 43 countries: a test of cultural relativity', *International Journal of Psychology,* **30**: 377–400.
90. Torrington, *International Human Resource Management.*
91. Calori, R. and Lawrence, P. (1992) 'Diversity still remains – views of European managers', *Long Range Planning,* **25**(2): 33–43.
92. Sloan, D.K. and Krone, K.J. (2000) 'Women managers and gendered values', *Women's Studies in Communication,* **23**(1): 111–30.
93. Prime, J., Jonsen, K., Carter, N. and Maznevski, M.L. (2008) 'Managers' perceptions of women and men leaders: a cross-cultural comparison', *International Journal of Cross Cultural Management,* **8**: 171–210.
94. van Emmerik, H., Euwema, M.C. and Wendt, H. (2008) 'Leadership behaviors around the world: the relative importance of gender versus cultural background', *International Journal of Cross Cultural Management,* **8**: 297–315.
95. Arvonen, J. and Lindell, M. (1996) 'The Nordic management style in a European context', *International Studies of Management and Organization,* **26**(3): 73–93.
96. Cummings, L.L., Harnett, D.L. and Stevens, O.J. (1971) 'Risk, fate, conciliation, and trust: an international study of attitudinal differences among executives', *Academy of Management Journal,* **14**: 285–304.

97. Sparrow, P.R. and Budhwar, P. (1998) 'Reappraising psychological contracting: lessons for the field of human-resource development from cross-cultural and occupational psychology research', *International Studies of Management and Organization*, **28**(4): 26–52.

98. Globokar, T. (1996) 'Intercultural management in Eastern Europe: an empirical study of a French–Slovenian plant', *International Studies of Management and Organization*, **26**(3): 47–60.

99. Michailova, S. (2002) 'When common sense becomes uncommon: participation and empowerment in Russian companies with Western participation', *Journal of World Business*, **37**(3): 180–7.

100. Hui, M.K., Au, K. and Fock, H. (2004) 'Empowerment effects across cultures', *Journal of International Business Studies*, **35**(1): 46–60.

101. Kozan, M.K. (1993) 'Cultural and industrialization level influences on leadership attitudes for Turkish managers', *International Studies of Management and Organization*, **23**(3): 7–18.

102. Pelled, 'Relational demography and perceptions of group conflict and performance: a field investigation'.

103. Haslam, S.A. and Platow, M.J. (2001) 'Your wish is our command: the role of shared identity in translating a leader's vision into followers' action', in Hogg, M.A. and Terry, D.J. (eds) *Social Identity Processes in Organizational Contexts*, pp. 213–28, Philadelphia, PA: Psychology Press.

104. Hartog, D., House, R.J., Hanges, R.J., Ruiz-Quntanilla, S.A. and Dorfman, R.W. (1999) 'Culture specific and cross culturally generalizable implicit leadership theories: are attributes of charismatic/transformational leadership universally endorsed?', *Leadership Quarterly*, **10**(2): 219–56.

105. Kouzes, J.M. and Posner, B.Z. (2007) *The Leadership Challenge*, Jossey-Bass.

106. Ergeneli, A., Gohar, R. and Temirbekova, Z. (2007) 'Transformational leadership: its relationship to culture value dimensions', *International Journal of Intercultural Relations*, **31**(6): 703–24.

107. Elenkov, D.S. and Manev, I.M. (2009) 'Senior expatriate leadership's effects on innovation and the role of cultural intelligence', *Journal of World Business*, **44**(4): 357–69.

108. Anakwe, U.P., Anandarajan, M. and Igbaria, M. (2000) 'Management practices across cultures: role of support in technology usage', *Journal of International Business Studies*, **31**(4): 653–66.

109. Sparrow and Budhwar, 'Reappraising psychological contracting'.

110. Caligiuri, P. and Tarique, I. (2009) 'Predicting effectiveness in global leadership activities', *Journal of World Business*, **44**(3): 336–46.

111. Czaplewski, A.J., Milliman, J. and Taylor, S. (2002) 'Cross-cultural performance feedback in multinational enterprises: opportunity for organizational learning', *Human Resource Planning*, **25**(3): 29–43.

112. Glastra, F., Schedler, P. and Kats, E. (1998) 'Employment equity policies in Canada and the Netherlands: enhancing minority employment between public controversy and market initiative', *Policy and Politics*, **26**(2): 163–76.

113. Fine, *Building Successful Multicultural Organizations*.

114. Ibid.

115. Schreiber, 'Muddles and huddles: facilitating a multicultural workforce through team management theory'.

116. Dadfar, H. and Gustavsson, P. (1992) 'Competition by effective management of cultural diversity: the case of international construction projects', *International Studies of Management and Organization*, **22**(4): 81–92.

117. Chevrier, S. (2003) 'Cross-cultural management in multinational project groups', *Journal of World Business*, **38**(2): 141–49.

118. Kumar, R., Rangan, U.S. and Rufín, C. (2005) 'Negotiating complexity and legitimacy in independent power project development', *Journal of World Business*, **40**(3): 302–30.

chapter nine

International Intercultural Communication

This chapter explores five different important international contexts for intercultural work communication. These are: working in virtual teams; offshore outsourcing, including the offshoring of call centres for telemarketing and after-sales to countries such as India; working and managing in international alliances, including joint ventures; working and managing in multinational companies and other multinational organizations; and international business-to-business relations.

9.1 TECHNOLOGY-MEDIATED COMMUNICATION, KNOWLEDGE TRANSFER AND CO-ORDINATION

In addition to intercultural work communication itself, three concerns arise to varying degrees in all the work contexts described in this chapter. These are the effects of technology-mediated communication and issues of knowledge transfer and co-ordination. This first section of the chapter describes these concerns and their implications.

Technology-mediated communication

Telephone conversations, electronic mail (e-mail), fax messages, text messaging on mobile phones, video- and audio-conferencing and voice mail are all examples of technology-mediated interpersonal communication. Low bandwidth tools such as e-mail and instant messenger programs are generally considered to have severe limitations compared with face-to-face communication. In the case of software development, for instance, one article noted: 'Disruption to a second, vital communication channel [the face-to-face channel not available when relying on mediated communication] can be surprisingly crippling; developers not located together have very little informal, spontaneous conversation across sites. One result is that the issues, big and small, that crop up on a nearly daily basis in any software project can go unrecognized or lie dormant and unresolved for extended periods.'[1]

Whatever its consequences, there has been and continues to be immense growth in the use of mediated interpersonal communication at work. This raises important questions about mediation's direct and indirect effects on communication and relationships, especially when the users are from different (sub)cultures. Media can be ranged along a continuum of 'social presence'. This is a matter of how well different media overcome various constraints of time and distance, transmit the social symbolic and non-verbal cues of human communication and convey ambiguous information.[2] Media high in social presence produce representations of objects, events and people that look and sound like the real thing, create a sense that two or more participants are physically together, and provide immediacy and intimacy, which are two important features of face-to-face communication. Face-to-face communication itself has the richest level of social presence, of course, followed by audio-visual, audio and written communication in that order.

High social presence has been found to enhance performance on tasks that are wide-ranging, complex and uncertain, such as tele-operations, where operators need to be able to extend their adaptive responses to another physical environment. Research subjects who watched a 15-minute infomercial in a visually immersive setting (cinema) experienced higher presence than those who watched it in a visually non-immersive setting (at-home television). They also expressed more confidence in their brand choices, showing that higher social presence can influence attitudes. Again, memory of images may be enhanced by high presence, though memory of the source of the images may be impaired. Unfortunately, recent research suggests that even the highest bandwidth ICT (information and communication technology) tool available today – videoconferencing – may have limited utility as a communication medium because it provides neither high-fidelity interactivity, as in face-to-face communication, nor the social benefits of co-location.[3]

A medium's social presence is determined by its formal and content features and by characteristics of the medium user. Media features include the number of human senses for which a medium provides stimulation, the quality of its visual display, and whether it uses stereoscopic images, subjective camera shots and changes of viewpoint and sound quality. Interactivity is another important media feature for presence. Major aspects of interactivity include the number of inputs from the user to which the medium responds, its speed of response ('real time' is ideal) and how closely the type of medium response corresponds to the type of user input. Characteristics of the media user that can affect social presence include his or her willingness to suspend disbelief and the amount of his or her prior experience with the medium. (Prior use of the medium reduces the amount of social presence experienced.)

Culture is another characteristic of the user that influences how CMC (computer-mediated communication) affects behaviour. There are findings that indicated that a team's cultural composition was a significant predictor of its performance on programming projects, although the type of programming task affected whether the relationship between individual cultural attributes and performance was strong or weak. Cultural

Box 9.1

An interesting finding is that computer users respond socially to their computers. For instance, they follow social rules concerning politeness and gender stereotypes, and evaluate a computer's performance in a tutoring task more favourably when another computer praises the tutor computer than when it praises itself.

attributes most strongly correlated to group performance included those related to attitudes about organizational hierarchy (high power distance reduced performance), organizational harmony (high perceived harmony increased performance), attitudes to trade-offs between future and current needs, and beliefs about how much influence individuals have on their fate (high internal locus of control increased performance).[4]

Not surprisingly, there is as yet little concrete information on how subcultural differences other than gender affect mediated communication. In theory, because communication media such as e-mail lack social context cues and participants may have a feeling of anonymity, people of lower social status may participate more equally than they do face-to-face. However, findings on gender differences do not support this contention. In on-line discussions, research found, men sent longer and more frequent messages than women, and Whites sent more messages than other cultural groups. Moreover, men were more willing to adopt the technology than women, and Whites were more willing than other cultural groups. Men presented more dominating behaviour online. The researcher concluded that online discussions parallel face-to-face interaction in respect of participation by different groups.[5] A meta-analysis of 50 studies involving a total of 63,889 users exploring gender differences in the use of CMC found that there was a small but significant gender effect on users' collaborative orientation. On average, female users had a significantly higher frequency of collaborative instances using CMC than males did; females also had a significantly higher frequency of challenging others and were more person-oriented. Males, on the other hand, used more authoritative statements. Male users enjoyed more about CMC environments than their female counterparts and were more confident in using CMC. Levels of apprehension, anxiety or difficulty did not, however, differ between genders.[6] Another piece of research found that, in a setting of participants with diverse linguistic backgrounds (an arbitrarily selected 6.5-hour chat session which elicited 3,092 contributions from 185 participants), the dominance of English was very strong. This feature may reduce participation by people with limited English language competence.[7]

In an experiment reported in Chapter 2, collectivist minorities were shown to be more susceptible to group majority influence than individualist minorities. However, all minorities in face-to-face groups experienced a higher level of majority influence than groups whose communication medium was computer-mediated (CMC), whether that was quasi face-to-face CMC (FtF CMC) like videoconferencing or distant CMC (dCMC) such as email. There was no significant difference found, however, between FtF CMC groups and dCMC groups. This finding implies that, in general, removal of some non-verbal cues (e.g., voice and facial expression) can result in significantly less social presence and conformance pressure, and, in turn, less majority influence. Such non-verbal cues, which are typically available in the FtF (face-to-face) unsupported setting, may enable group majorities to exercise the strongest influence on group minorities. Compared with FtF CMC, removing visual cues in a distributed CMC setting seemed not to reduce social presence so significantly as to impact majority influence. Majority influence was, however, manifested more strongly on Chinese (collectivist) minorities in heterogeneous groups than in homogeneous Chinese groups in a distributed CMC setting. In other words, despite collectivists' cultural inclination toward supporting and/or agreeing with ingroup members, when collectivistic majorities were restricted by the low social presence imposed by a communication medium, the influence of cultural similarity on a group decision-making outcome was limited.[8]

In a work context, it has been argued, culture can influence decision-making regarding distributed work. For example, decisions on what data to store in a database could depend on the degree of uncertainty avoidance of a culture, while who gets access to the data could depend on the culture's power distance level. Most empirical research has been carried out in relation to online marketing. One study examined the impact of culture on trust determinants in computer-mediated commerce transactions. The results showed that determinants of trust such as 'perceived importance of third-party seal' and 'perceived importance of positive referral' (labelled 'transference-based trust determinants' because the basis of trust is transferred from the vendor to a third party) were more positively related to consumer trust in e-vendors in a collectivistic/strong uncertainty avoidance/high long-term orientation/high context culture (labelled a Type II culture) than in an individualistic/weak uncertainty avoidance/low long-term orientation/low context culture (labelled a Type 1 culture). Contrary to expectations, however, trust determinants based on perceived security protection and perceived system reliability did not show stronger relations to consumer trust in e-vendors in a Type I culture than in a Type II culture. Perceived privacy concerns were seen to have a stronger effect on consumer trust in e-vendors in a Type I culture than in a Type II culture.[9] Another study found that potential user trust in information technology (IT) artefacts such as payroll software was enhanced when the artefact had higher quality navigational structure and greater visual appeal. The link between trust and such system quality attributes, of course, implies a limit on the effect of cultural distance on trust in these products. However, by comparing the trust of French and American potential users in e-commerce technologies, the study showed that not only did culture directly affect user trust in IT artefacts but it also moderated the extent to which navigational structure affected this form of trust.[10]

Regarding the effect of gender differences in responses to online marketing, one study focused on the relationship of trust in e-commerce and online word of mouth (consumer ratings of products offered for sale). The results showed that the effect of trust on intention to shop online was stronger for women than for men, that men valued their ability to post content online, whereas women valued the responsive participation of other consumers to the content they had posted, and that online word-of-mouth quality affected online trust differently across genders.[11]

Box 9.2

In a videoconference involving developers from the United States, France, and Germany, the Americans spent the first five to ten minutes worrying that not all participants were there yet. In contrast, the Europeans spent the time talking among themselves (across the video link) about the weather, sports, and other personal matters until the Americans decided that a quorum was present and business could begin. At the end of the videoconference, the Americans immediately disconnected the call. The French and Germans continued for another five minutes, wishing a departing French teammate well in his retirement, and reminiscing about good times. The Europeans viewed the American behaviour as rude and insensitive. The Americans viewed time as money, focusing on the cost of the videoconference. In other countries, entire videoconference calls are devoted to establishing relationships, without conducting the core of the task at all.

Source: Olson, J.S and Olson, G.M. (2003–4) 'Culture surprises in remote software development teams', *Queue*, 1(9): 52–9

Mediated communication creates the following opportunities and problems for intercultural communication at work:

■ People often experience an extended range of human contacts through electronic communication. Many of these additional contacts may be with people from different (sub)cultures. An example is the now common experience of European consumers interacting with staff of call centres in India.

■ Forms of social interaction change. New rules must be established, covering, for instance, what to disclose and what to conceal. Users must also realign working relationships. People can participate and withdraw from encounters intermittently. Electronic mediation affects greetings, feedback, turn management and sequencing, all of which this book has shown to be culturally influenced.

These changes alter the availability of techniques for improving intercultural communication; for instance, it has been shown that feedback is more necessary for successful intercultural than intracultural communication, but in electronic communication the proportion of feedback words is lower than in ordinary spoken interaction. Again, although in electronic communication considerable effort is expended on communication management, conversations nevertheless lack the 'orderliness' of comparable conversations face-to-face or by telephone. In computer-based communication there tends to be an intense need for response. A response is an endorsement that another person is willing to take the risk of interpreting the first person's message and, if necessary, supply the missing elements to make it understandable. A response can also be interpreted as a trusting behaviour, suggesting involvement, which conveys attraction, intimacy, attachment and affection.[12]

■ Users can and must adopt changed roles – new identities and senses of appropriate social standing. The need to manage personal and cultural identities is changed. In some cases, participants can, by not revealing their identities, avoid being stereotyped or victims of prejudice.

■ Power structures change in favour of employees who hold new skills or have control of information needed to perform work or receive its benefits. With changed power structures come changed expectations about language, deference and privilege.

■ Gibson and Gibbs (2006) suggested 'unpacking' the concept of virtuality into four characteristics, one of which is national diversity, the other three being geographic dispersion, electronic dependence and structural dynamism. They argued that all four involve mechanisms that hinder innovation but that many of these hindrances can be overcome by creating a psychologically safe communication climate. Interview and survey research largely confirmed these hypotheses.[13]

Business's concerns about privacy, referred to in Box 9.3, have generated interest in Enterprise 2.0 networks tailor-made for the corporate world. These work in much the same way as Facebook, but keep information off the public web and behind a corporate firewall. Benefits to organizations from virtual social networking include the following:

■ Staff can find data faster.
■ Duplication of knowledge-finding work is reduced.
■ Knowledge-sharing is increased.

Box 9.3

In a special report on social networking in January 2010, *The Economist* noted that Facebook was now the second most popular site on the internet after Google. It had over 350 million users – which, were it a nation, would make Facebook the world's third most populous after China and India. Its users were posting over 55 million updates a day on the site and sharing more than 3.5 billion pieces of content with one another every week. Some 70 per cent of its audience was outside the United States.

It was claimed that new social-networking offerings being developed for the corporate world would create huge benefits for businesses. Within companies, however, there was doubt about the benefits of online social networking in the office. A survey of 1,400 chief information officers conducted in 2009 by Robert Half Technology reported: 'The executives' biggest concern was that social networking would lead to social notworking, with employees using the sites to chat with friends instead of doing their jobs. Some bosses also fretted that the sites would be used to leak sensitive corporate information.'

However, 'as people become increasingly used to sharing and collaborating outside the workplace, they are coming to expect firms to be more open and collaborative places too.'

Source: The Economist, 28 January 2010

- Good ideas can emerge from anywhere in the organization.
- A more open/democratic workplace is created.
- The effect of existing IT systems, which are geared towards reinforcing separate silos rather than building bridges between them, is counteracted.
- Knowledge can be captured and experts within an organization identified.
- 'Social business intelligence' can be supplied. For instance, identifying people for a project team based on their expertise and their links to others may be facilitated.
- A big improvement over early knowledge-management systems is supported as virtual social networking combines content with commentary from people with know-how.

Problems organizations fear from virtual social networking include the following:

- What happens to personal data? Could it be used to spy on colleagues?
- Will informal networks spring up outside managerial control?
- There is fear of staff broadcasting politically incorrect comments. All comments can be traced to their originators, however, so people are careful.

Knowledge transfer

While high knowledge transferability can be seen as a 'double-edged sword' (it facilitates internal operations or those between offshore service providers and clients but it also means that knowledge can more easily be copied by outsiders), most interest has centred on increasing transferability.[14] There have been two lines of research on this topic. One is concerned with the characteristics of the knowledge, the other with the people and social systems in which the knowledge exists and in which transfer takes place or is required to take place.

Knowledge is increasingly seen as a sticky asset, in that it flows between locations only with difficulty. Knowledge stickiness impedes the transfer of knowledge necessary for executing processes from one set of personnel to another set of personnel. Knowledge stickiness is a positive function of the tacitness, ambiguity and social complexity of process knowledge and a negative function of its codifiability. In addition, Birkinshaw *et al*. (2002) found a 'neglected' dimension of knowledge that they called system embeddedness. This is the extent to which knowledge is a function of the social and physical system in which it exists. The system embeddedness of knowledge appears to be conceptually distinct from the tacit–articulate (also known as observability) dimension. In fact Birkinshaw *et al*. (2002) suggested that the interaction of these two orthogonal variables creates four categories of knowledge: isolated (where both observability (O) and system embeddedness (SE) are high), integrated (where both are low), transparent (where O is high but SE low) and opaque (where SE is high but O low). Transferability would be highest in the case of transparent knowledge, lowest in the case of opaque knowledge, where it may be obscure even to the unit that possesses it. Isolated and integrated knowledge would display intermediate levels of stickiness.[15] Certain other characteristics, however, make knowledge less sticky. Szulanski (1996) found the major barriers to internal knowledge transfer to be factors such as the recipient's lack of absorptive capacity and an arduous relationship between the source and the recipient, as much as ambiguity. Thus, a reduction in the level of these factors would reduce knowledge stickiness. Mechanisms that are useful in transferring sticky knowledge include close observation, process mapping and documentation.[16]

The second line of research into knowledge transfer has been concerned with how people and social systems affect it. Leung *et al*. (2005) considered that the effectiveness of cross-border knowledge transfer is directly related to the type of knowledge involved in the transfer process, but also that this transfer is moderated by the nature of the transacting cultural patterns and the cognitive styles of the individuals involved. Their model conceptualized four patterns of culture: vertical individualism, horizontal individualism, vertical collectivism and horizontal collectivism, as Chapter 2 explained. A series of propositions linked these cultural patterns to the ease or difficulty with which, other things being equal, knowledge is transferred. The greatest ease (in terms of speed and depth or viscosity) of knowledge transfer occurs when such transfers involve

Table 9.1   *Relative ease or difficulty of knowledge transfers between different types of culture*

Ease or difficulty of transfer	Types of transfer between cultures
Easiest	Vertical individualist to vertical individualist Vertical collectivist to vertical collectivist Horizontal individualist to horizontal individualist Horizontal collectivist to horizontal collectivist
Second easiest	Vertical individualist to horizontal individualist and vice versa Vertical collectivist to horizontal collectivist and vice versa
Third easiest	Vertical individualist to vertical collectivist and vice versa Horizontal individualist to horizontal collectivist and vice versa
Most difficult	Vertical individualist to horizontal individualist and vice versa Horizontal individualist to vertical collectivist and vice versa

Based on: Bhagat, B.L., Kedia, P.D., Harveston, H.C. and Triandis, H. (2002) 'Cultural variations in the cross-border transfer of organizational knowledge: an integrative framework', *Academy of Management Review*, **27**(2): 204–21

similar cultural contexts.[17] The degree of difficulty for each type of transfer depicted in Table 9.1 is a function of the difference between the approach to knowledge of the different cultural elements in each category. Individualism/collectivism, it is claimed, has more impact on information processing than verticality/horizontalism, although that does have some. Individualists prefer knowledge to be easily codified and to stand independent of the organizational context; collectivists put more emphasis on the context than the content and on what was mutually agreed upon than what precisely was communicated.[18]

Data on international acquisitions carried out by Finnish corporations showed that national cultural differences strongly affected knowledge transfer in international acquisitions.[19] Most empirical research on knowledge transfer has focused on communication between geographically and culturally distant locations where face-to-face communication cannot be the predominant mode. This topic is, therefore, the first of the contexts that are explored in this chapter. Further points about knowledge transfer will be made in subsequent sections.

Co-ordination

As Chapter 1 noted, co-ordination is fundamental to organization, and work communication is essential for co-ordination. In fact, there is a large literature that treats organizational design – and hence structure – as a response to the information processing needs created by the interdependence of organizations' constituent units. Interdependence is the inevitable consequence of the division of labour as it arises between those who carry out the divided work. Costly information processing requirements are generated by interdependence. These are the costs of communication and of decision-making.

Distinct patterns of interdependence give rise to different information processing requirements and 'task architectures': 'Variations in organizing modes are actually variations in the capacity of organizations to process information.'[20] Puranam *et al.* (2010) drew attention to a particular kind of interdependence, which they called epistemic interdependence: this means that in order to act in a way that maximizes his or her utility an agent (individual or unit) needs sufficiently accurate predictive knowledge about what another agent will do. 'Co-ordination problems are characterized by epistemic interdependence.' An example of a situation of epistemic interdependence, and thus of a potential co-ordination problem, might arise in a medical situation where a patient had more than one condition and some treatments for condition x would be harmful if condition y were being treated with certain medications. A business example, which has often arisen in the past, is the need of the advertising media schedulers to know when retail distribution will take place in relation to a new product launch. 'Whenever one agent's utility is maximized by acting on an accurate prediction of another agent's actions, there is a (potential) co-ordination problem. *A co-ordination failure* is fundamentally a failure to predict the actions of another in situations where such a prediction is essential for optimal action by oneself.' (In terms of the new product launch example, if the advertising breaks before retail distribution is achieved, much of the advertising expenditure may be wasted; while, if it breaks too long after the product is available at retail, low initial sales may result in retailers rejecting it.) Thus, 'Any setting in which actions are unobservable – either because they are taking place simultaneously, because of communication/information transmission constraints, or because of timing (it hasn't happened yet) – but must be predicted, can be modeled as a co-ordination problem.'[21] (This line of argument suggests that co-ordination issues are not the same as knowledge sharing issues. For instance, providing a system of appropriate signals or a history of interaction experiences [which is equivalent to common ground] is in place, co-ordination can occur without much shared knowledge: that, after all, is the way interpersonal interactions with strangers occur.)

The co-ordination problems caused by geographical distance and time lags and their implications for both organization and communication are common to both (the now rare) mono(sub)cultural and to intercultural (diverse) organizations. However, given that the ability sufficiently to predict another's behaviour is fundamental to co-ordination, it is clear that barriers to such prediction generated by (sub)cultural differences potentially increase the co-ordination 'problem'. Furthermore, research has shown that achieving co-ordination is an extremely important problem in the kinds of distributed settings that are the subject of this chapter, such as virtual teams, offshoring or multinational enterprises.

There is research to suggest that informal networks, horizontal communication and social networks are important for resolving co-ordination problems within organizations. For instance, a dataset of millions of electronic mail messages, calendar meetings and teleconferences for many thousands of employees of one multidivisional firm during three months of 2006 was analysed to investigate which boundaries between people least impeded communication. The findings were that most communication took place within strategic business units and functions – that is, within structural boundaries – and where pairs of individuals were collocated – in other words within spatial boundaries. Socio-demographic boundaries were much weaker – people were not much less likely to communicate with 'different others' than with similar others. A further finding was that particular categories of individuals were most likely to act as boundary spanners between distant groups in the company's social structure – these were women, mid- to high-level executives, and members of the executive management, sales and marketing functions.[22] These findings of the use and value of informal means of resolving co-ordination issues demonstrate the importance of effective intercultural communication in diverse organizations.

The jury is still out on the effects of CMC on intercultural relationships at work. Some hypothesized effects, such as that the CMC 'workplace' will be more democratic and less gender-biased, do not seem to be supported when research into actual usage is undertaken. The influence during groupwork of majorities (whether culture-based or not) on minorities does, however, appear to be lower when the groups communicate by CMC instead of face-to-face. Research into online marketing suggests that both culture and gender influence consumers' responses, and in particular their levels of trust in the marketing itself. CMC expands the range of contacts of many individuals, and so their need for intercultural communication skills. Forms of communication, roles, identities and (within organizations) power structures are all potentially affected. These consequences are likely to be increased with the growth of social networking both outside and within businesses.

Cultural differences in the approach to knowledge can create difficulties in knowledge transfer and help make knowledge 'sticky'. These differences are more marked between individualists and collectivists than between people differently located on a vertical–horizontal power dimension.

Many co-ordination issues are a function of how well individuals or units can predict other individuals' or units' behaviour. Cultural differences must affect the accuracy of such predictions, although research suggests that informal communication helps overcome the effects of such differences.

9.2 WORKING IN VIRTUAL TEAMS

The advantages to businesses of virtual teamworking include the ability to pass work-in-progress round the clock between the three main economic centres (Asia, Europe and North America), while even within the same time zone work-in-progress can be stored, which makes it possible to use time more efficiently. Paradoxically, one major barrier to virtual teamworking effectiveness is members' reluctance to share work-in-progress – for instance, software developers are often unwilling to pass over half-finished programs to others. As Pawar and Sharifi (1997) noted, by comparison with physically co-located teams, whose members 'are likely to have similar and comple-mentary educational and cultural backgrounds', members of virtual teams are more likely to vary in their education, culture, time orientation, language and expertise.[23]

A 2009 review article on virtual teams recorded a 'sizeable number' of studies that found a negative relationship between positive interpersonal climate and structural diversity (in the form of geographic dispersion, the existence of subgroups, and diver-sity with respect to culture, function, and age). The most consistently found relation-ships were the negative relationship between subgroups and trust, and the positive relationship between conflict and both cultural diversity and subgroups. Also found were positive relationships of communication quality with a positive interpersonal climate, media richness and interpersonal (as opposed to task-based) communica-ton. Evidence of a negative relationship between quality of communication and structural diversity was also found, but this was primarily with respect to geographic dispersion.[24]

There are problems of identity in virtual teamworking. Understanding what is going on in an interaction usually depends on knowing the identity of your interactor, but identity is ambiguous when team members are separated by time and borders, so that the cues generally used for identification are concealed. There is, for instance, the pos-sibility that any one interactor may adopt multiple virtual personas. Ferguson (2005) proposed that team members who only communicated via CMC and never came

Box 9.4

'In a multinational videoconference that intro-duced new development teammates to each other, individuals naturally assessed teammates by their dress and posture. We believe that had the team members travelled to meet face to face, they would have attempted to dress appropriately to the location where the meeting took place, alleviating some of the wrong first impressions generated at this event.'[a]

Becker et al. (2000), who pointed out the extensive use of gesture in design group meet-ings, noted that computing and communication technology were making possible new venues for carrying out design meetings, including dis-tributed meetings where either groupware or communication technologies were used. These, however, restricted the range of gestures that could be seen by other members of the group. One technology, for instance, desktop video conferencing, generally only allowed a head and shoulder shot to be transmitted.[b]

Sources: (a) Olson, J.S and Olson, G.M. (2003–4) 'Culture surprises in remote software development teams', *Queue*, **1**(9): 52–9

(b) Becker, M.M, Olson, J.S. and Olson, G.M. (2000) 'How does radical collocation help a team succeed?', *Proceedings of the 2000 ACM Conference on Computer supported Cooperative work, Philadelphia, Pennsylvania, United States*, 339–46

face-to-face with fellow team members and who knew from their virtual team's inception that the work team was only a temporary one were likely to view their virtual team members quite differently when compared with members of more traditional teams. 'This may be particularly so in a global virtual team where members are separated by time zones, language barriers, and cultural differences.' Identification with one's team or perceiving the team as an ingroup holds importance for organizational outcomes. Team members with a salient team identity tend to behave in a manner that benefits the group as whole rather than in a way that is self-interested. Therefore, the lack of team identity in globally distributed teams may lead to effort-withholding behaviours, which result in lowered team performance. When a team member acts in his/her own self-interest, it may often be at the expense of the team and even the organization. A small-scale study within one organization found that it may not be the 'virtuality' (computer-mediated communication, lack of face-to-face meetings, or lifespan of a team) that poses challenges to a virtual team, but rather its cultural diversity and the distance between members.[25]

Trust is clearly an issue for intercultural virtual teams. Much of the theoretical and empirical literature on interpersonal and organizational trust suggests that a lack of shared social context, such as occurs in global virtual teams, would result in low trust. Media richness and social presence theories also question the possibility of relationship development in virtual teams, since computer-based communication eliminates the types of communication cues needed to convey trust, warmth and other interpersonal affections. Without these cues individuals build stereotypical impressions of others based on limited information. Furthermore, cross-cultural variabilities such as individualism–collectivism suggest different needs, values and goals for the team, resulting in potentially differing levels of trust. The more cultures there are represented on a virtual team, the greater the tendency to establish strict control mechanisms. Some controls actually appear to signal to the team members that there is an absence of trust and, therefore, they can hamper its emergence. Institutional controls can also undermine trust when legal mechanisms give rise to rigidity in response to conflict and substitute high levels of formalization for more flexible conflict management.

A case study identified some communication behaviours and some actions that facilitated trust early in a group's life, including social communication (about personal rather than task matters) and communicating enthusiasm, coping with technical uncertainty and taking individual initiative. Later in a group's life predictable communication, substantive and timely responses, successful transition from social to procedural to task focus, positive leadership and phlegmatic responses to crises helped maintain trust. The case study report suggested that the trust initially created during the study was more like 'swift', depersonalized, action-based trust than long-term trust. Trusting behaviour based on swift trust may subsequently have provided a cognitive and emotional basis for longer-term trust.[26]

Pointing out that, whereas information technology-facilitated communication processes rely on technologically advanced systems to succeed, the ability to create a knowledge-sharing culture within a global virtual team rests on the existence (and maintenance) of intra-team respect, mutual trust, reciprocity and positive individual and group relationships, Zakaria *et al.* (2004) asked the question: 'How do organizations develop a knowledge sharing culture to promote effective organizational learning among culturally diverse team members?' Their findings suggested that the answer was that team members imported an understanding of knowledge-sharing cultures from other settings that they were familiar with; for their perceptions of their fellow team-members they used stereotypical impressions based on the initial use of category-driven information. A problem arises, of course, if individual team members' stereotypes are flawed, biased or incomplete, which, as Chapter 5 of this book showed, is not uncommon. An alternative view of the creation of knowledge-sharing cultures in culturally diverse teams is that members start from a position of crediting the other team members with adequate capability and also benevolence – positive beliefs about the emotional aspects of the other members' behaviour, such as their having a positive intention to exchange. This set of attitudes is, in effect, swift trust, which is less based on interpersonal relationships, and places greater stress on initial broad social structures and then on action. Here a potential problem is with culturally different expectations about work levels and outputs. Zakaria *et al.* (2004) concluded that team members need to maintain high levels of action regardless of their personal preferences.[27] The results on the beneficial effects of radical co-location described in Chapter 8 imply that supporting remote teams, whether intercultural or not, requires ways to provide 'constant awareness and easy transitions in and out of spontaneous meetings'.[28]

> Two issues have attracted most research attention in regard to virtual teams: identification with the team and trust between the dispersed team members. Cross-cultural differences, which lead to different needs, values and goals, can add to problems in these areas, and the managerial tendency to impose strict controls when the number of cultures represented is large adds a further trust-destroying dimension. On the other hand, lack of visual and non-verbal cues may sometimes reduce awareness of cultural difference, and swift trust developed early on may provide a basis for other kinds of trust later on.

9.3 OFFSHORING

Offshoring has become a strategic business model pursued by firms to decrease costs and focus on their core competencies. Although offshoring is not a new phenomenon, the current phase of offshoring is marked by the increased tradability of services enabled by ICT. In 2010, 40 per cent of US high-technology firms sent work offshore, and about 30 per cent of these firms that offshore sent IT work overseas.[29] Offshoring involves the geographic distribution of a process, typically to a low wage location, regardless of whether the process is in-house or outsourced (executed by a third party vendor).

Box 9.5

A study of six US-based, Fortune 500 firms involved in offshore outsourcing of services showed that these buying organizations initially experienced more complexity than anticipated in engaging with offshore suppliers in outsourcing relationships. To achieve success with these relationships, the buying organizations needed to embrace cultural differences, including the needs of their suppliers' employees.

Source: Tate, W.L., Ellram, L.M. and Brown, S.W. (2009) 'Offshore outsourcing of services: a stakeholder perspective', *Journal of Service Research*, **12**: 56–72

Offshore business services can be divided into two categories – content development and service provisioning. Content development involves generation of content to pre-defined specifications on a one-time basis, as in software development. The service provider is free to choose any method to create the output as long as it adheres to pre-specified agreements regarding the outcome. Service provisioning, on the other hand, involves ongoing delivery of services from a remote location and therefore implies the specification of not only the outputs but also the process by which the output is generated. Poor performance in offshored processes can result from knowledge sticki-ness and the consequent difficulty of transferring the knowledge required to execute the process. A second very important issue is that of co-ordination between the onsite and offshore locations. Interdependence across locations and the consequent need for co-ordination are much higher for service provisioning.

Co-ordination through ongoing (day by day) communication has severe limitations in the context of offshoring: limitations such as cost, information channel bandwidth constraints and time zone differences. A common approach to minimizing the need for ongoing communication is modularization – designing standard operating procedures, rules, plans and schedules that specify what each element must do so that their joint actions are co-ordinated. Set-up costs and flaws which mean that some interdependencies are missed are the weakness of modularization systems. Co-ordinating the residual inter-dependence that cannot be fully managed through modular interfaces is usually achieved through ongoing communication. As pointed out above, this has limitations.

A third means is to build 'common ground' – shared tacit knowledge – through enhancing observability of context, actions and outcomes across locations rather than direct communication (although ongoing communication itself helps to build common ground). For instance, staffing distributed teams with employees who have worked together before (in order to exploit their shared experiences) helps ensure that employees across locations know about each other's idiosyncratic work practices. Other examples include shared work-related training and/or cultural sensitivity train-ing to enable mutual knowledge of respective decision-making procedures; making actions transparent across locations by investment in technology tools; and using a

---

Box 9.6

A company undertaking web-based business research had its reports drafted in India using statistics researched and formulated there, then sent to the UK for copy editing. The UK copy editor used the 'Track changes' facility in Word and returned the document to the drafter. When the UK copy editor came across some-thing he/she did not understand or thought his/her amendment might be wrong, he/she high-lighted the area for further attention. The prob-lem was that the Indian drafter tended to accept all changes initiated in the UK without further consideration.

Another issue was that the company wanted to tag title each report to emphasize its news value and its client value. So, if, for instance, the main title was 'Orthopaedic procedures, France, 2012' there might be a tag title: 'French Government plans to boost market for hip replacement tissues'. Writing the tag titles was done in the UK. Without better co-ordination, that could mean it happened too late in the process, so the tag title was not fully reflected in the report.

Source: interview with an offshore production man-ager, author's research

shared vocabulary to facilitate interpreting communication across locations.[30] Cultural differences need to be accommodated for in applying these methods. The work context sometimes conceals cultural differences – on the surface people engaged in, for instance, software design or pharmaceutical development interact as if they think and feel similarly. It is therefore easy for participants in these shared activities to assume that they fully understand one another, when in reality significant misunderstandings occur. Since the purpose of these training or other exposures is to create common ground rather than to produce output, they are usually time-limited, and after the end of the period there is limited opportunity for misunderstandings to be corrected. The 'common' ground may not be common.

Despite this shortcoming, investment in creating common ground is widely used in high-end offshoring such as pharmaceutical R&D (Research and Development), and is effective. A survey of 42 IT, 54 back office and 30 call centre service providers in India (which accounts for 65 per cent of the global offshore IT industry and 46 per cent of the global BPO (business process outsourcing) industry) compared the three methods (modularization, ongoing communication and creating common ground). The alternatives were judged by performance measured across four categories which reflect most organizations' motives for offshoring – cost savings, service quality improvements, rapid growth and overall satisfaction with the service. All of them were shown to mitigate the co-ordination problems that interdependence creates in the context of offshoring. The researchers suggested that there is a tendency towards over-investment in communication channels at the expense of tacit means of building common ground.[31] Figure 9.1 depicts the alternative ways of achieving co-ordination of distributed work; research

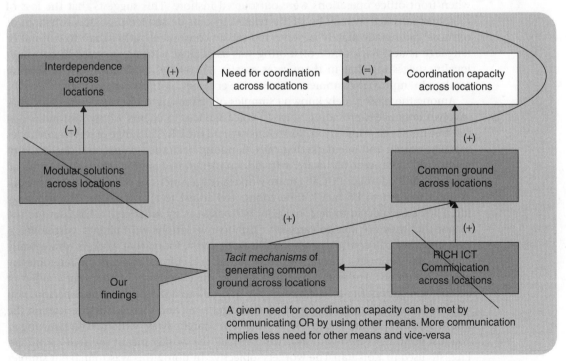

Figure 9.1   *Schematic representation of alternative co-ordination strategies. Reprinted with permission from Srikanth, K. and Puranam, P. (2010) 'Integrating distributed work: comparing task design, communication, and tacit co-ordination mechanisms',* SSRN Working Paper Series, *URL: http://ssrn.com/abstract=1125924*

identified more benefit from investment in 'tacit coordination' to create common ground than in modular solutions or rich communication channels.

'Our results point to the surprising conclusion that the primary role of ICTs in the offshored projects we studied was not as a substitute for collocated communication, but instead to enable tacit co-ordination by directly updating and maintaining "common ground" across locations. Common ground between two people is defined as "the sum of their mutual, common or joint knowledge, beliefs and suppositions".'[32] In the context of distributed software development, common ground refers to the joint knowledge across locations of who is working on what, what stage they are at, who is interdependent with whom, and information regarding the abilities and constraints facing participants in each location. In co-located settings, such common ground is created through normal face-to-face communication and the fact of being immersed in the same context. 'Our field interviews of software project managers indicates that through the use of specific kinds of ICT tools such as shared code repositories, configuration management systems and automated workflow tools such common ground could be generated without the need for direct communication between developers, which enabled them to co-ordinate their actions tacitly. Thus, our key finding is that ICT tools may enable the co-ordination of distributed activity, (such as in software services offshoring) not through providing channels for rich and direct communication, but by making rich communication unnecessary by directly building up a stock of common ground.'[33]

Whitaker et al. (2008) found a reduction in customer satisfaction when front office (i.e., customer interface) operations were offshored; these difficulties could be linked to cultural and language difficulties. On the other hand, a similar decrease was found when front office operations were outsourced inshore. This suggests that the loss of customer satisfaction may be partly related to outside service providers (offshore or onshore) failing adequately to serve and satisfy consumers, rather than to cultural or language issues. Back office offshoring was associated with an increase in customer loyalty, suggesting that in these cases greater efficiencies associated with offshoring resulted in improved customer service or lower prices, not just cost savings.[34]

Among the most widely known examples of offshoring is the call centre. The work involves employees providing voice-to-voice services to clients whose customers dial toll-free numbers, primarily in North America and the UK. The range of services includes market research and telemarketing calls, handling insurance claims, and dealing with credit card, computer hardware, network connections, banking, and other financial enquiries and complaints. Call centre workers learn American or British accents, work at night to cater to US or UK time zones, and adjust to an altered social and family life. They are expected to be conversant with day-to-day American or UK issues to the extent that they are able to carry on casual conversations with clients' customers. A case study of a call centre operation in Kolkata, India, found that workers 'strategically constructed identities – through accents, names, and cultural markers – to resemble the client [customer]'. For example, one described the experience of adopting a different accent while attending to clients on call: 'You talk to a person, a normal person, you will have a neutral accent. But as soon as you get a call and there is an American on the line or a British person, you go on to the accent straight away without even knowing it. You just go straight into your job.' (By 'normal' the worker meant the style of 'Indian English' used in Kolkata.) The workers' objective in doing this was to make it simpler for the customer to understand and accept them. They knew that they faced difficulty in being accepted by some customers.[35]

There are three recognized boundaries involved in outsourced offshoring, each of which creates barriers for communication and hence for knowledge sharing and

Box 9.7

The Managing Director (Asia) of a British-owned offshore operation was struggling with how to present the annual bonus to his staff. For the first time 50 per cent of the bonus was being awarded for team performance, a change imposed by the UK-based owners. 'They are going to hate this,' he said. 'Both the fact that their own individual bonus could be lower because someone else in the team has under-performed and the fact that some teams will be seen as having an advantage in terms of visibility. I hope it won't do more harm than good.'[a]

'Host-country management skills (middle management) [are very important] in bringing about the emergence of international offshoring. By shielding top management in the source country from routine problems faced by host country workers, the presence of middle managers improves the efficiency of the transmission of knowledge across countries.'[b]

Sources: (a) Author's research
(b) Antras, P., Garicano, L. and Rossi-Hansberg, E.A. (2006) 'Organizing offshoring: middle managers and communication costs', NBER Working Paper Series, Vol. w12196, URL: http://ssrn.com/abstract=900982, last accessed on 24 December 2010

co-ordination. In addition to the boundary of geography and distance discussed above, with their concomitants of time and distance that prevent face-to-face communication, there are those between firms and those between cultures. A study that investigated how co-ordination of work distributed between firms differed from that distributed within firms found that, although there were no mechanisms for co-ordination that were unique to the situation within or between firms, there was nevertheless a sharp distinction in how work was co-ordinated in the two cases. Distributed projects that involved multiple firms were always organized in such a way that the interface between firms was co-located; firms from different geographies worked together, but they did so by co-locating their employees, usually by the vendor firm locating personnel to work within the client firm. Distance was always 'internalized' within a firm. This internalization of distance appeared to be based on the superior prospects for co-ordinating distributed work enjoyed by intra-firm projects.[36] One reason may be that intra-firm common ground was chosen and maintained by authority (legitimated organizational power), which was not, obviously, available between organizations.

Cultural differences affect a range of the technologies for distributed work, including the use of video- versus audio-conferencing, brainstorming technologies and decision-support systems; speaker identification, distribution of e-mail and trust building are among the issues. In some cases, such as scientific research, the shared occupational culture (e.g., high-energy physics) may so dominate the national cultural differences as to minimize the effect of the latter. However, 'since cultural knowledge is so ingrained and automatic, it can surface when deadlines or other stressful conditions exist.' Suggested measures for dealing with these include making both parties aware of the issue (because culture is hidden), increasing co-workers' explicit knowledge about what the cultural values of their co-workers are and adjusting to suit others, as well as to understand them. In this way, it is hoped, an internet culture may emerge.[37]

Offshoring, especially of service provisioning, creates interdependencies that require high levels of co-ordination but also created obstacles to co-ordination from time differences, knowledge stickiness, costs and cultural differences. Rather than achieving co-ordination through ongoing communication or modularization, it has been suggested, methods that create and increase common ground between the personnel of the offshore supplier and client deserve more investment. Growth of common ground automatically reduces the negative consequences that may otherwise flow from cultural difference.

9.4 WORKING IN INTERNATIONAL ALLIANCES

An alliance is commonly defined as any voluntarily initiated co-operative agreement between firms that involves exchange, sharing, or co-development; it can include contributions by partners of capital, technology or firm-specific assets. At one extreme are 50/50 joint ventures; at the other, short-term product-marketing arrangements. Relationships between partners are a prominent issue in all co-operative alliances. The dynamics of these relationships become even more fundamental in a cross-cultural setting, in which international co-operative ventures encounter more opportunities (e.g., mutual learning, knowledge transfer and market entry) as well as greater challenges (e.g., institutional volatility, cultural barriers and property rights protection).[38]

The composition of an organization's top management team in terms of national diversity and international experience influences the choice of overseas expansion mode. Diverse top management teams are more likely to opt for international acquisitions or joint ventures, whereas top management teams with international experience tend to prefer greenfield investments.[39] A major reason for entering a joint venture on the part of firms in developing countries such as China and India is that the firms are seeking the transfer of knowledge. Where the knowledge they seek is tacit, embedded knowledge, data from 90 partner-seeking firms in China showed, it is complementary knowledge, rather than knowledge in the same area in which they already have knowledge of their own, that motivates their search.[40] This finding is one of several that link the literature on international alliances to that on knowledge transfer.

Most managerial research about mergers has assumed that cultural differences imply 'acculturative stress' (i.e., stress caused by the need to adjust to different others).[41] A study of European mergers confirmed that acculturative stress influenced performance in the merged firms. Cultural differences in beliefs about which factors had most effect on performance contributed to acculturative stress. For the French, for example, the most important factor was personal and societal responsibility. (The French place a high premium on concern for the health and well-being of employees, the local community and society at large.) For the British, the most important factor was performance and reward. (In British culture, individuals are achievement-driven and ambitious; they accept responsibility for their own work and therefore expect clear and objective standards of evaluation based on personal performance.[42])

Different cultural interpretations of a proper way to communicate content and relations during the integration phase following a cross-border acquisition can be fundamental to whether it succeeds or fails. In two qualitative studies conducted in Finland and France, Irrmann (2005) explored the intercultural dimension of communicative events at play during the integration phase (from 1997 to 2002) of two French–Finnish industrial and engineering groups. Both the French and the Finnish respondents considered their own organization as direct and informal and the other organization's culture hierarchical and formal. The researchers concluded that 'communication dissonance' or 'cultural dissonance' might be more significant than 'cultural distance'.[43] In a German–Japanese joint venture, it was found, the organizational culture that emerged from the 'negotiations' was affected by the meaning that those involved made of organizational events.[44] This meaning was culturally determined – that is, people's differing cultural backgrounds strongly influenced how they interpreted events.

The success of international alliances depends on the ability of both companies to work together after as well as during the merger, acquisition or set-up phase. In international business alliances, barriers to effective communication, and so to performance, result from underlying national and organizational cultural differences. Differences in the cultural backgrounds of partners cause problems in international joint ventures (IJVs), but one study showed that some differences were more disruptive than others. Cultural distance in uncertainty avoidance and long-term orientation reduced the survival chances of IJVs more than cultural distance in individualism, power distance or masculinity. Differences in uncertainty avoidance and long-term orientation may cause particular problems because these differences, which translate into differences in how IJV partners perceive and adapt to opportunities and threats in their environment, are more difficult to resolve than differences along the other three dimensions. Perhaps cultural differences regarding power distance, individualism and masculinity are more easily resolved because they are mainly reflected in different attitudes towards the management of personnel. Firms can make explicit agreements about personnel management before entering the partnership.[45]

A qualitative study of West European – Russian joint ventures found that cultural differences can have a key impact on operations and that cultural and operational differences can produce difficulties 'specific to this kind of partnership'. For instance, the Western Europeans felt a stronger pressure to achieve set targets within a given time frame. 'In contrast, while Russians are conscious of a goal to be reached, they do not seem to feel the time pressure or to be diligent in taking steps to achieve that goal.' Similarly, the Russians were inclined to present problems that arose to the Western partner with no suggestions for solutions, rather than to take the initiative to solve them. One Western manager in a manufacturing joint venture explained that it was difficult to show people that they had to make their own decisions and assume certain responsibilities. Russians' assumptions about a company and its functions may be 'drastically different' from West Europeans'. Until 1990 in Russia, the function of a company was not to make a profit by supplying a good or service; instead it was to serve a centralized and planned economy by complying with production standards. As a result business practices continued to differ in areas including price-setting, investment policies, cost analysis and control, quality control, and understanding the organizational structure. For example, one Russian joint-venture partner initially considered that the more people were employed, the greater the profit would be, on the grounds that labour is not a cost component to be included in the profit-and-loss statement. Russians were unaware of the management processes, systems and style that govern how a Western company functions. One manager described an instance when a mechanic appeared in the middle of a meeting of the board of directors.[46]

A study of a joint venture between India and other countries found that national culture distance more significantly predicted the efficiency and competitiveness of IJV (international joint venture) performance than organizational culture distance did, although the latter was a better predictor of satisfaction. Similarity on masculinity had a consistently positive effect on all performance measures, while cultural distance on the other national culture dimensions had a significant negative effect on satisfaction; it was only because these effects counterbalanced each other that the overall impact of national culture on the aggregate measures was limited.[47]

Methods of improving success rates of international alliances include flexibility over managerial practices, paying special attention to trust building, effective intercultural communication and attachments of boundary spanners:

■ Western managerial practices, such as goal-setting, performance-monitoring, conflict resolution and information sharing may need to be adapted. In three cross-border acquisitions by Western companies in South Korea, changes in human resource management and organizational culture were not only tolerated but even appreciated by the employees of Korean target firms. However, organizational culture changes encouraging more individualism and contradicting Confucian values were negatively perceived.[48]

■ Special attention must be paid to trust building. 'Co-operation between organizations creates mutual dependence and requires trust in order to succeed. This comes down to trust between the individuals who are involved in the alliance. Uncertainty about partners' motives, and a lack of detailed knowledge about how they operate, requires that a basis for trust be found for co-operation to get under way in the first place.'[49] Legal contracts play no significant role in this process. Methods of decision-making, conflict resolution and good interpersonal relationships have an important impact. Experienced managers in Russia advocated decision-making by consensus, rather than by voting majority or asserting ownership rights. Because the relations that really matter exist in the social fabric, the behavioural element of importance is the role of trust.[50] A study showed that trust enabled strategic managerial action to overcome the influence of business and institutional environments in cross-border ventures.[51] An important factor in whether trust develops in international alliances is that those affected perceive that they are treated with interactional justice – that is, whether they believe they are treated with dignity and respect and whether they are given adequate explanations about why procedures are used in a certain way or why outcomes are distributed in a certain fashion. An analysis of 152 international joint ventures suggested that perceived interactional justice was positively associated with decision effectiveness, interpersonal trust and inter-organizational attachment, and that interactional justice suppressed the negative influence of national cultural differences on inter-organizational attachment.[52]

More generally, initiating and fostering expectations that the relationship will continue, flexibility and information exchange between the partner firms are factors positively related to both trust and market performance in international partnerships. Interpersonal interactions to inculcate shared organizational beliefs also foster trust. A survey that included 12 Swedish cross-border mergers and acquisitions showed how national and cultural differences in mergers and acquisitions could best be overcome and the beliefs and values of the affected employees harmoniously integrated. It found these positive effects occurred when 'the buying firms rely on social controls. That is, by participating in such activities as introduction programs, training, cross-visits, retreats, celebrations and similar socialization rituals, employees will create, of their own volition, a joint organizational culture.'[53]

- Effective communication with international business partners is also key.[54] Direct contact is important in building the relationship. One manager in a Western European/Russian joint venture explained that he preferred to use his own poor Russian language rather than an interpreter. A good interface becomes very important. Russians 'appreciate a true friendship and distinguish this one from a mere forbearance born out of pure economic interests'.[55] In an American/Polish health care joint venture, there were four factors linked to success. These were high 'stakeholder strength' – that is, both parties' contributions were essential; reduced uncertainty because key decision-makers were acquainted through common business associations; a corporate culture that reflected religious affiliation (both parties were Roman Catholic organizations); and high trust, which in this case was also promoted by religious affiliation.[56]

- A study of 282 international co-operative ventures in China found that 'attachments' between boundary spanners within cross-cultural international co-operative ventures (ICVs) stimulated their performance and increased financial returns. 'Attachment' means that the parties' attitudes towards one another are positive; it is probably a precondition of trust, but trust also requires the parties to accept vulnerability (risk) based on those positive attitudes. 'Reliance and risk are two necessary conditions for trust but not for attachment.'[57] Thus, the finding that attachment itself promoted the ICV's performance is useful. Without personal attachment between boundary-spanning managers, opportunism tends to occur in these arrangements; it is hard to control by formal governance mechanisms. Personal attachment helps to suppress opportunism, boost trust and so counter dissolution. Attachment between individual boundary spanners in the ICVs was found to increase as their time working together (their overlap in tenure) increased.

    Other factors promoting attachment were goal congruity and low cultural distance between the parent firms; market disturbance and regulatory deterrence also seemed to operate as external pressures that increased cohesiveness.[58]

> Cultural differences in uncertainty avoidance and time orientation impact the success of international alliances such as joint ventures more than do cultural differences in power distance, individualism and masculinity. Differences have been found in the interpretation of events, in the factors that are believed to stimulate acculturative stress, in the perceived functions of a company and in business practices. Communication and interpretation differences also impact performance in international alliances. Adaptation of managerial practices, trust building, high standards of interactional justice, effective communication between the international partners, and attachments between boundary spanners all contribute to the success of international alliances.

9.5 COMMUNICATION ISSUES IN MULTINATIONAL ENTERPRISES (MNEs)

Both knowledge transfer and co-ordination, the two of work processes perhaps most dependent on communication, are extremely important for MNEs; in fact, Gupta and Govindarajan (2000) conceptualized multinational corporations as networks of transactions that are engaged in knowledge flows,[59] while Peng (2001) argued that MNCs (multinational companies) exist because of their capabilities to transfer and exploit knowledge more effectively. As a result, how to promote inter-unit communication in MNEs is a key question.[60] An early view that the success of knowledge transfer is exclusively a function of the characteristics of that knowledge is now discredited: 'To fully understand the process of knowledge transfer, it is important to include characteristics of the individuals involved in the transfer process as well as characteristics of the context in which knowledge transfer takes place.'[61] In international businesses, intercultural co-ordination within as well as across organizations is essential.

Welch *et al.* (2005) noted that in MNCs the need for control and co-ordination has driven the move towards language standardization, in the form of a common corporate language, with widespread effects on management processes. Despite their importance, however, language issues have been relatively ignored.[62] Most MNEs do in fact work in a common language – usually English. For some members, the common language will be their mother tongue; for many, it will be a second or third language. Charles (2007) argued that, although using a common language might appear to ease communication, the choice of language(s) used is a delicate issue, splitting the staff of MNEs into native/non-native speakers and thus requiring considerable people management skills.[63] BELF (Business English Lingua Franca – Charles' (2007) name for English as a common language in MNEs) is a mostly oral language. Through it power is wielded in multinationals, and perceptions of self and others created. Moreover, it is not a 'cultureless' language, but rather creates new operational cultures. Language choice thus has implications for management, human relations and employee satisfaction. Chen and Jackson (2008) raised the question of how language capability can affect knowledge transfer within MNEs. They argued that the challenge of language capability can cause communication barriers which may lead to conflict; and that language capability is compounded with the issue of cultural diversity, further raising barriers to the process of knowledge transfer.[64]

An ethnographic participant-observation study in the UK plant of a German MNC (whose findings were described in Box 5.3) led to the conclusions that culture and cohesion were opposed and that 'global strategies are always mediated by local circumstances, thus strengthening the arguments for recognising the interaction between management elites and local workforces, acknowledging cultural diversity and its impact on global business, and looking beyond simplistic notions of "national culture" towards diversity within national boundaries. ... The successful implementation of global corporate strategies works best not just with due acknowledgement of local workforce identities, but with positive engagement with local historical and cultural traditions.'[65]

Units within multi-unit organizations typically compete, either for markets or for resources or both. At the same time, they need to co-operate with each other if knowledge transfer optimization and its consequent benefits for the organization are to occur. 'This paradox has become a major challenge for multiunit organizations that seek to manage their internal knowledge flows.'[66] Tsai (2002) reported a study that showed that, within organizations with competing units, formal hierarchical structure, in the form of centralization, had a significant negative effect on knowledge sharing. The more control the headquarters exercised on its subunits, the less the subunits were willing to share knowledge with other units. 'Centralization may impose certain identifiable costs on an organization. These costs include: (1) a tendency for headquarters to intervene excessively or inappropriately, (2) increased time and effort devoted to influencing activities with a corresponding reduction in organizational productivity, (3) poor decision making resulting from the distortion of information associated with activities to influence, and (4) a loss of efficiency as the organization adapts its structure and policies to enhance control activities. Because of such costs, centralization can become an ineffective way to co-ordinate.'

Informal lateral relations, on the other hand, in the form of social interaction, were found to be more effective than centralization for achieving co-ordination of subunits in MNEs. They had a significant positive effect on knowledge sharing among units that competed with each other for market share (though not among units that competed with each other for internal resources).[67] Organizational units that interact with each other socially are likely to share knowledge with each other. The results confirm the importance of inter-unit social interaction as an effective co-ordination mechanism in a multi-unit organization. Social interaction allows individual units to accumulate social capital that can help them gain access to new knowledge or new information. The flows of information or knowledge through inter-unit networks require social interaction to promote trust and to reduce perceived uncertainty about providing new knowledge to other units (or acquiring new knowledge from other units). Knowledge sharing involves a complex social process that demands collaborative efforts. Social interaction is indispensable in this process as it can create trust and foster co-operation. Social interaction also helps break down barriers created by cultural differences.

There is a debate in the literature about the relative value of strong and weak ties for knowledge sharing. According to the weak-tie theory originally advanced by Granovetter (1973), distant and infrequent relationships (i.e., weak ties) are efficient for knowledge sharing because they provide access to novel information by bridging otherwise disconnected groups and individuals in an organization. Strong ties, in contrast, are likely to lead to redundant information because they tend to occur among a small group of actors in which everyone knows what the others know. Granovetter (1973) described the strength of a tie as a 'combination of the amount of time, the emotional intensity, the intimacy (mutual confiding) and the reciprocal services which characterize the tie'.[68] While there is substantial ambiguity built into this definition, it certainly seems likely that intercultural ties are generally weaker than intracultural ties, which would tend to imply that they are functional for knowledge sharing, or at least that other factors that might militate against intercultural ties for knowledge sharing would be to some degree counteracted.[69] A 1999 study found, however, that neither weak nor strong relationships between operating units were necessarily better for efficient sharing of knowledge among them. Weak and strong inter-unit ties had their respective strengths and weaknesses in facilitating search for and transfer of useful knowledge across organization subunits. The net effect on project completion time of having either weak or strong inter-unit ties was contingent on the complexity of the knowledge to be transferred across subunits. Strong inter-unit ties provided the highest relative net effect (or least negative effect) on completion time when the knowledge was highly complex, whereas weak inter-unit ties had the strongest positive effect on completion time when the knowledge was not complex.[70] Thus, while non-diverse organizations using complex knowledge may benefit from the strong ties that may result from intracultural relationships, diverse organizations using non-complex knowledge may benefit from the knowledge sharing that occurs in the weaker ties of intercultural relationships.

There is evidence, however, that strong ties that function as channels of knowledge sharing for complex knowledge across borders can be provided through expatriates. The empirical results of an exploratory case study showed that, when compared with other, more arm's-length, cross-border relationships, expatriate relationships had several typical characteristics that had direct consequences for knowledge sharing. First, expatriate relationships were, on average, richer and longer-term than arm's-length cross-border relationships, creating more opportunities for knowledge sharing. They also had a higher multiplying effect, spreading ties more effectively across new units.

Second, they were characterized by a higher level of trust and multiplexity, driven by shared experience, physical proximity and prolonged face-to-face interaction. Finally, a lengthened participation in the assignment unit typically led to a higher level of shared cognitive ground, effectively facilitating knowledge sharing. Expatriation may have a sustained effect on knowledge sharing within the multinational corporation (MNC), beyond the knowledge transfer perspective discussed in previous research.[71]

Nevertheless, knowledge sharing through expatriates is not unproblematic. From a sample of Finnish expatriates, the results revealed that expatriates were involved in transfers of several different types of knowledge, often requiring them to work across functions. This aspect of their knowledge-sharing task gave rise to difficulties. Knowledge-related and, to a lesser extent, organizational-related stickiness factors dominated those related to the social and relational contexts in explaining the difficulty of knowledge transfers from the expatriates' perspective.[72]

Factors that may influence communication in intra-MNC inter-unit relationships were tested on a sample of 308 dyadic relationships between Finnish and Chinese subsidiaries and their headquarters and sister units. The results indicated that the intensity (frequency and perceived importance) of inter-unit communication was related to the extent of subsidiary managers' participation in corporate training programmes, their fluency in the language in which the inter-unit communication took place, and, to some extent, to the use of expatriate managers.[73] Another finding concerning the transfer of knowledge across national borders within multinational enterprises is that it depends both on a common language necessary for communication and on the shared social knowledge necessary to understand and predict the behaviour of those engaged in the knowledge-transfer process. In a set of four case studies, it was found that knowledge transfer was more effective when technical and social knowledge were transferred together. Rich person-to-person contact in multinational teams provided an effective means of transferring social knowledge.[74] Finally, Noorderhaven and Harzing (2009) showed that social interaction between managers from different units of a multinational enterprise (MNE) supported knowledge sharing not only by forming a communication channel particularly conducive to the transfer of tacit, non-codified knowledge, but to an even greater degree by providing opportunities for social construction of knowledge in a learning dialogue. That is, knowledge was not only transferred when managers from different units interacted, it was also created by a synthesis of the parties' knowledge.[75]

Teams, too, can support intra-MNC knowledge transfer: based on a survey of 90 transnational product introductions Subramaniam and Venkatraman (2001) found that organizations had greater transnational product development capabilities when they used cross-national teams, teams with members who had prior overseas experience, or teams whose members communicated frequently with overseas managers in order to acquire information about tacit differences among countries.[76]

For MNCs that compete in knowledge-intensive industries, 'accessing knowledge and nurturing the innovative potential of R&D subsidiaries is vital for on-going competitiveness'. Overseas subsidiaries in high-technology sectors can become isolated, however. Analysis of a sample of 45 foreign-owned Austrian subsidiaries suggested that parent and subsidiary experience, the degree of early-stage research conducted by the subsidiary and the use of training and rotation practices by the subsidiary influenced communication frequency between the R&D subsidiary and various actors within the internal and the external networks, and this in turn acted to counter isolation.[77]

> Knowledge transfer and co-ordination are key functions performed by intercultural communication within MNCs. Informal lateral relations, expatriates' ties to both the local and the global organization and cross-national teams support these functions.

9.6 INTERNATIONAL BUSINESS-TO-BUSINESS (B2B) RELATIONS

Businesses do business with other businesses in order to obtain resources that they lack, whether those resources are of access to markets, raw materials, technology, finance, personnel or other factors. Those transactions with other firms are located on a continuum ranging from one-off transactions to very long-term relations lasting decades or more. Within cultures, the duration of the relationship is likely to be affected by the culture: in individualist, low uncertainty avoidance and short-term oriented cultures such relationships are likely to be of shorter duration than those within collectivist, high uncertainty avoidance and long-term oriented cultures. The closeness of the relationship as well as its durability may be affected by cultural factors, with individualists seeking more arm's-length relationships than collectivists. The existence and traditional importance of long-term, closely interwoven business groups in the collectivist countries of Asia, such as the *keiretsu* of Japan, by comparison with their absence from the individualist Anglo-American countries, go some way to confirm these arguments.

Research by the present author (Guirdham, 2009) brought out the significant and culturally influenced differences among business relations in five Asian countries – China, India, Japan, Taiwan and Singapore.[78] As important an influence as the societal culture was the business culture, defined as 'a set of business-related beliefs, attitudes, meanings and practices shared by a business community'. In Chinese business culture *guanxi* was a very important influence on business-to-business relations, as earlier researchers had also revealed. *Guanxi* is a more structured and sophisticated version of networking. It was described as pervasive in China, as modifying business objectives, at least in the short term, as varying across Chinese communities and as leading to a setting-aside of contracts and contractual commitments. It was equally important in Taiwan, where, in the words of one interviewee, a Taiwanese partner in a Taiwan venture capital firm, 'Everything depends on a close relationship with both business partners and customers.' In Japan, in contrast, the business-to-business relationships of large companies were increasingly impersonal, and even long-term inter-organizational relationships, such as those in business groups, had lost some of their importance. In India, interpersonal relationships between organizations were important: 'A lot depends on relationships, ... there is no sitting at home to do business deals – face-to-face means a lot – we socialize over business' (Indian, senior manager, private Indian bank). It was not, however, a *guanxi* system: 'With Indians, the relationship builds over time [but unlike in the Far East, it is not a prerequisite]' (successful Indian entrepreneur, internet-based business).

A model of business-to-business relationships founded on empirical findings from social-exchange theory, organizational theory and transaction theory has stimulated other research. Known as the KMV model, it postulates that relationship commitment is the sole first-order antecedent of the duration of B2B relations, where commitment is defined as the perceived importance of a relationship and implies a desire to continue a relationship assuming that it will bring future value or benefits. Trust has been shown by empirical research to be an antecedent of commitment. Trust is defined as the willingness to rely on an exchange partner in whom one has confidence; it includes an expectation about the other party's honesty and benevolence. According to the KMV model there are five antecedents of commitment and trust: benefits from the relationship, losses expected from ending the relationship and shared values increase commitment; trust is increased by high-quality communication and reduced by the opportunistic behaviour of the other party or parties.

Case study research by Friman *et al.* (2002) into international business relationships between service firms found support for this model. (It also rejected as influences on the duration of the relationship other plausible factors including fairness, perceived relationship effectiveness and prior beliefs regarding the likelihood that the exchanging partner will reciprocate acts of trust and commitment.[79]) It was thus suggested that the theory may be quite general, since it had been successfully used in previous analyses of other types of business-to-business relationships.[80] Given that commitment is closely related to 'shared values' between the trading partners, the inference that culture has a major impact is a reasonable one. This inference is supported by a finding that long-term commitment (or the lack of it) in cross-national business relationships is related to the social and structural bond between the partners, which in turn is related to their cultural orientation: cross-national business relationships between collectivists are more likely to be long-term than those between individualists.[81]

Intercultural B2B relations

The contention in the preceding paragraph of cultural influence on B2B relations raises questions about relationship duration and partner commitment in intercultural business relations. Is commitment likely to be lower and relationship duration less in intercultural business relations? The findings of a study that examined international B2B marketing channels comprised of channel members representing different cultural contexts showed that there is a relationship between culture and channel communication in international channels. When exporters from the low-context communication (LC) US culture dealt with foreign distributors from high-context communication (HC) cultures, 'old-fashioned' fax and telephone communication took place much more frequently than when the US exporters dealt with foreign distributors from LC cultures. The conclusions of the study disputed the prediction that cultural distance would be obviated in internet-based marketing channels, arguing that 'the need to augment the totally impersonal electronic communications flowing over the Internet via "old fashioned" but more comfortable modes of communications might be greater than ever in the new electronic marketing channels. The need to ask questions, get clarifications, and reassurances so as to achieve an acceptable comfort level will not suddenly disappear for channel members from HC cultures simply because they are electronically linked to a network.'[82]

Relationship quality, which is viewed as a higher-order construct composed of trust, commitment and satisfaction, has been described as of 'fundamental importance … in inter-organizational exchange' and this applies a fortiori to cross-border relationship quality. In a study of importing distributors trading with exporting manufacturers of industrial products, relationship quality was positively associated with transaction-specific investments and role performance, but also, and negatively, with psychic distance. Psychic distance is a set of elements inhibiting the flow of information to

Box 9.8

A Japanese manager from a Japanese trading company spoke in an interview of a lack of respect for the spirit of agreements among the Chinese. 'The SOEs [State-Owned Enterprises] break the rules. In fact, they have no written rules. For instance, they will pay for goods with letters of credit, then find some minute differ- ence from the contract and say they will not pay. They will pay in the end, because otherwise we would not deal with them again and they need us, but it wastes an awful lot of time.'

Source: Guirdham, M. (2009) *Culture and Business in Asia*, Basingstoke, UK: Palgrave Macmillan

and from a particular foreign market. It is defined as the traders' perception of differences between the operating environments of the exchange partners, and will usually include perceived cultural differences. The lower the degree of (perceived) dissimilarity, the lower the level of psychic distance surrounding the importer–exporter relationship and the better the quality of the relationship.[83]

Existing levels of trust had a positive effect on relationship performance outcomes achieved one year later, the study found. Importantly, trust took on greater importance in enhancing performance under conditions of high interdependence, whereas in circumstances of low interdependence trust had no discernible effect. The findings also indicated that exporter transaction-specific assets were positively related, and inter-firm psychic distance, internal uncertainty and opportunism were negatively related to importer trust. Opportunism is self-seeking with guile. It occurs when one party violates its appropriate or required role behaviour, leading to a transfer of wealth from the other party to the performer. Importer–exporter relationships create opportunities for opportunism because the supply-side markets are volatile and impossible for the importer to fully comprehend. The point is whether the importer perceives the exporter to behave opportunistically; if so, relationship commitment by the importer will be reduced.[84]

Much of the recent literature on inter-organizational relations provides evidence that relationship commitment can produce significant benefits for firms. What role does commitment play in international buyer–seller relationships? From a sample of 216 overseas distributor–manufacturer relationships, research findings suggested that exporter opportunism, as perceived by the importer, affected importer commitment, and that an importer's commitment had a positive impact on its performance in the relationship. Cultural sensitivity on the part of the exporter (as perceived by the importer) was indirectly associated with commitment by reducing perceived opportunism, but was also linked directly with commitment. 'This previously undisclosed finding shows that an exporter's cultural understanding of, and adjustment to, its import partner's local business practices has the ability to transform cross-border economic transactions into enduring relationships embedded in a social context by infusing them with behaviors that enable them to be perpetuated in the long run.'[85]

Among the factors identified by research as relevant to intercultural business-to-business relations are relationship commitment, trust, psychic distance and perceived opportunism. All these can be influenced by culture and cultural differences but are themselves related to whether cultural differences can be overcome.

9.7 CONCLUSION

This chapter has explored five key contexts within which intercultural communication in and between organizations takes place. These contexts were those of virtual teams, offshoring, international alliances, multinational enterprises and business-to-business relations. Coping with the consequences of computer-mediated communication is a vital skill in these contexts, while using intercultural communication to support knowledge sharing and co-ordination is also vitally important in all of them.

QUESTIONS AND EXERCISES

1. In egalitarian societies, it has been shown, new technologies that allow people to offer their ideas by typing them into a computer anonymously lead to more and better ideas being generated. Discuss the question of the possible outcomes from using these technologies in high power-distance cultures.
2. Rate broadcast television, broadcast radio, instant messaging, voice responsive interactive language learning programmes and internet videoconferencing for social presence.
3. What characteristics of the user of a medium affect the level of social presence occurring during its use?
4. In a negotiation being conducted by audio-conferencing, what consequences for people from high power-distance cultures might follow if the negotiators do not announce who they are before they speak?
5. Keep a record over a period of two weeks of the number of work-related pieces of information that you receive through informal communication channels at work.
6. Conduct an online discussion over a period of two weeks with the members of your class. Choose a topic that is likely to be neutral as far as obvious demographic differences are concerned. Ensure that individuals are identified only by a number. Afterwards, analyse the number and length of contributions by individual contributing by gender, first language and other differences found in published research into the topic. What patterns emerged?
7. Conduct the same discussion as in Question 6 face-to-face, recording the discussion. Analyse the contributions from this discussion in terms of majority/minority influence. (The majority may be a demographically or culturally or language-based one.) Reanalyse the data from Question 6 along the same lines and compare it with the face-to-face results.
8. Keep a log over a period of a week of the number of 'different others' that you meet face-to-face and their proportion of the total (limit this to people with whom you have at least one or two minutes' conversation); over the same period keep a log of the number of significant contacts you have online (limit these to those with whom you exchange at least one or two sentences). Compare the results for the percentage of different others you contact.
9. Explain the following statement from the text in your own words: 'Knowledge stickiness is a positive function of the tacitness, ambiguity and social complexity of process knowledge and a negative function of its codifiability.'
10. Why would knowledge transfer between a vertical individualist and a horizontal collectivist be more difficult than that between (a) a vertical individualist and a horizontal individualist and (b) a horizontal individualist and a vertical collectivist?
11. Decision-support systems (designed in the United States) embody algorithms that fit egalitarian, democratic participation. These systems allow for anonymous voting and

weighted decision analysis and other algorithms.[86] Discuss the question of the possible outcomes from using these technologies in collectivist cultures.

12. The text gives examples of a potential co-ordination problem resulting from epistemic interdependence. Give two more examples from different fields.

13. Discuss reasons why, as the research findings described in Section 9.1 show, structural and spatial boundaries might present greater obstacles to co-ordination than socio-demographic boundaries.

14. Becker *et al.* (2000), as referred to in Box 9.4, noted that lack of visibility of gesture in desktop videoconferencing could create problems of clarity for communication in design meetings. Would similar or other problems (or advantages) arise in meetings where gestures are primarily used for expressiveness rather than clarification? Give examples.

15. Research has found problems of autonomy–connectedness, inclusion–exclusion and empowerment–disempowerment in virtual teams. How would these problems map onto findings about the effects of cultural difference, prejudice and discrimination described earlier in this book?

16. Two people who are remote teammates on a development project, one from the USA, one from Greece, behave differently when they complete a task. The American immediately jumps into another task, whereas the Greek waits to be told what to do. If neither has cultural awareness, discuss the possible effects on their attitudes to one another.

17. You are a member of a virtual team working on a statistics-based report. The Indian team supplies the data and statistical analysis; the UK team supplies the client-need knowledge and the version of English demanded by the (mainly European) clients. What issues might arise? How might they be overcome?

18. Discuss the contention that investing in creating common ground is likely to be more productive for companies than expenditure in modularization or ongoing communication.

19. Role play the following scenario: An English-speaking Frenchman who has recently purchased a desktop computer telephones the manufacturer's helpdesk to complain that when on the internet he cannot adjust the screen size to enable him to see the whole screen. The Indian call centre operative has to explain that this is not a hardware problem but either a software or a server or similar problem. This is something the Frenchman does not want to hear! In enacting these roles bear in mind the findings on the cultural values of French and Indian people given in Chapter 2.

20. A study found that some differences in cultural values are more important than others for the survival of international joint ventures. Which differences were these and how can the findings be explained?

21. Summarize the research findings reported in the text on the effects of cultural differences on international joint ventures. How, in the light of these findings, can the prospects of success of international joint ventures be increased?

22. Consider an open discussion (in which personnel at all levels and from all departments take part) by videoconference within a large MNE that focuses on an issue of future development, with various positive and negative comments being exchanged. How might cultural influences affect responses to this situation?

NOTES AND REFERENCES

1. Herbsleb, J.D. and Moitra, D. (2001) 'Global software development', *IEEE Software*, March/April: 16–20.

2. Rice, R.E. (1992) 'Task analyzability, use of new medium and effectiveness: a multi-site exploration of media richness', *Organization Science*, **3**(4): 475–500.

3. Srikanth, K. (2008) 'Co-presence not communication: how ICT's really enable software services offshoring'. URL: http://ssrn.com/abstract=928072

4. Swigger, K., Alpaslan, F., Brazile, R. and Monticino, M. (2004) 'Effects of culture on computer-supported international collaborations', *International Journal of Human-Computer Studies*, **60**(3): 365–80.

5. Stewart, C.M., Shields, S.F. and Sen, N. (2002) 'A study of cultural and gender differences in Listservs', *Electronic Journal of Communication*, **8**(398). URL: http://www.cios.org/www/ejc/v8n398.htm

6. Li, Q. (2002) 'Computer-mediated communication and gender differences: a meta-analysis', *University of Calgary working paper*. URL: http://www.eric.ed.gov/PDFS/ED490640.pdf, last accessed on 24 December 2010.

7. Allwood, J. and Schroeder, R. (2000) 'Intercultural communication in a virtual environment', *Intercultural Communication*, **4**. URL: http://www.immi.se/intercultural/nr4/allwood.htm

8. Zhang, D., Lowry, P.B., Zhou, L. and Fu, X. (2007) 'The impact of individualism-collectivism, social presence, and group diversity on group decision making under majority influence', *Journal of Management Information Systems*, **23**(4): 53–8.

9. Kim, D.J. (2008) 'Self-perception-based versus transference-based trust determinants in computer-mediated transactions: a cross-cultural comparison study', *Journal of Management Information Systems*, **24**(4): 73–100.

10. Vance, A., Elie-dit-Cosaque, C. and Straub, D.W. (2008) 'Examining trust in information technology artifacts: the effects of system quality and culture', *Journal of Management Information Systems*, **24**(4): 13–45.

11. Awad, N.F. and Ragowsky, A. (2008) 'Establishing trust in electronic commerce through online word of mouth: an examination across genders', *Journal of Management Information Systems*, **24**(4): 101–21.

12. Suchan, J. and Hayzak, G. (2001) 'The communication characteristics of virtual teams: A case study', *IEEE Transactions on Professional Communication*, **44**(3): 174–86.

13. Gibson, C.B. and Gibbs, J.L. (2006) 'Unpacking the concept of virtuality: The effects of geographic dispersion, electronic dependence, dynamic structure, and national diversity on team innovation', *Administrative Science Quarterly*, **51**: 451–95.

14. Winter, S.G. (1987) 'Knowledge and competence as strategic assets', in Teece, D. (ed.) *The Competitive Challenge–Strategies for Industrial Innovation and Renewal*, Cambridge, MA: Ballinger.

15. Birkinshaw, J., Nobel, R. and Ridderstrale, J. (2002) 'Knowledge as a contingency variable: do the characteristics of knowledge predict organization structure?', *Organization Science*, **13**(3): 274–89.

16. Szulanski, G. (1996) 'Exploring internal stickiness: impediments to the transfer of best practice within the firm', *Strategic Management Journal*, **17**: 27–43.

17. Leung, K., Bhagat, R.S., Buchan, N.R., Erez, M. and Gibson, C.B. (2005) 'Culture and international business: recent advances and their implications for future research', *Journal of International Business Studies*, **36**: 357–78.

18. Bhagat, B.L., Kedia, P.D., Harveston, H.C. and Triandis, H. (2002) 'Cultural variations in the cross-border transfer of organizational knowledge: an integrative framework', *Academy of Management Review*, **27**(2): 204–21.

19. Sarala, R.M. and Vaara, E. (2009) 'Cultural differences, convergence, and crossvergence as explanations of knowledge transfer in international acquisitions', *Journal of International Business Studies*, doi:10.1057/jibs.2009.89.

20. Puranam, P., Goetting, M. and Knudsen, T. (2010) 'Interdependence, information processing and organization design: an epistemic perspective'. Available at SSRN: http://ssrn.com/abstract=1394459

21. Ibid.

22. Kleinbaum, A.M., Stuart, T.E. and Tushman, M. (2008) 'Communication (and co-ordination?) in a modern, complex organization', *Harvard Business School Entrepreneurial Management Working Paper No. 09–004*. Available at SSRN: http://ssrn.com/abstract=1162171.

23. Pawar, K.S. and Sharifi, S. (1997) 'Physical or virtual team collocation: Does it matter?', *International Journal of Production Economics*, **52**: 283–90.
24. Mortensen, M., Caya, O. and Pinsonneault, A. (2009) 'Virtual teams demystified: an integrative framework for understanding virtual teams and a synthesis of research', MIT Sloan Research Paper No. 4738–09. Available at SSRN: http://ssrn.com/abstract=1282095.
25. Ferguson, M.J. (2005) 'The role of group membership perception and team identity in a virtual team's use of influence tactics', *IACM 17th Annual Conference Paper*. Available at SSRN: http://ssrn.com/abstract=602047 (internal references omitted).
26. Suchan and Hayzak, 'The communication characteristics of virtual teams: a case study'.
27. Zakaria, N., Amelinckx, A. and Wilemon, D. (2004) 'Working together apart? Building a knowledge-sharing culture for global virtual teams', *Creativity and Innovation Management*, **13**: 15–29.
28. Teasley, S., Covi, L., Krishnan, M.S. and Olson, J.S. (2000) 'Computer supported cooperative work', *Proceedings of the 2000 ACM conference on Computer supported cooperative work*, Philadelphia, Pennsylvania, United States: 339–46.
29. Tambe, P. and Hitt, L.M. (2008) 'How does offshoring affect information technology workers?' Available at SSRN: http://ssrn.com/abstract=1259323.
30. Srikanth, K. and Puranam, P. (2007) 'Co-ordination in distributed organizations', URL: http://ssrn.com/abstract=939786.
31. Ibid.
32. Clark, H. (1996) *Using Language*, Cambridge, UK: Cambridge University Press.
33. Srikanth and Puranam, 'Co-ordination in distributed organizations'.
34. Whitaker, J., Krishnan, M.S. and Fornell, C. (2008) 'Does offshoring impact customer satisfaction?' Available at SSRN: http://ssrn.com/abstract=1010457.
35. Pal, M. and Buzzanell, P. (2008) 'The Indian call center experience: A case study in changing discourses of identity, identification, and career in a global context', *The Journal of Business Communication*, **45**(1): 31–60.
36. Srikanth and Puranam, 'Co-ordination in distributed organizations'.
37. Olson, J.S. and Olson, G.M. (2003–4) 'Culture surprises in remote software development teams', *Queue*, **1**(9): 52–9.
38. Luo, Y. (2001) 'Antecedents and consequences of personal attachment in cross-cultural cooperative ventures', *Administrative Science Quarterly*, **46**(2): 177–202.
39. Nielsen, B. B. and Nielsen, S. (2009) 'The impact of top management team nationality diversity and international experience on foreign entry mode'. Available at SSRN: http://ssrn.com/abstract=1511676.
40. Shenkar, O. and Li, J. (1999) 'Knowledge search in international cooperative ventures', *Organization Science*, **10**(2): 134–43.
41. Brannen, M.Y. and Salk, J.E. (2000) 'Partnering across borders: Negotiating organizational culture in a German-Japanese joint venture', *Human Relations*, **53**: 451–87.
42. Very, P., Lubatkin, M. and Calori, R. (1996) 'A cross-national assessment of acculturative stress in recent European mergers', *International Studies of Management and Organization*, **26**(1): 59–86.
43. Irrmann, O. (2005) 'Communication dissonance and pragmatic failures in strategic processes: The case of cross-border acquisitions', *Advances in Strategic Management*, **22**: 251–67.
44. Brannen, 'Partnering across borders'.
45. Barkema, H.G. and Vermeulen, F. (1997) 'What differences in the cultural backgrounds of partners are detrimental for international joint ventures?', *Journal of International Business Studies*, **28**(4): 845–69.
46. Aulakh, P.S., Kotabe, M. and Sahay, A. (1996) 'Trust and performance in cross-border marketing partnerships: a behavioral approach', *Journal of International Business Studies*, **27**(5): 1,005–32.
47. Pothukuchi, V.K., Damanpour, F., Choi, J., Chen, C. and Park, S.H. (2002) 'National and organizational culture differences and international joint venture performance', *Journal of International Business Studies*, **33**(2): 243–65.

48. Froese, F.J., Pak, Y.S. and Chong, L.C. (2008) 'Managing the human side of cross-border acquisitions in South Korea', *Journal of World Business*, **43**(1): 97–108.
49. Aulakh *et al.*, 'Trust and performance in cross-border marketing partnerships: a behavioral approach'.
50. Child, J., Chung, L. and Davies, H. (2003) 'The performance of cross-border units in China: a test of natural selection, strategic choice and contingency theories', *Journal of International Business Studies*, **34**(3): 242–54.
51. Griffith, D.A. (2002) 'The role of communication competencies in international business relationship development', *Journal of World Business*, **37**(4): 256–65.
52. Lu, Y. (2006) 'Toward the micro and macro-level consequences of interactional justice in cross-cultural joint ventures', *Human Relations*, **59**(8): 1,019–47.
53. Larsson, R. and Lubatkin, M. (2001) 'Achieving acculturation in mergers and acquisitions: an international case survey', *Human Relations*, **54**(12): 1,573–1,609.
54. Child *et al.*, 'The performance of cross-border units in China'.
55. Arino, A., Abramov, M., Skorobogatykh, I., Rykounina, I. and Vila, J. (1997) 'Partner selection and trust building in West European-Russian joint ventures: a Western perspective', *International Studies of Management & Organization*, **27**(1): 19–37.
56. Byers, K.M. and Lyles, M.A. (1994) 'An examination of a health care international joint venture in Poland', *International Studies of Management and Organization*, **24**(4): 31–47.
57. Luo, 'Antecedents and consequences of personal attachment in cross-cultural cooperative ventures'.
58. Inkpen, A.C. and Beamish, P.W. (1997) 'Knowledge, bargaining power, and the instability of international joint ventures', *Academy of Management Review*, **22**: 177–202.
59. Gupta, A.K. and Govindarajan, V. (2000) 'Knowledge flows within multinational corporations', *Strategic Management Journal*, **21**(4): 473–96.
60. Peng, M.W. (2001) 'The resource-based view and international business', *Journal of Management*, **27**(6): 803–29.
61. Minbaeva, D.B. (2007) 'Knowledge transfer in multinational corporations', *Management International Review*, **47**(4): 567–93.
62. Welch, D., Welch, L. and Piekkari, R. (2005) 'Speaking in tongues: The importance of language in international management processes', *International Studies of Management and Organization*, **35**(1): 10–27.
63. Charles, M. (2007) 'Language matters in global communication', *Journal of Business Communication*, **44**(3): 260–282.
64. Chen, C.Y. and Jackson, P.R. (2008) 'Lingua Franca, communication and knowledge transfer in MNEs'. Available at SSRN: http://ssrn.com/abstract=1374684.
65. Moore, F. and Rees, C. (2008) 'Culture against cohesion: Global corporate strategy and employee diversity in the UK plant of a German MNC', *Employee Relations*, **30**(2): 176–89.
66. Tsai, W. (2002) 'Social structure of "coopetition" within a multiunit organization: coordination, competition, and intraorganizational knowledge sharing', *Organization Science*, **13**(2): 179–90. (internal references omitted).
67. Ibid.
68. Granovetter, M.S. (1973) 'The strength of weak ties', *American Journal of Sociology*, **78**(6): 1,360– 80.
69. Lunan, R. and Barth, T. (2003) 'Managing the exploration vs. exploitation dilemma in transnational "bridging teams"', *Journal of World Business*, **38**(2): 110–26.
70. Hansen, M.T. (1999) 'The search-transfer problem: The role of weak ties in sharing knowledge across organization subunits', *Administrative Science Quarterly*, **44**(1): 82–111.
71. Mäkelä, K. (2007) 'Knowledge sharing through expatriate relationships: A social capital perspective', *International Studies of Management and Organization*, **37**(3): 108–25.
72. Riusala, K. and Smale, A. (2007) 'Predicting stickiness factors in the international transfer of knowledge through expatriates', *International Studies of Management and Organization*, **37**(3): 16–43.

73. Barner-Rasmussen, W. and Bjorkman, I. (2005) 'Surmounting interunit barriers: factors associated with interunit communication intensity in the multinational corporation', *International Studies of Management and Organization*, **35**(1): 28–46.

74. Buckley, P.J., Carter, M.J., Clegg, J. and Tan, H. (2005) 'Language and social knowledge in foreign-knowledge transfer to China', *International Studies of Management and Organization*, **35**(1): 47–65.

75. Noorderhaven, N. and Harzing, A.-W. (2009) 'Knowledge-sharing and social interaction within MNEs', *Journal of International Business Studies*, **40**: 719–41.

76. Subramaniam, M. and Venkatraman, N. (2001) 'Determinants of transnational new product development capability: testing the influence of transferring and deploying tacit overseas knowledge', *Strategic Management Journal*, **22**(4): 359–78.

77. Williams, C. and Nones, B. (2009) 'R&D subsidiary isolation in knowledge-intensive industries: evidence from Austria', *R&D Management*, **39**(2): 111–23.

78. Guirdham, M. (2009) *Culture and Business in Asia*, Basingstoke, UK: Palgrave Macmillan.

79. Friman, M., Gärling, T., Millett, B., Mattsson, J. and Johnston, R. (2002) 'An analysis of international business-to-business relationships based on the Commitment–Trust theory', *Industrial Marketing Management*, **31**: 403–9.

80. Morgan, M.R. and Hunt, S.D. (1994) 'The commitment–trust theory of relationship marketing', *Journal of Marketing*, **58**: 20–38.

81. Williams, J.D., Han, S.L. and Qualls, W.J. (1998) 'A conceptual model and study of cross-cultural business relationships', *Journal of Business Research*, **42**(2): 135–43.

82. Rosenbloom, B. and Larsen, T. (2003) 'Communication in international business-to-business marketing channels: does culture matter?', *Industrial Marketing Management*, **32**: 309–15.

83. Skarmeas, D., Katsikeas, C.S., Spyropoulou, S. and Salehi-Sangari, E. (2008) 'Market and supplier characteristics driving distributor relationship quality in international marketing channels of industrial products' *Industrial Marketing Management*, **37**(1): 23–36.

84. Katsikeas, C.S., Skarmeas, D. and Bello, D.C. (2009) 'Developing successful trust-based international exchange relationships', *Journal of International Business Studies*, **40**(1): 132–55.

85. Skarmeas, D., Katsikeas, C.S. and Schlegelmilch, B.B. (2002) 'Drivers of commitment and its impact on performance in cross-cultural buyer-seller relationships: the importer's perspective', *Journal of International Business Studies*, **33**: 757–83.

86. Nunamaker, J.F., Dennis, A.R., Valacich, J.S., Vogel, D.R. and George, J.F. (1991) 'Electronic meeting systems to support group work', *Communications of the ACM*, **34**(7): 40–61.

Scoring and Interpretation of Questionnaires

Q. 2.6   QUESTIONNAIRE ON OWN CULTURE

For questions 1, 2, 4, 6, 7, 8, 10, 11, 13, 15, 16, 17 and 19, score 1 for 'Strongly agree', 2 for 'Agree', 3 for 'Neither agree nor disagree', 4 for 'Disagree' and 5 for 'Strongly disagree'.

For questions 3, 5, 9, 12, 14, 18 and 20, score 5 for 'Strongly agree', 4 for 'Agree', 3 for 'Neither agree nor disagree', 2 for 'Disagree' and 1 for 'Strongly disagree'.

Questions 1 to 5 score universalism versus particularism: add your scores for the four questions; scores of 20 or above indicate a strongly universalistic culture; scores of 15 to 19 a moderately universalistic culture; scores of 5 or below a strongly particularistic culture; scores of 6 to 10 a moderately particularistic culture; scores between 10 and 15 are indeterminate.

Questions 6 and 7 score Trompenaars' version of individualism versus collectivism: add your scores for the two questions; scores of 7 and over indicate an individualistic culture; scores of 4 and below a collectivist culture; scores of 5 or 6 are indeterminate.

Questions 8, 9 and 10 score neutrality versus emotionalism: add your scores for the three questions; scores of 10 or above indicate a culture high in 'emotionalism'; scores of 5 or below one high in neutrality; scores between 6 and 9 are indeterminate.

Questions 11 and 12 score specificity versus diffuseness: add your scores for the two questions; scores of 7 and over indicate a specific culture; scores of 4 and below a diffuse culture; scores of 5 or 6 are indeterminate.

Questions 13 to 15 score achievement versus ascription as the basis for status: add your scores for the three questions; scores of 10 or above indicate an 'achievement' culture; scores of 5 or below indicate an ascription culture; scores between 6 and 9 are indeterminate.

Q. 3.18   QUESTIONNAIRE ON MANAGERS REQUESTS/ INSTRUCTIONS TO SUBORDINATES

For all questions, score 5 for 'Strongly agree', 4 for 'Agree', 3 for 'Neither agree nor disagree', 2 for 'Disagree' and 1 for 'Strongly disagree'.

This questionnaire scores different approaches to compliance gaining with subordinates, and is based on the research described in the related subsection of this chapter.

Questions 1 and 2 score the main methods used by US managers, reasoning and friendliness. Add your scores for the two questions. Scores of 7 or above indicate agreement with their approach, scores of 3 and below disagreement, scores of 4 to 6 are neutral.

Questions 3 and 4 score the methods used by Japanese managers in permanent employment. Add your scores for the two questions. Scores of 7 or above indicate agreement with their approach, scores of 3 and below disagreement, scores of 4 to 6 are neutral.

Q. 3.23 QUESTIONNAIRE ON CONFLICT HANDLING AT WORK

For questions 1, 4, 6, 7 and 8, score 5 for 'Strongly agree', 4 for 'Agree', 3 for 'Neither agree nor disagree', 2 for 'Disagree' and 1 for 'Strongly disagree'.

For questions 2, 3 and 5, score 1 for 'Strongly agree', 2 for 'Agree', 3 for 'Neither agree nor disagree', 4 for 'Disagree' and 5 for 'Strongly disagree'.

Add your scores for all questions. Your culture strongly favours a harmonising, collectivist kind of conflict management if your score is 33 or above, moderately favours it if your score is 25 to 32; scores of 8 or below and 9 to 16 indicate a culture that strongly or moderately favours a competitive, problem-solving individualist kind of conflict management; scores between 17 and 24 are indeterminate.

Q. 8.11 QUESTIONNAIRE ON NEGOTIATING STYLES

Questions 2, 4, 5, 6, and 7: score 5 for 'Strongly agree', 4 for 'Agree', 3 for 'Neither agree nor disagree', 2 for 'Disagree' and 1 for 'Strongly disagree'.

Questions 1, 3 and 8, score 1 for 'Strongly agree', 2 for 'Agree', 3 for 'Neither agree nor disagree', 4 for 'Disagree' and 5 for 'Strongly disagree'.

This questionnaire scores Western-style versus non-Western-style negotiating approaches. Scores above 32 indicate a strong cultural tendency to negotiate in a Western style (WSN); scores of 25 to 32 indicate moderate WSN; scores below 9 indicate a strong cultural tendency to negotiate in a non-Western style (NWSN); scores of 9 to 16 indicate moderate NWSN; scores of 17 to 24 are indeterminate. Scores on the individual items are also revealing.

Glossary of Terms as Used in this Book

Accommodation
Process of adapting communication to make it more similar to or more different from an interlocutor's

Achievement–ascription
Cultural value dimension which contrasts determining people's status from their achievements versus determining it from their position resulting from external factors such as inherited wealth

Ageism
Prejudice or discrimination on the grounds of age

Agency
The capacity of individuals and/or groups to act with intention

Anxiety
Fear of aspects of a communication episode, including its outcome

Appreciative Inquiry
An approach to communication that emphasizes having and displaying a positive regard for the interlocutor and treating communication as a process of discovery

Apprehension
Fear of communicating experienced beforehand

Attribution theory
A set of theories about how people decide what mainly caused (or is causing) another person's action

Authoritarianism
Orientation or belief system of high deference to those in authority; often associated with a rigid value system and prejudice against deviants. An individual trait, not a cultural value

B2B
Business-to-business relations; in this book mainly concerned with international B2B

Behavioural mirroring
The behaviour of reflecting back the verbal, non-verbal or paralinguistic style of an interlocutor

Biculturalism
Ability to orient fully to more than one culture

Boundary spanners
Individuals who provide liaison between different organizations or different units within the same organization. This activity may be part of their role (as in personal selling) or it may be something they just do.

CMC
computer-mediated communication

Co-cultures	Groups within a nation or culture (ethnic or religious, for example) treated as equivalents, not main and subordinate
Collectivism	Cultural value that prioritizes the group to which a person belongs over the individual him- or herself
Common ground	Knowledge (often tacit and based on shared experience) that facilitates intercultural communication
Communalism	A cultural value in which 'the supremacy of the community is culturally and socially entrenched, society is hierarchically ordered, life is sacrosanct, and religion is a way of life'; it is contended that communalism is distinct from collectivism and that some concepts of collectivism have confused the two
Communication	Message exchange between two or more people
Conforming/varied ideation	Suppression of divergent points of view and convergence towards normative views in decision-making, versus its opposite
Context	Those aspects of the environment of an encounter that are present in the minds of participants and may influence them; a context may be physical, social (such as the participants' work roles), relate to its purpose or to other aspects such as past encounters
Convergence	Process of adjusting communication style to be more like an interlocutor's
Conversational constraints	Concerns that influence a communicator's choice of conversational strategy – for example, for clarity or minimizing imposition
Co-ordination	Process of effectively combining the work of two or more individuals or groups, which is made more problematic by spatial and cultural distance
Cultural distance	The extent to which two cultures differ, based on an assumption that this can be measured
Cultural identity	That part of an individual's social identity that is based on his or her membership of one or more cultures
Cultural intelligence (CQ)	Theory that a combination of cognition, metacognition, motivation and behaviour strongly influences intercultural communication effectiveness, and that this combination can be measured and can be improved by training
Cultural relativism	The belief that all cultures are equally valid and that any culture's values and practices must in principle be understood from the point of view of its members
Culture	Socially constructed set of actions, ideas and objects that people share as members of an enduring, communicatively interacting social group; in this book 'culture' is generally applied only to whole social systems. The term 'subculture' is used for parts of social systems
Demographic profile	An individual's description in terms of ethnicity, age, gender, (dis)ability level, sexual orientation, nationality, education and socio-economic status

Discourses	All forms of social interaction, spoken or written, treated as constructing and performing reality, not just reflecting it. Different social groups, such as doctors, use different discourses
Discrimination	Any situation in which a group or individual is treated unfavourably on the basis of arbitrary grounds, especially prejudice
Distributive justice	The fairness with which rewards and punishments are allocated; perceived distributive justice is often as important as or more important than actual distributive justice. *See also procedural justice.*
Divergence	Process of adjusting communication style to be less like an interlocutor's
Diversity	Presence of, or stakeholding by, a range of groups of people differentiated by their demographic or cultural profile
Elaborated code	Communication style that explicitly verbalizes much of the message; it assumes little shared knowledge with the receiver
Embeddedness–autonomy	Cultural value related to individualism–collectivism and autonomy/conservatism, but which also contrasts openness to change with maintaining the status quo
Epistemic interdependence	Situation in which effective co-ordination of work depends on effective sharing of knowledge
Ethical relativism	The claim that there is no culture-free, universal morality and therefore no way of ranking moral views and practices as more or less right, at least across cultures
Ethics	Moral systems
Ethnicity	Membership of a population whose members believe that in some sense they share common descent and a common cultural heritage or tradition, and who are so regarded by others
Ethnic minority	Ethnic group, which, for reasons of relative numbers or history, often has subordinate status within a society
Ethnocentrism	Belief that one's own culture or ethnic group is superior to others
Ethnolinguistic identity	An individual's identity in terms of his or her ethnic/language group
Face	Social value people assume for themselves, the image they try to project; positive face is based on the need for others' approval; negative face on the need to be independent of others and their approval
Face-threatening acts	Speech acts that threaten the positive or negative 'face' of either the speaker or the hearer of a communication
Facework	Communication strategies and actions aimed at meeting the communicator's 'face' needs
Femininity	Cultural value that prioritizes modesty, compromise and co-operative success over assertiveness, competition and aggressive success
Gendering of organizations	Process by which a 'masculine' (or, rarely) 'feminine' culture is created within an organization

Globalization	Processes, facilitated by modern technology and communications, by which economic and business activity, employing capitalist means and values, are alleged to be becoming global and to drive out traditional cultures and values
Grounding	Process by which people establish and continuously update their shared understanding in conversations
Guanxi	Cultural Chinese system of networking
Harassment	Vexing by repeated attacks, which may be verbal and/or non-explicit
Heterogeneity, of workgroups	Workgroup composition that is mixed in terms of demographic profile
Hierarchy–egalitarianism	Cultural value system that contrasts a belief that people are equal with one that elevates some individuals to a right to greater power and status. In addition to equality, egalitarianism implies that people recognize one another as moral equals who share basic interests as human beings
High-context communication	Culturally endorsed communication style that assumes high levels of common ground and so uses elliptical speech
Human capital	A society's resources in terms both of its population's economic and social abilities and skills and also of its institutions (civil society)
Humanism/materialism	Cultural value system that contrasts prioritizing relationships and caring with prioritizing material success
Individualism	Cultural value that prioritizes the individual him- or herself over the group to which he or she belongs
Ingroup favouritism	The tendency of members of groups to favour the group to which they belong over other groups in allocating desired resources
Intercultural communication	Communication between members of two or more cultures, especially, but not only, when their cultural memberships are salient
Inter-group bias	Prejudice in favour of any group to which the bias-holder belongs or aspires
Inter-group communication	Communication between members of two or more groups when their group memberships are salient
Interlocutor	Participant in a dialogue or conversation
Interpersonal communication	Communication between two or more participants, either face-to-face or mediated
Joint venture	An enterprise set up by co-operation between two or more organizations; an international joint venture is set up by two or more organizations from different countries
Kinesics	Analyses of human movement
Knowledge stickiness	Characteristics of knowledge or its users that make it difficult to transfer within or between organizations
Learned helplessness	Theory that some people suffer from a sense of helplessness, learned from negative experiences

Locus of control	An individual's generalized expectations regarding the forces that determine rewards and punishments; 'internal' locus of control is usually contrasted with 'external', with implications for the individual's other attitudes and behaviour.
Low-context communication	Culturally endorsed communication style that assumes low levels of common ground and so uses verbally explicit speech
Marginalized groups	Within co-cultural communication theory, social groups that are excluded from full participation in their society
Masculinity	Cultural value that prioritizes assertiveness, competition and aggressive success over modesty, compromise and co-operative success
Mastery–harmony	Cultural value dimension that contrasts prioritizing controlling one's environment with prioritizing harmonizing with it; mastery is similar to masculinity but does not imply selfishness; harmony is related to uncertainty avoidance but does not imply an emphasis on controlling ambiguity
Mediating	Process of acting as a third party to facilitate two or more parties who are attempting to resolve a perceived divergence of interest
Mentoring	Process of providing a junior person with information, advice and support, often by a senior person from the same organization
Micro-inequities	Low-level discrimination practised against individuals or groups
Micropractices	Elements of communication that convey meaning through tiny signs; usually referred to as excluding some groups from full participation
Monochronic/polychronic time	Cultural value dimension contrasting a preference for doing one thing at a time with a preference for undertaking multiple activities simultaneously
Multinational enterprises (MNEs) and multinational companies (MNCs)	Organizations that operate in several countries simultaneously; usually applied only when production as well as marketing is operated multinationally
Negotiating	Process by which two or more parties attempt to resolve a perceived divergence of interest; often involves bargaining
Networks	Loose organizations of non-state actors characterized by voluntary, reciprocal, and horizontal patterns of communication and exchange. The central argument of 'network theory' is that actors, such as organizations, are embedded in networks of interconnected social relationships that offer opportunities for and constraints on behaviour
Neutrality–emotionalism	Cultural value dimension contrasting a preference for an appearance of emotional neutrality with a preference for open display of emotions
New racism	Prejudice that argues for the social and cultural relevance of biologically rooted characteristics and distinguishes groups of people from one another hierarchically on this basis
Offshoring	Transfer of work to another country to benefit from cost or other advantages there; it may or may not involve outsourcing

Organizational culture	A set of values and practices supposedly embedded in an organization; often in reality inculcated by top management
Outsourcing	Transfer of work to another organization to benefit from cost or other advantages
Paralinguistics	Study of ways of speaking that include turn-taking, voice tone, speed of speech and length of time that one speaker speaks; these have been shown to vary cross-culturally
Persistent injustice effect	Rejection of excuses or apologies by people who have suffered persistent injustice
Politeness	Facework adjusted to the perceived amount of face-threat involved in a communication
Power distance	Cultural value dimension that contrasts acceptance that power is distributed unequally with its opposite
Procedural justice	The fairness of the processes by which rewards or punishments are allocated; perceived procedural justice is often as important as or more important than actual procedural justice. *See also distributive justice*
Protestant Work Ethic	Belief system that stresses successful outcomes for anyone who works hard, and attributes failure to personal factors such as lack of effort and weakness of character
Proxemics	Analysis of human spatial distance preferences
Rapport management	Management of relationships during communication
Restricted code	Communication style that uses limited syntax and vocabulary, but relies extensively on non-verbal behaviour; it assumes a context of knowledge shared with the receiver
Rhetorical sensitivity	Tendency to adapt messages to audiences
Self-construal	Mental representation of the self, derived, at least in part, reflexively – that is, by interpreting how others seem, from their communication, to perceive the self. An independent self-construal is one in which an individual's mental representation of him- or her-self is as a self-reliant and mainly self-responsible individual; an interdependent self-construal is one in which an individual's mental representation of him- or herself is as someone reliant on and responsible to his or her group. Independent self-construals occur more often (but not exclusively) in individualist cultures; interdependent self-construals occur more often (but not exclusively) in collectivist cultures
Self-monitoring	Trait of self-observation and analysis
Semiotics	Study of signs and symbols
Social accounts	Explanations, apologies and excuses
Social distance	The gap perceived by one member of a society between him- or herself (or ingroup) and another member (or group) of the same society or a different society. It may be based on status, education, ethnicity or a number of other attributes. The use of the term 'distance' implies that the gap can be measured

Social Dominance Orientation	Belief in and support for a natural hierarchy among individuals and groups
Social loafing	Tendency to work less hard in a group than individually, partly because effort is less likely to bring personal reward
Specificity–diffuseness	Cultural value dimension of people's sense of what is in the public and private domains of life and of how separate these different domains should be
Speech acts	Communications treated as performing a function, such as promising, requesting or informing
Speech community	A group of people who share not just a language but a common vocabulary, way of speaking and some norms; a central concept in linguistics
Stakeholder approach	An attitude of organizations and institutions that gives weight to the interests of all groups affected by their actions, not, for instance, just shareholders of a company
Stereotypes	Stable set of beliefs or preconceived ideas that the members of a group share about the characteristics of a group of people
Strong/weak ties	Strong ties obtain between people who are in frequent contact with one another, in contrast to weak ties, in which contact is relatively distant and infrequent; a concept within network theory and linked to ease and difficulty of knowledge sharing
Subculture	Socially constructed set of actions, ideations and objects that people share as members of an enduring, communicatively interacting social group that is not a whole social system. Applies to gender, social class and so on
Subjective culture	A society's 'characteristic way of perceiving its social environment'; emphasizes psychological constructs
Topic–comment structure	Order in which a message is given – context first, then main point, or vice versa
Uncertainty	Inability to predict what strangers' attitudes, feelings, beliefs, values and behaviour will be or explain why they behave in the way they do
Uncertainty avoidance	Cultural value dimension that refers to the extent to which a culture prefers to avoid ambiguity and to the way in which it resolves uncertainty
Universalism/particularism	Cultural value dimension that contrasts a preference for drawing general principles versus a preference for the anecdotal or itemized
Values	'Concepts or beliefs that pertain to desirable end states or behaviours, transcend specific situations, guide selection or evaluation of behaviour and events and are ordered by relative importance', or broad tendencies to prefer certain states of affairs to others
Virtual teams	Groups of people working together who communicate only by CMC

Further Reading

PART I   CULTURE AND COMMUNICATION AT WORK

Adler, N.J. and Gunderson, A. (2007) *International Dimensions of Organizational Behaviour*, 5th edn, Cincinnati, Ohio: South-Western College Publishing.

Fiske, S. and Taylor, S. (2007) *Social Cognition: From Brains to Culture,* New York: McGraw Hill.

Alvesson, M. and Billing, Y.D. (2009) *Understanding Gender and Organizations,* 2nd edn, London: Sage.

Buchanan, D.A. and Huczynski, A.A. (2010) *Organizational Behaviour: An Introductory Text*, 7th edn, Harlow, Essex: Pearson Education.

Harrison, L.E. and Huntington, S.P. (eds) (2001) *Culture Matters: How Values Shape Human Progress*, New York: Basic Books.

Hofstede, G., Hofstede, G.J. and Minkov, M. (2010) *Cultures and Organizations: Software of the Mind*, 3rd edn, New York: McGraw Hill.

Littlejohn, S. and Foss, K. (2007) *Theories of Human Communication*, 9th edn, Wadsworth Publishing.

Guirdham, M. (2002) *Interactive Behaviour at Work*, 3rd edn, Harlow, Essex: Pearson Education.

Guirdham, M. (2009) *Culture and Business in Asia*, Basingstoke, Hants: Palgrave Macmillan.

PART II   INTERCULTURAL COMMUNICATION AT WORK

Samovar, L.A., Porter, R.E. and McDaniel, E.R. (2008) *Intercultural Communication: A Reader*, 12th edn, Boston, MA: Wadsworth.

Lustig, M.W. and Koester, J. (2009) *Intercultural Competence: Interpersonal Communication Across Cultures*, 6th edn, Pearson Education.

Chen, G.M. and Starosta, W.J. (2005) *Foundations of Intercultural Communication*, 2nd edn, Boston, MA: Allyn and Bacon.

Chaney, L.H. and Martin, J.S. (2011) *Intercultural Business Communication*, 5th edn, Pearson Education.

PART III EXTENSIONS AND APPLICATIONS

Jacob, N. (2003) *Intercultural Management*, London: Kogan Page.

Phatak, A., Bhagat, R. and Kashlak, R. (2008) *International Management: Managing in a Diverse and Dynamic Global Environment*, 2nd edn, New York: McGraw Hill.

Hickson, D.J. and Pugh, D. (2003) *Management Worldwide: Distinctive Styles Amid Globalization*, 2nd edn, Harmondsworth, Penguin Business.

Index